THE NEW AMERICAN SPLENDOR ANTHOLOGY

BY HARVEY PEKAR

FOUR WALLS EIGHT WINDOWS

NEW YORK/LONDON

PUBLISHED IN THE UNITED STATES BY
FOUR WALLS EIGHT WINDOWS
39 WEST 14TH STREET
NEW YORK, NEW YORK 10011

U.K. OFFICES:
FOUR WALLS EIGHT WINDOWS/TURNAROUND
UNIT 3, OLYMPIA TRADING ESTATE
COBURG ROAD, WOOD GREEN
LONDON N22 6TZ

FIRST PRINTING SEPTEMBER 1991.

LIBRARY OF CONGRESS CATALOGING-IN-PUBLICATION DATA:
PEKAR, HARVEY.
THE NEW AMERICAN SPLENDOR ANTHOLOGY BY HARVEY PEKAR.
ISBN: 0-941423-64-6
1: TITLE
PN6727. P4.4A6   1991
741.5'973--DC 20
91-2987   CIP

PRINTED IN CANADA

10 9 8 7 6 5

AMERICAN SPLENDOR

"PA-AYPER-REGGS!!"

STORY BY HARVEY PEKAR
ART BY R. CRUMB

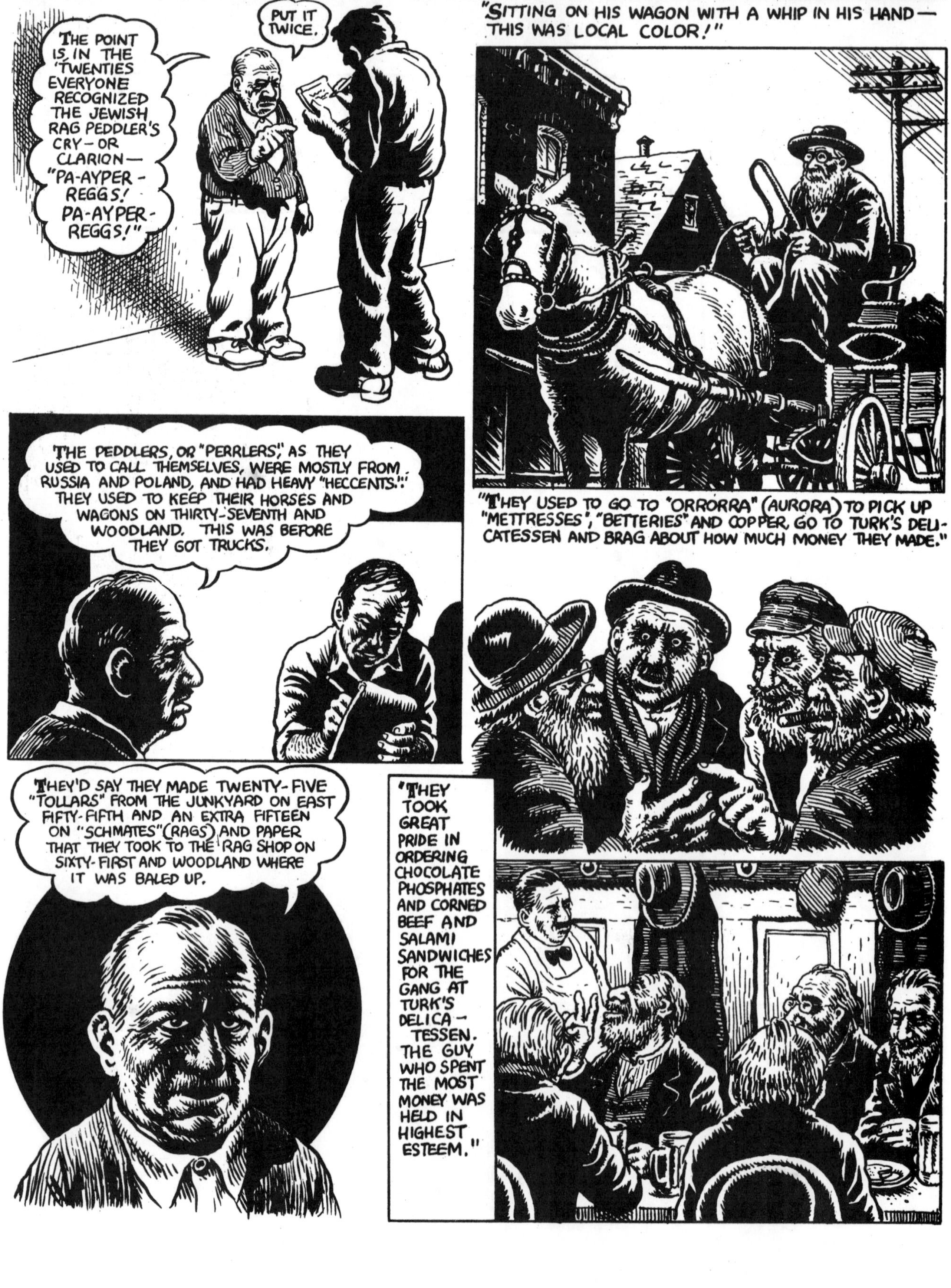
THE POINT IS IN THE 'TWENTIES EVERYONE RECOGNIZED THE JEWISH RAG PEDDLER'S CRY—OR CLARION—"PA-AYPER-REGGS! PA-AYPER-REGGS!"
PUT IT TWICE.
"SITTING ON HIS WAGON WITH A WHIP IN HIS HAND—THIS WAS LOCAL COLOR!"
"THEY USED TO GO TO "ORRORRA" (AURORA) TO PICK UP "METTRESSES", "BETTERIES" AND COPPER, GO TO TURK'S DELICATESSEN AND BRAG ABOUT HOW MUCH MONEY THEY MADE."
THE PEDDLERS, OR "PERRLERS," AS THEY USED TO CALL THEMSELVES, WERE MOSTLY FROM RUSSIA AND POLAND, AND HAD HEAVY "HECCENTS." THEY USED TO KEEP THEIR HORSES AND WAGONS ON THIRTY-SEVENTH AND WOODLAND. THIS WAS BEFORE THEY GOT TRUCKS.
THEY'D SAY THEY MADE TWENTY-FIVE "TOLLARS" FROM THE JUNKYARD ON EAST FIFTY-FIFTH AND AN EXTRA FIFTEEN ON "SCHMATES" (RAGS) AND PAPER THAT THEY TOOK TO THE RAG SHOP ON SIXTY-FIRST AND WOODLAND WHERE IT WAS BALED UP.
"THEY TOOK GREAT PRIDE IN ORDERING CHOCOLATE PHOSPHATES AND CORNED BEEF AND SALAMI SANDWICHES FOR THE GANG AT TURK'S DELICA-TESSEN. THE GUY WHO SPENT THE MOST MONEY WAS HELD IN HIGHEST ESTEEM."

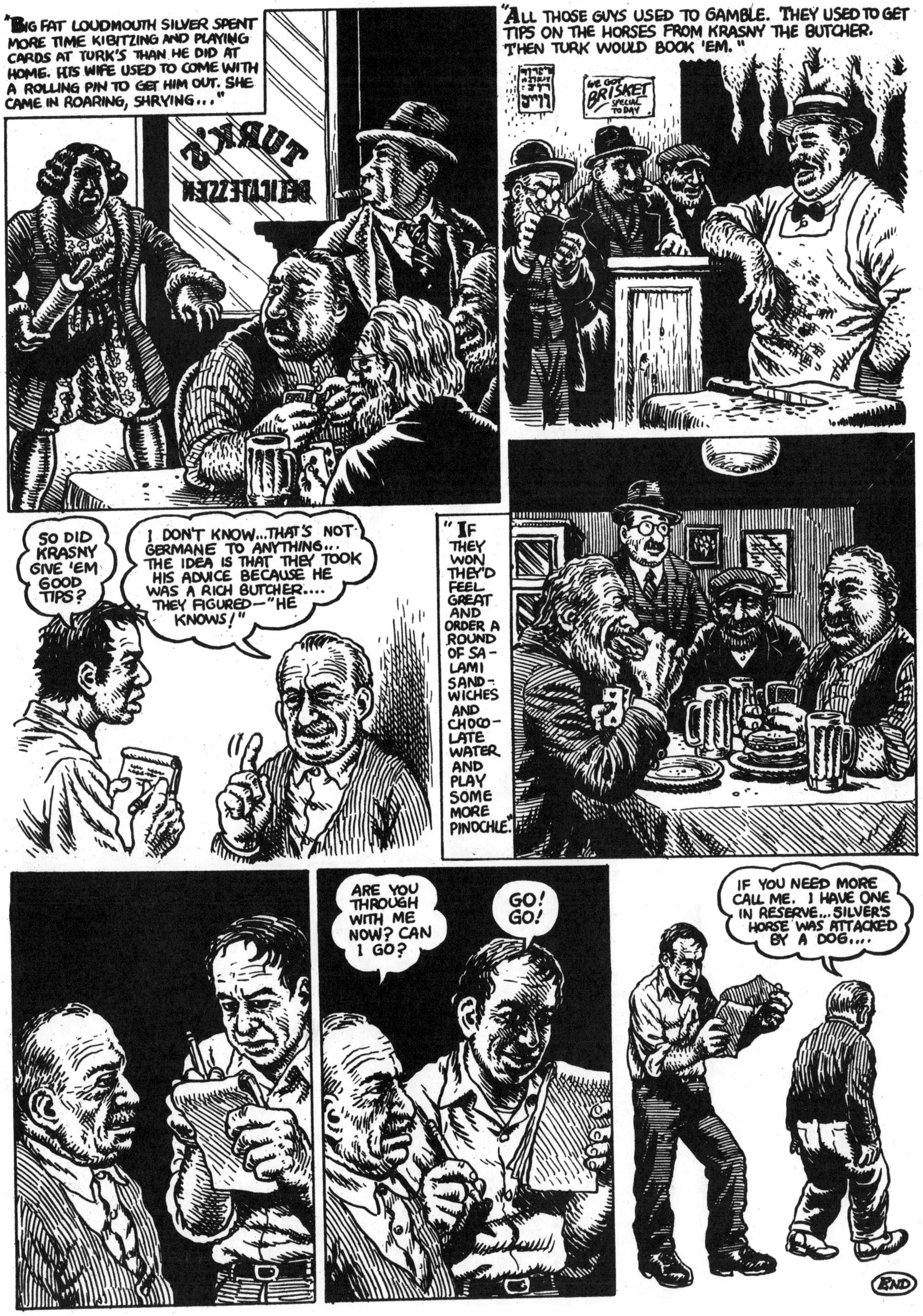
"BIG FAT LOUDMOUTH SILVER SPENT MORE TIME KIBITZING AND PLAYING CARDS AT TURK'S THAN HE DID AT HOME. HIS WIFE USED TO COME WITH A ROLLING PIN TO GET HIM OUT. SHE CAME IN ROARING, SHRYING..."
TURK'S DELICATESSEN
"ALL THOSE GUYS USED TO GAMBLE. THEY USED TO GET TIPS ON THE HORSES FROM KRASNY THE BUTCHER. THEN TURK WOULD BOOK 'EM."
WE GOT BRISKET SPECIAL TODAY
SO DID KRASNY GIVE 'EM GOOD TIPS?
I DON'T KNOW... THAT'S NOT GERMANE TO ANYTHING... THE IDEA IS THAT THEY TOOK HIS ADVICE BECAUSE HE WAS A RICH BUTCHER.... THEY FIGURED—"HE KNOWS!"
"IF THEY WON THEY'D FEEL GREAT AND ORDER A ROUND OF SALAMI SANDWICHES AND CHOCOLATE WATER AND PLAY SOME MORE PINOCHLE."
ARE YOU THROUGH WITH ME NOW? CAN I GO?
GO! GO!
IF YOU NEED MORE CALL ME. I HAVE ONE IN RESERVE... SILVER'S HORSE WAS ATTACKED BY A DOG....
END

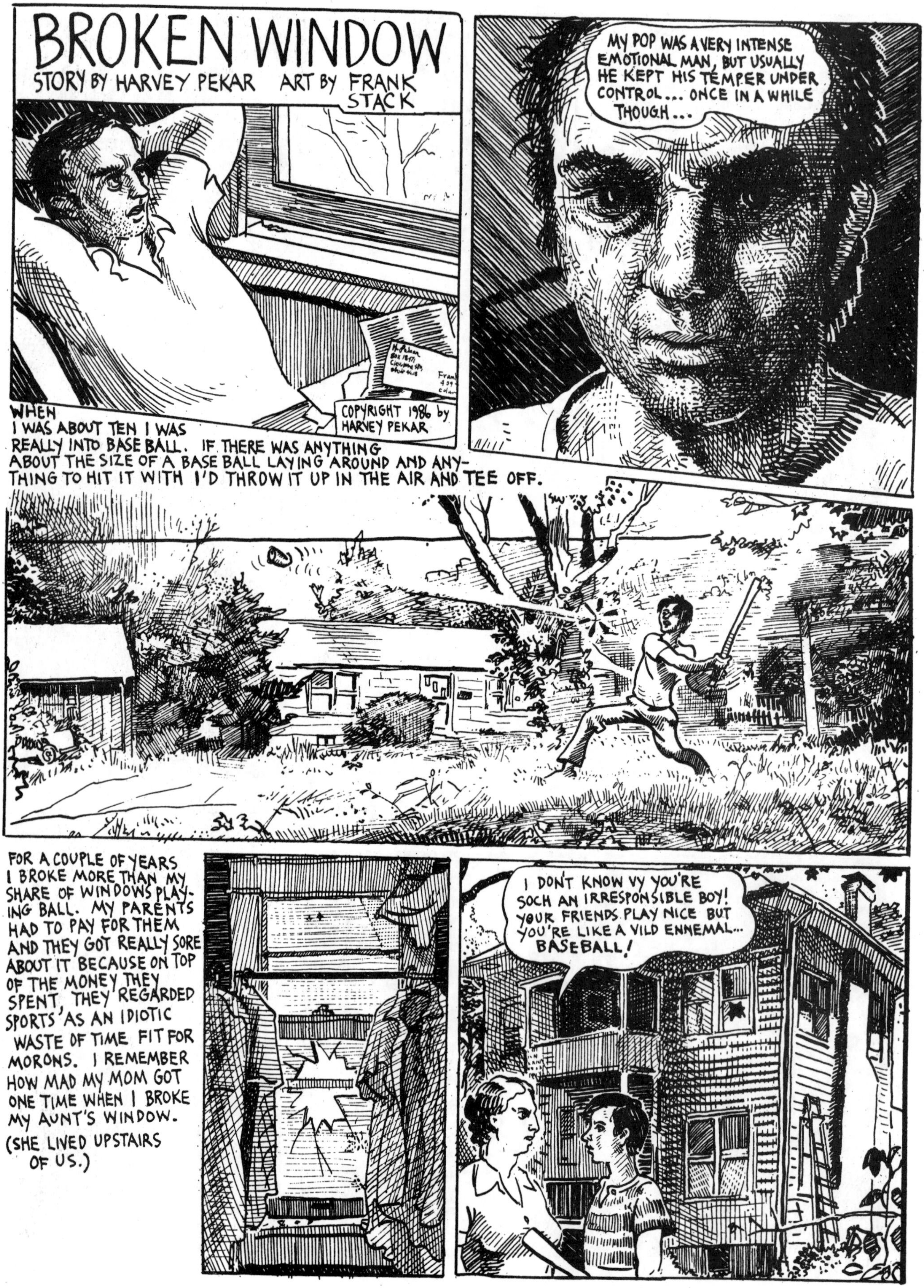
BROKEN WINDOW
STORY BY HARVEY PEKAR ART BY FRANK STACK
COPYRIGHT 1986 by HARVEY PEKAR
MY POP WAS A VERY INTENSE EMOTIONAL MAN, BUT USUALLY HE KEPT HIS TEMPER UNDER CONTROL... ONCE IN A WHILE THOUGH...
WHEN I WAS ABOUT TEN I WAS REALLY INTO BASE BALL. IF THERE WAS ANYTHING ABOUT THE SIZE OF A BASE BALL LAYING AROUND AND ANYTHING TO HIT IT WITH I'D THROW IT UP IN THE AIR AND TEE OFF.
FOR A COUPLE OF YEARS I BROKE MORE THAN MY SHARE OF WINDOWS PLAYING BALL. MY PARENTS HAD TO PAY FOR THEM AND THEY GOT REALLY SORE ABOUT IT BECAUSE ON TOP OF THE MONEY THEY SPENT, THEY REGARDED SPORTS AS AN IDIOTIC WASTE OF TIME FIT FOR MORONS. I REMEMBER HOW MAD MY MOM GOT ONE TIME WHEN I BROKE MY AUNT'S WINDOW.
(SHE LIVED UPSTAIRS OF US.)
I DON'T KNOW VY YOU'RE SOCH AN IRRESPONSIBLE BOY! YOUR FRIENDS PLAY NICE BUT YOU'RE LIKE A VILD ENNEMAL... BASEBALL!

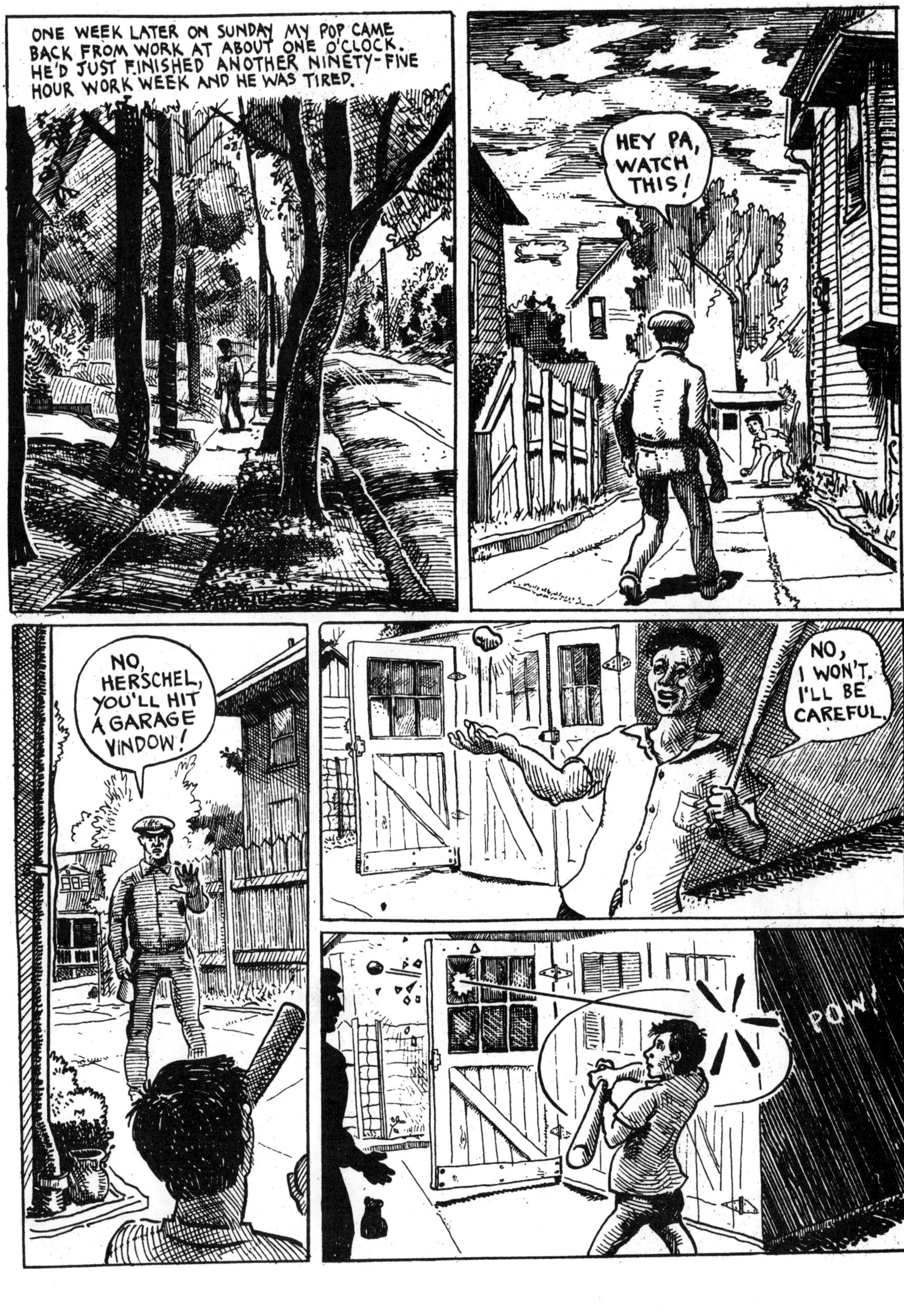
ONE WEEK LATER ON SUNDAY MY POP CAME BACK FROM WORK AT ABOUT ONE O'CLOCK. HE'D JUST FINISHED ANOTHER NINETY-FIVE HOUR WORK WEEK AND HE WAS TIRED.
HEY PA, WATCH THIS!
NO, HERSCHEL, YOU'LL HIT A GARAGE VINDOW!
NO, I WON'T. I'LL BE CAREFUL.
POW!

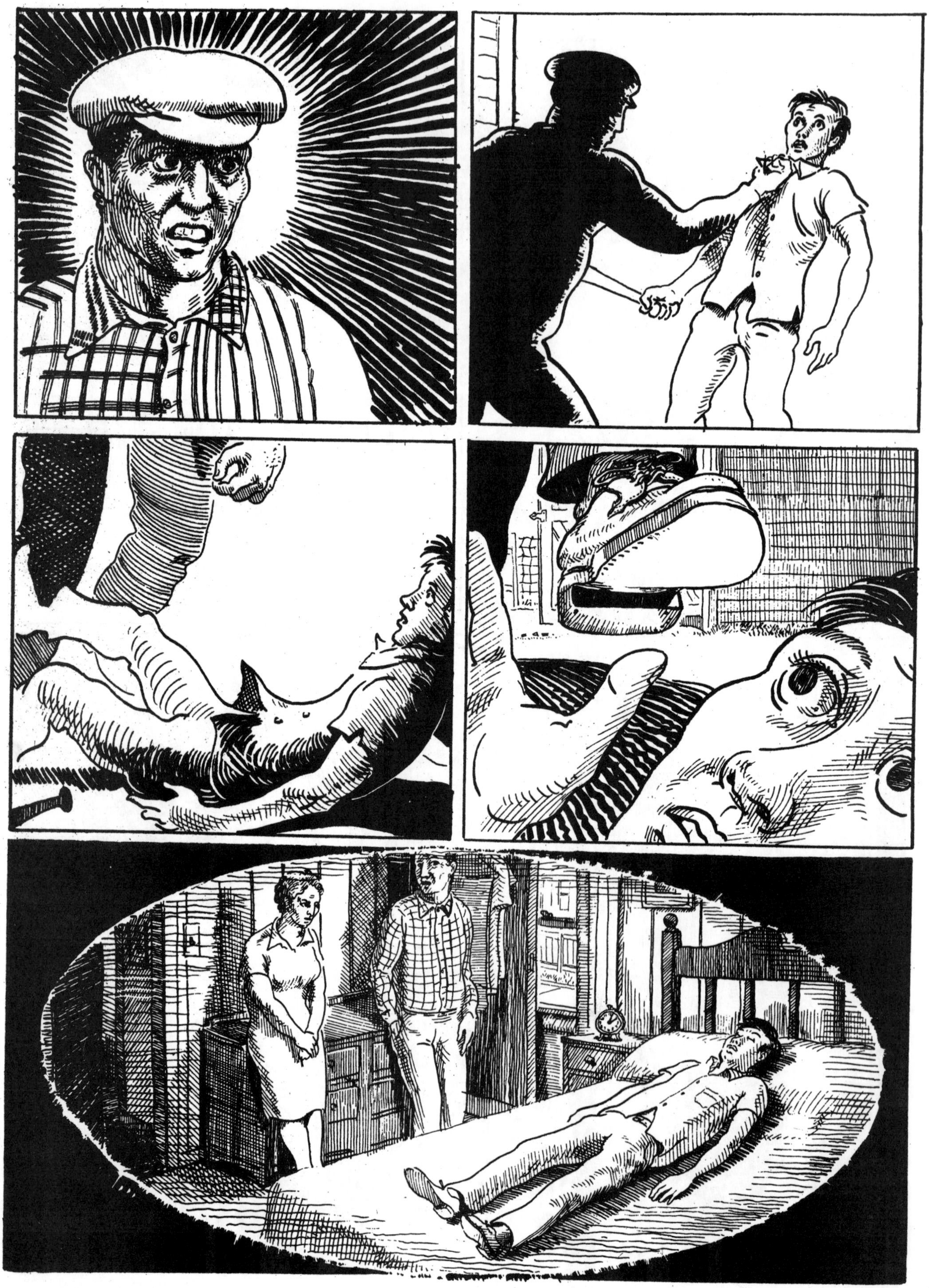

NO TIME SEEMS TO HAVE PASSED.

HOW DID I GET HERE?

I LOOK AT THE CLOCK

TWO O'CLOCK? I THOUGHT IT WAS ONE!

CAN I GO IN THE FRONT ROOM AND LISTEN TO THE INDIANS GAME? IT'S STARTED ALREADY.

YEH, SURE, HERSCHEL.

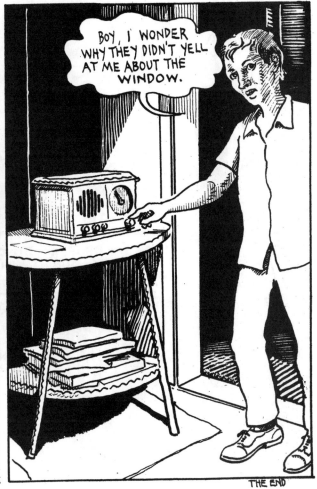

BOY, I WONDER WHY THEY DIDN'T YELL AT ME ABOUT THE WINDOW.

THE END

HYSTERIA

STORY BY: HARVEY PEKAR
ART BY: VAL MAYERIK & JAMES SHERMAN

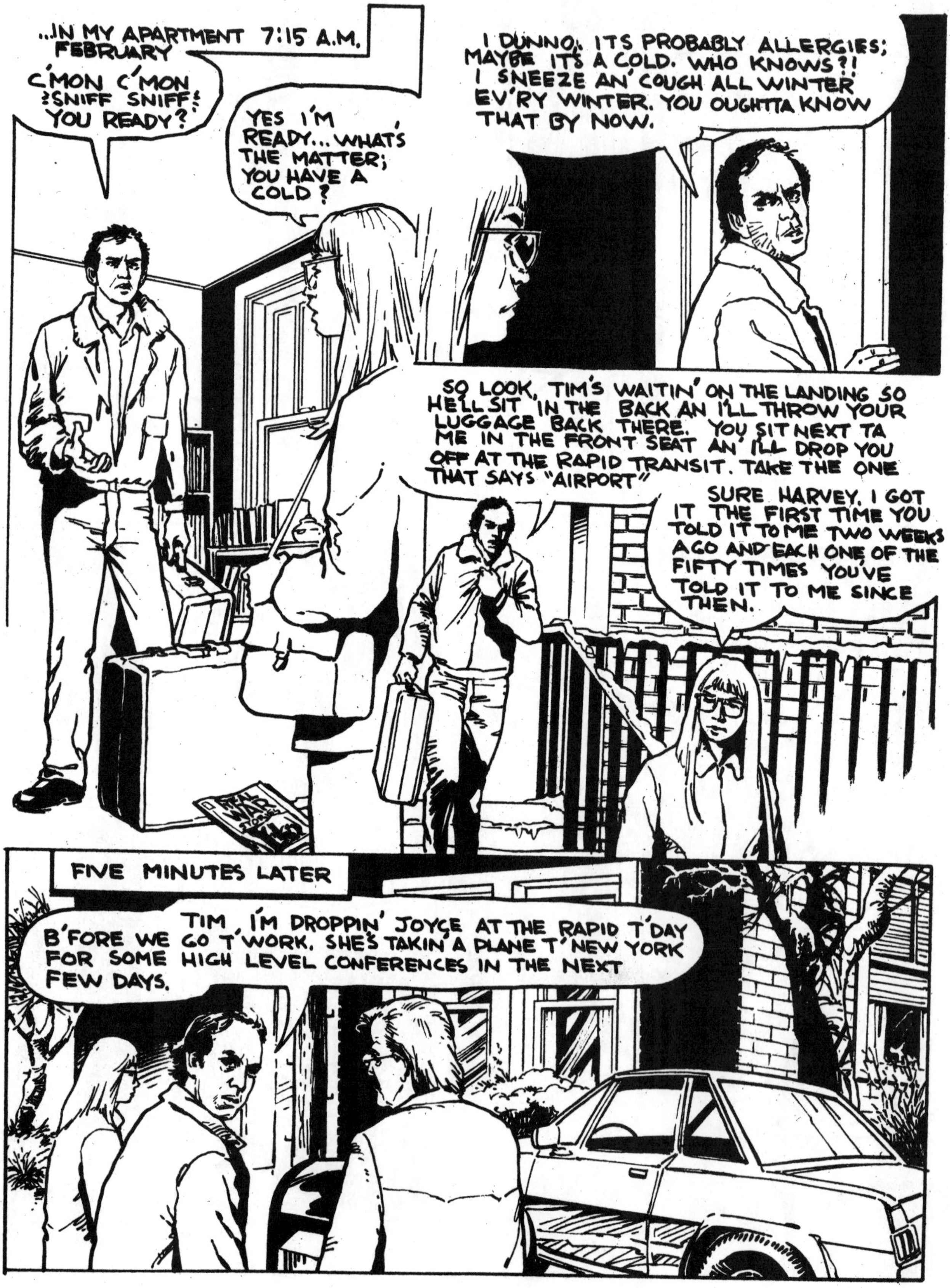
...IN MY APARTMENT 7:15 A.M. FEBRUARY
C'MON C'MON ≈SNIFF SNIFF≈ YOU READY?
YES I'M READY... WHAT'S THE MATTER; YOU HAVE A COLD?
I DUNNO. ITS PROBABLY ALLERGIES; MAYBE ITS A COLD. WHO KNOWS?! I SNEEZE AN' COUGH ALL WINTER EV'RY WINTER. YOU OUGHTTA KNOW THAT BY NOW.
SO LOOK, TIM'S WAITIN' ON THE LANDING SO HE'LL SIT IN THE BACK AN I'LL THROW YOUR LUGGAGE BACK THERE. YOU SIT NEXT TA ME IN THE FRONT SEAT AN' I'LL DROP YOU OFF AT THE RAPID TRANSIT. TAKE THE ONE THAT SAYS "AIRPORT"
SURE HARVEY, I GOT IT THE FIRST TIME YOU TOLD IT TO ME TWO WEEKS AGO AND EACH ONE OF THE FIFTY TIMES YOU'VE TOLD IT TO ME SINCE THEN.
FIVE MINUTES LATER
TIM, I'M DROPPIN' JOYCE AT THE RAPID T'DAY B'FORE WE GO T'WORK. SHE'S TAKIN' A PLANE T' NEW YORK FOR SOME HIGH LEVEL CONFERENCES IN THE NEXT FEW DAYS.

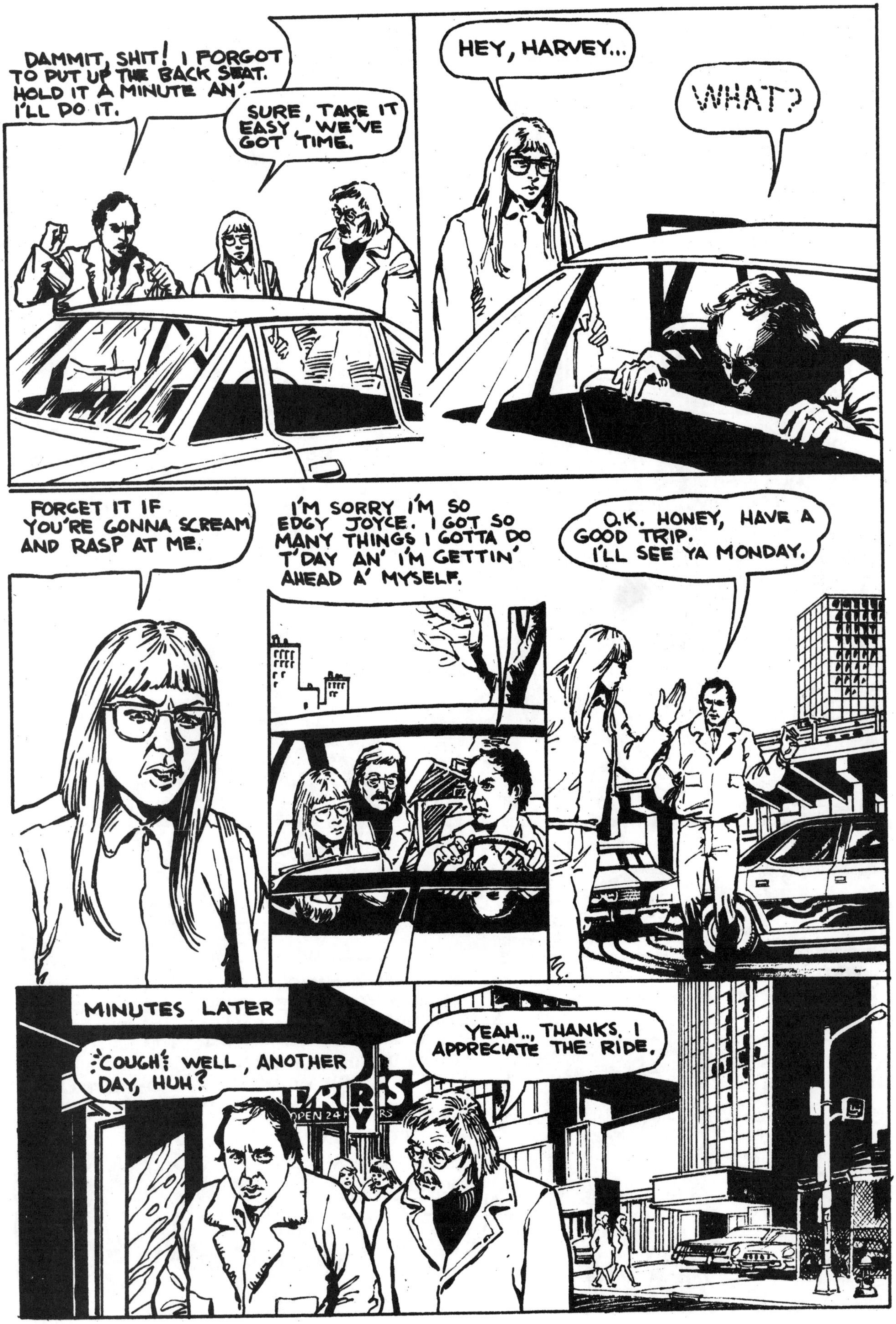
DAMMIT, SHIT! I FORGOT TO PUT UP THE BACK SEAT. HOLD IT A MINUTE AN' I'LL DO IT.
SURE, TAKE IT EASY, WE'VE GOT TIME.
HEY, HARVEY...
WHAT?
FORGET IT IF YOU'RE GONNA SCREAM AND RASP AT ME.
I'M SORRY I'M SO EDGY JOYCE. I GOT SO MANY THINGS I GOTTA DO T'DAY AN' I'M GETTIN' AHEAD A' MYSELF.
O.K. HONEY, HAVE A GOOD TRIP. I'LL SEE YA MONDAY.
MINUTES LATER
COUGH WELL, ANOTHER DAY, HUH?
YEAH.., THANKS. I APPRECIATE THE RIDE.
OPEN 24

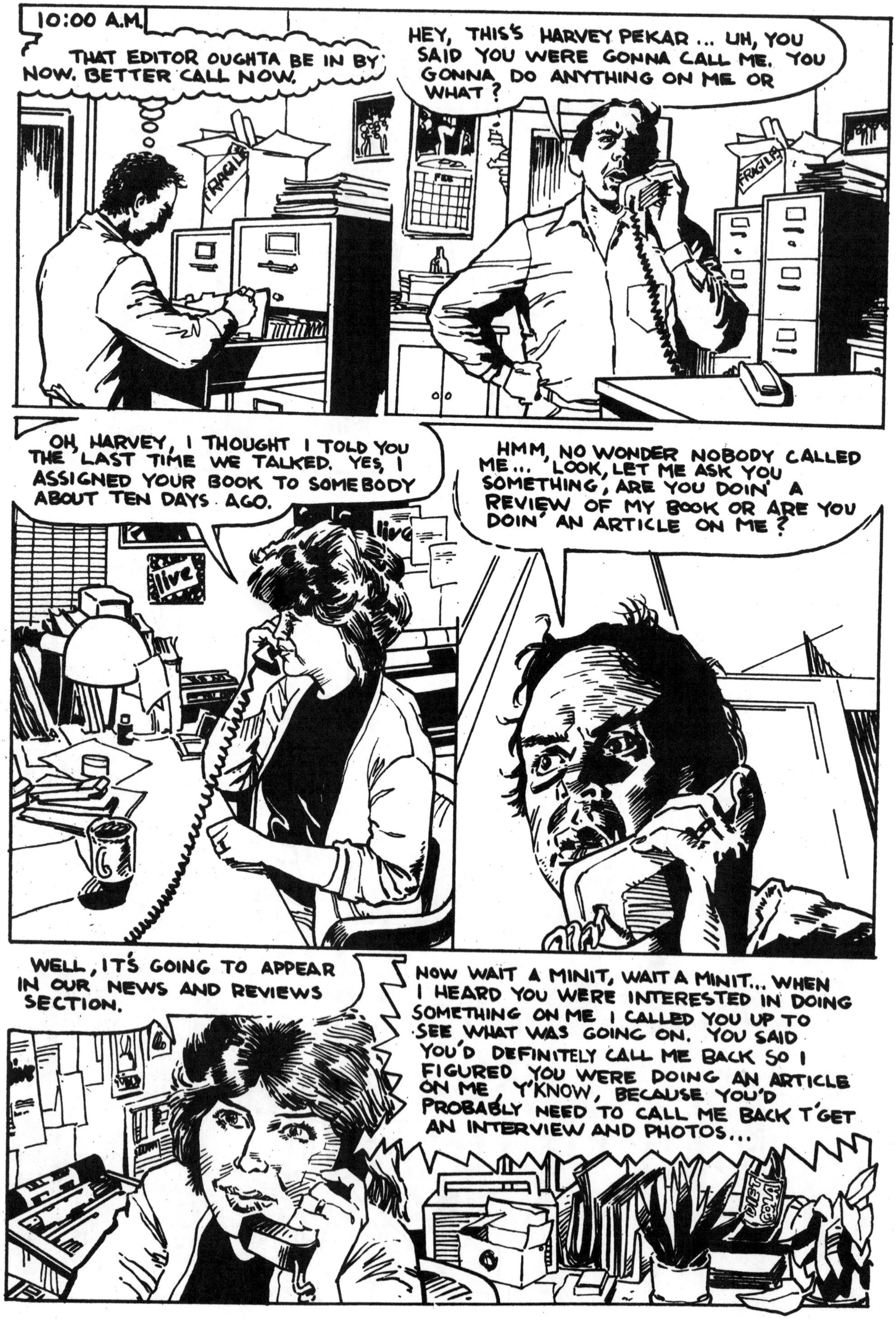
10:00 A.M.
THAT EDITOR OUGHTA BE IN BY NOW. BETTER CALL NOW.
HEY, THIS'S HARVEY PEKAR ... UH, YOU SAID YOU WERE GONNA CALL ME. YOU GONNA DO ANYTHING ON ME OR WHAT?
FRAGILE
OH, HARVEY, I THOUGHT I TOLD YOU THE LAST TIME WE TALKED. YES, I ASSIGNED YOUR BOOK TO SOMEBODY ABOUT TEN DAYS AGO.
live
HMM, NO WONDER NOBODY CALLED ME... LOOK, LET ME ASK YOU SOMETHING, ARE YOU DOIN' A REVIEW OF MY BOOK OR ARE YOU DOIN' AN ARTICLE ON ME?
WELL, IT'S GOING TO APPEAR IN OUR NEWS AND REVIEWS SECTION.
NOW WAIT A MINIT, WAIT A MINIT... WHEN I HEARD YOU WERE INTERESTED IN DOING SOMETHING ON ME I CALLED YOU UP TO SEE WHAT WAS GOING ON. YOU SAID YOU'D DEFINITELY CALL ME BACK SO I FIGURED YOU WERE DOING AN ARTICLE ON ME, Y'KNOW, BECAUSE YOU'D PROBABLY NEED TO CALL ME BACK T'GET AN INTERVIEW AND PHOTOS...
DIET COLA

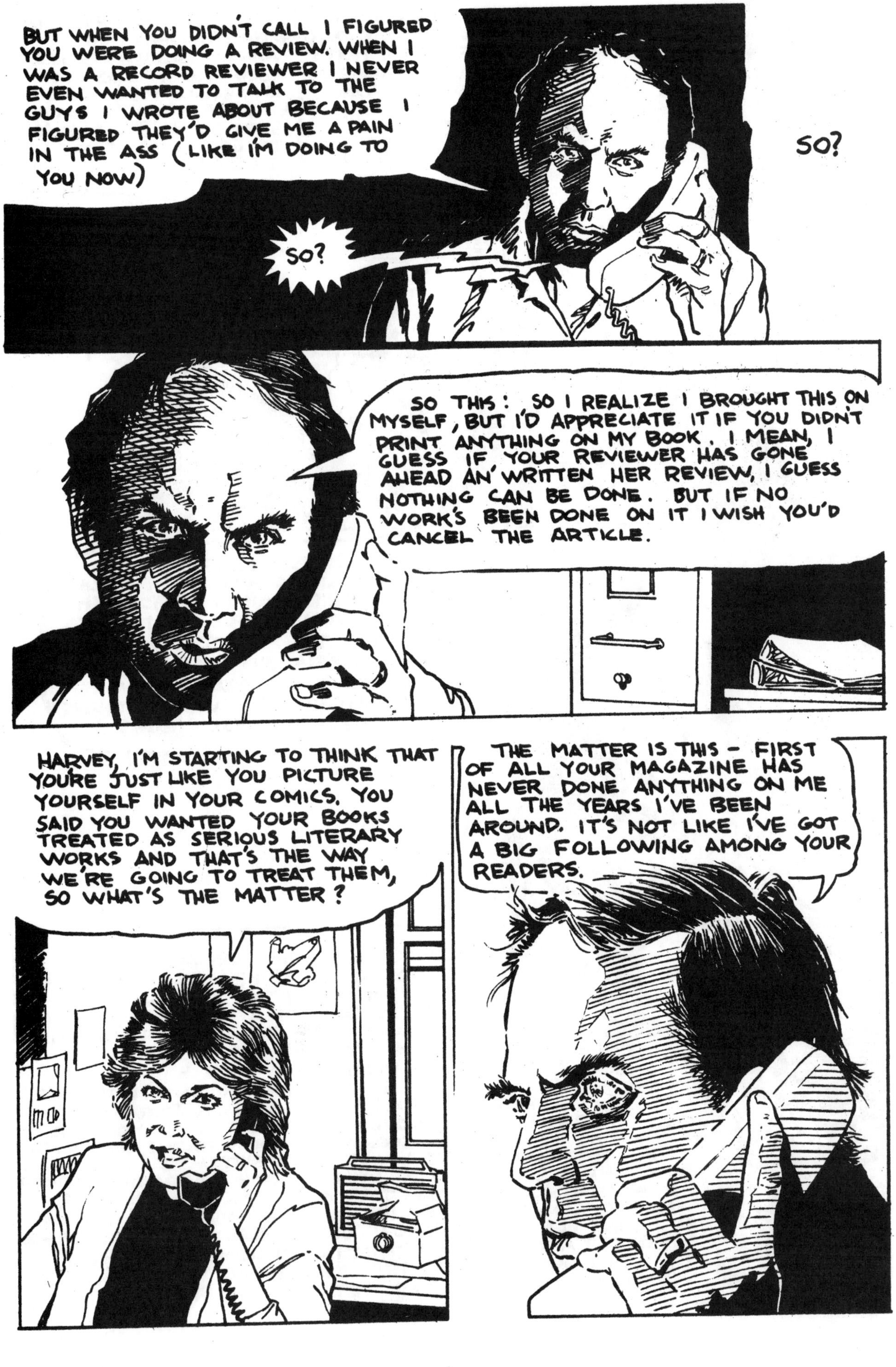
BUT WHEN YOU DIDN'T CALL I FIGURED YOU WERE DOING A REVIEW. WHEN I WAS A RECORD REVIEWER I NEVER EVEN WANTED TO TALK TO THE GUYS I WROTE ABOUT BECAUSE I FIGURED THEY'D GIVE ME A PAIN IN THE ASS (LIKE I'M DOING TO YOU NOW)
SO?
SO?
SO THIS: SO I REALIZE I BROUGHT THIS ON MYSELF, BUT I'D APPRECIATE IT IF YOU DIDN'T PRINT ANYTHING ON MY BOOK. I MEAN, I GUESS IF YOUR REVIEWER HAS GONE AHEAD AN' WRITTEN HER REVIEW, I GUESS NOTHING CAN BE DONE. BUT IF NO WORK'S BEEN DONE ON IT I WISH YOU'D CANCEL THE ARTICLE.
HARVEY, I'M STARTING TO THINK THAT YOU'RE JUST LIKE YOU PICTURE YOURSELF IN YOUR COMICS. YOU SAID YOU WANTED YOUR BOOKS TREATED AS SERIOUS LITERARY WORKS AND THAT'S THE WAY WE'RE GOING TO TREAT THEM, SO WHAT'S THE MATTER?
THE MATTER IS THIS - FIRST OF ALL YOUR MAGAZINE HAS NEVER DONE ANYTHING ON ME ALL THE YEARS I'VE BEEN AROUND. IT'S NOT LIKE I'VE GOT A BIG FOLLOWING AMONG YOUR READERS.

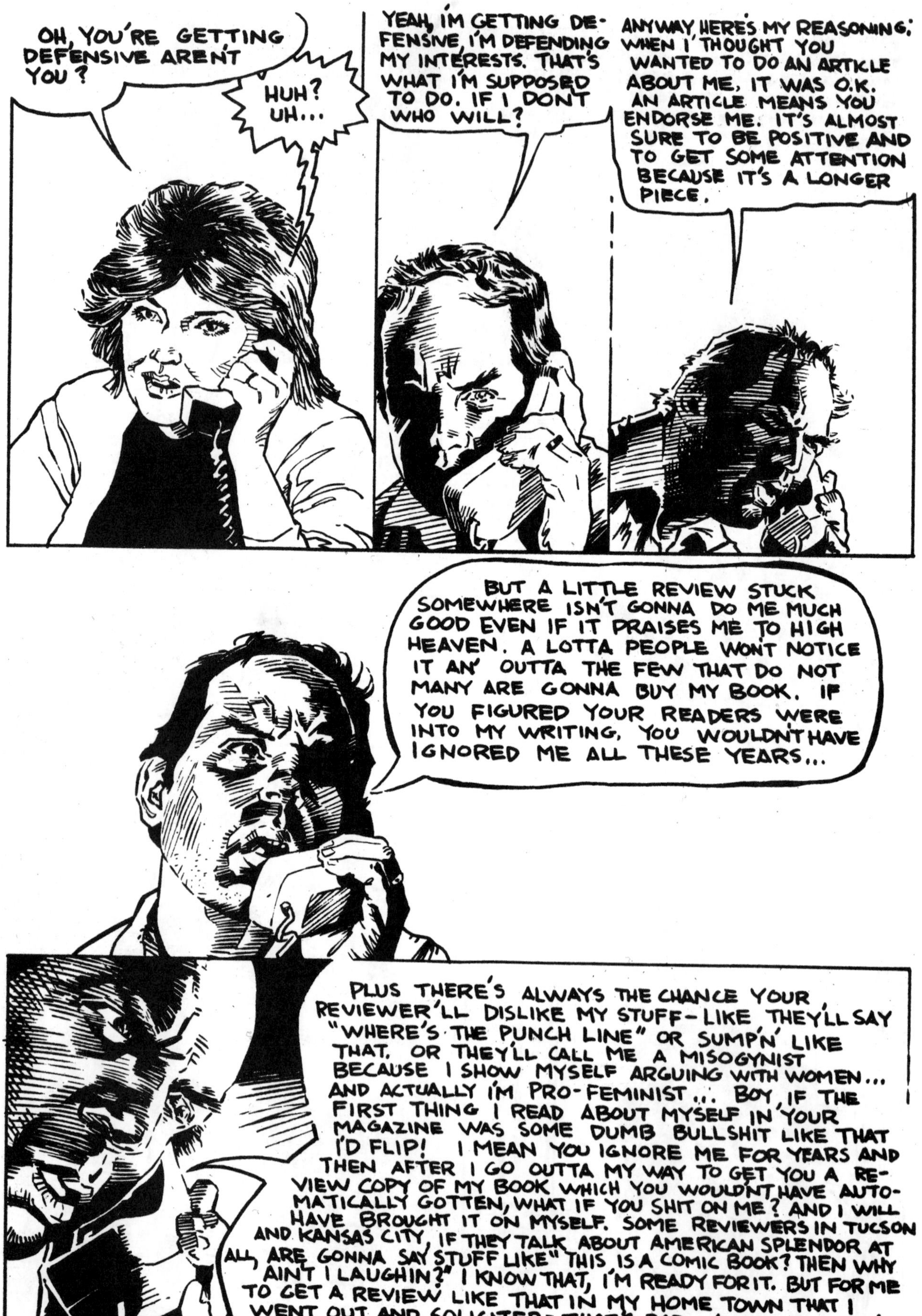
OH, YOU'RE GETTING DEFENSIVE AREN'T YOU ?
HUH? UH...
YEAH, I'M GETTING DEFENSIVE, I'M DEFENDING MY INTERESTS. THAT'S WHAT I'M SUPPOSED TO DO. IF I DON'T WHO WILL?
ANYWAY HERE'S MY REASONING: WHEN I THOUGHT YOU WANTED TO DO AN ARTICLE ABOUT ME, IT WAS O.K. AN ARTICLE MEANS YOU ENDORSE ME. IT'S ALMOST SURE TO BE POSITIVE AND TO GET SOME ATTENTION BECAUSE IT'S A LONGER PIECE.
BUT A LITTLE REVIEW STUCK SOMEWHERE ISN'T GONNA DO ME MUCH GOOD EVEN IF IT PRAISES ME TO HIGH HEAVEN. A LOTTA PEOPLE WON'T NOTICE IT AN' OUTTA THE FEW THAT DO NOT MANY ARE GONNA BUY MY BOOK. IF YOU FIGURED YOUR READERS WERE INTO MY WRITING, YOU WOULDN'T HAVE IGNORED ME ALL THESE YEARS...
PLUS THERE'S ALWAYS THE CHANCE YOUR REVIEWER'LL DISLIKE MY STUFF-LIKE THEY'LL SAY "WHERE'S THE PUNCH LINE" OR SUMP'N' LIKE THAT. OR THEY'LL CALL ME A MISOGYNIST BECAUSE I SHOW MYSELF ARGUING WITH WOMEN... AND ACTUALLY I'M PRO-FEMINIST... BOY, IF THE FIRST THING I READ ABOUT MYSELF IN YOUR MAGAZINE WAS SOME DUMB BULLSHIT LIKE THAT I'D FLIP! I MEAN YOU IGNORE ME FOR YEARS AND THEN AFTER I GO OUTTA MY WAY TO GET YOU A REVIEW COPY OF MY BOOK WHICH YOU WOULDN'T HAVE AUTOMATICALLY GOTTEN, WHAT IF YOU SHIT ON ME? AND I WILL HAVE BROUGHT IT ON MYSELF. SOME REVIEWERS IN TUCSON AND KANSAS CITY, IF THEY TALK ABOUT AMERICAN SPLENDOR AT ALL, ARE GONNA SAY STUFF LIKE "THIS IS A COMIC BOOK? THEN WHY AIN'T I LAUGHIN?" I KNOW THAT, I'M READY FOR IT. BUT FOR ME TO GET A REVIEW LIKE THAT IN MY HOME TOWN THAT I WENT OUT AND SOLICITED- THAT'S BAD. I'M JUST ASKIN' YOU TO TRY TO HELP ME GET OUTTA THIS MESS, BUT IF Y'CAN'T, Y'CAN'T.

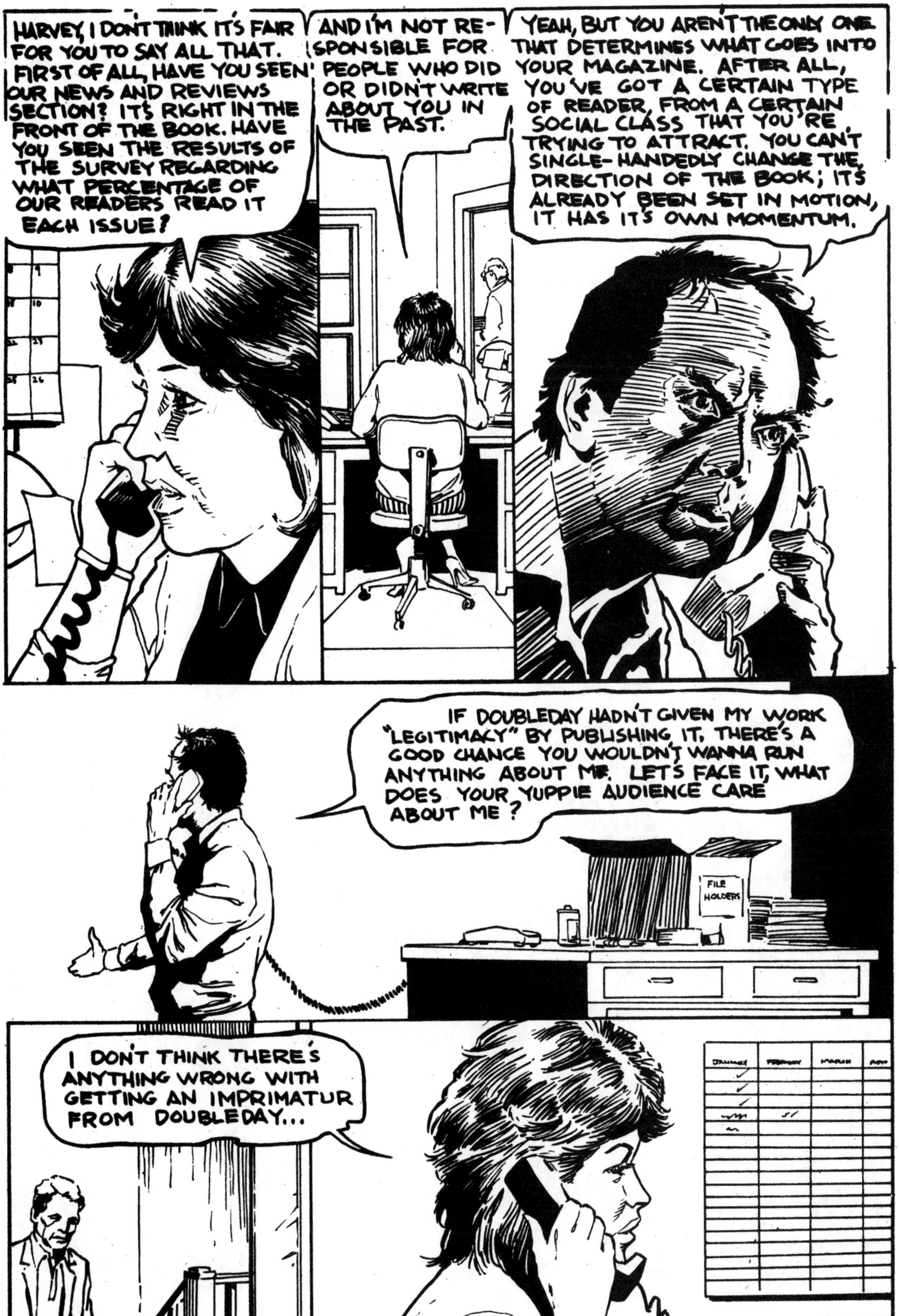
HARVEY, I DON'T THINK IT'S FAIR FOR YOU TO SAY ALL THAT. FIRST OF ALL, HAVE YOU SEEN OUR NEWS AND REVIEWS SECTION? IT'S RIGHT IN THE FRONT OF THE BOOK. HAVE YOU SEEN THE RESULTS OF THE SURVEY REGARDING WHAT PERCENTAGE OF OUR READERS READ IT EACH ISSUE?
AND I'M NOT RESPONSIBLE FOR PEOPLE WHO DID OR DIDN'T WRITE ABOUT YOU IN THE PAST.
YEAH, BUT YOU AREN'T THE ONLY ONE THAT DETERMINES WHAT GOES INTO YOUR MAGAZINE. AFTER ALL, YOU'VE GOT A CERTAIN TYPE OF READER, FROM A CERTAIN SOCIAL CLASS THAT YOU'RE TRYING TO ATTRACT. YOU CAN'T SINGLE-HANDEDLY CHANGE THE DIRECTION OF THE BOOK; IT'S ALREADY BEEN SET IN MOTION, IT HAS IT'S OWN MOMENTUM.
IF DOUBLEDAY HADN'T GIVEN MY WORK "LEGITIMACY" BY PUBLISHING IT, THERE'S A GOOD CHANCE YOU WOULDN'T WANNA RUN ANYTHING ABOUT ME. LET'S FACE IT, WHAT DOES YOUR YUPPIE AUDIENCE CARE ABOUT ME?
FILE HOLDERS
I DON'T THINK THERE'S ANYTHING WRONG WITH GETTING AN IMPRIMATUR FROM DOUBLEDAY...

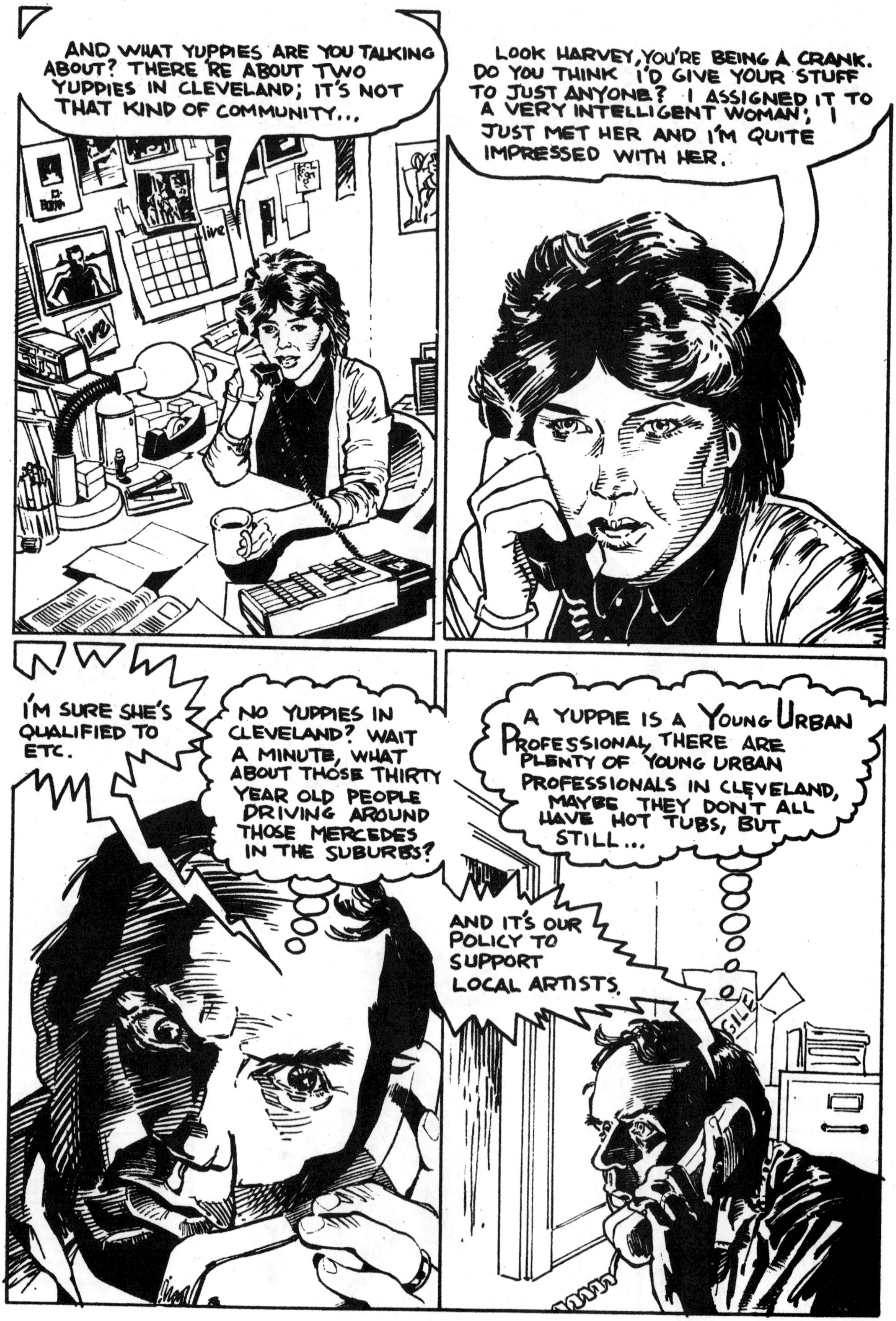
AND WHAT YUPPIES ARE YOU TALKING ABOUT? THERE'RE ABOUT TWO YUPPIES IN CLEVELAND; IT'S NOT THAT KIND OF COMMUNITY...
LOOK HARVEY, YOU'RE BEING A CRANK. DO YOU THINK I'D GIVE YOUR STUFF TO JUST ANYONE? I ASSIGNED IT TO A VERY INTELLIGENT WOMAN; I JUST MET HER AND I'M QUITE IMPRESSED WITH HER.
I'M SURE SHE'S QUALIFIED TO ETC.
NO YUPPIES IN CLEVELAND? WAIT A MINUTE, WHAT ABOUT THOSE THIRTY YEAR OLD PEOPLE DRIVING AROUND THOSE MERCEDES IN THE SUBURBS?
A YUPPIE IS A YOUNG URBAN PROFESSIONAL, THERE ARE PLENTY OF YOUNG URBAN PROFESSIONALS IN CLEVELAND, MAYBE THEY DON'T ALL HAVE HOT TUBS, BUT STILL...
AND IT'S OUR POLICY TO SUPPORT LOCAL ARTISTS.

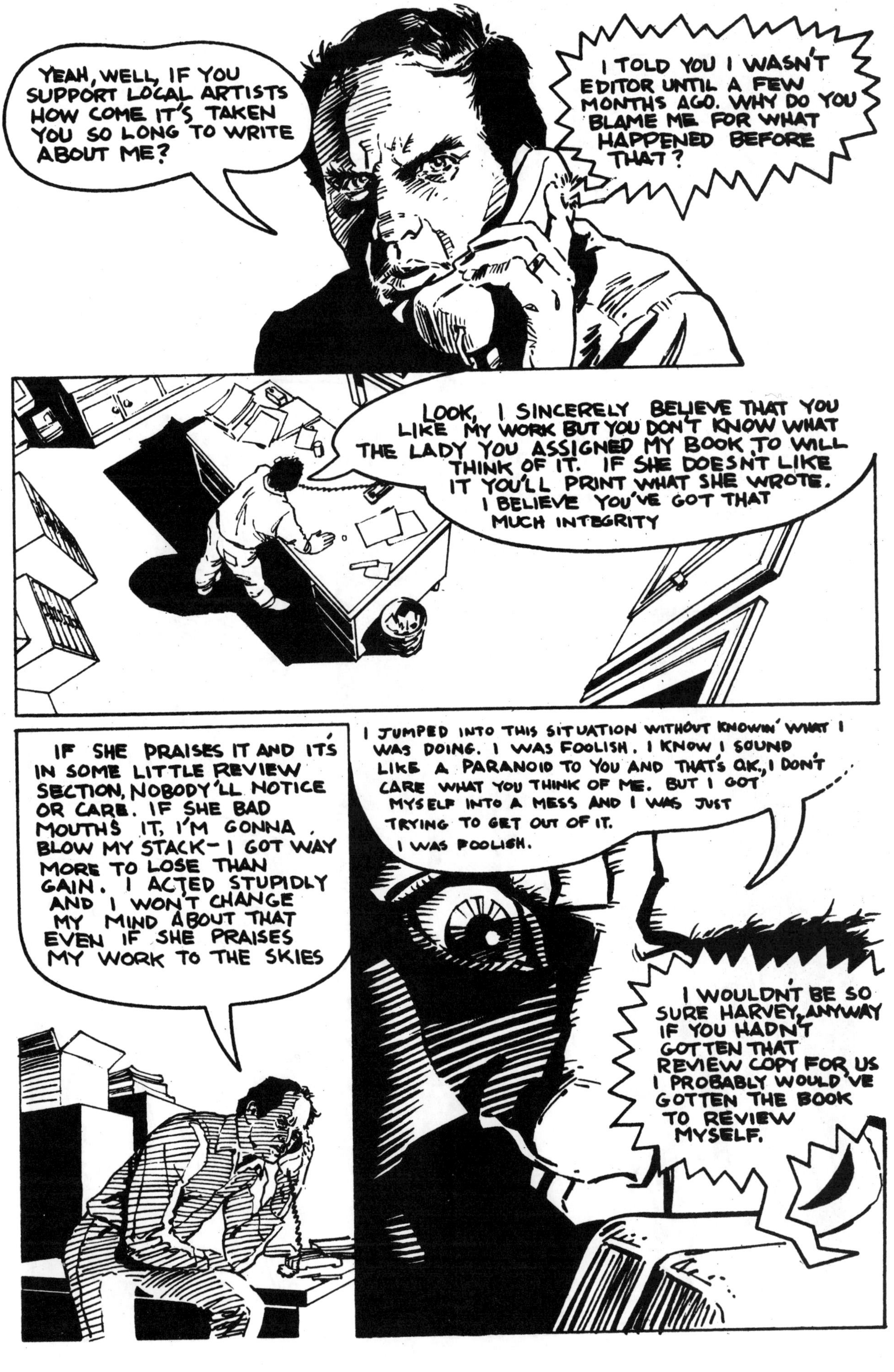
YEAH, WELL, IF YOU SUPPORT LOCAL ARTISTS HOW COME IT'S TAKEN YOU SO LONG TO WRITE ABOUT ME?
I TOLD YOU I WASN'T EDITOR UNTIL A FEW MONTHS AGO. WHY DO YOU BLAME ME FOR WHAT HAPPENED BEFORE THAT?
LOOK, I SINCERELY BELIEVE THAT YOU LIKE MY WORK BUT YOU DON'T KNOW WHAT THE LADY YOU ASSIGNED MY BOOK TO WILL THINK OF IT. IF SHE DOESN'T LIKE IT YOU'LL PRINT WHAT SHE WROTE. I BELIEVE YOU'VE GOT THAT MUCH INTEGRITY
IF SHE PRAISES IT AND ITS IN SOME LITTLE REVIEW SECTION, NOBODY'LL NOTICE OR CARE. IF SHE BAD MOUTHS IT, I'M GONNA BLOW MY STACK- I GOT WAY MORE TO LOSE THAN GAIN. I ACTED STUPIDLY AND I WON'T CHANGE MY MIND ABOUT THAT EVEN IF SHE PRAISES MY WORK TO THE SKIES
I JUMPED INTO THIS SITUATION WITHOUT KNOWIN' WHAT I WAS DOING. I WAS FOOLISH. I KNOW I SOUND LIKE A PARANOID TO YOU AND THAT'S O.K., I DON'T CARE WHAT YOU THINK OF ME. BUT I GOT MYSELF INTO A MESS AND I WAS JUST TRYING TO GET OUT OF IT. I WAS FOOLISH.
I WOULDN'T BE SO SURE HARVEY, ANYWAY IF YOU HADN'T GOTTEN THAT REVIEW COPY FOR US I PROBABLY WOULD'VE GOTTEN THE BOOK TO REVIEW MYSELF.

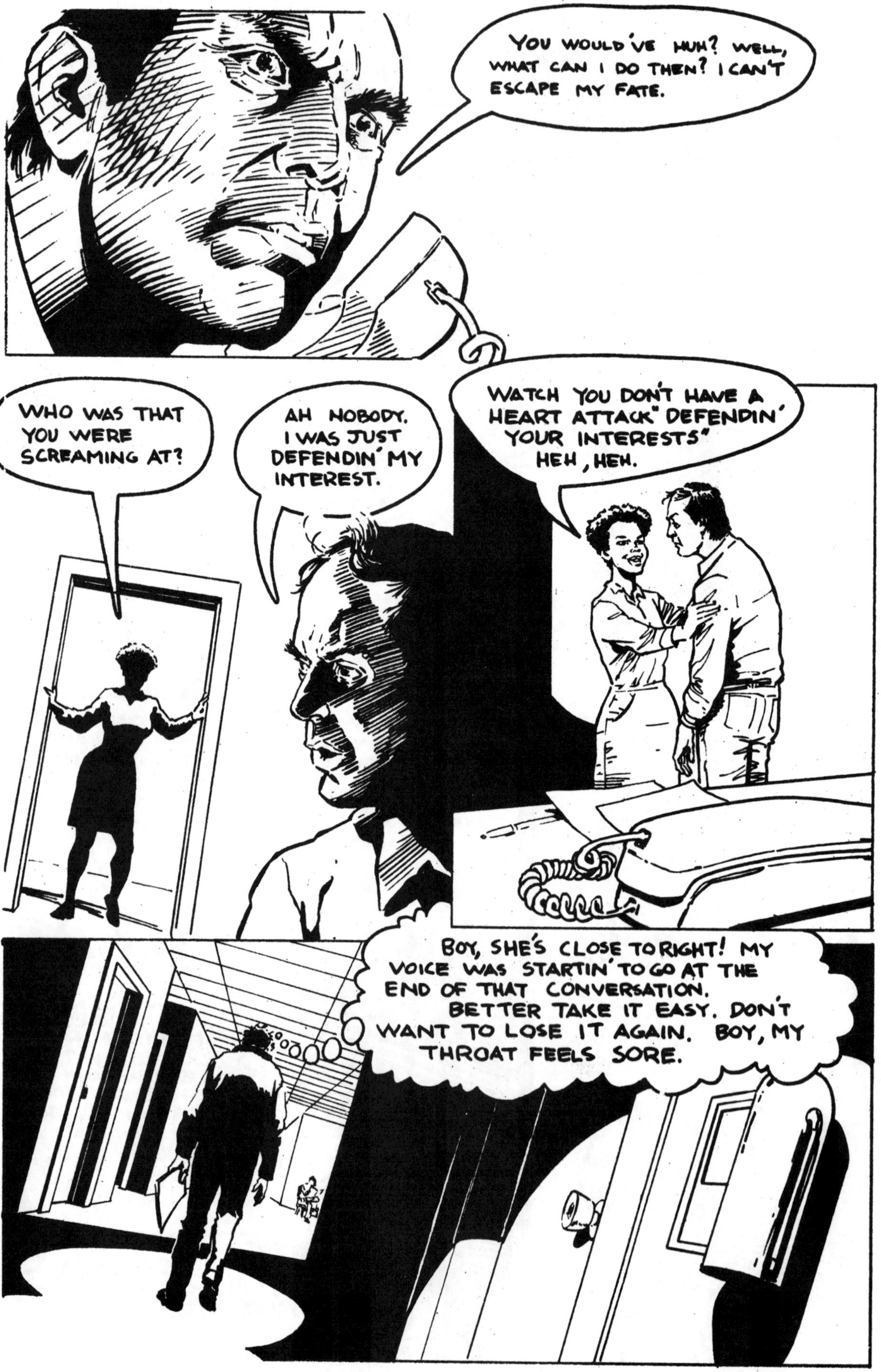
YOU WOULD'VE HUH? WELL, WHAT CAN I DO THEN? I CAN'T ESCAPE MY FATE.
WHO WAS THAT YOU WERE SCREAMING AT?
AH NOBODY. I WAS JUST DEFENDIN' MY INTEREST.
WATCH YOU DON'T HAVE A HEART ATTACK "DEFENDIN' YOUR INTERESTS" HEH, HEH.
BOY, SHE'S CLOSE TO RIGHT! MY VOICE WAS STARTIN' TO GO AT THE END OF THAT CONVERSATION. BETTER TAKE IT EASY. DON'T WANT TO LOSE IT AGAIN. BOY, MY THROAT FEELS SORE.

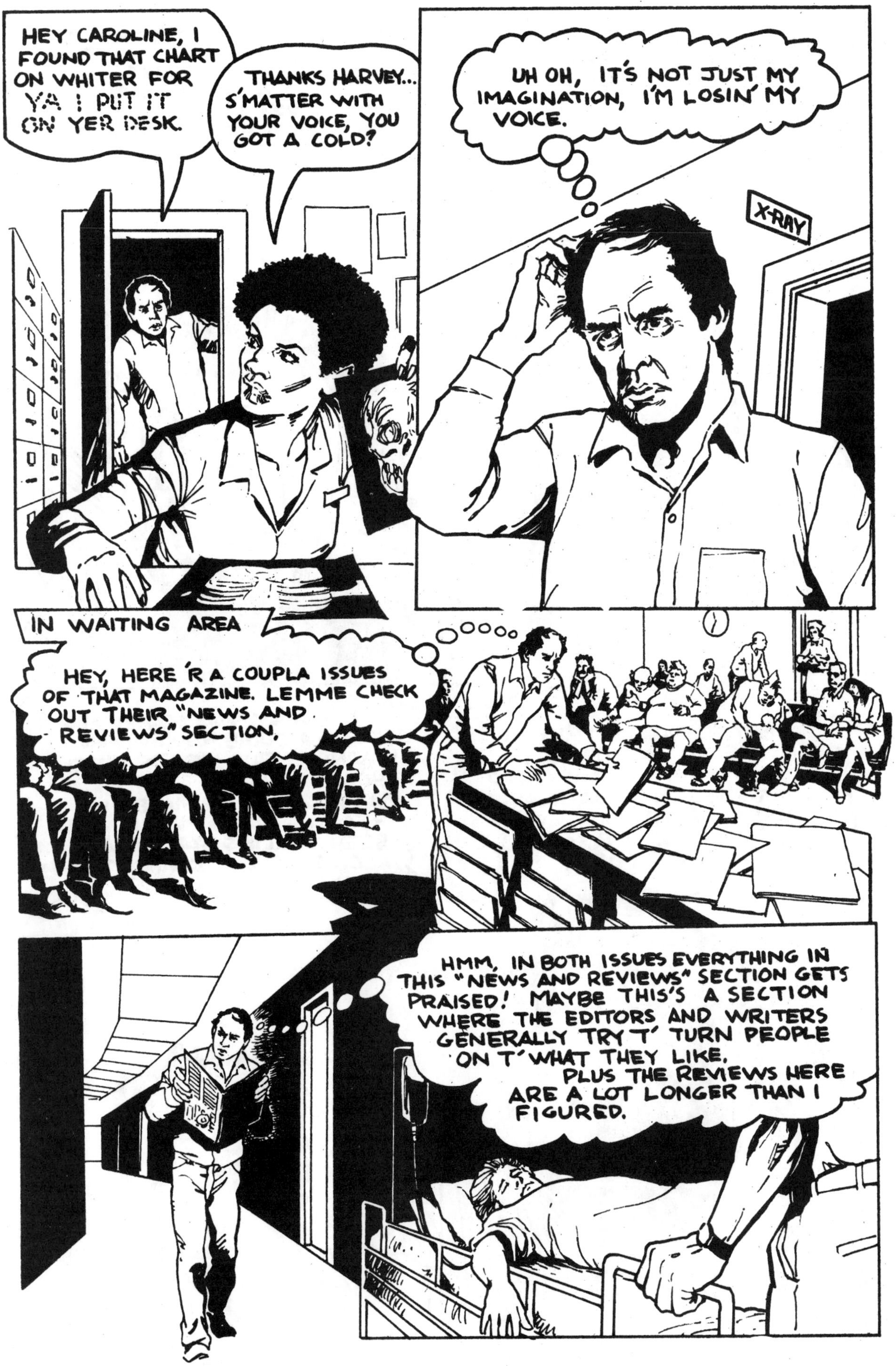
HEY CAROLINE, I FOUND THAT CHART ON WHITER FOR YA I PUT IT ON YER DESK.
THANKS HARVEY... S'MATTER WITH YOUR VOICE, YOU GOT A COLD?
UH OH, IT'S NOT JUST MY IMAGINATION, I'M LOSIN' MY VOICE.
X-RAY
IN WAITING AREA
HEY, HERE 'R A COUPLA ISSUES OF THAT MAGAZINE. LEMME CHECK OUT THEIR "NEWS AND REVIEWS" SECTION.
HMM, IN BOTH ISSUES EVERYTHING IN THIS "NEWS AND REVIEWS" SECTION GETS PRAISED! MAYBE THIS'S A SECTION WHERE THE EDITORS AND WRITERS GENERALLY TRY T' TURN PEOPLE ON T' WHAT THEY LIKE.
PLUS THE REVIEWS HERE ARE A LOT LONGER THAN I FIGURED.

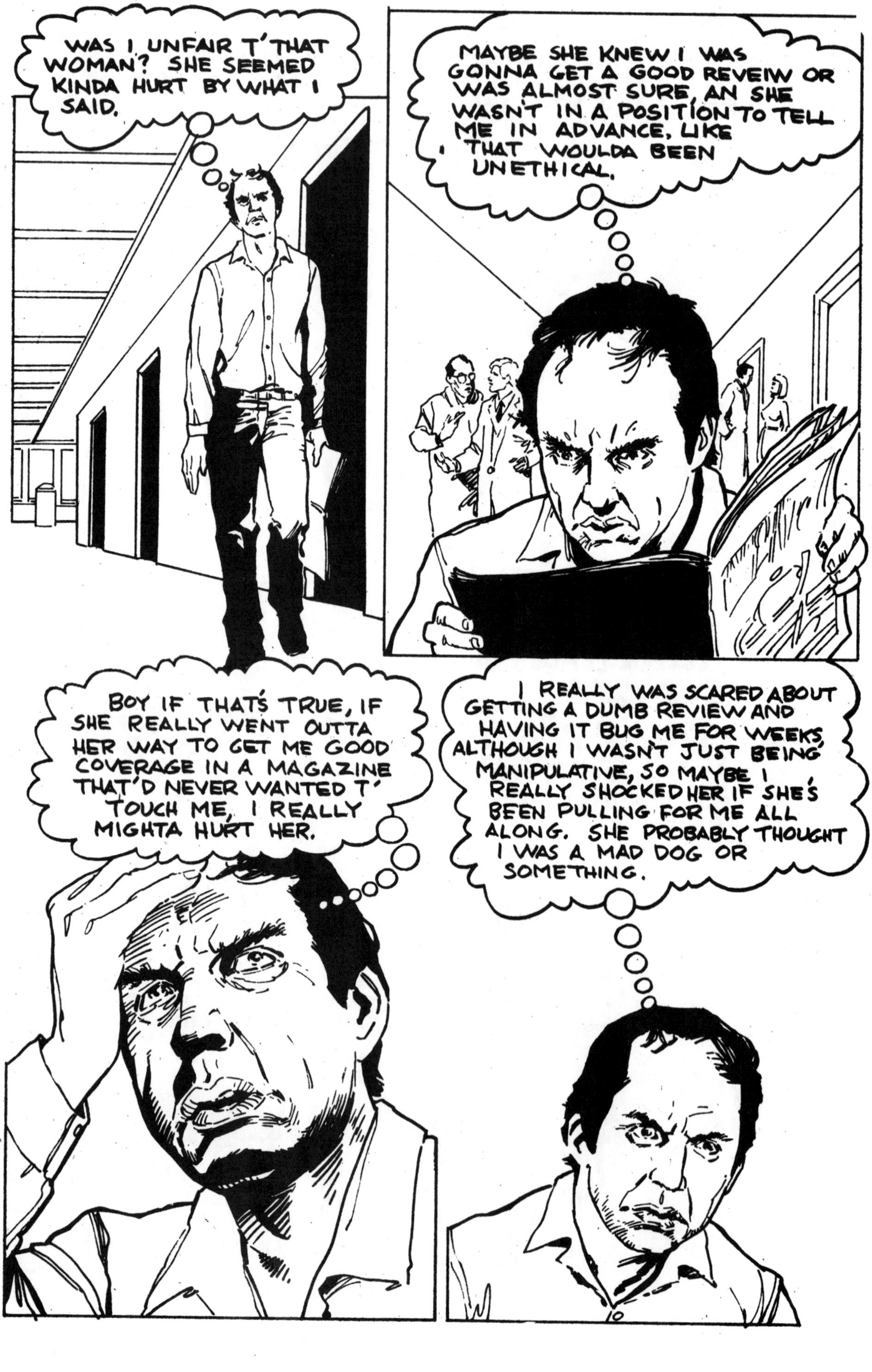
WAS I UNFAIR T'THAT WOMAN? SHE SEEMED KINDA HURT BY WHAT I SAID.
MAYBE SHE KNEW I WAS GONNA GET A GOOD REVEIW OR WAS ALMOST SURE, AN SHE WASN'T IN A POSITION TO TELL ME IN ADVANCE, LIKE THAT WOULDA BEEN UNETHICAL.
BOY IF THAT'S TRUE, IF SHE REALLY WENT OUTTA HER WAY TO GET ME GOOD COVERAGE IN A MAGAZINE THAT'D NEVER WANTED T' TOUCH ME, I REALLY MIGHTA HURT HER.
I REALLY WAS SCARED ABOUT GETTING A DUMB REVIEW AND HAVING IT BUG ME FOR WEEKS, ALTHOUGH I WASN'T JUST BEING MANIPULATIVE, SO MAYBE I REALLY SHOCKED HER IF SHE'S BEEN PULLING FOR ME ALL ALONG. SHE PROBABLY THOUGHT I WAS A MAD DOG OR SOMETHING.

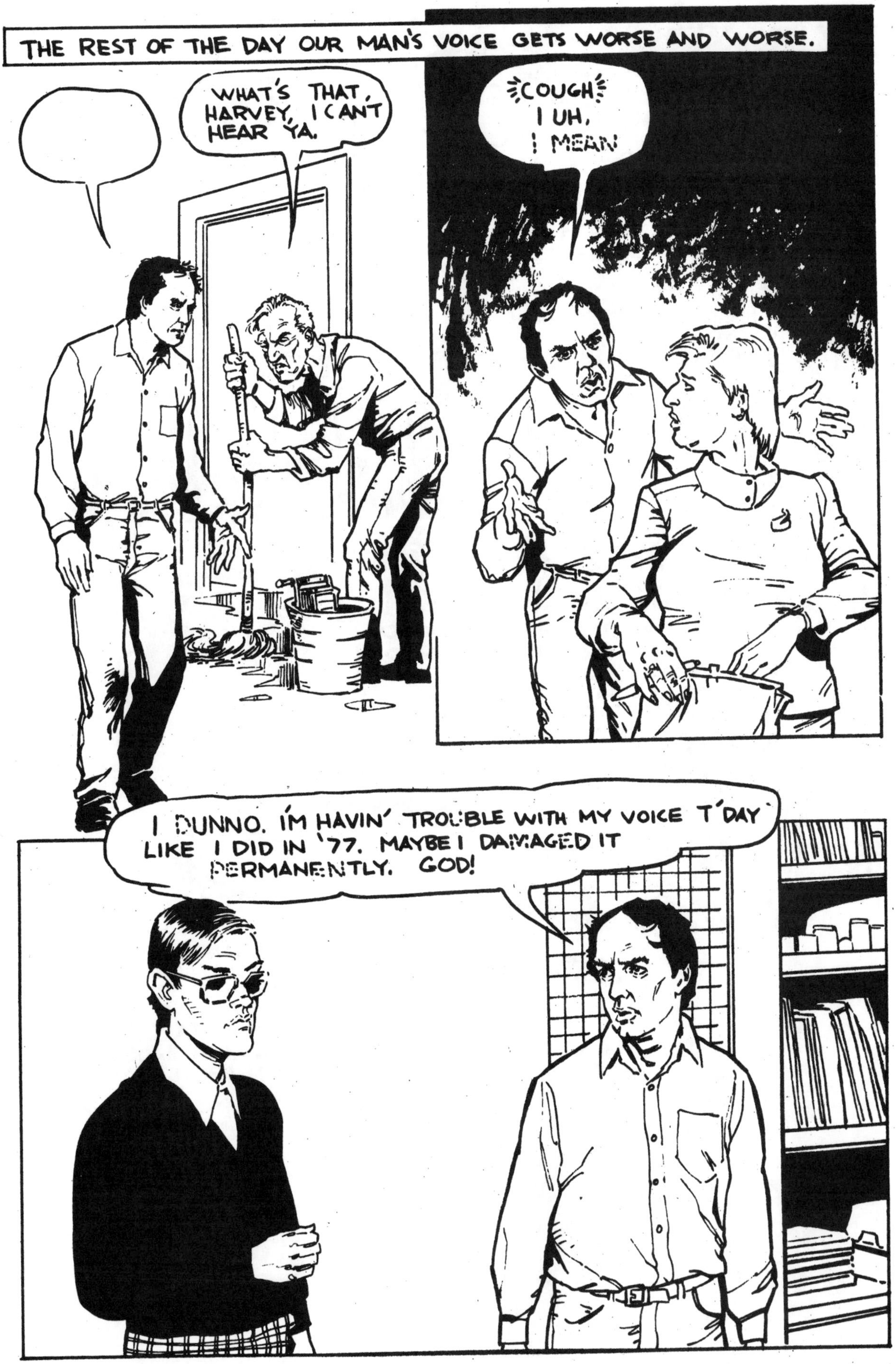
THE REST OF THE DAY OUR MAN'S VOICE GETS WORSE AND WORSE.
WHAT'S THAT, HARVEY, I CAN'T HEAR YA.
COUGH I UH, I MEAN
I DUNNO. I'M HAVIN' TROUBLE WITH MY VOICE T'DAY LIKE I DID IN '77. MAYBE I DAMAGED IT PERMANENTLY. GOD!

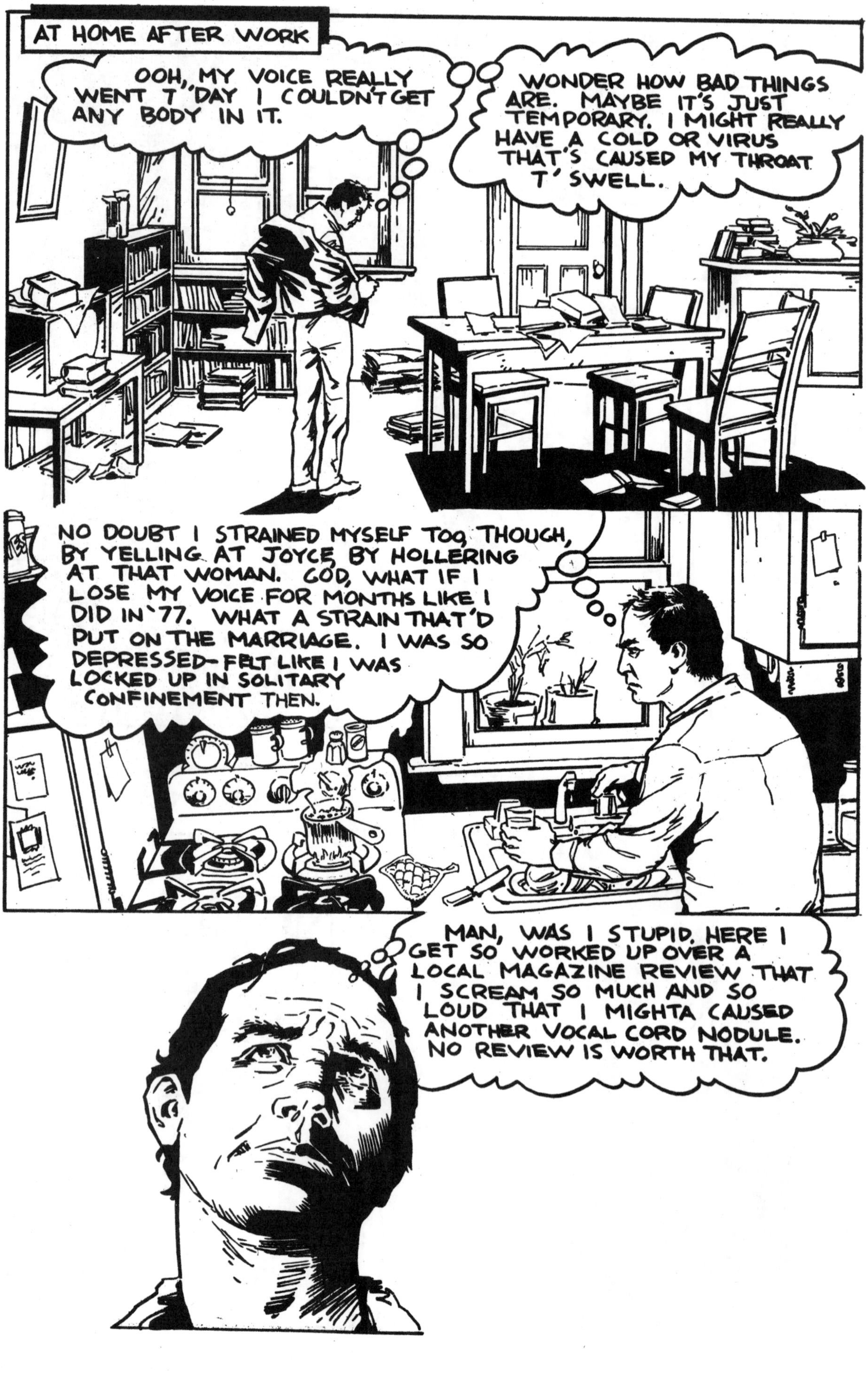
AT HOME AFTER WORK
OOH, MY VOICE REALLY WENT T'DAY I COULDN'T GET ANY BODY IN IT.
WONDER HOW BAD THINGS ARE. MAYBE IT'S JUST TEMPORARY. I MIGHT REALLY HAVE A COLD OR VIRUS THAT'S CAUSED MY THROAT T'SWELL.
NO DOUBT I STRAINED MYSELF TOO, THOUGH, BY YELLING AT JOYCE BY HOLLERING AT THAT WOMAN. GOD, WHAT IF I LOSE MY VOICE FOR MONTHS LIKE I DID IN '77. WHAT A STRAIN THAT'D PUT ON THE MARRIAGE. I WAS SO DEPRESSED– FELT LIKE I WAS LOCKED UP IN SOLITARY CONFINEMENT THEN.
MAN, WAS I STUPID. HERE I GET SO WORKED UP OVER A LOCAL MAGAZINE REVIEW THAT I SCREAM SO MUCH AND SO LOUD THAT I MIGHTA CAUSED ANOTHER VOCAL CORD NODULE. NO REVIEW IS WORTH THAT.

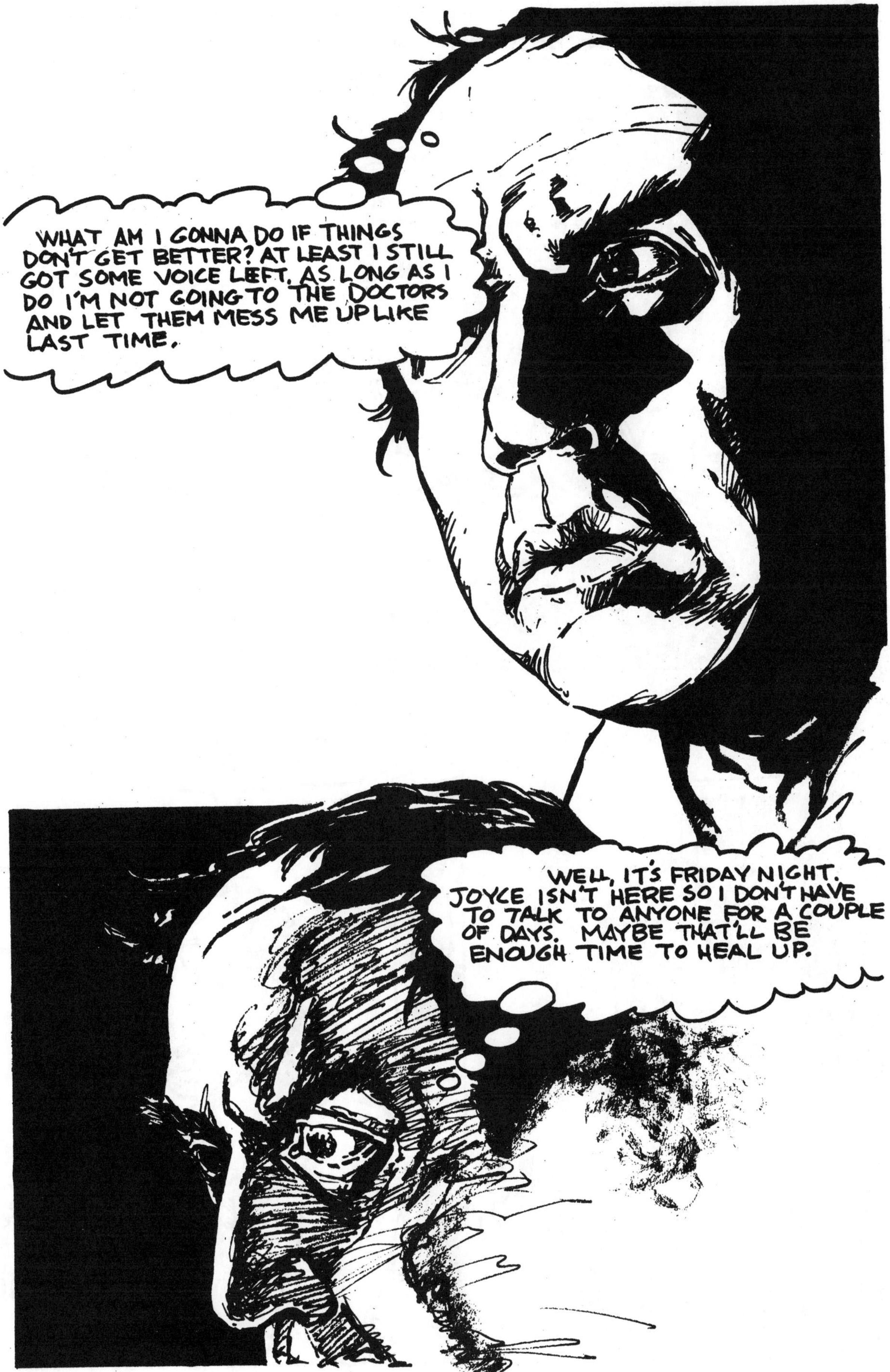
WHAT AM I GONNA DO IF THINGS DON'T GET BETTER? AT LEAST I STILL GOT SOME VOICE LEFT. AS LONG AS I DO I'M NOT GOING TO THE DOCTORS AND LET THEM MESS ME UP LIKE LAST TIME.
WELL, IT'S FRIDAY NIGHT. JOYCE ISN'T HERE SO I DON'T HAVE TO TALK TO ANYONE FOR A COUPLE OF DAYS. MAYBE THAT'LL BE ENOUGH TIME TO HEAL UP.

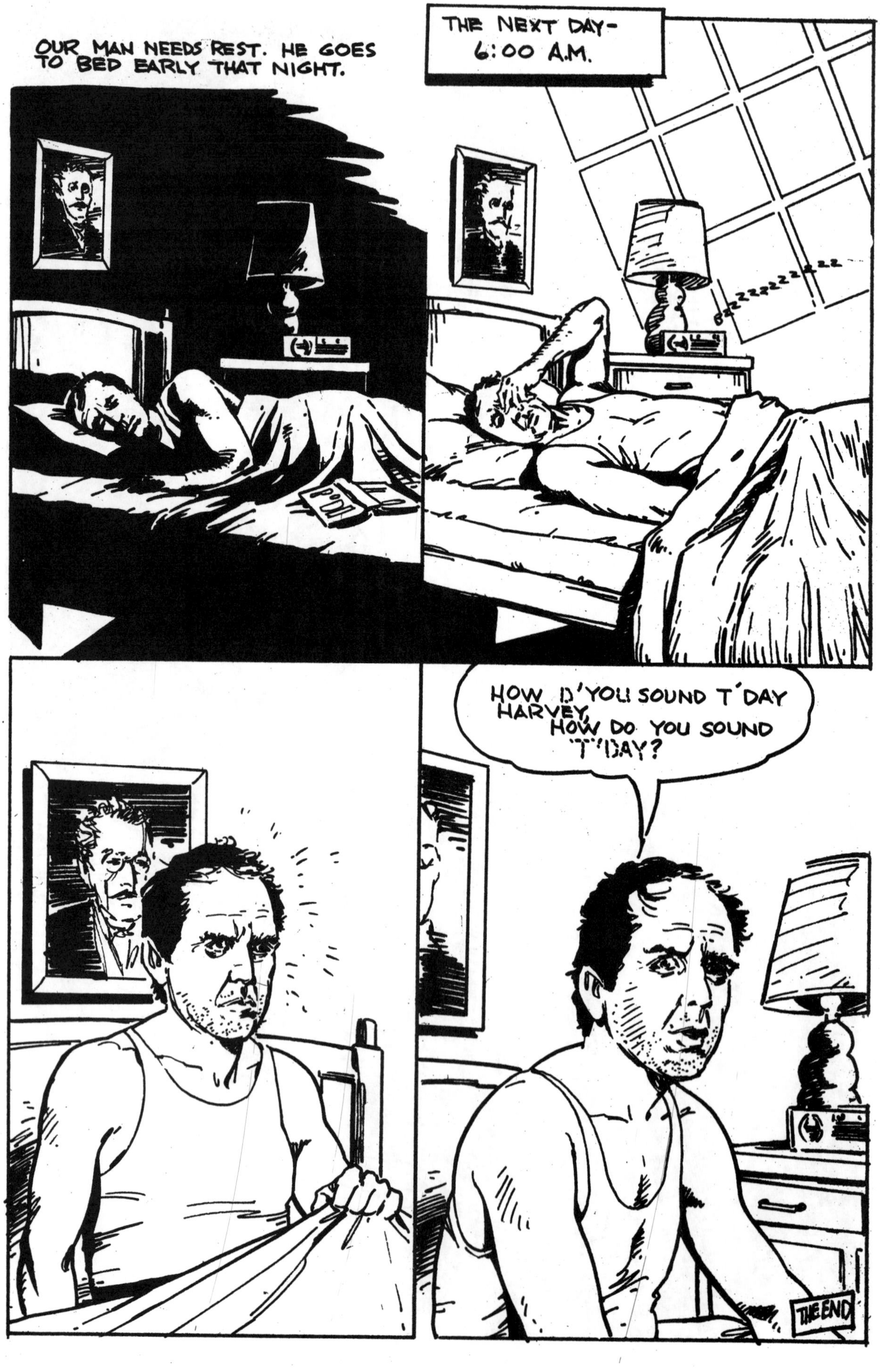
OUR MAN NEEDS REST. HE GOES TO BED EARLY THAT NIGHT.
THE NEXT DAY- 6:00 A.M.
HOW D'YOU SOUND T'DAY HARVEY, HOW DO YOU SOUND T'DAY?
THE END

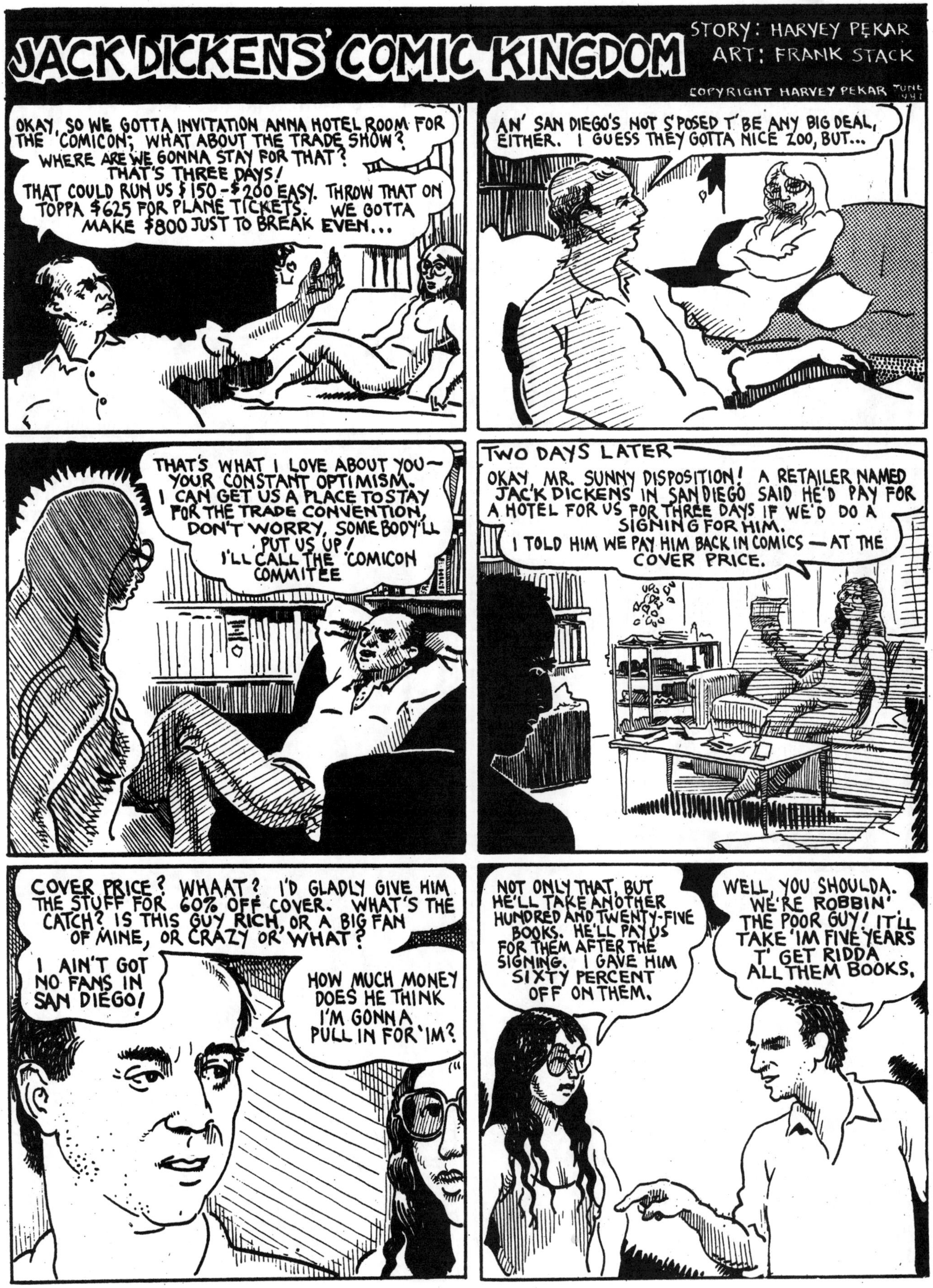

JACK DICKENS' COMIC KINGDOM
STORY: HARVEY PEKAR
ART: FRANK STACK
COPYRIGHT HARVEY PEKAR
OKAY, SO WE GOTTA INVITATION ANNA HOTEL ROOM FOR THE 'COMICON'; WHAT ABOUT THE TRADE SHOW? WHERE ARE WE GONNA STAY FOR THAT? THAT'S THREE DAYS! THAT COULD RUN US $150-$200 EASY. THROW THAT ON TOPPA $625 FOR PLANE TICKETS. WE GOTTA MAKE $800 JUST TO BREAK EVEN...
AN' SAN DIEGO'S NOT S'POSED T' BE ANY BIG DEAL, EITHER. I GUESS THEY GOTTA NICE ZOO, BUT...
THAT'S WHAT I LOVE ABOUT YOU— YOUR CONSTANT OPTIMISM. I CAN GET US A PLACE TO STAY FOR THE TRADE CONVENTION. DON'T WORRY, SOMEBODY'LL PUT US UP! I'LL CALL THE 'COMICON' COMMITEE
TWO DAYS LATER
OKAY, MR. SUNNY DISPOSITION! A RETAILER NAMED JACK DICKENS IN SAN DIEGO SAID HE'D PAY FOR A HOTEL FOR US FOR THREE DAYS IF WE'D DO A SIGNING FOR HIM. I TOLD HIM WE PAY HIM BACK IN COMICS — AT THE COVER PRICE.
COVER PRICE? WHAAT? I'D GLADLY GIVE HIM THE STUFF FOR 60% OFF COVER. WHAT'S THE CATCH? IS THIS GUY RICH, OR A BIG FAN OF MINE, OR CRAZY OR WHAT?
I AIN'T GOT NO FANS IN SAN DIEGO!
HOW MUCH MONEY DOES HE THINK I'M GONNA PULL IN FOR 'IM?
NOT ONLY THAT, BUT HE'LL TAKE ANOTHER HUNDRED AND TWENTY-FIVE BOOKS. HE'LL PAY US FOR THEM AFTER THE SIGNING. I GAVE HIM SIXTY PERCENT OFF ON THEM.
WELL, YOU SHOULDA. WE'RE ROBBIN' THE POOR GUY! IT'LL TAKE 'IM FIVE YEARS T' GET RIDDA ALL THEM BOOKS.

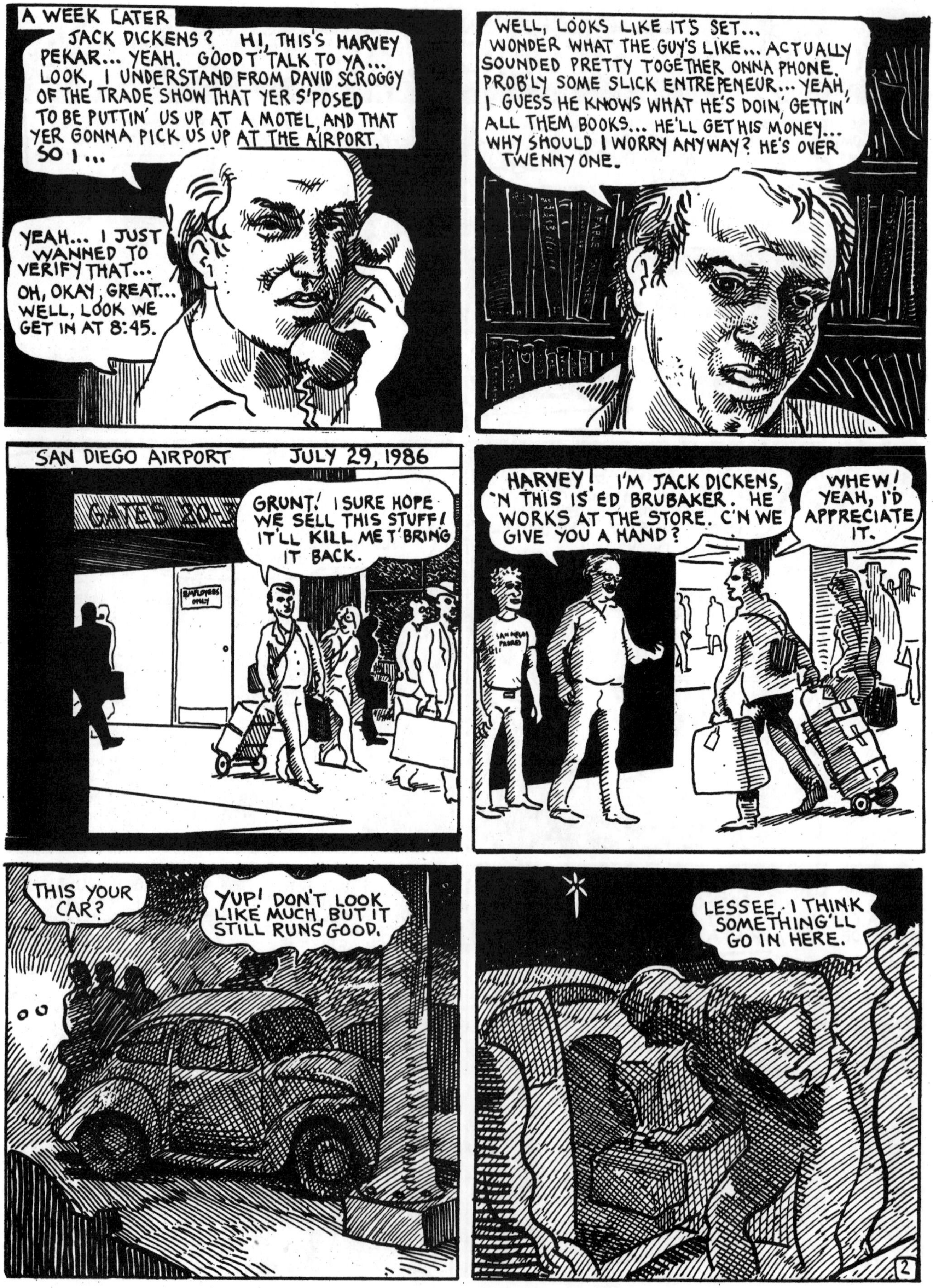
A WEEK LATER
JACK DICKENS? HI, THIS'S HARVEY PEKAR... YEAH. GOOD T' TALK TO YA... LOOK, I UNDERSTAND FROM DAVID SCROGGY OF THE TRADE SHOW THAT YER S'POSED TO BE PUTTIN' US UP AT A MOTEL, AND THAT YER GONNA PICK US UP AT THE AIRPORT, SO I...
YEAH... I JUST WANNED TO VERIFY THAT... OH, OKAY, GREAT... WELL, LOOK WE GET IN AT 8:45.
WELL, LOOKS LIKE IT'S SET... WONDER WHAT THE GUY'S LIKE... ACTUALLY SOUNDED PRETTY TOGETHER ONNA PHONE. PROB'LY SOME SLICK ENTREPENEUR... YEAH, I GUESS HE KNOWS WHAT HE'S DOIN', GETTIN' ALL THEM BOOKS... HE'LL GET HIS MONEY... WHY SHOULD I WORRY ANYWAY? HE'S OVER TWENNY ONE.
SAN DIEGO AIRPORT JULY 29, 1986
GRUNT! I SURE HOPE WE SELL THIS STUFF! IT'LL KILL ME T' BRING IT BACK.
HARVEY! I'M JACK DICKENS, 'N THIS IS ED BRUBAKER. HE WORKS AT THE STORE. C'N WE GIVE YOU A HAND?
WHEW! YEAH, I'D APPRECIATE IT.
THIS YOUR CAR?
YUP! DON'T LOOK LIKE MUCH, BUT IT STILL RUNS GOOD.
LESSEE, I THINK SOMETHING'LL GO IN HERE.
2

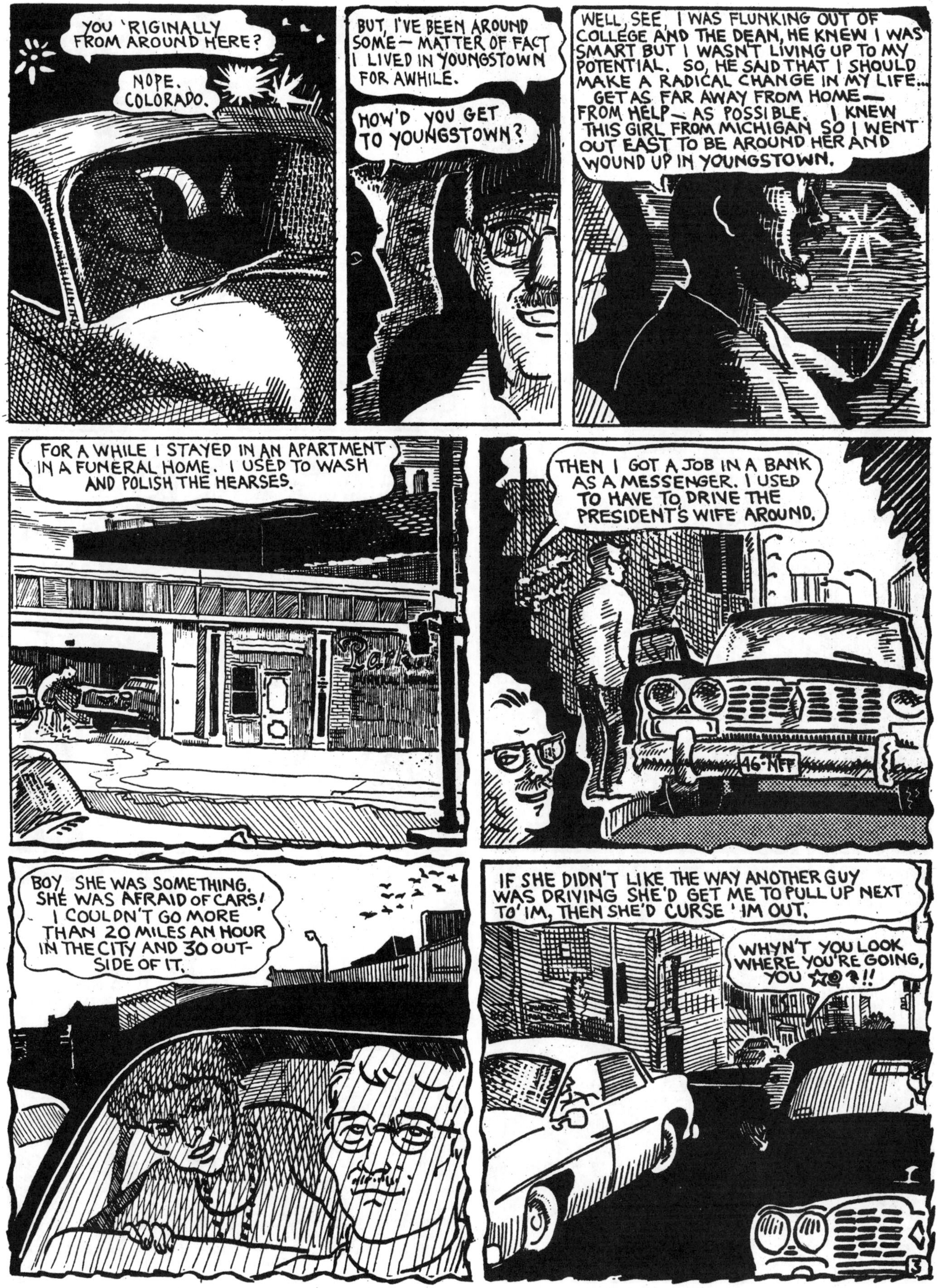
YOU 'RIGINALLY FROM AROUND HERE?
NOPE. COLORADO.
BUT, I'VE BEEN AROUND SOME— MATTER OF FACT I LIVED IN YOUNGSTOWN FOR AWHILE.
HOW'D YOU GET TO YOUNGSTOWN?
WELL, SEE, I WAS FLUNKING OUT OF COLLEGE AND THE DEAN, HE KNEW I WAS SMART BUT I WASN'T LIVING UP TO MY POTENTIAL. SO, HE SAID THAT I SHOULD MAKE A RADICAL CHANGE IN MY LIFE... GET AS FAR AWAY FROM HOME— FROM HELP— AS POSSIBLE. I KNEW THIS GIRL FROM MICHIGAN SO I WENT OUT EAST TO BE AROUND HER AND WOUND UP IN YOUNGSTOWN.
FOR A WHILE I STAYED IN AN APARTMENT IN A FUNERAL HOME. I USED TO WASH AND POLISH THE HEARSES.
THEN I GOT A JOB IN A BANK AS A MESSENGER. I USED TO HAVE TO DRIVE THE PRESIDENT'S WIFE AROUND.
46-NFF
BOY, SHE WAS SOMETHING. SHE WAS AFRAID OF CARS! I COULDN'T GO MORE THAN 20 MILES AN HOUR IN THE CITY AND 30 OUTSIDE OF IT.
IF SHE DIDN'T LIKE THE WAY ANOTHER GUY WAS DRIVING SHE'D GET ME TO PULL UP NEXT TO 'IM, THEN SHE'D CURSE 'IM OUT.
WHYN'T YOU LOOK WHERE YOU'RE GOING, YOU ☆@?!!
3

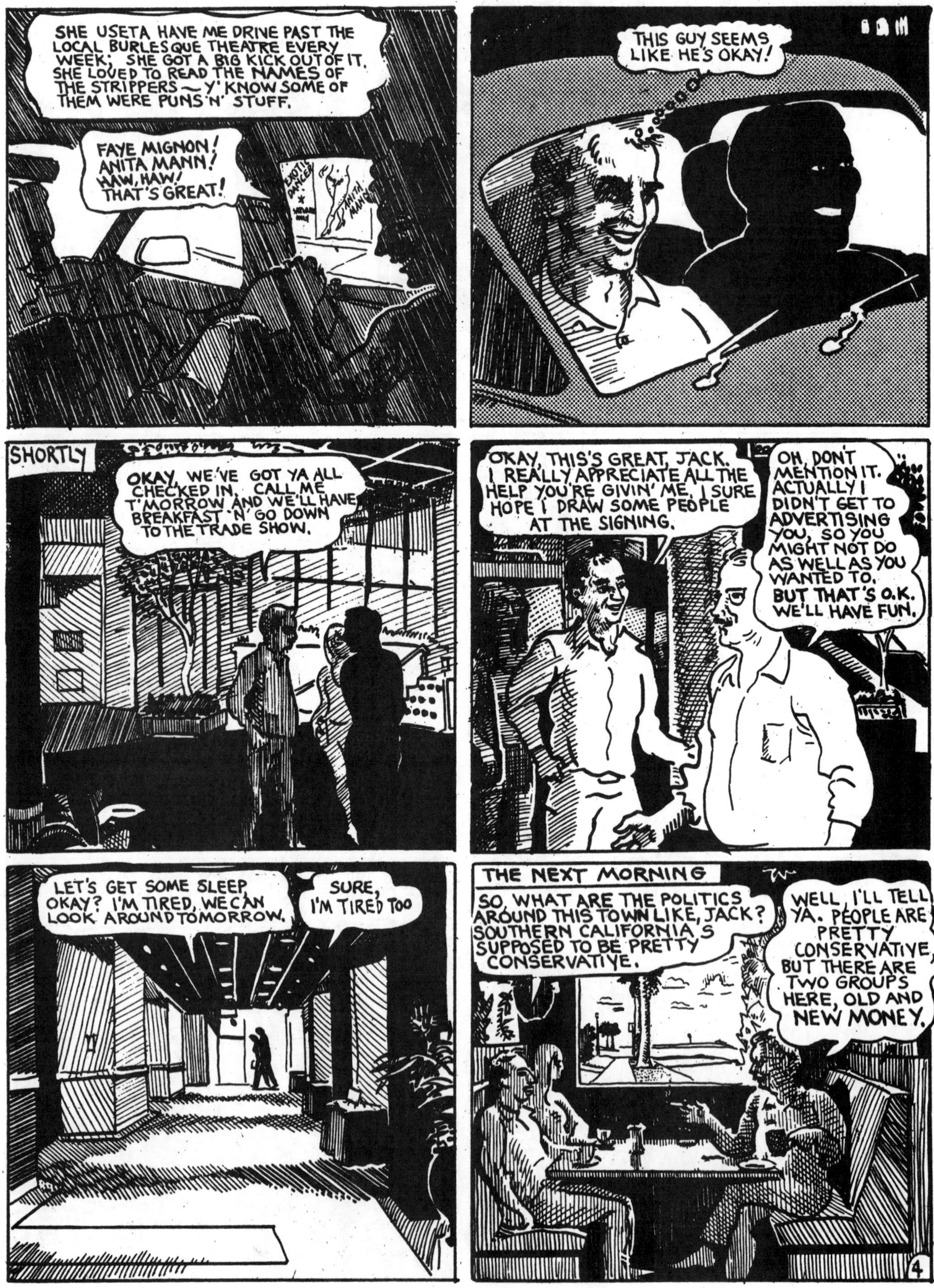
SHE USETA HAVE ME DRIVE PAST THE LOCAL BURLESQUE THEATRE EVERY WEEK; SHE GOT A BIG KICK OUT OF IT. SHE LOVED TO READ THE NAMES OF THE STRIPPERS ~ Y' KNOW SOME OF THEM WERE PUNS 'N' STUFF.
FAYE MIGNON! ANITA MANN! HAW, HAW! THAT'S GREAT!
EXOTIC DANCER
ANITA MANN
THIS GUY SEEMS LIKE HE'S OKAY!
SHORTLY
OKAY, WE'VE GOT YA ALL CHECKED IN. CALL ME T'MORROW AND WE'LL HAVE BREAKFAST 'N' GO DOWN TO THE TRADE SHOW.
OKAY, THIS'S GREAT, JACK. I REALLY APPRECIATE ALL THE HELP YOU'RE GIVIN' ME. I SURE HOPE I DRAW SOME PEOPLE AT THE SIGNING.
OH, DON'T MENTION IT. ACTUALLY I DIDN'T GET TO ADVERTISING YOU, SO YOU MIGHT NOT DO AS WELL AS YOU WANTED TO. BUT THAT'S O.K. WE'LL HAVE FUN.
LET'S GET SOME SLEEP OKAY? I'M TIRED, WE CAN LOOK AROUND TOMORROW.
SURE, I'M TIRED TOO
THE NEXT MORNING
SO, WHAT ARE THE POLITICS AROUND THIS TOWN LIKE, JACK? SOUTHERN CALIFORNIA'S SUPPOSED TO BE PRETTY CONSERVATIVE.
WELL, I'LL TELL YA. PEOPLE ARE PRETTY CONSERVATIVE, BUT THERE ARE TWO GROUPS HERE, OLD AND NEW MONEY.
4

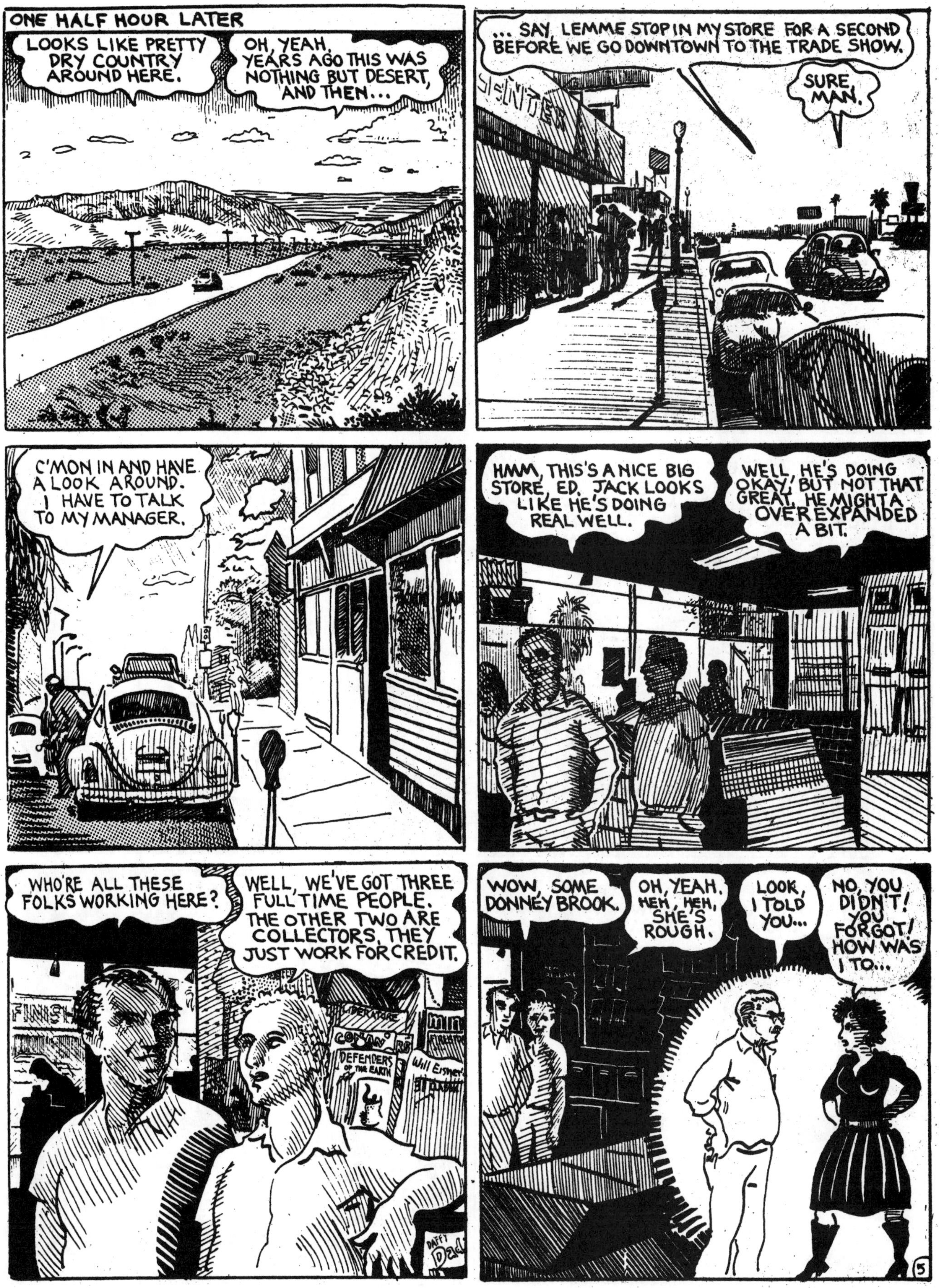
ONE HALF HOUR LATER
LOOKS LIKE PRETTY DRY COUNTRY AROUND HERE.
OH, YEAH, YEARS AGO THIS WAS NOTHING BUT DESERT, AND THEN...
... SAY, LEMME STOP IN MY STORE FOR A SECOND BEFORE WE GO DOWNTOWN TO THE TRADE SHOW.
SURE, MAN.
C'MON IN AND HAVE A LOOK AROUND. I HAVE TO TALK TO MY MANAGER.
HMM, THIS'S A NICE BIG STORE, ED. JACK LOOKS LIKE HE'S DOING REAL WELL.
WELL, HE'S DOING OKAY, BUT NOT THAT GREAT. HE MIGHTA OVER EXPANDED A BIT.
WHO'RE ALL THESE FOLKS WORKING HERE?
WELL, WE'VE GOT THREE FULL TIME PEOPLE. THE OTHER TWO ARE COLLECTORS, THEY JUST WORK FOR CREDIT.
DEFENDERS OF THE EARTH
WOW, SOME DONNEY BROOK.
OH, YEAH, HEH, HEH, SHE'S ROUGH.
LOOK, I TOLD YOU...
NO, YOU DIDN'T! YOU FORGOT! HOW WAS I TO...

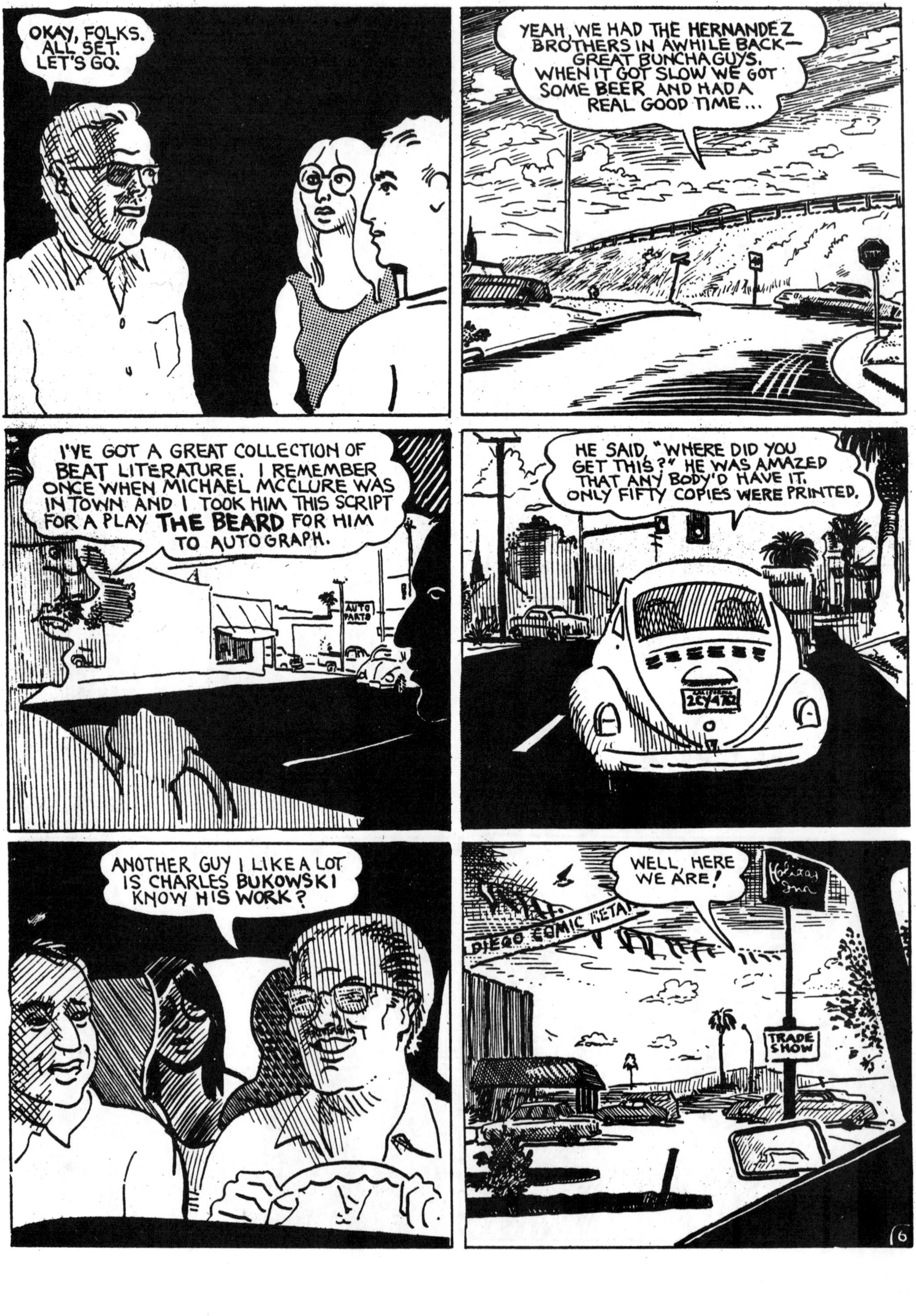
OKAY, FOLKS. ALL SET. LET'S GO.
YEAH, WE HAD THE HERNANDEZ BROTHERS IN AWHILE BACK— GREAT BUNCHA GUYS. WHEN IT GOT SLOW WE GOT SOME BEER AND HAD A REAL GOOD TIME...
I'VE GOT A GREAT COLLECTION OF BEAT LITERATURE. I REMEMBER ONCE WHEN MICHAEL McCLURE WAS IN TOWN AND I TOOK HIM THIS SCRIPT FOR A PLAY THE BEARD FOR HIM TO AUTOGRAPH.
AUTO PARTS
HE SAID, "WHERE DID YOU GET THIS?" HE WAS AMAZED THAT ANY BODY'D HAVE IT. ONLY FIFTY COPIES WERE PRINTED.
ANOTHER GUY I LIKE A LOT IS CHARLES BUKOWSKI KNOW HIS WORK?
WELL, HERE WE ARE!
DIEGO COMIC RETAI
TRADE SHOW

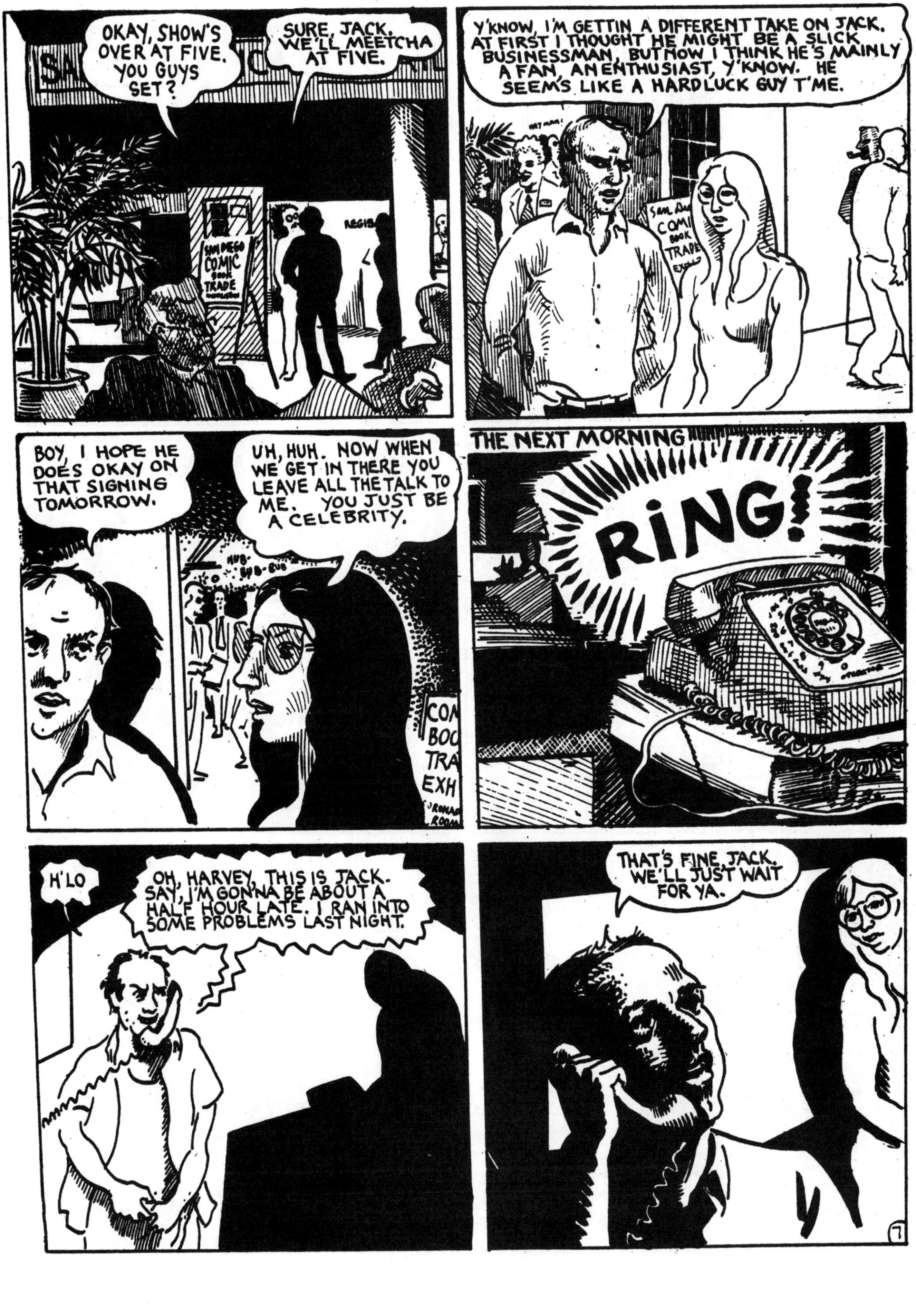
OKAY, SHOW'S OVER AT FIVE. YOU GUYS SET?
SURE, JACK. WE'LL MEETCHA AT FIVE.
Y'KNOW, I'M GETTIN A DIFFERENT TAKE ON JACK. AT FIRST I THOUGHT HE MIGHT BE A SLICK BUSINESSMAN, BUT NOW I THINK HE'S MAINLY A FAN, AN ENTHUSIAST, Y'KNOW. HE SEEMS LIKE A HARDLUCK GUY T'ME.
BOY, I HOPE HE DOES OKAY ON THAT SIGNING TOMORROW.
UH, HUH. NOW WHEN WE GET IN THERE YOU LEAVE ALL THE TALK TO ME. YOU JUST BE A CELEBRITY.
THE NEXT MORNING
RING!
H'LO
OH, HARVEY, THIS IS JACK. SAY, I'M GONNA BE ABOUT A HALF HOUR LATE. I RAN INTO SOME PROBLEMS LAST NIGHT.
THAT'S FINE JACK. WE'LL JUST WAIT FOR YA.

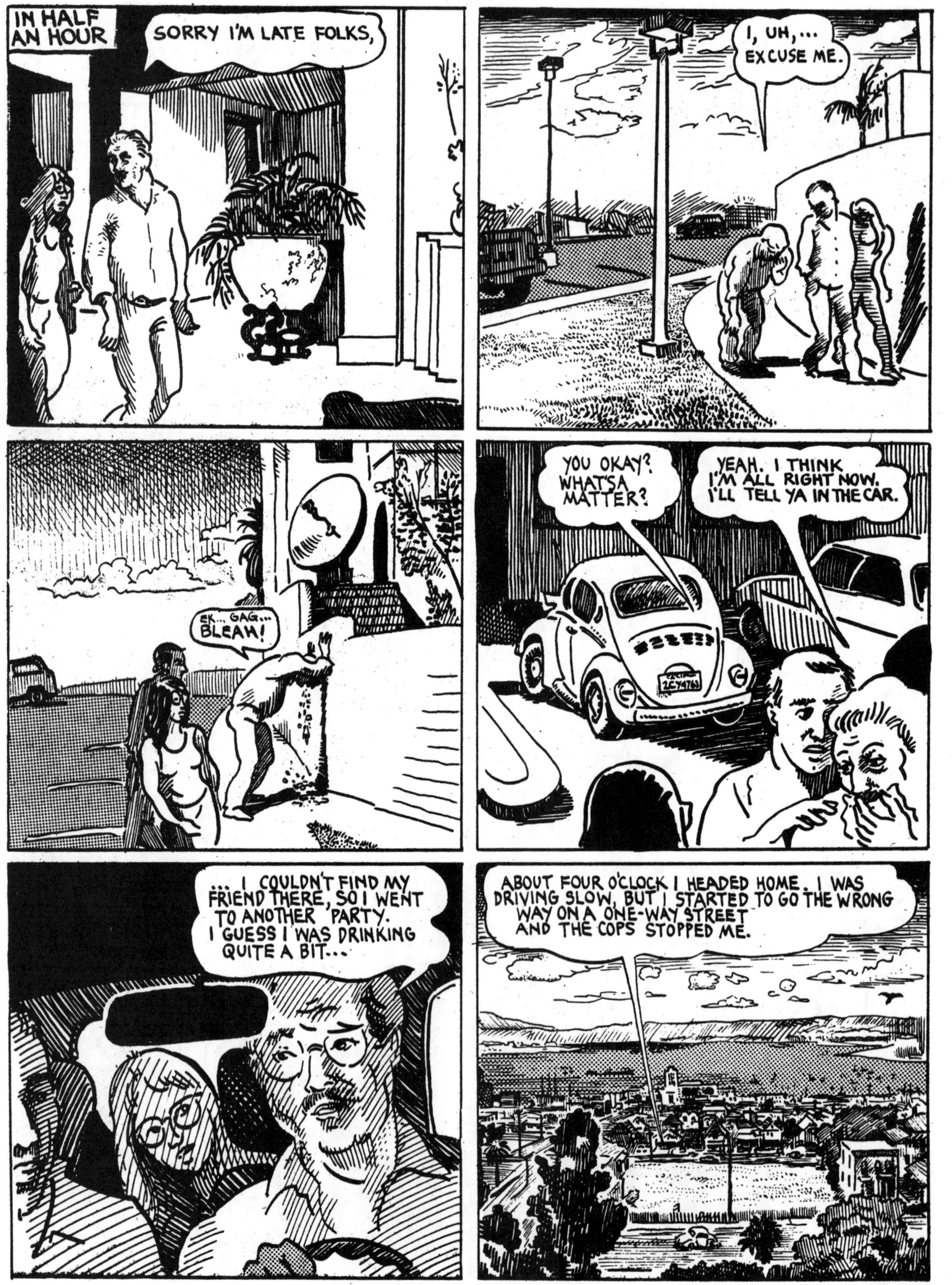
IN HALF AN HOUR
SORRY I'M LATE FOLKS,
I, UH,... EXCUSE ME.
EK... GAG... BLEAH!
YOU OKAY? WHAT'SA MATTER?
YEAH. I THINK I'M ALL RIGHT NOW. I'LL TELL YA IN THE CAR.
... I COULDN'T FIND MY FRIEND THERE, SO I WENT TO ANOTHER PARTY. I GUESS I WAS DRINKING QUITE A BIT...
ABOUT FOUR O'CLOCK I HEADED HOME. I WAS DRIVING SLOW, BUT I STARTED TO GO THE WRONG WAY ON A ONE-WAY STREET AND THE COPS STOPPED ME.

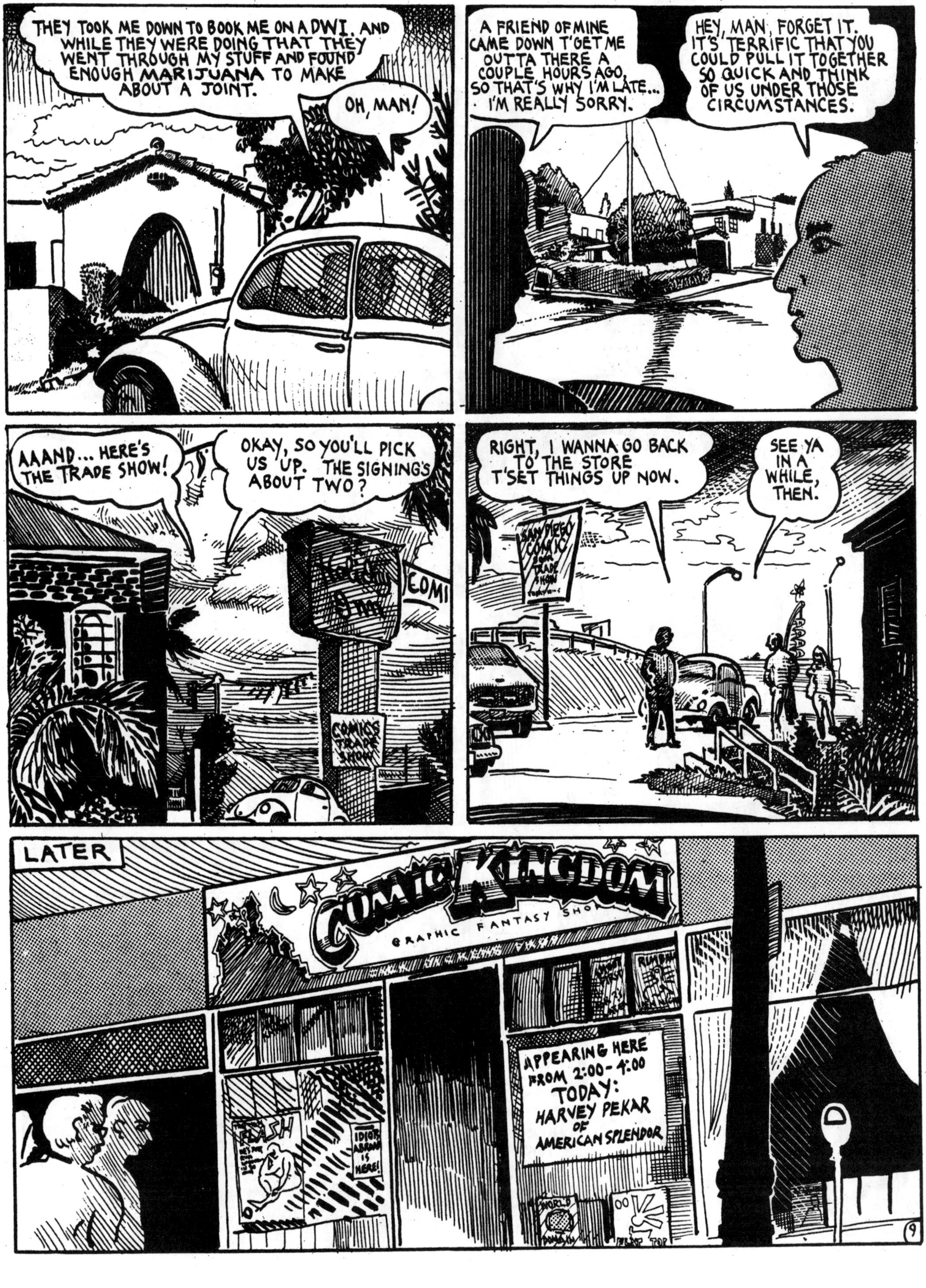
THEY TOOK ME DOWN TO BOOK ME ON A DWI. AND WHILE THEY WERE DOING THAT THEY WENT THROUGH MY STUFF AND FOUND ENOUGH MARIJUANA TO MAKE ABOUT A JOINT.
OH, MAN!
A FRIEND OF MINE CAME DOWN T'GET ME OUTTA THERE A COUPLE HOURS AGO, SO THAT'S WHY I'M LATE... I'M REALLY SORRY.
HEY, MAN, FORGET IT. IT'S TERRIFIC THAT YOU COULD PULL IT TOGETHER SO QUICK AND THINK OF US UNDER THOSE CIRCUMSTANCES.
AAAND... HERE'S THE TRADE SHOW!
OKAY, SO YOU'LL PICK US UP. THE SIGNING'S ABOUT TWO?
COMICS TRADE SHOW
RIGHT, I WANNA GO BACK TO THE STORE T'SET THINGS UP NOW.
SEE YA IN A WHILE, THEN.
LATER
COMIC KINGDOM
GRAPHIC FANTASY SHOP
APPEARING HERE FROM 2:00-4:00 TODAY: HARVEY PEKAR OF AMERICAN SPLENDOR
FLASH
IDIOT'S ABROAD IS HERE!

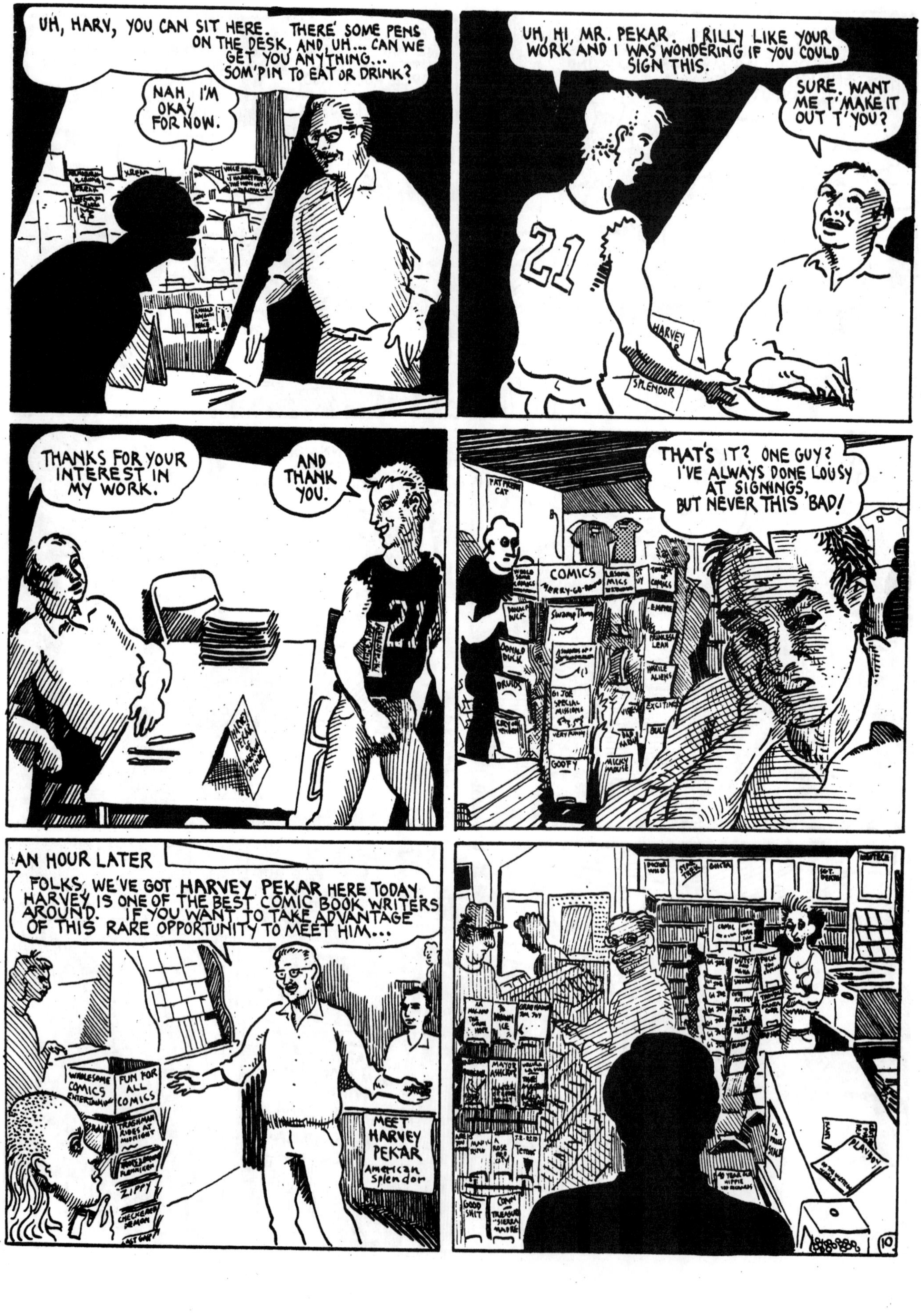

UH, HARV, YOU CAN SIT HERE. THERE' SOME PENS ON THE DESK, AND, UH... CAN WE GET YOU ANYTHING... SOM'PIN TO EAT OR DRINK?
NAH, I'M OKAY FOR NOW.
UH, HI, MR. PEKAR. I RILLY LIKE YOUR WORK AND I WAS WONDERING IF YOU COULD SIGN THIS.
SURE. WANT ME T'MAKE IT OUT T'YOU?
THANKS FOR YOUR INTEREST IN MY WORK.
AND THANK YOU.
THAT'S IT? ONE GUY? I'VE ALWAYS DONE LOUSY AT SIGNINGS, BUT NEVER THIS 'BAD!
COMICS
GOOFY
AN HOUR LATER
FOLKS, WE'VE GOT HARVEY PEKAR HERE TODAY. HARVEY IS ONE OF THE BEST COMIC BOOK WRITERS AROUND. IF YOU WANT TO TAKE ADVANTAGE OF THIS RARE OPPORTUNITY TO MEET HIM...
WHOLESOME COMICS
FUN FOR ALL COMICS
MEET HARVEY PEKAR American Splendor
ZIPPY
PLAYBOY

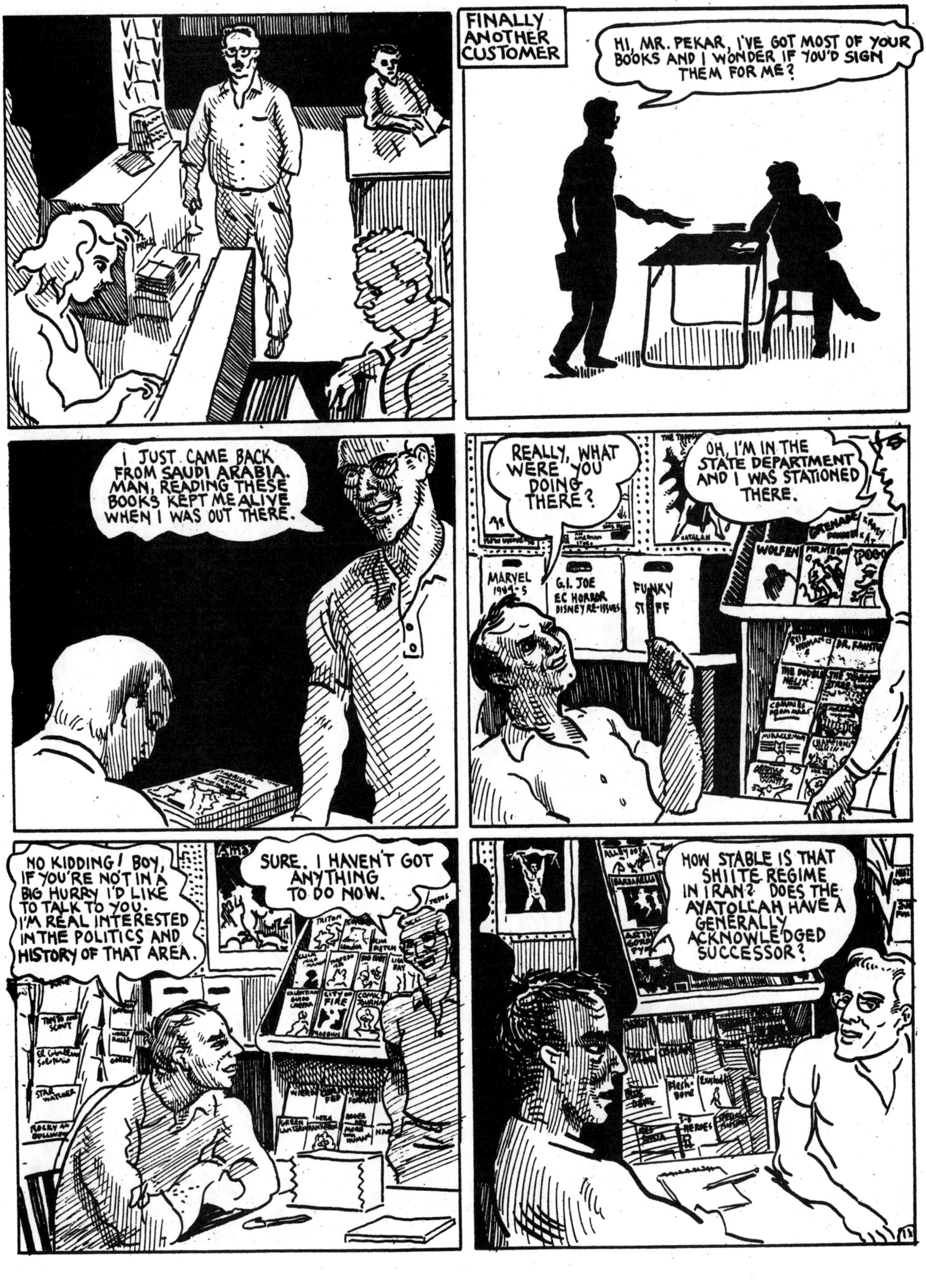
FINALLY ANOTHER CUSTOMER
HI, MR. PEKAR, I'VE GOT MOST OF YOUR BOOKS AND I WONDER IF YOU'D SIGN THEM FOR ME?
I JUST CAME BACK FROM SAUDI ARABIA. MAN, READING THESE BOOKS KEPT ME ALIVE WHEN I WAS OUT THERE.
REALLY, WHAT WERE YOU DOING THERE?
OH, I'M IN THE STATE DEPARTMENT AND I WAS STATIONED THERE.
MARVEL 1949-5
G.I. JOE
EC HORROR
DISNEY RE-ISSUES
FUNKY STUFF
WOLFEN
POGO
DR. FAUSTUS
THE DOUBLE HELIX
NO KIDDING! BOY, IF YOU'RE NOT IN A BIG HURRY I'D LIKE TO TALK TO YOU. I'M REAL INTERESTED IN THE POLITICS AND HISTORY OF THAT AREA.
SURE. I HAVEN'T GOT ANYTHING TO DO NOW.
CITY OF FIRE
STAR WATCHER
HOW STABLE IS THAT SHIITE REGIME IN IRAN? DOES THE AYATOLLAH HAVE A GENERALLY ACKNOWLEDGED SUCCESSOR?
3-D HEROES
13

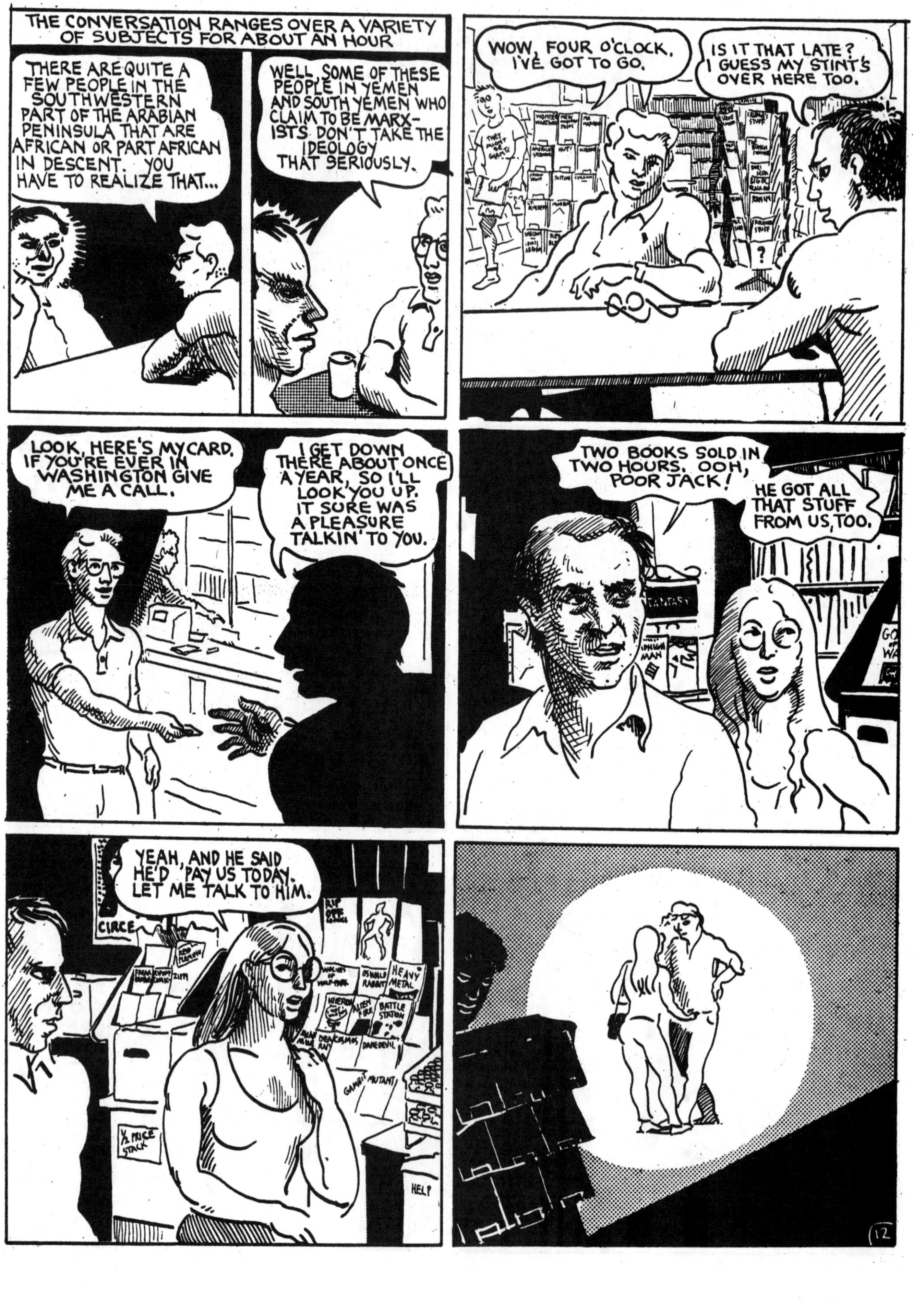

THE CONVERSATION RANGES OVER A VARIETY OF SUBJECTS FOR ABOUT AN HOUR
THERE ARE QUITE A FEW PEOPLE IN THE SOUTHWESTERN PART OF THE ARABIAN PENINSULA THAT ARE AFRICAN OR PART AFRICAN IN DESCENT. YOU HAVE TO REALIZE THAT...
WELL, SOME OF THESE PEOPLE IN YEMEN AND SOUTH YEMEN WHO CLAIM TO BE MARX-ISTS DON'T TAKE THE IDEOLOGY THAT SERIOUSLY.
WOW, FOUR O'CLOCK. I'VE GOT TO GO.
IS IT THAT LATE? I GUESS MY STINT'S OVER HERE TOO.
LOOK, HERE'S MY CARD. IF YOU'RE EVER IN WASHINGTON GIVE ME A CALL.
I GET DOWN THERE ABOUT ONCE A YEAR, SO I'LL LOOK YOU UP. IT SURE WAS A PLEASURE TALKIN' TO YOU.
TWO BOOKS SOLD IN TWO HOURS. OOH, POOR JACK!
HE GOT ALL THAT STUFF FROM US, TOO.
YEAH, AND HE SAID HE'D PAY US TODAY. LET ME TALK TO HIM.
CIRCE
HEAVY METAL
OSWALD RABBIT
ALIEN FIRE
BATTLE STATION
DAREDEVIL
GAMBIT
MUTANT
½ PRICE STACK
HELP

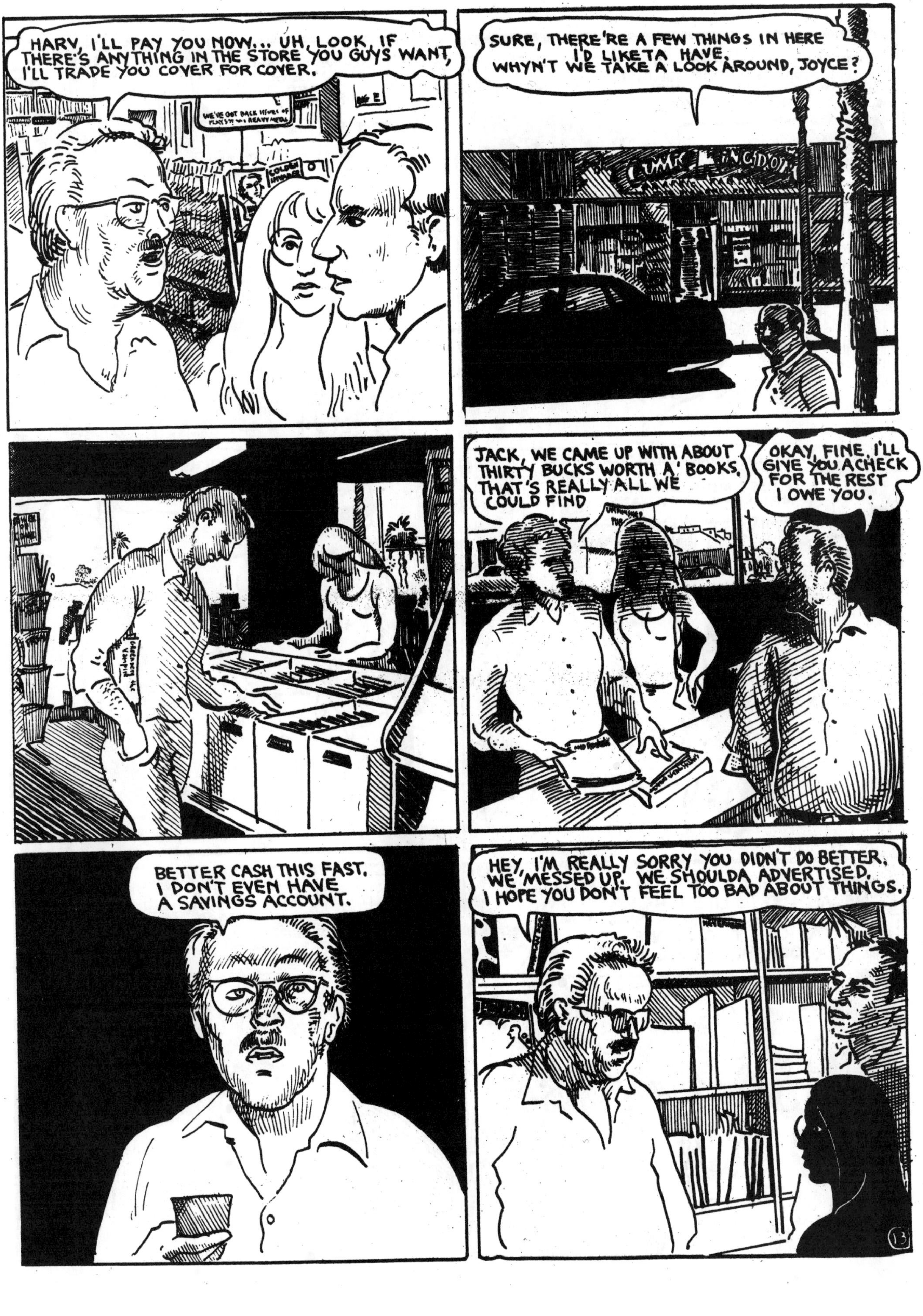
HARV, I'LL PAY YOU NOW... UH, LOOK, IF THERE'S ANYTHING IN THE STORE YOU GUYS WANT, I'LL TRADE YOU COVER FOR COVER.
SURE, THERE'RE A FEW THINGS IN HERE I'D LIKETA HAVE. WHYN'T WE TAKE A LOOK AROUND, JOYCE?
JACK, WE CAME UP WITH ABOUT THIRTY BUCKS WORTH A' BOOKS, THAT'S REALLY ALL WE COULD FIND
OKAY, FINE. I'LL GIVE YOU A CHECK FOR THE REST I OWE YOU.
BETTER CASH THIS FAST. I DON'T EVEN HAVE A SAVINGS ACCOUNT.
HEY, I'M REALLY SORRY YOU DIDN'T DO BETTER. WE MESSED UP. WE SHOULDA ADVERTISED. I HOPE YOU DON'T FEEL TOO BAD ABOUT THINGS.

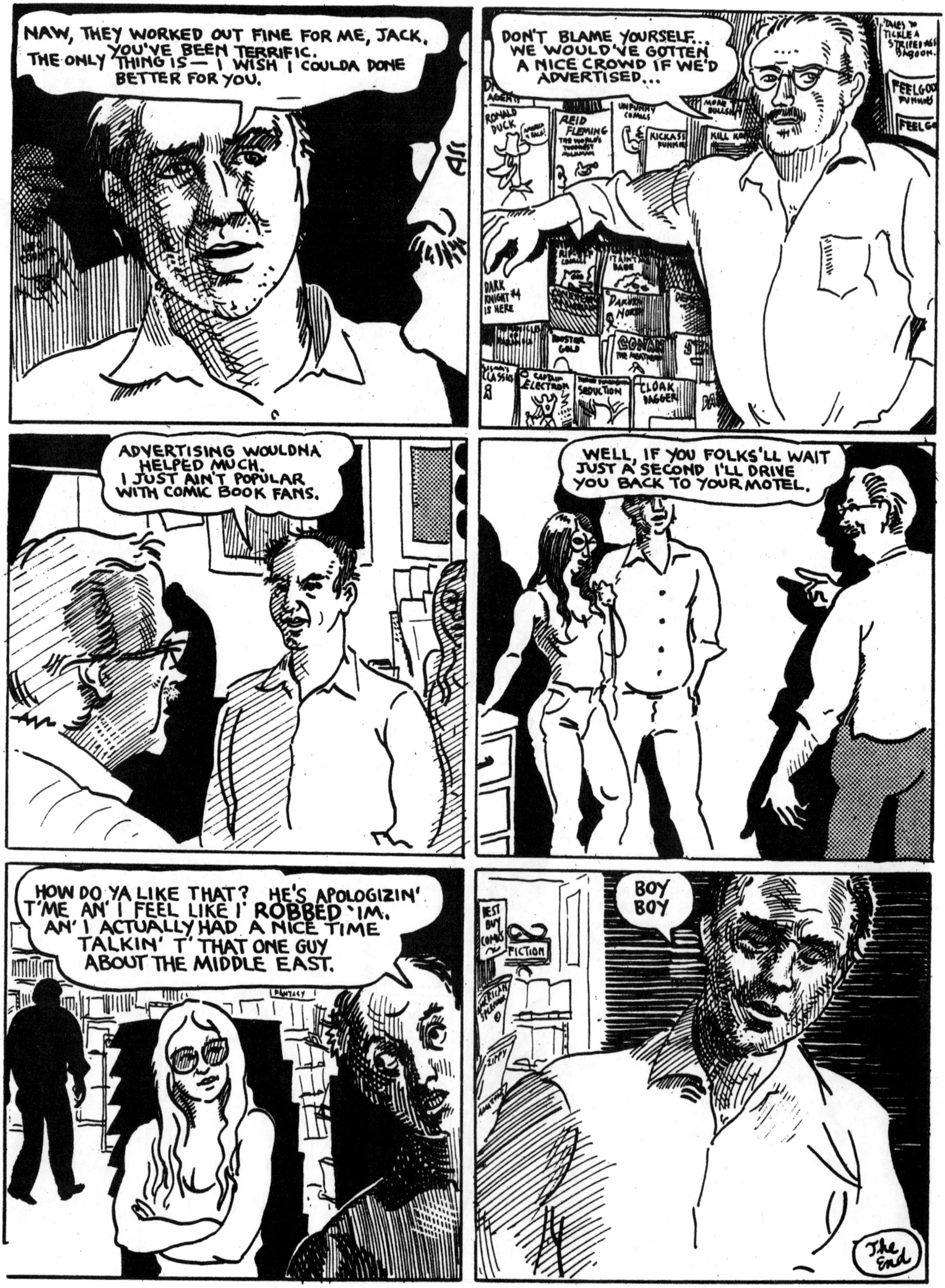
NAW, THEY WORKED OUT FINE FOR ME, JACK. YOU'VE BEEN TERRIFIC. THE ONLY THING IS— I WISH I COULDA DONE BETTER FOR YOU.
DON'T BLAME YOURSELF... WE WOULD'VE GOTTEN A NICE CROWD IF WE'D ADVERTISED...
ADVERTISING WOULDNA HELPED MUCH. I JUST AIN'T POPULAR WITH COMIC BOOK FANS.
WELL, IF YOU FOLKS'LL WAIT JUST A SECOND I'LL DRIVE YOU BACK TO YOUR MOTEL.
HOW DO YA LIKE THAT? HE'S APOLOGIZIN' T'ME AN' I FEEL LIKE I' ROBBED 'IM. AN' I ACTUALLY HAD A NICE TIME TALKIN' T' THAT ONE GUY ABOUT THE MIDDLE EAST.
BOY BOY
The End

Late Night With David Letterman

Story By Harvey Pekar
Drawings By Gerry Shamray

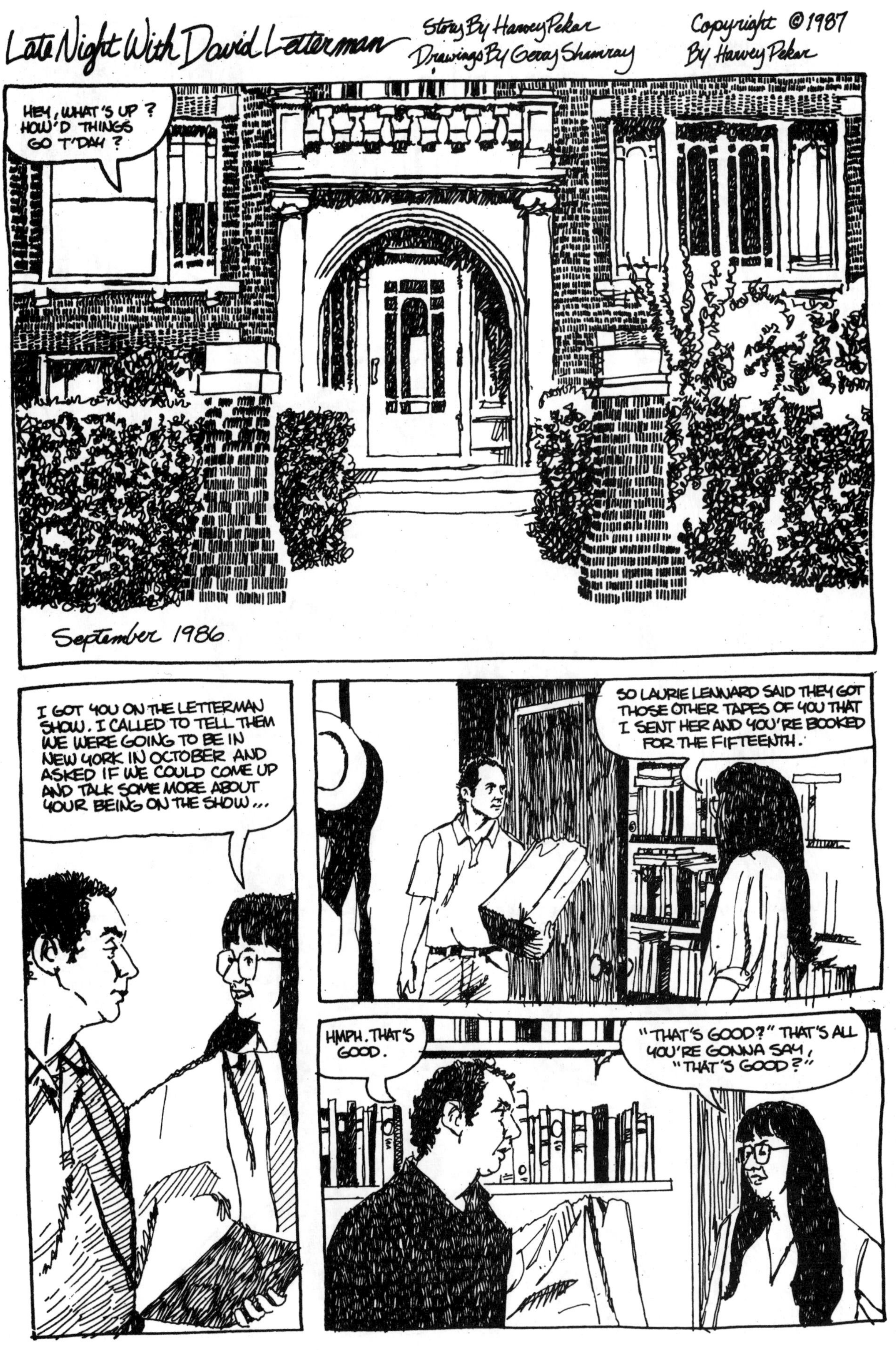
HEY, WHAT'S UP ? HOW'D THINGS GO T'DAY ?
September 1986
I GOT YOU ON THE LETTERMAN SHOW. I CALLED TO TELL THEM WE WERE GOING TO BE IN NEW YORK IN OCTOBER AND ASKED IF WE COULD COME UP AND TALK SOME MORE ABOUT YOUR BEING ON THE SHOW...
SO LAURIE LENNARD SAID THEY GOT THOSE OTHER TAPES OF YOU THAT I SENT HER AND YOU'RE BOOKED FOR THE FIFTEENTH.
HMPH. THAT'S GOOD.
"THAT'S GOOD?" THAT'S ALL YOU'RE GONNA SAY, "THAT'S GOOD?"

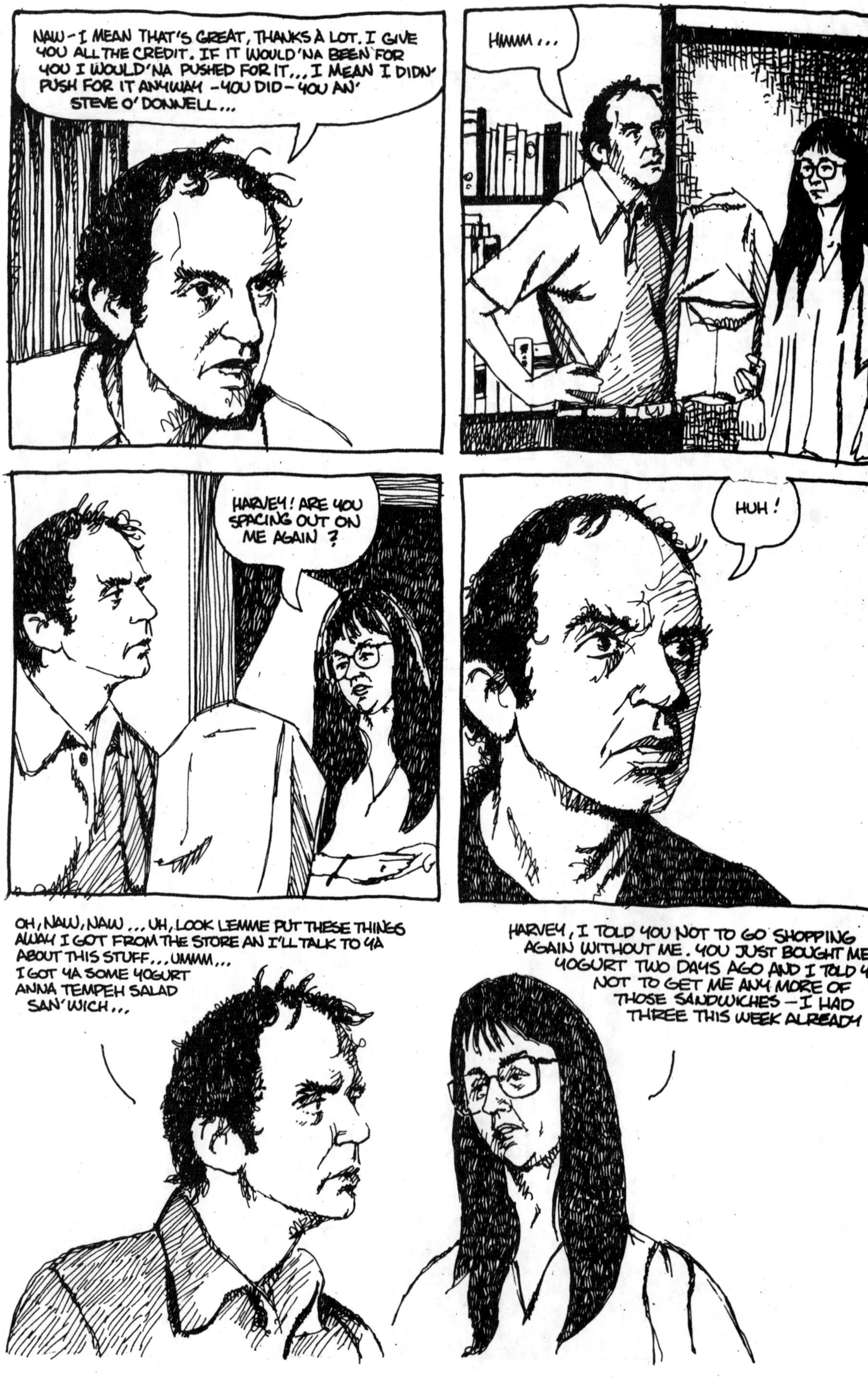
NAW - I MEAN THAT'S GREAT, THANKS A LOT. I GIVE YOU ALL THE CREDIT. IF IT WOULD'NA BEEN FOR YOU I WOULD'NA PUSHED FOR IT... I MEAN I DIDN' PUSH FOR IT ANYWAY -YOU DID - YOU AN' STEVE O'DONNELL...
HMMM...
HARVEY! ARE YOU SPACING OUT ON ME AGAIN ?
HUH !
OH, NAW, NAW... UH, LOOK LEMME PUT THESE THINGS AWAY I GOT FROM THE STORE AN I'LL TALK TO YA ABOUT THIS STUFF... UMMM... I GOT YA SOME YOGURT ANNA TEMPEH SALAD SAN'WICH...
HARVEY, I TOLD YOU NOT TO GO SHOPPING AGAIN WITHOUT ME. YOU JUST BOUGHT ME YOGURT TWO DAYS AGO AND I TOLD YOU NOT TO GET ME ANY MORE OF THOSE SANDWICHES - I HAD THREE THIS WEEK ALREADY

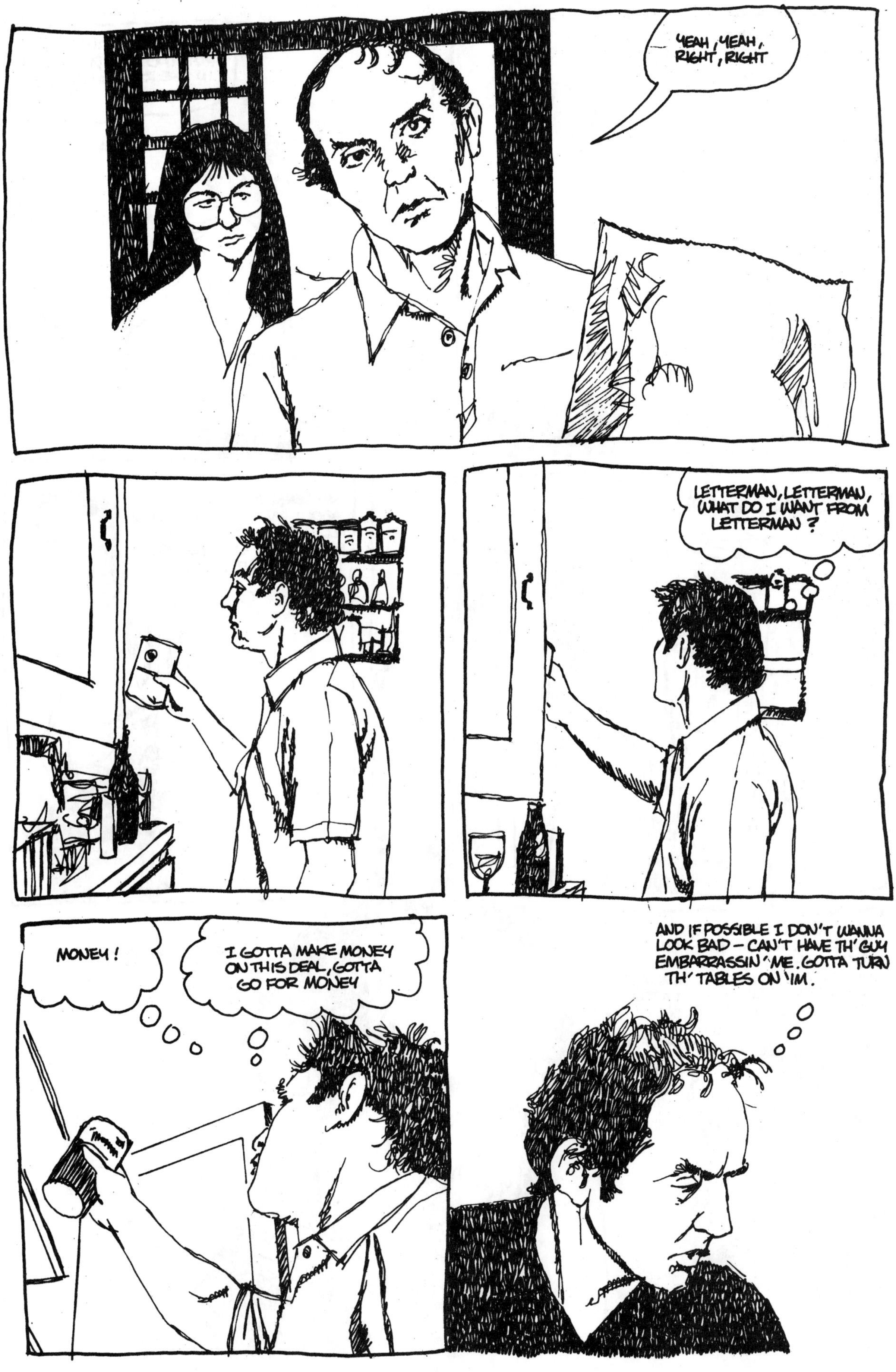
YEAH, YEAH, RIGHT, RIGHT
LETTERMAN, LETTERMAN, WHAT DO I WANT FROM LETTERMAN?
MONEY!
I GOTTA MAKE MONEY ON THIS DEAL, GOTTA GO FOR MONEY
AND IF POSSIBLE I DON'T WANNA LOOK BAD - CAN'T HAVE TH' GUY EMBARRASSIN' ME. GOTTA TURN TH' TABLES ON 'IM.

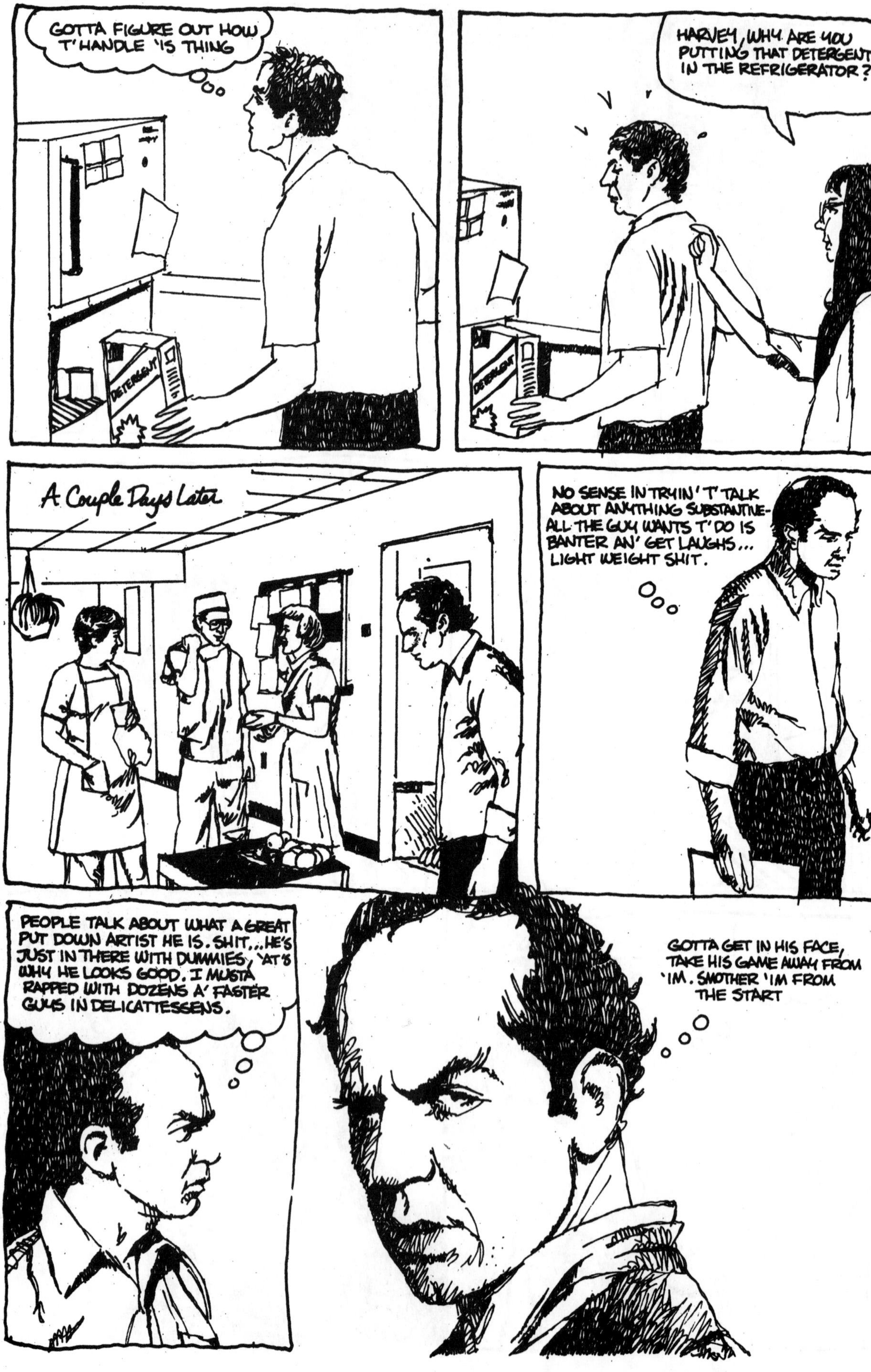
GOTTA FIGURE OUT HOW T'HANDLE 'IS THING
HARVEY, WHY ARE YOU PUTTING THAT DETERGENT IN THE REFRIGERATOR?
A Couple Days Later
NO SENSE IN TRYIN' T' TALK ABOUT ANYTHING SUBSTANTIVE- ALL THE GUY WANTS T'DO IS BANTER AN' GET LAUGHS... LIGHT WEIGHT SHIT.
PEOPLE TALK ABOUT WHAT A GREAT PUT DOWN ARTIST HE IS. SHIT... HE'S JUST IN THERE WITH DUMMIES, 'AT'S WHY HE LOOKS GOOD. I MUSTA RAPPED WITH DOZENS A' FASTER GUYS IN DELICATTESSENS.
GOTTA GET IN HIS FACE, TAKE HIS GAME AWAY FROM 'IM. SMOTHER 'IM FROM THE START

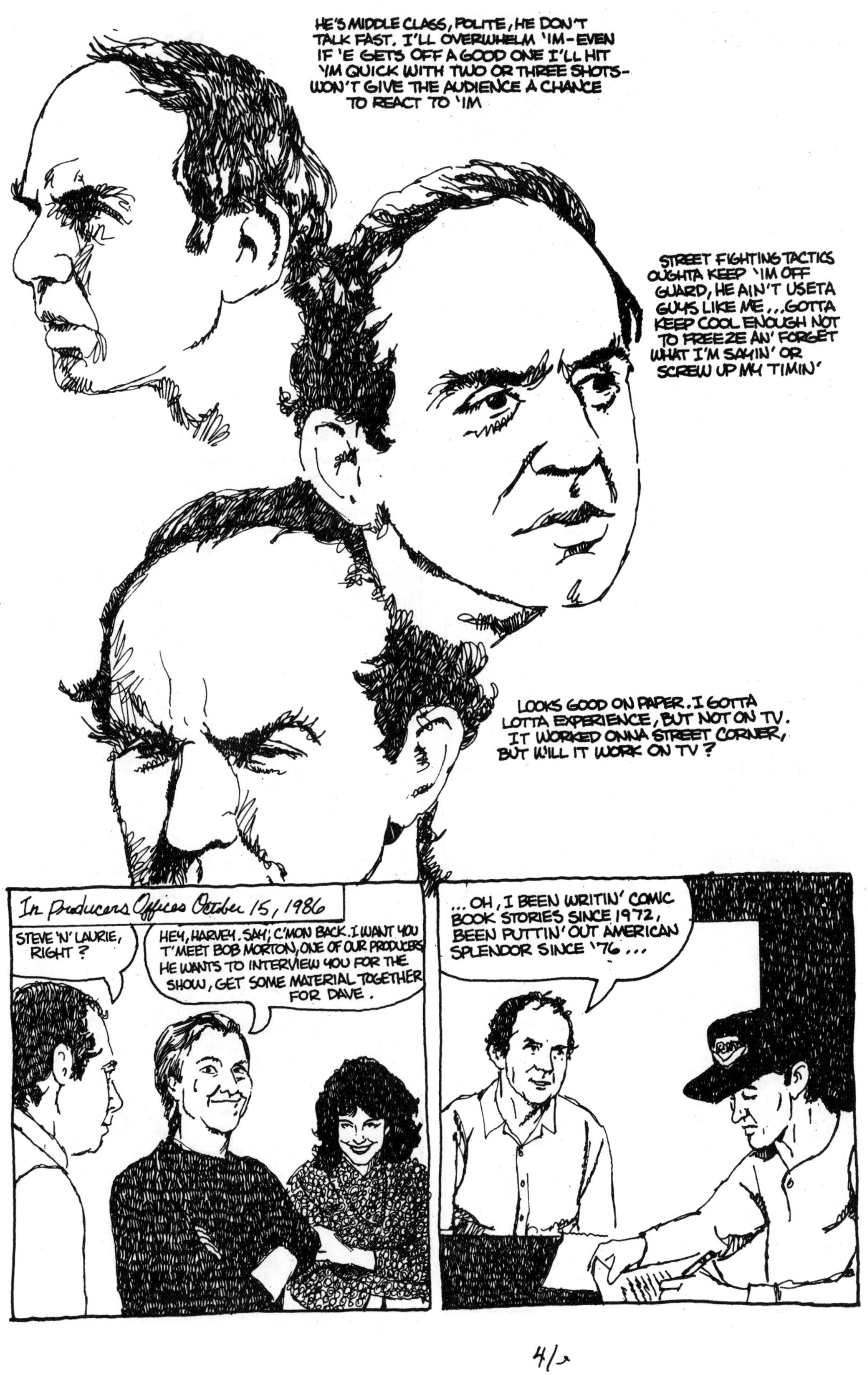

HE'S MIDDLE CLASS, POLITE, HE DON'T TALK FAST. I'LL OVERWHELM 'IM - EVEN IF 'E GETS OFF A GOOD ONE I'LL HIT 'IM QUICK WITH TWO OR THREE SHOTS - WON'T GIVE THE AUDIENCE A CHANCE TO REACT TO 'IM
STREET FIGHTING TACTICS OUGHTA KEEP 'IM OFF GUARD, HE AIN'T USETA GUYS LIKE ME... GOTTA KEEP COOL ENOUGH NOT TO FREEZE AN' FORGET WHAT I'M SAYIN' OR SCREW UP MY TIMIN'
LOOKS GOOD ON PAPER. I GOTTA LOTTA EXPERIENCE, BUT NOT ON TV. IT WORKED ONNA STREET CORNER, BUT WILL IT WORK ON TV?
In Producers Offices October 15, 1986
STEVE 'N' LAURIE, RIGHT?
HEY, HARVEY. SAY, C'MON BACK. I WANT YOU T'MEET BOB MORTON, ONE OF OUR PRODUCERS. HE WANTS TO INTERVIEW YOU FOR THE SHOW, GET SOME MATERIAL TOGETHER FOR DAVE.
...OH, I BEEN WRITIN' COMIC BOOK STORIES SINCE 1972, BEEN PUTTIN' OUT AMERICAN SPLENDOR SINCE '76...

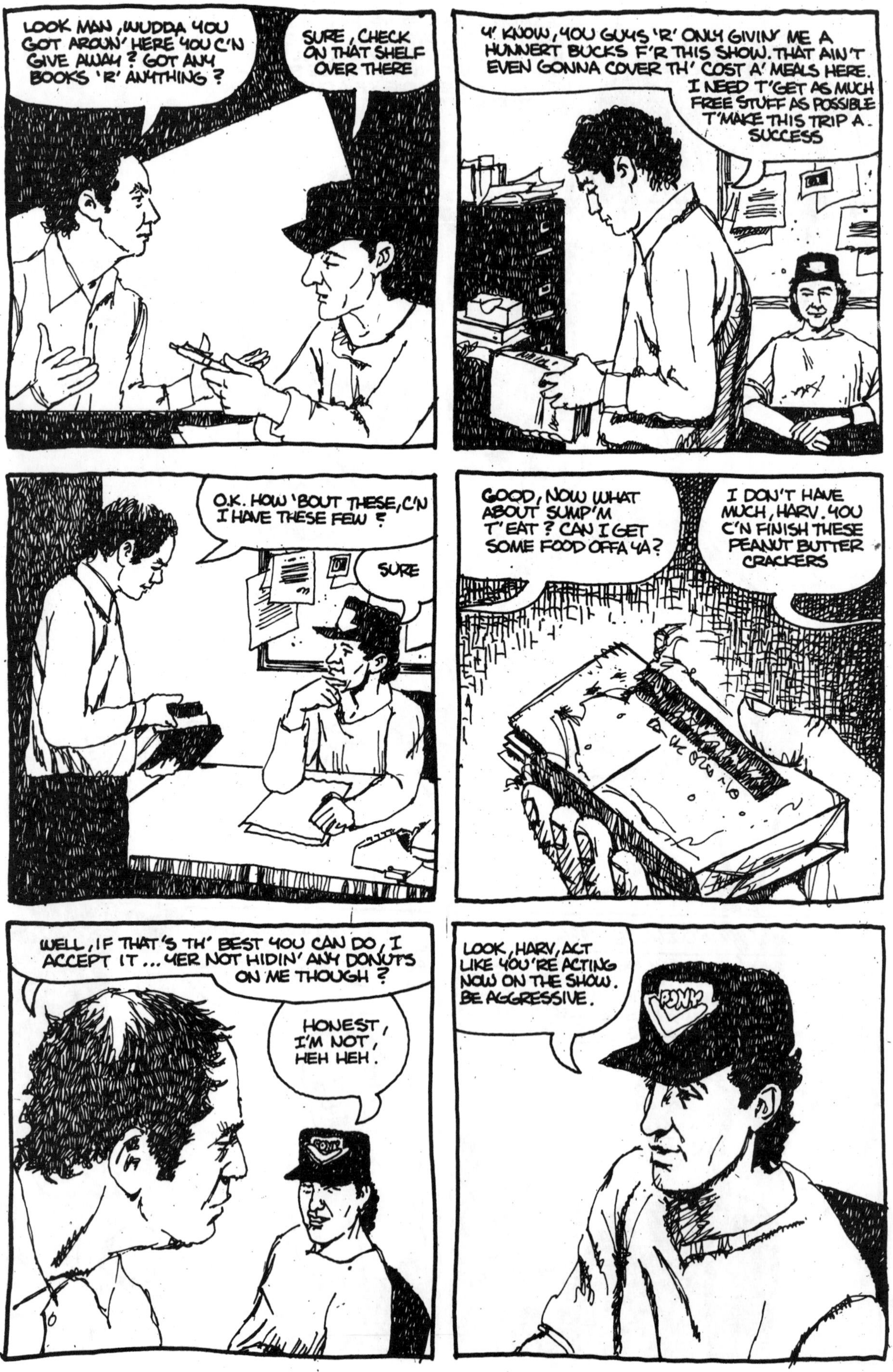
LOOK MAN, WUDDA YOU GOT AROUN' HERE YOU C'N GIVE AWAY? GOT ANY BOOKS 'R' ANYTHING?
SURE, CHECK ON THAT SHELF OVER THERE
Y' KNOW, YOU GUYS 'R' ONLY GIVIN' ME A HUNNERT BUCKS F'R THIS SHOW. THAT AIN'T EVEN GONNA COVER TH' COST A' MEALS HERE.
I NEED T'GET AS MUCH FREE STUFF AS POSSIBLE T'MAKE THIS TRIP A SUCCESS
O.K. HOW 'BOUT THESE, C'N I HAVE THESE FEW?
SURE
GOOD, NOW WHAT ABOUT SUMP'M T'EAT? CAN I GET SOME FOOD OFFA YA?
I DON'T HAVE MUCH, HARV. YOU C'N FINISH THESE PEANUT BUTTER CRACKERS
WELL, IF THAT'S TH' BEST YOU CAN DO, I ACCEPT IT... YER NOT HIDIN' ANY DONUTS ON ME THOUGH?
HONEST, I'M NOT, HEH HEH.
LOOK, HARV, ACT LIKE YOU'RE ACTING NOW ON THE SHOW. BE AGGRESSIVE.

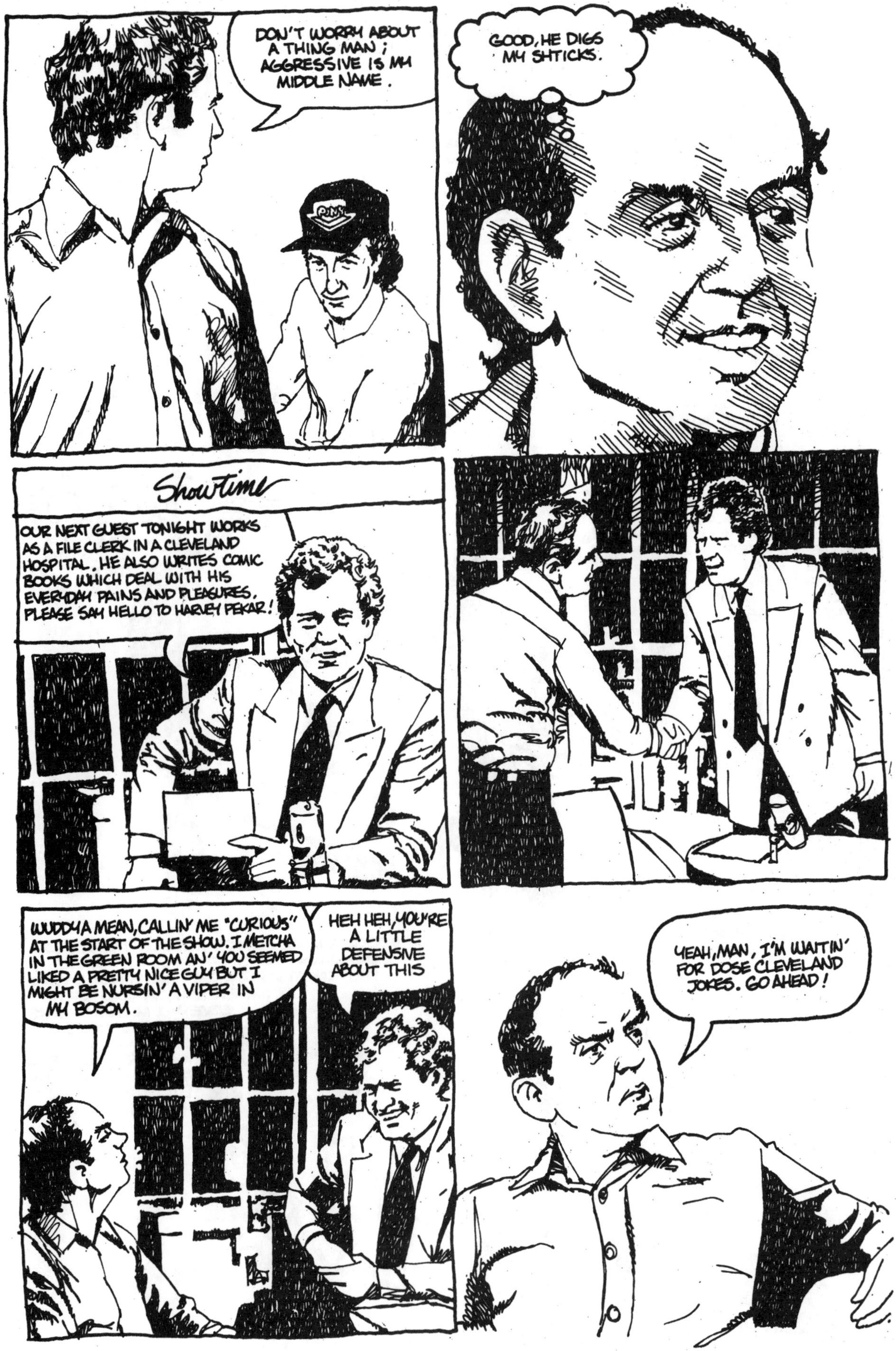
DON'T WORRY ABOUT A THING MAN; AGGRESSIVE IS MY MIDDLE NAME.
GOOD, HE DIGS MY SHTICKS.
Showtime
OUR NEXT GUEST TONIGHT WORKS AS A FILE CLERK IN A CLEVELAND HOSPITAL. HE ALSO WRITES COMIC BOOKS WHICH DEAL WITH HIS EVERYDAY PAINS AND PLEASURES. PLEASE SAY HELLO TO HARVEY PEKAR!
WUDDYA MEAN, CALLIN' ME "CURIOUS" AT THE START OF THE SHOW. I METCHA IN THE GREEN ROOM AN' YOU SEEMED LIKED A PRETTY NICE GUY BUT I MIGHT BE NURSIN' A VIPER IN MY BOSOM.
HEH HEH, YOU'RE A LITTLE DEFENSIVE ABOUT THIS
YEAH, MAN, I'M WAITIN' FOR DOSE CLEVELAND JOKES. GO AHEAD!

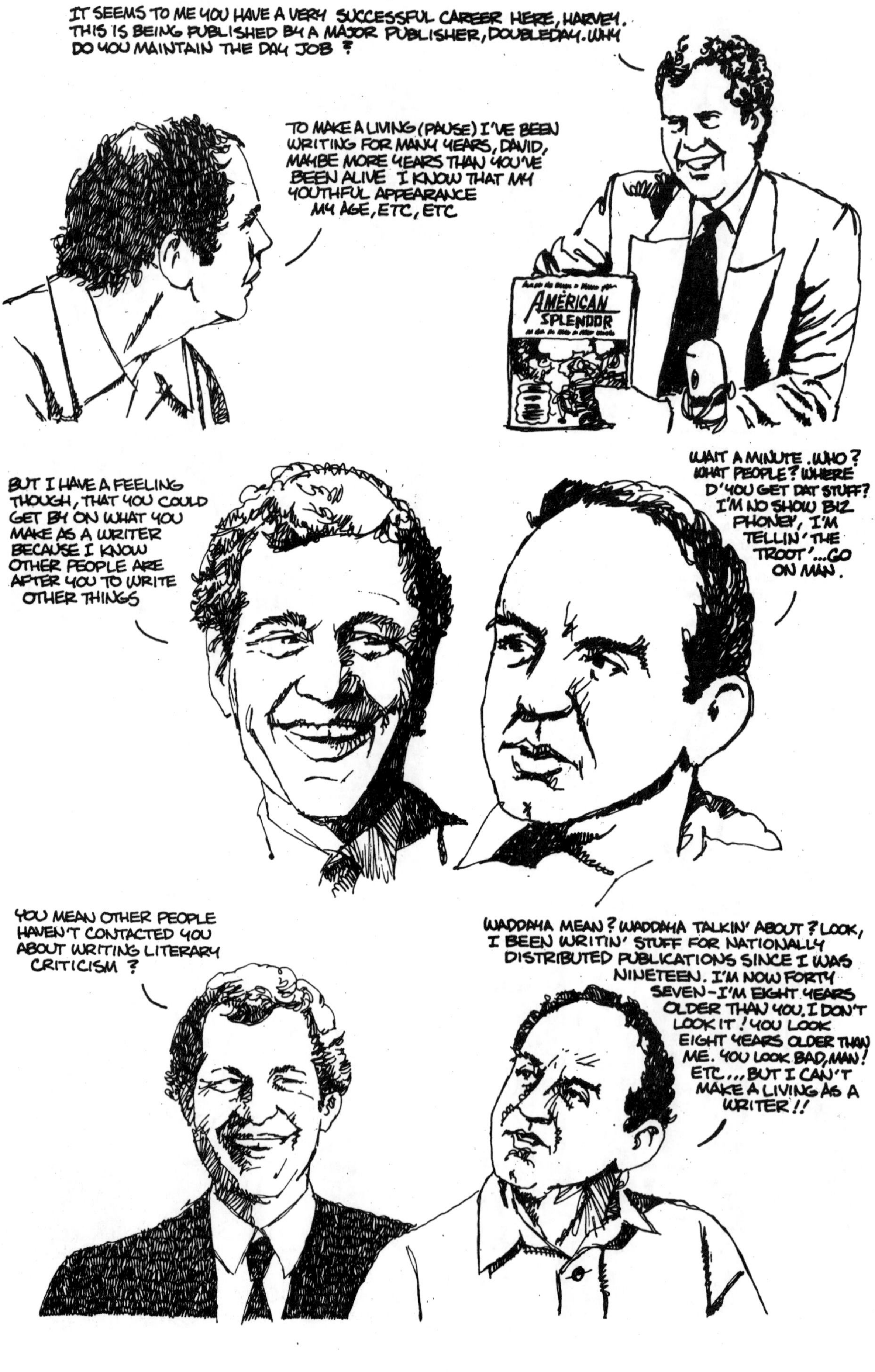
IT SEEMS TO ME YOU HAVE A VERY SUCCESSFUL CAREER HERE, HARVEY. THIS IS BEING PUBLISHED BY A MAJOR PUBLISHER, DOUBLEDAY. WHY DO YOU MAINTAIN THE DAY JOB ?
TO MAKE A LIVING (PAUSE) I'VE BEEN WRITING FOR MANY YEARS, DAVID, MAYBE MORE YEARS THAN YOU'VE BEEN ALIVE I KNOW THAT MY YOUTHFUL APPEARANCE MY AGE, ETC, ETC
AMERICAN SPLENDOR
BUT I HAVE A FEELING THOUGH, THAT YOU COULD GET BY ON WHAT YOU MAKE AS A WRITER BECAUSE I KNOW OTHER PEOPLE ARE AFTER YOU TO WRITE OTHER THINGS
WAIT A MINUTE. WHO? WHAT PEOPLE? WHERE D'YOU GET DAT STUFF? I'M NO SHOW BIZ PHONEY, I'M TELLIN' THE TROOT'...GO ON MAN.
YOU MEAN OTHER PEOPLE HAVEN'T CONTACTED YOU ABOUT WRITING LITERARY CRITICISM ?
WADDAYA MEAN? WADDAYA TALKIN' ABOUT? LOOK, I BEEN WRITIN' STUFF FOR NATIONALLY DISTRIBUTED PUBLICATIONS SINCE I WAS NINETEEN. I'M NOW FORTY SEVEN-I'M EIGHT YEARS OLDER THAN YOU. I DON'T LOOK IT! YOU LOOK EIGHT YEARS OLDER THAN ME. YOU LOOK BAD, MAN! ETC..., BUT I CAN'T MAKE A LIVING AS A WRITER!!

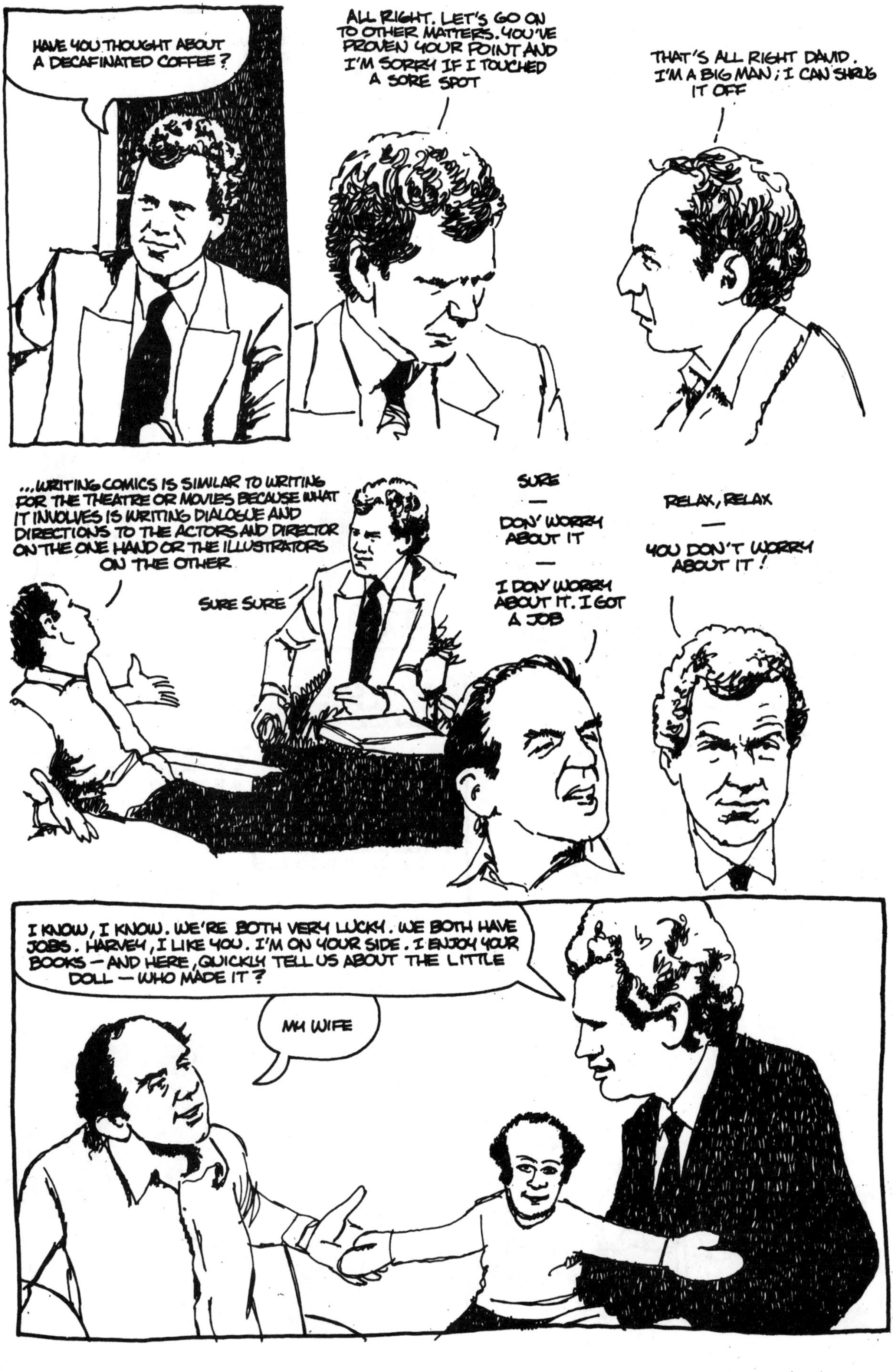

HAVE YOU THOUGHT ABOUT A DECAFINATED COFFEE ?
ALL RIGHT. LET'S GO ON TO OTHER MATTERS. YOU'VE PROVEN YOUR POINT AND I'M SORRY IF I TOUCHED A SORE SPOT
THAT'S ALL RIGHT DAVID. I'M A BIG MAN; I CAN SHRUG IT OFF
...WRITING COMICS IS SIMILAR TO WRITING FOR THE THEATRE OR MOVIES BECAUSE WHAT IT INVOLVES IS WRITING DIALOGUE AND DIRECTIONS TO THE ACTORS AND DIRECTOR ON THE ONE HAND OR THE ILLUSTRATORS ON THE OTHER
SURE SURE
SURE — DON' WORRY ABOUT IT
I DON' WORRY ABOUT IT. I GOT A JOB
RELAX, RELAX — YOU DON'T WORRY ABOUT IT!
I KNOW, I KNOW. WE'RE BOTH VERY LUCKY. WE BOTH HAVE JOBS. HARVEY, I LIKE YOU. I'M ON YOUR SIDE. I ENJOY YOUR BOOKS — AND HERE, QUICKLY TELL US ABOUT THE LITTLE DOLL — WHO MADE IT ?
MY WIFE

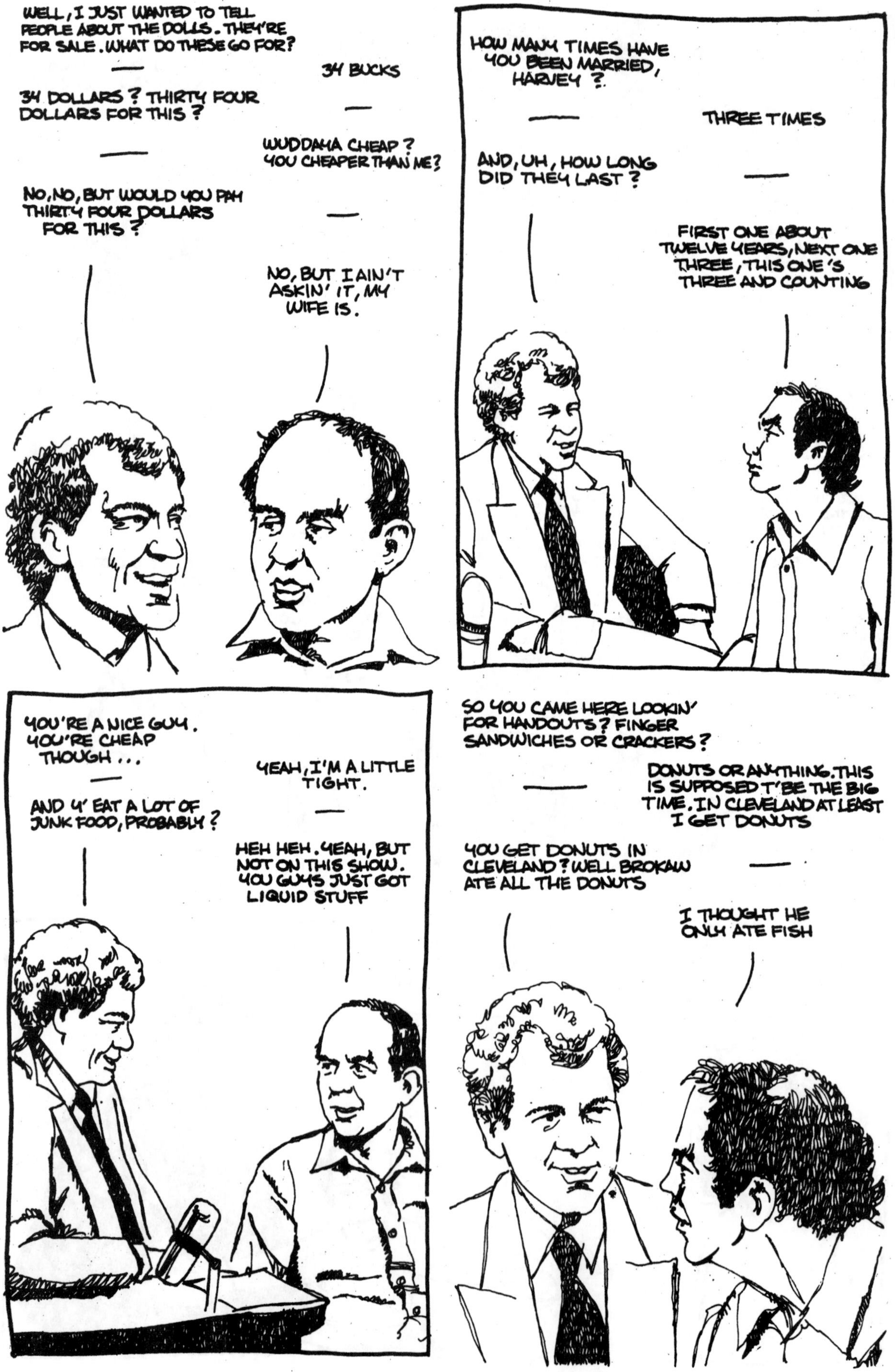

WELL, I JUST WANTED TO TELL PEOPLE ABOUT THE DOLLS. THEY'RE FOR SALE. WHAT DO THESE GO FOR?
34 BUCKS
34 DOLLARS? THIRTY FOUR DOLLARS FOR THIS?
WUDDAYA CHEAP? YOU CHEAPER THAN ME?
NO, NO, BUT WOULD YOU PAY THIRTY FOUR DOLLARS FOR THIS?
NO, BUT I AIN'T ASKIN' IT, MY WIFE IS.
HOW MANY TIMES HAVE YOU BEEN MARRIED, HARVEY?
THREE TIMES
AND, UH, HOW LONG DID THEY LAST?
FIRST ONE ABOUT TWELVE YEARS, NEXT ONE THREE, THIS ONE'S THREE AND COUNTING
YOU'RE A NICE GUY. YOU'RE CHEAP THOUGH...
YEAH, I'M A LITTLE TIGHT.
AND Y' EAT A LOT OF JUNK FOOD, PROBABLY?
HEH HEH. YEAH, BUT NOT ON THIS SHOW. YOU GUYS JUST GOT LIQUID STUFF
SO YOU CAME HERE LOOKIN' FOR HANDOUTS? FINGER SANDWICHES OR CRACKERS?
DONUTS OR ANYTHING. THIS IS SUPPOSED T'BE THE BIG TIME. IN CLEVELAND AT LEAST I GET DONUTS
YOU GET DONUTS IN CLEVELAND? WELL BROKAW ATE ALL THE DONUTS
I THOUGHT HE ONLY ATE FISH

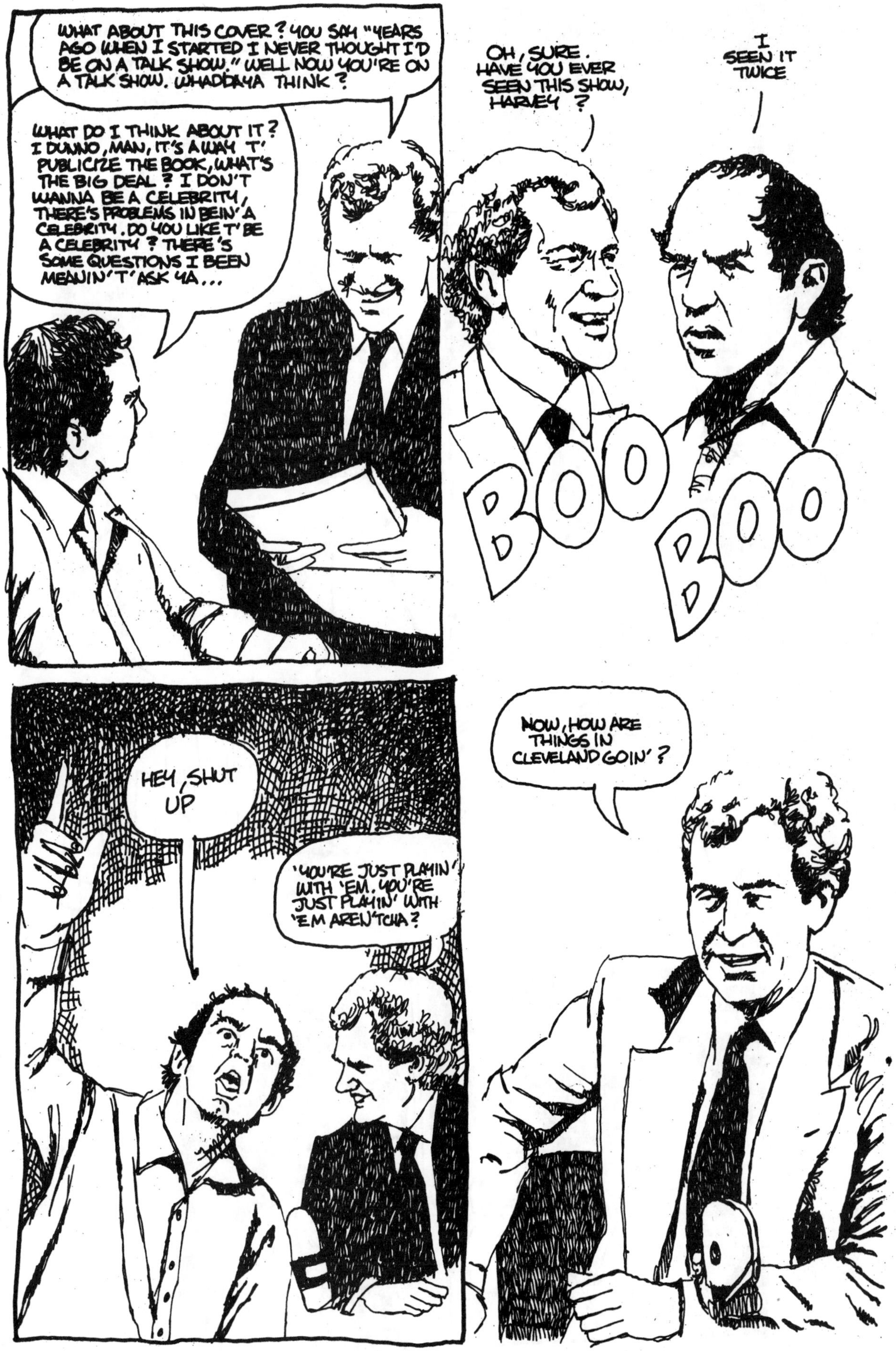
WHAT ABOUT THIS COVER? YOU SAY "YEARS AGO WHEN I STARTED I NEVER THOUGHT I'D BE ON A TALK SHOW." WELL NOW YOU'RE ON A TALK SHOW. WHADDAYA THINK?
WHAT DO I THINK ABOUT IT? I DUNNO, MAN, IT'S A WAY T' PUBLICIZE THE BOOK, WHAT'S THE BIG DEAL? I DON'T WANNA BE A CELEBRITY, THERE'S PROBLEMS IN BEIN' A CELEBRITY. DO YOU LIKE T' BE A CELEBRITY? THERE'S SOME QUESTIONS I BEEN MEANIN' T'ASK YA...
OH, SURE. HAVE YOU EVER SEEN THIS SHOW, HARVEY?
I SEEN IT TWICE
BOO
BOO
HEY, SHUT UP
'YOU'RE JUST PLAYIN' WITH 'EM. YOU'RE JUST PLAYIN' WITH 'EM AREN'TCHA?
NOW, HOW ARE THINGS IN CLEVELAND GOIN'?

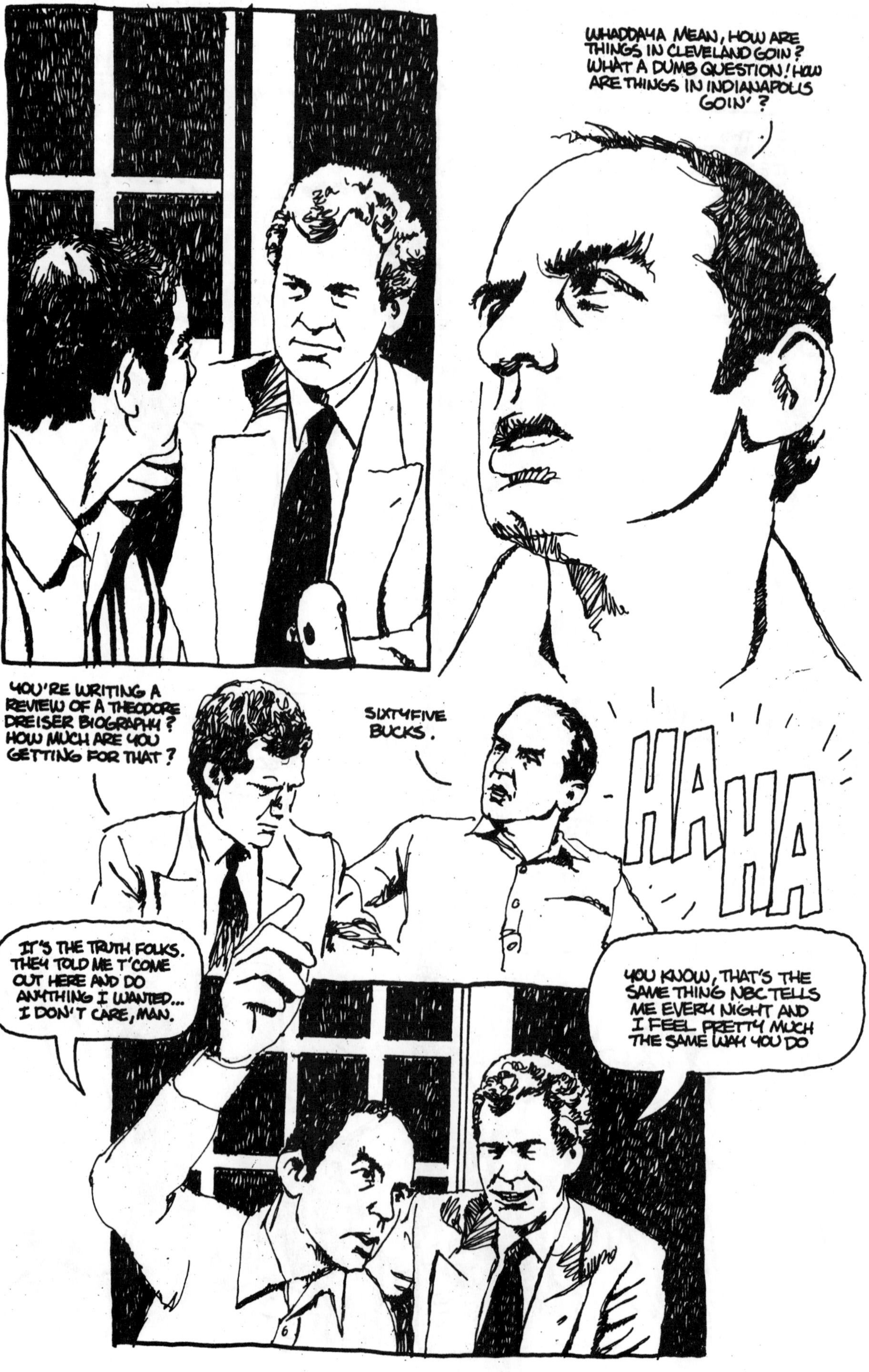
WHADDAYA MEAN, HOW ARE THINGS IN CLEVELAND GOIN? WHAT A DUMB QUESTION! HOW ARE THINGS IN INDIANAPOLIS GOIN'?
YOU'RE WRITING A REVIEW OF A THEODORE DREISER BIOGRAPHY? HOW MUCH ARE YOU GETTING FOR THAT?
SIXTYFIVE BUCKS.
HA HA HA
IT'S THE TRUTH FOLKS. THEY TOLD ME T'COME OUT HERE AND DO ANYTHING I WANTED... I DON'T CARE, MAN.
YOU KNOW, THAT'S THE SAME THING NBC TELLS ME EVERY NIGHT AND I FEEL PRETTY MUCH THE SAME WAY YOU DO

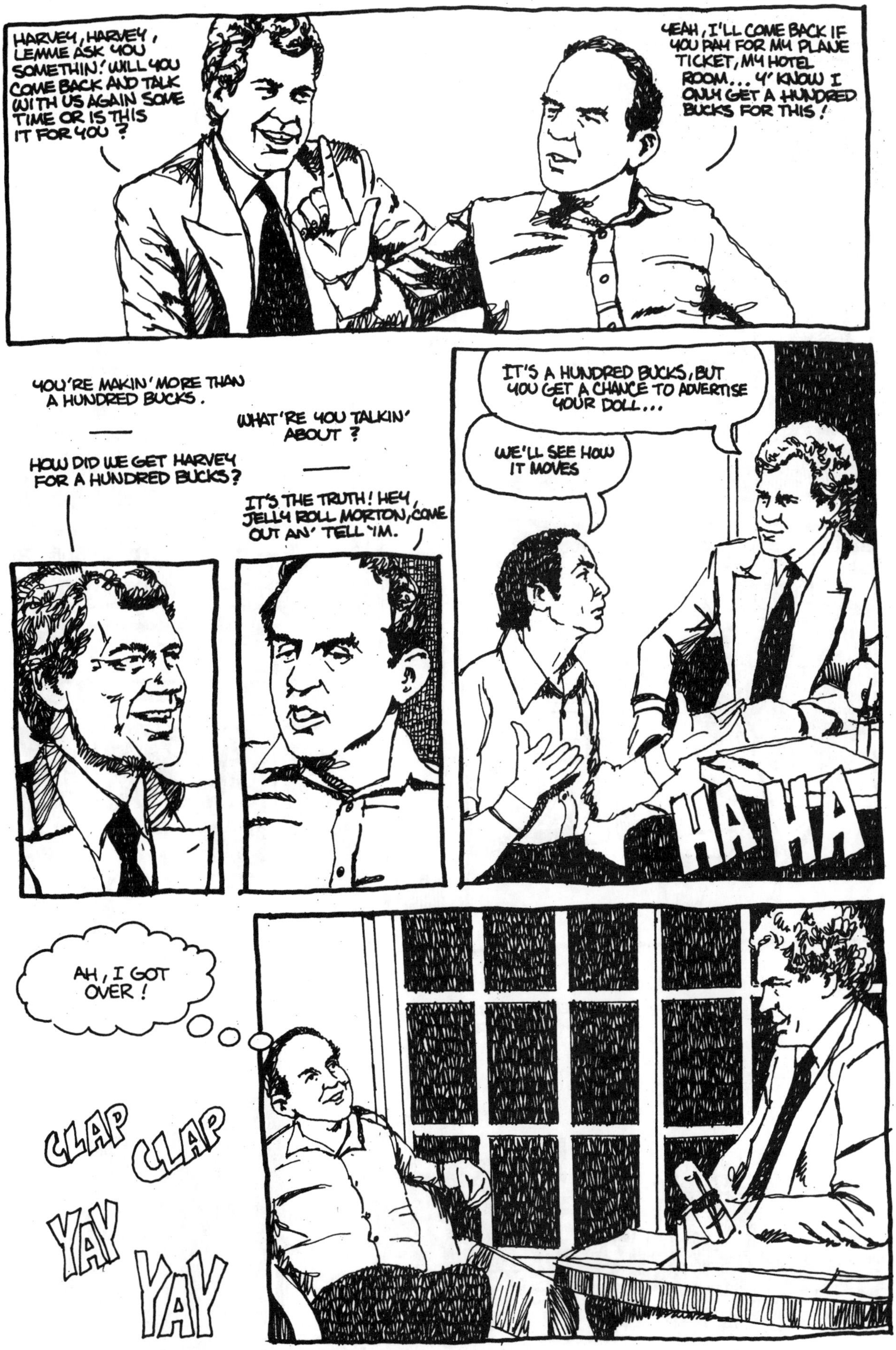
HARVEY, HARVEY, LEMME ASK YOU SOMETHIN'! WILL YOU COME BACK AND TALK WITH US AGAIN SOME TIME OR IS THIS IT FOR YOU?
YEAH, I'LL COME BACK IF YOU PAY FOR MY PLANE TICKET, MY HOTEL ROOM... Y'KNOW I ONLY GET A HUNDRED BUCKS FOR THIS!
YOU'RE MAKIN' MORE THAN A HUNDRED BUCKS.
HOW DID WE GET HARVEY FOR A HUNDRED BUCKS?
WHAT'RE YOU TALKIN' ABOUT?
IT'S THE TRUTH! HEY, JELLY ROLL MORTON, COME OUT AN' TELL 'IM.
IT'S A HUNDRED BUCKS, BUT YOU GET A CHANCE TO ADVERTISE YOUR DOLL...
WE'LL SEE HOW IT MOVES
HA HA
AH, I GOT OVER!
CLAP CLAP
YAY YAY

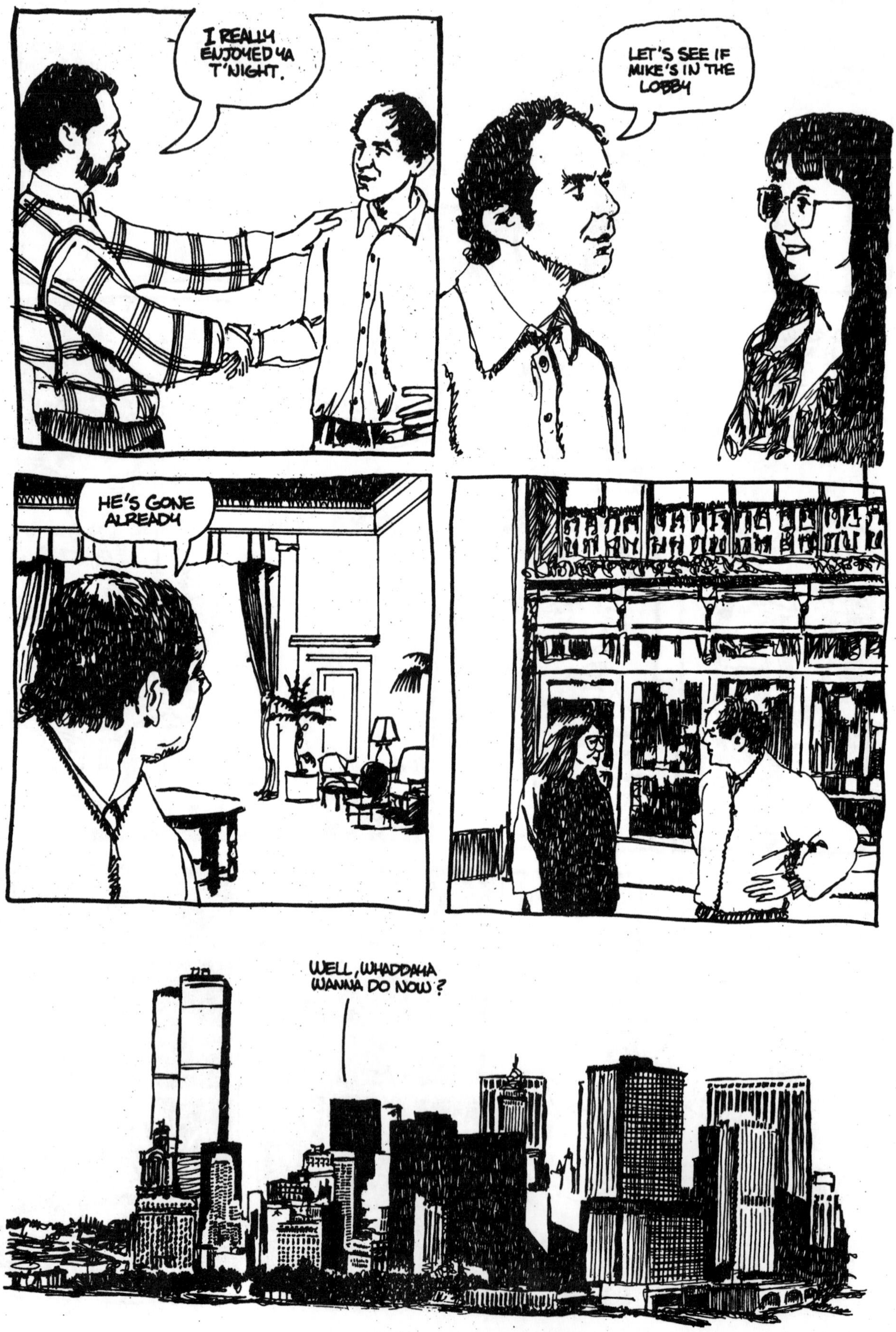
I REALLY ENJOYED YA T'NIGHT.
LET'S SEE IF MIKE'S IN THE LOBBY
HE'S GONE ALREADY
WELL, WHADDAHA WANNA DO NOW?
End

NEW YORK: CITY WITH A HEART

STORY BY HARVEY PEKAR
ART BY DREW FRIEDMAN

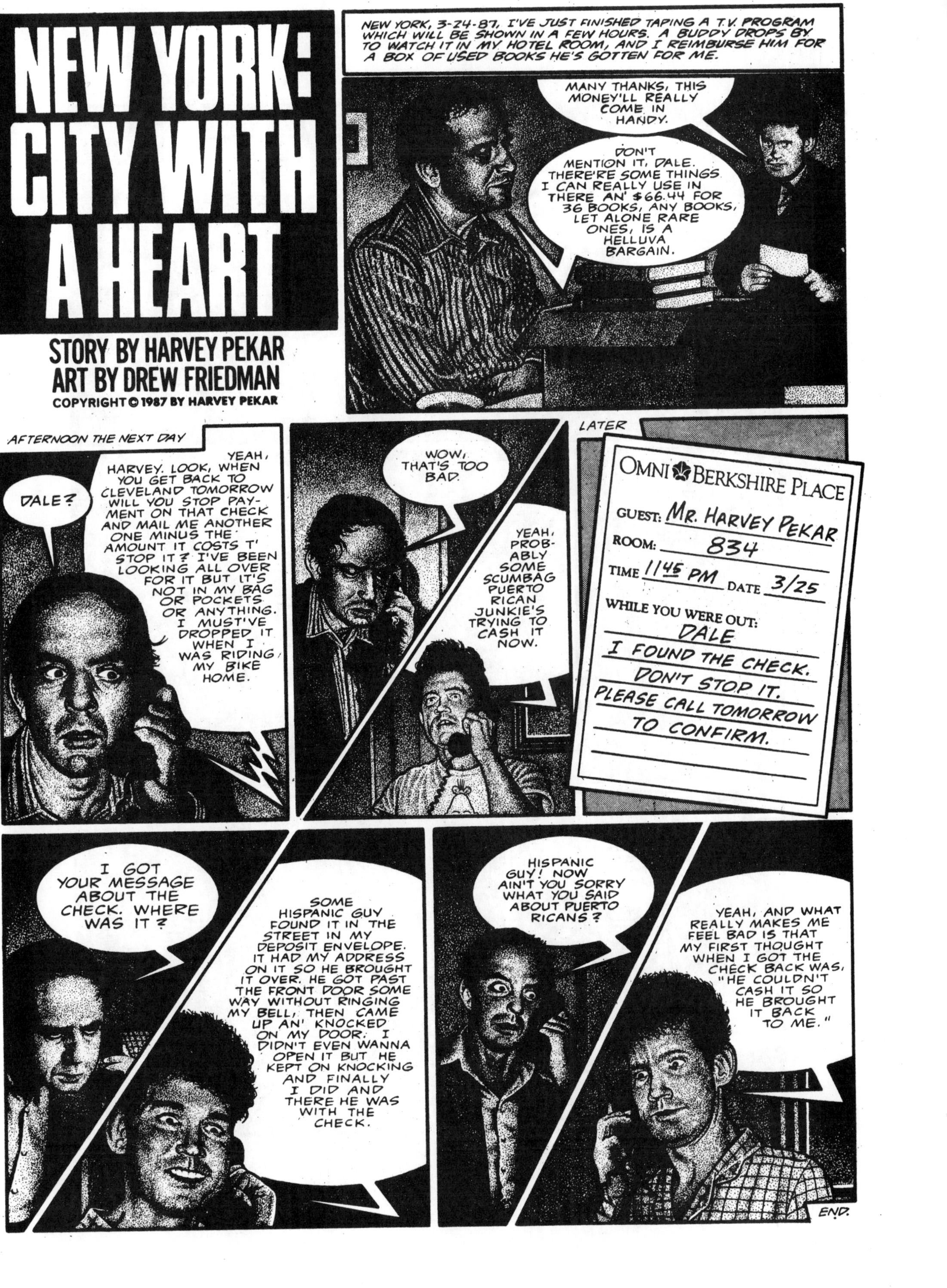
NEW YORK, 3-24-87, I'VE JUST FINISHED TAPING A T.V. PROGRAM WHICH WILL BE SHOWN IN A FEW HOURS. A BUDDY DROPS BY TO WATCH IT IN MY HOTEL ROOM, AND I REIMBURSE HIM FOR A BOX OF USED BOOKS HE'S GOTTEN FOR ME.
MANY THANKS, THIS MONEY'LL REALLY COME IN HANDY.
DON'T MENTION IT, DALE. THERE'RE SOME THINGS I CAN REALLY USE IN THERE AN' $66.44 FOR 36 BOOKS, ANY BOOKS, LET ALONE RARE ONES, IS A HELLUVA BARGAIN.
AFTERNOON THE NEXT DAY
DALE?
YEAH, HARVEY. LOOK, WHEN YOU GET BACK TO CLEVELAND TOMORROW WILL YOU STOP PAYMENT ON THAT CHECK AND MAIL ME ANOTHER ONE MINUS THE AMOUNT IT COSTS T' STOP IT? I'VE BEEN LOOKING ALL OVER FOR IT BUT IT'S NOT IN MY BAG OR POCKETS OR ANYTHING. I MUST'VE DROPPED IT WHEN I WAS RIDING MY BIKE HOME.
WOW, THAT'S TOO BAD.
YEAH, PROBABLY SOME SCUMBAG PUERTO RICAN JUNKIE'S TRYING TO CASH IT NOW.
LATER
OMNI BERKSHIRE PLACE
GUEST: MR. HARVEY PEKAR
ROOM: 834
TIME 11:45 PM DATE 3/25
WHILE YOU WERE OUT: DALE
I FOUND THE CHECK. DON'T STOP IT. PLEASE CALL TOMORROW TO CONFIRM.
I GOT YOUR MESSAGE ABOUT THE CHECK. WHERE WAS IT?
SOME HISPANIC GUY FOUND IT IN THE STREET IN MY DEPOSIT ENVELOPE. IT HAD MY ADDRESS ON IT SO HE BROUGHT IT OVER. HE GOT PAST THE FRONT DOOR SOME WAY WITHOUT RINGING MY BELL, THEN CAME UP AN' KNOCKED ON MY DOOR. I DIDN'T EVEN WANNA OPEN IT BUT HE KEPT ON KNOCKING AND FINALLY I DID AND THERE HE WAS WITH THE CHECK.
HISPANIC GUY! NOW AIN'T YOU SORRY WHAT YOU SAID ABOUT PUERTO RICANS?
YEAH, AND WHAT REALLY MAKES ME FEEL BAD IS THAT MY FIRST THOUGHT WHEN I GOT THE CHECK BACK WAS, "HE COULDN'T CASH IT SO HE BROUGHT IT BACK TO ME."
END.

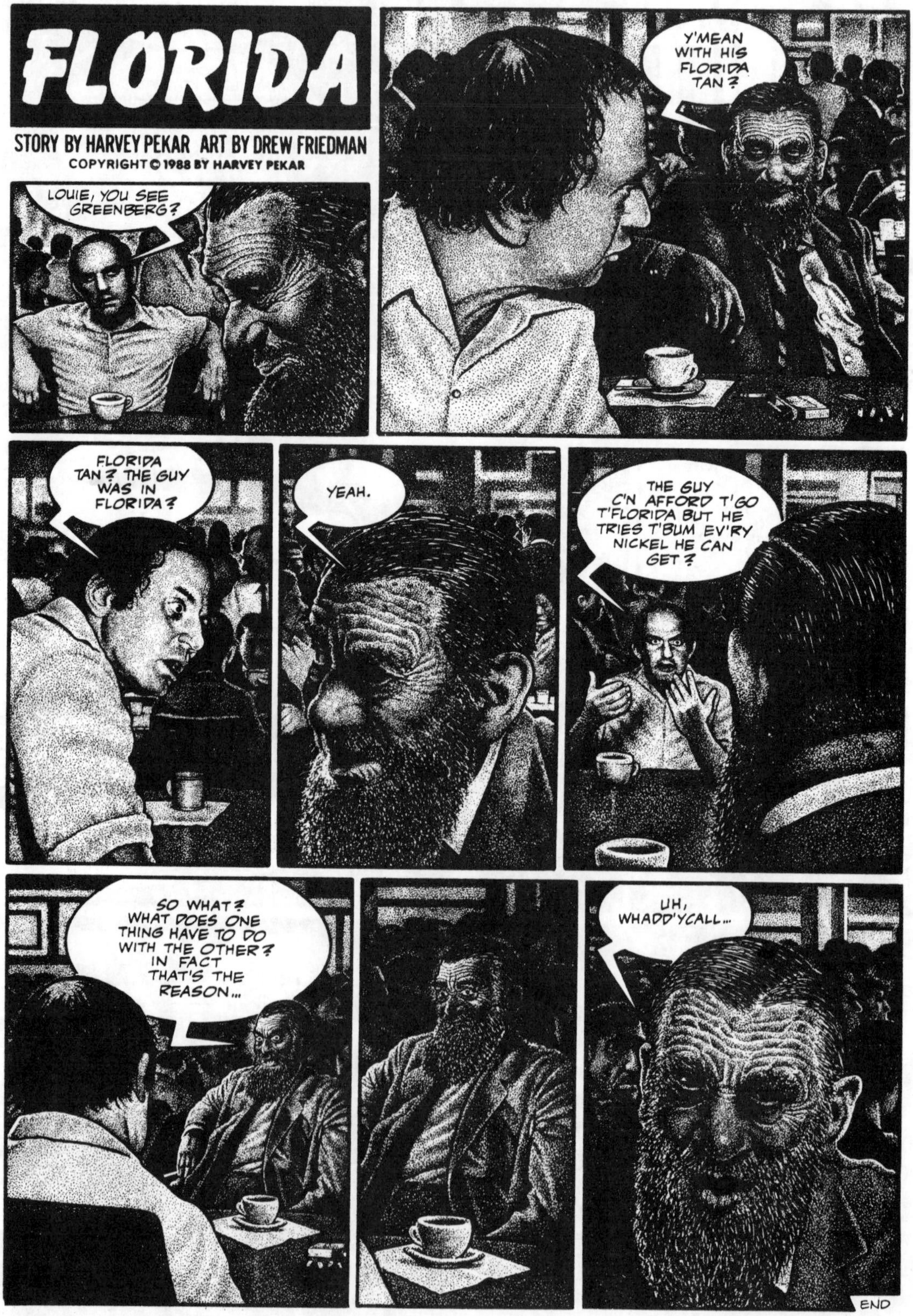
FLORIDA
STORY BY HARVEY PEKAR ART BY DREW FRIEDMAN
COPYRIGHT © 1988 BY HARVEY PEKAR
LOUIE, YOU SEE GREENBERG?
Y'MEAN WITH HIS FLORIDA TAN?
FLORIDA TAN? THE GUY WAS IN FLORIDA?
YEAH.
THE GUY C'N AFFORD T'GO T'FLORIDA BUT HE TRIES T'BUM EV'RY NICKEL HE CAN GET?
SO WHAT? WHAT DOES ONE THING HAVE TO DO WITH THE OTHER? IN FACT THAT'S THE REASON...
UH, WHADD'YCALL...
END

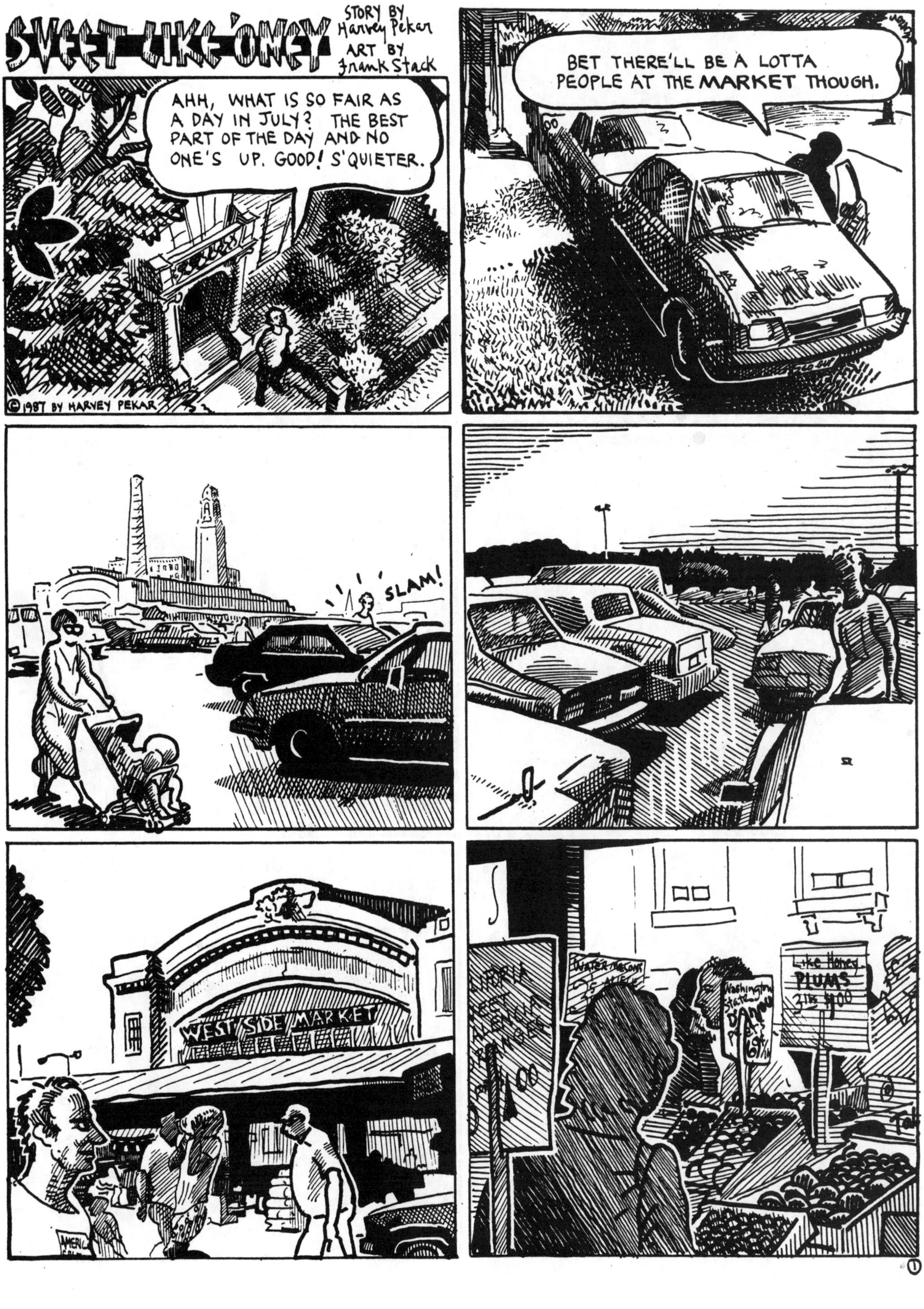
SWEET LIKE 'ONEY
STORY BY Harvey Pekar
ART BY Frank Stack
AHH, WHAT IS SO FAIR AS A DAY IN JULY? THE BEST PART OF THE DAY AND NO ONE'S UP. GOOD! S'QUIETER.
© 1987 BY HARVEY PEKAR
BET THERE'LL BE A LOTTA PEOPLE AT THE MARKET THOUGH.
SLAM!
WEST SIDE MARKET
WATERMELONS
Washington State
Like Honey
PLUMS
3 lbs $1.00

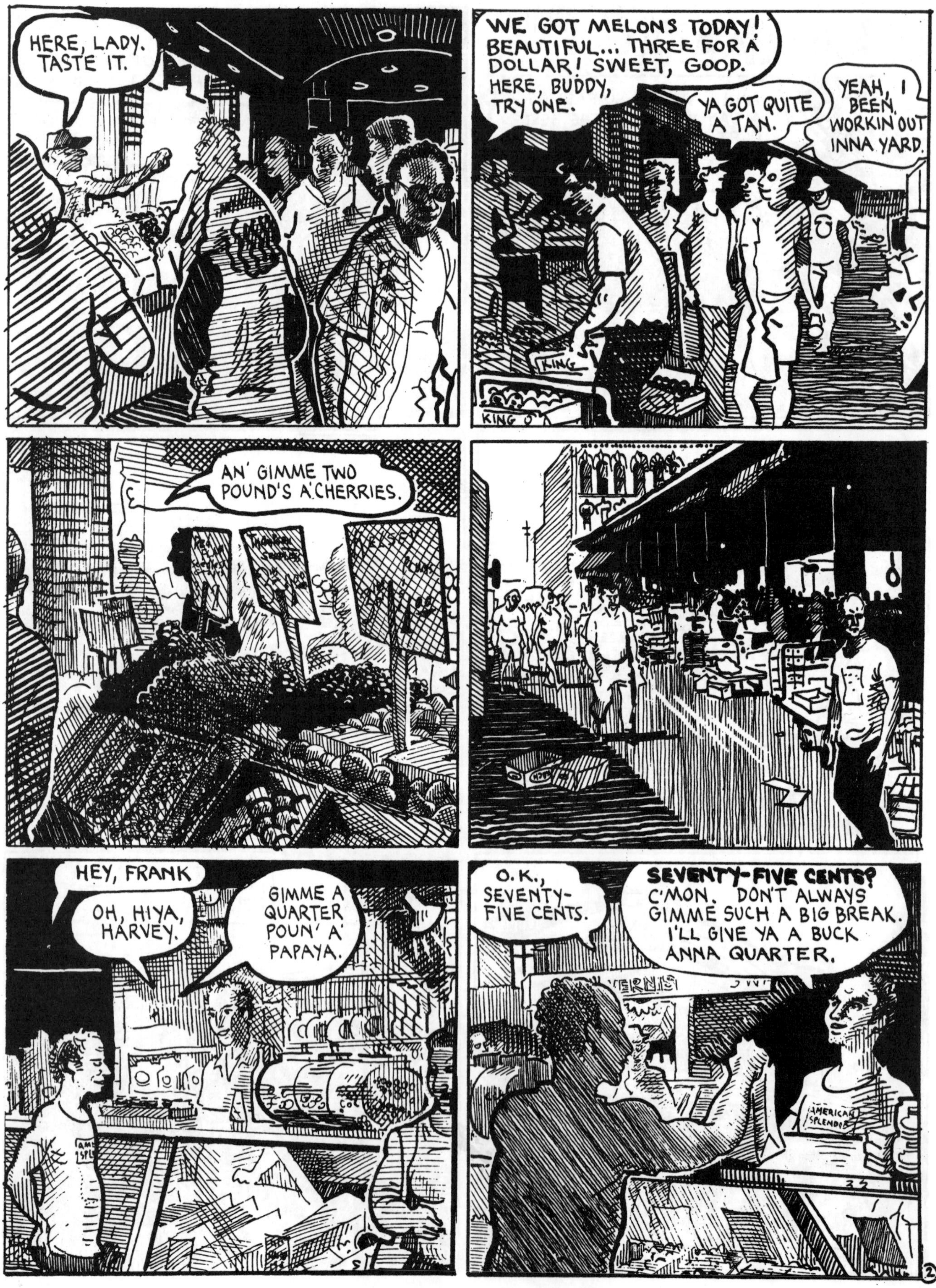
HERE, LADY. TASTE IT.
WE GOT MELONS TODAY! BEAUTIFUL... THREE FOR A DOLLAR! SWEET, GOOD. HERE, BUDDY, TRY ONE.
YA GOT QUITE A TAN.
YEAH, I BEEN WORKIN' OUT INNA YARD.
KING
AN' GIMME TWO POUND'S A' CHERRIES.
HEY, FRANK
OH, HIYA, HARVEY.
GIMME A QUARTER POUN' A' PAPAYA.
O.K., SEVENTY-FIVE CENTS.
SEVENTY-FIVE CENTS? C'MON. DON'T ALWAYS GIMME SUCH A BIG BREAK. I'LL GIVE YA A BUCK ANNA QUARTER.
AMERICAN SPLENDOR

NAW, NAW, HARVEY, IT'S $3.00 A POUND. I CHARGE YOU THE SAME PRICE I'D CHARGE ANYBODY.

OH, YEAH? WELL, GIMME ANOTHER QUARTER POUND THEN. I LOVE THAT STUFF.

SAY, DID YOU SEE THIS OLLIE NORTH GUY ON T.V.? SURE LOOKS LIKE HE'S WON THE HEARTS AND MINDS OF THE COUNTRY. PEOPLE ARE NUTS ABOUT HIM.

THEY'RE SO STUPID. HERE'S THIS GUY WHO SAYS HE'S FOR SETTING UP SECRET GOVERNMENT AGENCIES THAT AREN'T ACCOUNTABLE TO CONGRESS OR THE PUBLIC OR ANYONE AND PEOPLE DON'T PAY ANY ATTENTION TO WHAT HE'S SAYING.

THEY HEAR THAT MOM AND APPLE PIE AND PATRIOTISM STUFF AND THEY THINK THE GUY'S JUST TERRIFIC. THEY WANT HIM FOR A SON-IN-LAW! AN' HERE HE'S IN FAVOR OF SUBVERTING DEMOCRACY!

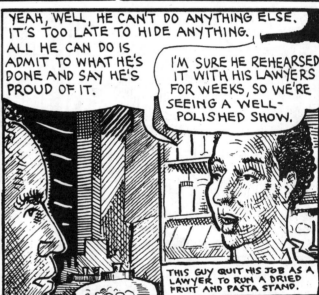

YEAH, WELL, HE CAN'T DO ANYTHING ELSE. IT'S TOO LATE TO HIDE ANYTHING. ALL HE CAN DO IS ADMIT TO WHAT HE'S DONE AND SAY HE'S PROUD OF IT.

I'M SURE HE REHEARSED IT WITH HIS LAWYERS FOR WEEKS, SO WE'RE SEEING A WELL-POLISHED SHOW.

THIS GUY QUIT HIS JOB AS A LAWYER TO RUN A DRIED FRUIT AND PASTA STAND.

IT LOOKS LIKE THEY'RE GONNA TRY AN' PIN EV'RYTHING ON THIS GUY CASEY.

THAT WAS CONVENIENT A' HIM T'DIE...

I NEVER WAS INTO CONSPIRACY THEORIES, BUT THE WAY CASEY DIED... IT SEEMS SUSPICIOUS, Y'KNOW.

NORTH SAYS HE TOLD ALL THIS STUFF TO CASEY, AN' REAGAN SAYS CASEY DIDN'T TELL HIM ANYTHING. SO THE BUCK STOPS WITH A DEAD MAN.

9

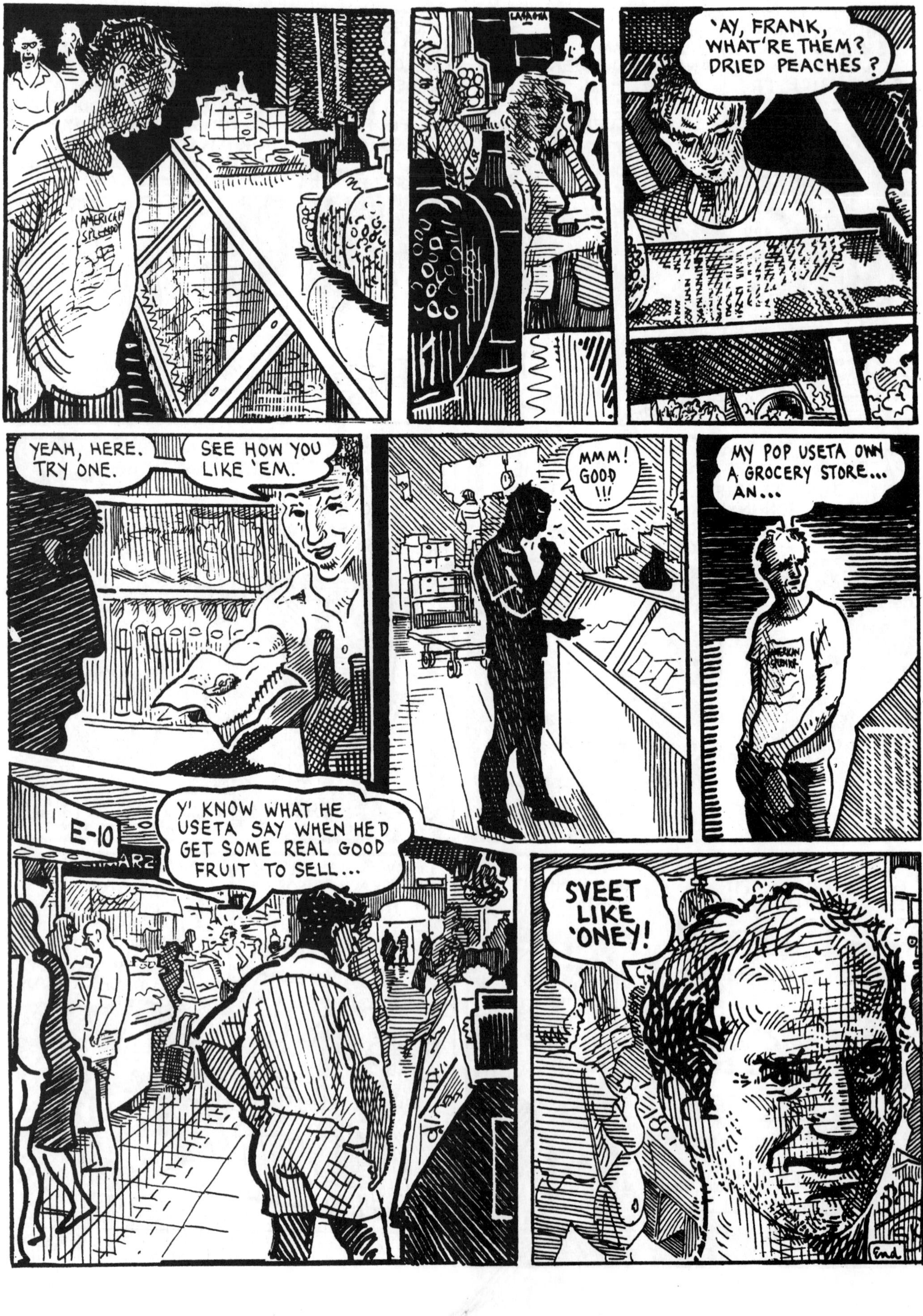

'AY, FRANK, WHAT'RE THEM? DRIED PEACHES?
YEAH, HERE. TRY ONE.
SEE HOW YOU LIKE 'EM.
MMM! GOOD !!!
MY POP USETA OWN A GROCERY STORE... AN...
Y' KNOW WHAT HE USETA SAY WHEN HE'D GET SOME REAL GOOD FRUIT TO SELL...
E-10
SVEET LIKE 'ONEY!
End

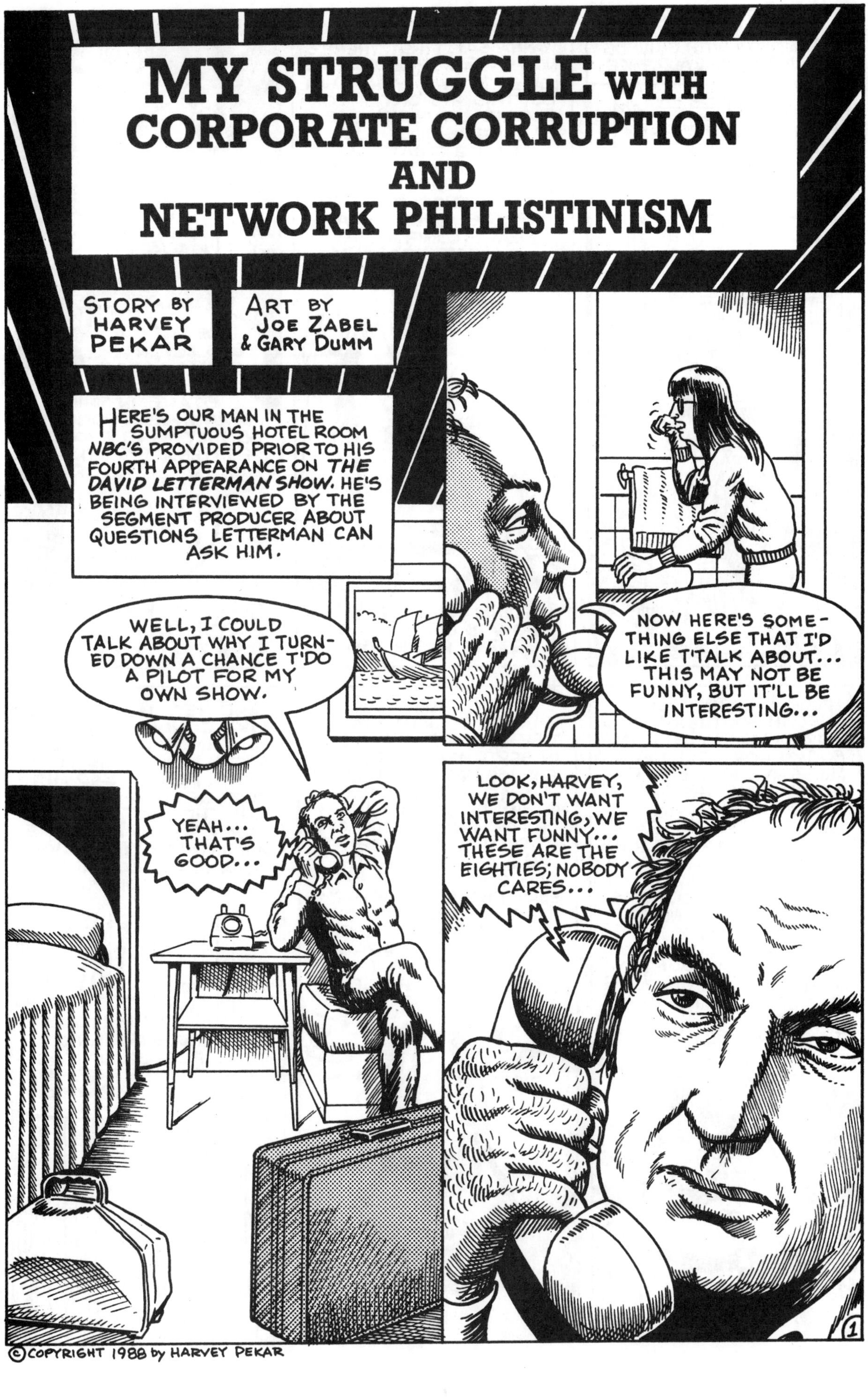
MY STRUGGLE WITH CORPORATE CORRUPTION AND NETWORK PHILISTINISM
STORY BY HARVEY PEKAR
ART BY JOE ZABEL & GARY DUMM
HERE'S OUR MAN IN THE SUMPTUOUS HOTEL ROOM NBC'S PROVIDED PRIOR TO HIS FOURTH APPEARANCE ON THE DAVID LETTERMAN SHOW. HE'S BEING INTERVIEWED BY THE SEGMENT PRODUCER ABOUT QUESTIONS LETTERMAN CAN ASK HIM.
WELL, I COULD TALK ABOUT WHY I TURNED DOWN A CHANCE T'DO A PILOT FOR MY OWN SHOW.
YEAH... THAT'S GOOD...
NOW HERE'S SOMETHING ELSE THAT I'D LIKE T'TALK ABOUT... THIS MAY NOT BE FUNNY, BUT IT'LL BE INTERESTING...
LOOK, HARVEY, WE DON'T WANT INTERESTING, WE WANT FUNNY... THESE ARE THE EIGHTIES; NOBODY CARES...
1

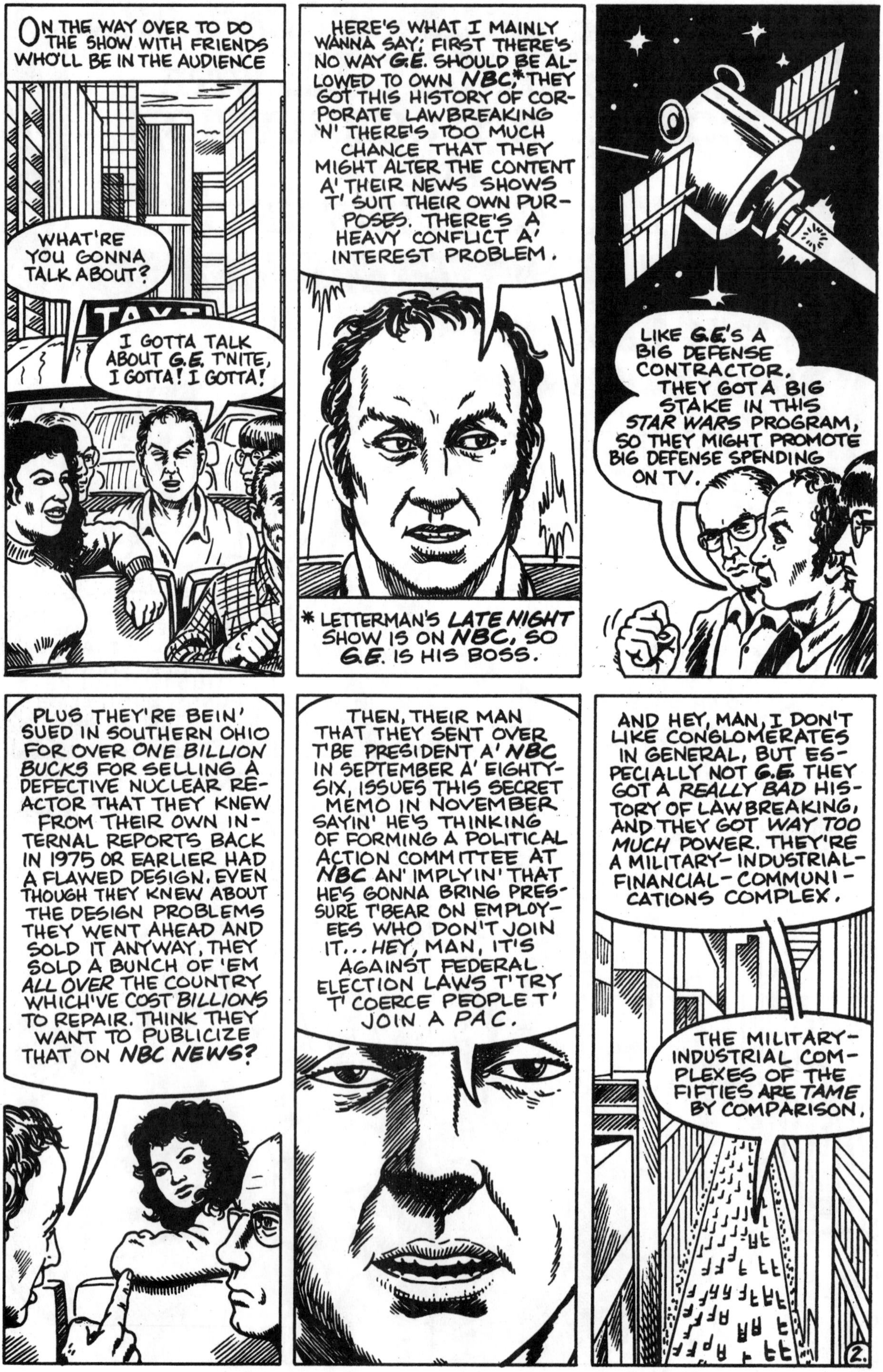
ON THE WAY OVER TO DO THE SHOW WITH FRIENDS WHO'LL BE IN THE AUDIENCE
WHAT'RE YOU GONNA TALK ABOUT?
TAXI
I GOTTA TALK ABOUT G.E. T'NITE, I GOTTA! I GOTTA!
HERE'S WHAT I MAINLY WANNA SAY; FIRST THERE'S NO WAY G.E. SHOULD BE ALLOWED TO OWN NBC;* THEY GOT THIS HISTORY OF CORPORATE LAWBREAKING 'N' THERE'S TOO MUCH CHANCE THAT THEY MIGHT ALTER THE CONTENT A' THEIR NEWS SHOWS T' SUIT THEIR OWN PURPOSES. THERE'S A HEAVY CONFLICT A' INTEREST PROBLEM.
* LETTERMAN'S LATE NIGHT SHOW IS ON NBC, SO G.E. IS HIS BOSS.
LIKE G.E.'S A BIG DEFENSE CONTRACTOR. THEY GOT A BIG STAKE IN THIS STAR WARS PROGRAM, SO THEY MIGHT PROMOTE BIG DEFENSE SPENDING ON TV.
PLUS THEY'RE BEIN' SUED IN SOUTHERN OHIO FOR OVER ONE BILLION BUCKS FOR SELLING A DEFECTIVE NUCLEAR REACTOR THAT THEY KNEW FROM THEIR OWN INTERNAL REPORTS BACK IN 1975 OR EARLIER HAD A FLAWED DESIGN. EVEN THOUGH THEY KNEW ABOUT THE DESIGN PROBLEMS THEY WENT AHEAD AND SOLD IT ANYWAY, THEY SOLD A BUNCH OF 'EM ALL OVER THE COUNTRY WHICH'VE COST BILLIONS TO REPAIR. THINK THEY WANT TO PUBLICIZE THAT ON NBC NEWS?
THEN, THEIR MAN THAT THEY SENT OVER T'BE PRESIDENT A' NBC IN SEPTEMBER A' EIGHTY-SIX, ISSUES THIS SECRET MEMO IN NOVEMBER SAYIN' HE'S THINKING OF FORMING A POLITICAL ACTION COMMITTEE AT NBC AN' IMPLYIN' THAT HE'S GONNA BRING PRESSURE T'BEAR ON EMPLOYEES WHO DON'T JOIN IT... HEY, MAN, IT'S AGAINST FEDERAL ELECTION LAWS T'TRY T' COERCE PEOPLE T' JOIN A PAC.
AND HEY, MAN, I DON'T LIKE CONGLOMERATES IN GENERAL, BUT ESPECIALLY NOT G.E. THEY GOT A REALLY BAD HISTORY OF LAWBREAKING, AND THEY GOT WAY TOO MUCH POWER. THEY'RE A MILITARY-INDUSTRIAL-FINANCIAL-COMMUNICATIONS COMPLEX.
THE MILITARY-INDUSTRIAL COMPLEXES OF THE FIFTIES ARE TAME BY COMPARISON.

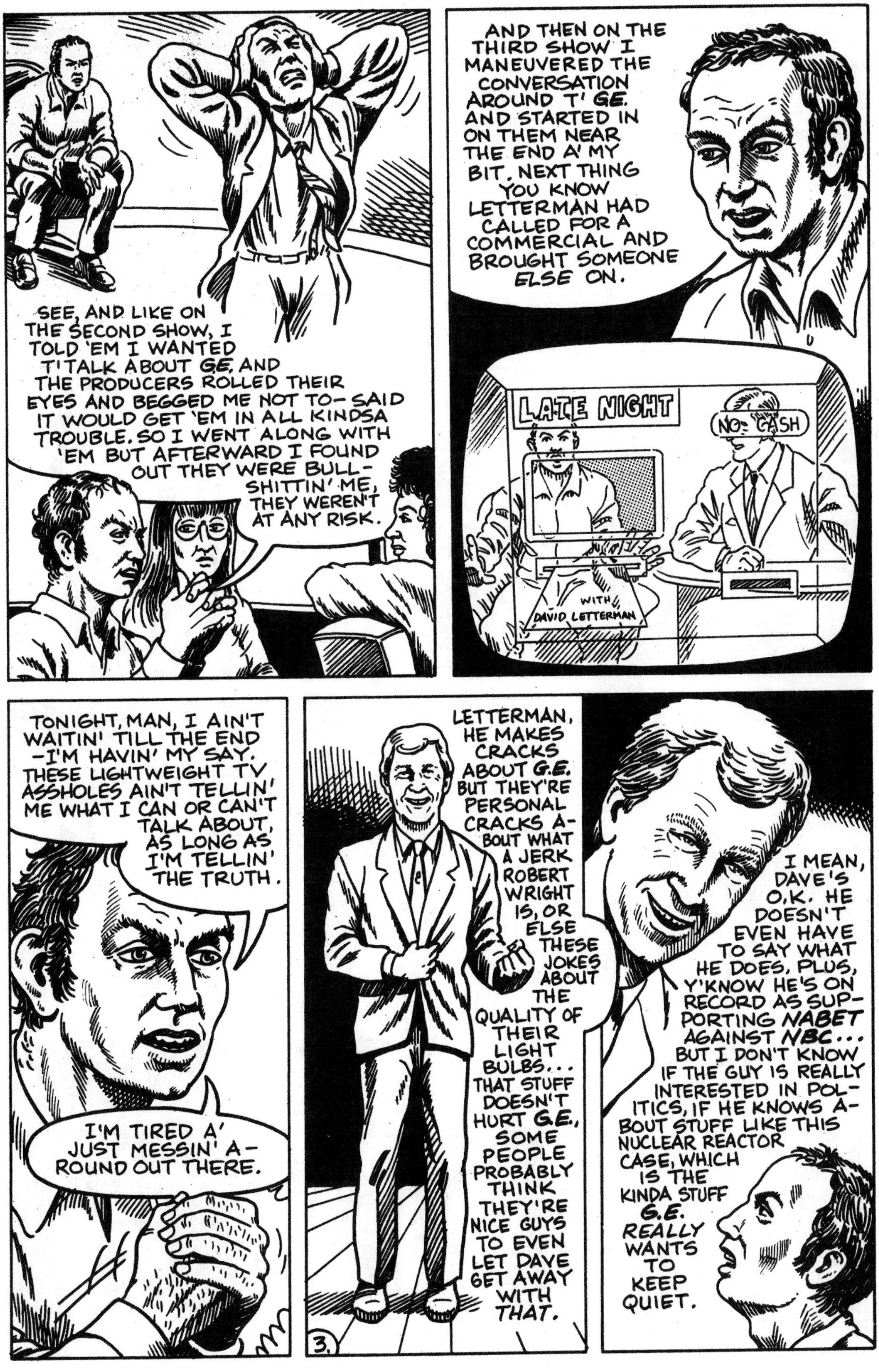
SEE, AND LIKE ON THE SECOND SHOW, I TOLD 'EM I WANTED T' TALK ABOUT GE, AND THE PRODUCERS ROLLED THEIR EYES AND BEGGED ME NOT TO– SAID IT WOULD GET 'EM IN ALL KINDSA TROUBLE. SO I WENT ALONG WITH 'EM BUT AFTERWARD I FOUND OUT THEY WERE BULL-SHITTIN' ME, THEY WEREN'T AT ANY RISK.
AND THEN ON THE THIRD SHOW I MANEUVERED THE CONVERSATION AROUND T' GE. AND STARTED IN ON THEM NEAR THE END A' MY BIT. NEXT THING YOU KNOW LETTERMAN HAD CALLED FOR A COMMERCIAL AND BROUGHT SOMEONE ELSE ON.
LATE NIGHT
NO CASH
WITH DAVID LETTERMAN
TONIGHT, MAN, I AIN'T WAITIN' TILL THE END –I'M HAVIN' MY SAY. THESE LIGHTWEIGHT TV ASSHOLES AIN'T TELLIN' ME WHAT I CAN OR CAN'T TALK ABOUT, AS LONG AS I'M TELLIN' THE TRUTH.
I'M TIRED A' JUST MESSIN' A-ROUND OUT THERE.
LETTERMAN, HE MAKES CRACKS ABOUT G.E. BUT THEY'RE PERSONAL CRACKS A-BOUT WHAT A JERK ROBERT WRIGHT IS, OR ELSE THESE JOKES ABOUT THE QUALITY OF THEIR LIGHT BULBS... THAT STUFF DOESN'T HURT G.E., SOME PEOPLE PROBABLY THINK THEY'RE NICE GUYS TO EVEN LET DAVE GET AWAY WITH THAT.
I MEAN, DAVE'S O.K. HE DOESN'T EVEN HAVE TO SAY WHAT HE DOES, PLUS, Y'KNOW HE'S ON RECORD AS SUP-PORTING NABET AGAINST NBC... BUT I DON'T KNOW IF THE GUY IS REALLY INTERESTED IN POL-ITICS, IF HE KNOWS A-BOUT STUFF LIKE THIS NUCLEAR REACTOR CASE, WHICH IS THE KINDA STUFF G.E. REALLY WANTS TO KEEP QUIET.

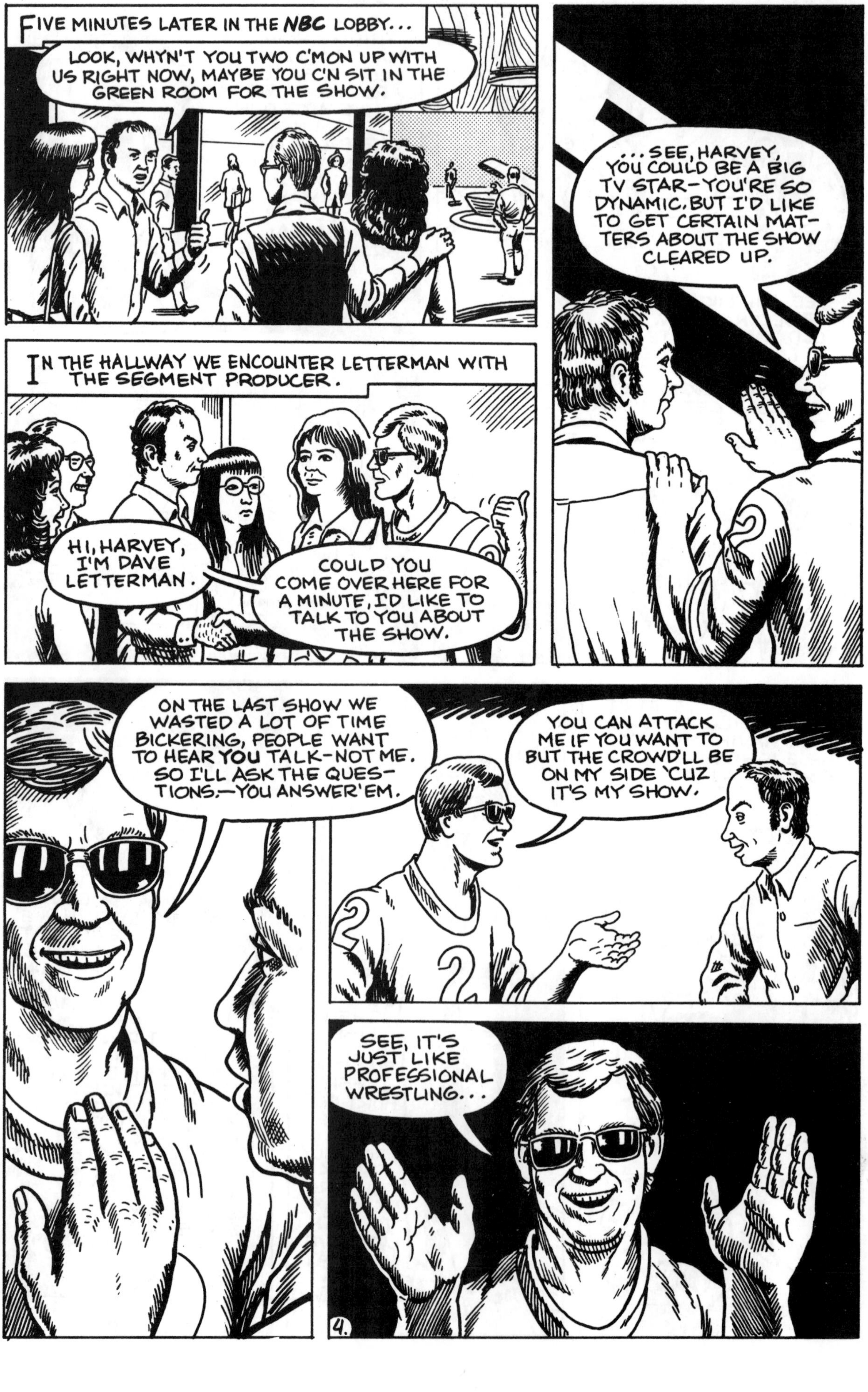
FIVE MINUTES LATER IN THE NBC LOBBY...
LOOK, WHYN'T YOU TWO C'MON UP WITH US RIGHT NOW, MAYBE YOU C'N SIT IN THE GREEN ROOM FOR THE SHOW.
IN THE HALLWAY WE ENCOUNTER LETTERMAN WITH THE SEGMENT PRODUCER.
HI, HARVEY, I'M DAVE LETTERMAN.
COULD YOU COME OVER HERE FOR A MINUTE, I'D LIKE TO TALK TO YOU ABOUT THE SHOW.
...SEE, HARVEY, YOU COULD BE A BIG TV STAR–YOU'RE SO DYNAMIC, BUT I'D LIKE TO GET CERTAIN MATTERS ABOUT THE SHOW CLEARED UP.
ON THE LAST SHOW WE WASTED A LOT OF TIME BICKERING, PEOPLE WANT TO HEAR YOU TALK–NOT ME. SO I'LL ASK THE QUESTIONS.–YOU ANSWER 'EM.
YOU CAN ATTACK ME IF YOU WANT TO BUT THE CROWD'LL BE ON MY SIDE 'CUZ IT'S MY SHOW.
SEE, IT'S JUST LIKE PROFESSIONAL WRESTLING...

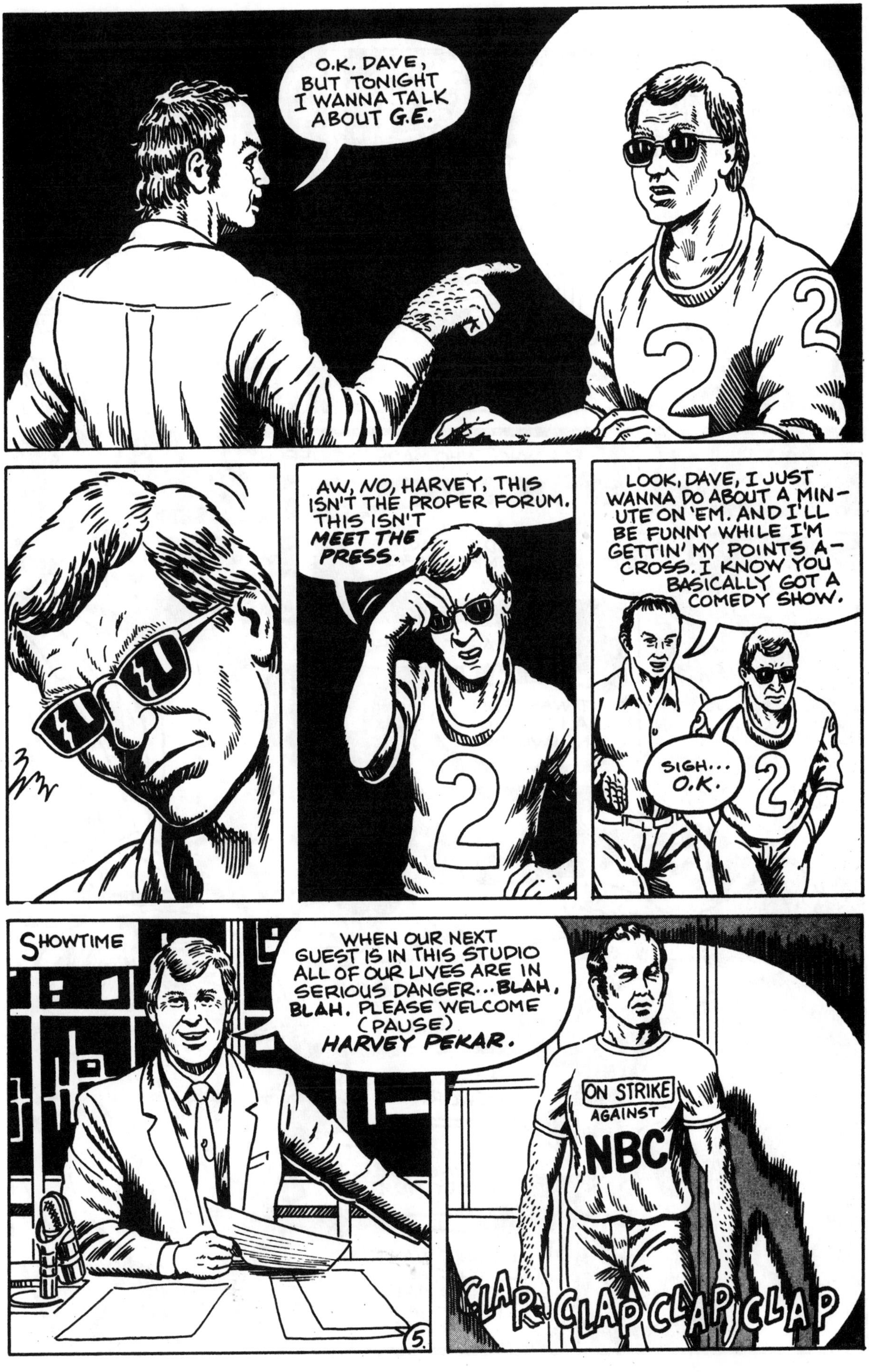
O.K. DAVE, BUT TONIGHT I WANNA TALK ABOUT G.E.
AW, NO, HARVEY, THIS ISN'T THE PROPER FORUM. THIS ISN'T MEET THE PRESS.
LOOK, DAVE, I JUST WANNA DO ABOUT A MIN-UTE ON 'EM. AND I'LL BE FUNNY WHILE I'M GETTIN' MY POINTS A-CROSS. I KNOW YOU BASICALLY GOT A COMEDY SHOW.
SIGH... O.K.
SHOWTIME
WHEN OUR NEXT GUEST IS IN THIS STUDIO ALL OF OUR LIVES ARE IN SERIOUS DANGER... BLAH, BLAH. PLEASE WELCOME (PAUSE) HARVEY PEKAR.
ON STRIKE AGAINST NBC
CLAP CLAP CLAP CLAP CLAP
5.

AFTER A FEW MINUTES OF TRIVIAL BULLSHIT:

HARVEY, IT'S BEEN BROUGHT TO MY ATTENTION THAT YOU'VE BEEN OFFERED YOUR OWN TELEVISION SHOW. IS THAT TRUE?

FOLKS, LEMME TELL YOU, THAT'S THE TRUTH. I DON'T WANT TO TELL YOU WHAT NETWORK. IT WAS AN OFFER TO DO A PILOT.

FOR WHO? WHO MADE THE OFFER?

I DON'T WANNA TELL YOU BECAUSE I TURNED IT DOWN. I DON'T WANNA EMBARRASS ANYBODY.

WAS IT A CABLE DEAL?

IT WAS FOR ANOTHER NETWORK.

WAS IT A.B.C.? I BET IT WAS A.B.C.

IT WAS ANOTHER NETWORK.

THEY'VE GOT NOTHING. A.B.C. IS REALLY HURTING.

I DON'T WANT TO TELL YOU, THEY WERE NICE ENOUGH TO MAKE THE OFFER, I DON'T WANT TO SPIT ON THEM.

6.

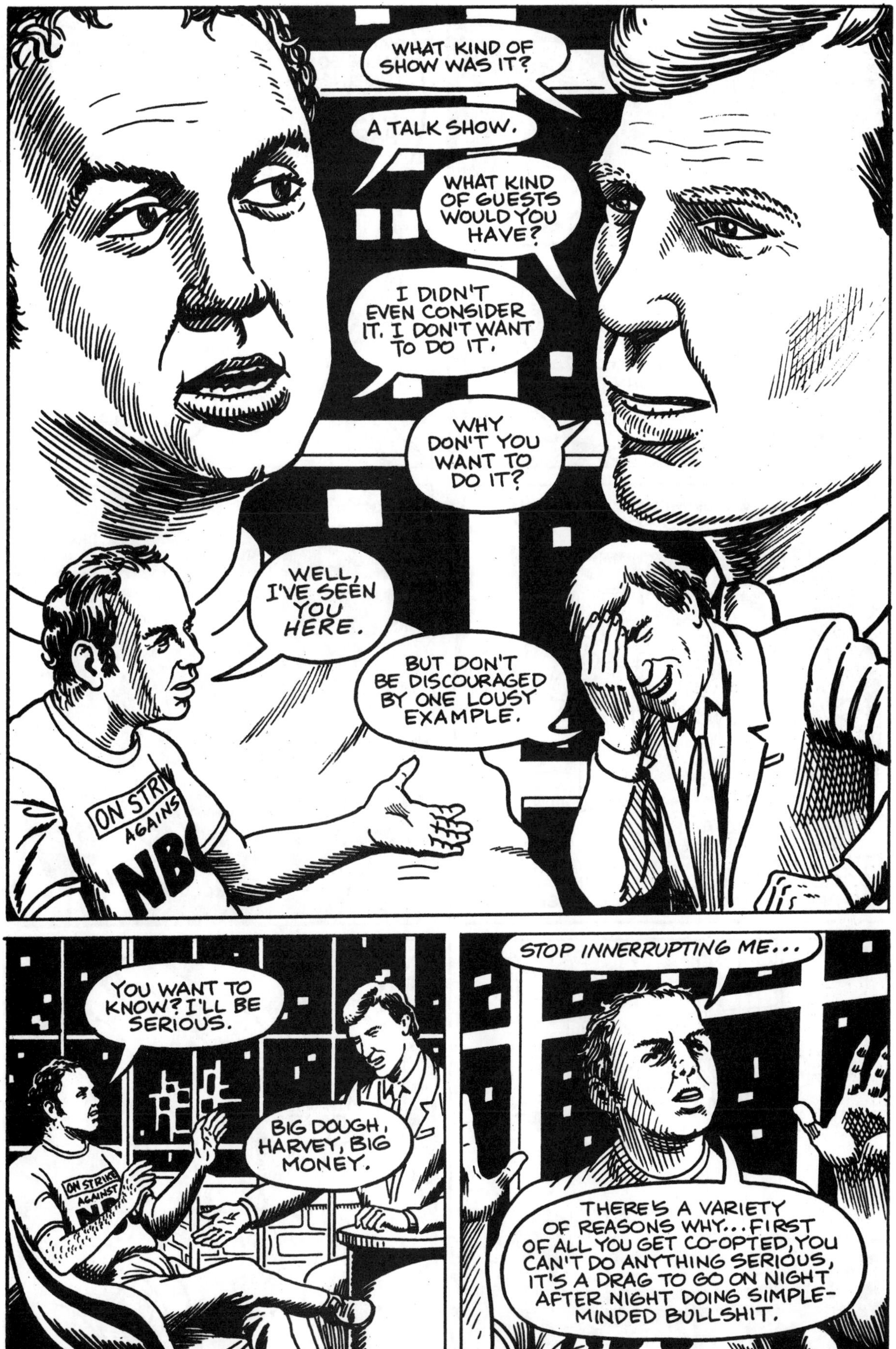
WHAT KIND OF SHOW WAS IT?
A TALK SHOW.
WHAT KIND OF GUESTS WOULD YOU HAVE?
I DIDN'T EVEN CONSIDER IT. I DON'T WANT TO DO IT.
WHY DON'T YOU WANT TO DO IT?
WELL, I'VE SEEN YOU HERE.
BUT DON'T BE DISCOURAGED BY ONE LOUSY EXAMPLE.
ON STRIKE AGAINST NBC
YOU WANT TO KNOW? I'LL BE SERIOUS.
BIG DOUGH, HARVEY, BIG MONEY.
STOP INNERRUPTING ME...
THERE'S A VARIETY OF REASONS WHY... FIRST OF ALL YOU GET CO-OPTED, YOU CAN'T DO ANYTHING SERIOUS, IT'S A DRAG TO GO ON NIGHT AFTER NIGHT DOING SIMPLE-MINDED BULLSHIT.

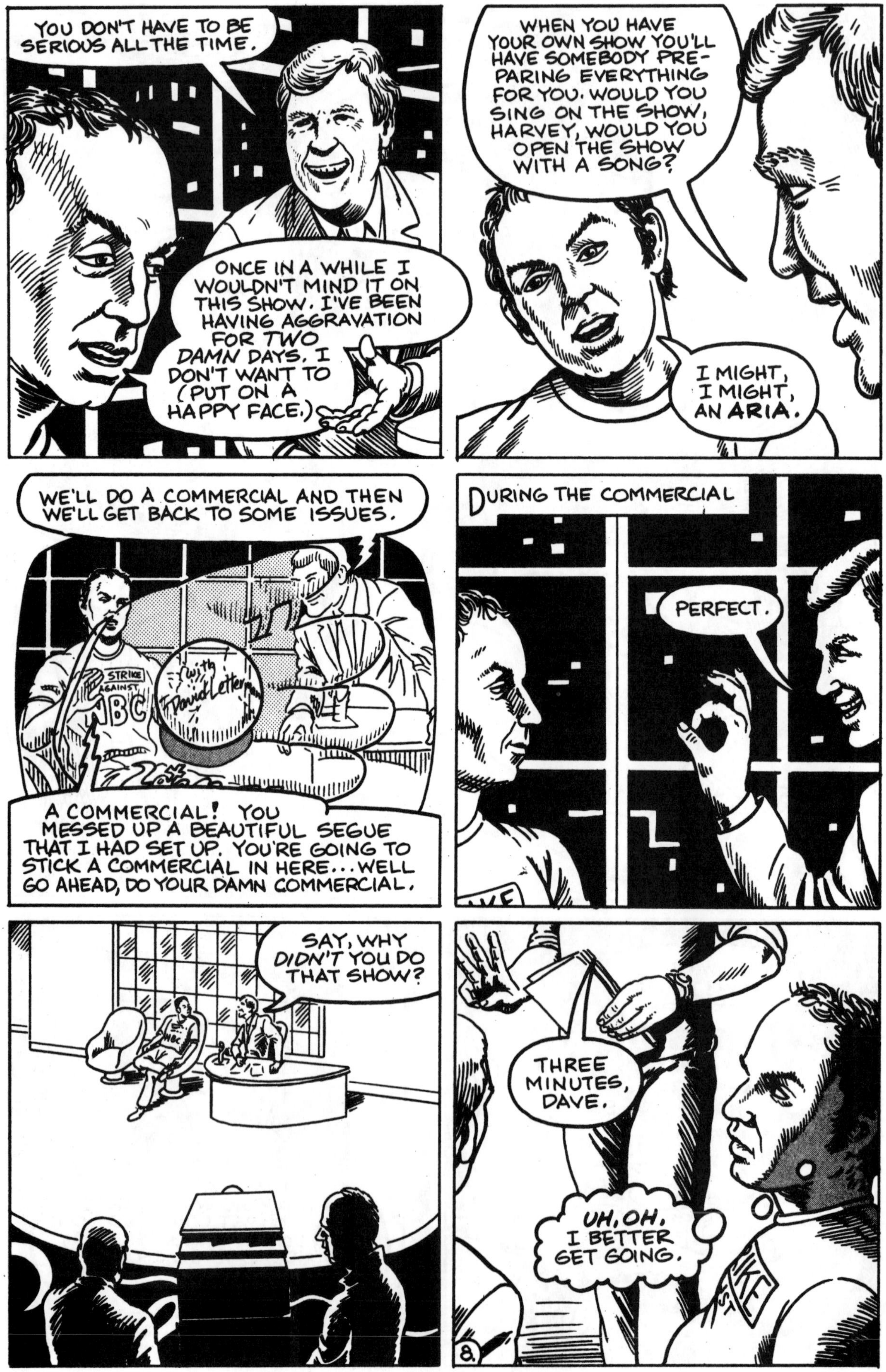
YOU DON'T HAVE TO BE SERIOUS ALL THE TIME.
ONCE IN A WHILE I WOULDN'T MIND IT ON THIS SHOW. I'VE BEEN HAVING AGGRAVATION FOR TWO DAMN DAYS. I DON'T WANT TO (PUT ON A HAPPY FACE.)
WHEN YOU HAVE YOUR OWN SHOW YOU'LL HAVE SOMEBODY PRE-PARING EVERYTHING FOR YOU. WOULD YOU SING ON THE SHOW, HARVEY, WOULD YOU OPEN THE SHOW WITH A SONG?
I MIGHT, I MIGHT, AN ARIA.
WE'LL DO A COMMERCIAL AND THEN WE'LL GET BACK TO SOME ISSUES.
STRIKE AGAINST NBC
with David Letterman
A COMMERCIAL! YOU MESSED UP A BEAUTIFUL SEGUE THAT I HAD SET UP. YOU'RE GOING TO STICK A COMMERCIAL IN HERE... WELL GO AHEAD, DO YOUR DAMN COMMERCIAL.
DURING THE COMMERCIAL
PERFECT.
SAY, WHY DIDN'T YOU DO THAT SHOW?
THREE MINUTES, DAVE.
UH, OH, I BETTER GET GOING.
8.

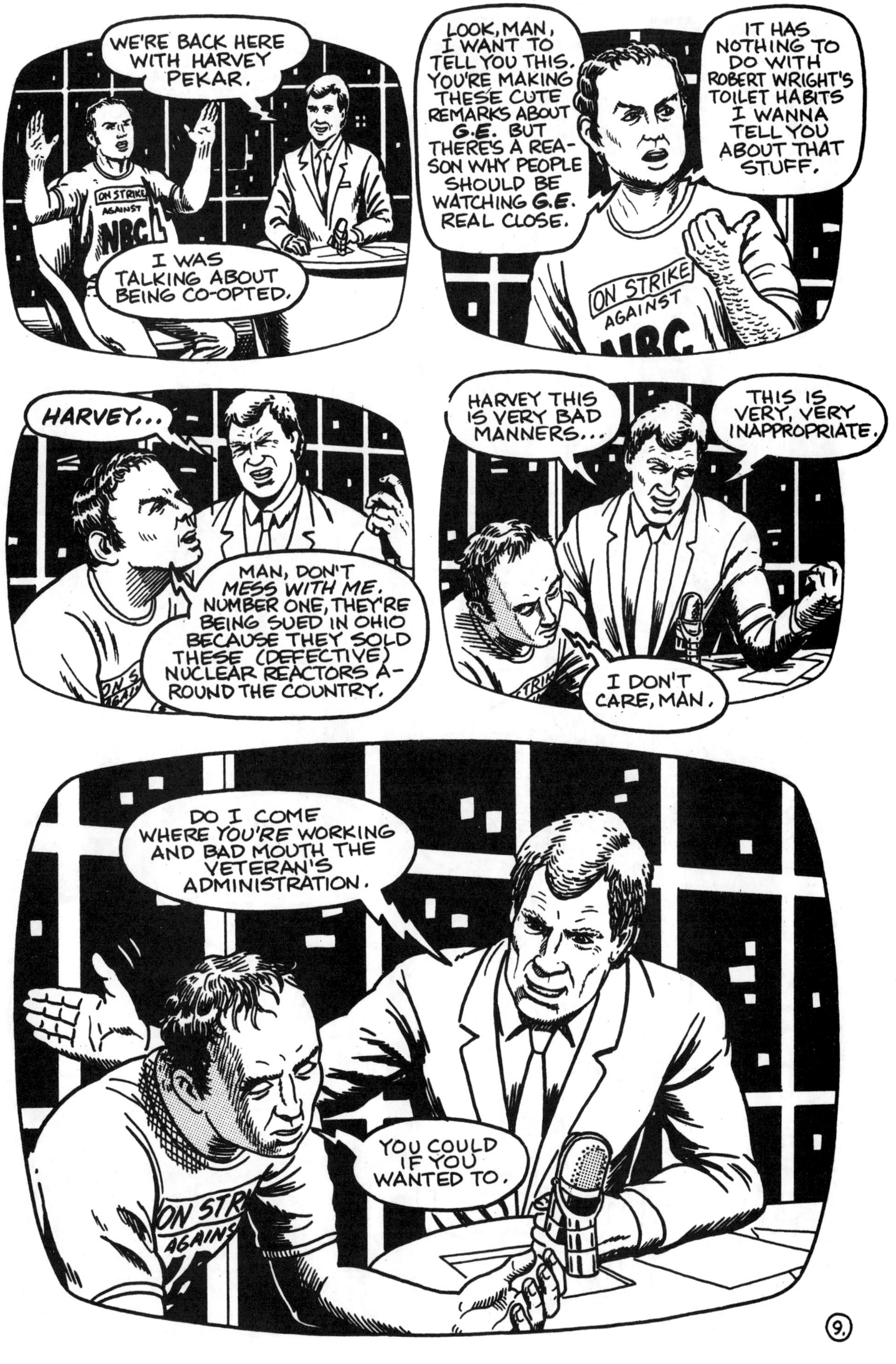
WE'RE BACK HERE WITH HARVEY PEKAR.
I WAS TALKING ABOUT BEING CO-OPTED.
ON STRIKE AGAINST NBC
LOOK, MAN, I WANT TO TELL YOU THIS. YOU'RE MAKING THESE CUTE REMARKS ABOUT G.E. BUT THERE'S A REASON WHY PEOPLE SHOULD BE WATCHING G.E. REAL CLOSE.
IT HAS NOTHING TO DO WITH ROBERT WRIGHT'S TOILET HABITS I WANNA TELL YOU ABOUT THAT STUFF.
ON STRIKE AGAINST
HARVEY...
MAN, DON'T MESS WITH ME. NUMBER ONE, THEY'RE BEING SUED IN OHIO BECAUSE THEY SOLD THESE (DEFECTIVE) NUCLEAR REACTORS AROUND THE COUNTRY.
HARVEY THIS IS VERY BAD MANNERS...
THIS IS VERY, VERY INAPPROPRIATE.
I DON'T CARE, MAN.
DO I COME WHERE YOU'RE WORKING AND BAD MOUTH THE VETERAN'S ADMINISTRATION.
YOU COULD IF YOU WANTED TO.
ON STR AGAINS

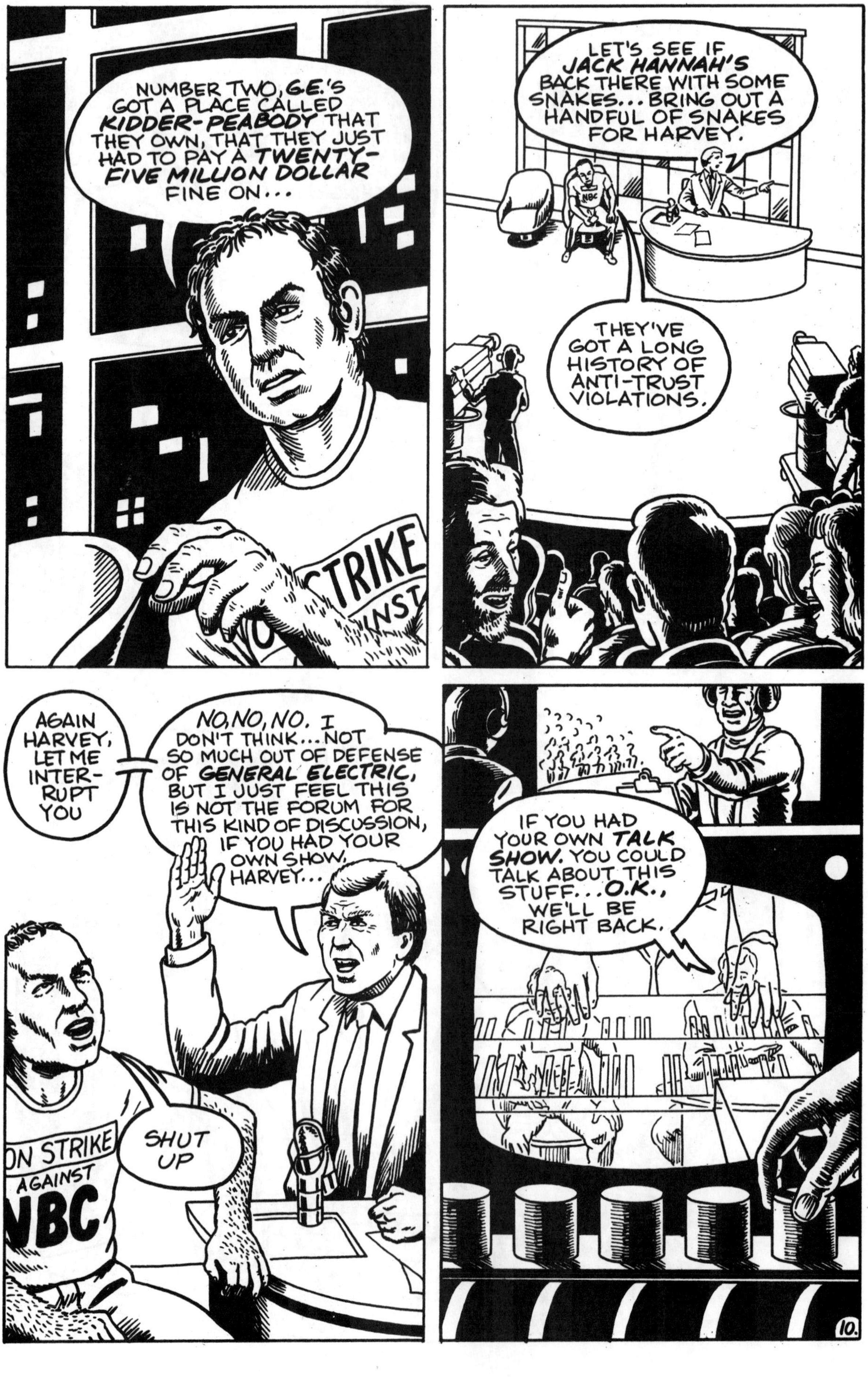
NUMBER TWO, G.E.'S GOT A PLACE CALLED KIDDER-PEABODY THAT THEY OWN, THAT THEY JUST HAD TO PAY A TWENTY-FIVE MILLION DOLLAR FINE ON...
STRIKE
INST
LET'S SEE IF JACK HANNAH'S BACK THERE WITH SOME SNAKES... BRING OUT A HANDFUL OF SNAKES FOR HARVEY.
NBC
THEY'VE GOT A LONG HISTORY OF ANTI-TRUST VIOLATIONS.
AGAIN HARVEY, LET ME INTER-RUPT YOU
NO, NO, NO. I DON'T THINK... NOT SO MUCH OUT OF DEFENSE OF GENERAL ELECTRIC, BUT I JUST FEEL THIS IS NOT THE FORUM FOR THIS KIND OF DISCUSSION, IF YOU HAD YOUR OWN SHOW, HARVEY...
SHUT UP
ON STRIKE AGAINST NBC
IF YOU HAD YOUR OWN TALK SHOW. YOU COULD TALK ABOUT THIS STUFF... O.K., WE'LL BE RIGHT BACK.

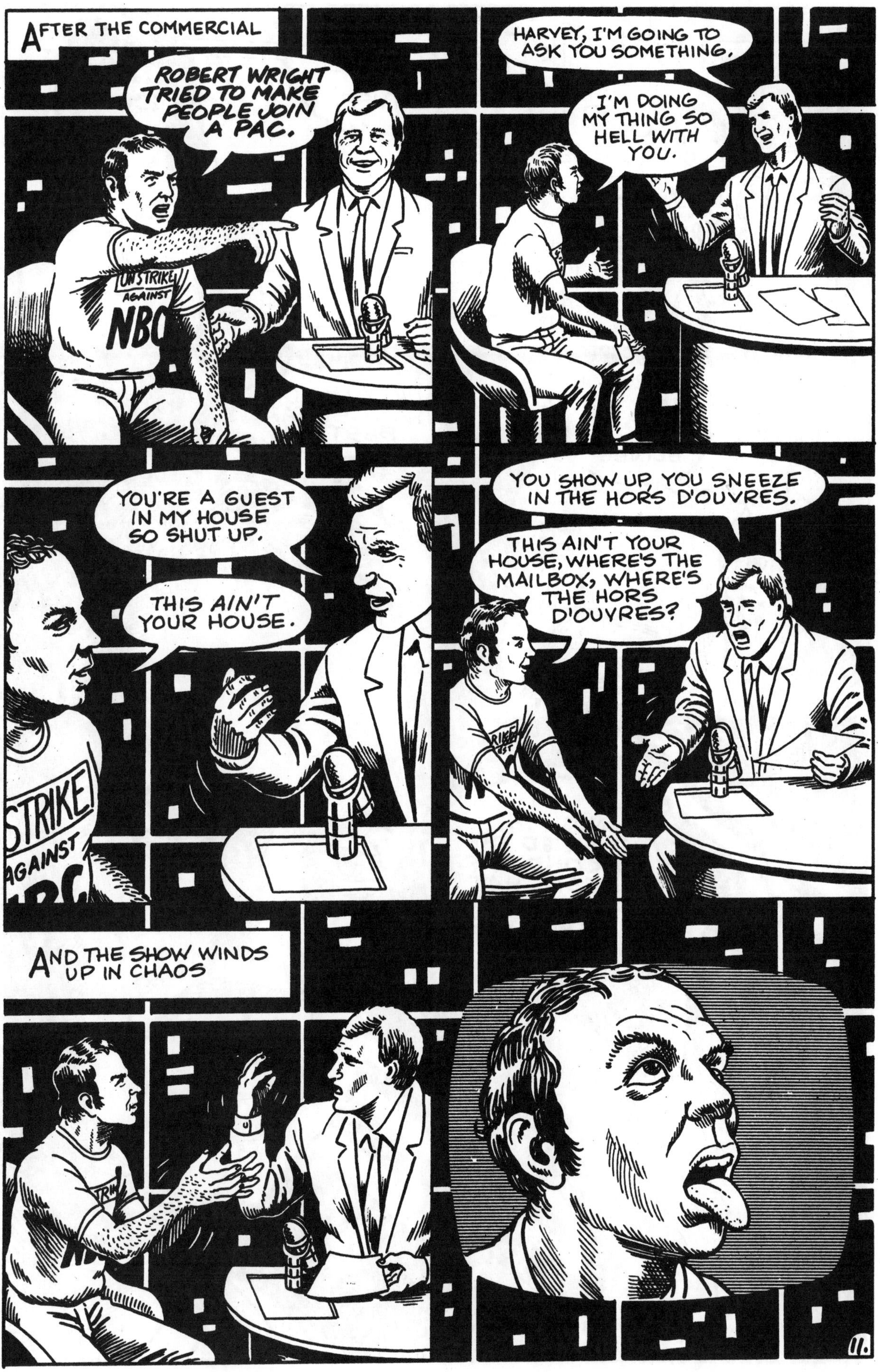
AFTER THE COMMERCIAL
ROBERT WRIGHT TRIED TO MAKE PEOPLE JOIN A PAC.
ON STRIKE AGAINST NBC
HARVEY, I'M GOING TO ASK YOU SOMETHING.
I'M DOING MY THING SO HELL WITH YOU.
YOU'RE A GUEST IN MY HOUSE SO SHUT UP.
THIS AIN'T YOUR HOUSE.
STRIKE! AGAINST
YOU SHOW UP, YOU SNEEZE IN THE HORS D'OUVRES.
THIS AIN'T YOUR HOUSE, WHERE'S THE MAILBOX, WHERE'S THE HORS D'OUVRES?
AND THE SHOW WINDS UP IN CHAOS
11.

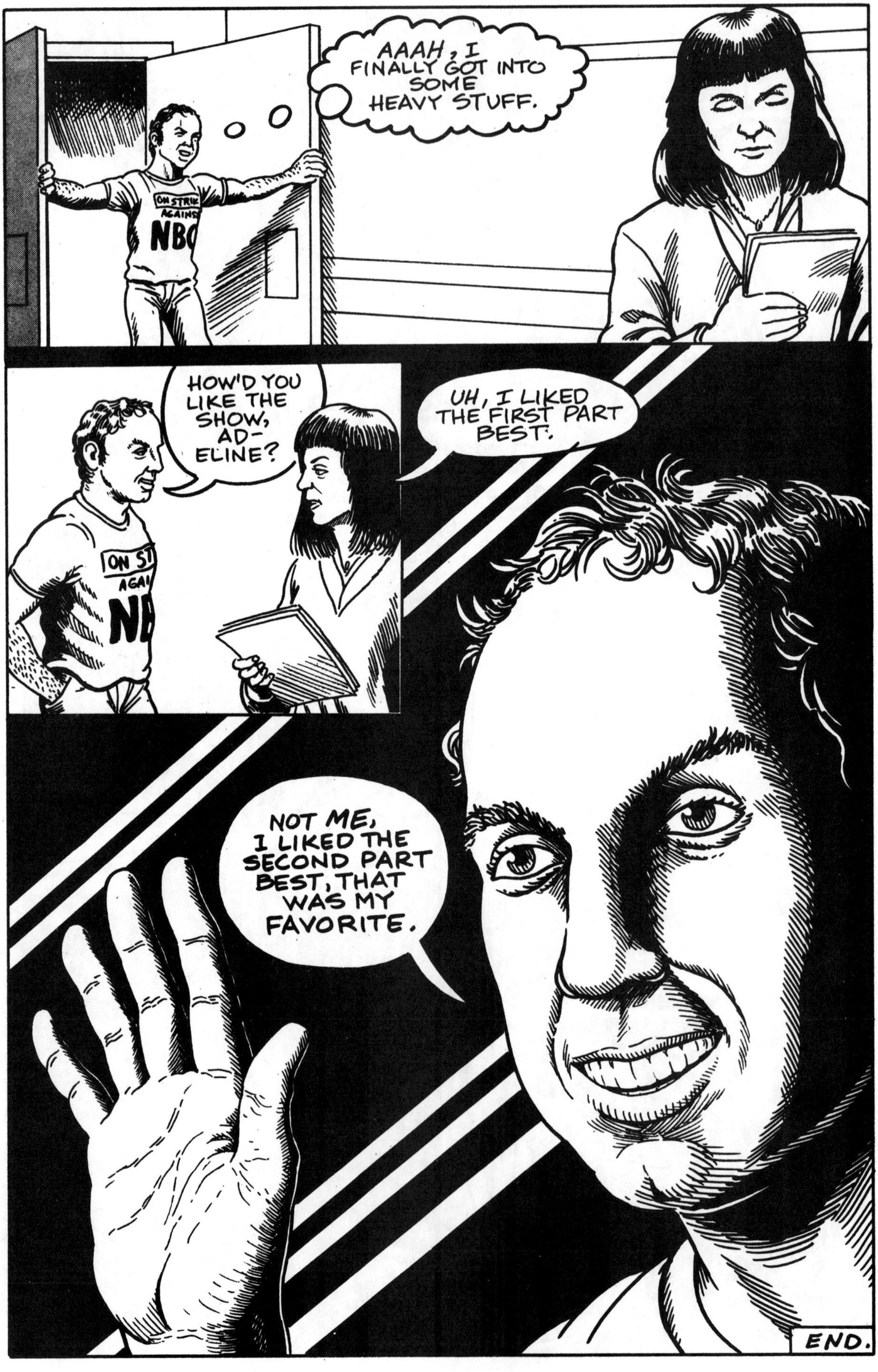
AAAH, I FINALLY GOT INTO SOME HEAVY STUFF.
ON STRIKE AGAINST NBC
HOW'D YOU LIKE THE SHOW, AD-ELINE?
UH, I LIKED THE FIRST PART BEST.
NOT ME, I LIKED THE SECOND PART BEST, THAT WAS MY FAVORITE.
END.

ALTERATIONS

STORY BY HARVEY PEKAR
ART BY VAL MAYERIK

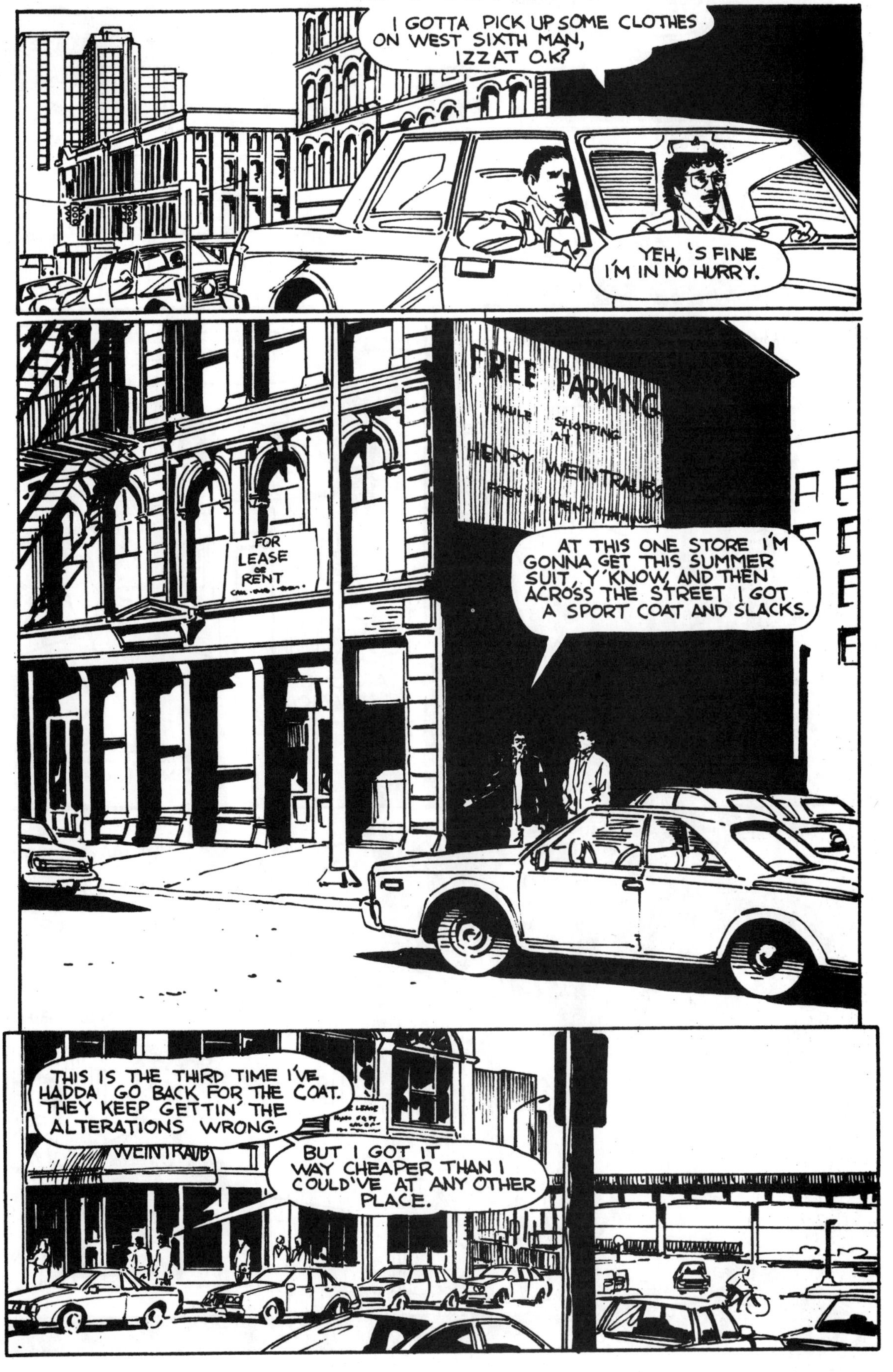
I GOTTA PICK UP SOME CLOTHES ON WEST SIXTH MAN, IZZAT O.K?
YEH, 'S FINE I'M IN NO HURRY.
FREE PARKING
WHILE SHOPPING AT
HENRY WEINTRAUB'S
FOR LEASE OR RENT
AT THIS ONE STORE I'M GONNA GET THIS SUMMER SUIT, Y'KNOW, AND THEN ACROSS THE STREET I GOT A SPORT COAT AND SLACKS.
THIS IS THE THIRD TIME I'VE HADDA GO BACK FOR THE COAT. THEY KEEP GETTIN' THE ALTERATIONS WRONG.
WEINTRAUB
BUT I GOT IT WAY CHEAPER THAN I COULD'VE AT ANY OTHER PLACE.

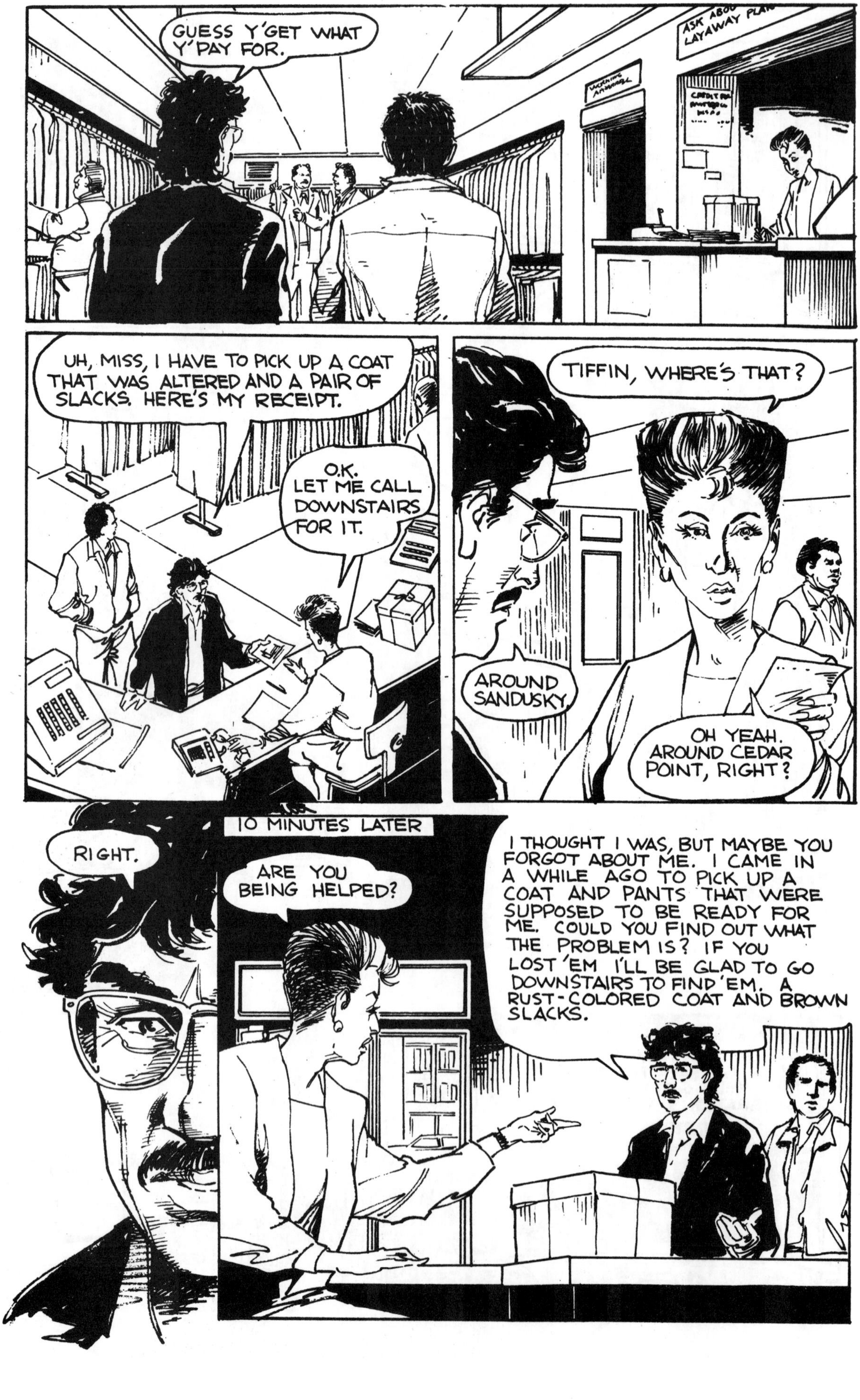
GUESS Y'GET WHAT Y'PAY FOR.
UH, MISS, I HAVE TO PICK UP A COAT THAT WAS ALTERED AND A PAIR OF SLACKS. HERE'S MY RECEIPT.
O.K. LET ME CALL DOWNSTAIRS FOR IT.
TIFFIN, WHERE'S THAT?
AROUND SANDUSKY.
OH YEAH. AROUND CEDAR POINT, RIGHT?
RIGHT.
10 MINUTES LATER
ARE YOU BEING HELPED?
I THOUGHT I WAS, BUT MAYBE YOU FORGOT ABOUT ME. I CAME IN A WHILE AGO TO PICK UP A COAT AND PANTS THAT WERE SUPPOSED TO BE READY FOR ME. COULD YOU FIND OUT WHAT THE PROBLEM IS? IF YOU LOST 'EM I'LL BE GLAD TO GO DOWNSTAIRS TO FIND 'EM. A RUST-COLORED COAT AND BROWN SLACKS.

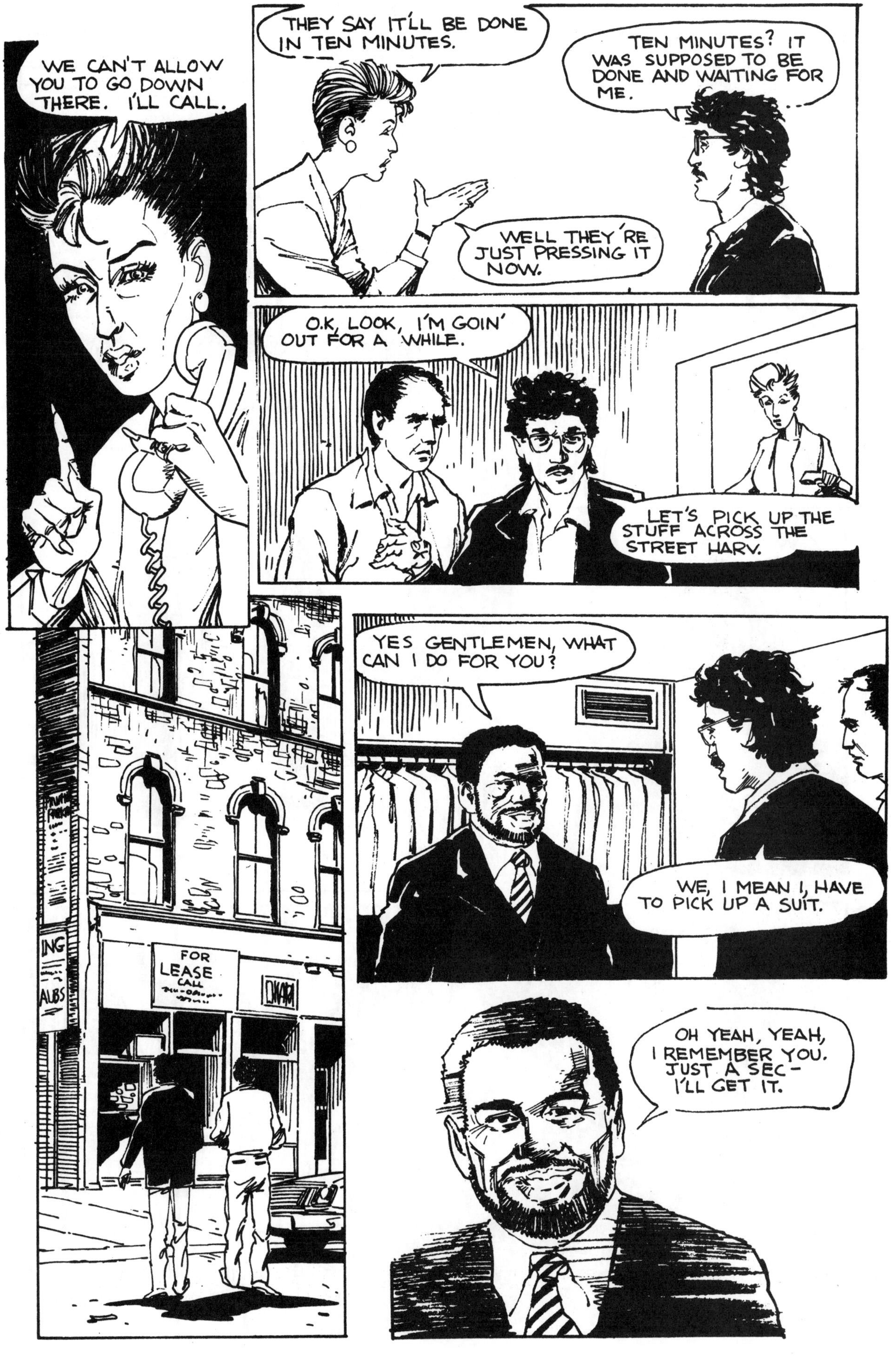

WE CAN'T ALLOW YOU TO GO DOWN THERE. I'LL CALL.
THEY SAY IT'LL BE DONE IN TEN MINUTES.
TEN MINUTES? IT WAS SUPPOSED TO BE DONE AND WAITING FOR ME.
WELL THEY'RE JUST PRESSING IT NOW.
O.K, LOOK, I'M GOIN' OUT FOR A WHILE.
LET'S PICK UP THE STUFF ACROSS THE STREET HARV.
FOR LEASE CALL
YES GENTLEMEN, WHAT CAN I DO FOR YOU?
WE, I MEAN I, HAVE TO PICK UP A SUIT.
OH YEAH, YEAH, I REMEMBER YOU. JUST A SEC - I'LL GET IT.

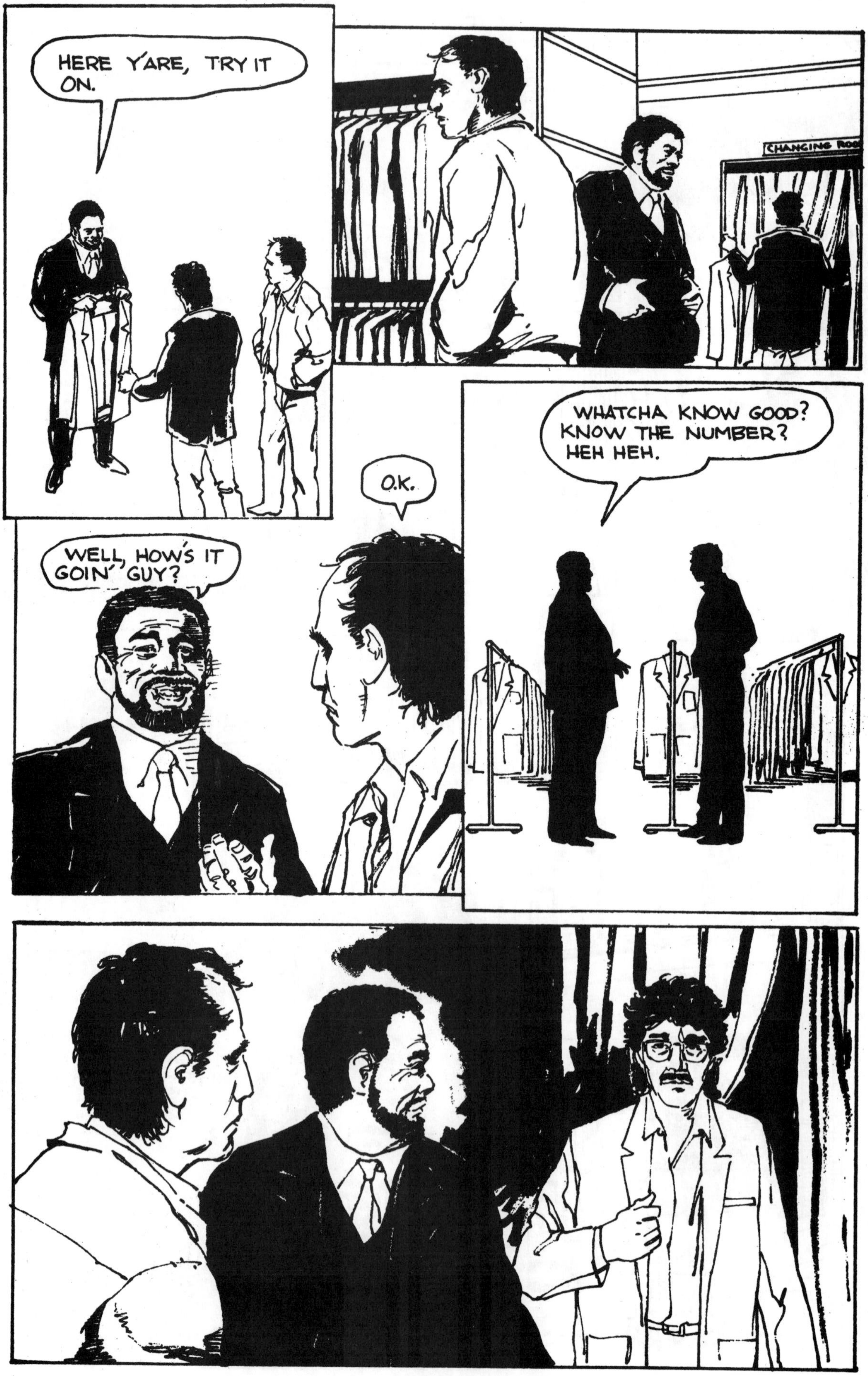
HERE YARE, TRY IT ON.
WELL, HOW'S IT GOIN' GUY?
O.K.
WHATCHA KNOW GOOD? KNOW THE NUMBER? HEH HEH.

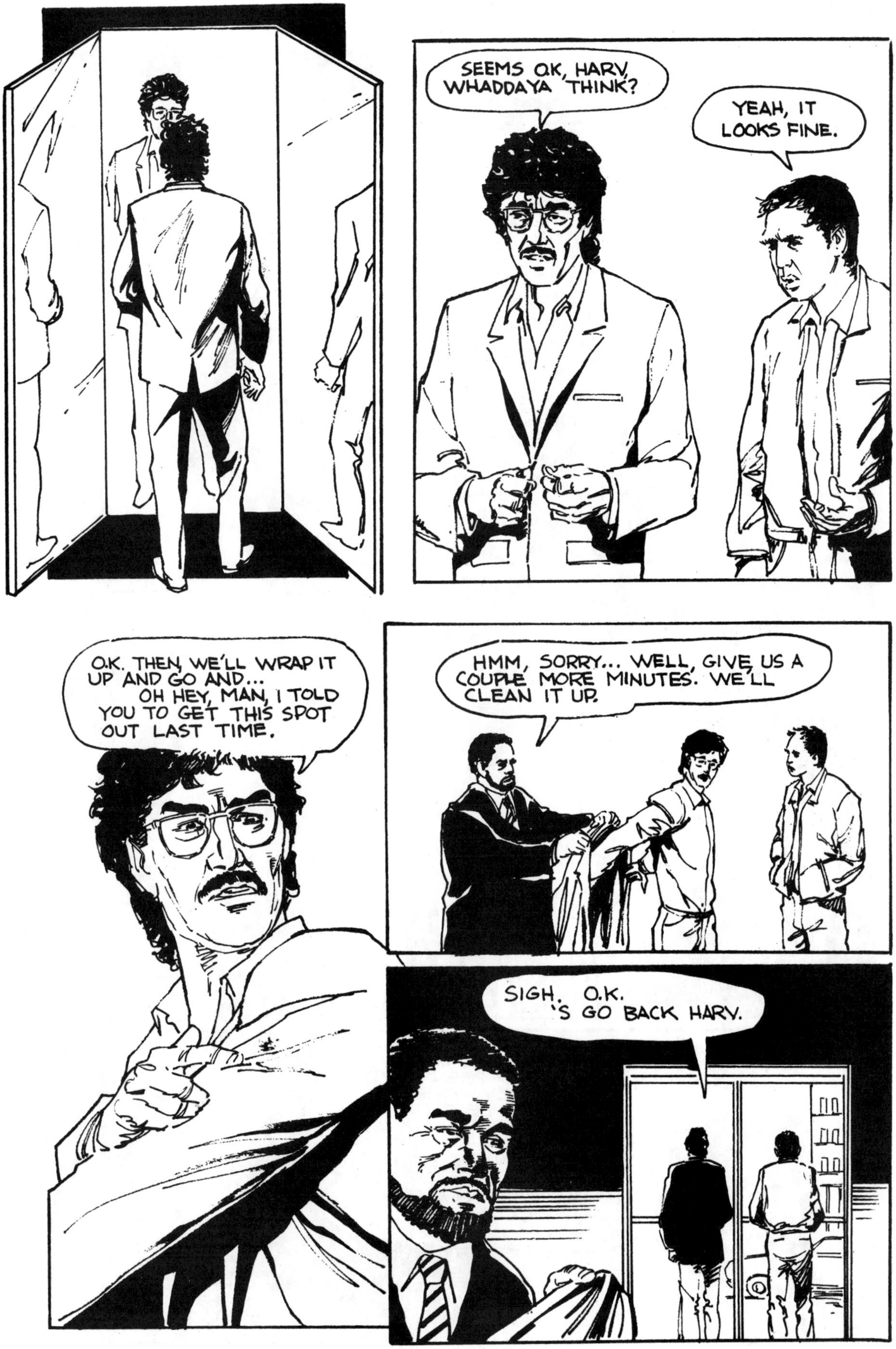
SEEMS O.K., HARV, WHADDAYA THINK?
YEAH, IT LOOKS FINE.
O.K. THEN, WE'LL WRAP IT UP AND GO AND... OH HEY, MAN, I TOLD YOU TO GET THIS SPOT OUT LAST TIME.
HMM, SORRY... WELL, GIVE US A COUPLE MORE MINUTES. WE'LL CLEAN IT UP.
SIGH. O.K. 'S GO BACK HARV.

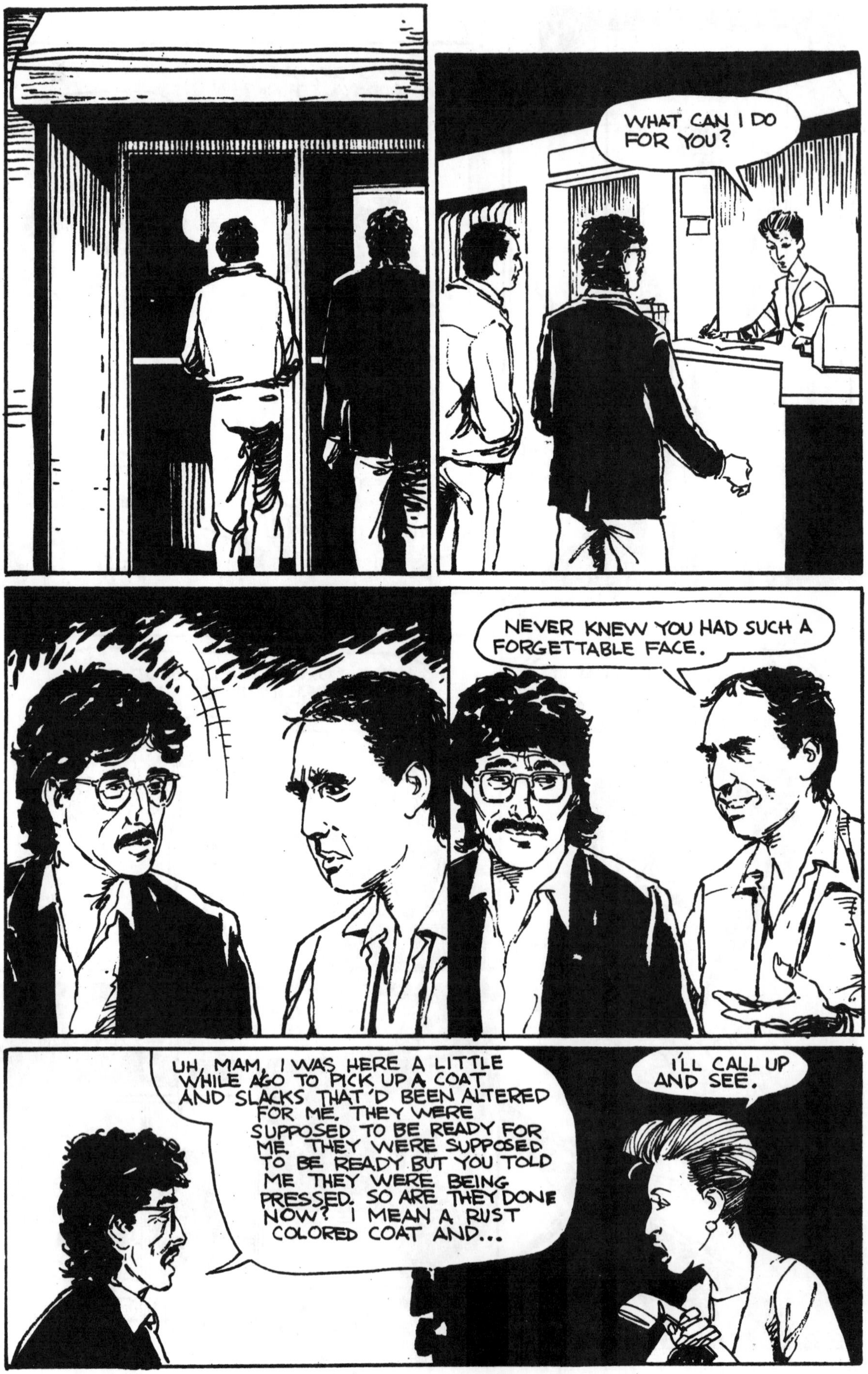
WHAT CAN I DO FOR YOU?
NEVER KNEW YOU HAD SUCH A FORGETTABLE FACE.
UH, MAM, I WAS HERE A LITTLE WHILE AGO TO PICK UP A COAT AND SLACKS THAT'D BEEN ALTERED FOR ME. THEY WERE SUPPOSED TO BE READY FOR ME. THEY WERE SUPPOSED TO BE READY BUT YOU TOLD ME THEY WERE BEING PRESSED. SO ARE THEY DONE NOW? I MEAN A RUST COLORED COAT AND...
I'LL CALL UP AND SEE.

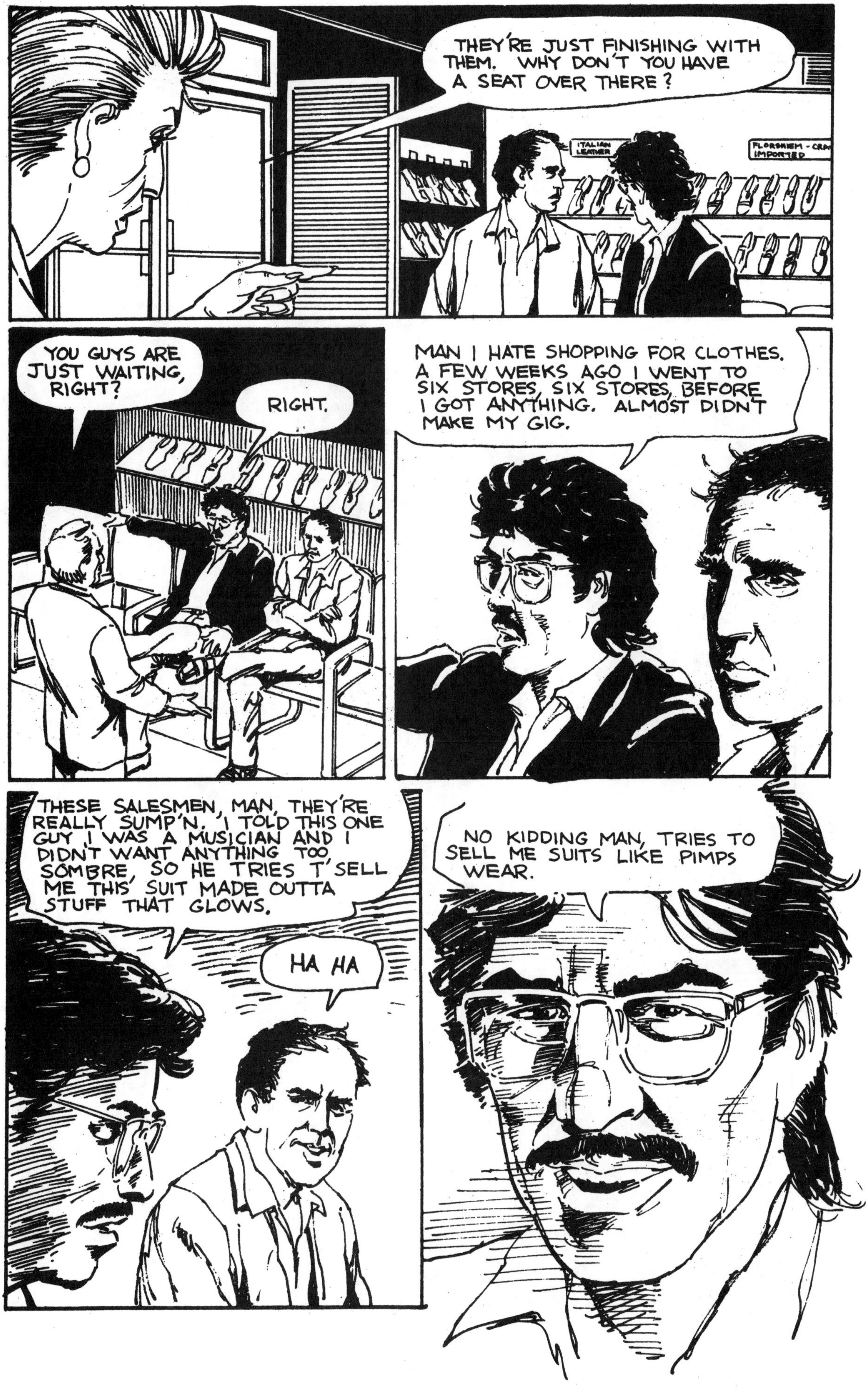
THEY'RE JUST FINISHING WITH THEM. WHY DON'T YOU HAVE A SEAT OVER THERE?
ITALIAN LEATHER
FLORSHIEM - CRA
IMPORTED
YOU GUYS ARE JUST WAITING, RIGHT?
RIGHT.
MAN I HATE SHOPPING FOR CLOTHES. A FEW WEEKS AGO I WENT TO SIX STORES, SIX STORES, BEFORE I GOT ANYTHING. ALMOST DIDN'T MAKE MY GIG.
THESE SALESMEN, MAN, THEY'RE REALLY SUMP'N. I TOLD THIS ONE GUY I WAS A MUSICIAN AND I DIDN'T WANT ANYTHING TOO SOMBRE, SO HE TRIES T'SELL ME THIS SUIT MADE OUTTA STUFF THAT GLOWS.
HA HA
NO KIDDING MAN, TRIES TO SELL ME SUITS LIKE PIMPS WEAR.

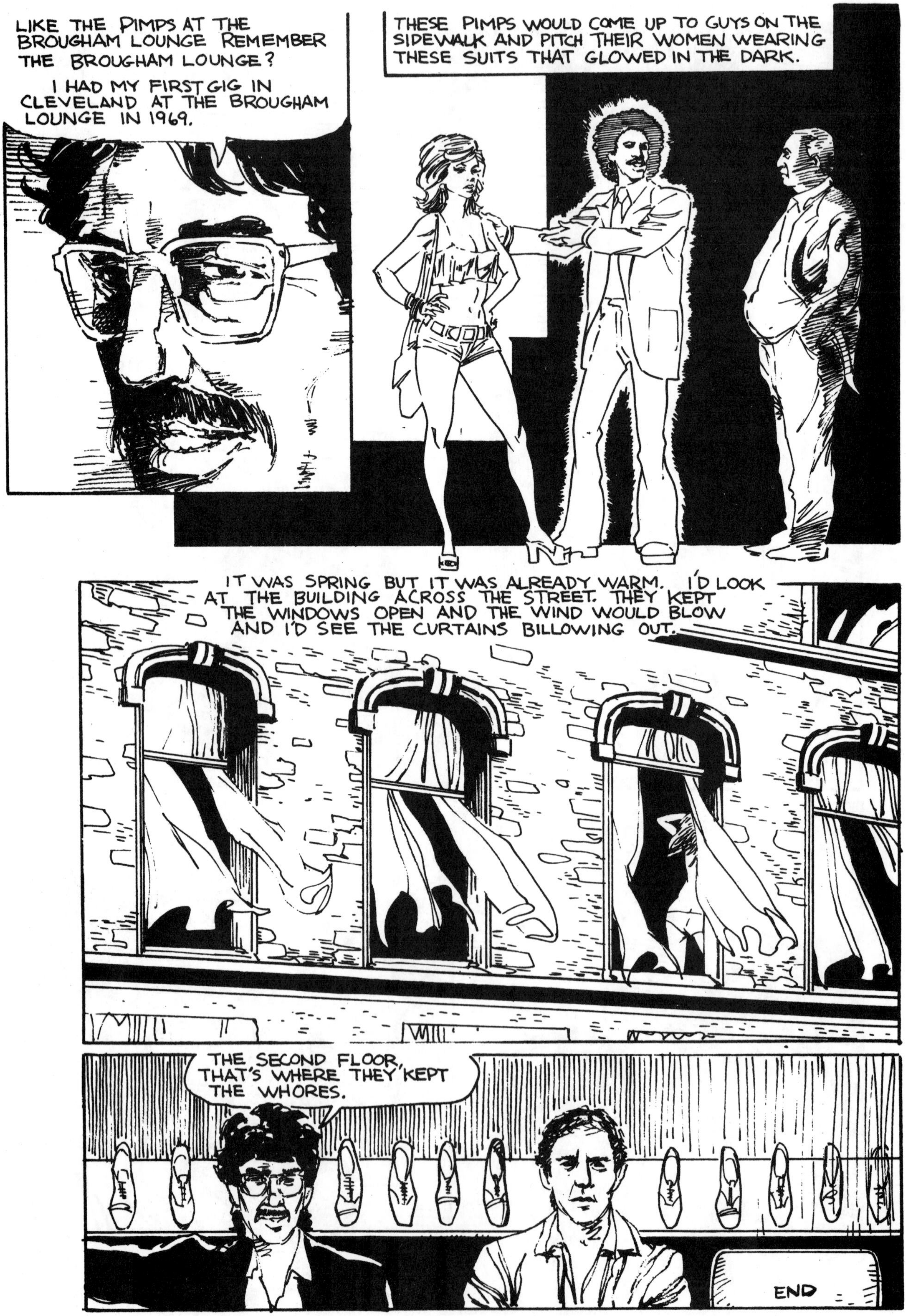
LIKE THE PIMPS AT THE BROUGHAM LOUNGE REMEMBER THE BROUGHAM LOUNGE?
I HAD MY FIRST GIG IN CLEVELAND AT THE BROUGHAM LOUNGE IN 1969.
THESE PIMPS WOULD COME UP TO GUYS ON THE SIDEWALK AND PITCH THEIR WOMEN WEARING THESE SUITS THAT GLOWED IN THE DARK.
IT WAS SPRING BUT IT WAS ALREADY WARM. I'D LOOK AT THE BUILDING ACROSS THE STREET. THEY KEPT THE WINDOWS OPEN AND THE WIND WOULD BLOW AND I'D SEE THE CURTAINS BILLOWING OUT.
THE SECOND FLOOR, THAT'S WHERE THEY KEPT THE WHORES.
END

PRESIDENT'S DAY

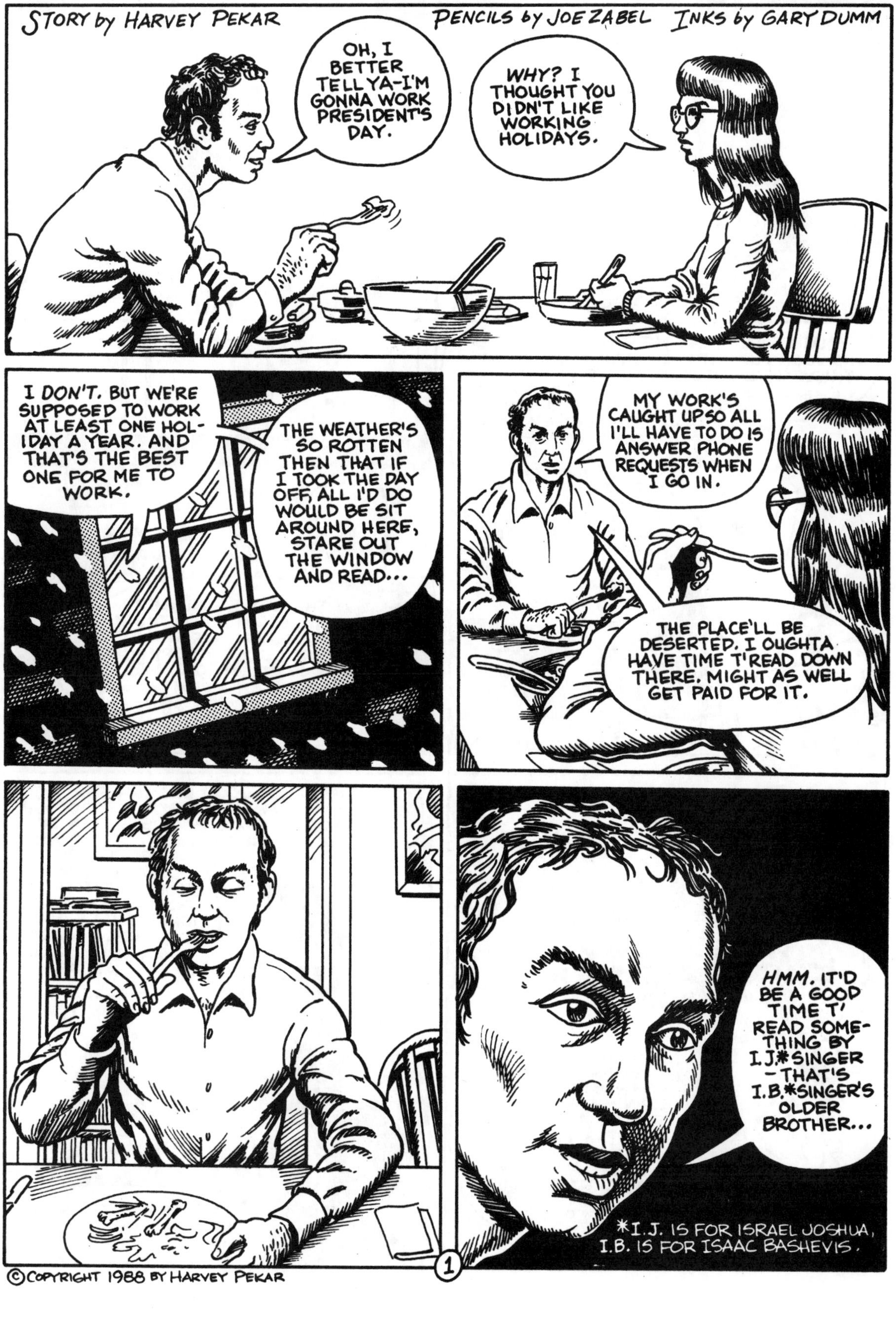
STORY by HARVEY PEKAR
PENCILS by JOE ZABEL
INKS by GARY DUMM
OH, I BETTER TELL YA–I'M GONNA WORK PRESIDENT'S DAY.
WHY? I THOUGHT YOU DIDN'T LIKE WORKING HOLIDAYS.
I DON'T. BUT WE'RE SUPPOSED TO WORK AT LEAST ONE HOLIDAY A YEAR. AND THAT'S THE BEST ONE FOR ME TO WORK.
THE WEATHER'S SO ROTTEN THEN THAT IF I TOOK THE DAY OFF, ALL I'D DO WOULD BE SIT AROUND HERE, STARE OUT THE WINDOW AND READ...
MY WORK'S CAUGHT UP SO ALL I'LL HAVE TO DO IS ANSWER PHONE REQUESTS WHEN I GO IN.
THE PLACE'LL BE DESERTED. I OUGHTA HAVE TIME T'READ DOWN THERE. MIGHT AS WELL GET PAID FOR IT.
HMM. IT'D BE A GOOD TIME T' READ SOMETHING BY I.J.* SINGER – THAT'S I.B.* SINGER'S OLDER BROTHER...
*I.J. IS FOR ISRAEL JOSHUA, I.B. IS FOR ISAAC BASHEVIS.

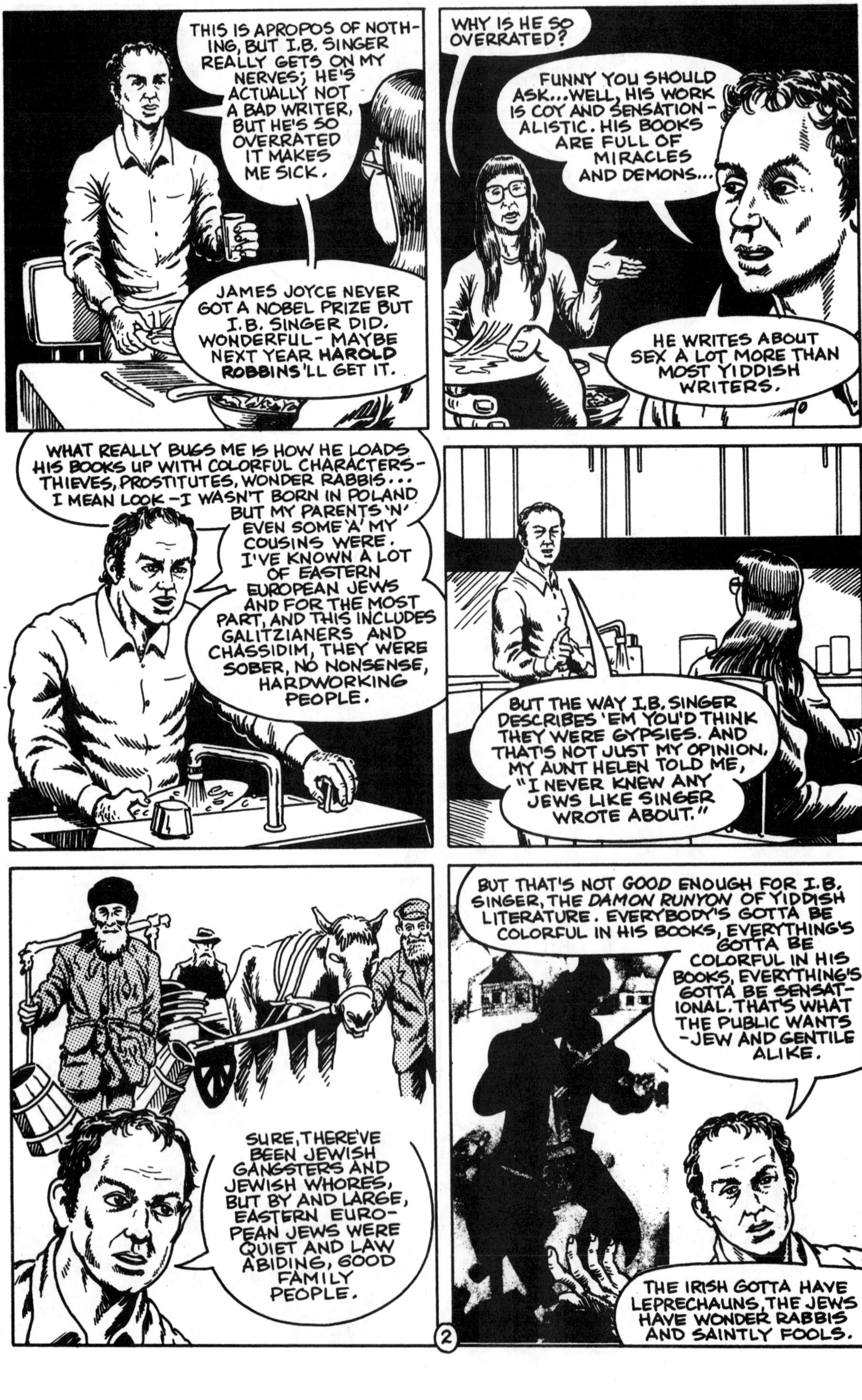
THIS IS APROPOS OF NOTHING, BUT I.B. SINGER REALLY GETS ON MY NERVES; HE'S ACTUALLY NOT A BAD WRITER, BUT HE'S SO OVERRATED IT MAKES ME SICK.
JAMES JOYCE NEVER GOT A NOBEL PRIZE BUT I.B. SINGER DID. WONDERFUL- MAYBE NEXT YEAR HAROLD ROBBINS'LL GET IT.
WHY IS HE SO OVERRATED?
FUNNY YOU SHOULD ASK...WELL, HIS WORK IS COY AND SENSATIONALISTIC. HIS BOOKS ARE FULL OF MIRACLES AND DEMONS...
HE WRITES ABOUT SEX A LOT MORE THAN MOST YIDDISH WRITERS.
WHAT REALLY BUGS ME IS HOW HE LOADS HIS BOOKS UP WITH COLORFUL CHARACTERS- THIEVES, PROSTITUTES, WONDER RABBIS... I MEAN LOOK -I WASN'T BORN IN POLAND BUT MY PARENTS 'N' EVEN SOME 'A' MY COUSINS WERE. I'VE KNOWN A LOT OF EASTERN EUROPEAN JEWS AND FOR THE MOST PART, AND THIS INCLUDES GALITZIANERS AND CHASSIDIM, THEY WERE SOBER, NO NONSENSE, HARDWORKING PEOPLE.
BUT THE WAY I.B. SINGER DESCRIBES 'EM YOU'D THINK THEY WERE GYPSIES. AND THAT'S NOT JUST MY OPINION, MY AUNT HELEN TOLD ME, "I NEVER KNEW ANY JEWS LIKE SINGER WROTE ABOUT."
SURE, THERE'VE BEEN JEWISH GANGSTERS AND JEWISH WHORES, BUT BY AND LARGE, EASTERN EUROPEAN JEWS WERE QUIET AND LAW ABIDING, GOOD FAMILY PEOPLE.
BUT THAT'S NOT GOOD ENOUGH FOR I.B. SINGER, THE DAMON RUNYON OF YIDDISH LITERATURE. EVERYBODY'S GOTTA BE COLORFUL IN HIS BOOKS, EVERYTHING'S GOTTA BE COLORFUL IN HIS BOOKS, EVERYTHING'S GOTTA BE SENSATIONAL. THAT'S WHAT THE PUBLIC WANTS -JEW AND GENTILE ALIKE.
THE IRISH GOTTA HAVE LEPRECHAUNS, THE JEWS HAVE WONDER RABBIS AND SAINTLY FOOLS.

I.B.'S A SLICK P.R. MAN, TOO. I SEE HIM ON T.V. HE COMES ON LIKE A CARICATURE OF THE SIMPLE, KINDLY, OLD JEWISH GRANDFATHER, HUMBLE, JUST A "KLEINE MENSCH," YOU KNOW, A TEVYE. JUST PLAIN FOLKS. SURE.

SO I GOT THIS FEELING MAYBE HIS OLDER BROTHER I.J. SINGER IS A BETTER WRITER. FOR SOME REASON I WANNA BELIEVE THAT.

I MEAN AFTER ALL, I.J. WAS A SOCIALIST. I THINK HE HAD A LOT MORE POLITICAL AWARENESS AND GUTS THAN I.B.

I STARTED TO READ THIS ONE NOVEL BY I.J., *THE BROTHERS ASHKENAZI*, BUT I DIDN'T GET TOO FAR IN IT FOR SOME REASON. BUT Y'KNOW, IT STARTED OFF SOLID— REMINDED ME A BIT OF THOMAS MANN'S WORK— AT LEAST THERE WEREN'T A BUNCHA MIRACLES IN IT, AS FAR AS I GOT, ANYWAY.

I'LL FINISH IT ONE DAY, BUT ON PRESIDENT'S DAY, I THINK I WANNA READ *YOSHE KALB* BY I.J. I BEEN MEANING TO GET TO IT FOR A LONG TIME. I DUNNO. I GOT A FEELING IT MIGHT BE I.J.'S BEST.

7:00 A.M. PRESIDENT'S DAY

HONEY, I GOTTA GO NOW. TAKE CARE A' YERSELF T'DAY, HUH?

MMM. IT'S SO *COLD* OUT THERE. YOU SURE YOU DON'T WANT TO TAKE THE CAR. I'LL TAKE THE BUS.

NAW, I'LL WALK. YOU GOT THAT DOCTOR'S APPOINTMENT T'DAY, BETTER I SHOULD FREEZE THAN YOU.

O.K... BUT I HATE TO THINK OF YOU OUTSIDE IN THAT ZERO WEATHER.

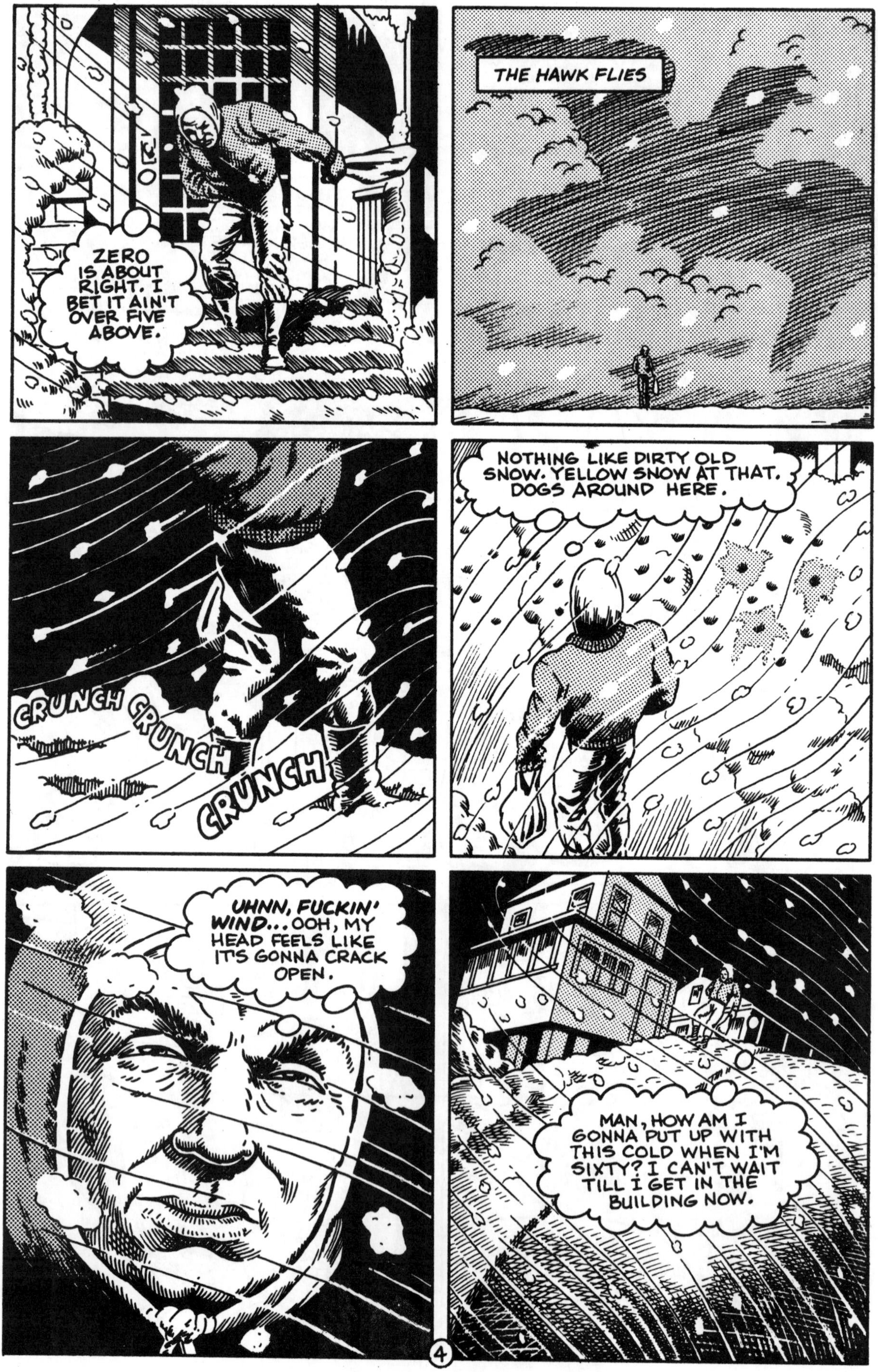
ZERO IS ABOUT RIGHT. I BET IT AIN'T OVER FIVE ABOVE.
THE HAWK FLIES
CRUNCH CRUNCH CRUNCH CRUNCH
NOTHING LIKE DIRTY OLD SNOW. YELLOW SNOW AT THAT. DOGS AROUND HERE.
UHNN, FUCKIN' WIND... OOH, MY HEAD FEELS LIKE IT'S GONNA CRACK OPEN.
MAN, HOW AM I GONNA PUT UP WITH THIS COLD WHEN I'M SIXTY? I CAN'T WAIT TILL I GET IN THE BUILDING NOW.

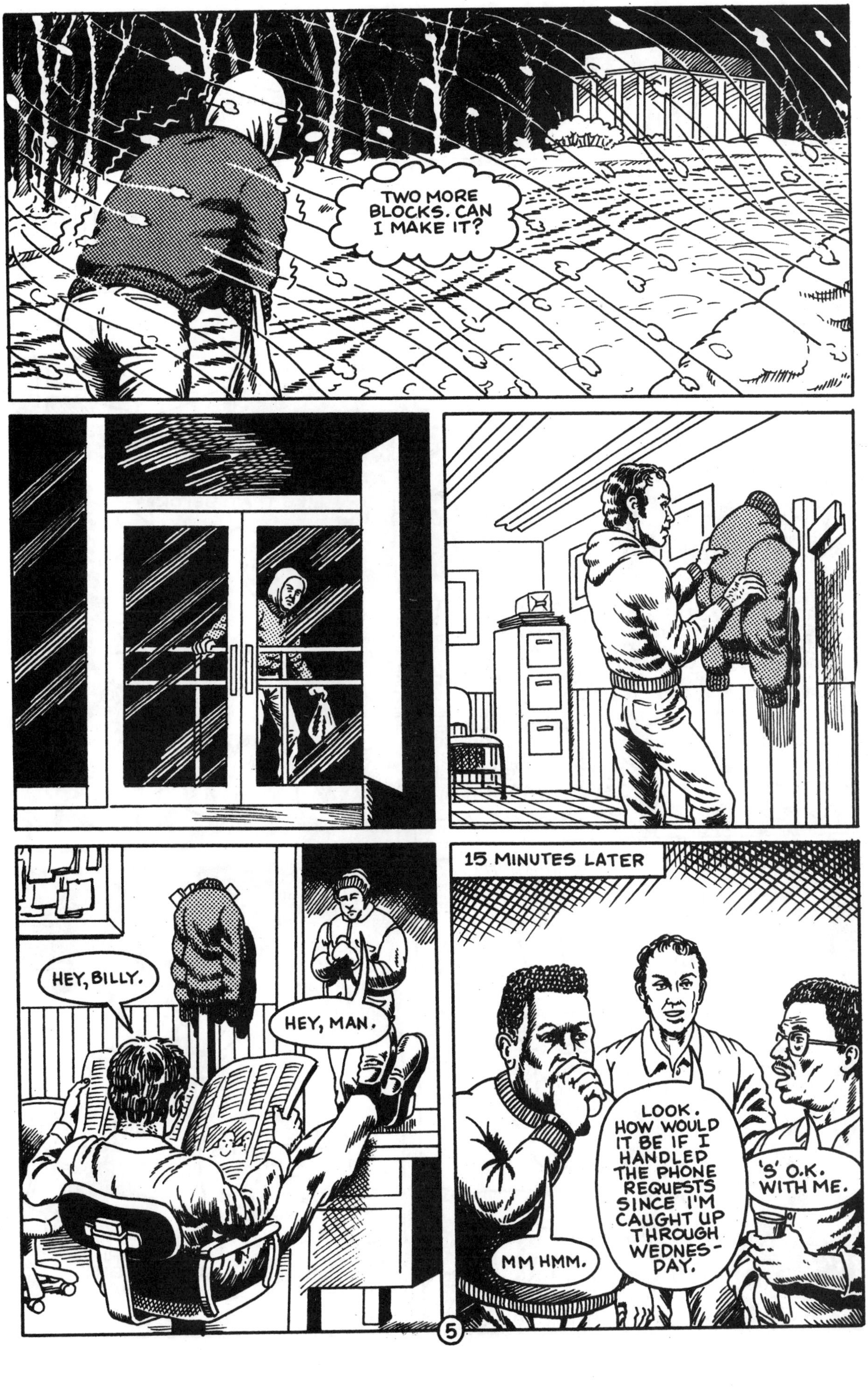
TWO MORE BLOCKS. CAN I MAKE IT?
HEY, BILLY.
HEY, MAN.
15 MINUTES LATER
LOOK. HOW WOULD IT BE IF I HANDLED THE PHONE REQUESTS SINCE I'M CAUGHT UP THROUGH WEDNES-DAY.
MM HMM.
'S' O.K. WITH ME.

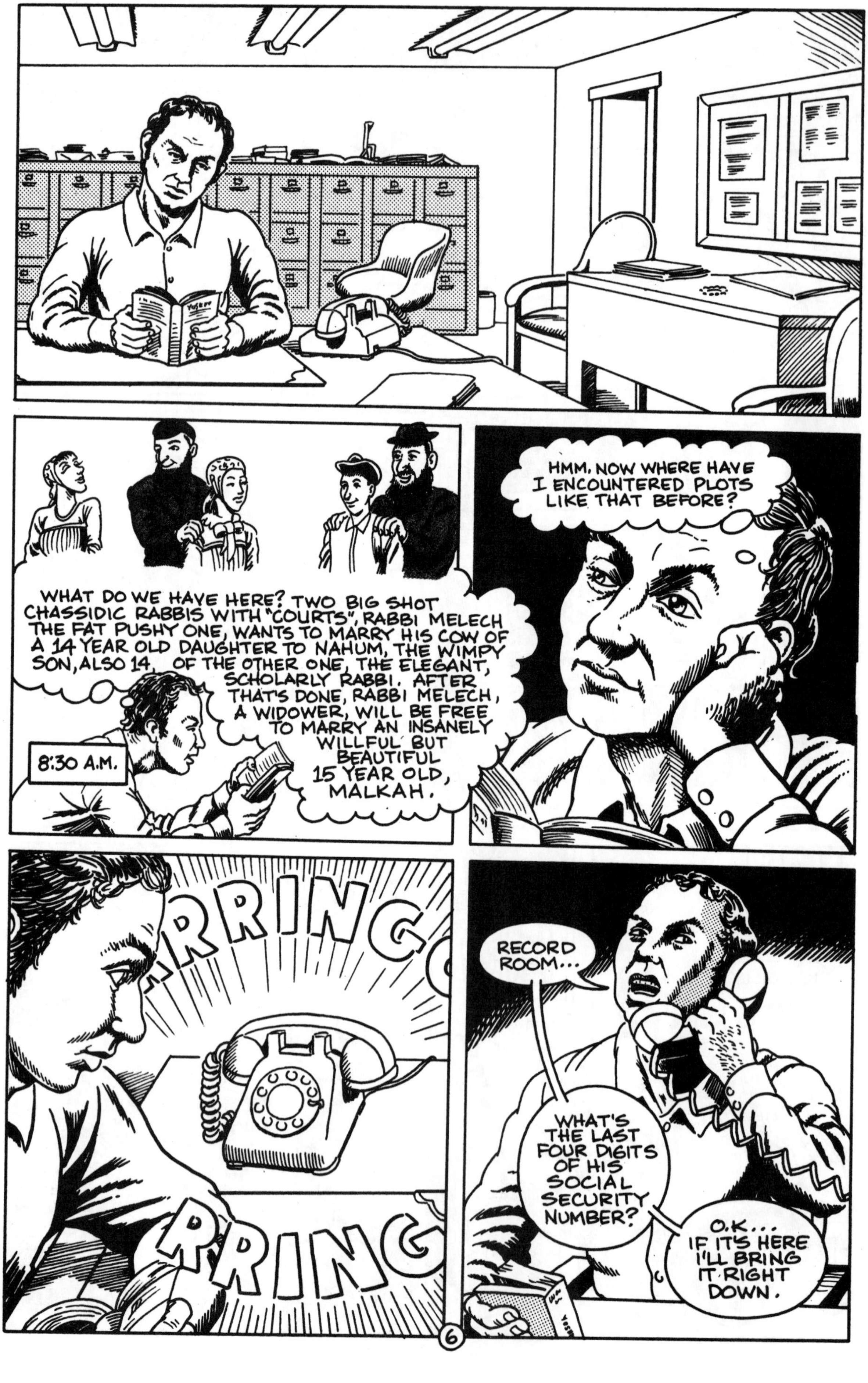
WHAT DO WE HAVE HERE? TWO BIG SHOT CHASSIDIC RABBIS WITH "COURTS", RABBI MELECH THE FAT PUSHY ONE, WANTS TO MARRY HIS COW OF A 14 YEAR OLD DAUGHTER TO NAHUM, THE WIMPY SON, ALSO 14, OF THE OTHER ONE, THE ELEGANT, SCHOLARLY RABBI. AFTER THAT'S DONE, RABBI MELECH, A WIDOWER, WILL BE FREE TO MARRY AN INSANELY WILLFUL BUT BEAUTIFUL 15 YEAR OLD, MALKAH.
8:30 A.M.
HMM. NOW WHERE HAVE I ENCOUNTERED PLOTS LIKE THAT BEFORE?
RRING
RRING
RECORD ROOM...
WHAT'S THE LAST FOUR DIGITS OF HIS SOCIAL SECURITY NUMBER?
O.K... IF IT'S HERE I'LL BRING IT RIGHT DOWN.

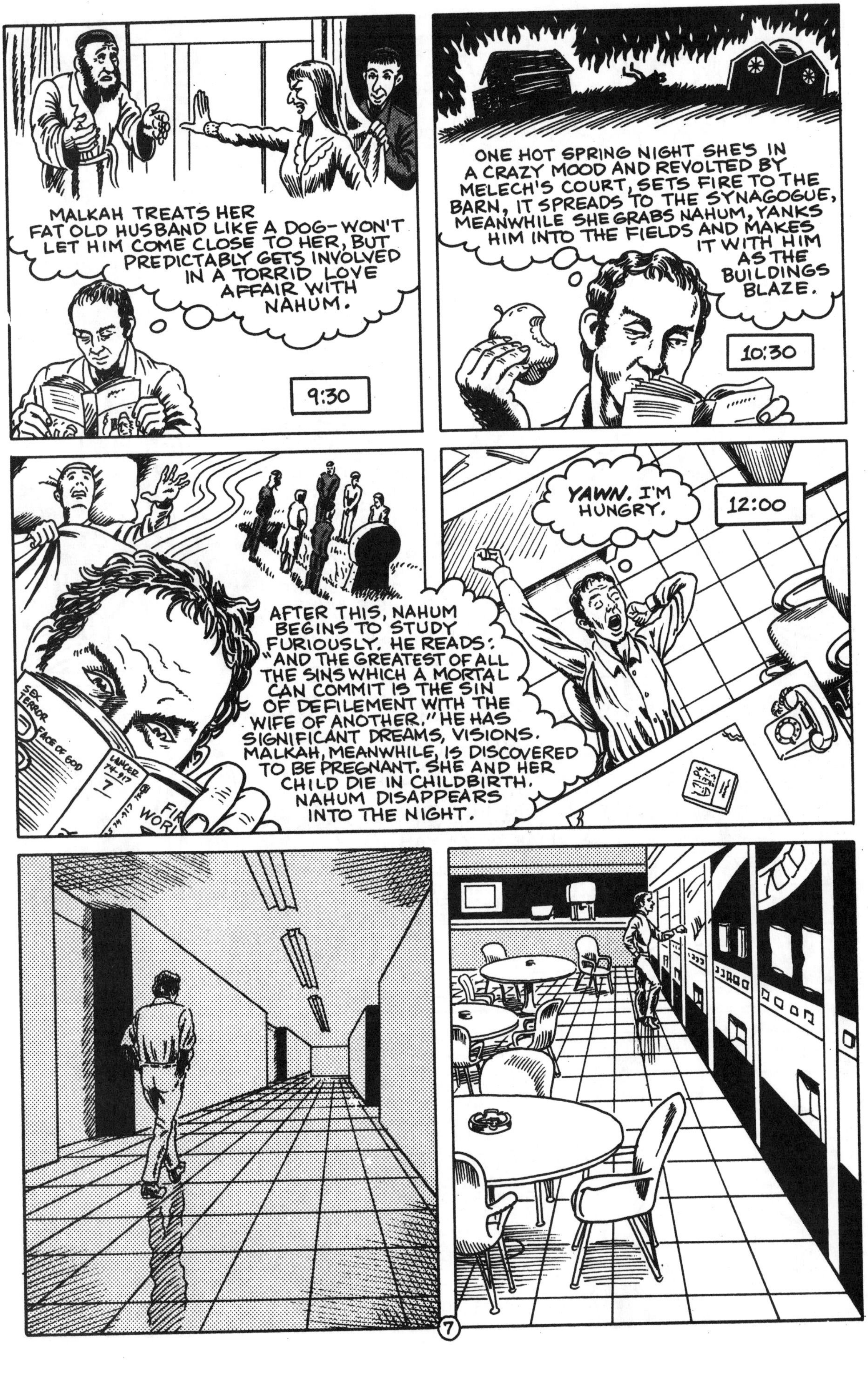
MALKAH TREATS HER FAT OLD HUSBAND LIKE A DOG- WON'T LET HIM COME CLOSE TO HER, BUT PREDICTABLY GETS INVOLVED IN A TORRID LOVE AFFAIR WITH NAHUM.
9:30
ONE HOT SPRING NIGHT SHE'S IN A CRAZY MOOD AND REVOLTED BY MELECH'S COURT, SETS FIRE TO THE BARN, IT SPREADS TO THE SYNAGOGUE, MEANWHILE SHE GRABS NAHUM, YANKS HIM INTO THE FIELDS AND MAKES IT WITH HIM AS THE BUILDINGS BLAZE.
10:30
AFTER THIS, NAHUM BEGINS TO STUDY FURIOUSLY. HE READS: "AND THE GREATEST OF ALL THE SINS WHICH A MORTAL CAN COMMIT IS THE SIN OF DEFILEMENT WITH THE WIFE OF ANOTHER." HE HAS SIGNIFICANT DREAMS, VISIONS. MALKAH, MEANWHILE, IS DISCOVERED TO BE PREGNANT. SHE AND HER CHILD DIE IN CHILDBIRTH. NAHUM DISAPPEARS INTO THE NIGHT.
SEX
TERROR
FACE OF GOD
YAWN. I'M HUNGRY.
12:00

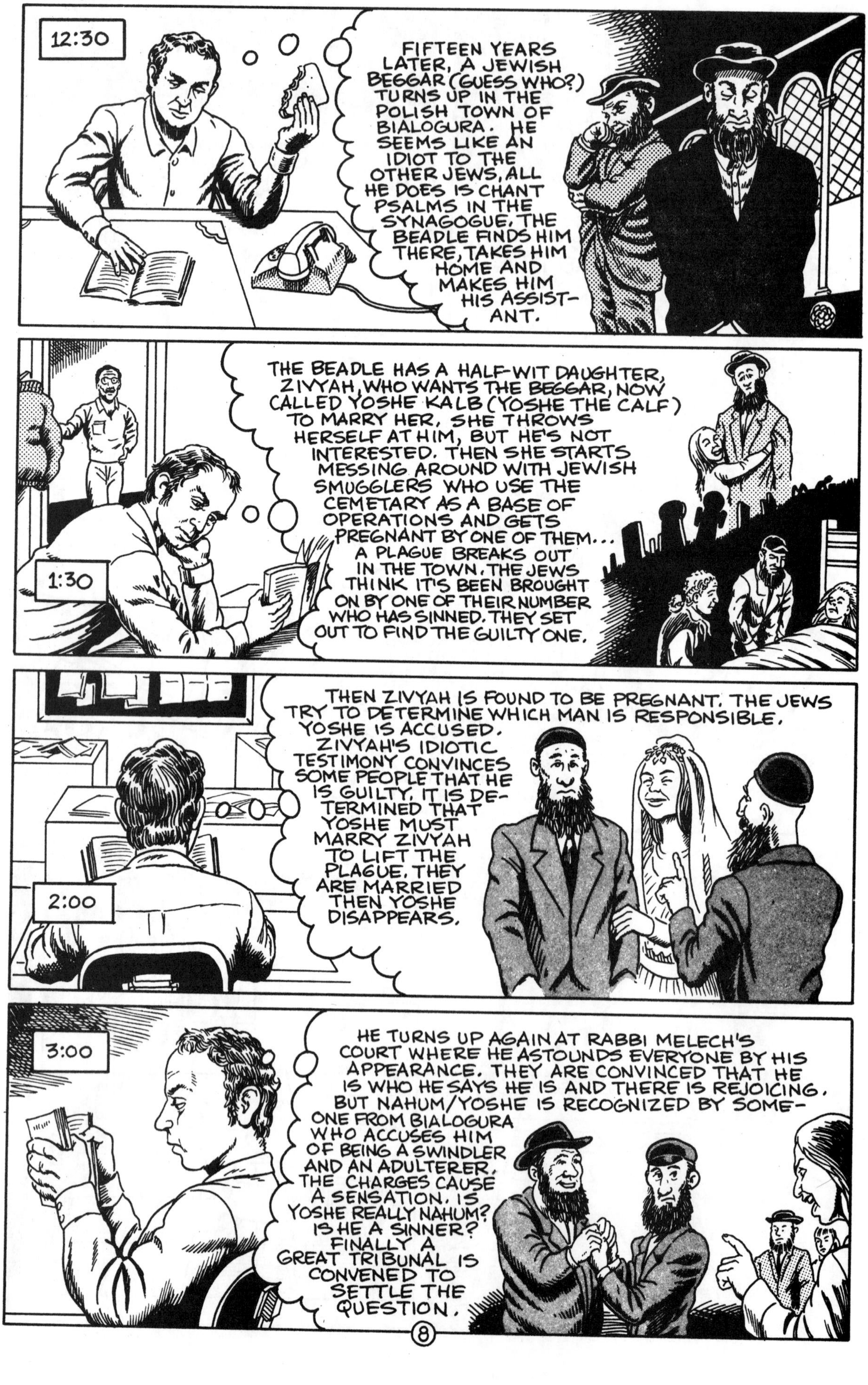
12:30
FIFTEEN YEARS LATER, A JEWISH BEGGAR (GUESS WHO?) TURNS UP IN THE POLISH TOWN OF BIALOGURA. HE SEEMS LIKE AN IDIOT TO THE OTHER JEWS, ALL HE DOES IS CHANT PSALMS IN THE SYNAGOGUE. THE BEADLE FINDS HIM THERE, TAKES HIM HOME AND MAKES HIM HIS ASSIST-ANT.
1:30
THE BEADLE HAS A HALF-WIT DAUGHTER, ZIVYAH, WHO WANTS THE BEGGAR, NOW CALLED YOSHE KALB (YOSHE THE CALF) TO MARRY HER. SHE THROWS HERSELF AT HIM, BUT HE'S NOT INTERESTED. THEN SHE STARTS MESSING AROUND WITH JEWISH SMUGGLERS WHO USE THE CEMETARY AS A BASE OF OPERATIONS AND GETS PREGNANT BY ONE OF THEM... A PLAGUE BREAKS OUT IN THE TOWN. THE JEWS THINK IT'S BEEN BROUGHT ON BY ONE OF THEIR NUMBER WHO HAS SINNED. THEY SET OUT TO FIND THE GUILTY ONE.
2:00
THEN ZIVYAH IS FOUND TO BE PREGNANT. THE JEWS TRY TO DETERMINE WHICH MAN IS RESPONSIBLE. YOSHE IS ACCUSED. ZIVYAH'S IDIOTIC TESTIMONY CONVINCES SOME PEOPLE THAT HE IS GUILTY. IT IS DE-TERMINED THAT YOSHE MUST MARRY ZIVYAH TO LIFT THE PLAGUE. THEY ARE MARRIED THEN YOSHE DISAPPEARS.
3:00
HE TURNS UP AGAIN AT RABBI MELECH'S COURT WHERE HE ASTOUNDS EVERYONE BY HIS APPEARANCE. THEY ARE CONVINCED THAT HE IS WHO HE SAYS HE IS AND THERE IS REJOICING. BUT NAHUM/YOSHE IS RECOGNIZED BY SOME-ONE FROM BIALOGURA WHO ACCUSES HIM OF BEING A SWINDLER AND AN ADULTERER. THE CHARGES CAUSE A SENSATION. IS YOSHE REALLY NAHUM? IS HE A SINNER? FINALLY A GREAT TRIBUNAL IS CONVENED TO SETTLE THE QUESTION.

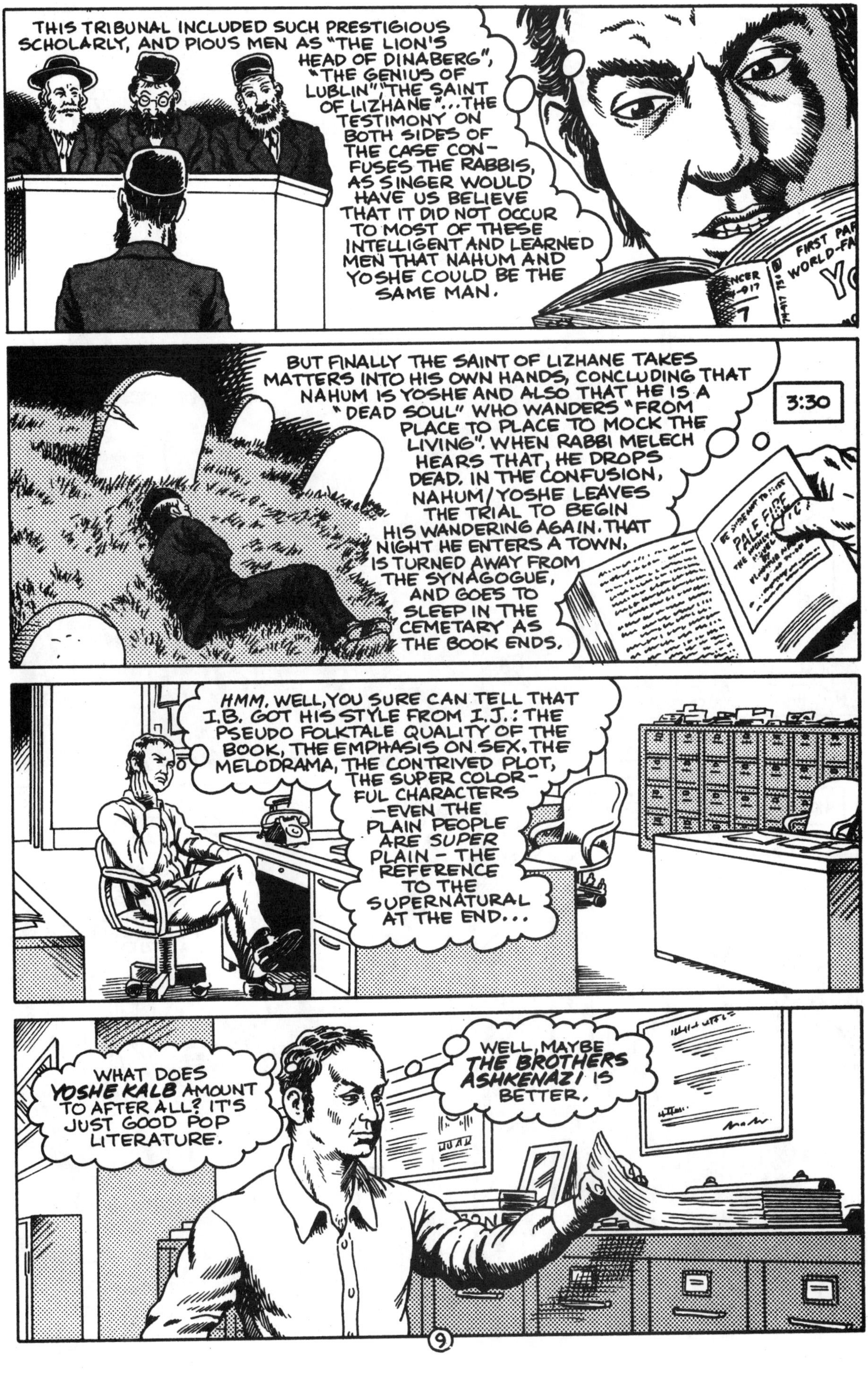
THIS TRIBUNAL INCLUDED SUCH PRESTIGIOUS SCHOLARLY, AND PIOUS MEN AS "THE LION'S HEAD OF DINABERG", "THE GENIUS OF LUBLIN" "THE SAINT OF LIZHANE"... THE TESTIMONY ON BOTH SIDES OF THE CASE CONFUSES THE RABBIS, AS SINGER WOULD HAVE US BELIEVE THAT IT DID NOT OCCUR TO MOST OF THESE INTELLIGENT AND LEARNED MEN THAT NAHUM AND YOSHE COULD BE THE SAME MAN.
BUT FINALLY THE SAINT OF LIZHANE TAKES MATTERS INTO HIS OWN HANDS, CONCLUDING THAT NAHUM IS YOSHE AND ALSO THAT HE IS A "DEAD SOUL" WHO WANDERS "FROM PLACE TO PLACE TO MOCK THE LIVING". WHEN RABBI MELECH HEARS THAT, HE DROPS DEAD. IN THE CONFUSION, NAHUM/YOSHE LEAVES THE TRIAL TO BEGIN HIS WANDERING AGAIN. THAT NIGHT HE ENTERS A TOWN, IS TURNED AWAY FROM THE SYNAGOGUE, AND GOES TO SLEEP IN THE CEMETARY AS THE BOOK ENDS.
3:30
PALE FIRE
HMM. WELL, YOU SURE CAN TELL THAT I.B. GOT HIS STYLE FROM I.J.: THE PSEUDO FOLKTALE QUALITY OF THE BOOK, THE EMPHASIS ON SEX, THE MELODRAMA, THE CONTRIVED PLOT, THE SUPER COLORFUL CHARACTERS —EVEN THE PLAIN PEOPLE ARE SUPER PLAIN — THE REFERENCE TO THE SUPERNATURAL AT THE END...
WHAT DOES YOSHE KALB AMOUNT TO AFTER ALL? IT'S JUST GOOD POP LITERATURE.
WELL, MAYBE THE BROTHERS ASHKENAZI IS BETTER.

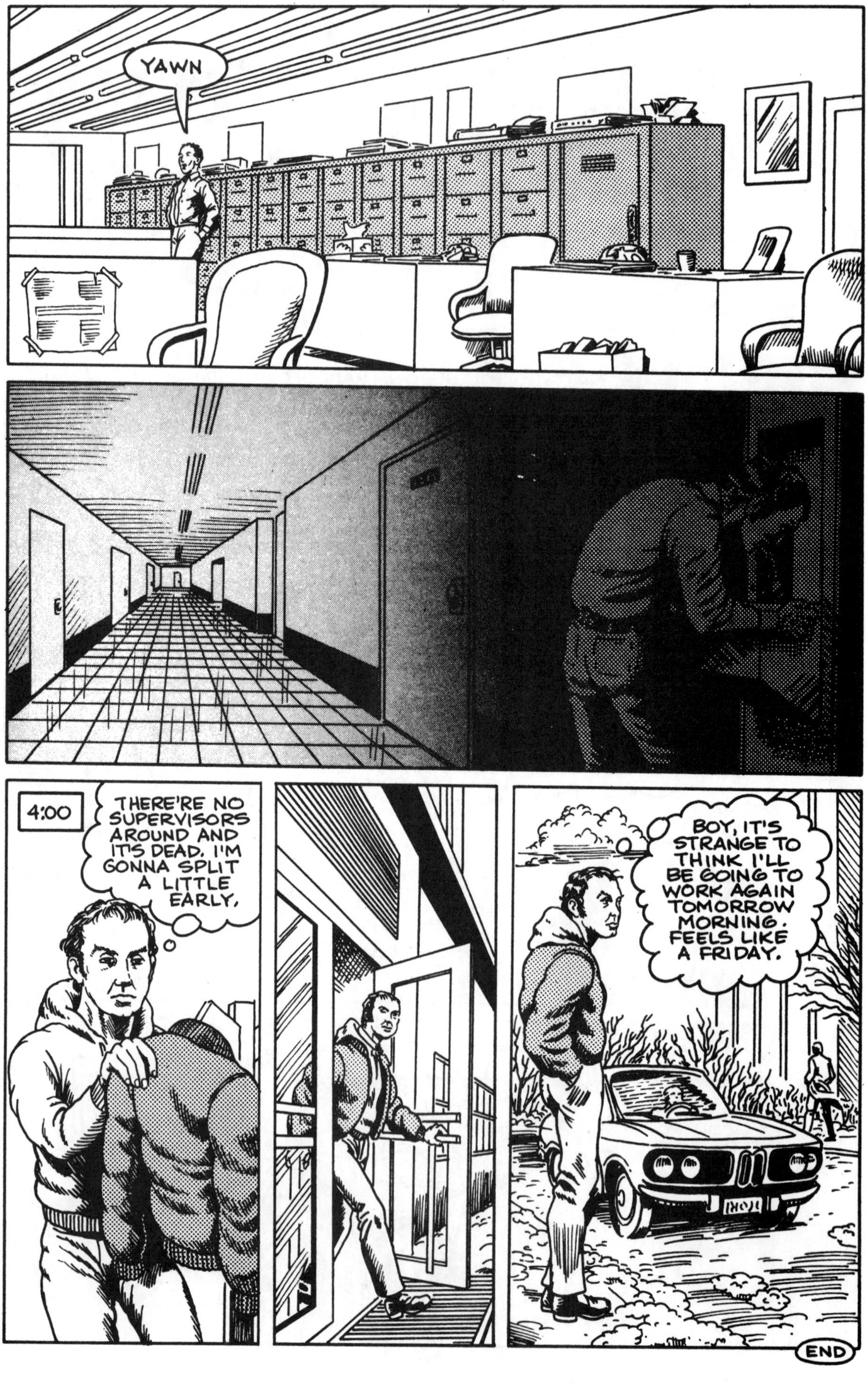
YAWN
4:00
THERE'RE NO SUPERVISORS AROUND AND IT'S DEAD. I'M GONNA SPLIT A LITTLE EARLY.
BOY, IT'S STRANGE TO THINK I'LL BE GOING TO WORK AGAIN TOMORROW MORNING. FEELS LIKE A FRIDAY.
END

I DON'T WANNA SEEM JUDG-MENTAL, BUT...

STORY BY HARVEY PEKAR ART-REBECCA HUNTINGTON

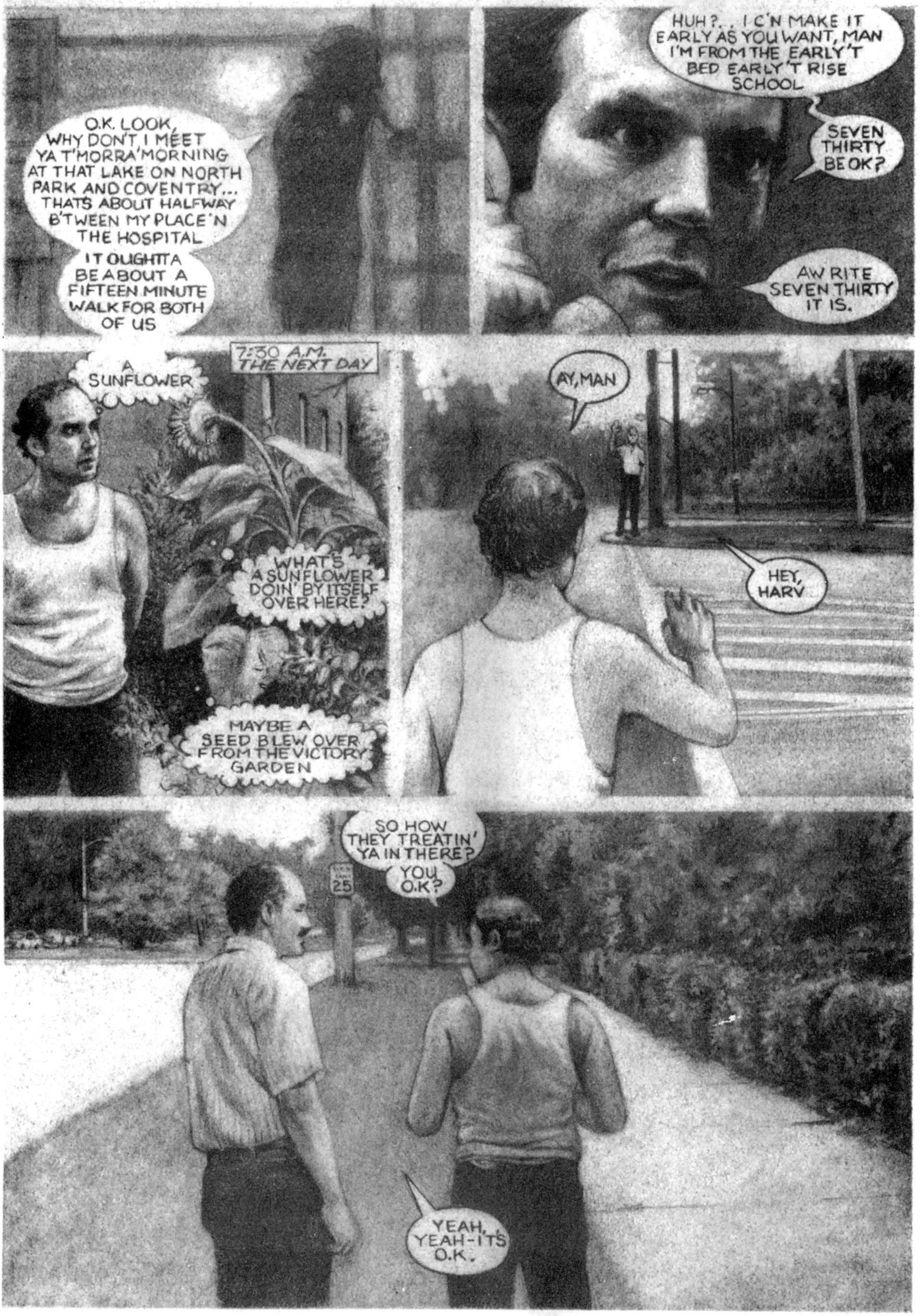
O.K. LOOK, WHY DON'T I MEET YA T'MORRA'MORNING AT THAT LAKE ON NORTH PARK AND COVENTRY... THATS ABOUT HALFWAY B'TWEEN MY PLACE'N THE HOSPITAL
IT OUGHTTA BE ABOUT A FIFTEEN MINUTE WALK FOR BOTH OF US
HUH?... I C'N MAKE IT EARLY AS YOU WANT, MAN I'M FROM THE EARLY 'T BED EARLY 'T RISE SCHOOL
SEVEN THIRTY BE OK?
AW RITE SEVEN THIRTY IT IS.
7:30 A.M. THE NEXT DAY
A SUNFLOWER
WHAT'S A SUNFLOWER DOIN' BY ITSELF OVER HERE?
MAYBE A SEED BLEW OVER FROM THE VICTORY GARDEN
AY, MAN
HEY, HARV
SO HOW THEY TREATIN' YA IN THERE?
YOU O.K?
25
YEAH, YEAH-IT'S O.K.

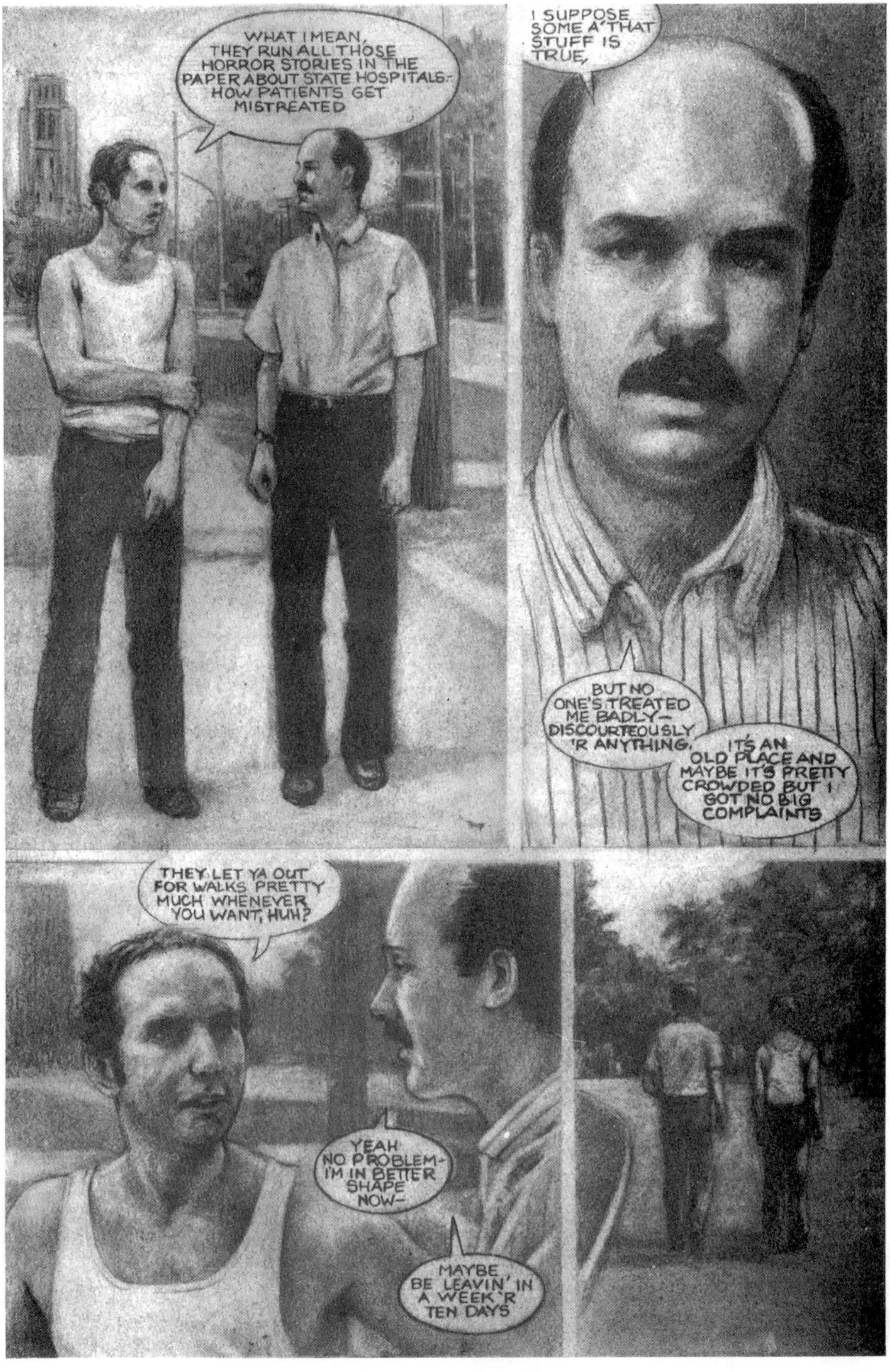
WHAT I MEAN, THEY RUN ALL THOSE HORROR STORIES IN THE PAPER ABOUT STATE HOSPITALS- HOW PATIENTS GET MISTREATED
I SUPPOSE SOME A' THAT STUFF IS TRUE,
BUT NO ONE'S TREATED ME BADLY- DISCOURTEOUSLY 'R ANYTHING.
IT'S AN OLD PLACE AND MAYBE IT'S PRETTY CROWDED BUT I GOT NO BIG COMPLAINTS
THEY LET YA OUT FOR WALKS PRETTY MUCH WHENEVER YOU WANT, HUH?
YEAH NO PROBLEM- I'M IN BETTER SHAPE NOW-
MAYBE BE LEAVIN' IN A WEEK 'R TEN DAYS

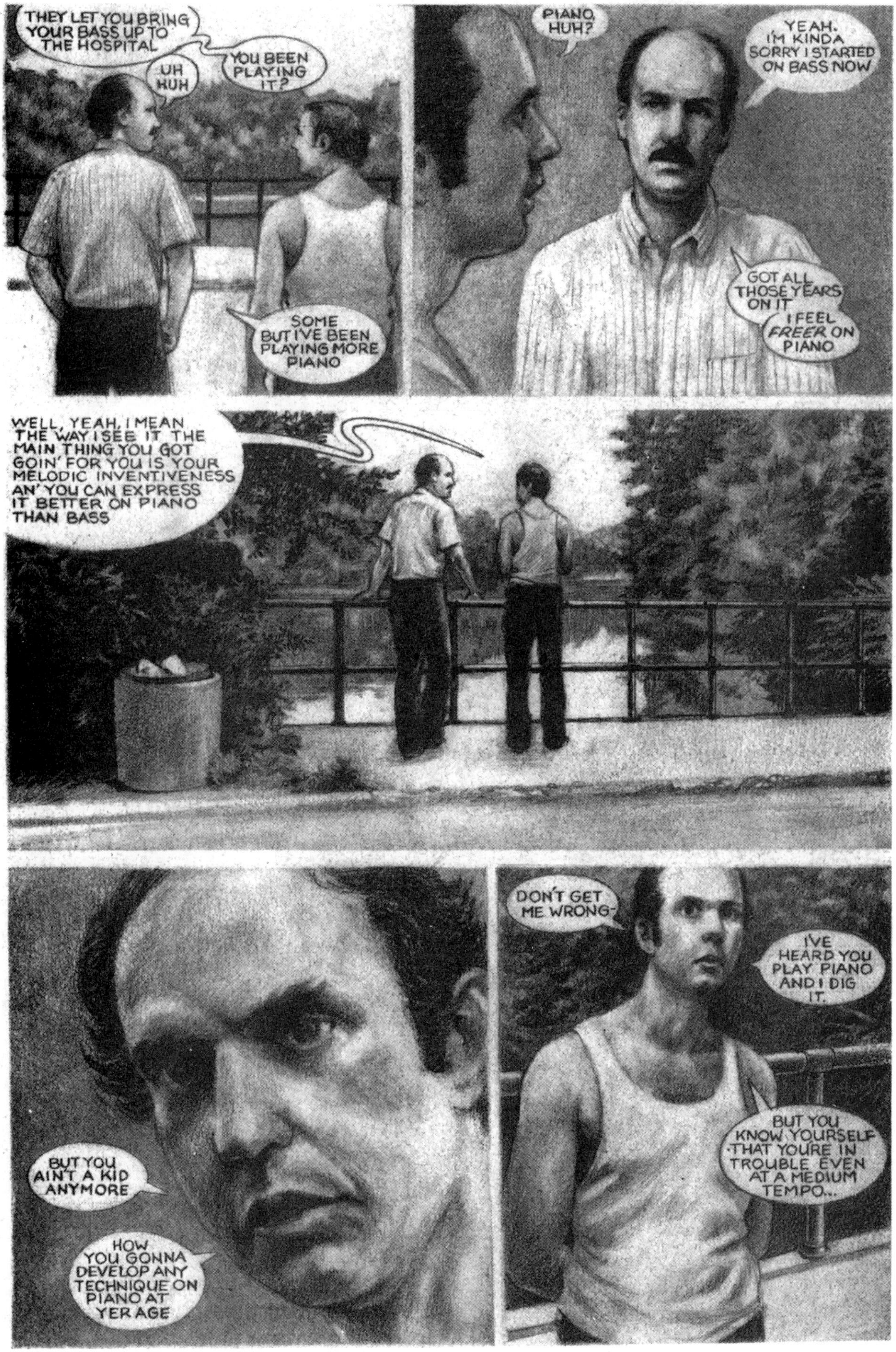
THEY LET YOU BRING YOUR BASS UP TO THE HOSPITAL
UH HUH
YOU BEEN PLAYING IT?
SOME BUT IVE BEEN PLAYING MORE PIANO
PIANO, HUH?
YEAH. I'M KINDA SORRY I STARTED ON BASS NOW
GOT ALL THOSE YEARS ON IT
I FEEL FREER ON PIANO
WELL, YEAH, I MEAN THE WAY I SEE IT THE MAIN THING YOU GOT GOIN' FOR YOU IS YOUR MELODIC INVENTIVENESS AN' YOU CAN EXPRESS IT BETTER ON PIANO THAN BASS
DON'T GET ME WRONG-
I'VE HEARD YOU PLAY PIANO AND I DIG IT.
BUT YOU KNOW YOURSELF THAT YOURE IN TROUBLE EVEN AT A MEDIUM TEMPO...
BUT YOU AIN'T A KID ANYMORE
HOW YOU GONNA DEVELOP ANY TECHNIQUE ON PIANO AT YER AGE

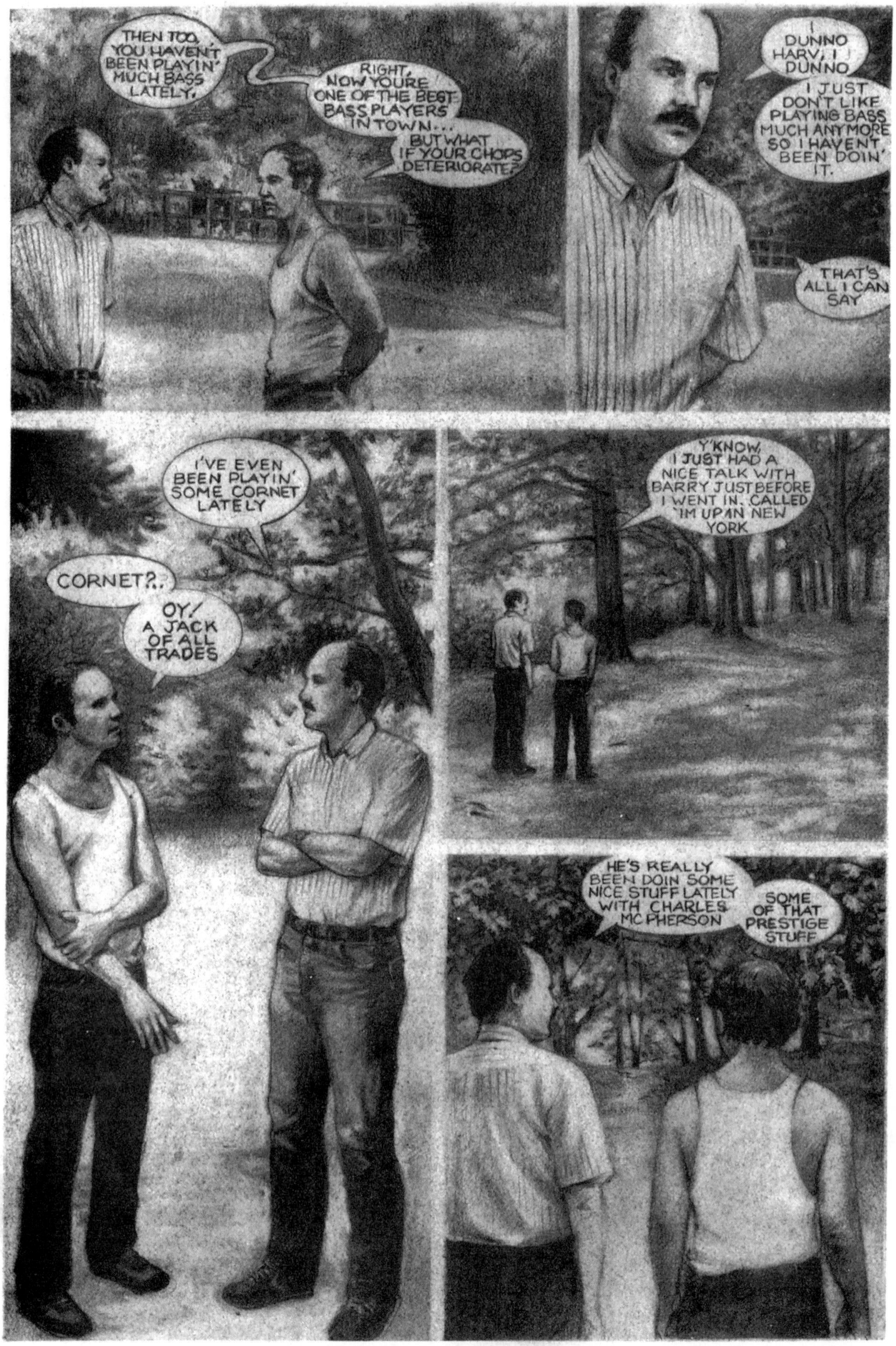
THEN TOO, YOU HAVEN'T BEEN PLAYIN' MUCH BASS LATELY.
RIGHT, NOW YOU'RE ONE OF THE BEST BASS PLAYERS IN TOWN...
BUT WHAT IF YOUR CHOPS DETERIORATE?
I DUNNO HARV, I DUNNO
I JUST DON'T LIKE PLAYING BASS MUCH ANYMORE SO I HAVEN'T BEEN DOIN' IT.
THAT'S ALL I CAN SAY
I'VE EVEN BEEN PLAYIN' SOME CORNET LATELY
CORNET?..
OY! A JACK OF ALL TRADES
Y'KNOW, I JUST HAD A NICE TALK WITH BARRY JUST BEFORE I WENT IN. CALLED 'IM UP 'N NEW YORK
HE'S REALLY BEEN DOIN SOME NICE STUFF LATELY WITH CHARLES MC PHERSON
SOME OF THAT PRESTIGE STUFF

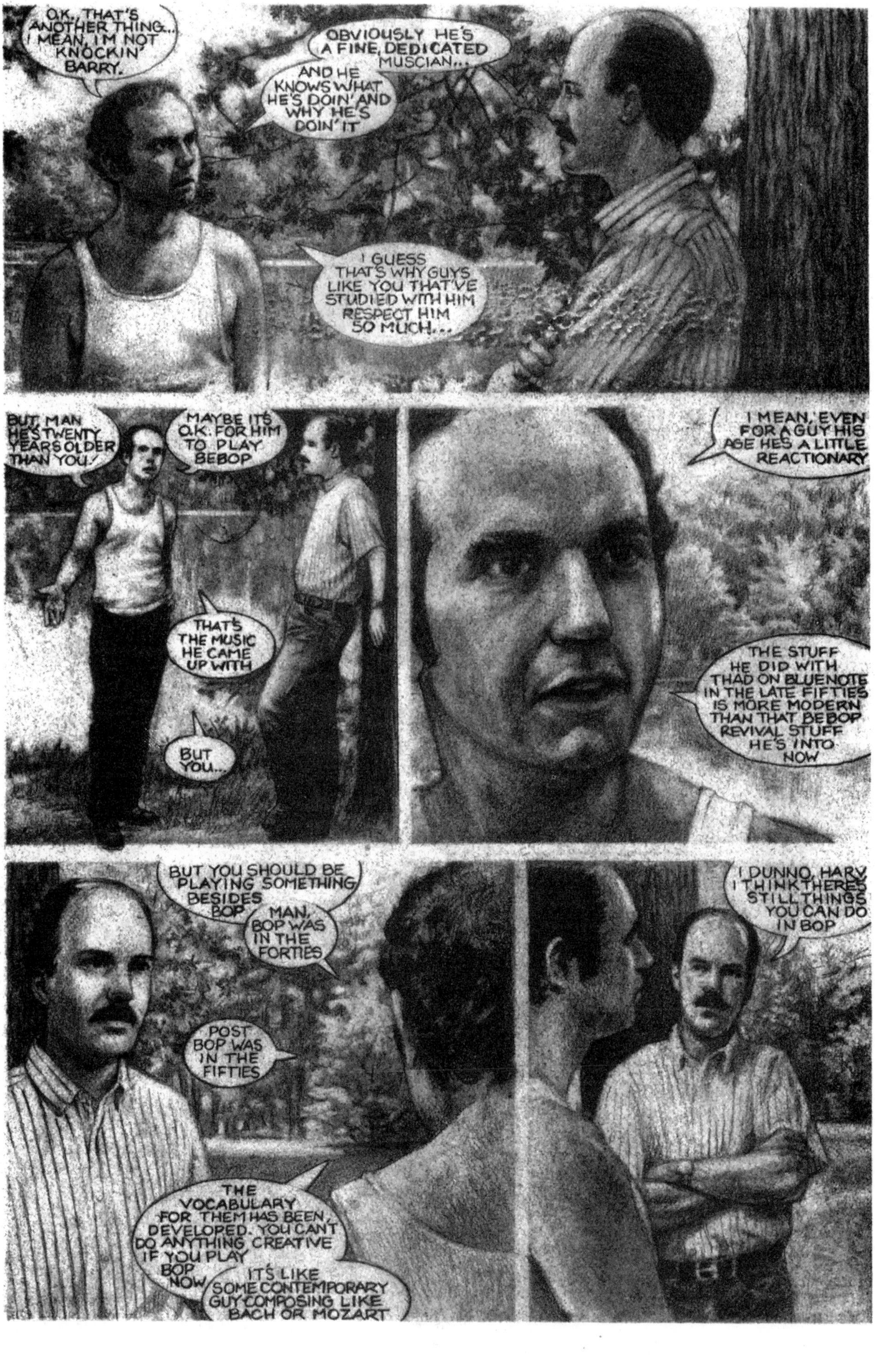
O.K., THAT'S ANOTHER THING... I MEAN, I'M NOT KNOCKIN' BARRY.
OBVIOUSLY HE'S A FINE, DEDICATED MUSCIAN...
AND HE KNOWS WHAT HE'S DOIN' AND WHY HE'S DOIN' IT
I GUESS THAT'S WHY GUYS LIKE YOU THAT'VE STUDIED WITH HIM RESPECT HIM SO MUCH...
BUT, MAN HE'S TWENTY YEARS OLDER THAN YOU!
MAYBE IT'S O.K. FOR HIM TO PLAY BEBOP
THAT'S THE MUSIC HE CAME UP WITH
BUT YOU...
I MEAN, EVEN FOR A GUY HIS AGE HE'S A LITTLE REACTIONARY
THE STUFF HE DID WITH THAD ON BLUENOTE IN THE LATE FIFTIES IS MORE MODERN THAN THAT BEBOP REVIVAL STUFF HE'S INTO NOW
BUT YOU SHOULD BE PLAYING SOMETHING BESIDES BOP
MAN, BOP WAS IN THE FORTIES
POST BOP WAS IN THE FIFTIES
THE VOCABULARY FOR THEM HAS BEEN DEVELOPED. YOU CAN'T DO ANYTHING CREATIVE IF YOU PLAY BOP NOW
IT'S LIKE SOME CONTEMPORARY GUY COMPOSING LIKE BACH OR MOZART
I DUNNO, HARV I THINK THERE'S STILL THINGS YOU CAN DO IN BOP

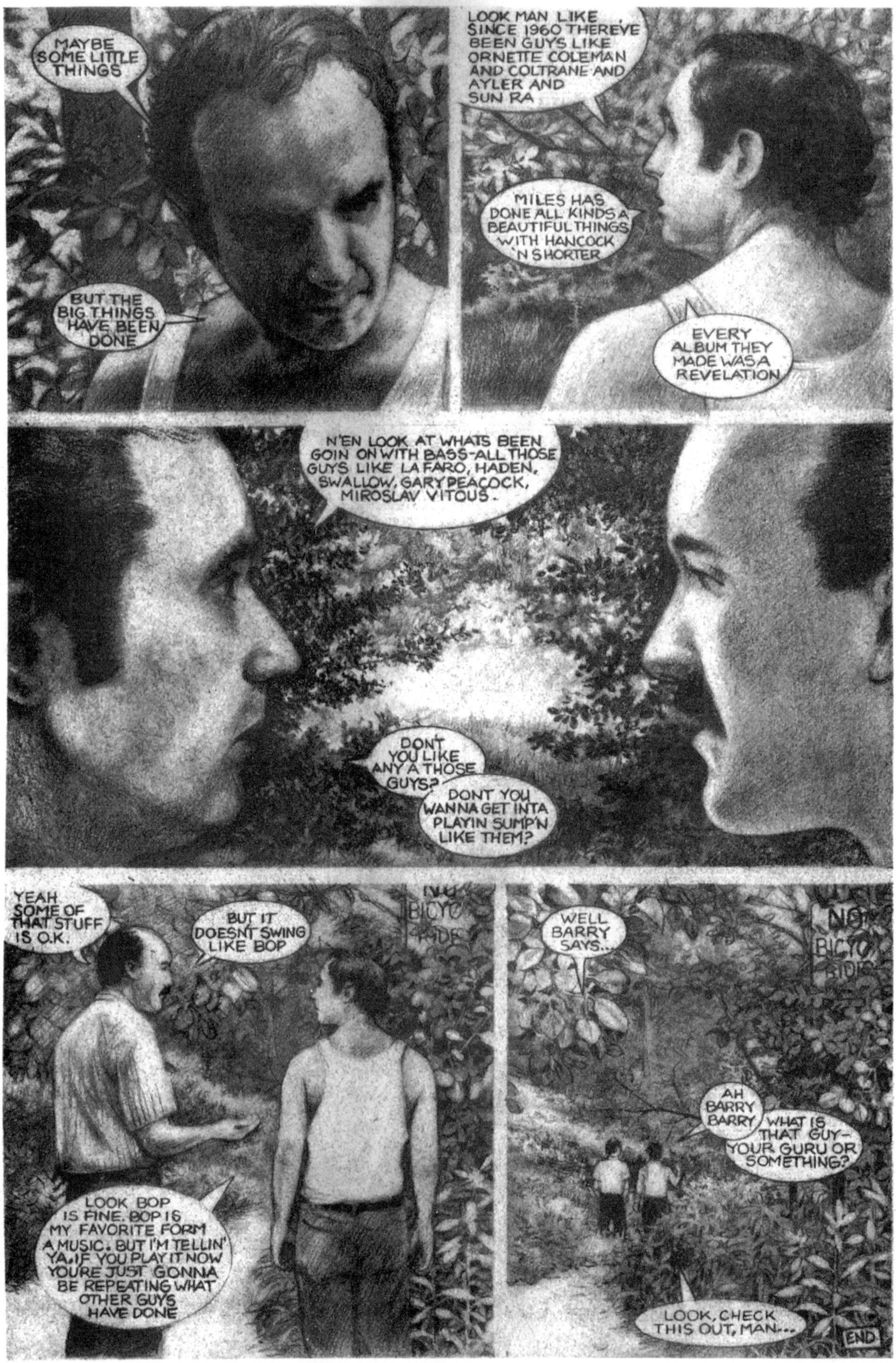
MAYBE SOME LITTLE THINGS
BUT THE BIG THINGS HAVE BEEN DONE
LOOK MAN LIKE , SINCE 1960 THEREVE BEEN GUYS LIKE ORNETTE COLEMAN AND COLTRANE AND AYLER AND SUN RA
MILES HAS DONE ALL KINDS A BEAUTIFUL THINGS WITH HANCOCK 'N SHORTER
EVERY ALBUM THEY MADE WAS A REVELATION
N'EN LOOK AT WHATS BEEN GOIN ON WITH BASS-ALL THOSE GUYS LIKE LA FARO, HADEN, SWALLOW, GARY PEACOCK, MIROSLAV VITOUS.
DONT YOU LIKE ANY A THOSE GUYS?
DONT YOU WANNA GET INTA PLAYIN SUMP'N LIKE THEM?
YEAH SOME OF THAT STUFF IS O.K.
BUT IT DOESNT SWING LIKE BOP
LOOK BOP IS FINE. BOP IS MY FAVORITE FORM A MUSIC. BUT I'M TELLIN' YA, IF YOU PLAY IT NOW YOU'RE JUST GONNA BE REPEATING WHAT OTHER GUYS HAVE DONE
WELL BARRY SAYS...
AH BARRY BARRY
WHAT IS THAT GUY- YOUR GURU OR SOMETHING?
LOOK, CHECK THIS OUT, MAN...
END

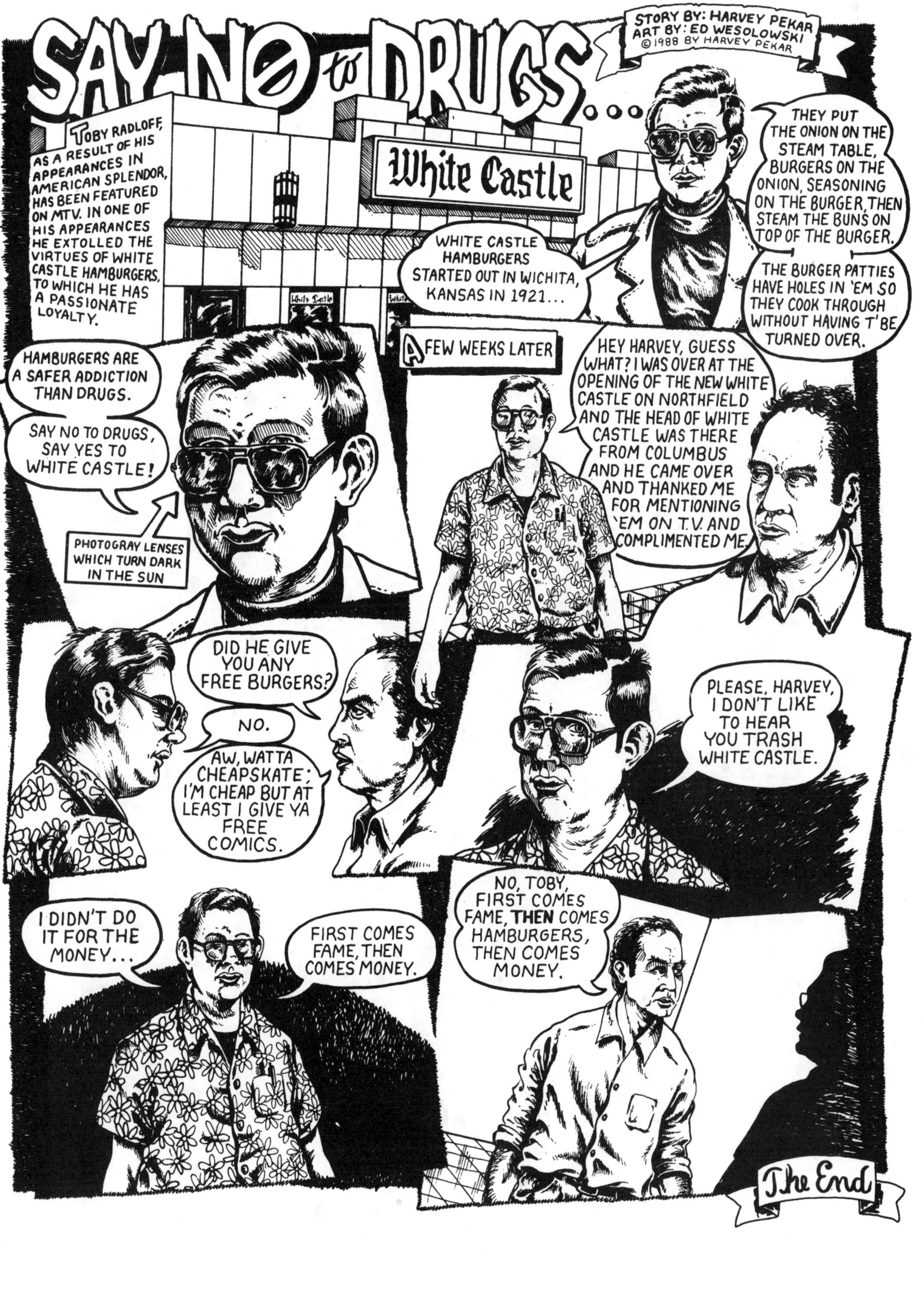

SAY NO to DRUGS...
STORY BY: HARVEY PEKAR
ART BY: ED WESOLOWSKI
© 1988 BY HARVEY PEKAR
TOBY RADLOFF, AS A RESULT OF HIS APPEARANCES IN AMERICAN SPLENDOR, HAS BEEN FEATURED ON MTV. IN ONE OF HIS APPEARANCES HE EXTOLLED THE VIRTUES OF WHITE CASTLE HAMBURGERS, TO WHICH HE HAS A PASSIONATE LOYALTY.
White Castle
WHITE CASTLE HAMBURGERS STARTED OUT IN WICHITA, KANSAS IN 1921...
THEY PUT THE ONION ON THE STEAM TABLE, BURGERS ON THE ONION, SEASONING ON THE BURGER, THEN STEAM THE BUNS ON TOP OF THE BURGER.
THE BURGER PATTIES HAVE HOLES IN 'EM SO THEY COOK THROUGH WITHOUT HAVING T' BE TURNED OVER.
HAMBURGERS ARE A SAFER ADDICTION THAN DRUGS.
SAY NO TO DRUGS, SAY YES TO WHITE CASTLE!
PHOTOGRAY LENSES WHICH TURN DARK IN THE SUN
A FEW WEEKS LATER
HEY HARVEY, GUESS WHAT? I WAS OVER AT THE OPENING OF THE NEW WHITE CASTLE ON NORTHFIELD AND THE HEAD OF WHITE CASTLE WAS THERE FROM COLUMBUS AND HE CAME OVER AND THANKED ME FOR MENTIONING 'EM ON T.V. AND COMPLIMENTED ME.
DID HE GIVE YOU ANY FREE BURGERS?
NO.
AW, WATTA CHEAPSKATE; I'M CHEAP BUT AT LEAST I GIVE YA FREE COMICS.
PLEASE, HARVEY, I DON'T LIKE TO HEAR YOU TRASH WHITE CASTLE.
I DIDN'T DO IT FOR THE MONEY...
FIRST COMES FAME, THEN COMES MONEY.
NO, TOBY, FIRST COMES FAME, THEN COMES HAMBURGERS, THEN COMES MONEY.
The End

BUSTING DR. GESUNDHEIDT'S BALLS

RABBI'S VIFE

STORY BY HARVEY PEKAR ART BY DREW FRIEDMAN

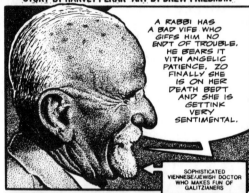

A RABBI HAS A BAD VIFE WHO GIFFS HIM NO ENDT OF TROUBLE, HE BEARS IT VITH ANGELIC PATIENCE, ZO FINALLY SHE IS ON HER DEATH BEDT AND SHE IS GETTINK VERY SENTIMENTAL.

SOPHISTICATED VIENNESE/JEWISH DOCTOR WHO MAKES FUN OF GALITZIANERS

SHE SAYS, "OH, VOT ARE YOU GOING TO DO AFTER I'M GONE? YOU'LL FIND ANUZZER WOMAN AND CARRY ON... BOO HOO, BOO HOO."

UH, I BEG YER PARDON BUT WERE YOU EVER ONNA STAGE?

HUH? NO, I VASN'T... SO ANY VAY...

THE REASON I ASK IS BECAUSE YOU'RE TELLING THIS STORY WITH A GREAT DEAL OF EMOTION.

SO ANY VAY -- Z'RABBI SAYS TO HIS VIFE, "DON'T BE SILLY. VOT ARE YOU VORRYINK ABOUT ZUCH QUESTIONS? VY DON'T YOU DIE FIRST?"

HAW HAW!

LEMME GET THIS NOW. THERE WAS ANOTHER RABBI IN TH' ROOM AN' HE SAID TO THE SICK RABBI...

NO, NO. VOT ARE YOU TALKING ABOUDT, ZERE VAS ONLY ONE RABBI AND HE VASN'T SICK-- HIS VIFE VAS SICK.

OHH, NOW I GET IT! YEAH, YEAH!

YEAH, I GOT IT NOW. SEE, I GOT CARRIED AWAY WITH HOW YOU WERE TELLIN' TH' STORY AN' I LOST MY TRAIN A' THOUGHT, BUT I GOT IT NOW!

COPYRIGHT © 1988 BY HARVEY PEKAR

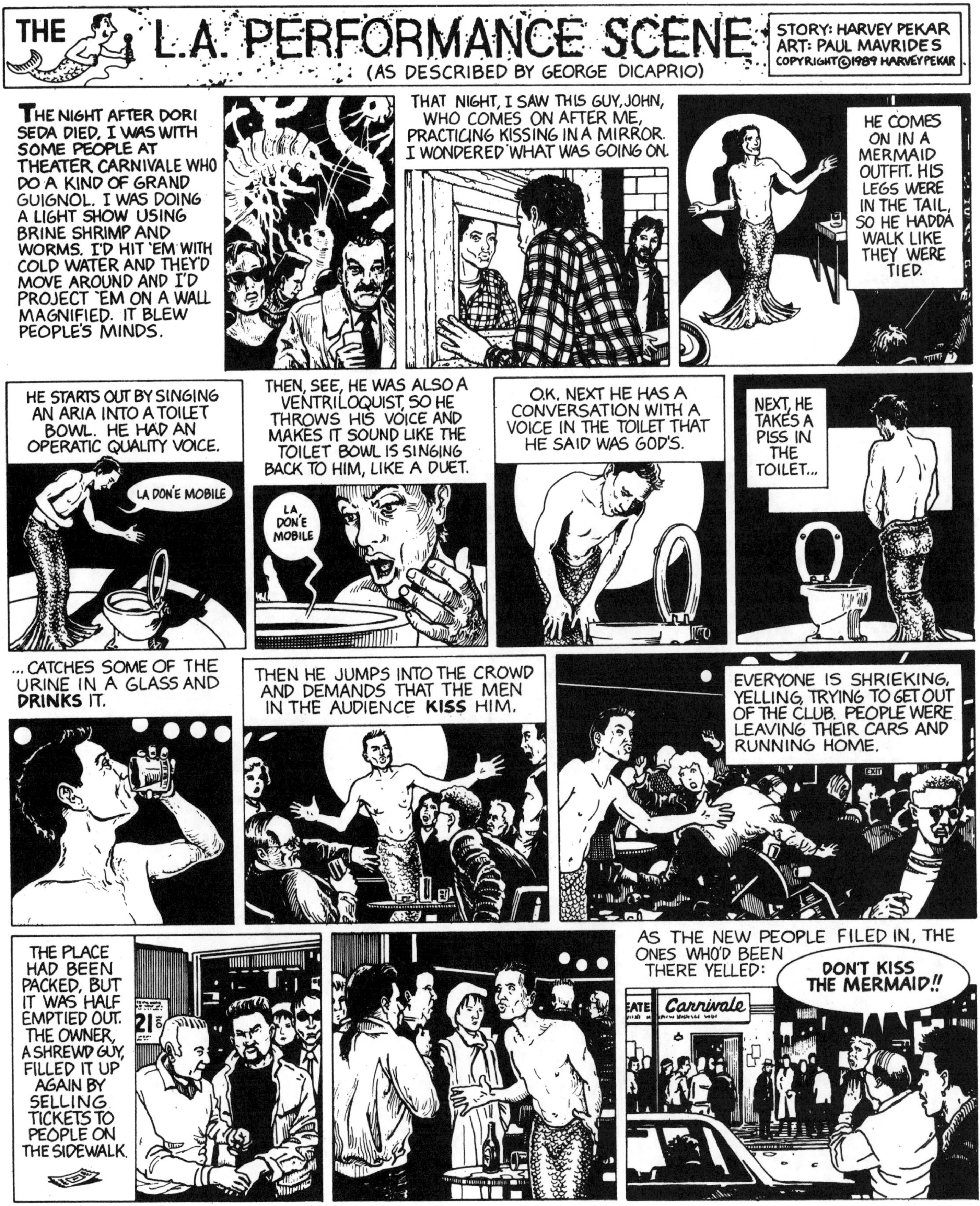
THE L.A. PERFORMANCE SCENE
(AS DESCRIBED BY GEORGE DICAPRIO)
STORY: HARVEY PEKAR
ART: PAUL MAVRIDES
COPYRIGHT © 1989 HARVEY PEKAR
THE NIGHT AFTER DORI SEDA DIED, I WAS WITH SOME PEOPLE AT THEATER CARNIVALE WHO DO A KIND OF GRAND GUIGNOL. I WAS DOING A LIGHT SHOW USING BRINE SHRIMP AND WORMS. I'D HIT 'EM WITH COLD WATER AND THEY'D MOVE AROUND AND I'D PROJECT 'EM ON A WALL MAGNIFIED. IT BLEW PEOPLE'S MINDS.
THAT NIGHT, I SAW THIS GUY, JOHN, WHO COMES ON AFTER ME, PRACTICING KISSING IN A MIRROR. I WONDERED WHAT WAS GOING ON.
HE COMES ON IN A MERMAID OUTFIT. HIS LEGS WERE IN THE TAIL, SO HE HADDA WALK LIKE THEY WERE TIED.
HE STARTS OUT BY SINGING AN ARIA INTO A TOILET BOWL. HE HAD AN OPERATIC QUALITY VOICE.
LA DON'E MOBILE
THEN, SEE, HE WAS ALSO A VENTRILOQUIST, SO HE THROWS HIS VOICE AND MAKES IT SOUND LIKE THE TOILET BOWL IS SINGING BACK TO HIM, LIKE A DUET.
LA, DON'E MOBILE
O.K. NEXT HE HAS A CONVERSATION WITH A VOICE IN THE TOILET THAT HE SAID WAS GOD'S.
NEXT, HE TAKES A PISS IN THE TOILET...
...CATCHES SOME OF THE URINE IN A GLASS AND DRINKS IT.
THEN HE JUMPS INTO THE CROWD AND DEMANDS THAT THE MEN IN THE AUDIENCE KISS HIM.
EVERYONE IS SHRIEKING, YELLING, TRYING TO GET OUT OF THE CLUB. PEOPLE WERE LEAVING THEIR CARS AND RUNNING HOME.
EXIT
THE PLACE HAD BEEN PACKED, BUT IT WAS HALF EMPTIED OUT. THE OWNER, A SHREWD GUY, FILLED IT UP AGAIN BY SELLING TICKETS TO PEOPLE ON THE SIDEWALK.
AS THE NEW PEOPLE FILED IN, THE ONES WHO'D BEEN THERE YELLED:
DON'T KISS THE MERMAID!!
Carrivale

ADAM PUKES ON HALLOWEEN

story by Harvey Pekar
art by Frank Stack

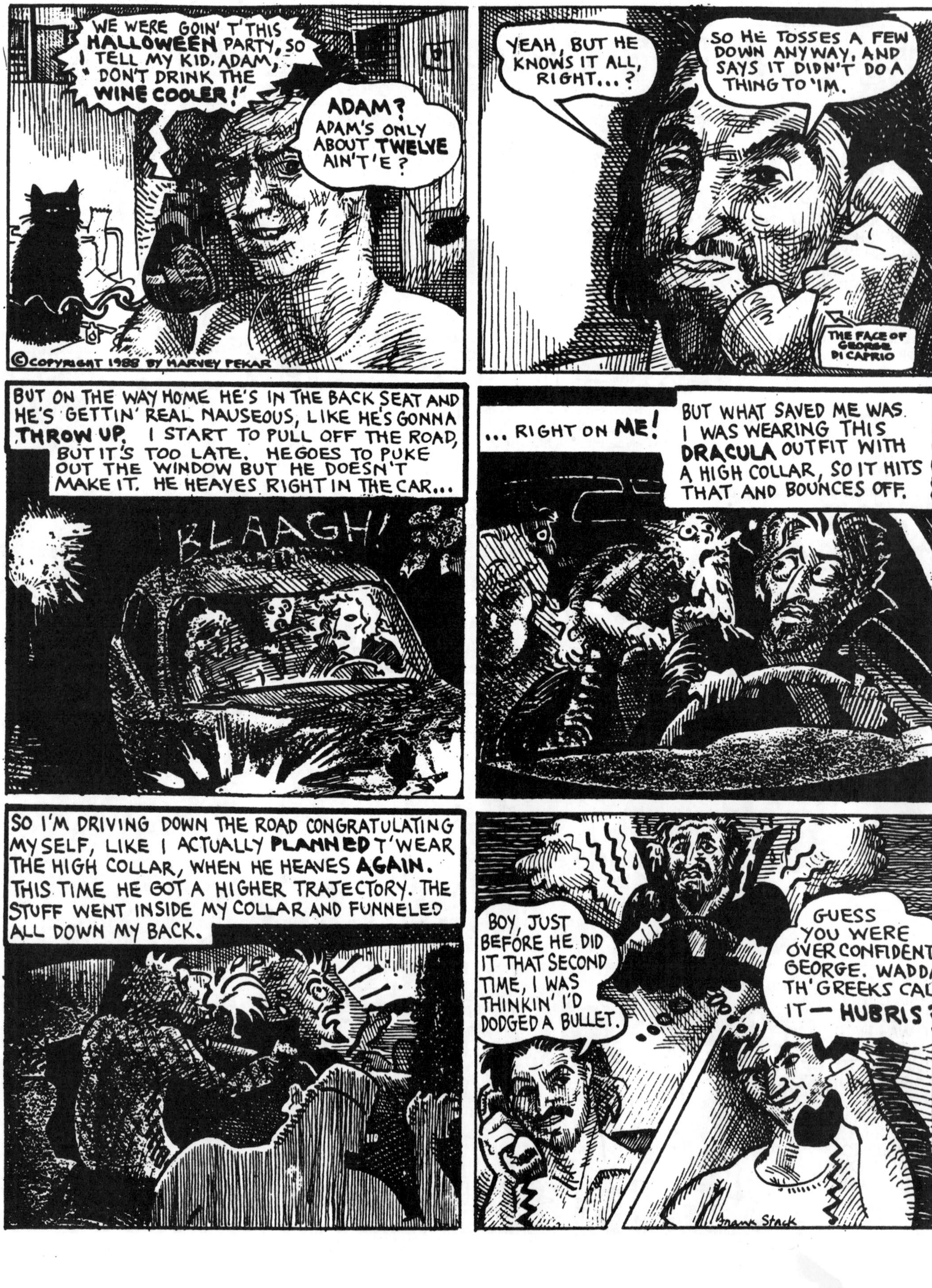

WE WERE GOIN' T'THIS HALLOWEEN PARTY, SO I TELL MY KID, ADAM, "DON'T DRINK THE WINE COOLER!"
ADAM? ADAM'S ONLY ABOUT TWELVE AIN'T'E?
©COPYRIGHT 1988 BY HARVEY PEKAR
YEAH, BUT HE KNOWS IT ALL, RIGHT...?
SO HE TOSSES A FEW DOWN ANYWAY, AND SAYS IT DIDN'T DO A THING TO 'IM.
THE FACE OF GEORGE DI CAPRIO
BUT ON THE WAY HOME HE'S IN THE BACK SEAT AND HE'S GETTIN' REAL NAUSEOUS, LIKE HE'S GONNA THROW UP. I START TO PULL OFF THE ROAD, BUT IT'S TOO LATE. HE GOES TO PUKE OUT THE WINDOW BUT HE DOESN'T MAKE IT. HE HEAVES RIGHT IN THE CAR...
BLAAGH!
... RIGHT ON ME!
BUT WHAT SAVED ME WAS I WAS WEARING THIS DRACULA OUTFIT WITH A HIGH COLLAR, SO IT HITS THAT AND BOUNCES OFF.
SO I'M DRIVING DOWN THE ROAD CONGRATULATING MYSELF, LIKE I ACTUALLY PLANNED T'WEAR THE HIGH COLLAR, WHEN HE HEAVES AGAIN. THIS TIME HE GOT A HIGHER TRAJECTORY. THE STUFF WENT INSIDE MY COLLAR AND FUNNELED ALL DOWN MY BACK.
BOY, JUST BEFORE HE DID IT THAT SECOND TIME, I WAS THINKIN' I'D DODGED A BULLET.
GUESS YOU WERE OVERCONFIDENT, GEORGE. WADDA TH'GREEKS CALL IT— HUBRIS?
Frank Stack

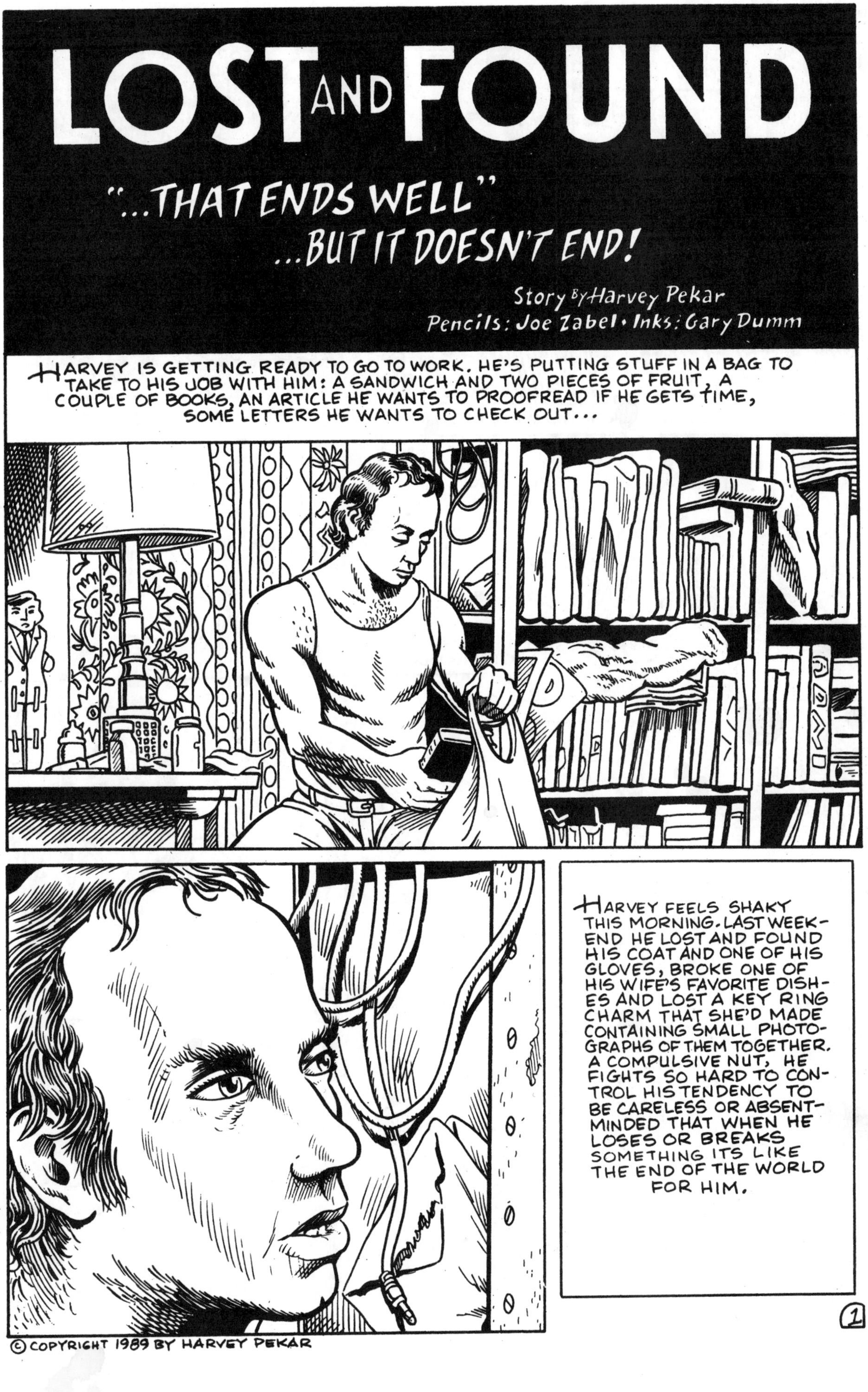
LOST AND FOUND
"...THAT ENDS WELL"
...BUT IT DOESN'T END!
Story By Harvey Pekar
Pencils: Joe Zabel • Inks: Gary Dumm
HARVEY IS GETTING READY TO GO TO WORK. HE'S PUTTING STUFF IN A BAG TO TAKE TO HIS JOB WITH HIM: A SANDWICH AND TWO PIECES OF FRUIT, A COUPLE OF BOOKS, AN ARTICLE HE WANTS TO PROOFREAD IF HE GETS TIME, SOME LETTERS HE WANTS TO CHECK OUT...
HARVEY FEELS SHAKY THIS MORNING. LAST WEEKEND HE LOST AND FOUND HIS COAT AND ONE OF HIS GLOVES, BROKE ONE OF HIS WIFE'S FAVORITE DISHES AND LOST A KEY RING CHARM THAT SHE'D MADE CONTAINING SMALL PHOTOGRAPHS OF THEM TOGETHER. A COMPULSIVE NUT, HE FIGHTS SO HARD TO CONTROL HIS TENDENCY TO BE CARELESS OR ABSENT-MINDED THAT WHEN HE LOSES OR BREAKS SOMETHING ITS LIKE THE END OF THE WORLD FOR HIM.

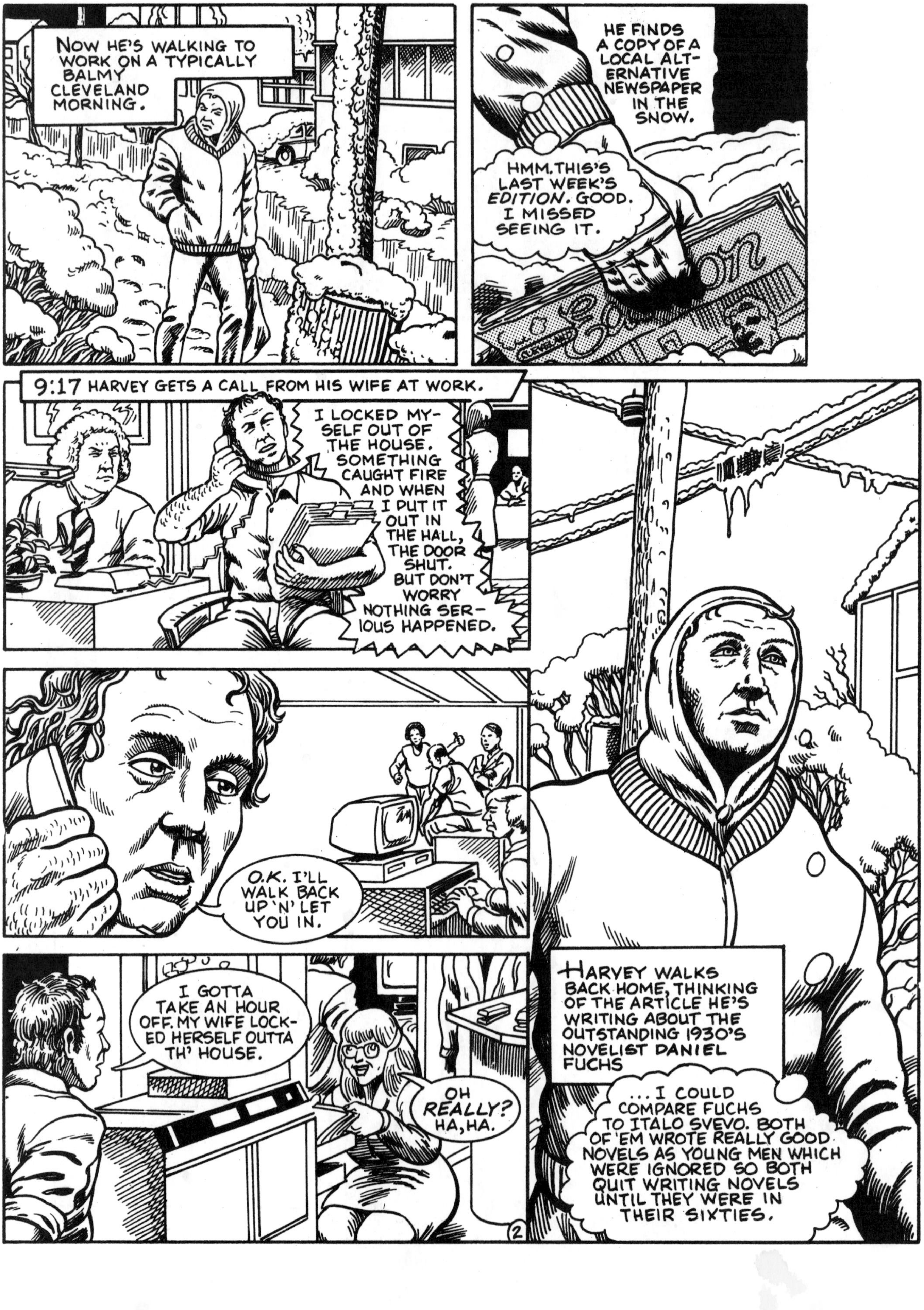
NOW HE'S WALKING TO WORK ON A TYPICALLY BALMY CLEVELAND MORNING.
HE FINDS A COPY OF A LOCAL ALTERNATIVE NEWSPAPER IN THE SNOW.
HMM. THIS'S LAST WEEK'S EDITION. GOOD. I MISSED SEEING IT.
9:17 HARVEY GETS A CALL FROM HIS WIFE AT WORK.
I LOCKED MYSELF OUT OF THE HOUSE. SOMETHING CAUGHT FIRE AND WHEN I PUT IT OUT IN THE HALL, THE DOOR SHUT. BUT DON'T WORRY NOTHING SERIOUS HAPPENED.
O.K. I'LL WALK BACK UP 'N' LET YOU IN.
I GOTTA TAKE AN HOUR OFF. MY WIFE LOCKED HERSELF OUTTA TH' HOUSE.
OH REALLY? HA, HA.
HARVEY WALKS BACK HOME, THINKING OF THE ARTICLE HE'S WRITING ABOUT THE OUTSTANDING 1930'S NOVELIST DANIEL FUCHS
... I COULD COMPARE FUCHS TO ITALO SVEVO. BOTH OF 'EM WROTE REALLY GOOD NOVELS AS YOUNG MEN WHICH WERE IGNORED SO BOTH QUIT WRITING NOVELS UNTIL THEY WERE IN THEIR SIXTIES.
2

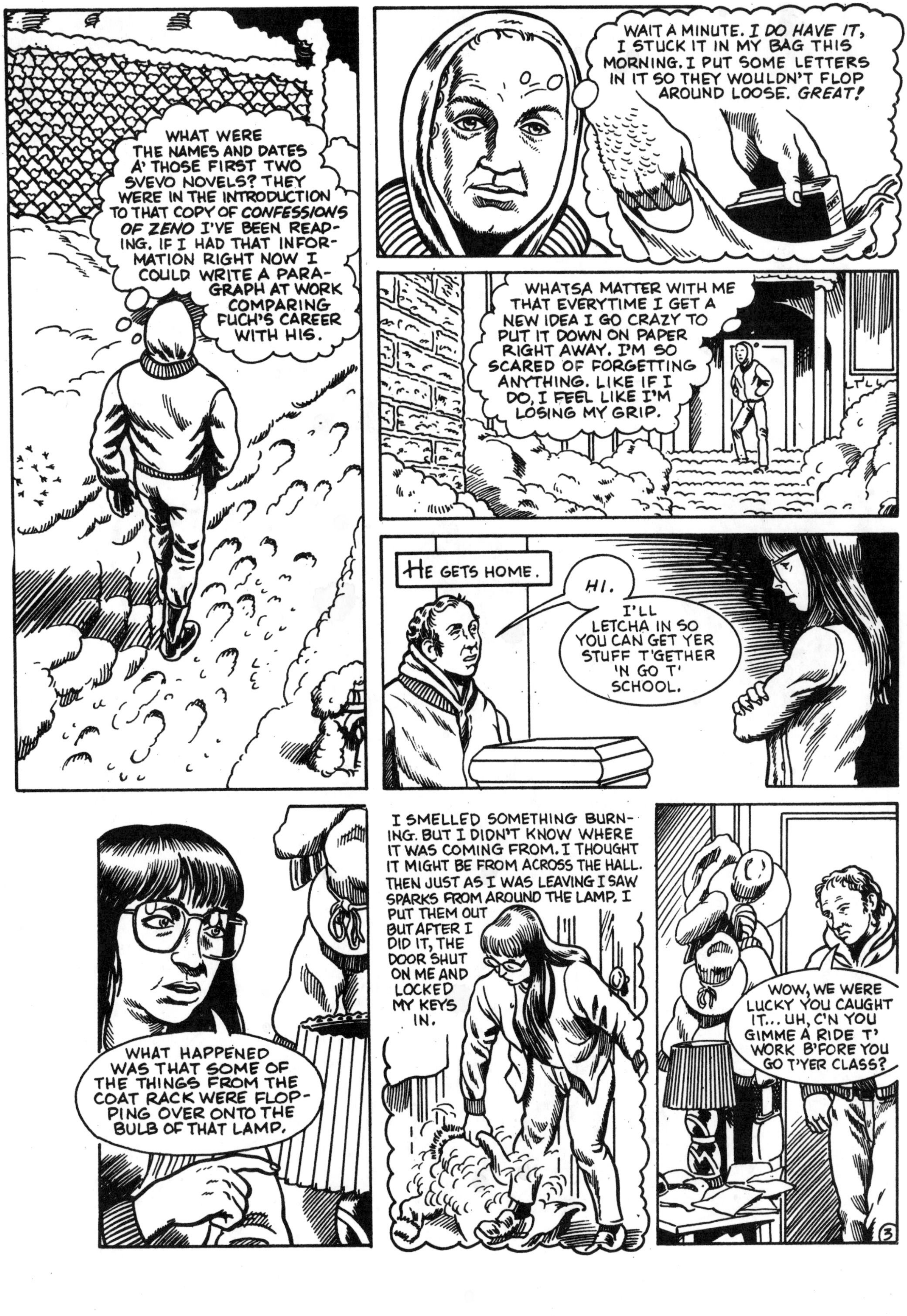
WHAT WERE THE NAMES AND DATES A' THOSE FIRST TWO SVEVO NOVELS? THEY WERE IN THE INTRODUCTION TO THAT COPY OF CONFESSIONS OF ZENO I'VE BEEN READING. IF I HAD THAT INFORMATION RIGHT NOW I COULD WRITE A PARAGRAPH AT WORK COMPARING FUCH'S CAREER WITH HIS.
WAIT A MINUTE. I DO HAVE IT, I STUCK IT IN MY BAG THIS MORNING. I PUT SOME LETTERS IN IT SO THEY WOULDN'T FLOP AROUND LOOSE. GREAT!
WHATSA MATTER WITH ME THAT EVERYTIME I GET A NEW IDEA I GO CRAZY TO PUT IT DOWN ON PAPER RIGHT AWAY. I'M SO SCARED OF FORGETTING ANYTHING. LIKE IF I DO, I FEEL LIKE I'M LOSING MY GRIP.
HE GETS HOME.
HI.
I'LL LETCHA IN SO YOU CAN GET YER STUFF T'GETHER 'N GO T' SCHOOL.
WHAT HAPPENED WAS THAT SOME OF THE THINGS FROM THE COAT RACK WERE FLOPPING OVER ONTO THE BULB OF THAT LAMP.
I SMELLED SOMETHING BURNING. BUT I DIDN'T KNOW WHERE IT WAS COMING FROM. I THOUGHT IT MIGHT BE FROM ACROSS THE HALL. THEN JUST AS I WAS LEAVING I SAW SPARKS FROM AROUND THE LAMP. I PUT THEM OUT BUT AFTER I DID IT, THE DOOR SHUT ON ME AND LOCKED MY KEYS IN.
WOW, WE WERE LUCKY YOU CAUGHT IT... UH, C'N YOU GIMME A RIDE T' WORK B'FORE YOU GO T'YER CLASS?

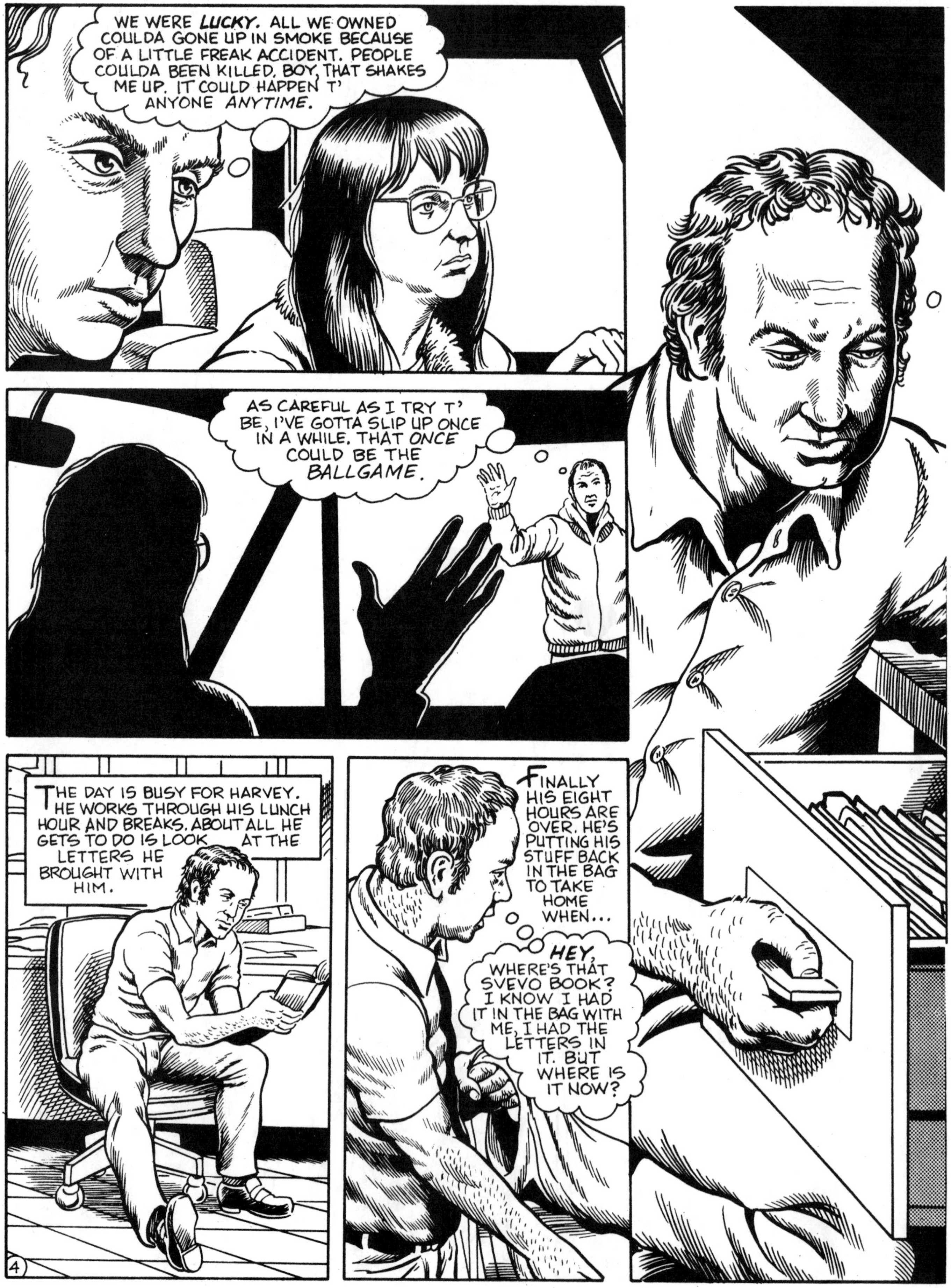

WE WERE LUCKY. ALL WE OWNED COULDA GONE UP IN SMOKE BECAUSE OF A LITTLE FREAK ACCIDENT. PEOPLE COULDA BEEN KILLED, BOY, THAT SHAKES ME UP. IT COULD HAPPEN T' ANYONE ANYTIME.
AS CAREFUL AS I TRY T' BE, I'VE GOTTA SLIP UP ONCE IN A WHILE. THAT ONCE COULD BE THE BALLGAME.
THE DAY IS BUSY FOR HARVEY. HE WORKS THROUGH HIS LUNCH HOUR AND BREAKS. ABOUT ALL HE GETS TO DO IS LOOK AT THE LETTERS HE BROUGHT WITH HIM.
FINALLY HIS EIGHT HOURS ARE OVER. HE'S PUTTING HIS STUFF BACK IN THE BAG TO TAKE HOME WHEN...
HEY, WHERE'S THAT SVEVO BOOK? I KNOW I HAD IT IN THE BAG WITH ME, I HAD THE LETTERS IN IT. BUT WHERE IS IT NOW?

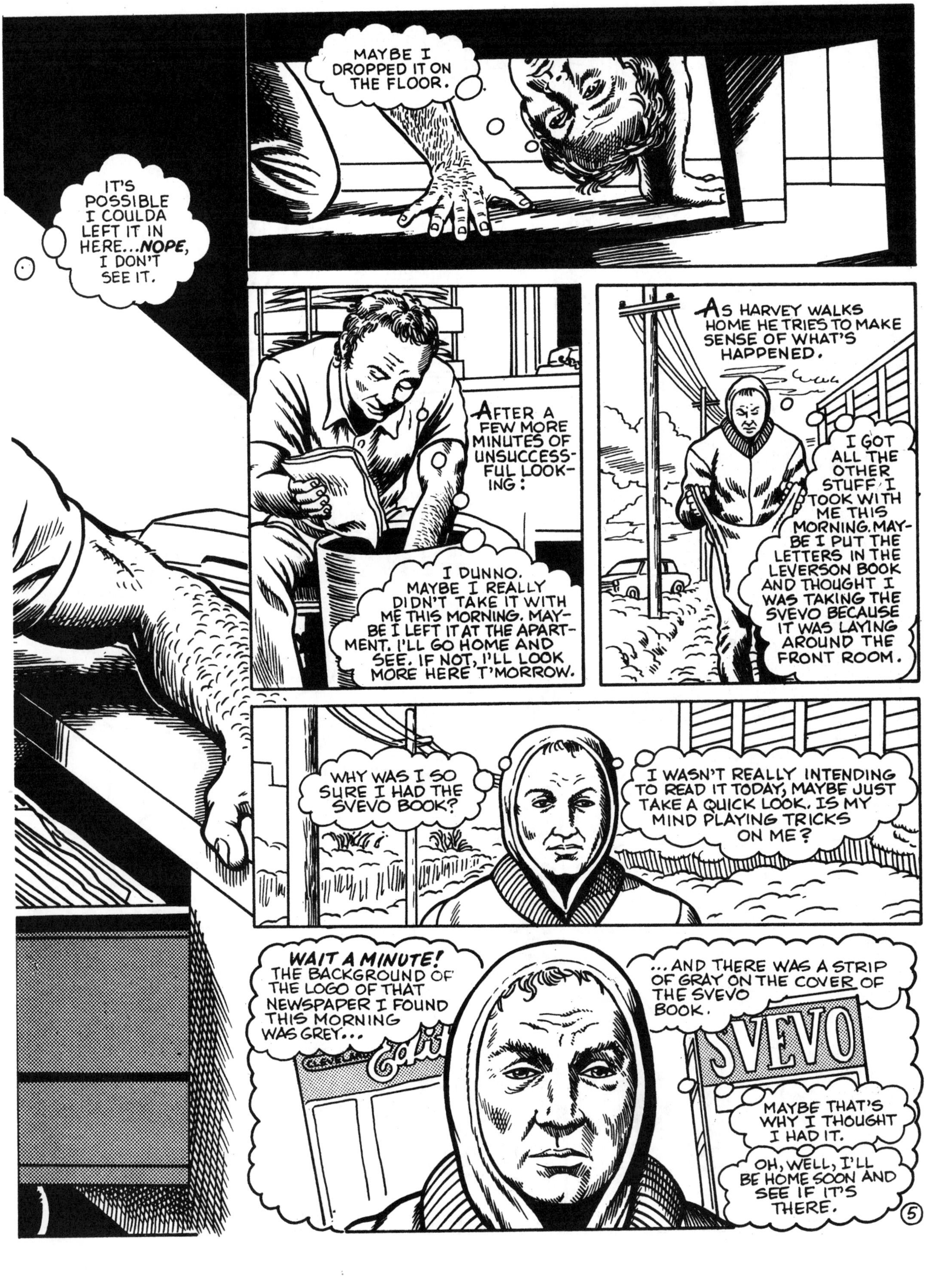
MAYBE I DROPPED IT ON THE FLOOR.
IT'S POSSIBLE I COULDA LEFT IT IN HERE...NOPE, I DON'T SEE IT.
AFTER A FEW MORE MINUTES OF UNSUCCESSFUL LOOKING:
I DUNNO. MAYBE I REALLY DIDN'T TAKE IT WITH ME THIS MORNING. MAYBE I LEFT IT AT THE APARTMENT. I'LL GO HOME AND SEE. IF NOT, I'LL LOOK MORE HERE T'MORROW.
AS HARVEY WALKS HOME HE TRIES TO MAKE SENSE OF WHAT'S HAPPENED.
I GOT ALL THE OTHER STUFF I TOOK WITH ME THIS MORNING. MAYBE I PUT THE LETTERS IN THE LEVERSON BOOK AND THOUGHT I WAS TAKING THE SVEVO BECAUSE IT WAS LAYING AROUND THE FRONT ROOM.
WHY WAS I SO SURE I HAD THE SVEVO BOOK?
I WASN'T REALLY INTENDING TO READ IT TODAY, MAYBE JUST TAKE A QUICK LOOK. IS MY MIND PLAYING TRICKS ON ME?
WAIT A MINUTE! THE BACKGROUND OF THE LOGO OF THAT NEWSPAPER I FOUND THIS MORNING WAS GREY...
...AND THERE WAS A STRIP OF GRAY ON THE COVER OF THE SVEVO BOOK.
SVEVO
MAYBE THAT'S WHY I THOUGHT I HAD IT.
OH, WELL, I'LL BE HOME SOON AND SEE IF IT'S THERE.

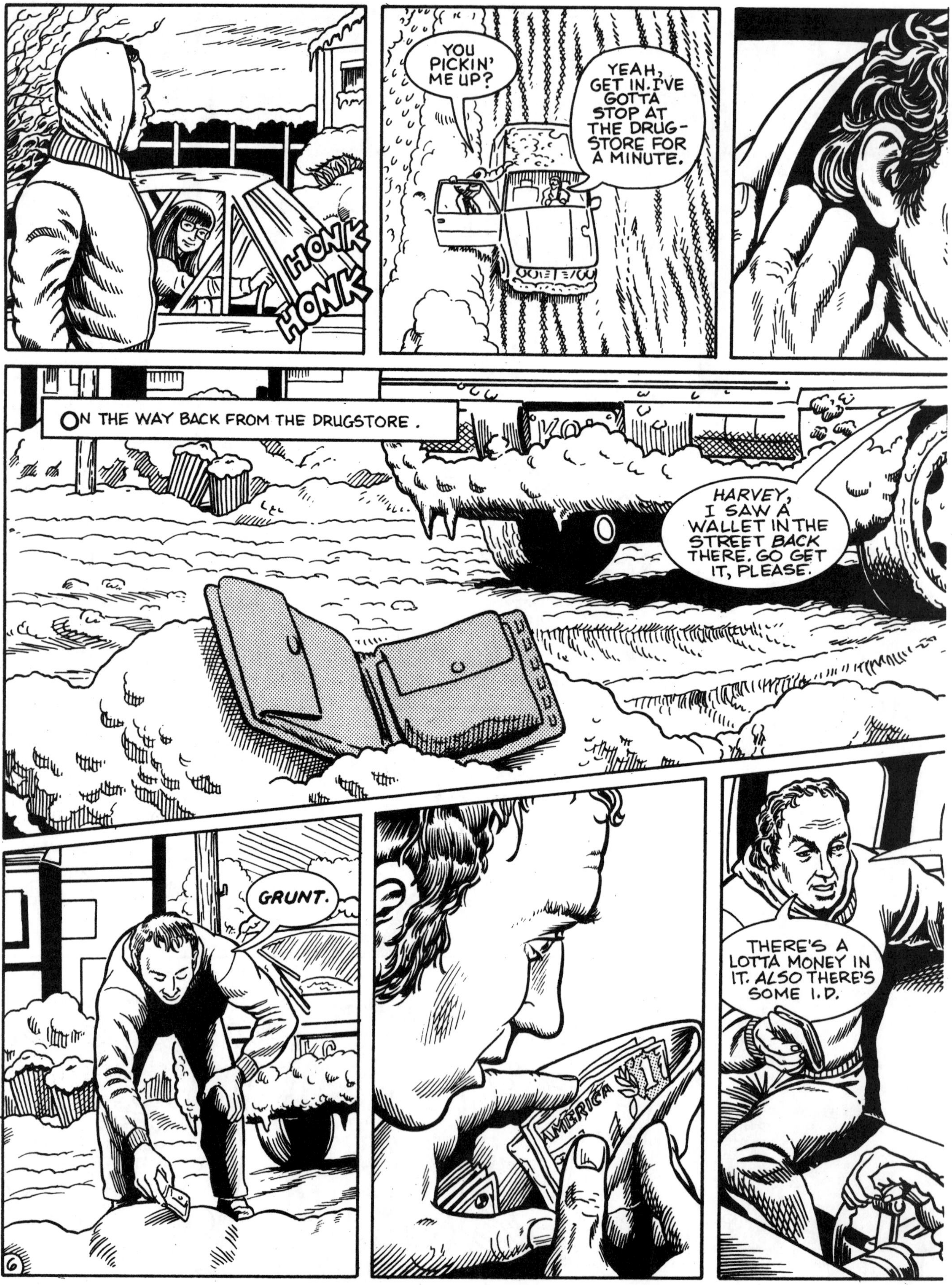
HONK HONK
YOU PICKIN' ME UP?
YEAH, GET IN. I'VE GOTTA STOP AT THE DRUG-STORE FOR A MINUTE.
ON THE WAY BACK FROM THE DRUGSTORE.
HARVEY, I SAW A WALLET IN THE STREET *BACK* THERE. GO GET IT, PLEASE.
GRUNT.
THERE'S A LOTTA MONEY IN IT. *ALSO* THERE'S SOME I.D.

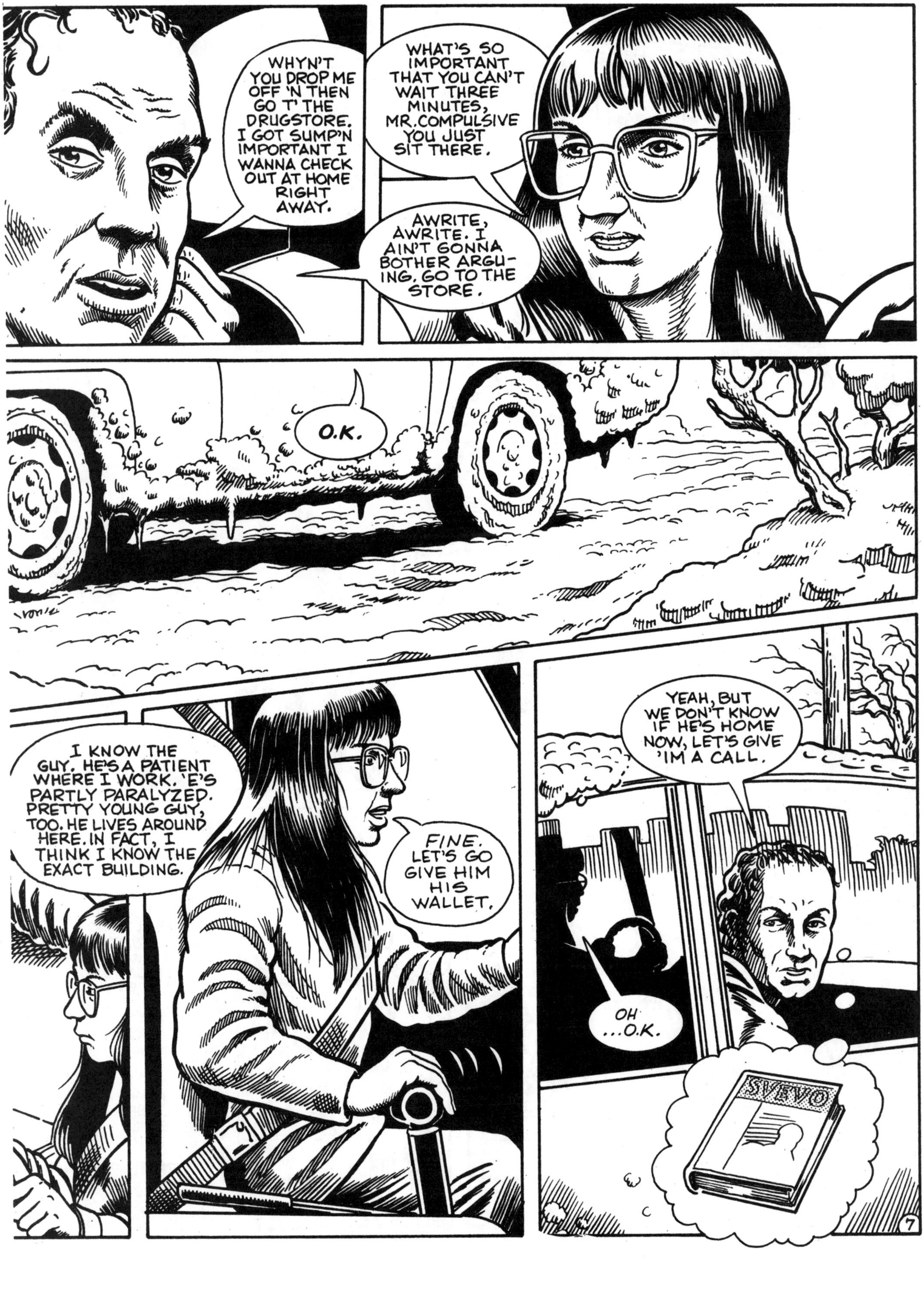
WHYN'T YOU DROP ME OFF 'N THEN GO T' THE DRUGSTORE. I GOT SUMP'N IMPORTANT I WANNA CHECK OUT AT HOME RIGHT AWAY.
WHAT'S SO IMPORTANT THAT YOU CAN'T WAIT THREE MINUTES, MR. COMPULSIVE YOU JUST SIT THERE.
AWRITE, AWRITE. I AIN'T GONNA BOTHER ARGUING. GO TO THE STORE.
O.K.
I KNOW THE GUY. HE'S A PATIENT WHERE I WORK. 'E'S PARTLY PARALYZED. PRETTY YOUNG GUY, TOO. HE LIVES AROUND HERE. IN FACT, I THINK I KNOW THE EXACT BUILDING.
FINE. LET'S GO GIVE HIM HIS WALLET.
YEAH, BUT WE DON'T KNOW IF HE'S HOME NOW, LET'S GIVE 'IM A CALL.
OH ...O.K.
SVEVO

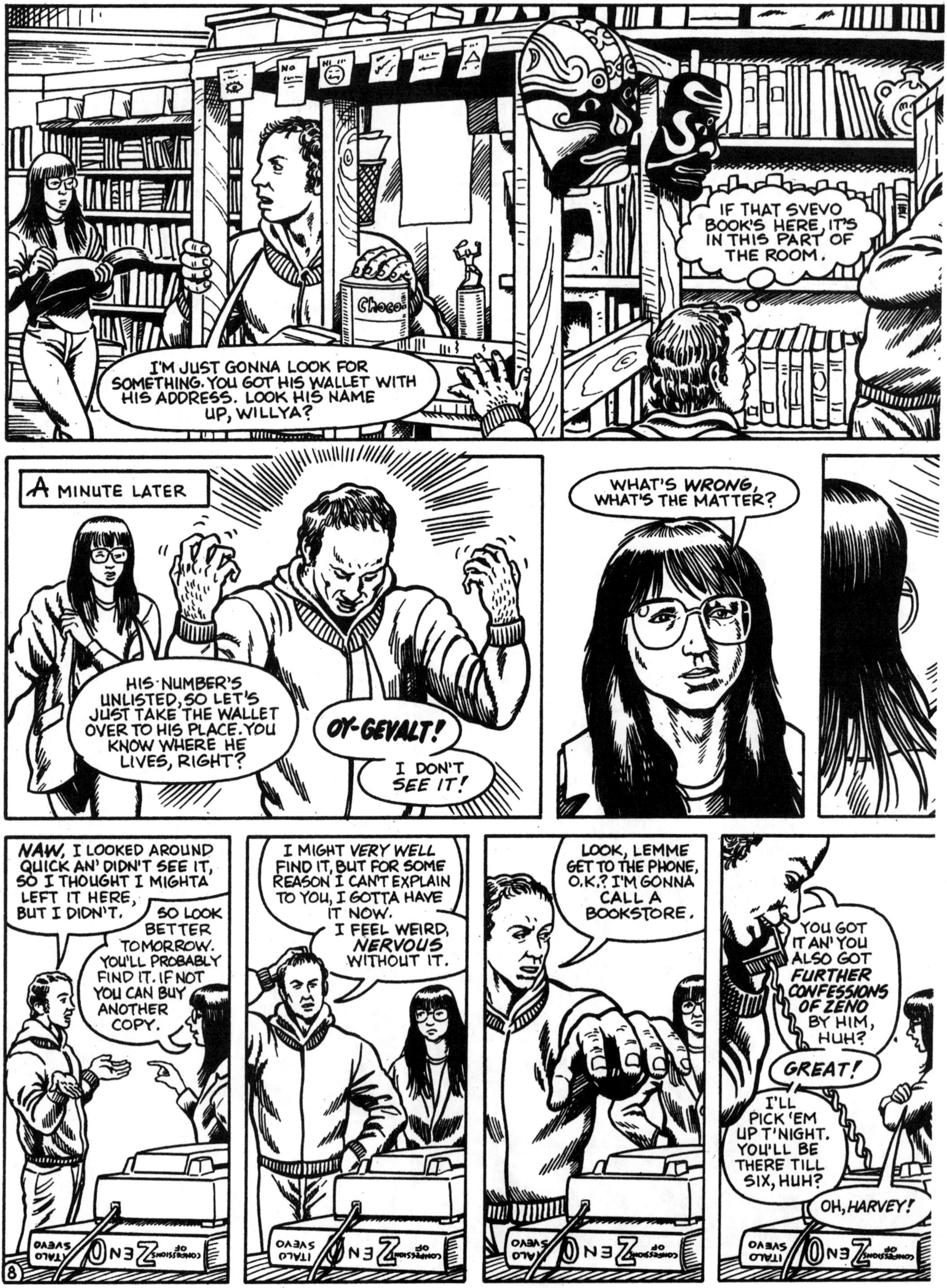
IF THAT SVEVO BOOK'S HERE, IT'S IN THIS PART OF THE ROOM.
I'M JUST GONNA LOOK FOR SOMETHING. YOU GOT HIS WALLET WITH HIS ADDRESS. LOOK HIS NAME UP, WILLYA?
A MINUTE LATER
HIS NUMBER'S UNLISTED, SO LET'S JUST TAKE THE WALLET OVER TO HIS PLACE. YOU KNOW WHERE HE LIVES, RIGHT?
OY-GEVALT!
I DON'T SEE IT!
WHAT'S WRONG, WHAT'S THE MATTER?
NAW, I LOOKED AROUND QUICK AN' DIDN'T SEE IT, SO I THOUGHT I MIGHTA LEFT IT HERE, BUT I DIDN'T.
SO LOOK BETTER TOMORROW. YOU'LL PROBABLY FIND IT. IF NOT YOU CAN BUY ANOTHER COPY.
I MIGHT VERY WELL FIND IT, BUT FOR SOME REASON I CAN'T EXPLAIN TO YOU, I GOTTA HAVE IT NOW.
I FEEL WEIRD, NERVOUS WITHOUT IT.
LOOK, LEMME GET TO THE PHONE, O.K.? I'M GONNA CALL A BOOKSTORE.
YOU GOT IT AN' YOU ALSO GOT FURTHER CONFESSIONS OF ZENO BY HIM, HUH?
GREAT!
I'LL PICK 'EM UP T'NIGHT. YOU'LL BE THERE TILL SIX, HUH?
OH, HARVEY!

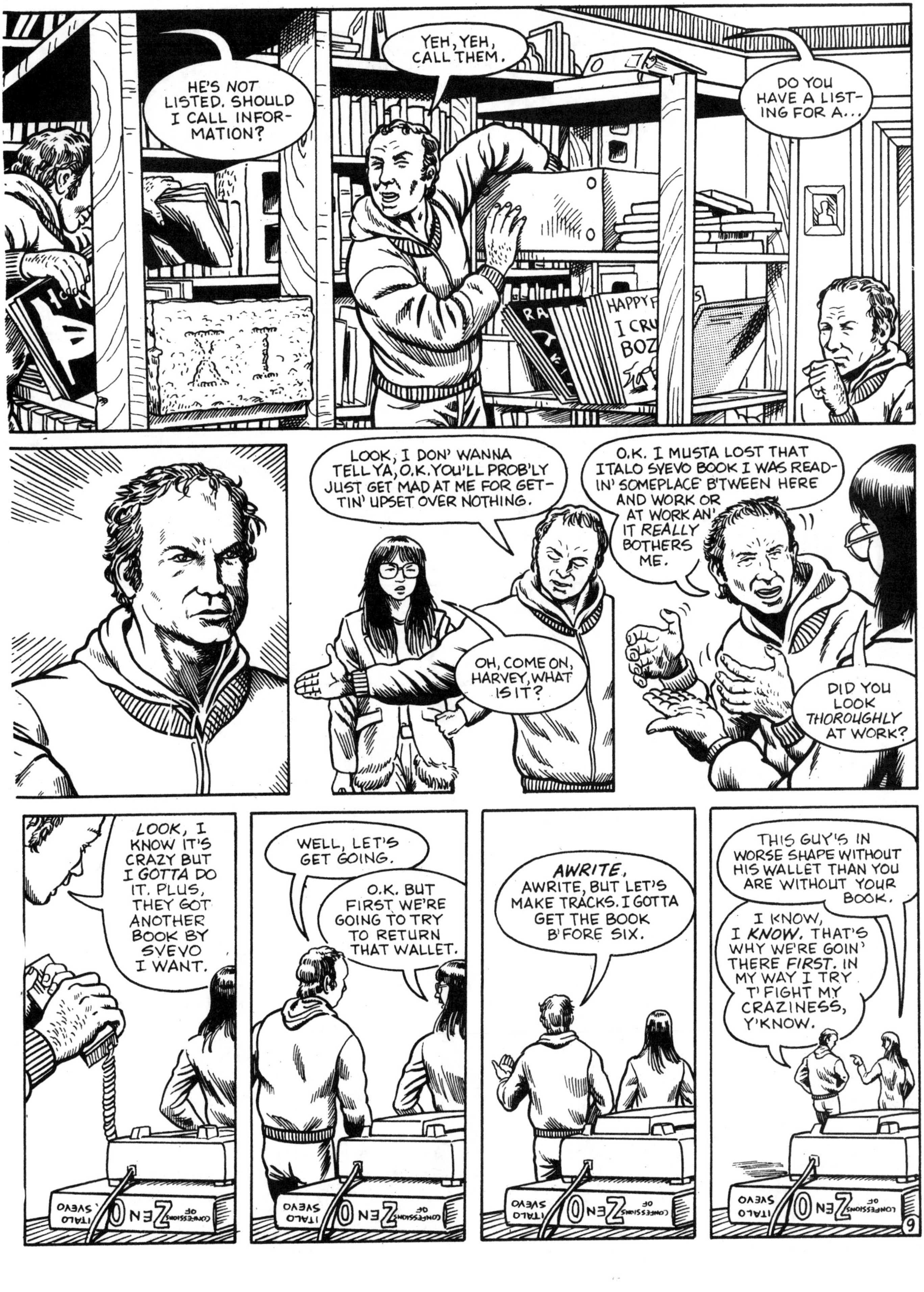

HE'S NOT LISTED. SHOULD I CALL INFORMATION?
YEH, YEH, CALL THEM.
DO YOU HAVE A LISTING FOR A...
LOOK, I DON' WANNA TELL YA, O.K. YOU'LL PROB'LY JUST GET MAD AT ME FOR GETTIN' UPSET OVER NOTHING.
OH, COME ON, HARVEY, WHAT IS IT?
O.K. I MUSTA LOST THAT ITALO SVEVO BOOK I WAS READIN' SOMEPLACE B'TWEEN HERE AND WORK OR AT WORK AN' IT REALLY BOTHERS ME.
DID YOU LOOK THOROUGHLY AT WORK?
LOOK, I KNOW IT'S CRAZY BUT I GOTTA DO IT. PLUS, THEY GOT ANOTHER BOOK BY SVEVO I WANT.
WELL, LET'S GET GOING.
O.K. BUT FIRST WE'RE GOING TO TRY TO RETURN THAT WALLET.
AWRITE, AWRITE, BUT LET'S MAKE TRACKS. I GOTTA GET THE BOOK B'FORE SIX.
THIS GUY'S IN WORSE SHAPE WITHOUT HIS WALLET THAN YOU ARE WITHOUT YOUR BOOK.
I KNOW, I KNOW. THAT'S WHY WE'RE GOIN' THERE FIRST. IN MY WAY I TRY T' FIGHT MY CRAZINESS, Y'KNOW.
CONFESSIONS OF ZENO ITALO SVEVO

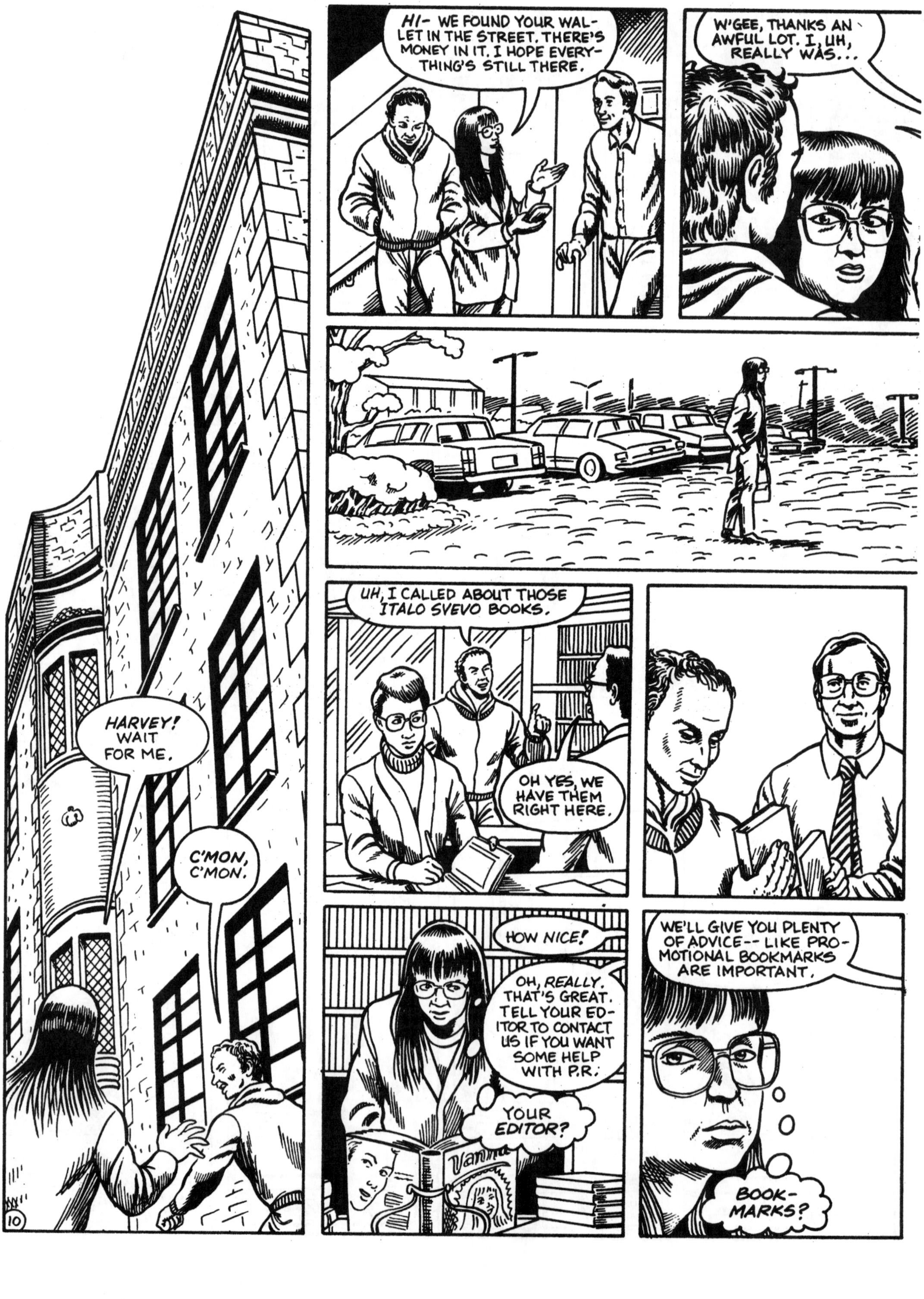
HARVEY! WAIT FOR ME.
C'MON, C'MON.
HI- WE FOUND YOUR WALLET IN THE STREET. THERE'S MONEY IN IT. I HOPE EVERYTHING'S STILL THERE.
W'GEE, THANKS AN AWFUL LOT. I, UH, REALLY WAS...
UH, I CALLED ABOUT THOSE ITALO SVEVO BOOKS.
OH YES, WE HAVE THEM RIGHT HERE.
HOW NICE!
OH, REALLY. THAT'S GREAT. TELL YOUR EDITOR TO CONTACT US IF YOU WANT SOME HELP WITH P.R.
YOUR EDITOR?
WE'LL GIVE YOU PLENTY OF ADVICE-- LIKE PROMOTIONAL BOOKMARKS ARE IMPORTANT.
BOOK-MARKS?

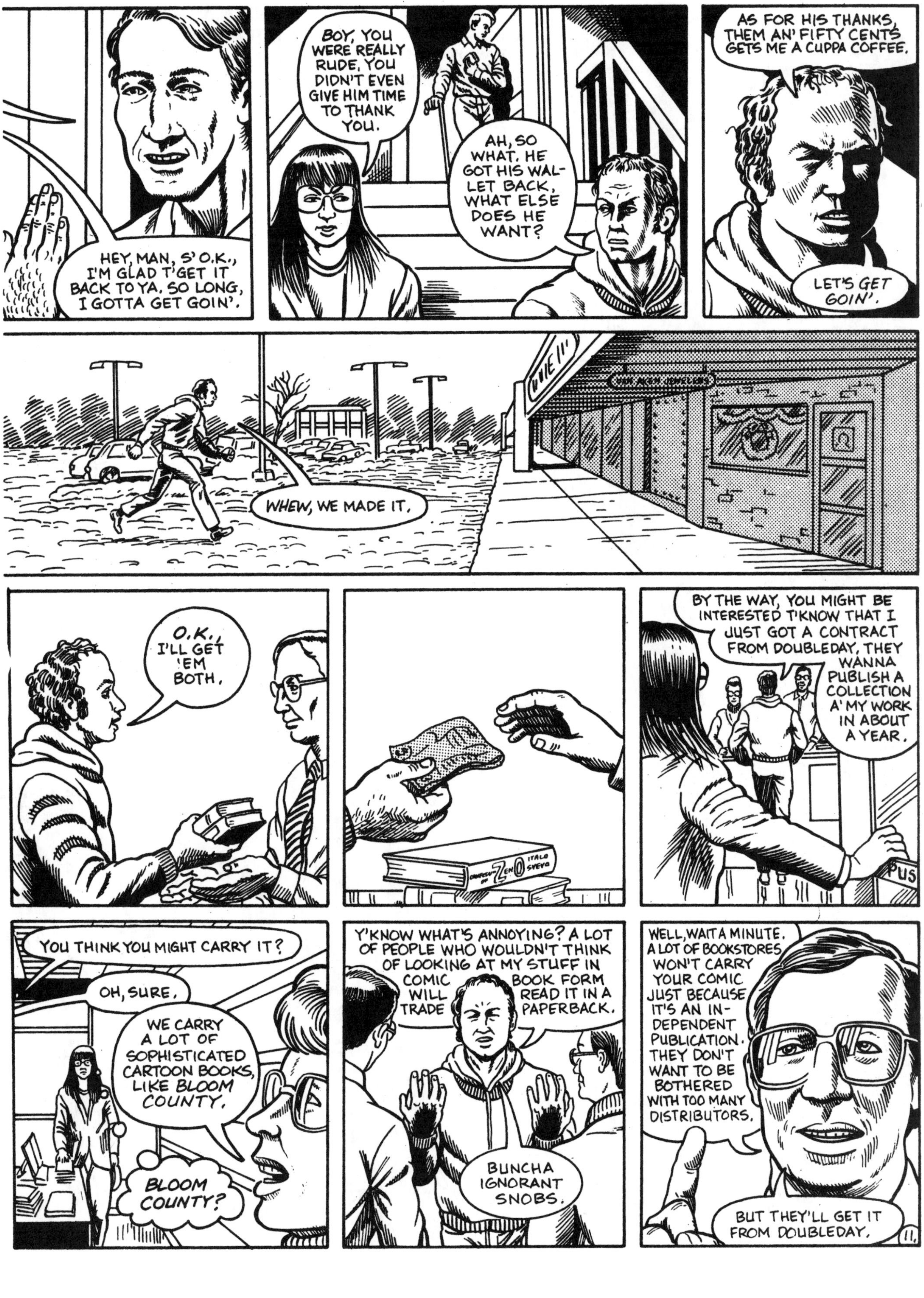

HEY, MAN, S'O.K., I'M GLAD T'GET IT BACK TO YA. SO LONG, I GOTTA GET GOIN'.
BOY, YOU WERE REALLY RUDE. YOU DIDN'T EVEN GIVE HIM TIME TO THANK YOU.
AH, SO WHAT. HE GOT HIS WALLET BACK, WHAT ELSE DOES HE WANT?
AS FOR HIS THANKS, THEM AN' FIFTY CENTS GETS ME A CUPPA COFFEE.
LET'S GET GOIN'.
WHEW, WE MADE IT.
O.K., I'LL GET 'EM BOTH.
ZENO
ITALO SVEVO
BY THE WAY, YOU MIGHT BE INTERESTED T'KNOW THAT I JUST GOT A CONTRACT FROM DOUBLEDAY. THEY WANNA PUBLISH A COLLECTION A' MY WORK IN ABOUT A YEAR.
PUS
YOU THINK YOU MIGHT CARRY IT?
OH, SURE.
WE CARRY A LOT OF SOPHISTICATED CARTOON BOOKS, LIKE BLOOM COUNTY.
BLOOM COUNTY?
Y'KNOW WHAT'S ANNOYING? A LOT OF PEOPLE WHO WOULDN'T THINK OF LOOKING AT MY STUFF IN COMIC BOOK FORM WILL TRADE READ IT IN A PAPERBACK.
BUNCHA IGNORANT SNOBS.
WELL, WAIT A MINUTE. A LOT OF BOOKSTORES WON'T CARRY YOUR COMIC JUST BECAUSE IT'S AN INDEPENDENT PUBLICATION. THEY DON'T WANT TO BE BOTHERED WITH TOO MANY DISTRIBUTORS.
BUT THEY'LL GET IT FROM DOUBLEDAY.

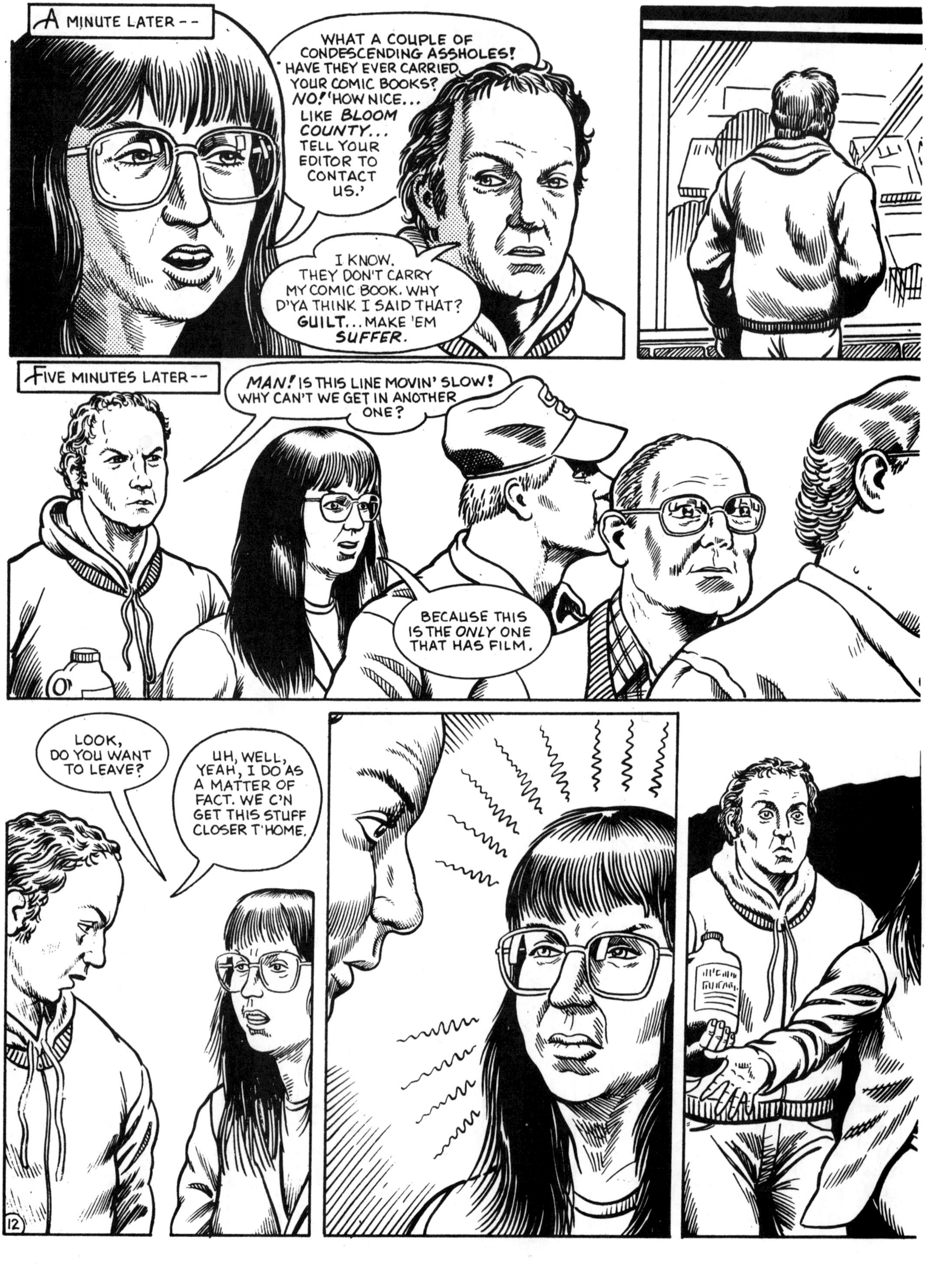

A MINUTE LATER--
WHAT A COUPLE OF CONDESCENDING ASSHOLES! HAVE THEY EVER CARRIED YOUR COMIC BOOKS? NO! 'HOW NICE... LIKE BLOOM COUNTY... TELL YOUR EDITOR TO CONTACT US.'
I KNOW. THEY DON'T CARRY MY COMIC BOOK. WHY D'YA THINK I SAID THAT? GUILT... MAKE 'EM SUFFER.
FIVE MINUTES LATER--
MAN! IS THIS LINE MOVIN' SLOW! WHY CAN'T WE GET IN ANOTHER ONE?
BECAUSE THIS IS THE ONLY ONE THAT HAS FILM.
LOOK, DO YOU WANT TO LEAVE?
UH, WELL, YEAH, I DO AS A MATTER OF FACT. WE C'N GET THIS STUFF CLOSER T'HOME.

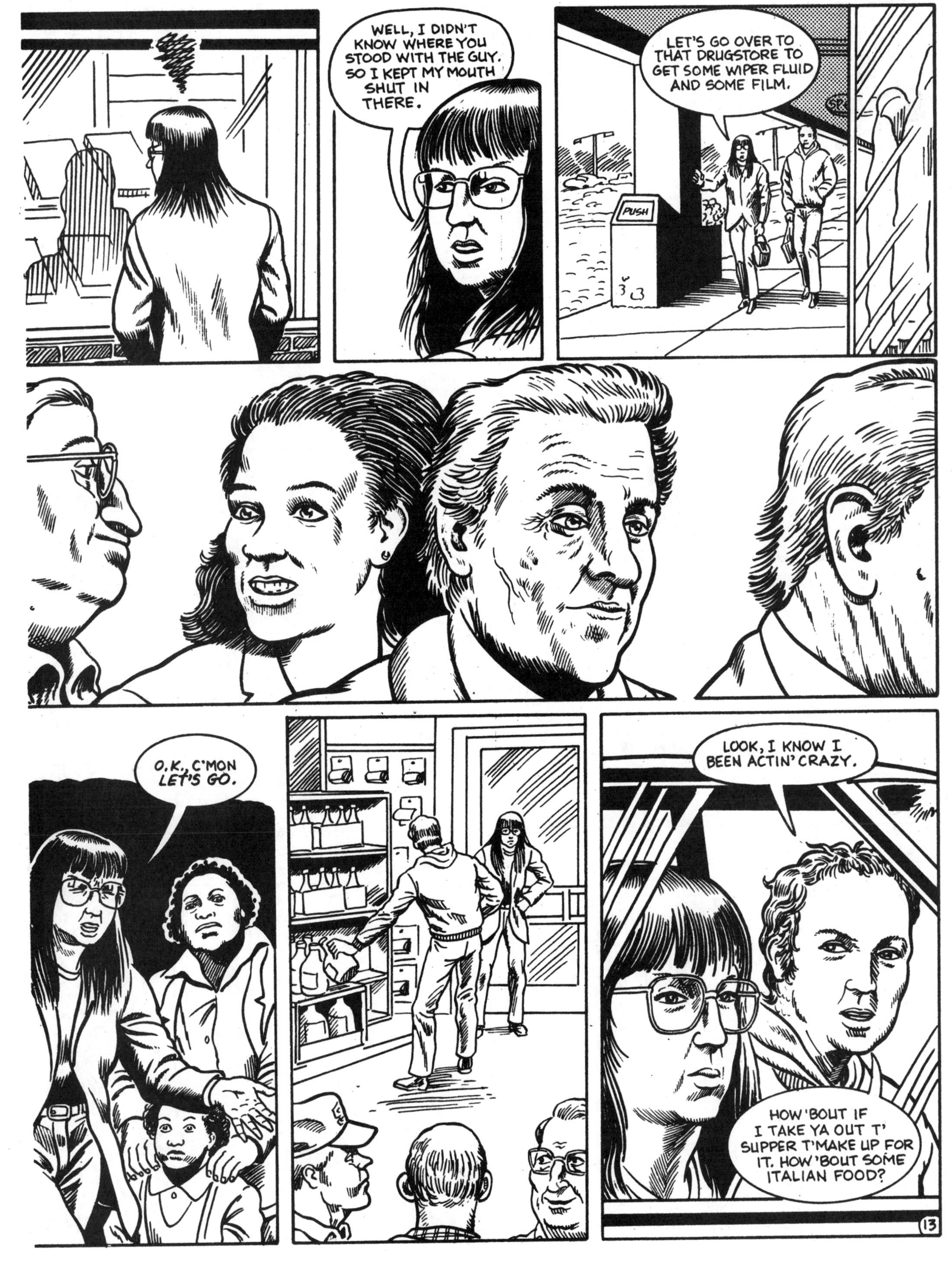
WELL, I DIDN'T KNOW WHERE YOU STOOD WITH THE GUY. SO I KEPT MY MOUTH SHUT IN THERE.
LET'S GO OVER TO THAT DRUGSTORE TO GET SOME WIPER FLUID AND SOME FILM.
PUSH
O.K., C'MON LET'S GO.
LOOK, I KNOW I BEEN ACTIN' CRAZY.
HOW 'BOUT IF I TAKE YA OUT T' SUPPER T'MAKE UP FOR IT. HOW 'BOUT SOME ITALIAN FOOD?

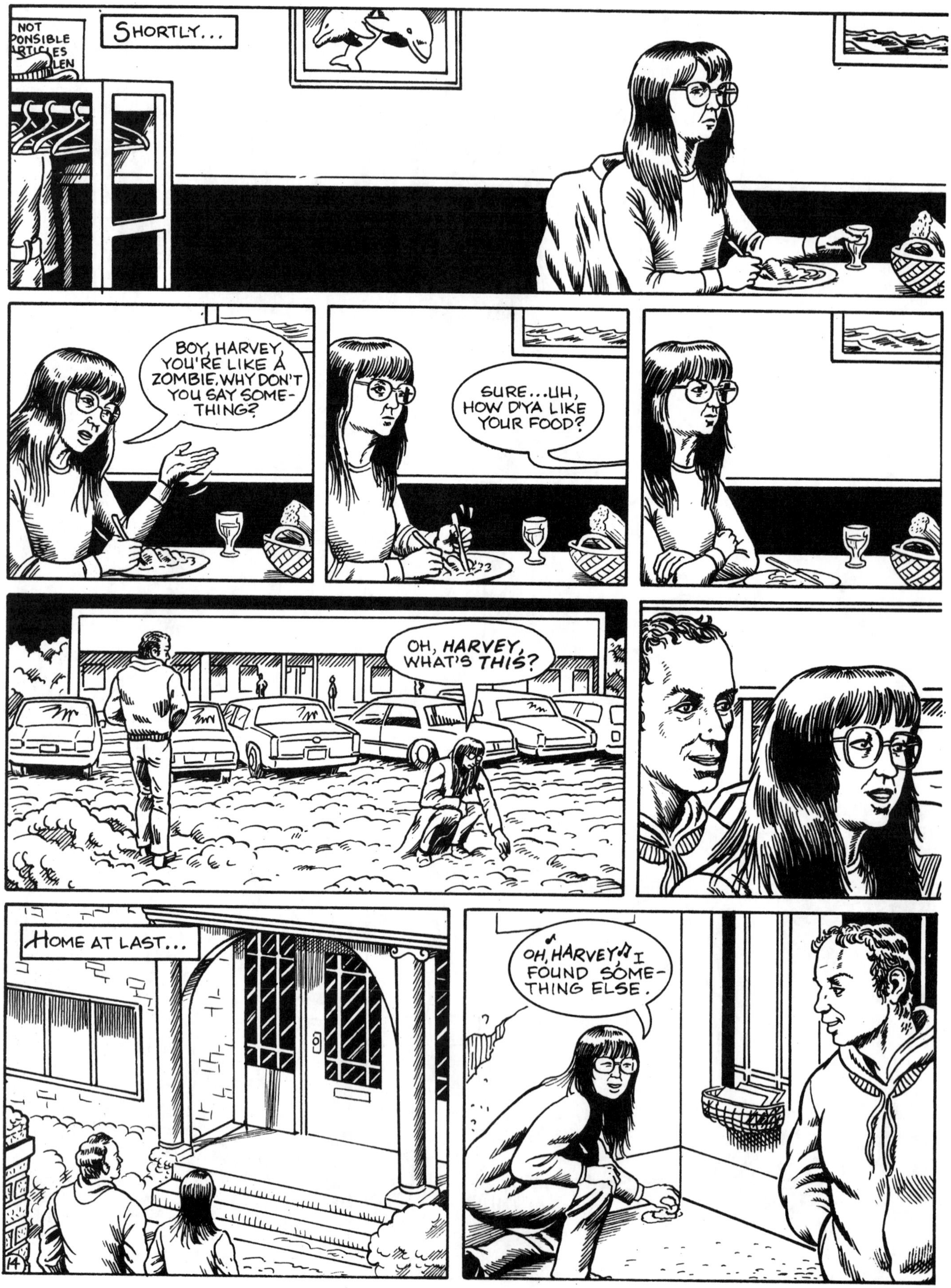
NOT
SHORTLY...
BOY, HARVEY, YOU'RE LIKE A ZOMBIE, WHY DON'T YOU SAY SOMETHING?
SURE...UH, HOW D'YA LIKE YOUR FOOD?
OH, HARVEY, WHAT'S THIS?
HOME AT LAST...
OH, HARVEY, I FOUND SOMETHING ELSE.

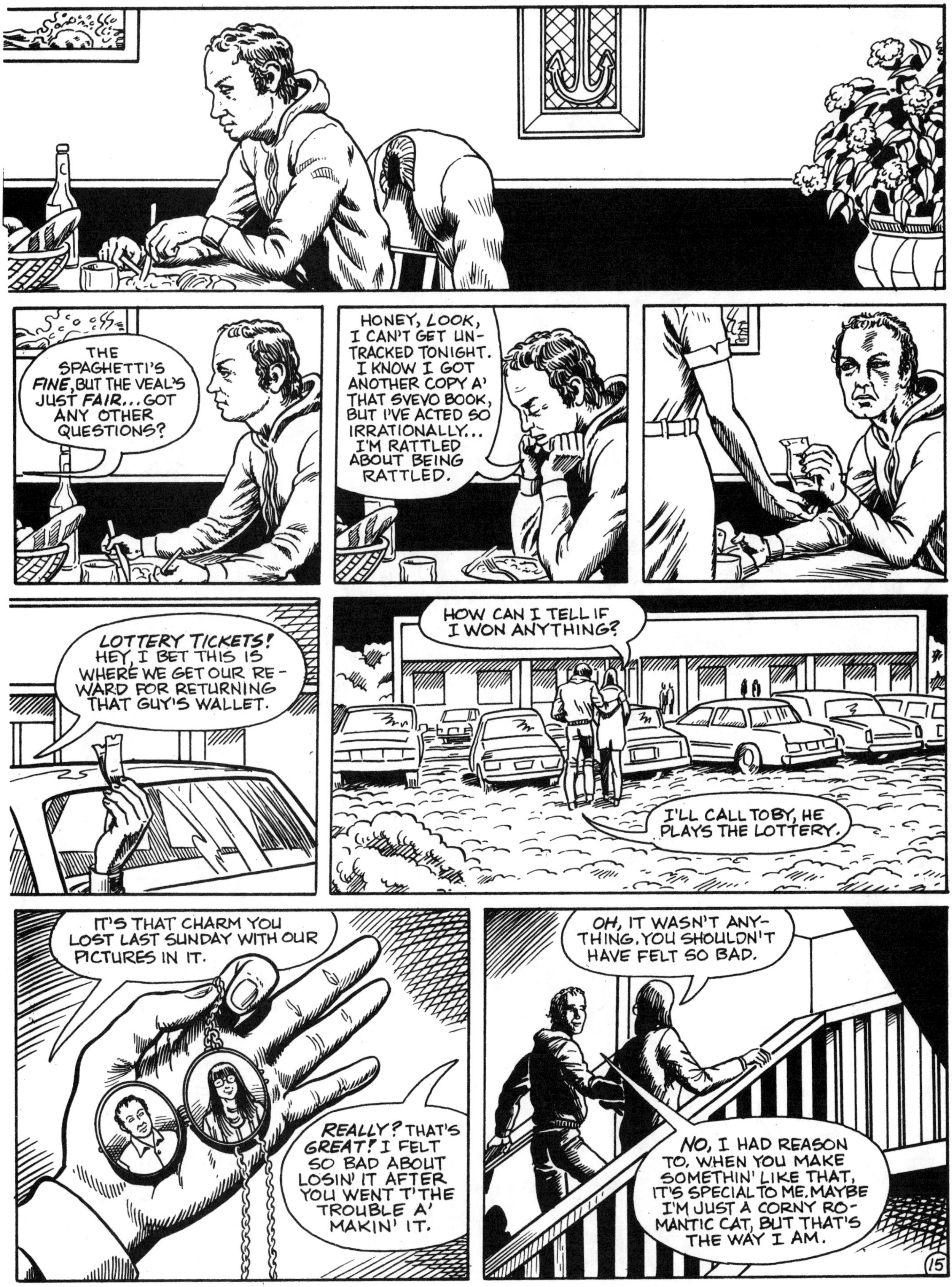

THE SPAGHETTI'S FINE, BUT THE VEAL'S JUST FAIR... GOT ANY OTHER QUESTIONS?
HONEY, LOOK, I CAN'T GET UNTRACKED TONIGHT. I KNOW I GOT ANOTHER COPY A' THAT SVEVO BOOK, BUT I'VE ACTED SO IRRATIONALLY... I'M RATTLED ABOUT BEING RATTLED.
LOTTERY TICKETS! HEY, I BET THIS IS WHERE WE GET OUR REWARD FOR RETURNING THAT GUY'S WALLET.
HOW CAN I TELL IF I WON ANYTHING?
I'LL CALL TOBY, HE PLAYS THE LOTTERY.
IT'S THAT CHARM YOU LOST LAST SUNDAY WITH OUR PICTURES IN IT.
REALLY? THAT'S GREAT! I FELT SO BAD ABOUT LOSIN' IT AFTER YOU WENT T'THE TROUBLE A' MAKIN' IT.
OH, IT WASN'T ANYTHING. YOU SHOULDN'T HAVE FELT SO BAD.
NO, I HAD REASON TO. WHEN YOU MAKE SOMETHIN' LIKE THAT, IT'S SPECIAL TO ME. MAYBE I'M JUST A CORNY ROMANTIC CAT, BUT THAT'S THE WAY I AM.

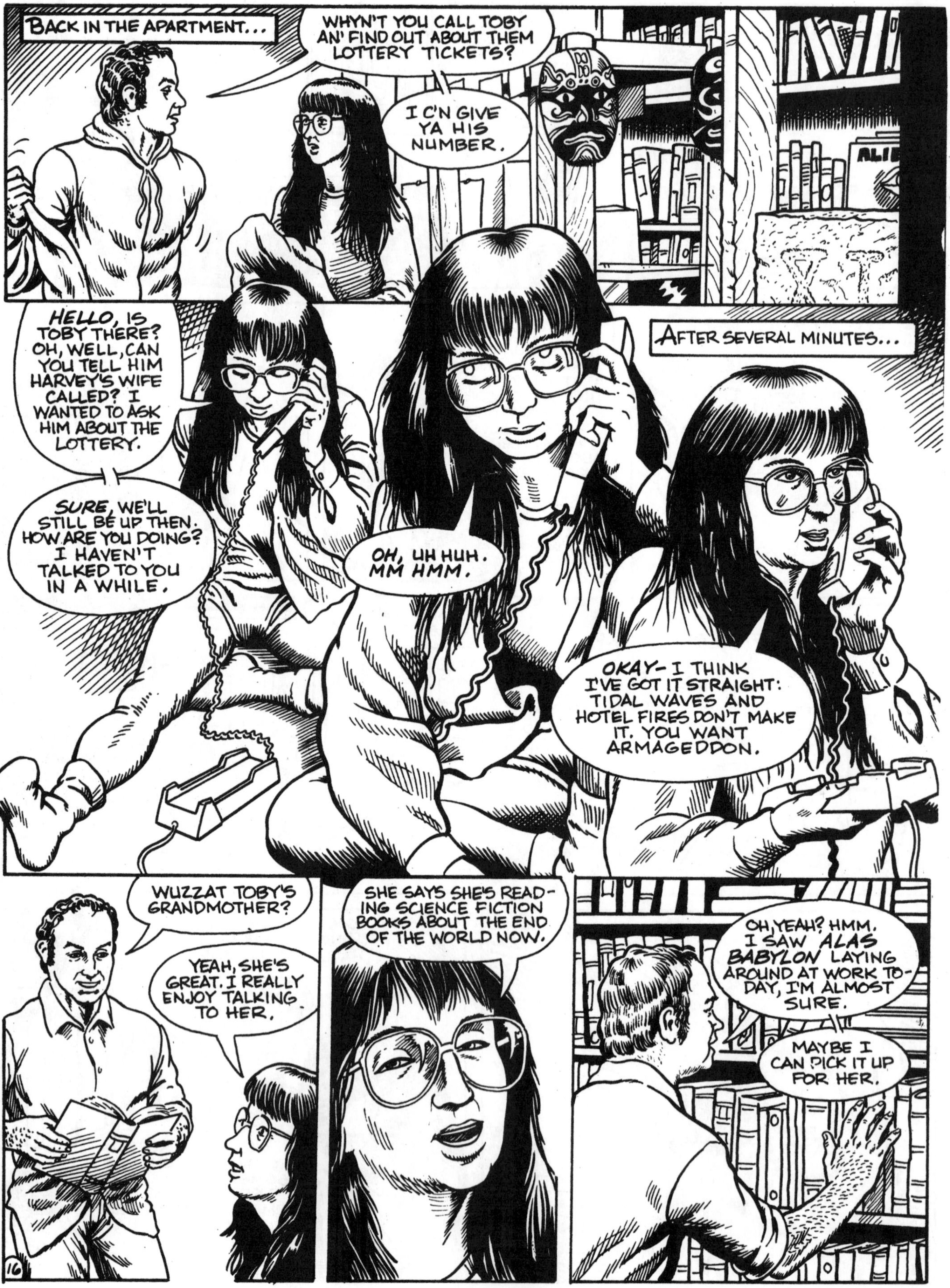
BACK IN THE APARTMENT...
WHYN'T YOU CALL TOBY AN' FIND OUT ABOUT THEM LOTTERY TICKETS?
I C'N GIVE YA HIS NUMBER.
HELLO, IS TOBY THERE? OH, WELL, CAN YOU TELL HIM HARVEY'S WIFE CALLED? I WANTED TO ASK HIM ABOUT THE LOTTERY.
SURE, WE'LL STILL BE UP THEN. HOW ARE YOU DOING? I HAVEN'T TALKED TO YOU IN A WHILE.
OH, UH HUH. MM HMM.
AFTER SEVERAL MINUTES...
OKAY- I THINK I'VE GOT IT STRAIGHT: TIDAL WAVES AND HOTEL FIRES DON'T MAKE IT. YOU WANT ARMAGEDDON.
WUZZAT TOBY'S GRANDMOTHER?
YEAH, SHE'S GREAT. I REALLY ENJOY TALKING TO HER.
SHE SAYS SHE'S READING SCIENCE FICTION BOOKS ABOUT THE END OF THE WORLD NOW.
OH, YEAH? HMM. I SAW ALAS BABYLON LAYING AROUND AT WORK TODAY, I'M ALMOST SURE.
MAYBE I CAN PICK IT UP FOR HER.
16

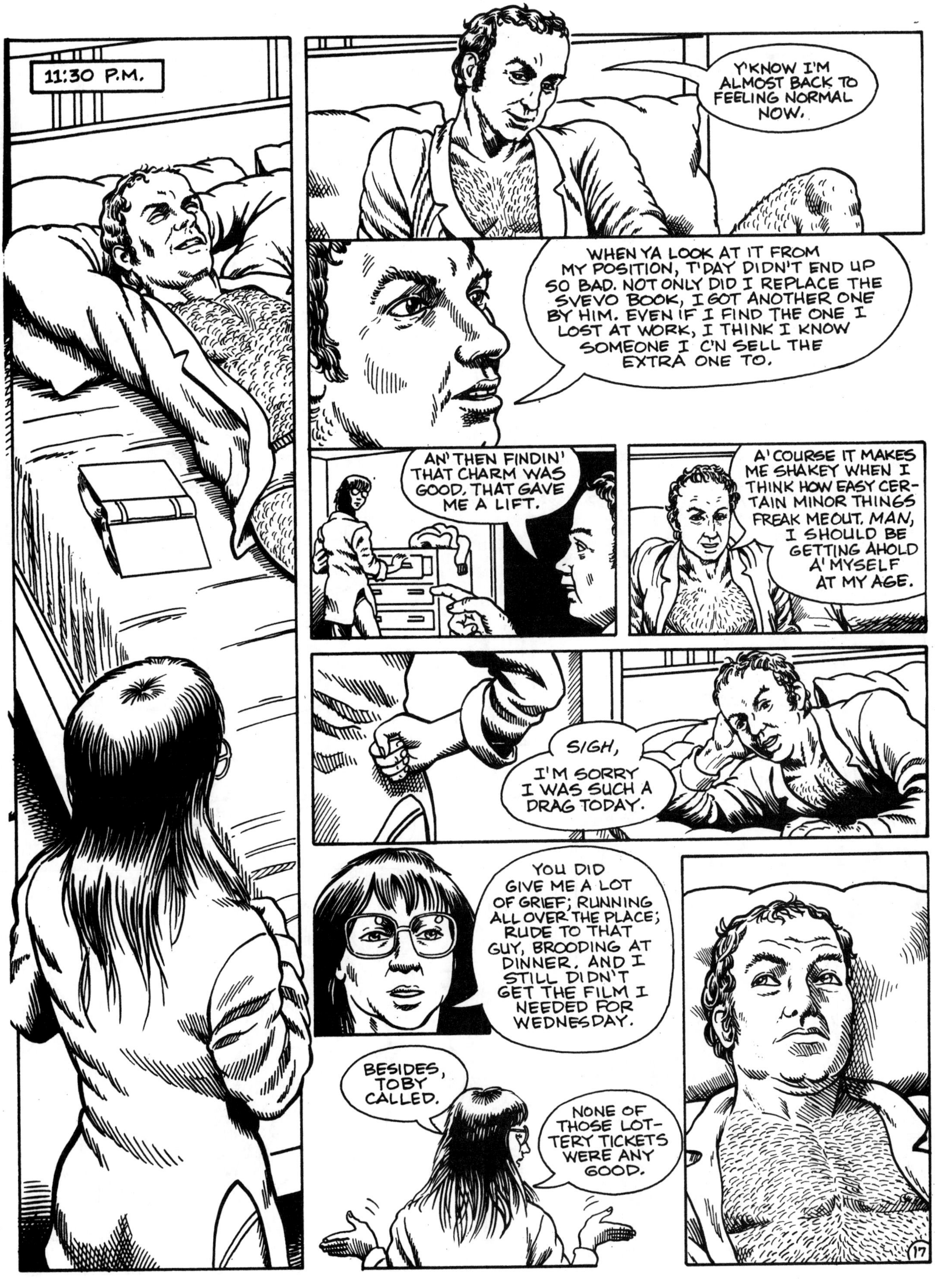

11:30 P.M.
Y'KNOW I'M ALMOST BACK TO FEELING NORMAL NOW.
WHEN YA LOOK AT IT FROM MY POSITION, T'DAY DIDN'T END UP SO BAD. NOT ONLY DID I REPLACE THE SVEVO BOOK, I GOT ANOTHER ONE BY HIM. EVEN IF I FIND THE ONE I LOST AT WORK, I THINK I KNOW SOMEONE I C'N SELL THE EXTRA ONE TO.
AN' THEN FINDIN' THAT CHARM WAS GOOD. THAT GAVE ME A LIFT.
A' COURSE IT MAKES ME SHAKEY WHEN I THINK HOW EASY CERTAIN MINOR THINGS FREAK ME OUT. MAN, I SHOULD BE GETTING AHOLD A' MYSELF AT MY AGE.
SIGH,
I'M SORRY I WAS SUCH A DRAG TODAY.
YOU DID GIVE ME A LOT OF GRIEF; RUNNING ALL OVER THE PLACE; RUDE TO THAT GUY, BROODING AT DINNER. AND I STILL DIDN'T GET THE FILM I NEEDED FOR WEDNESDAY.
BESIDES, TOBY CALLED.
NONE OF THOSE LOTTERY TICKETS WERE ANY GOOD.

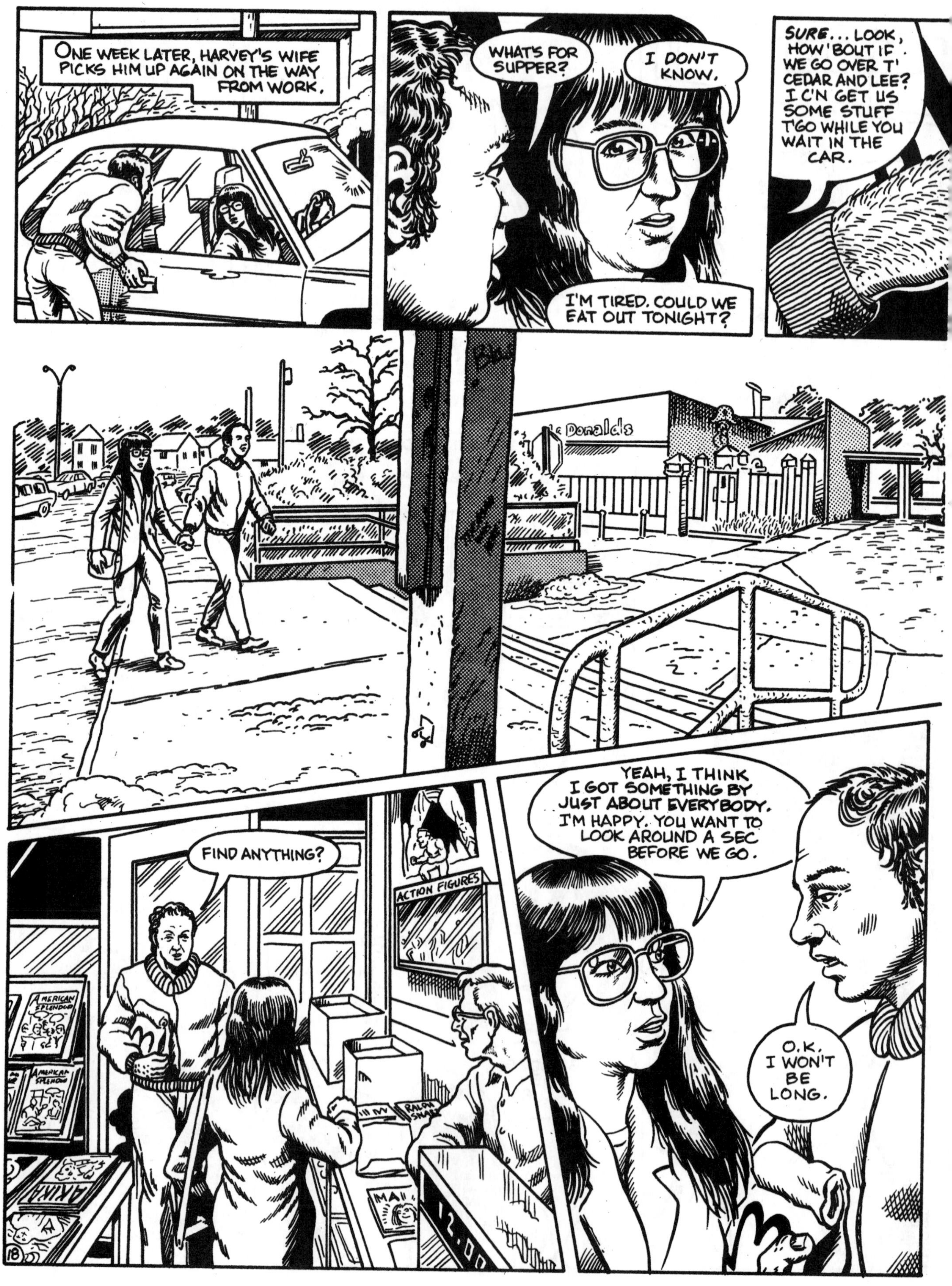

ONE WEEK LATER, HARVEY'S WIFE PICKS HIM UP AGAIN ON THE WAY FROM WORK.
WHAT'S FOR SUPPER?
I DON'T KNOW.
I'M TIRED. COULD WE EAT OUT TONIGHT?
SURE... LOOK, HOW 'BOUT IF WE GO OVER T' CEDAR AND LEE? I C'N GET US SOME STUFF T'GO WHILE YOU WAIT IN THE CAR.
McDonalds
FIND ANYTHING?
ACTION FIGURES
AMERICAN SPLENDOR
AMERICAN SPLENDOR
YEAH, I THINK I GOT SOMETHING BY JUST ABOUT EVERYBODY. I'M HAPPY. YOU WANT TO LOOK AROUND A SEC BEFORE WE GO.
O.K. I WON'T BE LONG.

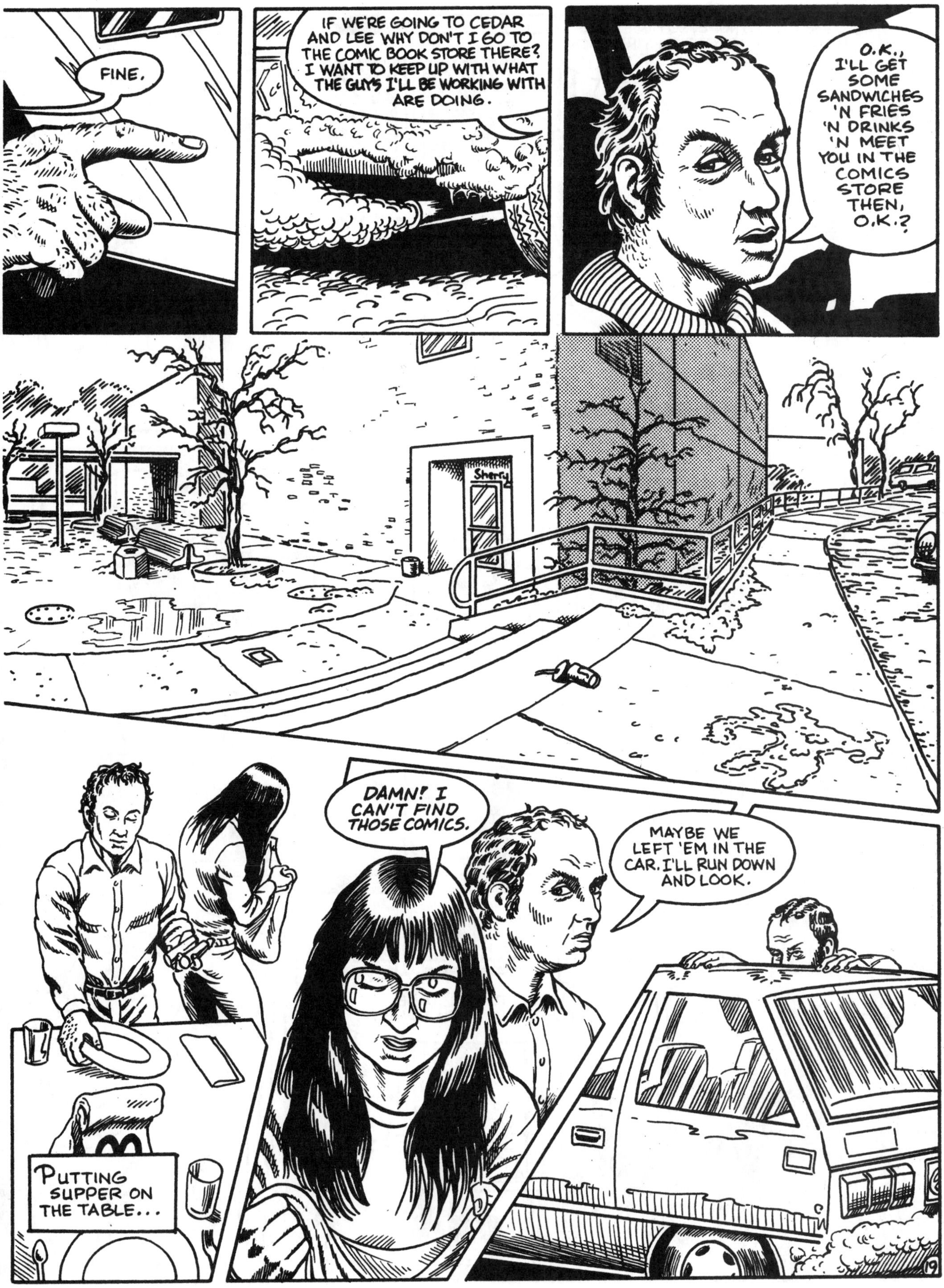
FINE.
IF WE'RE GOING TO CEDAR AND LEE WHY DON'T I GO TO THE COMIC BOOK STORE THERE? I WANT TO KEEP UP WITH WHAT THE GUYS I'LL BE WORKING WITH ARE DOING.
O.K., I'LL GET SOME SANDWICHES 'N FRIES 'N DRINKS 'N MEET YOU IN THE COMICS STORE THEN, O.K.?
PUTTING SUPPER ON THE TABLE...
DAMN! I CAN'T FIND THOSE COMICS.
MAYBE WE LEFT 'EM IN THE CAR. I'LL RUN DOWN AND LOOK.
19

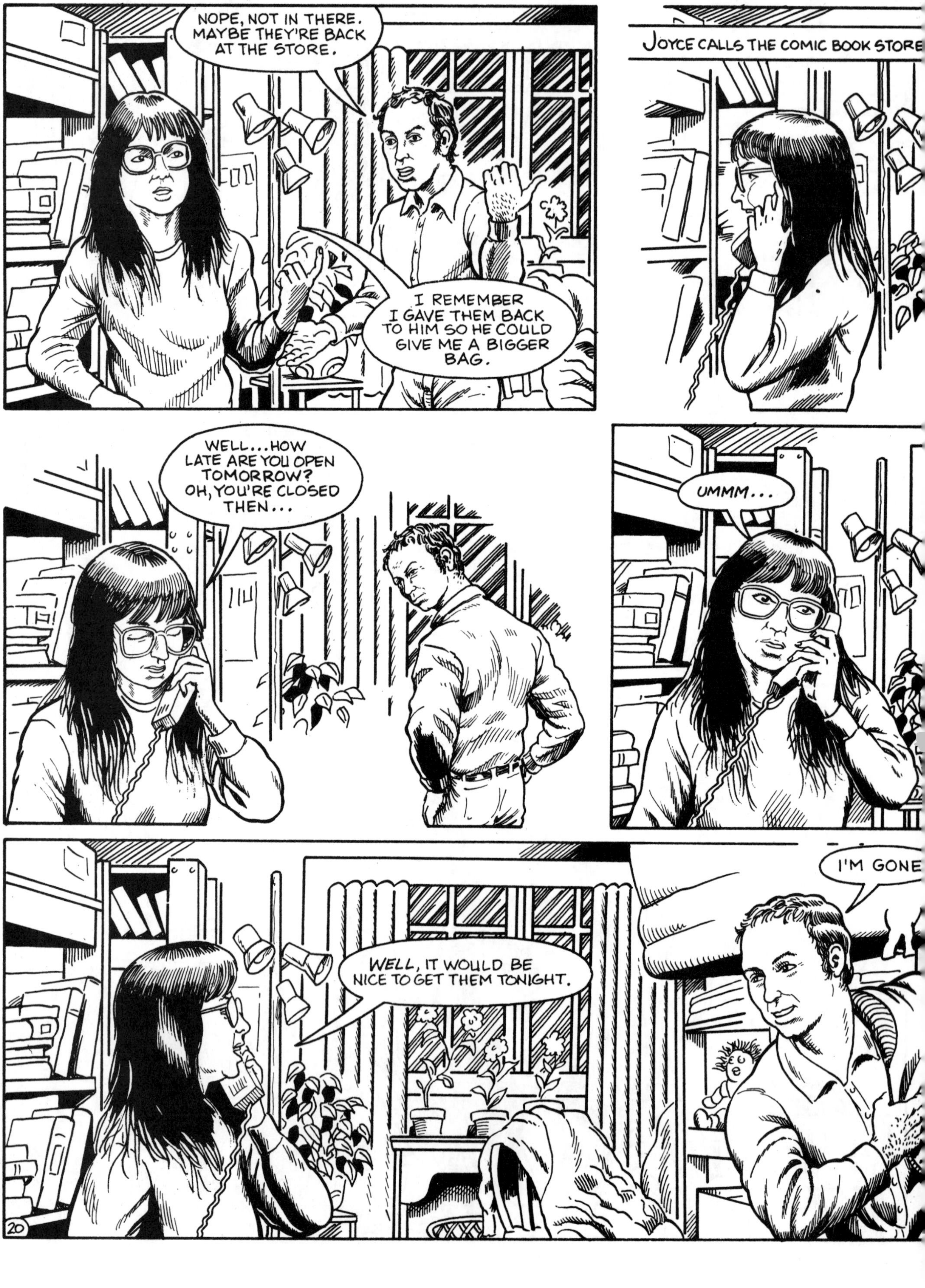
NOPE, NOT IN THERE. MAYBE THEY'RE BACK AT THE STORE.
I REMEMBER I GAVE THEM BACK TO HIM SO HE COULD GIVE ME A BIGGER BAG.
JOYCE CALLS THE COMIC BOOK STORE
WELL... HOW LATE ARE YOU OPEN TOMORROW? OH, YOU'RE CLOSED THEN...
UMMM...
WELL, IT WOULD BE NICE TO GET THEM TONIGHT.
I'M GONE
20

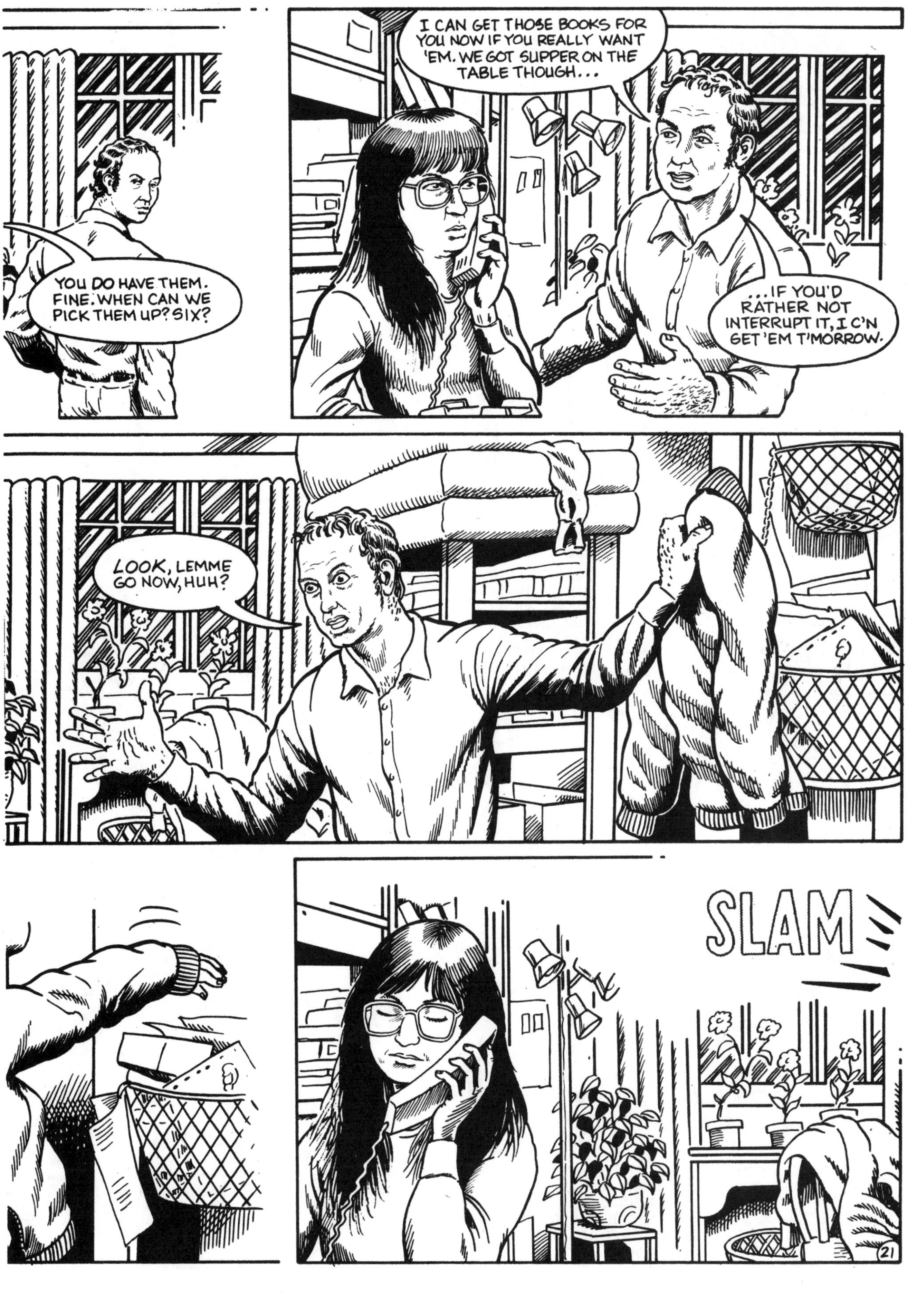
YOU DO HAVE THEM. FINE. WHEN CAN WE PICK THEM UP? SIX?
I CAN GET THOSE BOOKS FOR YOU NOW IF YOU REALLY WANT 'EM. WE GOT SUPPER ON THE TABLE THOUGH...
...IF YOU'D RATHER NOT INTERRUPT IT, I C'N GET 'EM T'MORROW.
LOOK, LEMME GO NOW, HUH?
SLAM

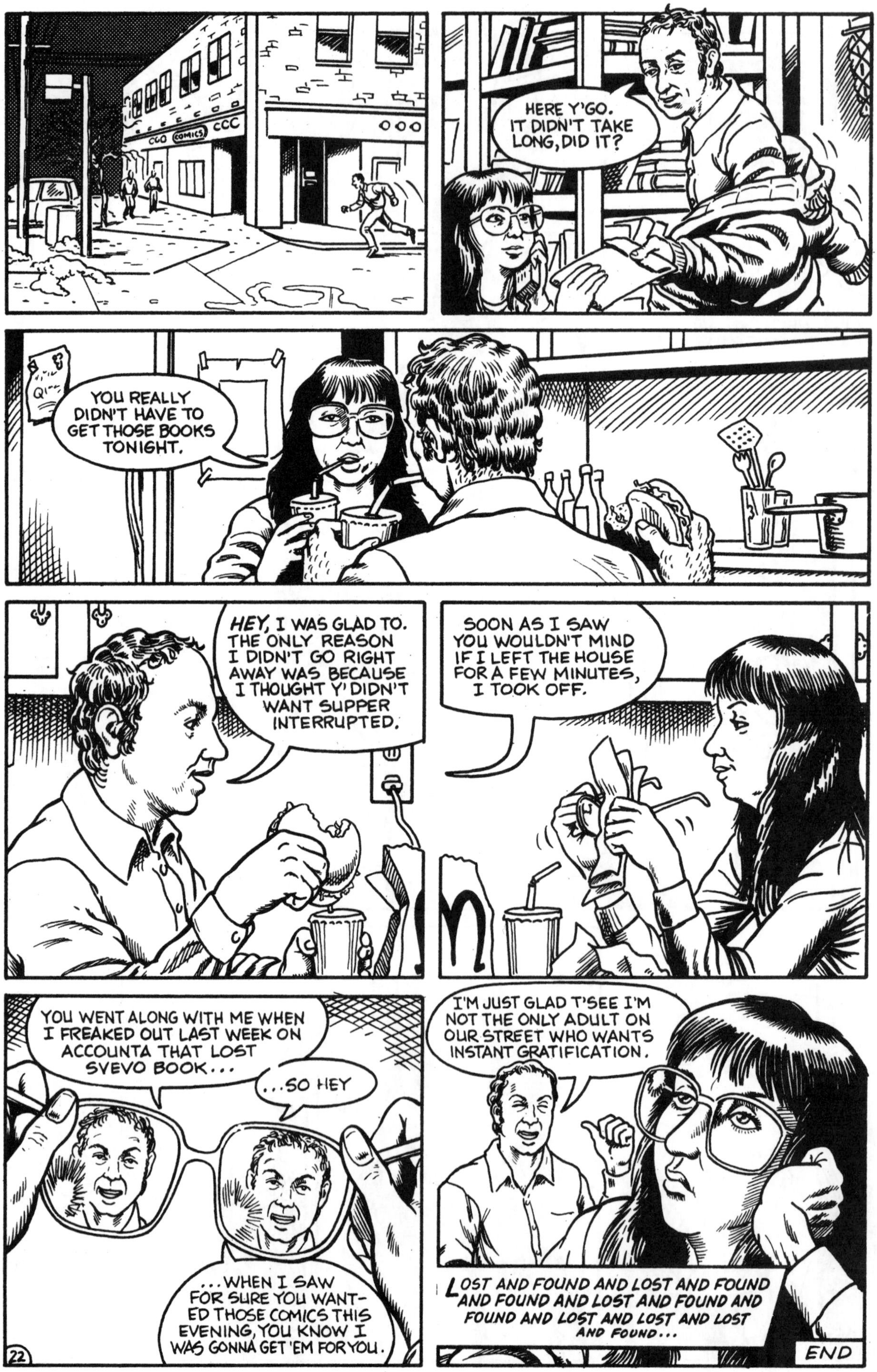
COMICS
HERE Y'GO.
IT DIDN'T TAKE LONG, DID IT?
YOU REALLY DIDN'T HAVE TO GET THOSE BOOKS TONIGHT.
HEY, I WAS GLAD TO. THE ONLY REASON I DIDN'T GO RIGHT AWAY WAS BECAUSE I THOUGHT Y' DIDN'T WANT SUPPER INTERRUPTED.
SOON AS I SAW YOU WOULDN'T MIND IF I LEFT THE HOUSE FOR A FEW MINUTES, I TOOK OFF.
YOU WENT ALONG WITH ME WHEN I FREAKED OUT LAST WEEK ON ACCOUNTA THAT LOST SVEVO BOOK...
...SO HEY
...WHEN I SAW FOR SURE YOU WANTED THOSE COMICS THIS EVENING, YOU KNOW I WAS GONNA GET 'EM FOR YOU.
I'M JUST GLAD T'SEE I'M NOT THE ONLY ADULT ON OUR STREET WHO WANTS INSTANT GRATIFICATION.
LOST AND FOUND AND LOST AND FOUND AND FOUND AND LOST AND FOUND AND FOUND AND LOST AND LOST AND LOST AND FOUND...
END

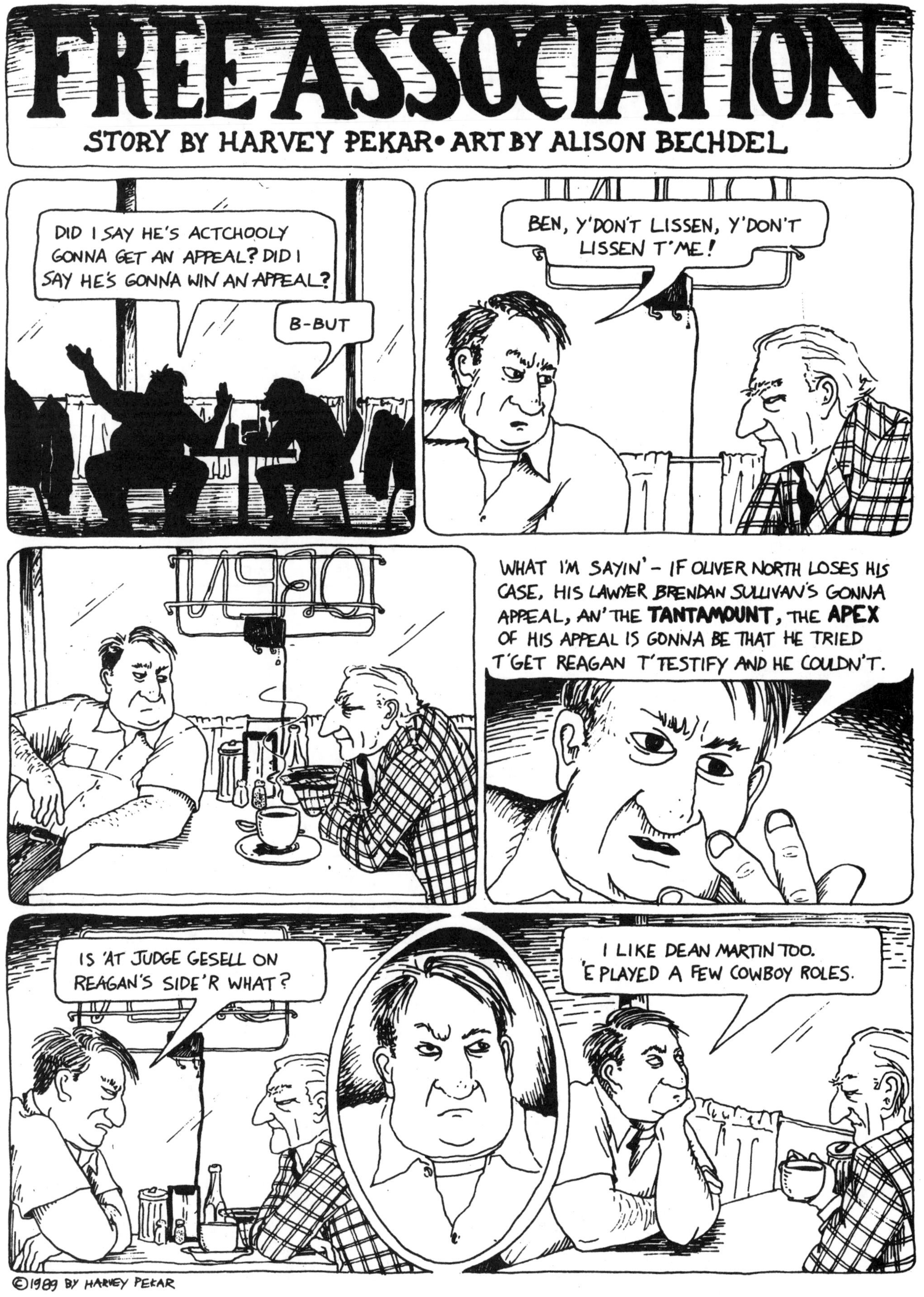
FREE ASSOCIATION
STORY BY HARVEY PEKAR • ART BY ALISON BECHDEL
DID I SAY HE'S ACTCHOOLY GONNA GET AN APPEAL? DID I SAY HE'S GONNA WIN AN APPEAL?
B-BUT
BEN, Y'DON'T LISSEN, Y'DON'T LISSEN T'ME!
WHAT I'M SAYIN' - IF OLIVER NORTH LOSES HIS CASE, HIS LAWYER BRENDAN SULLIVAN'S GONNA APPEAL, AN' THE TANTAMOUNT, THE APEX OF HIS APPEAL IS GONNA BE THAT HE TRIED T'GET REAGAN T'TESTIFY AND HE COULDN'T.
IS 'AT JUDGE GESELL ON REAGAN'S SIDE'R WHAT?
I LIKE DEAN MARTIN TOO. 'E PLAYED A FEW COWBOY ROLES.

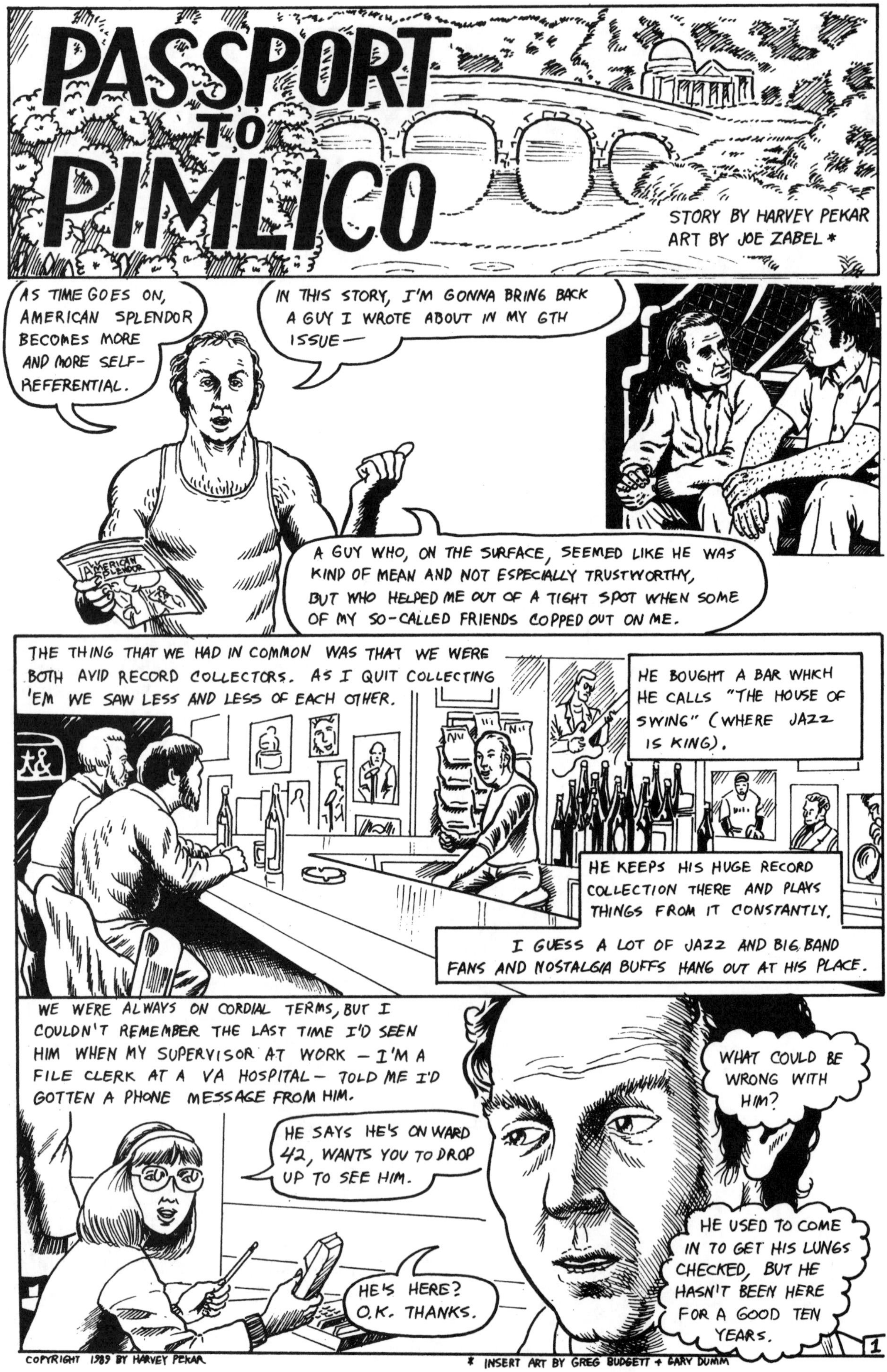
PASSPORT TO PIMLICO
STORY BY HARVEY PEKAR
ART BY JOE ZABEL *
AS TIME GOES ON, AMERICAN SPLENDOR BECOMES MORE AND MORE SELF-REFERENTIAL.
IN THIS STORY, I'M GONNA BRING BACK A GUY I WROTE ABOUT IN MY 6TH ISSUE—
A GUY WHO, ON THE SURFACE, SEEMED LIKE HE WAS KIND OF MEAN AND NOT ESPECIALLY TRUSTWORTHY, BUT WHO HELPED ME OUT OF A TIGHT SPOT WHEN SOME OF MY SO-CALLED FRIENDS COPPED OUT ON ME.
AMERICAN SPLENDOR
THE THING THAT WE HAD IN COMMON WAS THAT WE WERE BOTH AVID RECORD COLLECTORS. AS I QUIT COLLECTING 'EM WE SAW LESS AND LESS OF EACH OTHER.
HE BOUGHT A BAR WHICH HE CALLS "THE HOUSE OF SWING" (WHERE JAZZ IS KING).
HE KEEPS HIS HUGE RECORD COLLECTION THERE AND PLAYS THINGS FROM IT CONSTANTLY.
I GUESS A LOT OF JAZZ AND BIG BAND FANS AND NOSTALGIA BUFFS HANG OUT AT HIS PLACE.
WE WERE ALWAYS ON CORDIAL TERMS, BUT I COULDN'T REMEMBER THE LAST TIME I'D SEEN HIM WHEN MY SUPERVISOR AT WORK — I'M A FILE CLERK AT A VA HOSPITAL — TOLD ME I'D GOTTEN A PHONE MESSAGE FROM HIM.
HE SAYS HE'S ON WARD 42, WANTS YOU TO DROP UP TO SEE HIM.
HE'S HERE? O.K. THANKS.
WHAT COULD BE WRONG WITH HIM?
HE USED TO COME IN TO GET HIS LUNGS CHECKED, BUT HE HASN'T BEEN HERE FOR A GOOD TEN YEARS.
1

* INSERT ART BY GREG BUDGETT + GARY DUMM

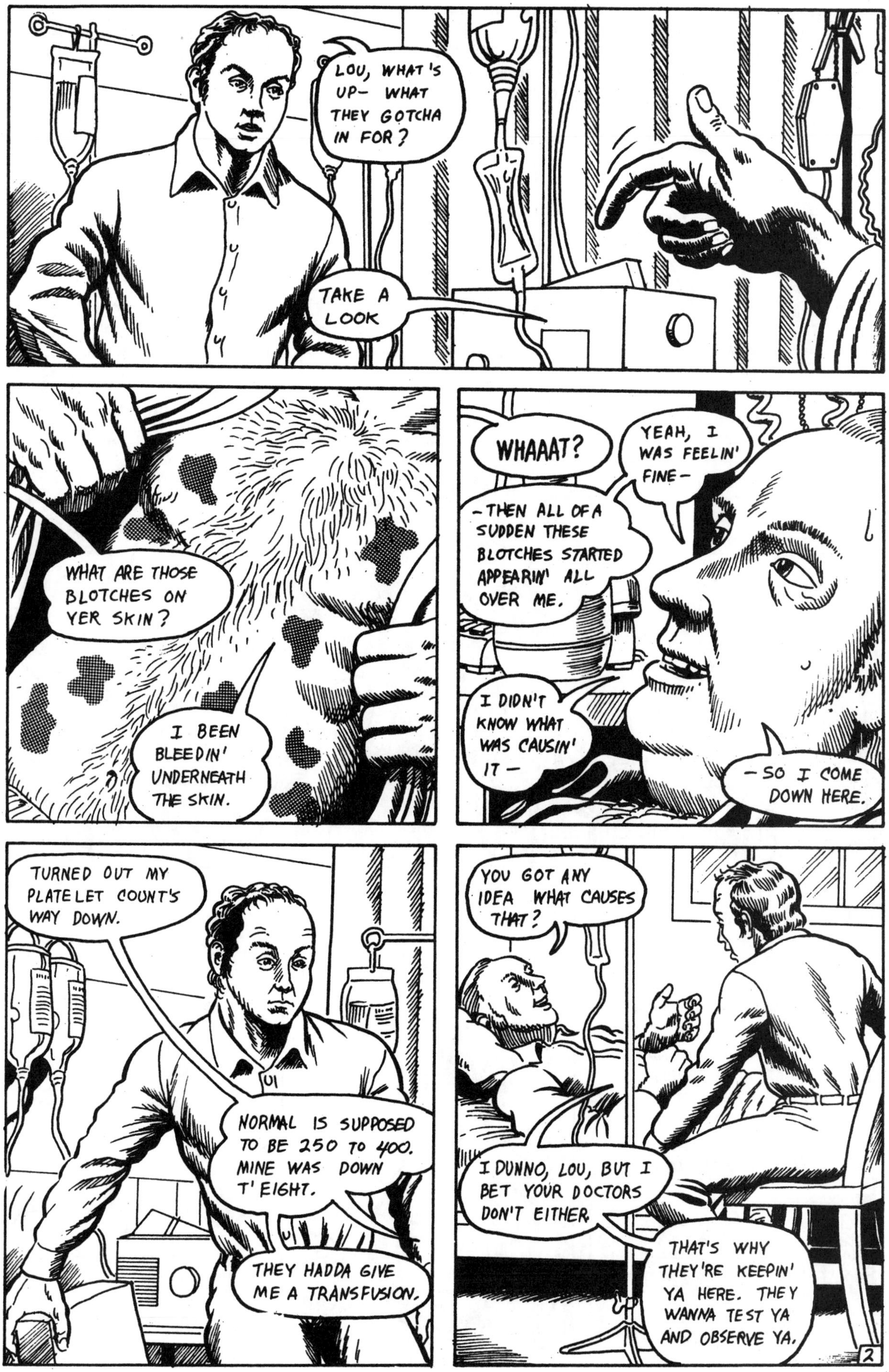
LOU, WHAT'S UP- WHAT THEY GOTCHA IN FOR?
TAKE A LOOK
WHAT ARE THOSE BLOTCHES ON YER SKIN?
I BEEN BLEEDIN' UNDERNEATH THE SKIN.
WHAAAT?
YEAH, I WAS FEELIN' FINE-
-THEN ALL OF A SUDDEN THESE BLOTCHES STARTED APPEARIN' ALL OVER ME.
I DIDN'T KNOW WHAT WAS CAUSIN' IT-
-SO I COME DOWN HERE.
TURNED OUT MY PLATELET COUNT'S WAY DOWN.
NORMAL IS SUPPOSED TO BE 250 TO 400. MINE WAS DOWN T' EIGHT.
THEY HADDA GIVE ME A TRANSFUSION.
YOU GOT ANY IDEA WHAT CAUSES THAT?
I DUNNO, LOU, BUT I BET YOUR DOCTORS DON'T EITHER.
THAT'S WHY THEY'RE KEEPIN' YA HERE. THEY WANNA TEST YA AND OBSERVE YA.
2

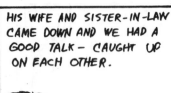

PROBABLY TOO MANY DEWARS + SODA.

LOU SEEMED LIKE HE WAS FEELING HALFWAY DECENT.

HIS WIFE AND SISTER-IN-LAW CAME DOWN AND WE HAD A GOOD TALK— CAUGHT UP ON EACH OTHER.

LOU'S GOTTA DO SOMETHING ABOUT HIS CHOLESTEROL TOO, IT'S WAY TOO HIGH.

AFTER FIFTEEN MINUTES—

WELL, LOOK, I BETTER GET BACK T' WORK.

AS IT HAPPENS, I'M GOIN' TO CHICAGO FOR THREE DAYS TO A COMIC CONVENTION—

BUT IF YER HERE WHEN I GET BACK, I'LL DROP BY.

GOODBYE LINDA.

BYE BARBARA.

THAT NIGHT I DISCUSSED LOU WITH MY WIFE.

WHAT D'YOU THINK IT COULD BE?

I DON'T KNOW— MAYBE LEUKEMIA.

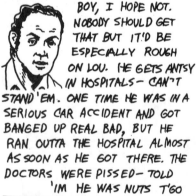

BOY, I HOPE NOT. NOBODY SHOULD GET THAT BUT IT'D BE ESPECIALLY ROUGH ON LOU. HE GETS ANTSY IN HOSPITALS— CAN'T STAND 'EM. ONE TIME HE WAS IN A SERIOUS CAR ACCIDENT AND GOT BANGED UP REAL BAD, BUT HE RAN OUTTA THE HOSPITAL ALMOST AS SOON AS HE GOT THERE. THE DOCTORS WERE PISSED— TOLD 'IM HE WAS NUTS T'GO SO SOON.

I GOT BACK FROM CHICAGO AND WENT TO SEE WHAT WAS HAPPENING WITH LOU.

YOU GOT A PATIENT HERE NAMED KALLIE?

HE CHECKED OUT YESTERDAY.

HMMM. DIDN'T SEEM TO STAY LONG; MAYBE HE'S O.K. —

— BUT THERE'S ALWAYS THE CHANCE HE SPLIT 'CAUSE HE DIDN'T HAVE THE PATIENCE TO STAY.

3

SEVERAL DAYS LATER

RRINNG!

H'LO RECORD ROOM. HARVEY SPEAKIN'

HARVEY, THIS IS LOU. I'M BACK INNA HOSPITAL. C'MON UP 'N' SEE ME.

FIVE MINUTES LATER

WHAT HAPPENED?

I HADDA RELAPSE, STARTED BLEEDIN' AGAIN.

DID THEY EVER FIGURE OUT WHAT YOUR PROBLEM WAS?

THEY'RE 99% SURE IT WAS A TOXIC REACTION T'ALCOHOL.

THEY WANNED ME T'STAY 'N' DO SOME MORE TESTS BUT I HADDA GET OUT.

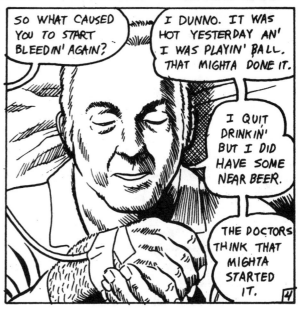

SO WHAT CAUSED YOU TO START BLEEDIN' AGAIN?

I DUNNO. IT WAS HOT YESTERDAY AN' I WAS PLAYIN' BALL. THAT MIGHTA DONE IT.

I QUIT DRINKIN' BUT I DID HAVE SOME NEAR BEER.

THE DOCTORS THINK THAT MIGHTA STARTED IT.

4

LOU HAD ANOTHER TRANSFUSION AND SEEMED PRETTY RELAXED SO WE TALKED ABOUT A LOT OF THINGS, THE SUBJECT GOT AROUND TO RECORD COLLECTING, WHICH HE WAS STILL INTO.

YEAH, I GOT RIDDA MOSTA MY STUFF TO THIS DEALER IN DETROIT—

BUT I STILL GOT ABOUT 1500 L.P.S LEFT.

OH YEAH, WHAT KINDA STUFF IS IT?

I SAW A CHANCE TO SCORE A LITTLE DOUGH. THE HOSPITAL ISN'T THE MOST APPROPRIATE PLACE TO MAKE A DEAL, BUT A BUCK IS A BUCK:

WELL, ACTUALLY SOME IS PRETTY NICE. THERE'S SOME RARE THINGS THAT ARE JUST IN SO-SO SHAPE SO THEY GOT PASSED UP—

—AN' THEN SOME REAL OBSCURE L.P.S...

PROBABLY THERE'S SUMP'N THERE YOU CAN USE...

IN 1500 OR SO L.P.S YOU SHOULD BE ABLE TO FIND AT LEAST A FEW, EVEN T'USE FOR TRADING.

I'M ONLY ASKIN' A BUCK A PIECE.

YEAH, I'M INNERESTED. WHY DON'T WE GET T'GETHER AFTER I GET OUT? I'M NOT GONNA BE HERE MUCH LONGER.

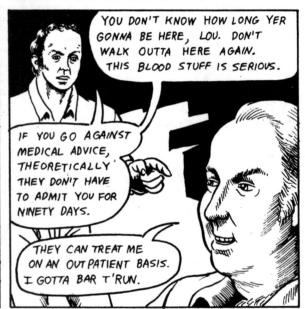

YOU DON'T KNOW HOW LONG YER GONNA BE HERE, LOU. DON'T WALK OUTTA HERE AGAIN. THIS BLOOD STUFF IS SERIOUS.

IF YOU GO AGAINST MEDICAL ADVICE, THEORETICALLY THEY DON'T HAVE TO ADMIT YOU FOR NINETY DAYS.

THEY CAN TREAT ME ON AN OUTPATIENT BASIS. I GOTTA BAR T'RUN.

SURE ENOUGH, LOU SPLIT AGAINST MEDICAL ADVICE. BUT I CALLED HIM AND HE SEEMED TO BE O.K. HE WAS BEING TREATED AS AN OUTPATIENT... AFTER A WHILE THE SUBJECT SHIFTED TO RECORDS AGAIN.

SO LOU, YOU WANNA STOP DOWN 'N' LOOK AT THESE L.P.S? ALL I'M ASKIN IS A BUCK A SIDE.

O.K., HOW 'BOUT SUNDAY AFTERNOON; YOU GONNA BE HOME?

SUNDAY AFTERNOON

O.K. YOU GOT SIX A' THESE SPECIAL EUROPEAN SIDES AT $3 APIECE—

—AN' 40 REGULAR ONES AT A DOLLAR APIECE. THEN HOW'S $55 SOUND?

MMKAY.

5

THE MIDDLE OF THE NEXT WEEK.

HARVEY, I FOUND MY NOTEBOOK BURIED UNDER A PILE OF YOUR BOOKS. I CAN'T FIND ANYTHING. I'VE GOT NO ROOM FOR ANYTHING. YOUR STUFF IS EVERYWHERE.

I DON'T FEEL LIKE I EVEN LIVE HERE

THE ARGUMENT BETWEEN ME AND MY WIFE ABOUT WHO GOT HOW MUCH STORAGE ROOM — WE BOTH COLLECTED AND SAVED A LOT OF STUFF — WAS A LONGSTANDING AND NASTY ONE. THIS TIME I HAD TO DO SOMETHING TO "EASE THE TENSION."

O.K. I'LL TELL YOU WHAT. I'LL GET RIDDA MY 78'S.*

SURE

REMEMBRANCE OF THINGS PAST

CITIES OF THE PLAIN

THE CAPTIVE

THE SWEET CHEAT GONE

THE PAST RECAPTURED

I KNOW I'VE TOLD YOU THAT BEFORE, BUT I'LL DO IT NOW EVEN IF I HAVE TO GIVE 'EM AWAY.

* 78'S ARE 78 RPM RECORDS, THE OLD KIND THAT SPIN FAST AND BREAK EASY.

6

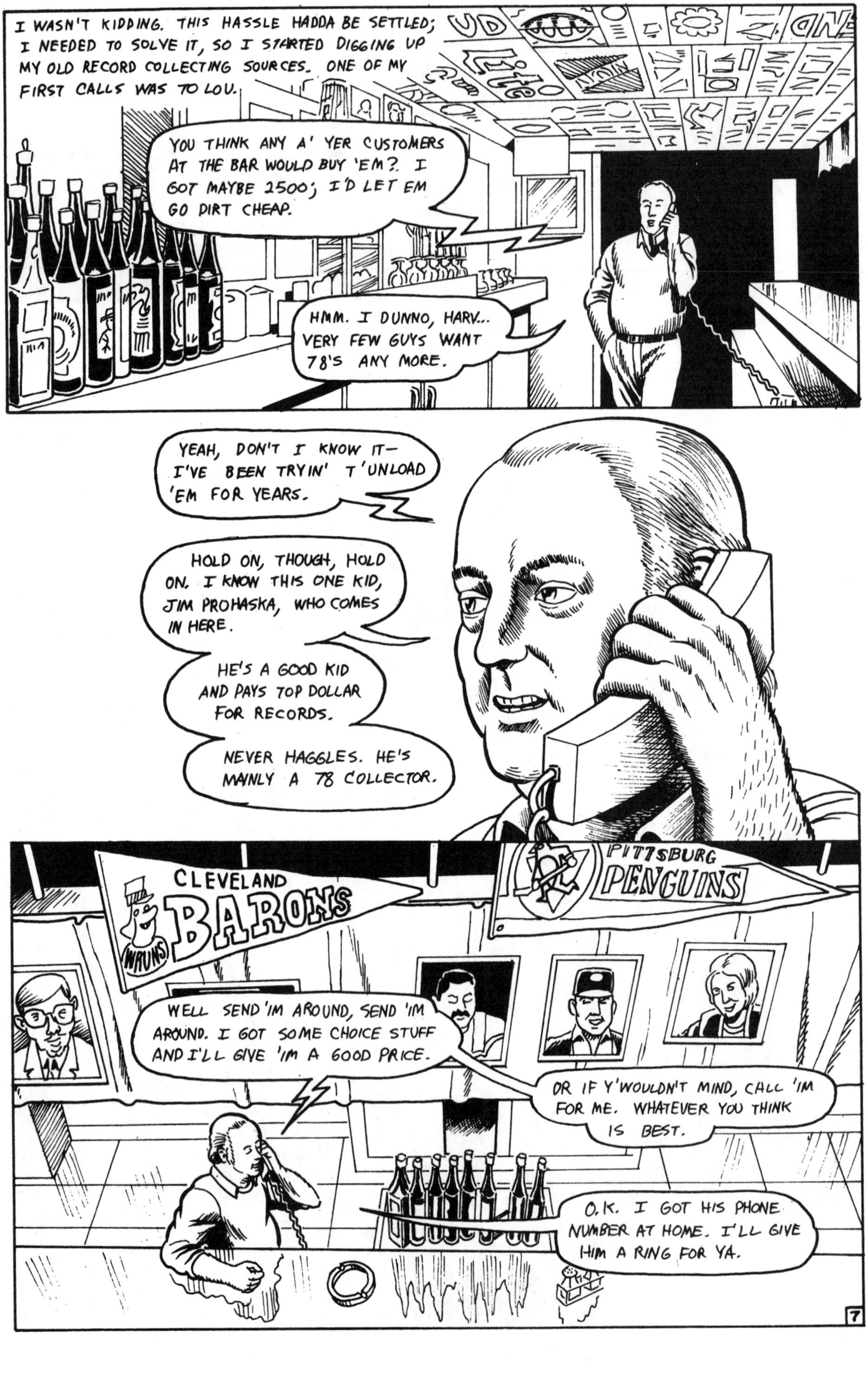
I WASN'T KIDDING. THIS HASSLE HADDA BE SETTLED; I NEEDED TO SOLVE IT, SO I STARTED DIGGING UP MY OLD RECORD COLLECTING SOURCES. ONE OF MY FIRST CALLS WAS TO LOU.
Lite
YOU THINK ANY A' YER CUSTOMERS AT THE BAR WOULD BUY 'EM? I GOT MAYBE 2500; I'D LET EM GO DIRT CHEAP.
HMM. I DUNNO, HARV... VERY FEW GUYS WANT 78'S ANY MORE.
YEAH, DON'T I KNOW IT— I'VE BEEN TRYIN' T'UNLOAD 'EM FOR YEARS.
HOLD ON, THOUGH, HOLD ON. I KNOW THIS ONE KID, JIM PROHASKA, WHO COMES IN HERE.
HE'S A GOOD KID AND PAYS TOP DOLLAR FOR RECORDS.
NEVER HAGGLES. HE'S MAINLY A 78 COLLECTOR.
CLEVELAND BARONS
WRUNS
PITTSBURG PENGUINS
WELL SEND 'IM AROUND, SEND 'IM AROUND. I GOT SOME CHOICE STUFF AND I'LL GIVE 'IM A GOOD PRICE.
OR IF Y'WOULDN'T MIND, CALL 'IM FOR ME. WHATEVER YOU THINK IS BEST.
O.K. I GOT HIS PHONE NUMBER AT HOME. I'LL GIVE HIM A RING FOR YA.

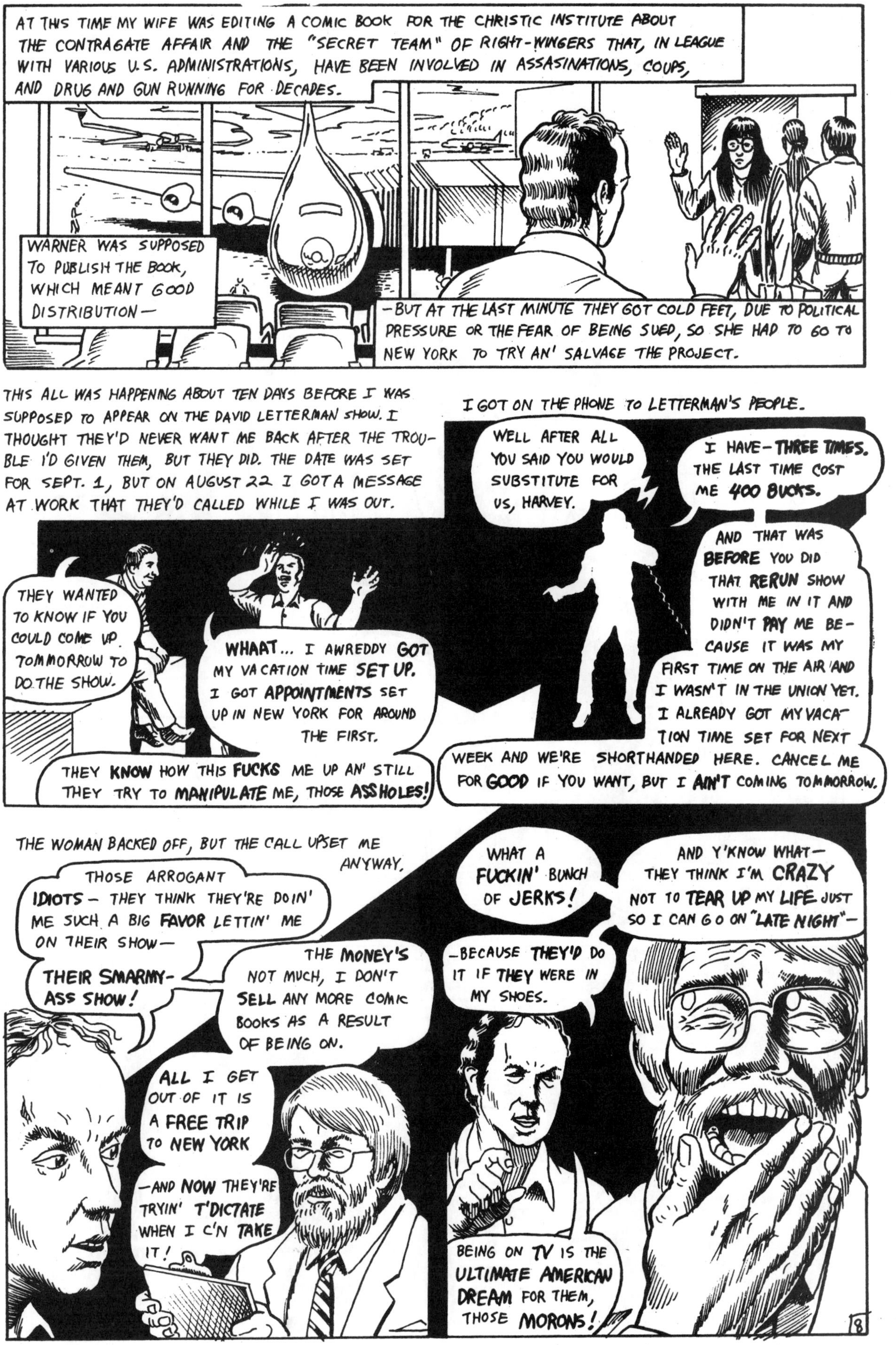

AT THIS TIME MY WIFE WAS EDITING A COMIC BOOK FOR THE CHRISTIC INSTITUTE ABOUT THE CONTRAGATE AFFAIR AND THE "SECRET TEAM" OF RIGHT-WINGERS THAT, IN LEAGUE WITH VARIOUS U.S. ADMINISTRATIONS, HAVE BEEN INVOLVED IN ASSASINATIONS, COUPS, AND DRUG AND GUN RUNNING FOR DECADES.
WARNER WAS SUPPOSED TO PUBLISH THE BOOK, WHICH MEANT GOOD DISTRIBUTION—
—BUT AT THE LAST MINUTE THEY GOT COLD FEET, DUE TO POLITICAL PRESSURE OR THE FEAR OF BEING SUED, SO SHE HAD TO GO TO NEW YORK TO TRY AN' SALVAGE THE PROJECT.
THIS ALL WAS HAPPENING ABOUT TEN DAYS BEFORE I WAS SUPPOSED TO APPEAR ON THE DAVID LETTERMAN SHOW. I THOUGHT THEY'D NEVER WANT ME BACK AFTER THE TROUBLE I'D GIVEN THEM, BUT THEY DID. THE DATE WAS SET FOR SEPT. 1, BUT ON AUGUST 22 I GOT A MESSAGE AT WORK THAT THEY'D CALLED WHILE I WAS OUT.
THEY WANTED TO KNOW IF YOU COULD COME UP TOMMORROW TO DO THE SHOW.
WHAAT... I AWREDDY GOT MY VACATION TIME SET UP. I GOT APPOINTMENTS SET UP IN NEW YORK FOR AROUND THE FIRST.
THEY KNOW HOW THIS FUCKS ME UP AN' STILL THEY TRY TO MANIPULATE ME, THOSE ASSHOLES!
I GOT ON THE PHONE TO LETTERMAN'S PEOPLE.
WELL AFTER ALL YOU SAID YOU WOULD SUBSTITUTE FOR US, HARVEY.
I HAVE— THREE TIMES. THE LAST TIME COST ME 400 BUCKS.
AND THAT WAS BEFORE YOU DID THAT RERUN SHOW WITH ME IN IT AND DIDN'T PAY ME BECAUSE IT WAS MY FIRST TIME ON THE AIR AND I WASN'T IN THE UNION YET. I ALREADY GOT MY VACATION TIME SET FOR NEXT WEEK AND WE'RE SHORTHANDED HERE. CANCEL ME FOR GOOD IF YOU WANT, BUT I AIN'T COMING TOMMORROW.
THE WOMAN BACKED OFF, BUT THE CALL UPSET ME ANYWAY.
THOSE ARROGANT IDIOTS— THEY THINK THEY'RE DOIN' ME SUCH A BIG FAVOR LETTIN' ME ON THEIR SHOW—
THEIR SMARMY-ASS SHOW!
THE MONEY'S NOT MUCH, I DON'T SELL ANY MORE COMIC BOOKS AS A RESULT OF BEING ON.
ALL I GET OUT OF IT IS A FREE TRIP TO NEW YORK
—AND NOW THEY'RE TRYIN' T'DICTATE WHEN I C'N TAKE IT!
WHAT A FUCKIN' BUNCH OF JERKS!
AND Y'KNOW WHAT— THEY THINK I'M CRAZY NOT TO TEAR UP MY LIFE JUST SO I CAN GO ON "LATE NIGHT"—
—BECAUSE THEY'D DO IT IF THEY WERE IN MY SHOES.
BEING ON TV IS THE ULTIMATE AMERICAN DREAM FOR THEM, THOSE MORONS!
8

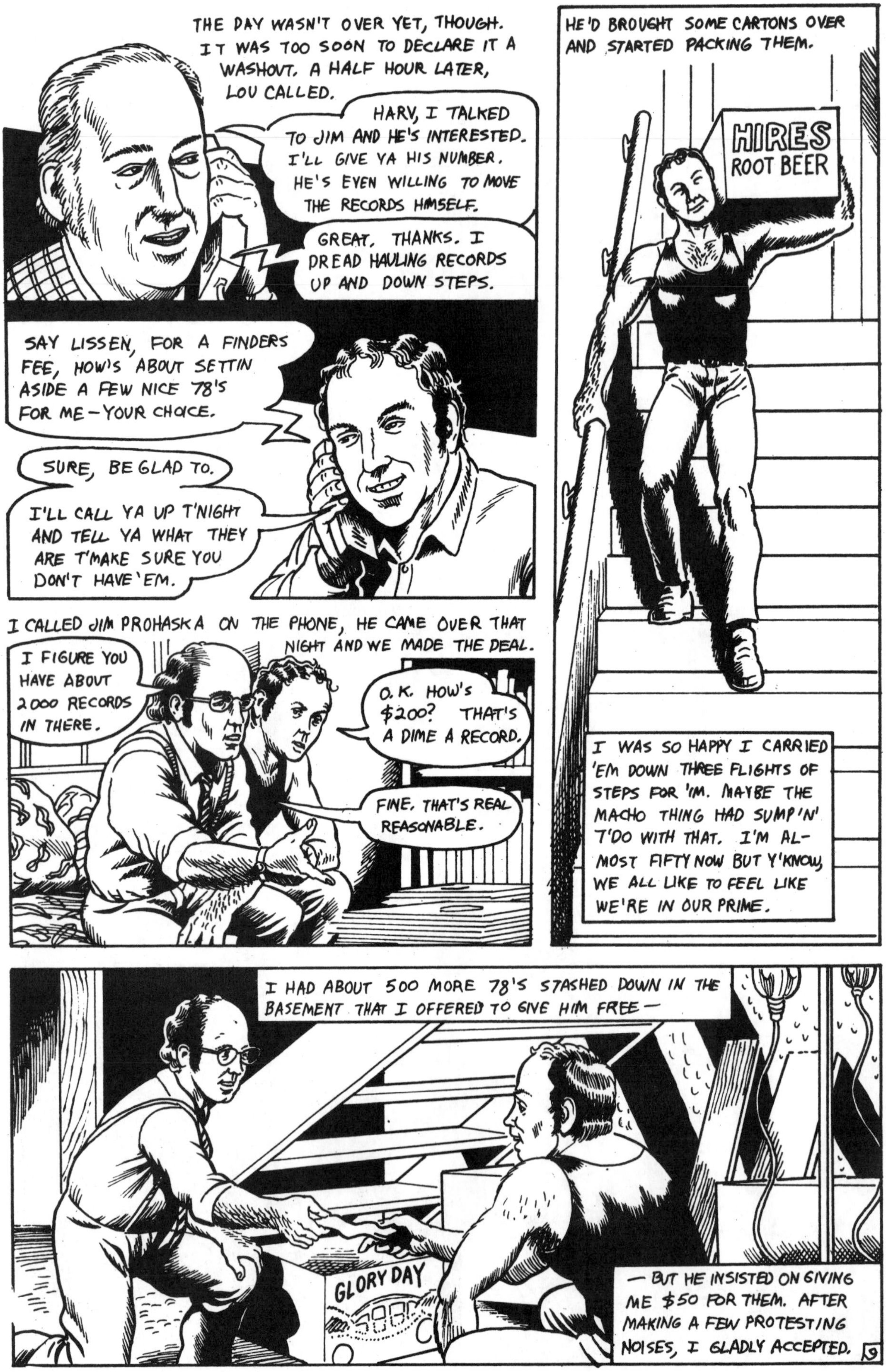
THE DAY WASN'T OVER YET, THOUGH. IT WAS TOO SOON TO DECLARE IT A WASHOUT. A HALF HOUR LATER, LOU CALLED.
HARV, I TALKED TO JIM AND HE'S INTERESTED. I'LL GIVE YA HIS NUMBER. HE'S EVEN WILLING TO MOVE THE RECORDS HIMSELF.
GREAT, THANKS. I DREAD HAULING RECORDS UP AND DOWN STEPS.
SAY LISSEN, FOR A FINDERS FEE, HOW'S ABOUT SETTIN ASIDE A FEW NICE 78'S FOR ME—YOUR CHOICE.
SURE, BE GLAD TO.
I'LL CALL YA UP T'NIGHT AND TELL YA WHAT THEY ARE T'MAKE SURE YOU DON'T HAVE 'EM.
I CALLED JIM PROHASKA ON THE PHONE, HE CAME OVER THAT NIGHT AND WE MADE THE DEAL.
I FIGURE YOU HAVE ABOUT 2000 RECORDS IN THERE.
O.K. HOW'S $200? THAT'S A DIME A RECORD.
FINE, THAT'S REAL REASONABLE.
HE'D BROUGHT SOME CARTONS OVER AND STARTED PACKING THEM.
HIRES ROOT BEER
I WAS SO HAPPY I CARRIED 'EM DOWN THREE FLIGHTS OF STEPS FOR 'IM. MAYBE THE MACHO THING HAD SUMP'N' T'DO WITH THAT. I'M ALMOST FIFTY NOW BUT Y'KNOW, WE ALL LIKE TO FEEL LIKE WE'RE IN OUR PRIME.
I HAD ABOUT 500 MORE 78'S STASHED DOWN IN THE BASEMENT THAT I OFFERED TO GIVE HIM FREE—
GLORY DAY
—BUT HE INSISTED ON GIVING ME $50 FOR THEM. AFTER MAKING A FEW PROTESTING NOISES, I GLADLY ACCEPTED.

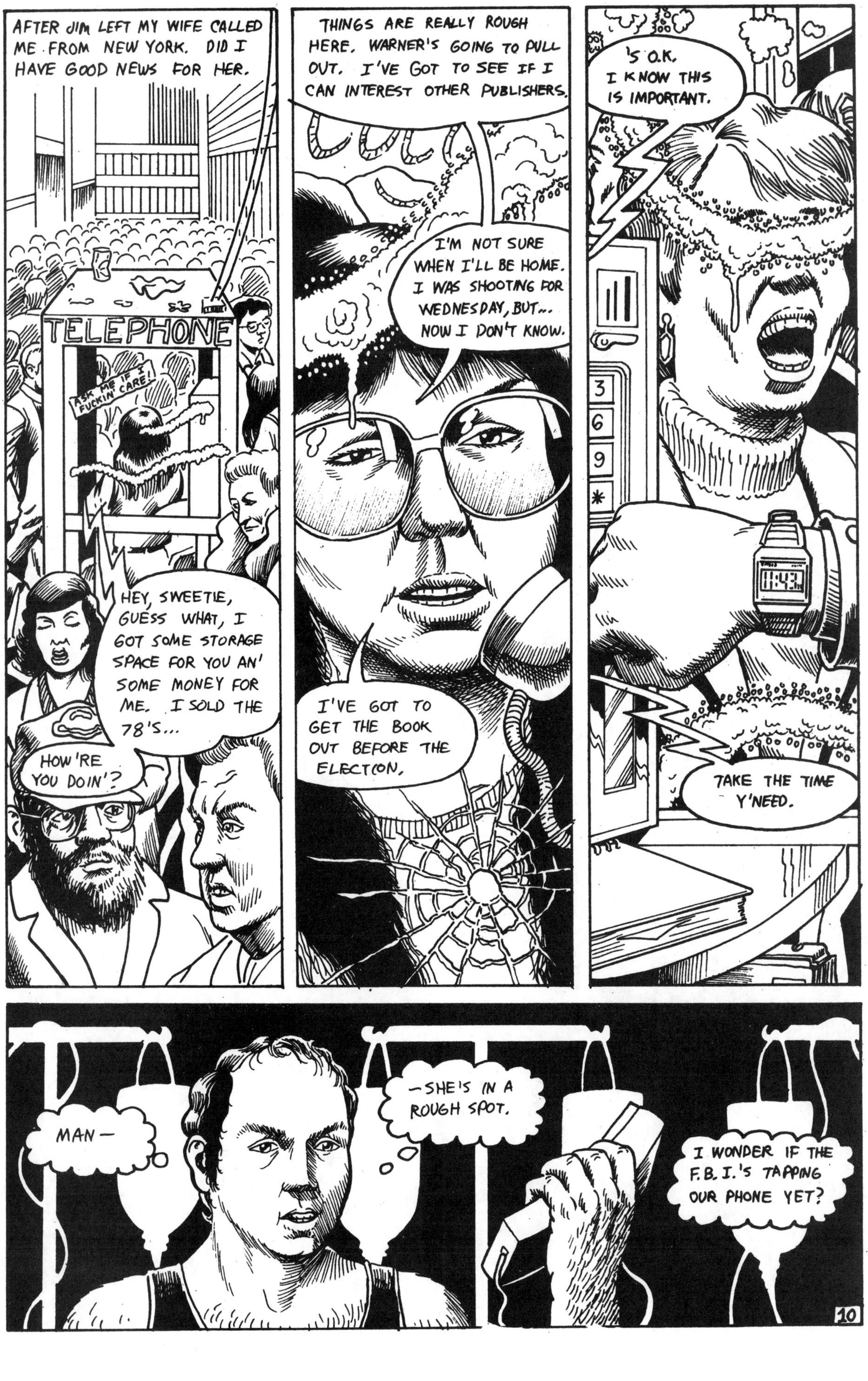
AFTER JIM LEFT MY WIFE CALLED ME FROM NEW YORK. DID I HAVE GOOD NEWS FOR HER.
TELEPHONE
ASK ME IF I FUCKIN' CARE!
HEY, SWEETIE, GUESS WHAT, I GOT SOME STORAGE SPACE FOR YOU AN' SOME MONEY FOR ME. I SOLD THE 78'S...
HOW'RE YOU DOIN'?
THINGS ARE REALLY ROUGH HERE. WARNER'S GOING TO PULL OUT. I'VE GOT TO SEE IF I CAN INTEREST OTHER PUBLISHERS.
I'M NOT SURE WHEN I'LL BE HOME. I WAS SHOOTING FOR WEDNESDAY, BUT... NOW I DON'T KNOW.
I'VE GOT TO GET THE BOOK OUT BEFORE THE ELECTION.
'S O.K. I KNOW THIS IS IMPORTANT.
11:43
TAKE THE TIME Y'NEED.
MAN—
—SHE'S IN A ROUGH SPOT.
I WONDER IF THE F.B.I.'S TAPPING OUR PHONE YET?

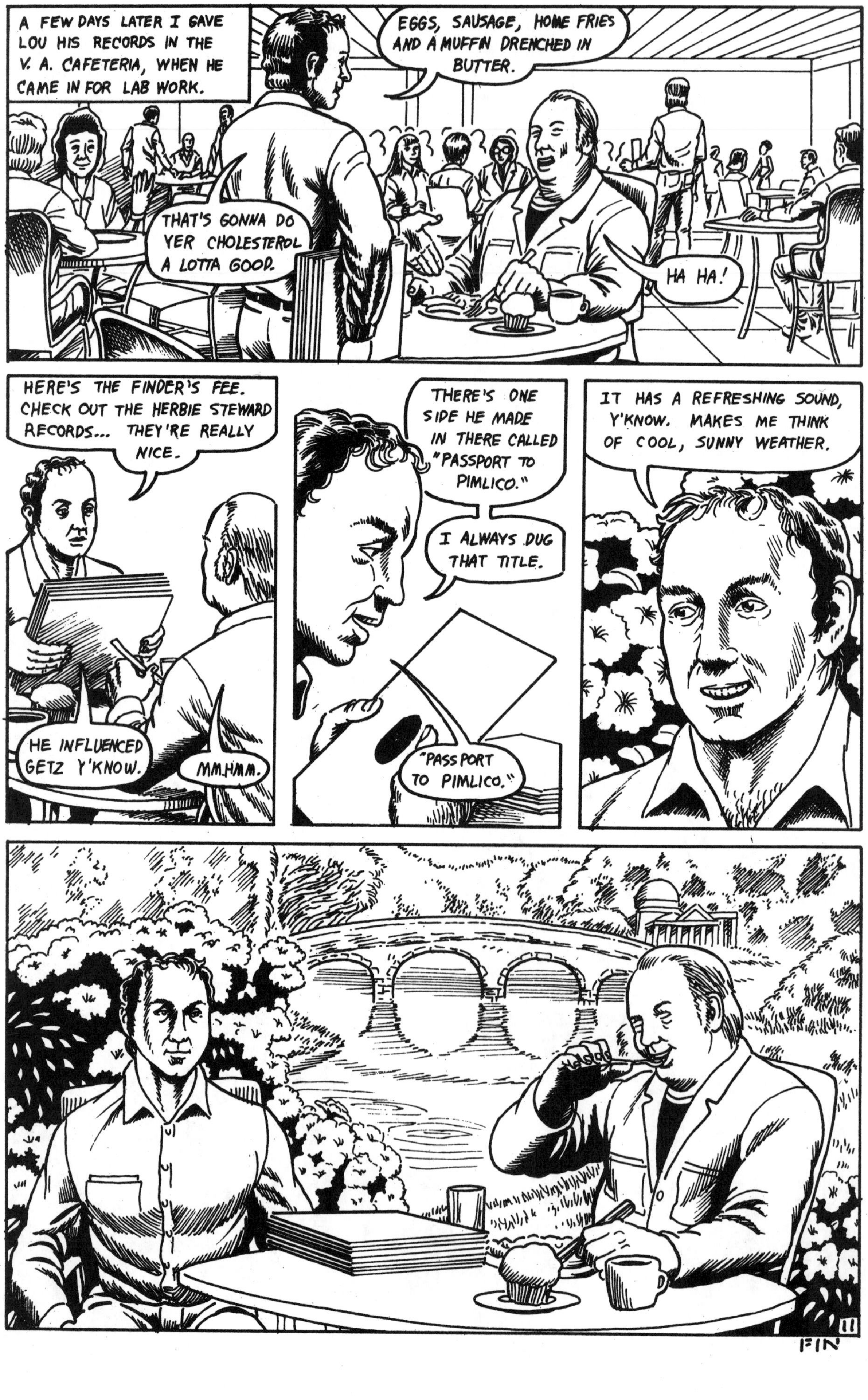
A FEW DAYS LATER I GAVE LOU HIS RECORDS IN THE V. A. CAFETERIA, WHEN HE CAME IN FOR LAB WORK.
EGGS, SAUSAGE, HOME FRIES AND A MUFFIN DRENCHED IN BUTTER.
THAT'S GONNA DO YER CHOLESTEROL A LOTTA GOOD.
HA HA!
HERE'S THE FINDER'S FEE. CHECK OUT THE HERBIE STEWARD RECORDS... THEY'RE REALLY NICE.
HE INFLUENCED GETZ Y'KNOW.
MM.HMM.
THERE'S ONE SIDE HE MADE IN THERE CALLED "PASSPORT TO PIMLICO."
I ALWAYS DUG THAT TITLE.
"PASSPORT TO PIMLICO."
IT HAS A REFRESHING SOUND, Y'KNOW. MAKES ME THINK OF COOL, SUNNY WEATHER.

FIN

PRE-DAWN RIDE

I'LL BE COMING IN AT 6:22 IN THE MORNING. IF YOU WANT I CAN TAKE THE RAPID TRANSIT HOME.

Story BY HARVEY PEKAR

Art BY GARY DUMM

ASSISTED BY LAURA DARNELL DUMM

NAW, NAW, THAT'S O.K. Y'GOTTA TRANSFER FROM THE RAPID TO THE BUS WITH YOUR BAGS— THAT'S TOO MUCH OF A HASSLE. I'LL GO T'SLEEP A LITTLE EARLIER T'NIGHT—I SHOULD BE O.K. I'LL PICK YA UP, LEAVE YA OFF AT HOME, 'N'EN GO T'WORK.

4:30 A.M.

I'M WIDE AWAKE. MIGHT AS WELL GET UP NOW.

1.

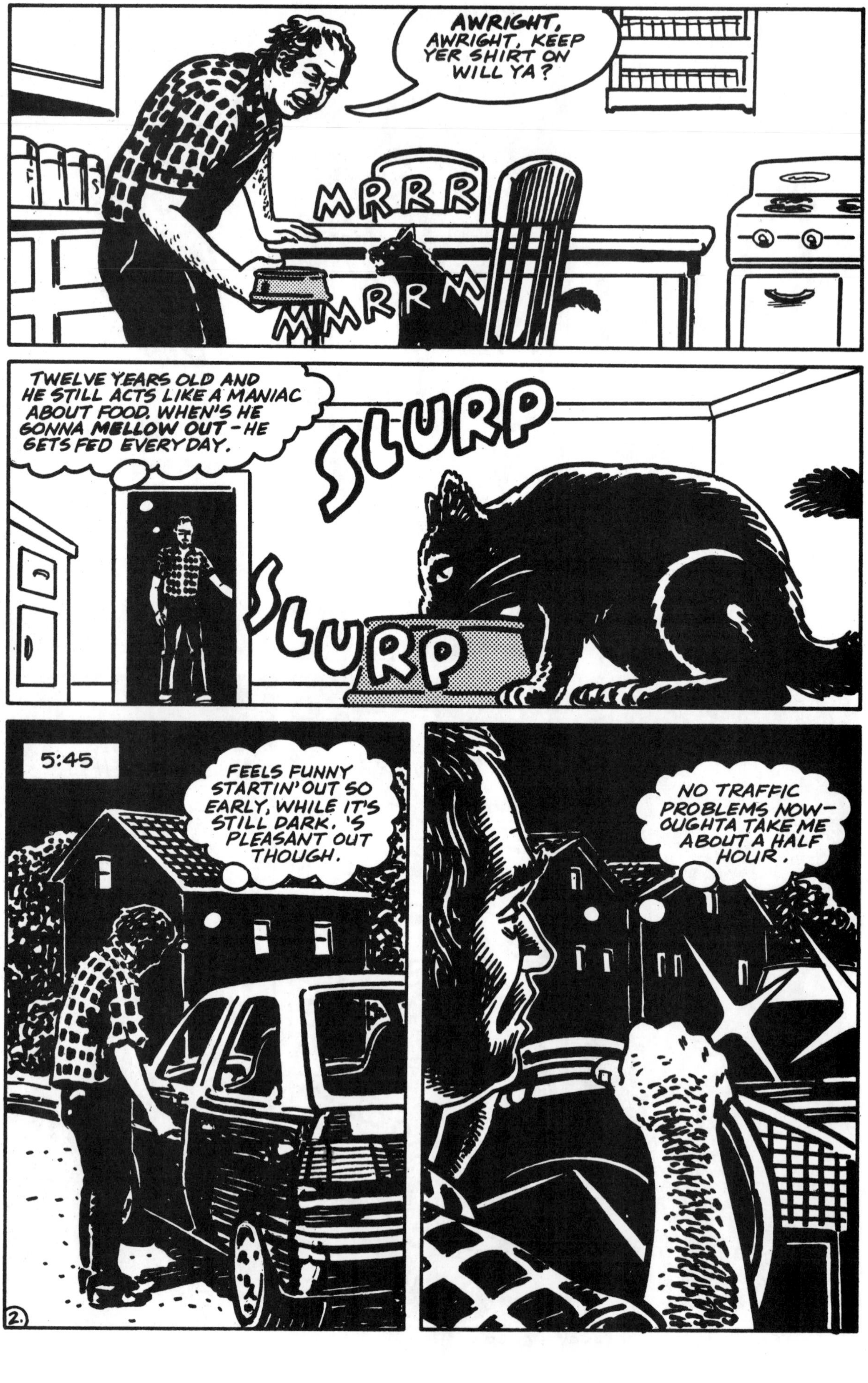
AWRIGHT, AWRIGHT, KEEP YER SHIRT ON WILL YA?
MRRR
MMRRM
TWELVE YEARS OLD AND HE STILL ACTS LIKE A MANIAC ABOUT FOOD. WHEN'S HE GONNA MELLOW OUT - HE GETS FED EVERYDAY.
SLURP
SLURP
5:45
FEELS FUNNY STARTIN' OUT SO EARLY, WHILE IT'S STILL DARK. 'S PLEASANT OUT THOUGH.
NO TRAFFIC PROBLEMS NOW- OUGHTA TAKE ME ABOUT A HALF HOUR.
2.

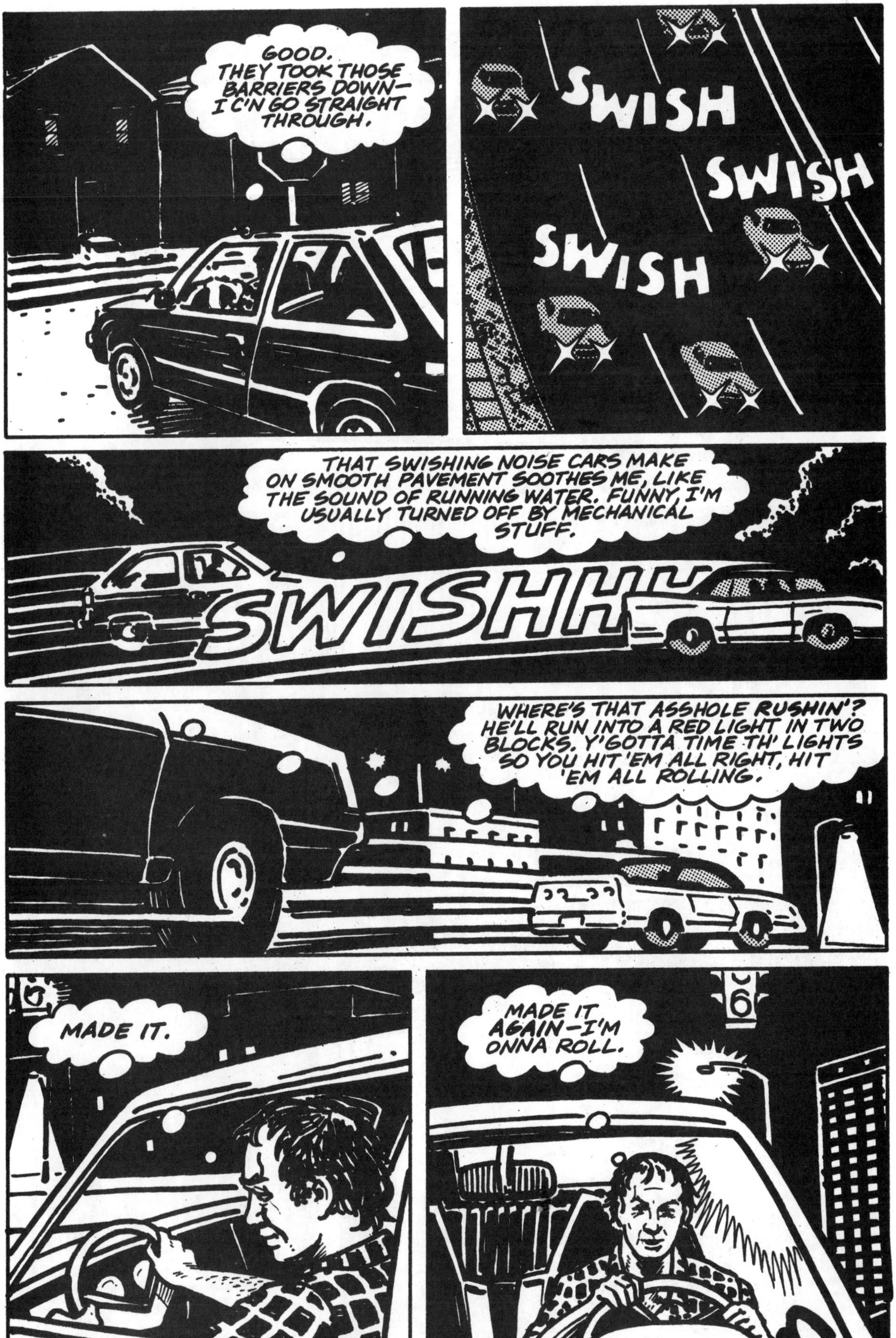
GOOD. THEY TOOK THOSE BARRIERS DOWN— I C'N GO STRAIGHT THROUGH.
SWISH
SWISH
SWISH
THAT SWISHING NOISE CARS MAKE ON SMOOTH PAVEMENT SOOTHES ME, LIKE THE SOUND OF RUNNING WATER. FUNNY, I'M USUALLY TURNED OFF BY MECHANICAL STUFF.
SWISHH
WHERE'S THAT ASSHOLE RUSHIN'? HE'LL RUN INTO A RED LIGHT IN TWO BLOCKS. Y'GOTTA TIME TH' LIGHTS SO YOU HIT 'EM ALL RIGHT, HIT 'EM ALL ROLLING.
MADE IT.
MADE IT AGAIN—I'M ONNA ROLL.
3.

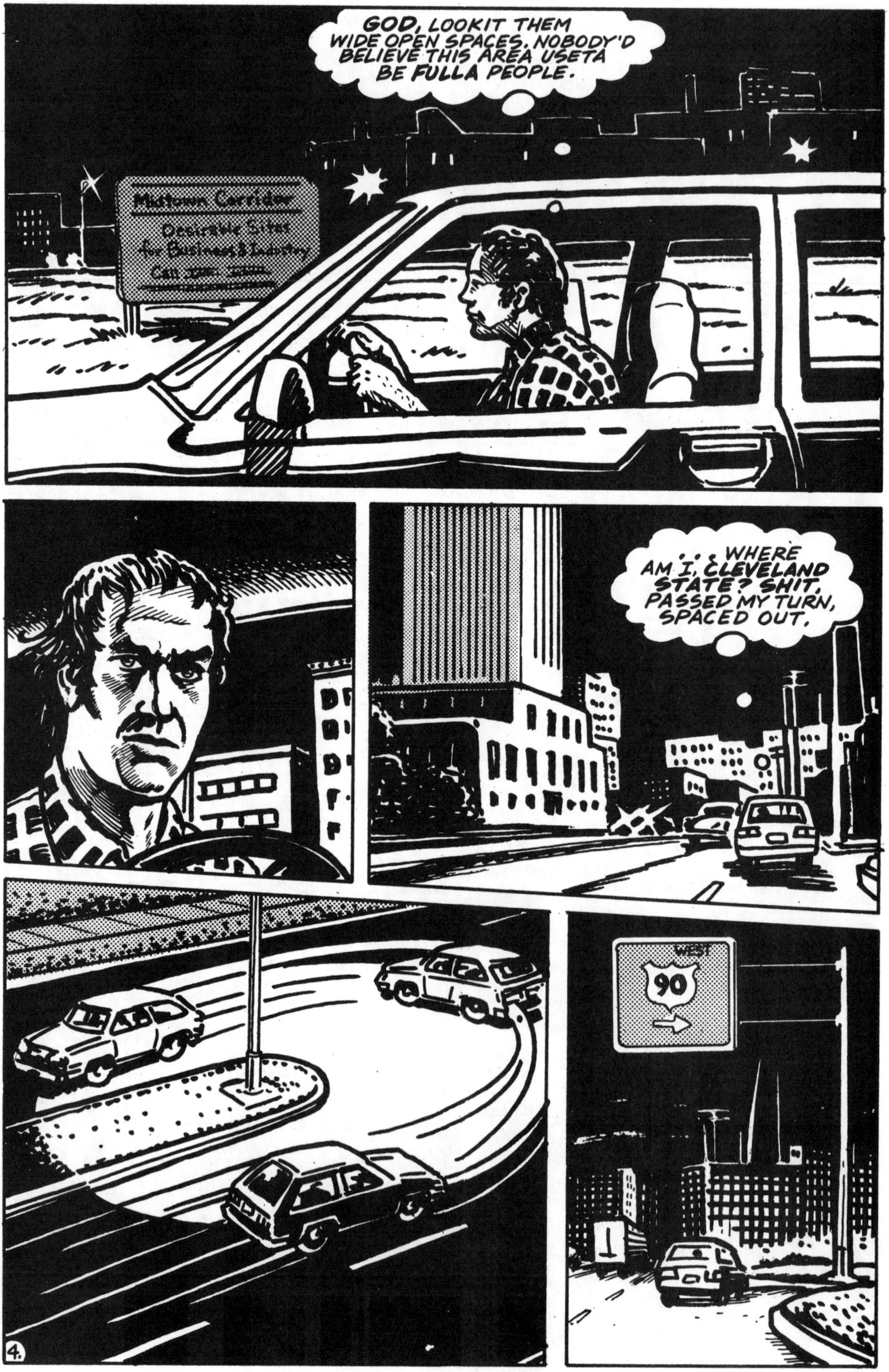
GOD, LOOKIT THEM WIDE OPEN SPACES. NOBODY'D BELIEVE THIS AREA USETA BE FULLA PEOPLE.
Midtown Corridor
Desirable Sites for Business & Industry
...WHERE AM I, CLEVELAND STATE? SHIT, PASSED MY TURN, SPACED OUT.
WEST
90

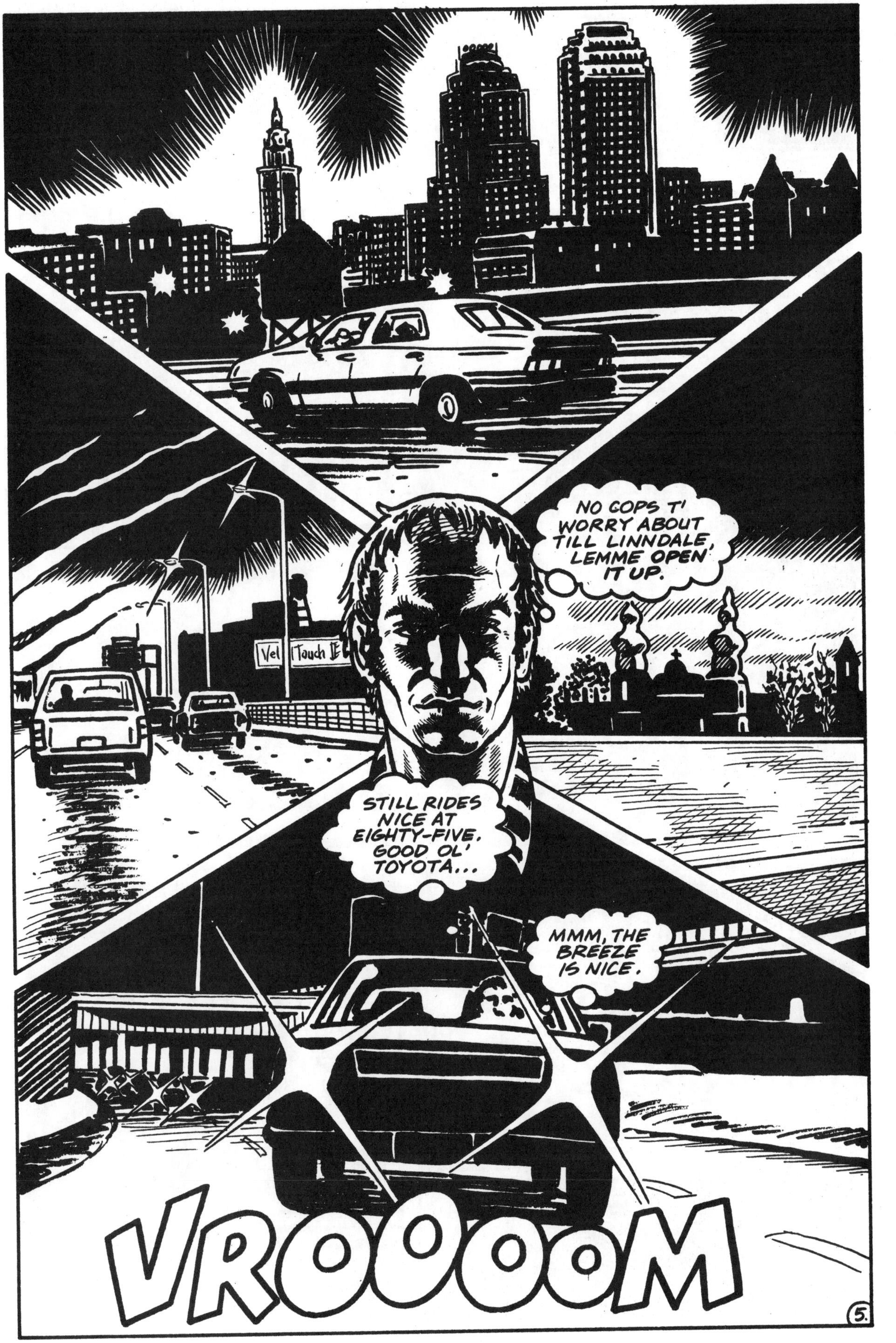
NO COPS T' WORRY ABOUT TILL LINNDALE, LEMME OPEN IT UP.
STILL RIDES NICE AT EIGHTY-FIVE. GOOD OL' TOYOTA...
MMM, THE BREEZE IS NICE.
VROOOOOM
5.

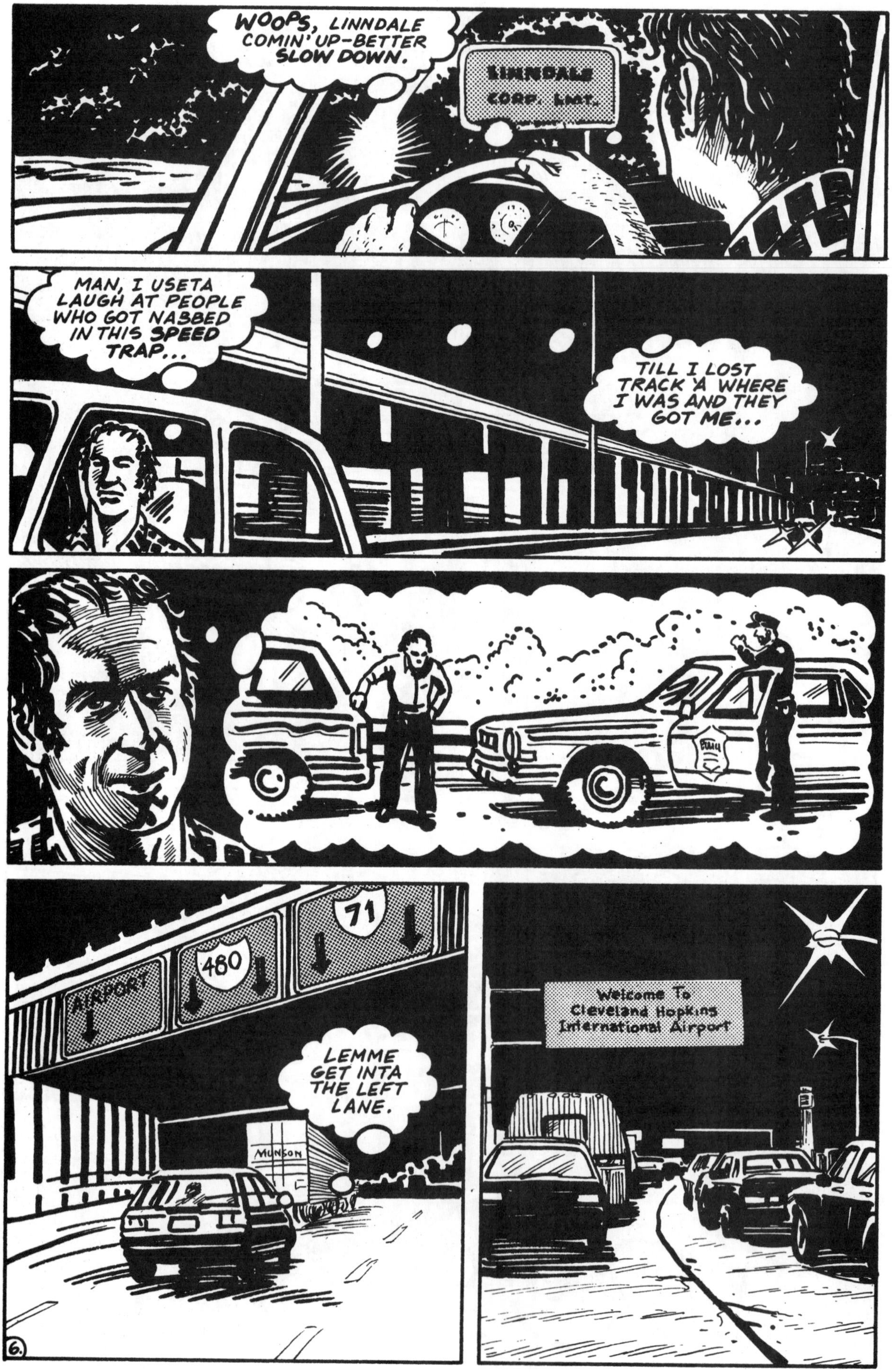
WOOPS, LINNDALE COMIN' UP–BETTER SLOW DOWN.
LINNDALE CORP. LMT.
MAN, I USETA LAUGH AT PEOPLE WHO GOT NABBED IN THIS SPEED TRAP...
TILL I LOST TRACK 'A WHERE I WAS AND THEY GOT ME...
AIRPORT
480
71
LEMME GET INTA THE LEFT LANE.
MUNSON
Welcome To Cleveland Hopkins International Airport

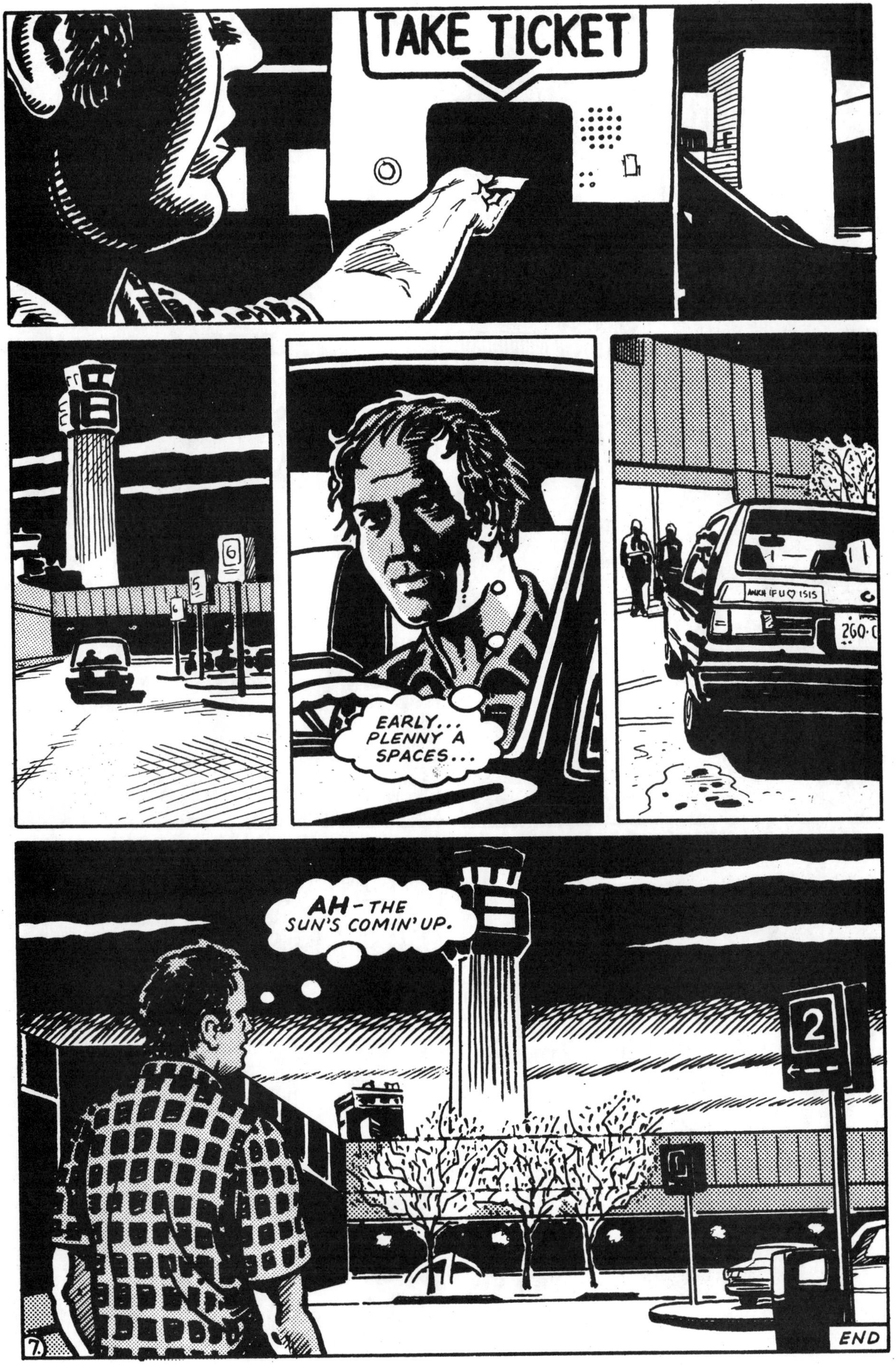
TAKE TICKET
EARLY... PLENNY A SPACES...
AH - THE SUN'S COMIN' UP.
7.
END

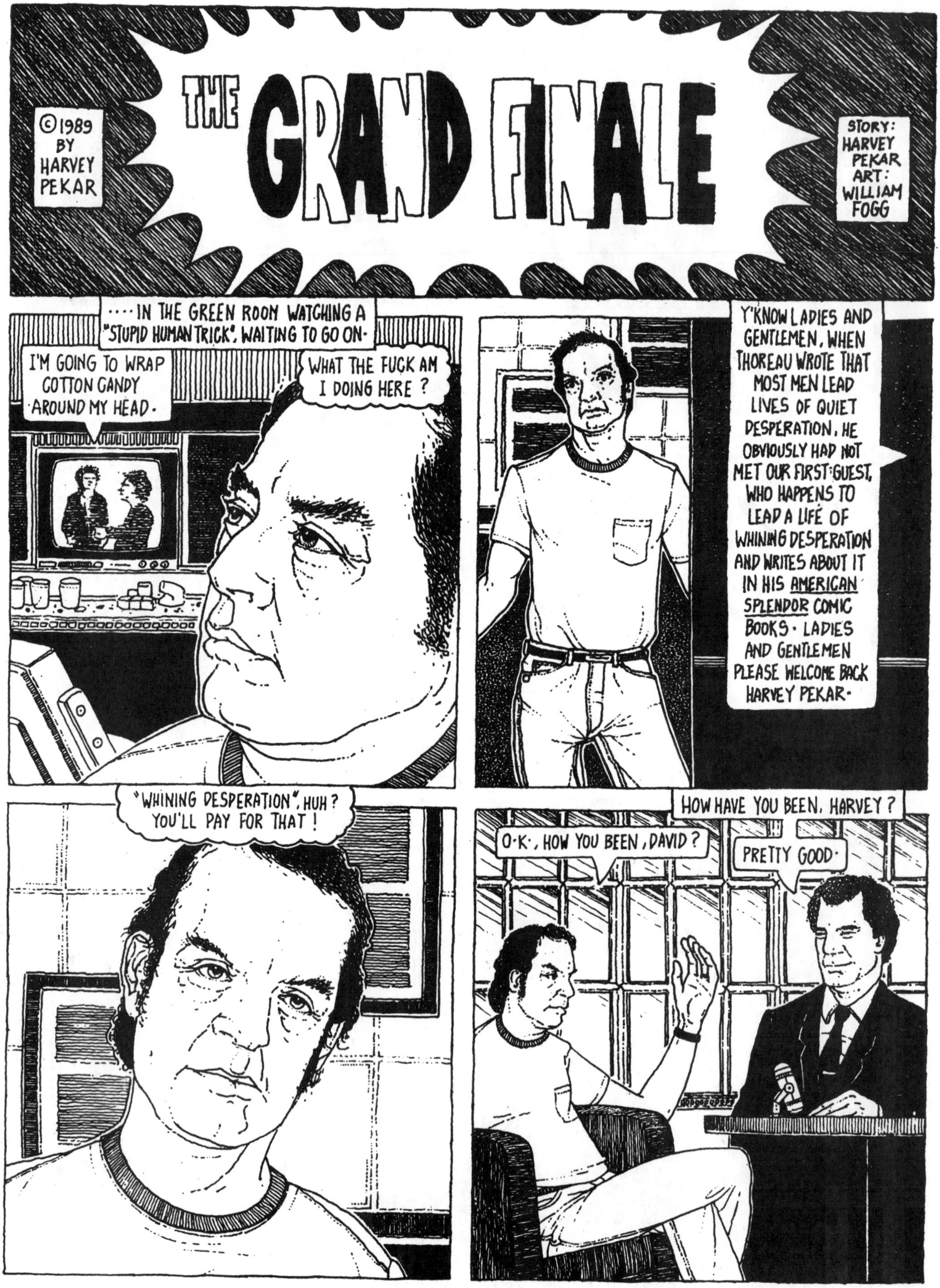
THE GRAND FINALE
©1989 BY HARVEY PEKAR
STORY: HARVEY PEKAR ART: WILLIAM FOGG
....IN THE GREEN ROOM WATCHING A "STUPID HUMAN TRICK", WAITING TO GO ON.
I'M GOING TO WRAP COTTON CANDY AROUND MY HEAD.
WHAT THE FUCK AM I DOING HERE ?
Y'KNOW LADIES AND GENTLEMEN, WHEN THOREAU WROTE THAT MOST MEN LEAD LIVES OF QUIET DESPERATION, HE OBVIOUSLY HAD NOT MET OUR FIRST GUEST, WHO HAPPENS TO LEAD A LIFE OF WHINING DESPERATION AND WRITES ABOUT IT IN HIS AMERICAN SPLENDOR COMIC BOOKS. LADIES AND GENTLEMEN PLEASE WELCOME BACK HARVEY PEKAR.
"WHINING DESPERATION", HUH ? YOU'LL PAY FOR THAT !
HOW HAVE YOU BEEN, HARVEY ?
O.K., HOW YOU BEEN, DAVID ?
PRETTY GOOD.

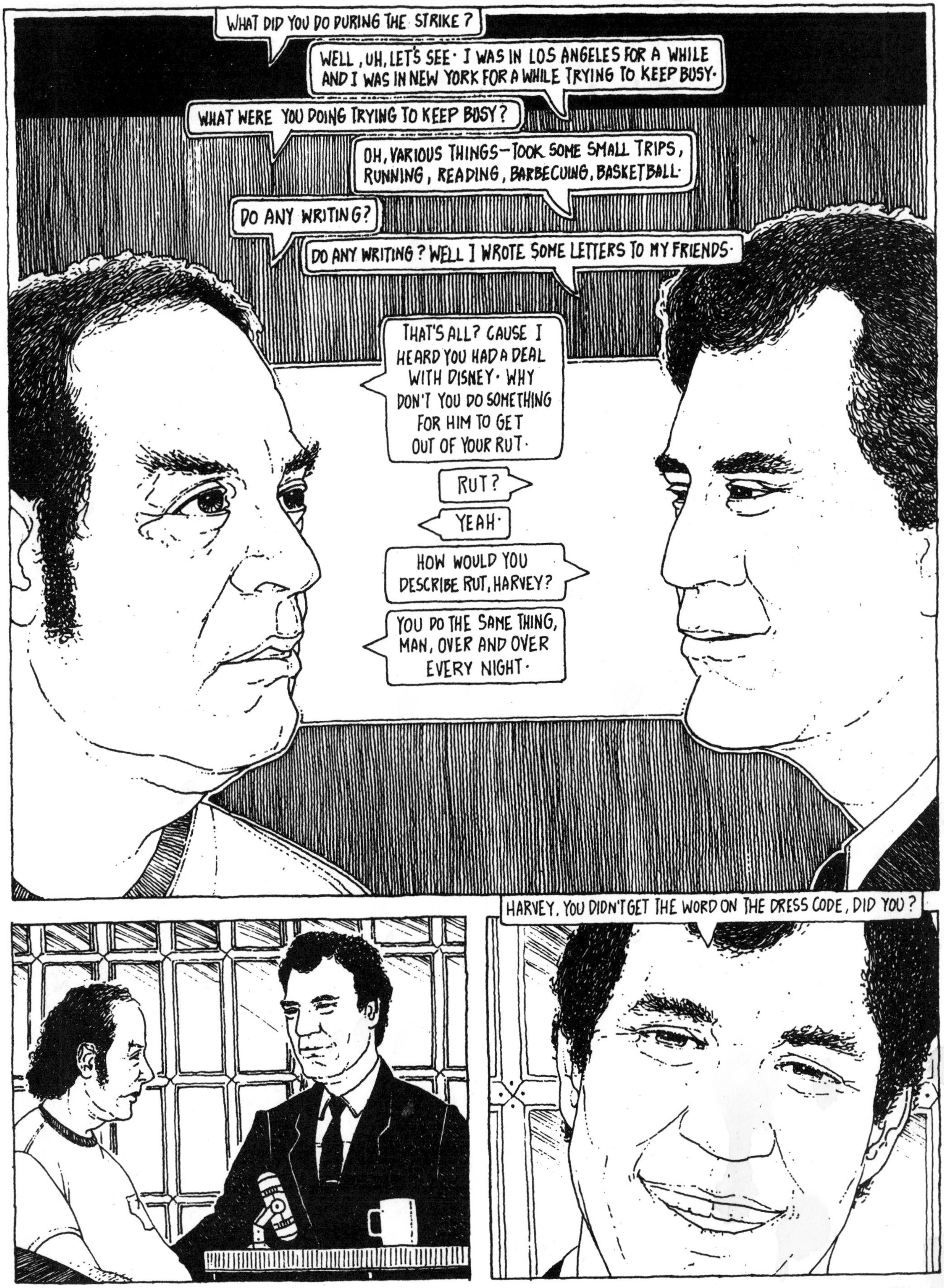
WHAT DID YOU DO DURING THE STRIKE?
WELL, UH, LET'S SEE. I WAS IN LOS ANGELES FOR A WHILE AND I WAS IN NEW YORK FOR A WHILE TRYING TO KEEP BUSY.
WHAT WERE YOU DOING TRYING TO KEEP BUSY?
OH, VARIOUS THINGS—TOOK SOME SMALL TRIPS, RUNNING, READING, BARBECUING, BASKETBALL.
DO ANY WRITING?
DO ANY WRITING? WELL I WROTE SOME LETTERS TO MY FRIENDS.
THAT'S ALL? CAUSE I HEARD YOU HAD A DEAL WITH DISNEY. WHY DON'T YOU DO SOMETHING FOR HIM TO GET OUT OF YOUR RUT.
RUT?
YEAH.
HOW WOULD YOU DESCRIBE RUT, HARVEY?
YOU DO THE SAME THING, MAN, OVER AND OVER EVERY NIGHT.
HARVEY, YOU DIDN'T GET THE WORD ON THE DRESS CODE, DID YOU?

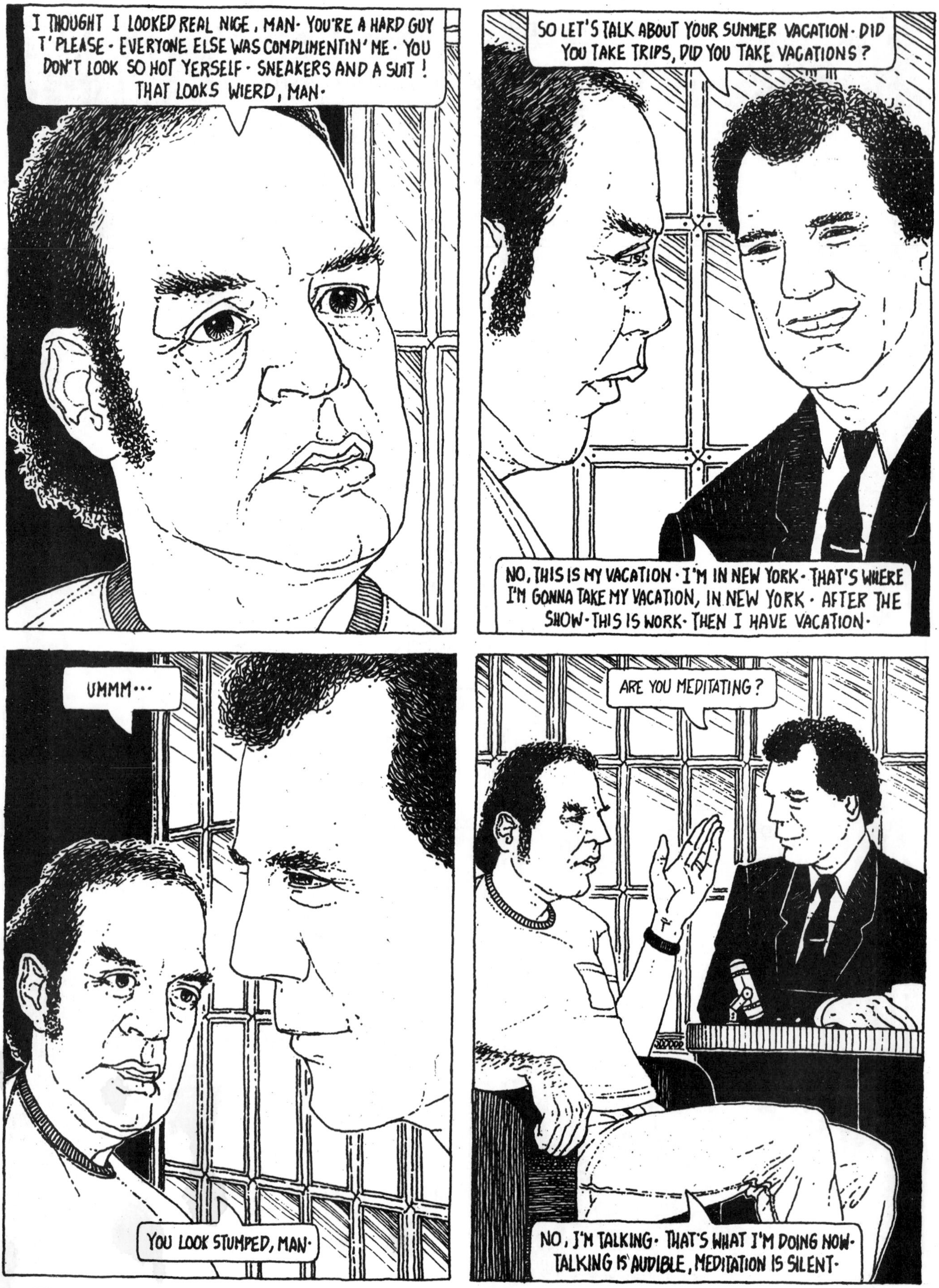
I THOUGHT I LOOKED REAL NICE, MAN. YOU'RE A HARD GUY T' PLEASE. EVERYONE ELSE WAS COMPLIMENTIN' ME. YOU DON'T LOOK SO HOT YERSELF. SNEAKERS AND A SUIT! THAT LOOKS WIERD, MAN.
SO LET'S TALK ABOUT YOUR SUMMER VACATION. DID YOU TAKE TRIPS, DID YOU TAKE VACATIONS?
NO, THIS IS MY VACATION. I'M IN NEW YORK. THAT'S WHERE I'M GONNA TAKE MY VACATION, IN NEW YORK. AFTER THE SHOW. THIS IS WORK. THEN I HAVE VACATION.
UMMM...
YOU LOOK STUMPED, MAN.
ARE YOU MEDITATING?
NO, I'M TALKING. THAT'S WHAT I'M DOING NOW. TALKING IS AUDIBLE, MEDITATION IS SILENT.

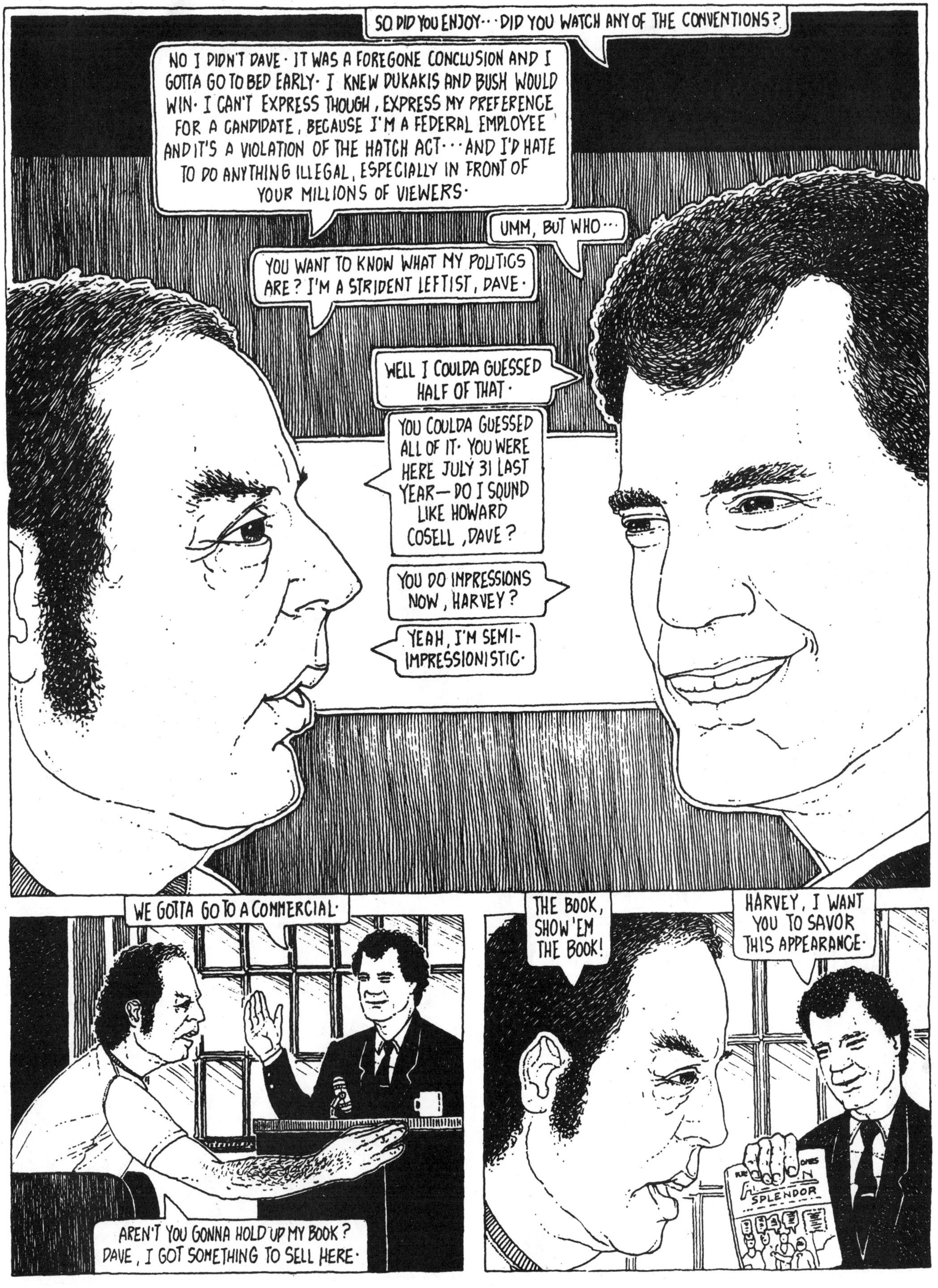
SO DID YOU ENJOY... DID YOU WATCH ANY OF THE CONVENTIONS?
NO I DIDN'T DAVE. IT WAS A FOREGONE CONCLUSION AND I GOTTA GO TO BED EARLY. I KNEW DUKAKIS AND BUSH WOULD WIN. I CAN'T EXPRESS THOUGH, EXPRESS MY PREFERENCE FOR A CANDIDATE, BECAUSE I'M A FEDERAL EMPLOYEE AND IT'S A VIOLATION OF THE HATCH ACT... AND I'D HATE TO DO ANYTHING ILLEGAL, ESPECIALLY IN FRONT OF YOUR MILLIONS OF VIEWERS.
UMM, BUT WHO...
YOU WANT TO KNOW WHAT MY POLITICS ARE? I'M A STRIDENT LEFTIST, DAVE.
WELL I COULDA GUESSED HALF OF THAT.
YOU COULDA GUESSED ALL OF IT. YOU WERE HERE JULY 31 LAST YEAR—DO I SOUND LIKE HOWARD COSELL, DAVE?
YOU DO IMPRESSIONS NOW, HARVEY?
YEAH, I'M SEMI-IMPRESSIONISTIC.
WE GOTTA GO TO A COMMERCIAL.
AREN'T YOU GONNA HOLD UP MY BOOK? DAVE, I GOT SOMETHING TO SELL HERE.
THE BOOK, SHOW 'EM THE BOOK!
HARVEY, I WANT YOU TO SAVOR THIS APPEARANCE.
SPLENDOR

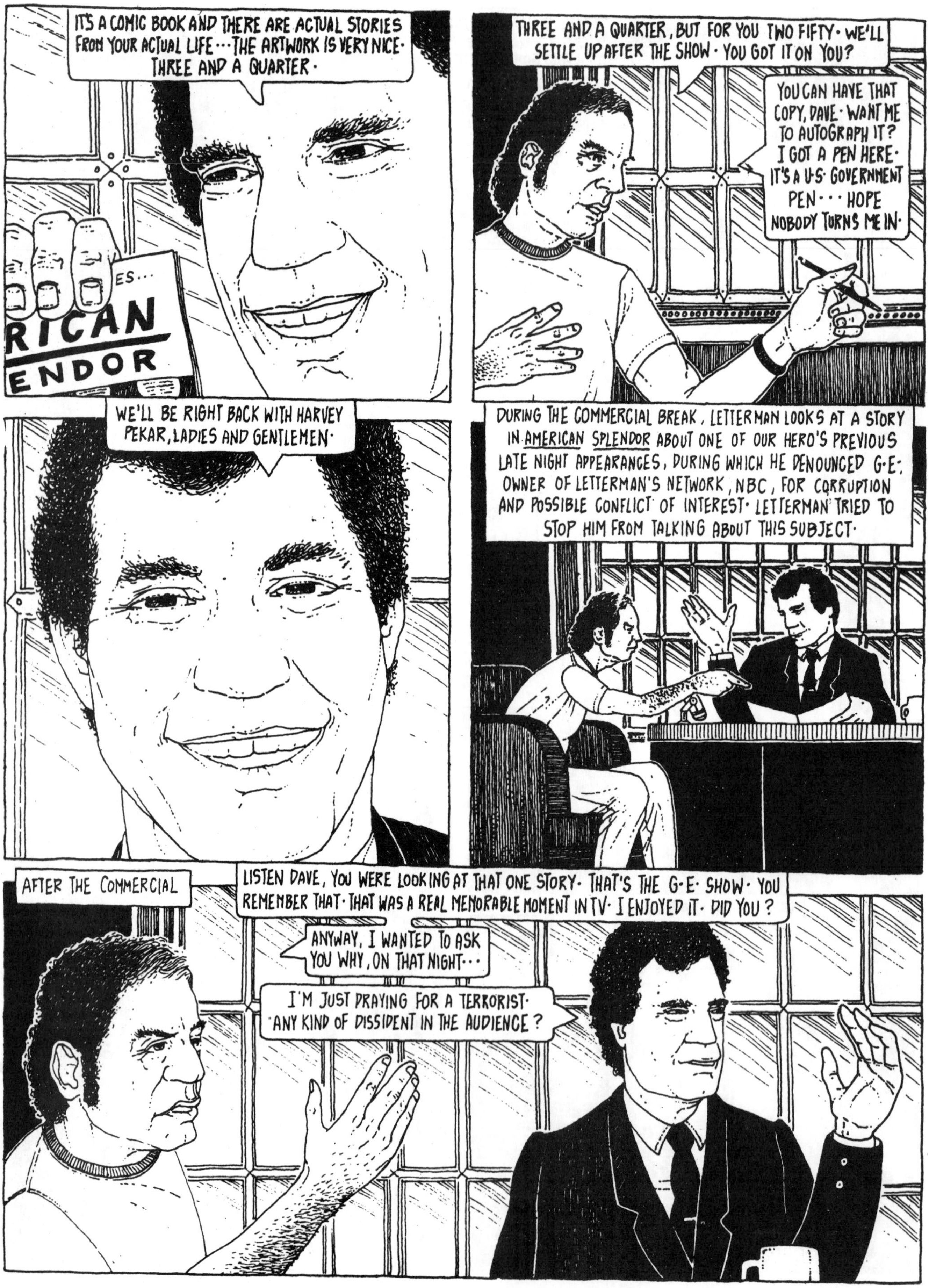
IT'S A COMIC BOOK AND THERE ARE ACTUAL STORIES FROM YOUR ACTUAL LIFE··· THE ARTWORK IS VERY NICE· THREE AND A QUARTER·
ES...
RICAN
ENDOR
THREE AND A QUARTER, BUT FOR YOU TWO FIFTY· WE'LL SETTLE UP AFTER THE SHOW· YOU GOT IT ON YOU?
YOU CAN HAVE THAT COPY, DAVE· WANT ME TO AUTOGRAPH IT? I GOT A PEN HERE· IT'S A U·S· GOVERNMENT PEN··· HOPE NOBODY TURNS ME IN·
WE'LL BE RIGHT BACK WITH HARVEY PEKAR, LADIES AND GENTLEMEN·
DURING THE COMMERCIAL BREAK, LETTERMAN LOOKS AT A STORY IN AMERICAN SPLENDOR ABOUT ONE OF OUR HERO'S PREVIOUS LATE NIGHT APPEARANCES, DURING WHICH HE DENOUNCED G·E·, OWNER OF LETTERMAN'S NETWORK, NBC, FOR CORRUPTION AND POSSIBLE CONFLICT OF INTEREST· LETTERMAN TRIED TO STOP HIM FROM TALKING ABOUT THIS SUBJECT·
AFTER THE COMMERCIAL
LISTEN DAVE, YOU WERE LOOKING AT THAT ONE STORY· THAT'S THE G·E· SHOW· YOU REMEMBER THAT· THAT WAS A REAL MEMORABLE MOMENT IN TV· I ENJOYED IT· DID YOU?
ANYWAY, I WANTED TO ASK YOU WHY, ON THAT NIGHT···
I'M JUST PRAYING FOR A TERRORIST· ANY KIND OF DISSIDENT IN THE AUDIENCE?

LISTEN, THIS IS YOUR HOUSE, DAVID, YOU SHOULD TREAT ME WELL. YOU'VE GOT THIS DELUSION THAT THIS IS YOUR HOUSE; WHY DON'T YOU TREAT ME WELL. YOU THINK YOU OWN THE R.C.A. BUILDING. TREAT ME WELL, DAVID.

IS HARVEY'S NURSE IN THE GREEN ROOM? SEE IF IT'S TIME FOR THE MEDICATION.

YOU'RE A COP-OUT, MAN!

ANYWAY, I'M SERIOUS; I WANTED TO ASK YOU WHY...

NO, WAIT A MINUTE, LEMME SHOW YOU SOMETHING.

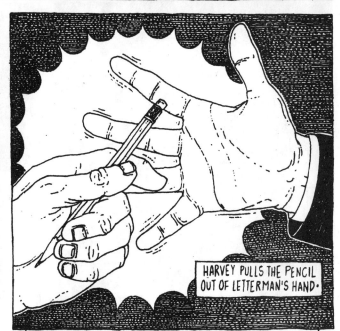

HARVEY PULLS THE PENCIL OUT OF LETTERMAN'S HAND.

ANYWAY, I WANTED TO ASK YOU WHY, WHY YOU DEFENDED G.E. I THOUGHT THAT WAS REALLY DUMB BECAUSE IT MADE YOU LOOK LIKE A SHILL FOR G.E. AND I WAS REALLY SURPRISED TO HEAR YOU DO THAT.

FIRST OF ALL, HARVEY, WHAT YOU ARE SAYING IS NOT TRUE; SECOND OF ALL, THIS IS NOT THE PLACE TO SAY IT. IF YOU WANT TO TALK ABOUT THIS, GO SOMEWHERE ELSE BECAUSE YOU'RE NOT TALKING ABOUT IT HERE ON THE SHOW.

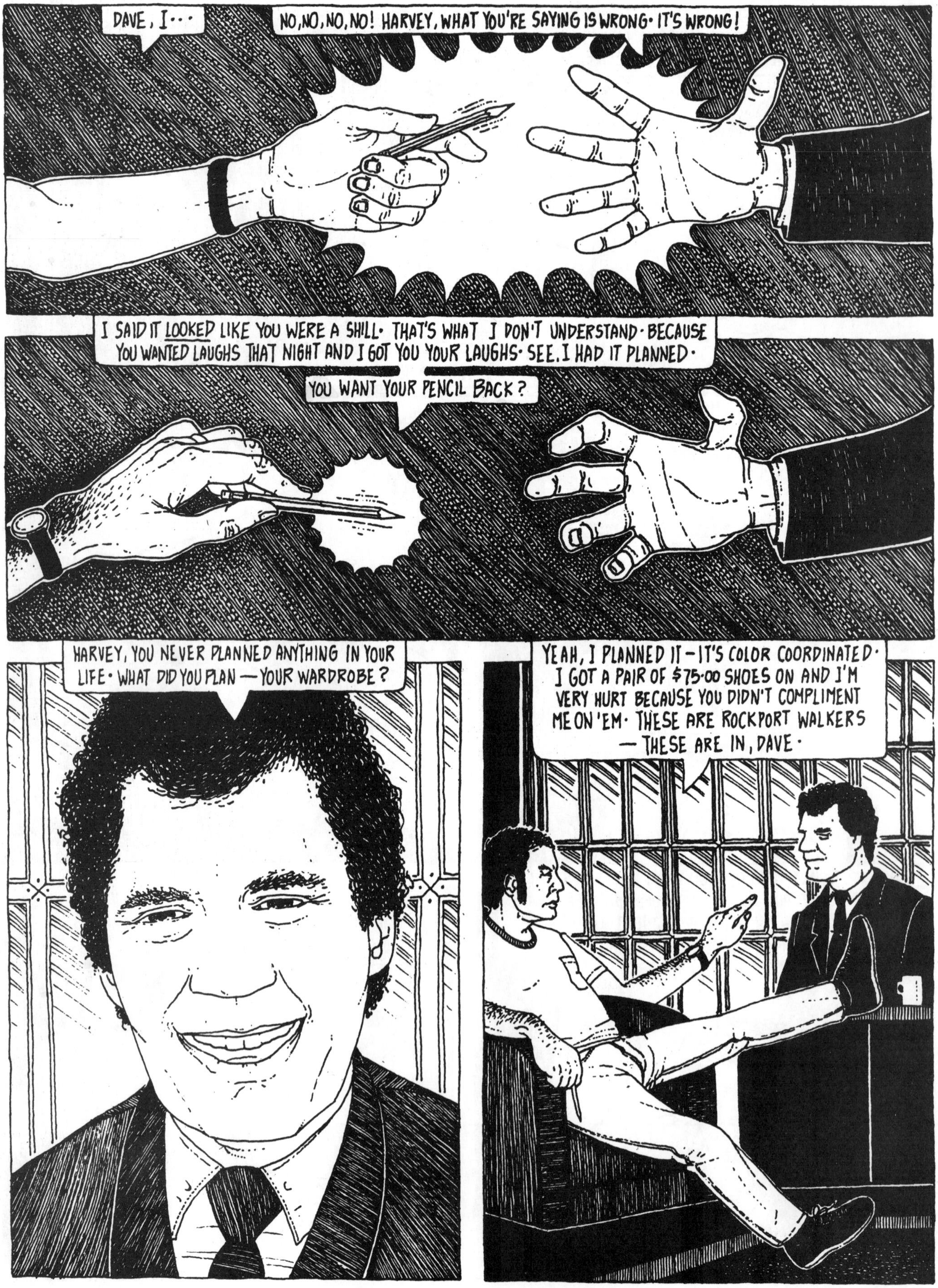
DAVE, I···
NO, NO, NO, NO! HARVEY, WHAT YOU'RE SAYING IS WRONG· IT'S WRONG!
I SAID IT LOOKED LIKE YOU WERE A SHILL· THAT'S WHAT I DON'T UNDERSTAND· BECAUSE YOU WANTED LAUGHS THAT NIGHT AND I GOT YOU YOUR LAUGHS· SEE, I HAD IT PLANNED·
YOU WANT YOUR PENCIL BACK?
HARVEY, YOU NEVER PLANNED ANYTHING IN YOUR LIFE· WHAT DID YOU PLAN — YOUR WARDROBE?
YEAH, I PLANNED IT — IT'S COLOR COORDINATED· I GOT A PAIR OF $75·00 SHOES ON AND I'M VERY HURT BECAUSE YOU DIDN'T COMPLIMENT ME ON 'EM· THESE ARE ROCKPORT WALKERS — THESE ARE IN, DAVE·

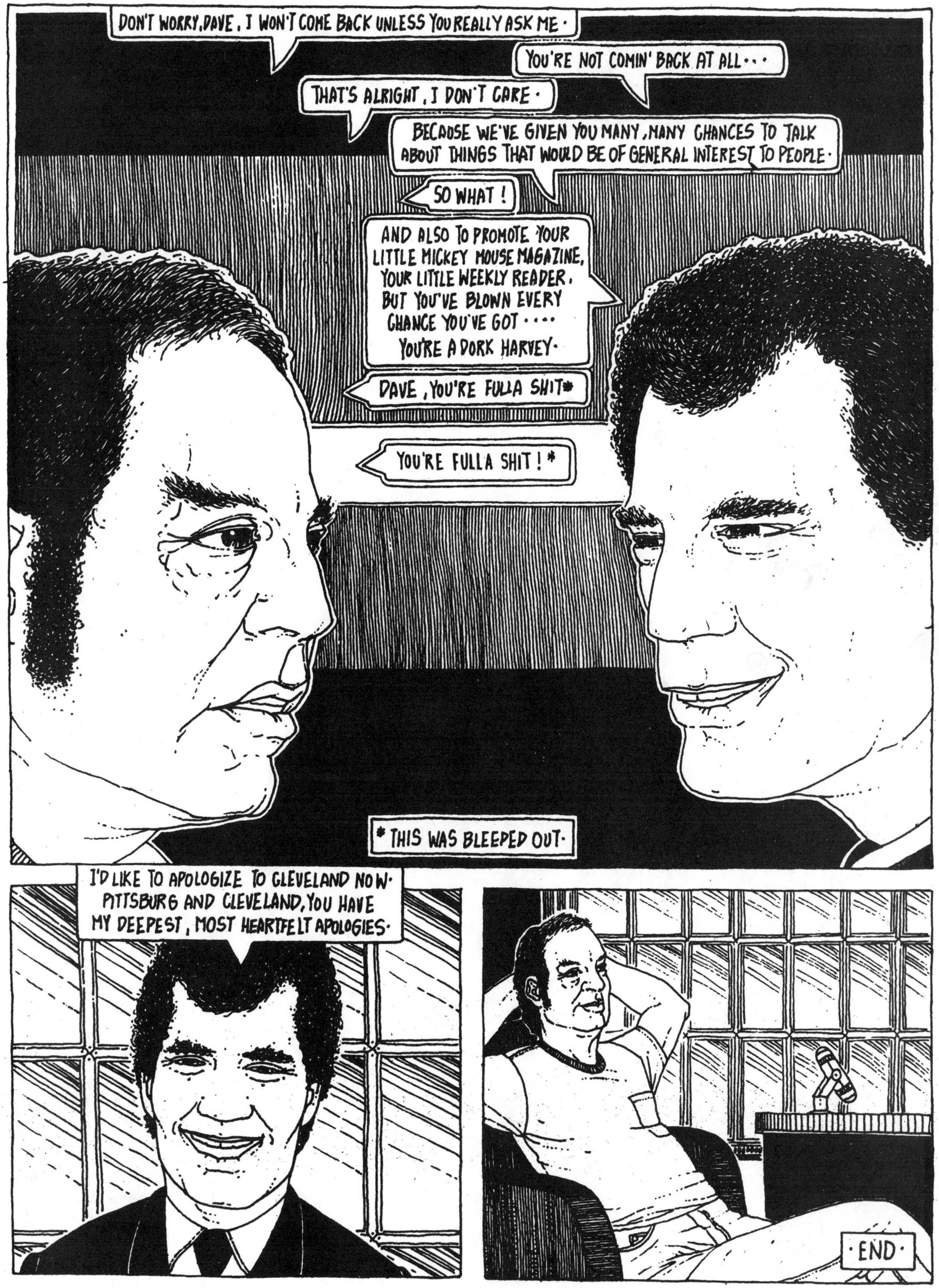
DON'T WORRY, DAVE. I WON'T COME BACK UNLESS YOU REALLY ASK ME.
YOU'RE NOT COMIN' BACK AT ALL...
THAT'S ALRIGHT. I DON'T CARE.
BECAUSE WE'VE GIVEN YOU MANY, MANY CHANCES TO TALK ABOUT THINGS THAT WOULD BE OF GENERAL INTEREST TO PEOPLE.
SO WHAT!
AND ALSO TO PROMOTE YOUR LITTLE MICKEY MOUSE MAGAZINE, YOUR LITTLE WEEKLY READER. BUT YOU'VE BLOWN EVERY CHANCE YOU'VE GOT.... YOU'RE A DORK HARVEY.
DAVE, YOU'RE FULLA SHIT*
YOU'RE FULLA SHIT!*
* THIS WAS BLEEPED OUT.
I'D LIKE TO APOLOGIZE TO CLEVELAND NOW. PITTSBURG AND CLEVELAND, YOU HAVE MY DEEPEST, MOST HEARTFELT APOLOGIES.
·END·

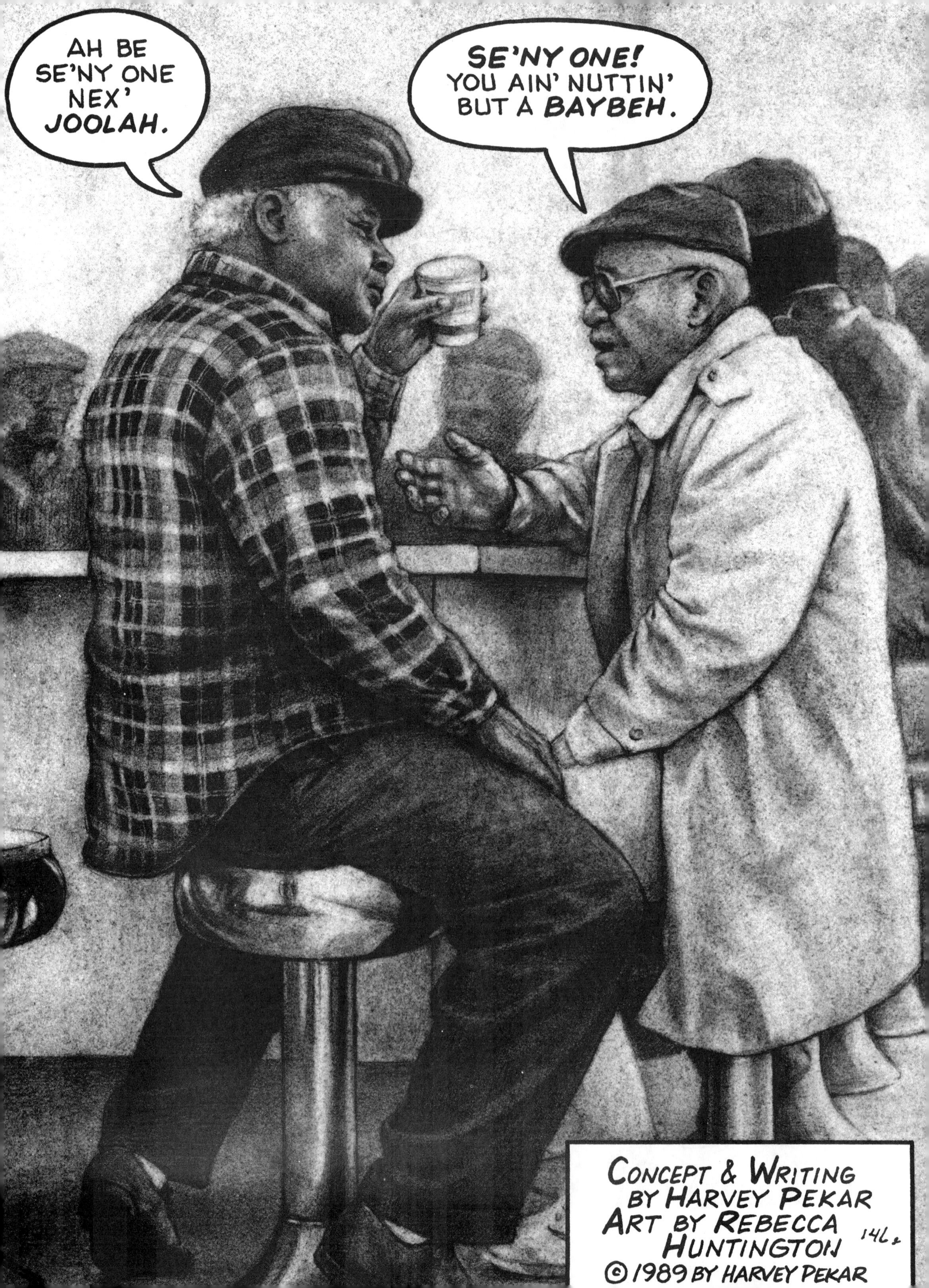
AH BE SE'NY ONE NEX' JOOLAH.
SE'NY ONE! YOU AIN' NUTTIN' BUT A BAYBEH.
CONCEPT & WRITING BY HARVEY PEKAR
ART BY REBECCA HUNTINGTON
© 1989 BY HARVEY PEKAR

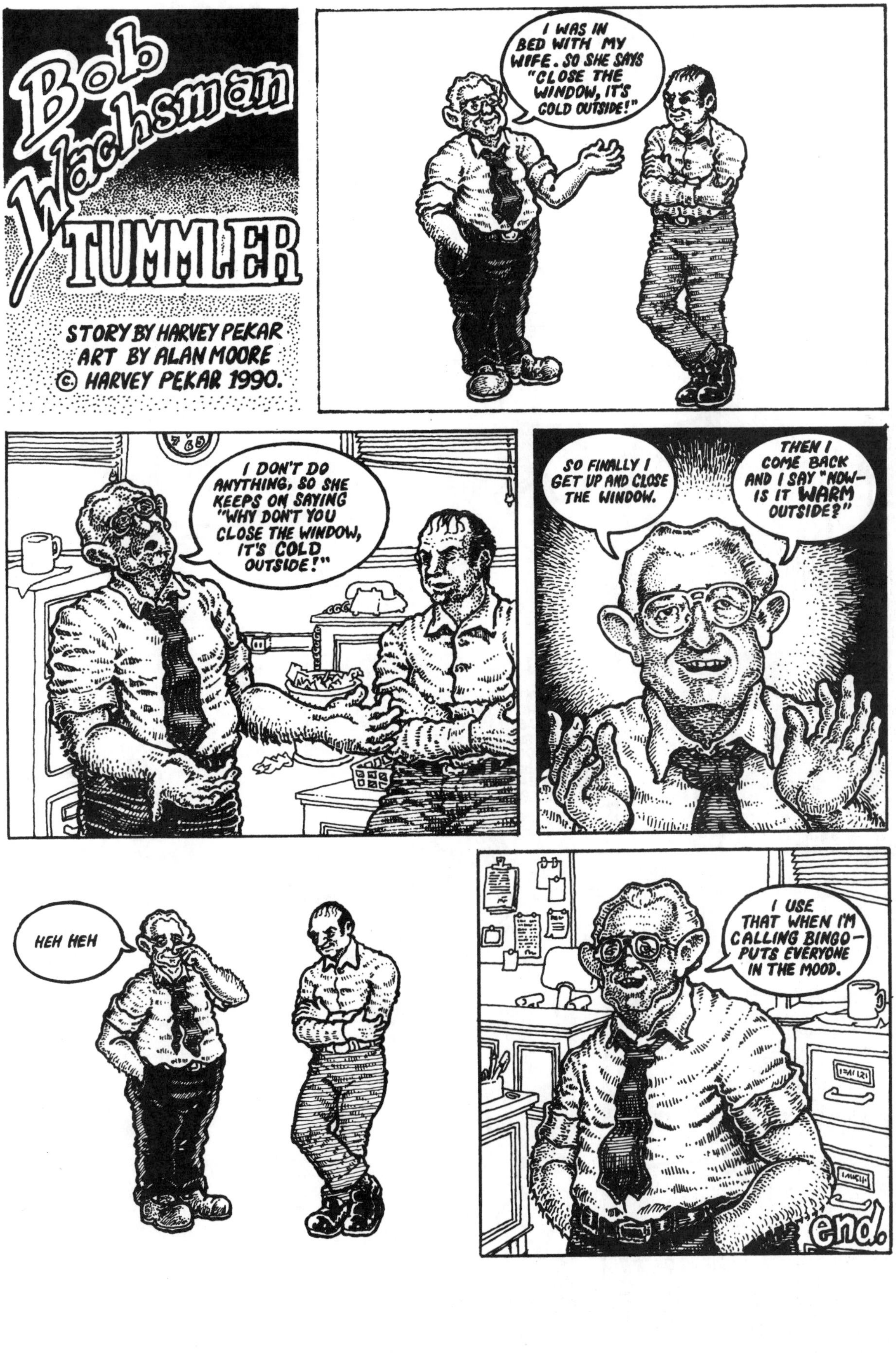
Bob Wachsman
TUMMLER
STORY BY HARVEY PEKAR
ART BY ALAN MOORE
© HARVEY PEKAR 1990.
I WAS IN BED WITH MY WIFE. SO SHE SAYS "CLOSE THE WINDOW, IT'S COLD OUTSIDE!"
I DON'T DO ANYTHING, SO SHE KEEPS ON SAYING "WHY DON'T YOU CLOSE THE WINDOW, IT'S COLD OUTSIDE!"
SO FINALLY I GET UP AND CLOSE THE WINDOW.
THEN I COME BACK AND I SAY "NOW- IS IT WARM OUTSIDE?"
HEH HEH
I USE THAT WHEN I'M CALLING BINGO- PUTS EVERYONE IN THE MOOD.
end.

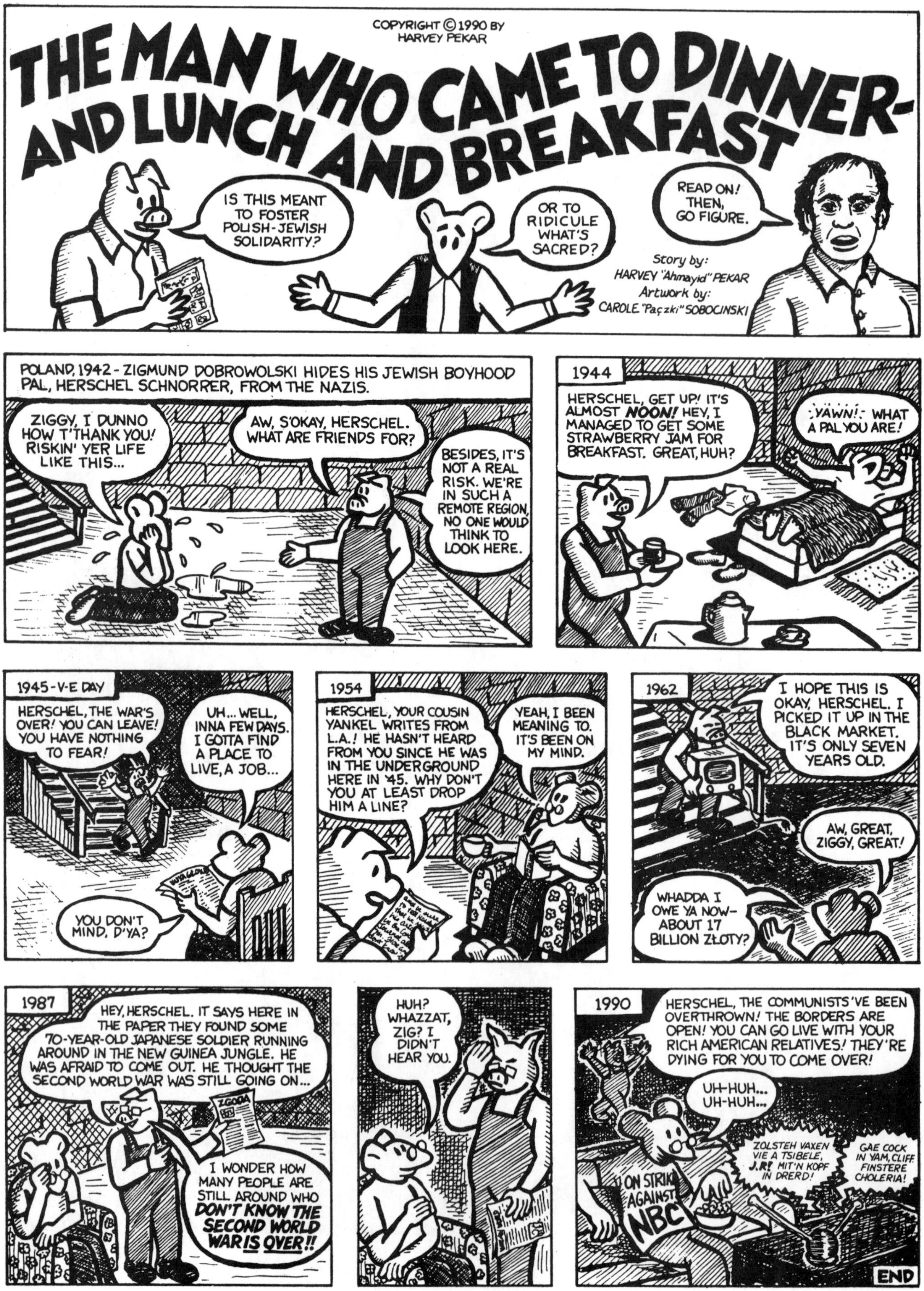
COPYRIGHT © 1990 BY
HARVEY PEKAR
THE MAN WHO CAME TO DINNER- AND LUNCH AND BREAKFAST
IS THIS MEANT TO FOSTER POLISH-JEWISH SOLIDARITY?
OR TO RIDICULE WHAT'S SACRED?
READ ON! THEN, GO FIGURE.
Story by:
HARVEY "Ahmayid" PEKAR
Artwork by:
CAROLE "Pa̧czki" SOBOCINSKI
POLAND, 1942 - ZIGMUND DOBROWOLSKI HIDES HIS JEWISH BOYHOOD PAL, HERSCHEL SCHNORRER, FROM THE NAZIS.
ZIGGY, I DUNNO HOW T'THANK YOU! RISKIN' YER LIFE LIKE THIS...
AW, S'OKAY, HERSCHEL. WHAT ARE FRIENDS FOR?
BESIDES, IT'S NOT A REAL RISK. WE'RE IN SUCH A REMOTE REGION, NO ONE WOULD THINK TO LOOK HERE.
1944
HERSCHEL, GET UP! IT'S ALMOST NOON! HEY, I MANAGED TO GET SOME STRAWBERRY JAM FOR BREAKFAST. GREAT, HUH?
:YAWN!: WHAT A PAL YOU ARE!
1945 - V-E DAY
HERSCHEL, THE WAR'S OVER! YOU CAN LEAVE! YOU HAVE NOTHING TO FEAR!
UH... WELL, INNA FEW DAYS. I GOTTA FIND A PLACE TO LIVE, A JOB...
YOU DON'T MIND, D'YA?
1954
HERSCHEL, YOUR COUSIN YANKEL WRITES FROM L.A.! HE HASN'T HEARD FROM YOU SINCE HE WAS IN THE UNDERGROUND HERE IN '45. WHY DON'T YOU AT LEAST DROP HIM A LINE?
YEAH, I BEEN MEANING TO. IT'S BEEN ON MY MIND.
1962
I HOPE THIS IS OKAY, HERSCHEL. I PICKED IT UP IN THE BLACK MARKET. IT'S ONLY SEVEN YEARS OLD.
AW, GREAT, ZIGGY, GREAT!
WHADDA I OWE YA NOW- ABOUT 17 BILLION ZŁOTY?
1987
HEY, HERSCHEL. IT SAYS HERE IN THE PAPER THEY FOUND SOME 70-YEAR-OLD JAPANESE SOLDIER RUNNING AROUND IN THE NEW GUINEA JUNGLE. HE WAS AFRAID TO COME OUT. HE THOUGHT THE SECOND WORLD WAR WAS STILL GOING ON...
ZGODA
I WONDER HOW MANY PEOPLE ARE STILL AROUND WHO DON'T KNOW THE SECOND WORLD WAR IS OVER!!
HUH? WHAZZAT, ZIG? I DIDN'T HEAR YOU.
1990
HERSCHEL, THE COMMUNISTS'VE BEEN OVERTHROWN! THE BORDERS ARE OPEN! YOU CAN GO LIVE WITH YOUR RICH AMERICAN RELATIVES! THEY'RE DYING FOR YOU TO COME OVER!
UH-HUH... UH-HUH...
ON STRIKE AGAINST NBC
ZOLSTEH VAXEN VIE A TSIBELE, J.R! MIT'N KOPF IN DRERD!
GAE COCK IN YAM, CLIFF. FINSTERE CHOLERIA!
END

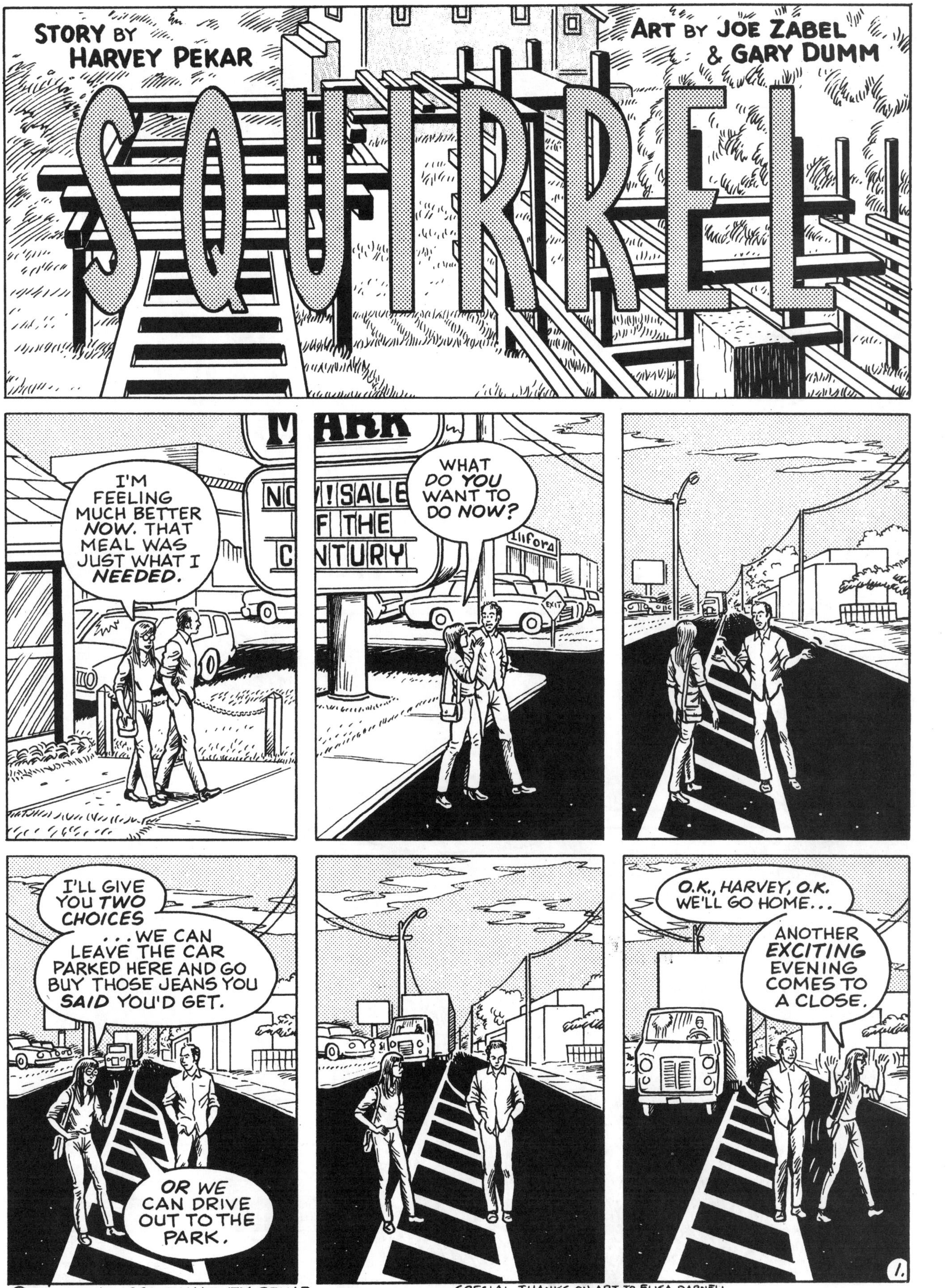
STORY BY
HARVEY PEKAR
ART BY JOE ZABEL
& GARY DUMM
SQUIRREL
I'M FEELING MUCH BETTER NOW. THAT MEAL WAS JUST WHAT I NEEDED.
NOW! SALE OF THE CENTURY
WHAT DO YOU WANT TO DO NOW?
EXIT
I'LL GIVE YOU TWO CHOICES
. . . WE CAN LEAVE THE CAR PARKED HERE AND GO BUY THOSE JEANS YOU SAID YOU'D GET.
OR WE CAN DRIVE OUT TO THE PARK.
O.K., HARVEY, O.K. WE'LL GO HOME...
ANOTHER EXCITING EVENING COMES TO A CLOSE.
1.

SPECIAL THANKS ON ART TO ELISA DARNELL

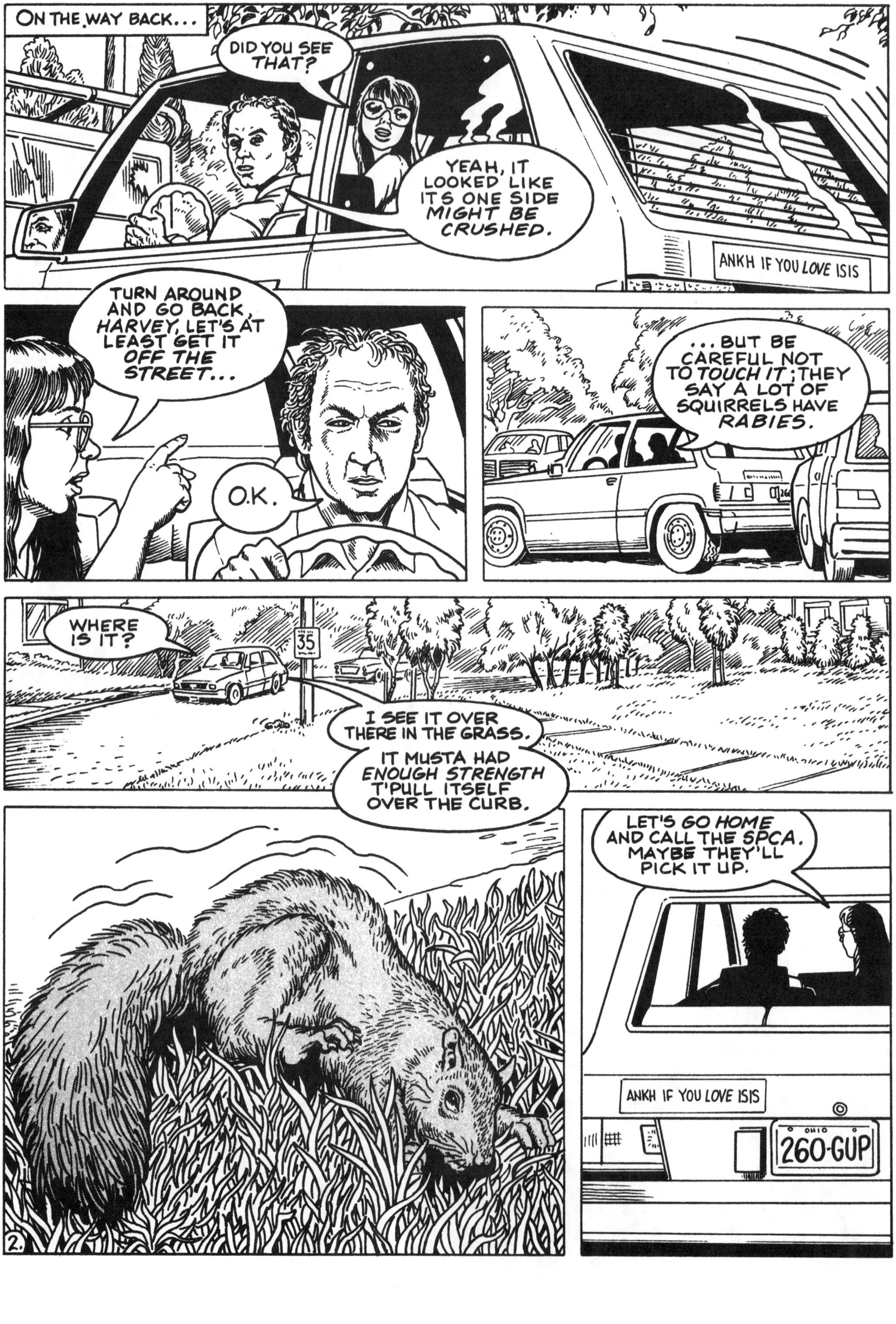
ON THE WAY BACK...
DID YOU SEE THAT?
YEAH, IT LOOKED LIKE IT'S ONE SIDE MIGHT BE CRUSHED.
ANKH IF YOU LOVE ISIS
TURN AROUND AND GO BACK, HARVEY, LET'S AT LEAST GET IT OFF THE STREET...
O.K.
...BUT BE CAREFUL NOT TO TOUCH IT; THEY SAY A LOT OF SQUIRRELS HAVE RABIES.
WHERE IS IT?
35
I SEE IT OVER THERE IN THE GRASS.
IT MUSTA HAD ENOUGH STRENGTH T'PULL ITSELF OVER THE CURB.
LET'S GO HOME AND CALL THE SPCA. MAYBE THEY'LL PICK IT UP.
ANKH IF YOU LOVE ISIS
OHIO
260-GUP

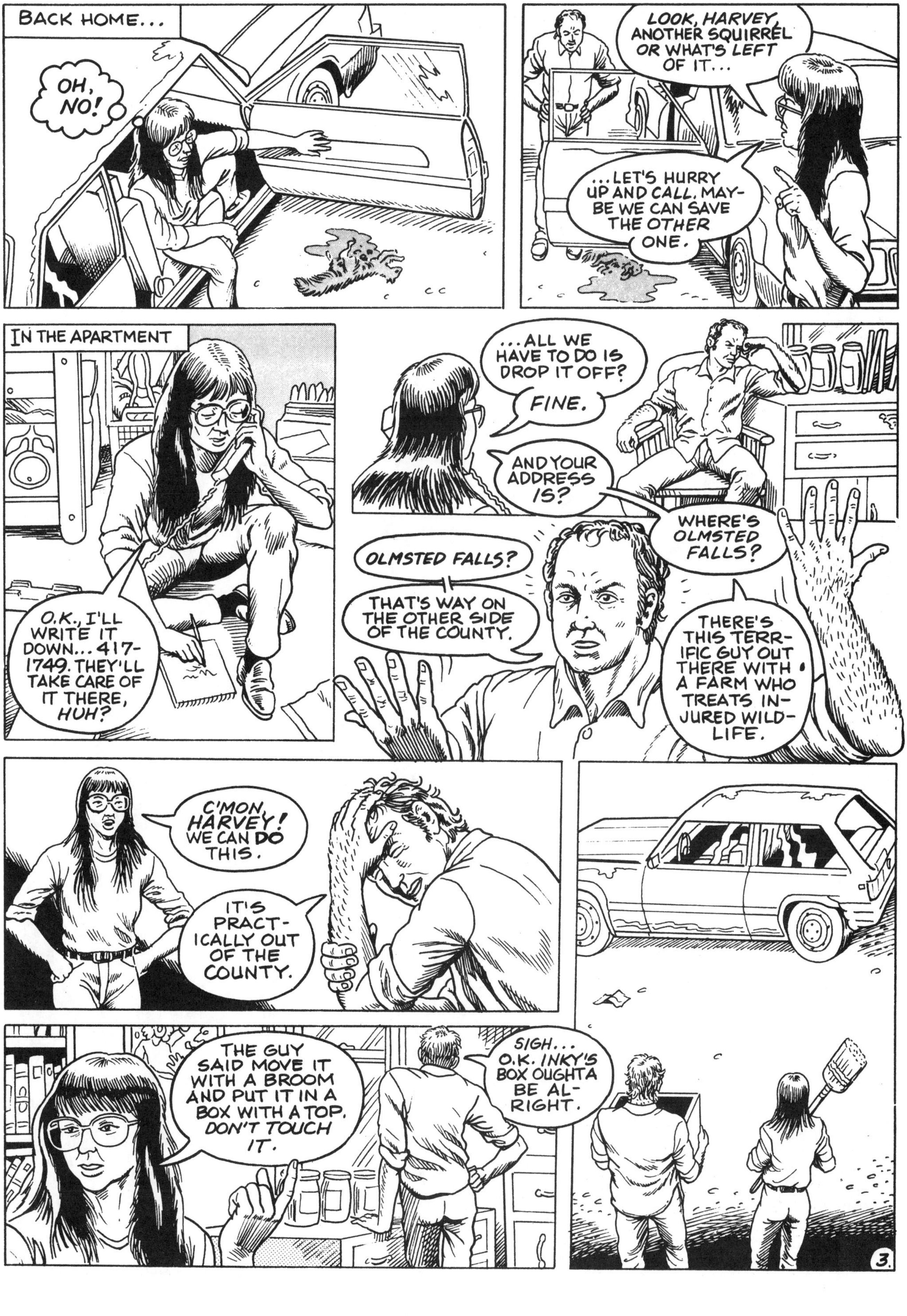
BACK HOME...
OH, NO!
LOOK, HARVEY, ANOTHER SQUIRREL OR WHAT'S LEFT OF IT...
...LET'S HURRY UP AND CALL. MAY-BE WE CAN SAVE THE OTHER ONE.
IN THE APARTMENT
O.K., I'LL WRITE IT DOWN... 417-1749. THEY'LL TAKE CARE OF IT THERE, HUH?
...ALL WE HAVE TO DO IS DROP IT OFF?
FINE.
AND YOUR ADDRESS IS?
WHERE'S OLMSTED FALLS?
OLMSTED FALLS?
THAT'S WAY ON THE OTHER SIDE OF THE COUNTY.
THERE'S THIS TERR-IFIC GUY OUT THERE WITH A FARM WHO TREATS IN-JURED WILD-LIFE.
C'MON, HARVEY! WE CAN DO THIS.
IT'S PRACT-ICALLY OUT OF THE COUNTY.
THE GUY SAID MOVE IT WITH A BROOM AND PUT IT IN A BOX WITH A TOP. DON'T TOUCH IT.
SIGH... O.K. INKY'S BOX OUGHTA BE AL-RIGHT.
3.

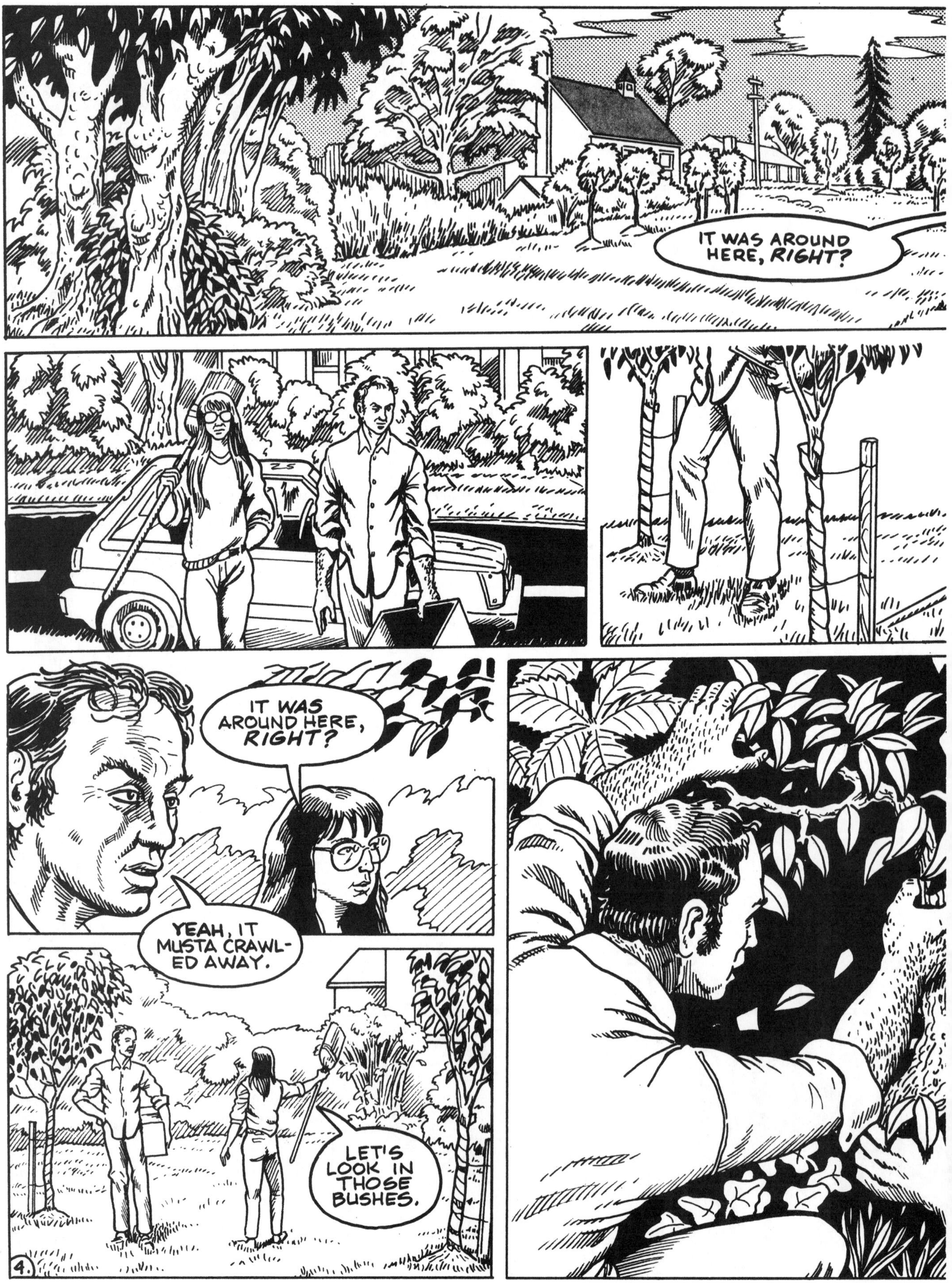
IT WAS AROUND HERE, RIGHT?
IT WAS AROUND HERE, RIGHT?
YEAH, IT MUSTA CRAWL-ED AWAY.
LET'S LOOK IN THOSE BUSHES.

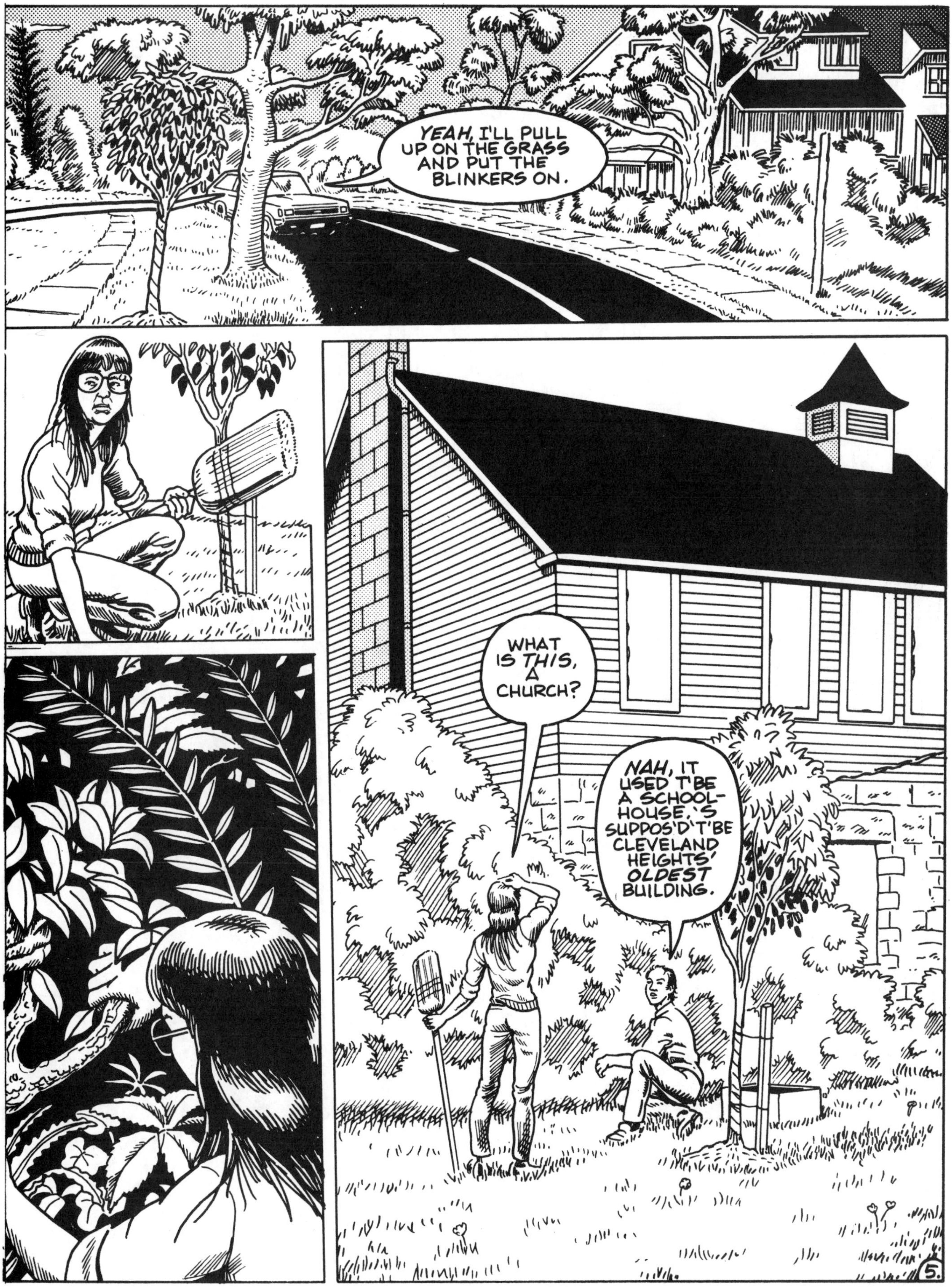
YEAH, I'LL PULL UP ON THE GRASS AND PUT THE BLINKERS ON.
WHAT IS THIS, A CHURCH?
NAH, IT USED T'BE A SCHOOL-HOUSE. 'S SUPPOS'D T'BE CLEVELAND HEIGHTS' OLDEST BUILDING.

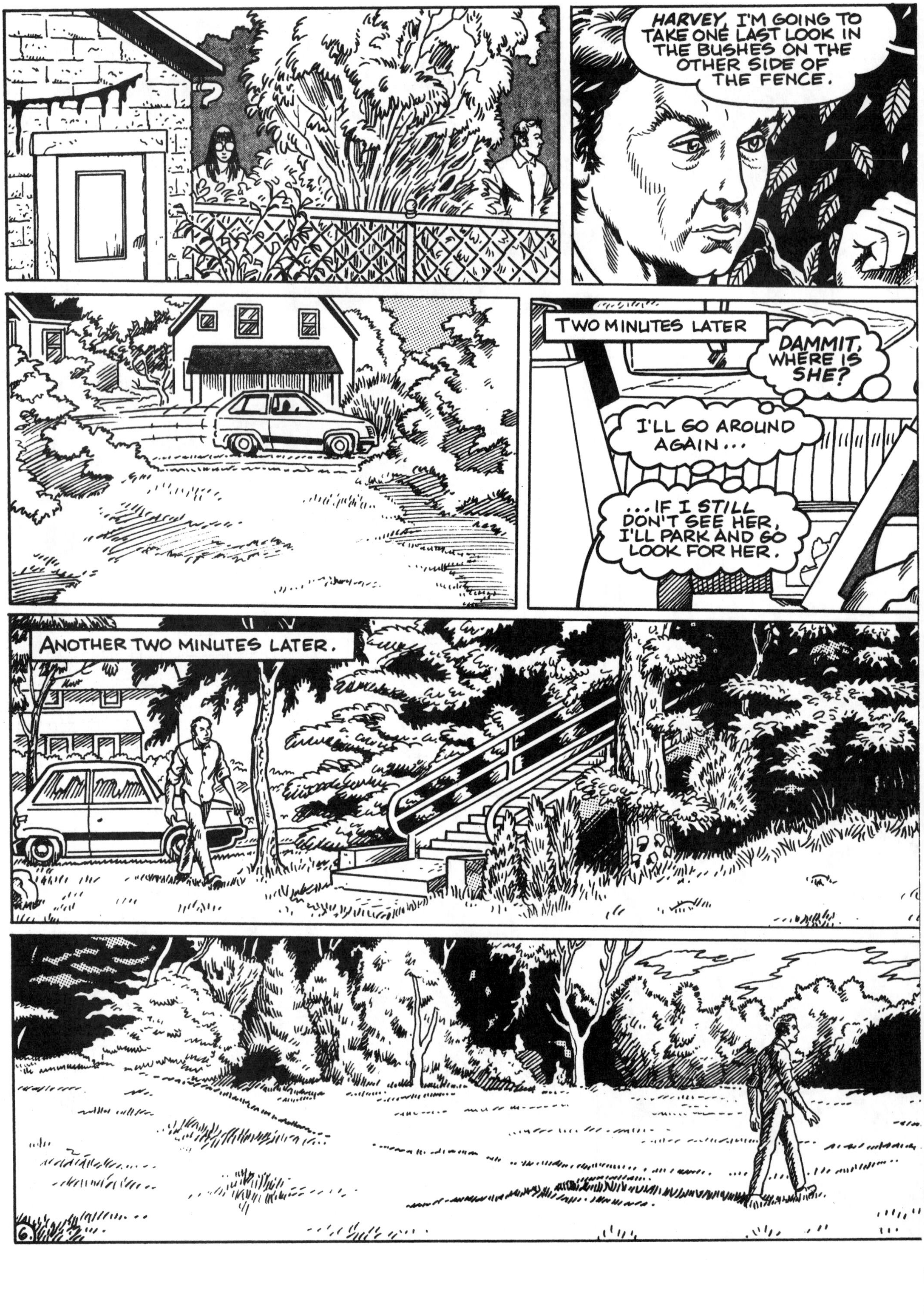
HARVEY, I'M GOING TO TAKE ONE LAST LOOK IN THE BUSHES ON THE OTHER SIDE OF THE FENCE.
TWO MINUTES LATER
DAMMIT, WHERE IS SHE?
I'LL GO AROUND AGAIN...
...IF I STILL DON'T SEE HER, I'LL PARK AND GO LOOK FOR HER.
ANOTHER TWO MINUTES LATER.

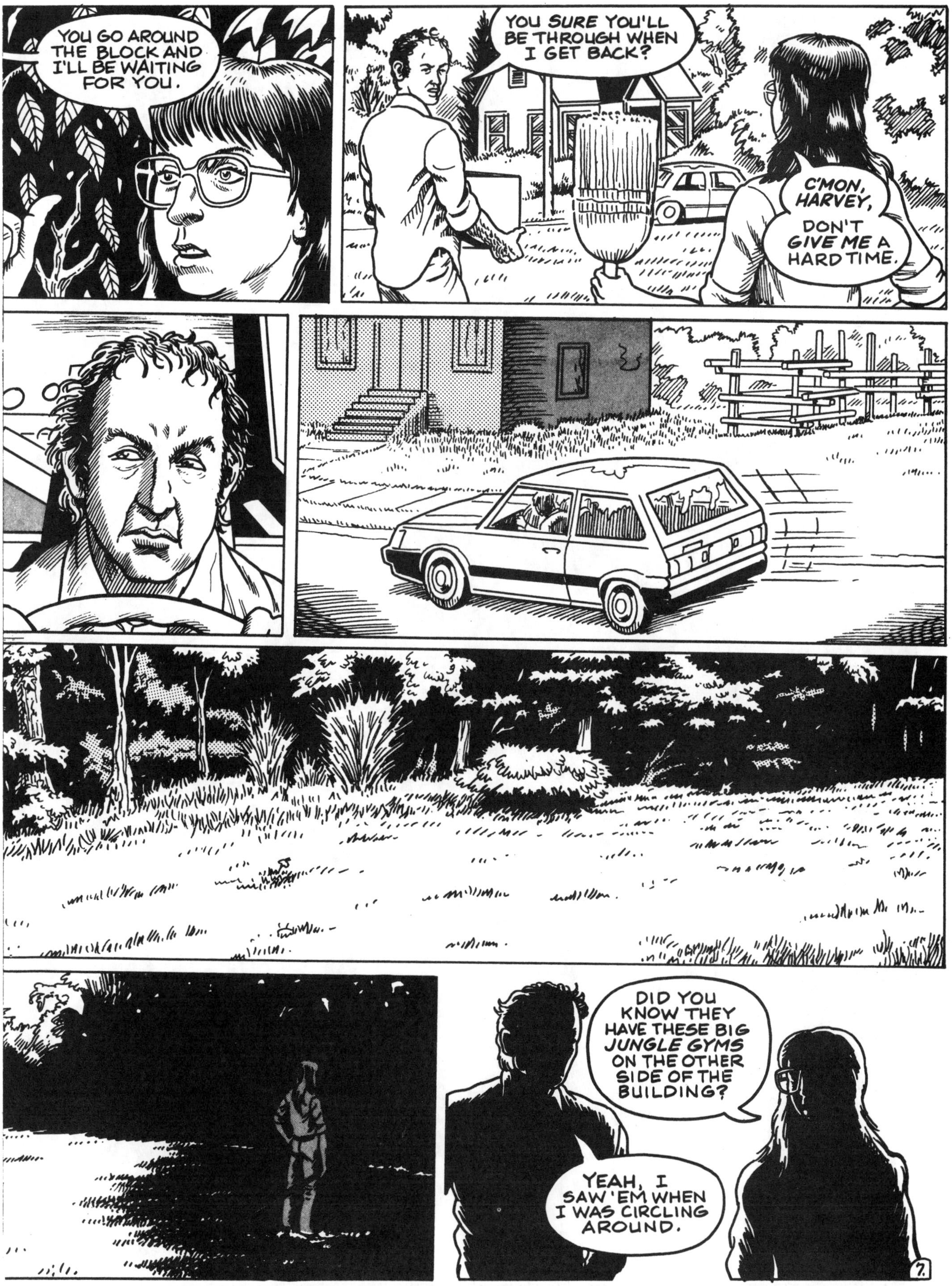
YOU GO AROUND THE BLOCK AND I'LL BE WAITING FOR YOU.
YOU SURE YOU'LL BE THROUGH WHEN I GET BACK?
C'MON, HARVEY,
DON'T GIVE ME A HARD TIME.
DID YOU KNOW THEY HAVE THESE BIG JUNGLE GYMS ON THE OTHER SIDE OF THE BUILDING?
YEAH, I SAW 'EM WHEN I WAS CIRCLING AROUND.
7.

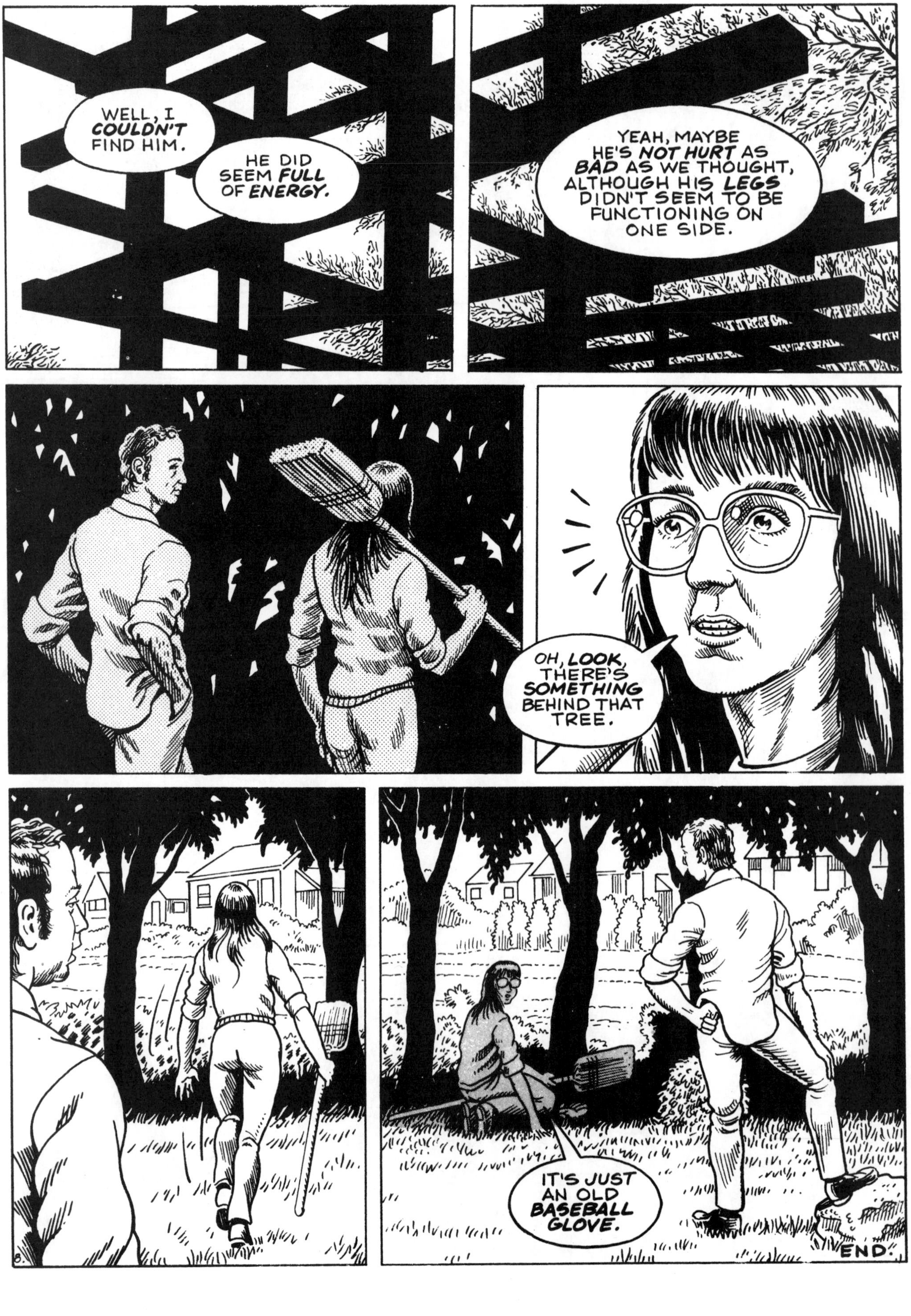
WELL, I COULDN'T FIND HIM.
HE DID SEEM FULL OF ENERGY.
YEAH, MAYBE HE'S NOT HURT AS BAD AS WE THOUGHT, ALTHOUGH HIS LEGS DIDN'T SEEM TO BE FUNCTIONING ON ONE SIDE.
OH, LOOK, THERE'S SOMETHING BEHIND THAT TREE.
IT'S JUST AN OLD BASEBALL GLOVE.
END.

WOUNDED IN ACTION

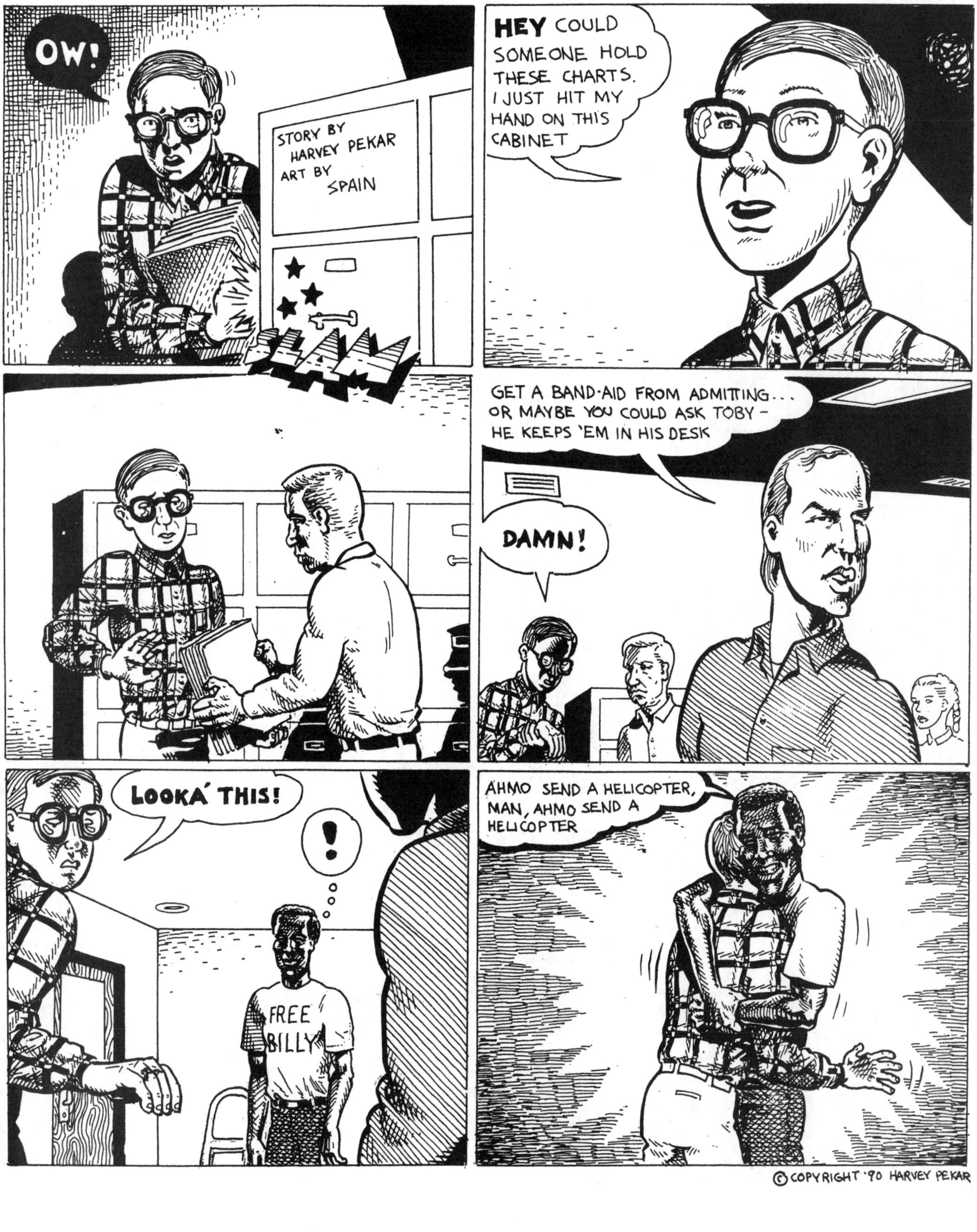
OW!
STORY BY HARVEY PEKAR ART BY SPAIN
SLAM
HEY COULD SOMEONE HOLD THESE CHARTS. I JUST HIT MY HAND ON THIS CABINET
GET A BAND-AID FROM ADMITTING... OR MAYBE YOU COULD ASK TOBY - HE KEEPS 'EM IN HIS DESK
DAMN!
LOOKA' THIS!
!
FREE BILLY
AHMO SEND A HELICOPTER, MAN, AHMO SEND A HELICOPTER

WEEKEND

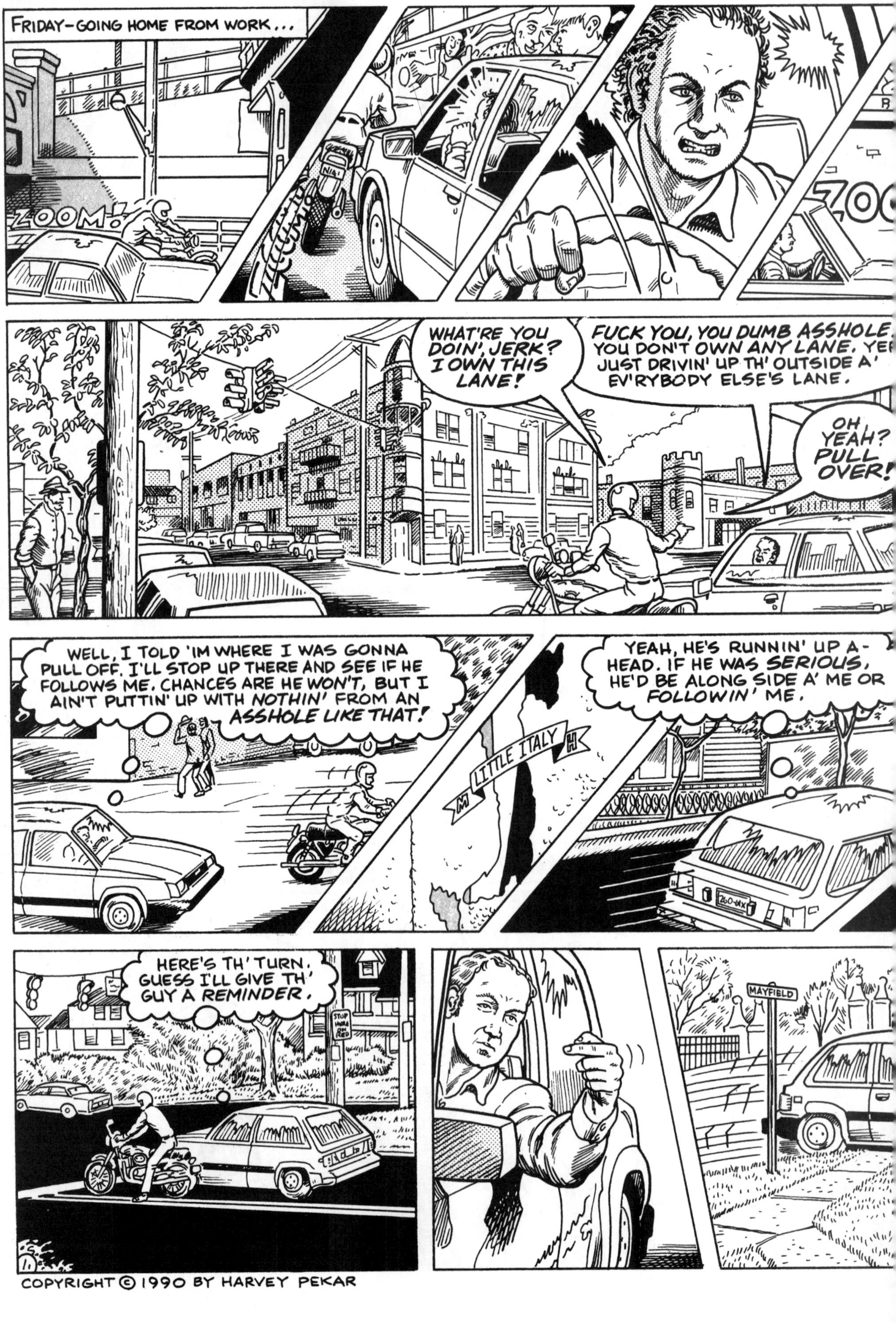
FRIDAY–GOING HOME FROM WORK...
ZOOM!
WHAT'RE YOU DOIN', JERK? I OWN THIS LANE!
FUCK YOU, YOU DUMB ASSHOLE. YOU DON'T OWN ANY LANE. YE
JUST DRIVIN' UP TH' OUTSIDE A' EV'RYBODY ELSE'S LANE.
OH YEAH? PULL OVER!
WELL, I TOLD 'IM WHERE I WAS GONNA PULL OFF. I'LL STOP UP THERE AND SEE IF HE FOLLOWS ME. CHANCES ARE HE WON'T, BUT I AIN'T PUTTIN' UP WITH NOTHIN' FROM AN ASSHOLE LIKE THAT!
LITTLE ITALY
YEAH, HE'S RUNNIN' UP A-HEAD. IF HE WAS SERIOUS, HE'D BE ALONG SIDE A' ME OR FOLLOWIN' ME.
HERE'S TH' TURN. GUESS I'LL GIVE TH' GUY A REMINDER.
MAYFIELD

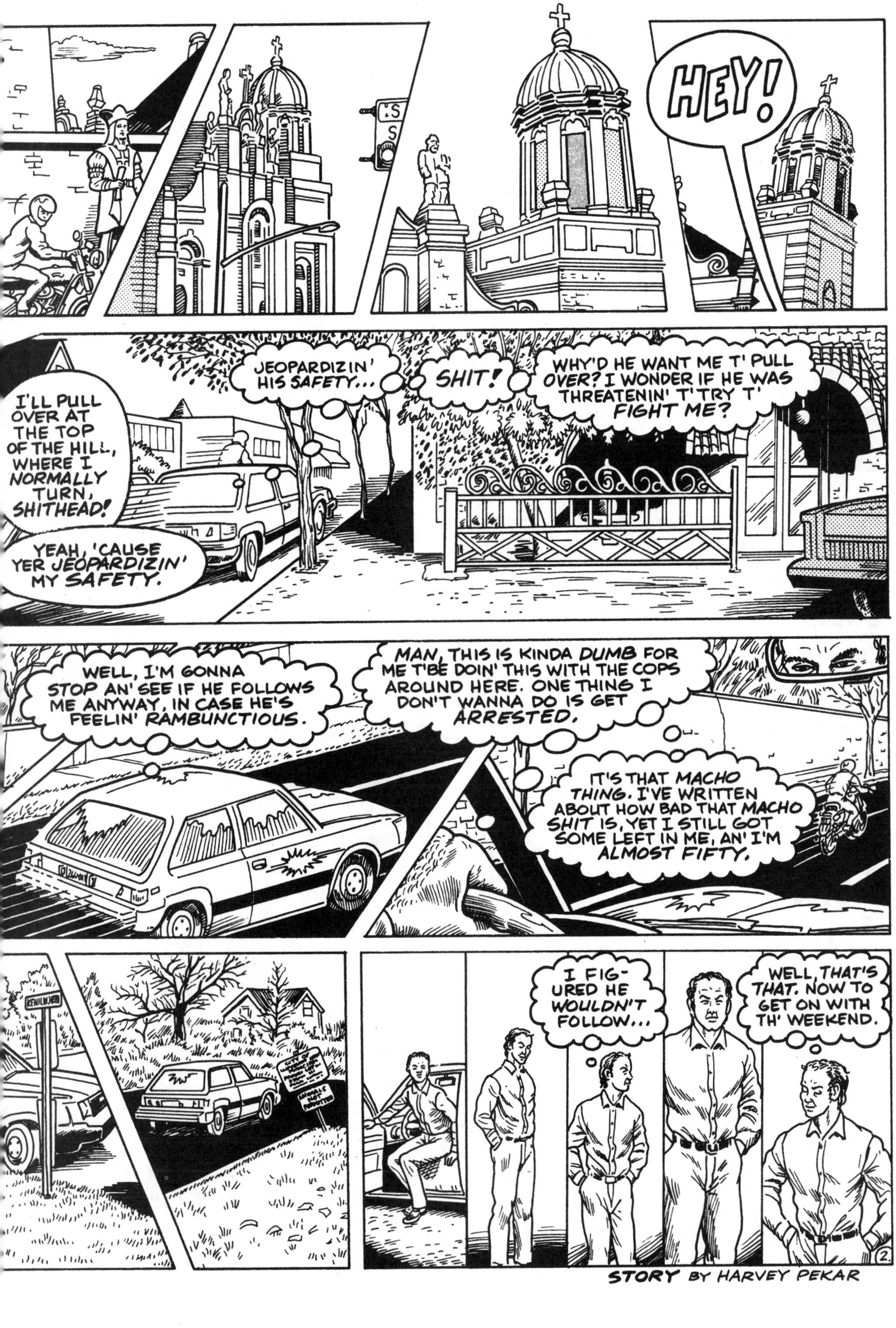
HEY!
I'LL PULL OVER AT THE TOP OF THE HILL, WHERE I NORMALLY TURN, SHITHEAD!
YEAH, 'CAUSE YER JEOPARDIZIN' MY SAFETY.
JEOPARDIZIN' HIS SAFETY...
SHIT!
WHY'D HE WANT ME T' PULL OVER? I WONDER IF HE WAS THREATENIN' T' TRY T' FIGHT ME?
WELL, I'M GONNA STOP AN' SEE IF HE FOLLOWS ME ANYWAY, IN CASE HE'S FEELIN' RAMBUNCTIOUS.
MAN, THIS IS KINDA DUMB FOR ME T'BE DOIN' THIS WITH THE COPS AROUND HERE. ONE THING I DON'T WANNA DO IS GET ARRESTED.
IT'S THAT MACHO THING. I'VE WRITTEN ABOUT HOW BAD THAT MACHO SHIT IS, YET I STILL GOT SOME LEFT IN ME, AN' I'M ALMOST FIFTY.
I FIGURED HE WOULDN'T FOLLOW...
WELL, THAT'S THAT. NOW TO GET ON WITH TH' WEEKEND.

STORY BY HARVEY PEKAR

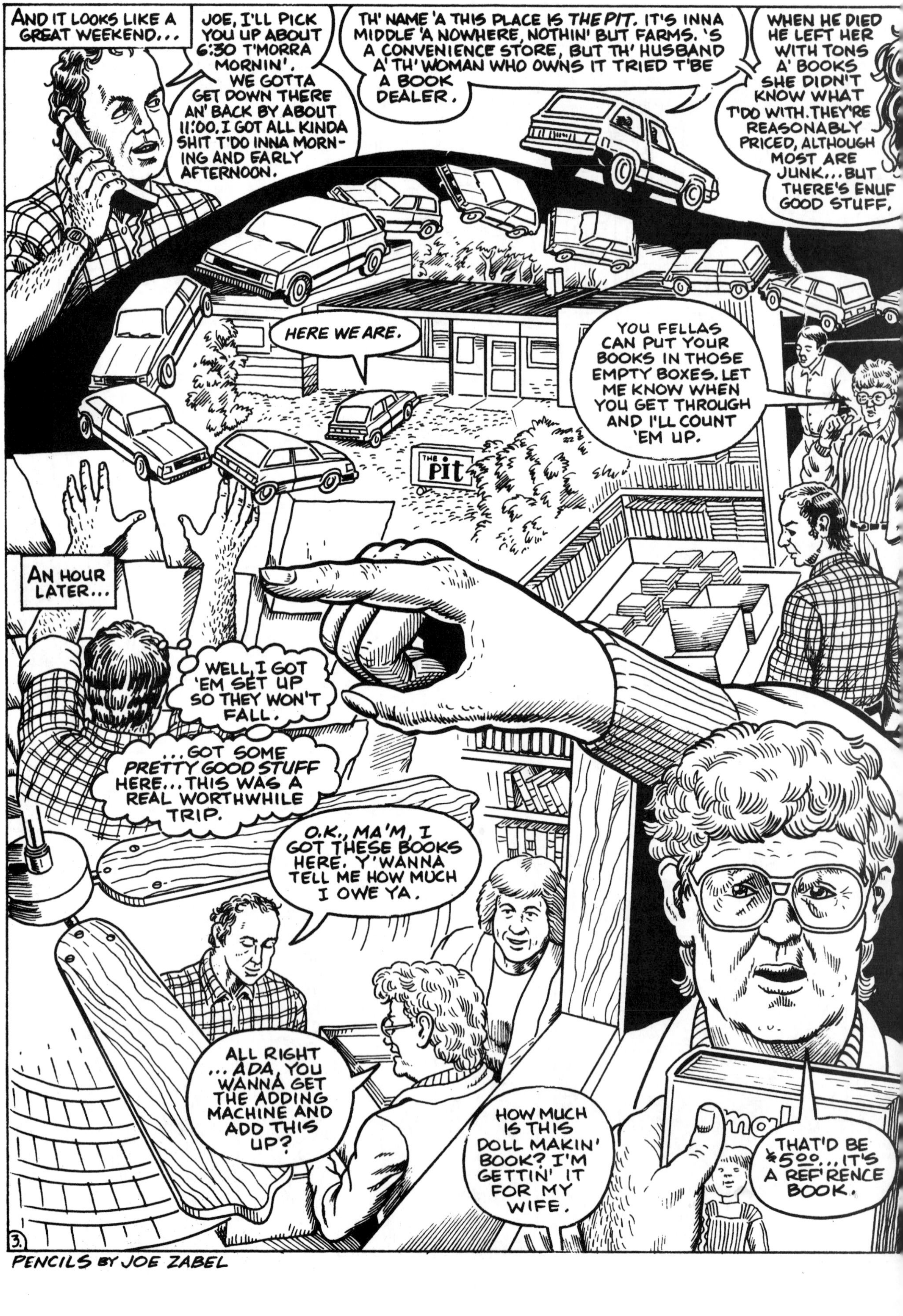
AND IT LOOKS LIKE A GREAT WEEKEND...
JOE, I'LL PICK YOU UP ABOUT 6:30 T'MORRA MORNIN'. WE GOTTA GET DOWN THERE AN' BACK BY ABOUT 11:00. I GOT ALL KINDA SHIT T'DO INNA MORNING AND EARLY AFTERNOON.
TH' NAME 'A THIS PLACE IS THE PIT. IT'S INNA MIDDLE 'A NOWHERE, NOTHIN' BUT FARMS. 'S A CONVENIENCE STORE, BUT TH' HUSBAND A'TH' WOMAN WHO OWNS IT TRIED T'BE A BOOK DEALER.
WHEN HE DIED HE LEFT HER WITH TONS A' BOOKS SHE DIDN'T KNOW WHAT T'DO WITH. THEY'RE REASONABLY PRICED, ALTHOUGH MOST ARE JUNK... BUT THERE'S ENUF GOOD STUFF.
HERE WE ARE.
THE PIT
YOU FELLAS CAN PUT YOUR BOOKS IN THOSE EMPTY BOXES. LET ME KNOW WHEN YOU GET THROUGH AND I'LL COUNT 'EM UP.
AN HOUR LATER...
WELL, I GOT 'EM SET UP SO THEY WON'T FALL.
...GOT SOME PRETTY GOOD STUFF HERE... THIS WAS A REAL WORTHWHILE TRIP.
O.K., MA'M, I GOT THESE BOOKS HERE. Y'WANNA TELL ME HOW MUCH I OWE YA.
ALL RIGHT ...ADA, YOU WANNA GET THE ADDING MACHINE AND ADD THIS UP?
HOW MUCH IS THIS DOLL MAKIN' BOOK? I'M GETTIN' IT FOR MY WIFE.
THAT'D BE $5.00... IT'S A REF'RENCE BOOK.
3.

PENCILS BY JOE ZABEL

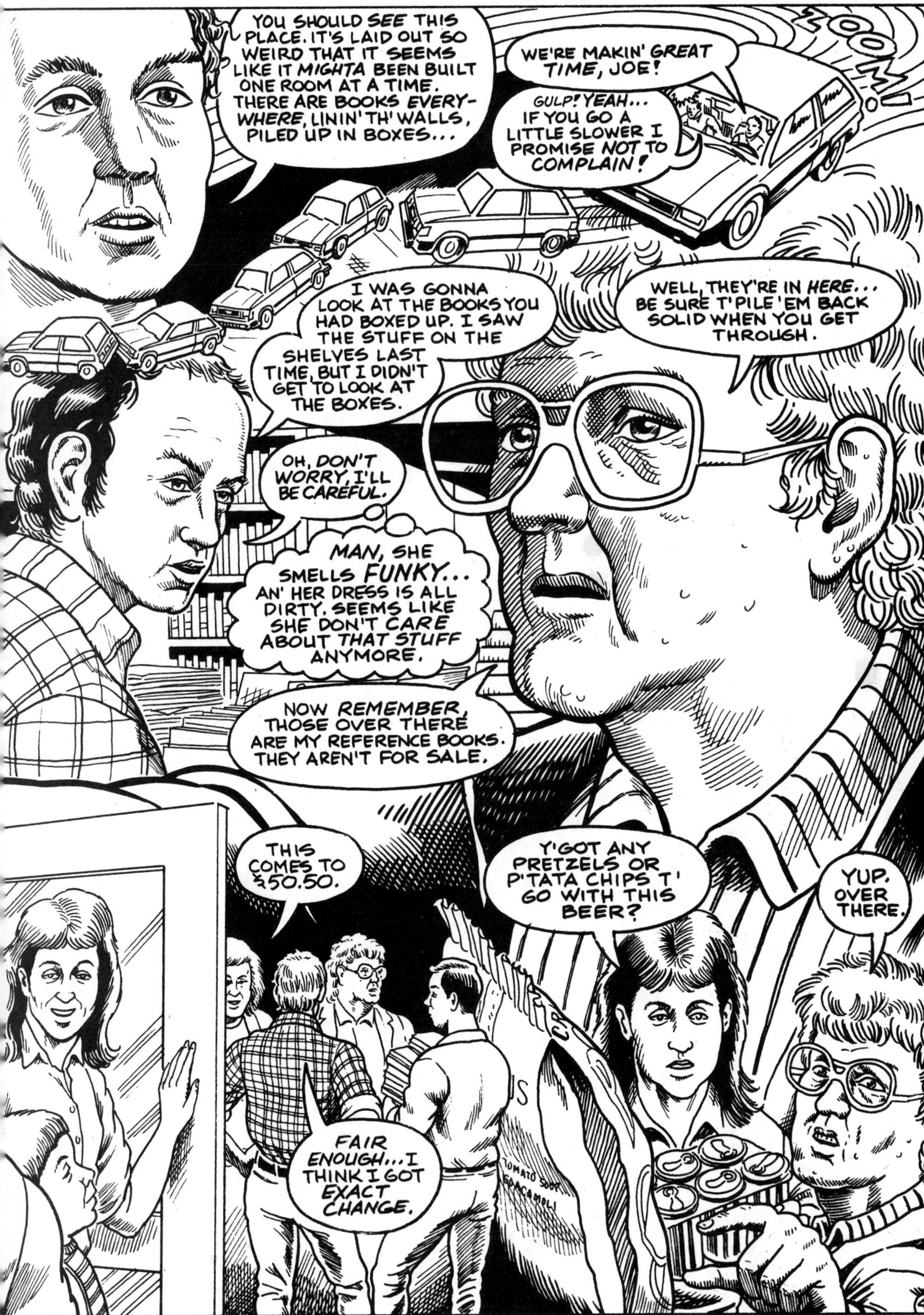
YOU SHOULD SEE THIS PLACE. IT'S LAID OUT SO WEIRD THAT IT SEEMS LIKE IT MIGHTA BEEN BUILT ONE ROOM AT A TIME. THERE ARE BOOKS EVERY-WHERE, LININ' TH' WALLS, PILED UP IN BOXES...
WE'RE MAKIN' GREAT TIME, JOE!
ZOOOM
GULP! YEAH... IF YOU GO A LITTLE SLOWER I PROMISE NOT TO COMPLAIN!
I WAS GONNA LOOK AT THE BOOKS YOU HAD BOXED UP. I SAW THE STUFF ON THE SHELVES LAST TIME, BUT I DIDN'T GET TO LOOK AT THE BOXES.
WELL, THEY'RE IN HERE... BE SURE T'PILE 'EM BACK SOLID WHEN YOU GET THROUGH.
OH, DON'T WORRY, I'LL BE CAREFUL.
MAN, SHE SMELLS FUNKY... AN' HER DRESS IS ALL DIRTY. SEEMS LIKE SHE DON'T CARE ABOUT THAT STUFF ANYMORE.
NOW REMEMBER, THOSE OVER THERE ARE MY REFERENCE BOOKS. THEY AREN'T FOR SALE.
THIS COMES TO $50.50.
Y'GOT ANY PRETZELS OR P'TATA CHIPS T' GO WITH THIS BEER?
YUP. OVER THERE.
FAIR ENOUGH... I THINK I GOT EXACT CHANGE.
TOMATO SOUP
GUACAMOLI
4.

INKS & LETTERS BY GARY DUMM

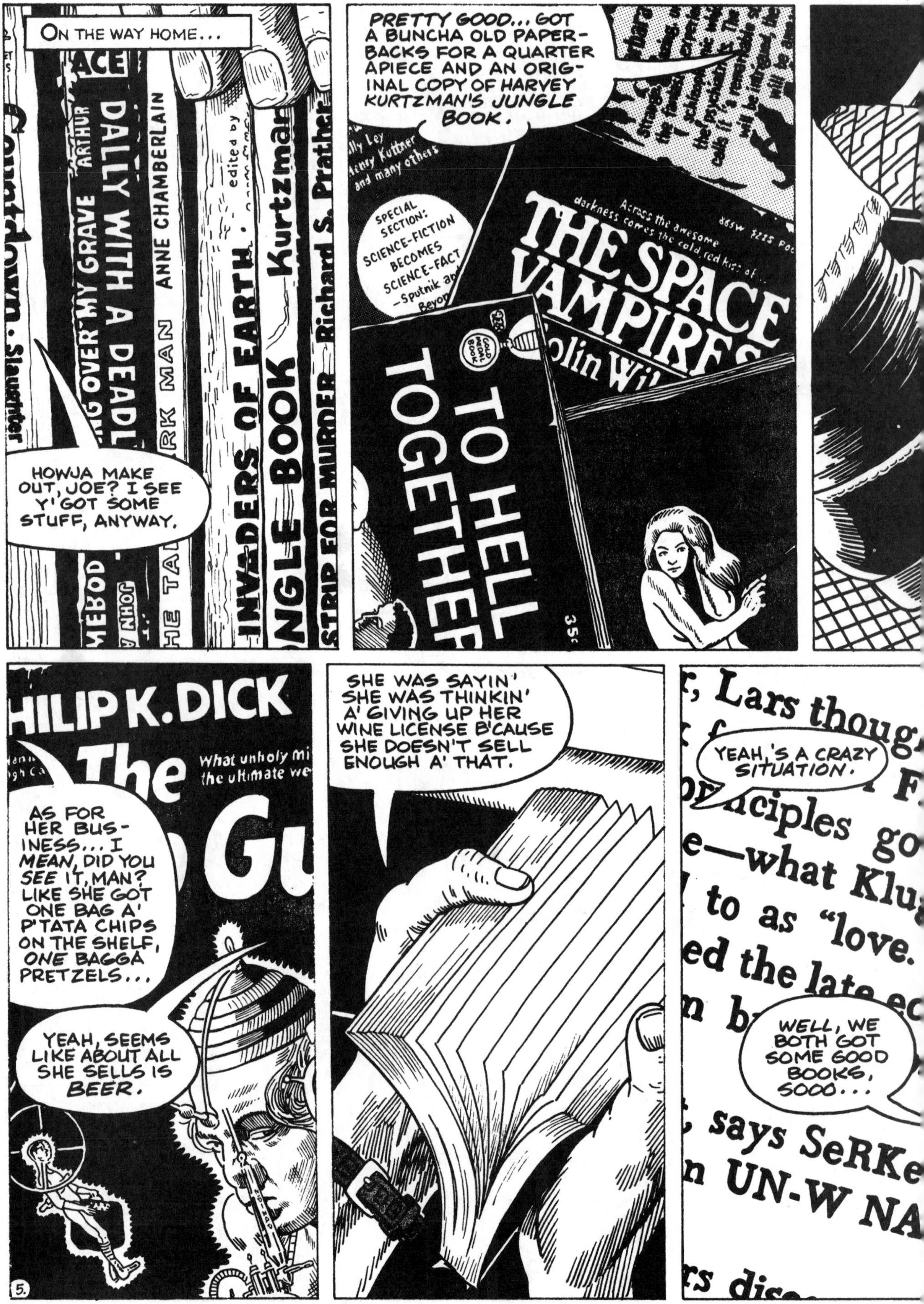
ON THE WAY HOME...
HOWJA MAKE OUT, JOE? I SEE Y'GOT SOME STUFF, ANYWAY.
PRETTY GOOD... GOT A BUNCHA OLD PAPERBACKS FOR A QUARTER APIECE AND AN ORIGINAL COPY OF HARVEY KURTZMAN'S JUNGLE BOOK.
AS FOR HER BUSINESS... I MEAN, DID YOU SEE IT, MAN? LIKE SHE GOT ONE BAG A' P'TATA CHIPS ON THE SHELF, ONE BAGGA PRETZELS...
YEAH, SEEMS LIKE ABOUT ALL SHE SELLS IS BEER.
SHE WAS SAYIN' SHE WAS THINKIN' A' GIVING UP HER WINE LICENSE B'CAUSE SHE DOESN'T SELL ENOUGH A' THAT.
YEAH, 'S A CRAZY SITUATION.
WELL, WE BOTH GOT SOME GOOD BOOKS, SOOO...
5.

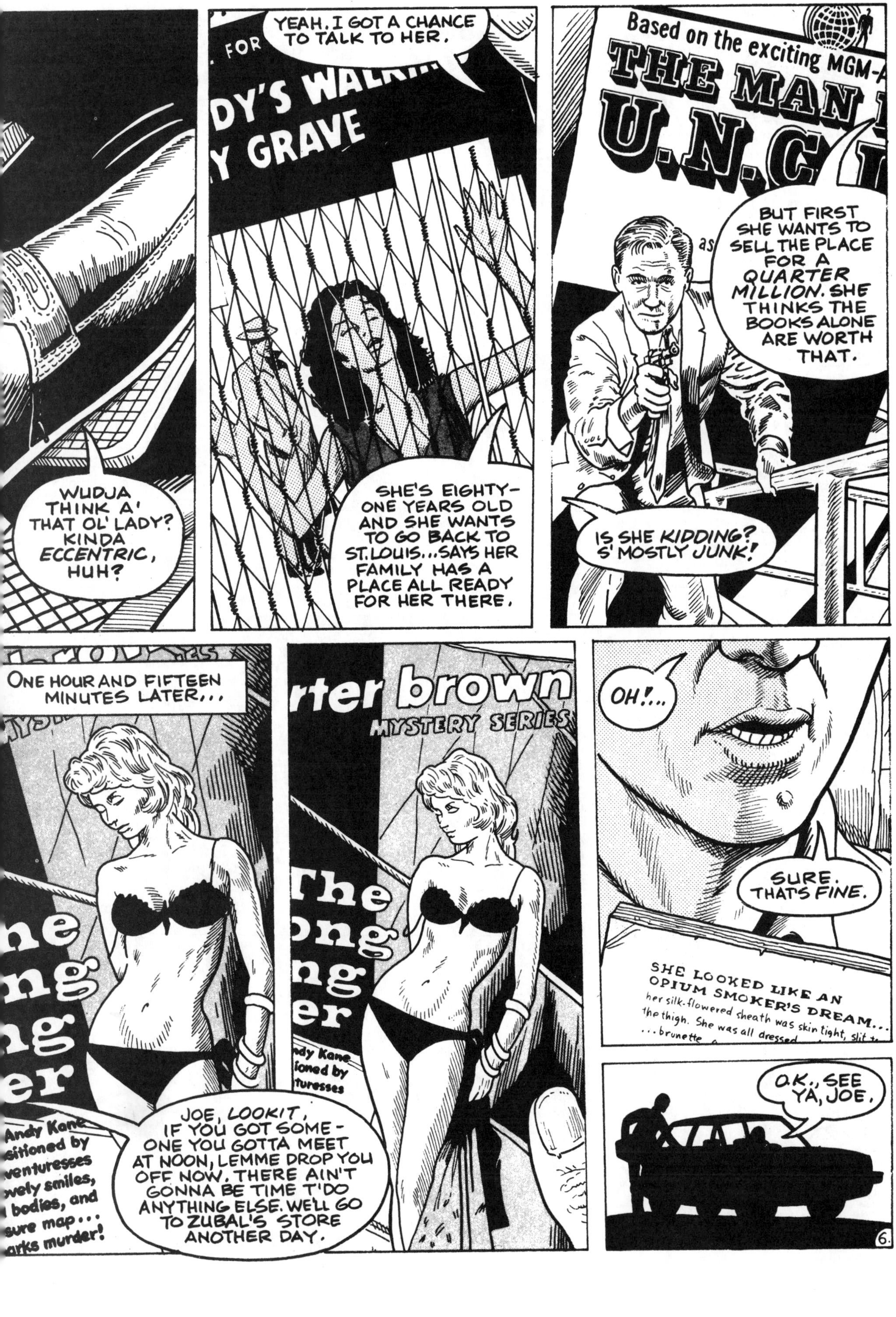
WUDJA THINK A' THAT OL' LADY? KINDA ECCENTRIC, HUH?
YEAH, I GOT A CHANCE TO TALK TO HER.
SHE'S EIGHTY-ONE YEARS OLD AND SHE WANTS TO GO BACK TO ST. LOUIS... SAYS HER FAMILY HAS A PLACE ALL READY FOR HER THERE.
Based on the exciting MGM-A
BUT FIRST SHE WANTS TO SELL THE PLACE FOR A QUARTER MILLION. SHE THINKS THE BOOKS ALONE ARE WORTH THAT.
IS SHE KIDDING? S' MOSTLY JUNK!
ONE HOUR AND FIFTEEN MINUTES LATER...
MYSTERY SERIES
JOE, LOOKIT, IF YOU GOT SOMEONE YOU GOTTA MEET AT NOON, LEMME DROP YOU OFF NOW. THERE AIN'T GONNA BE TIME T'DO ANYTHING ELSE. WE'LL GO TO ZUBAL'S STORE ANOTHER DAY.
OH!...
SURE. THAT'S FINE.
SHE LOOKED LIKE AN OPIUM SMOKER'S DREAM...
her silk-flowered sheath was skin tight, slit to the thigh. She was all dressed
O.K., SEE YA, JOE.

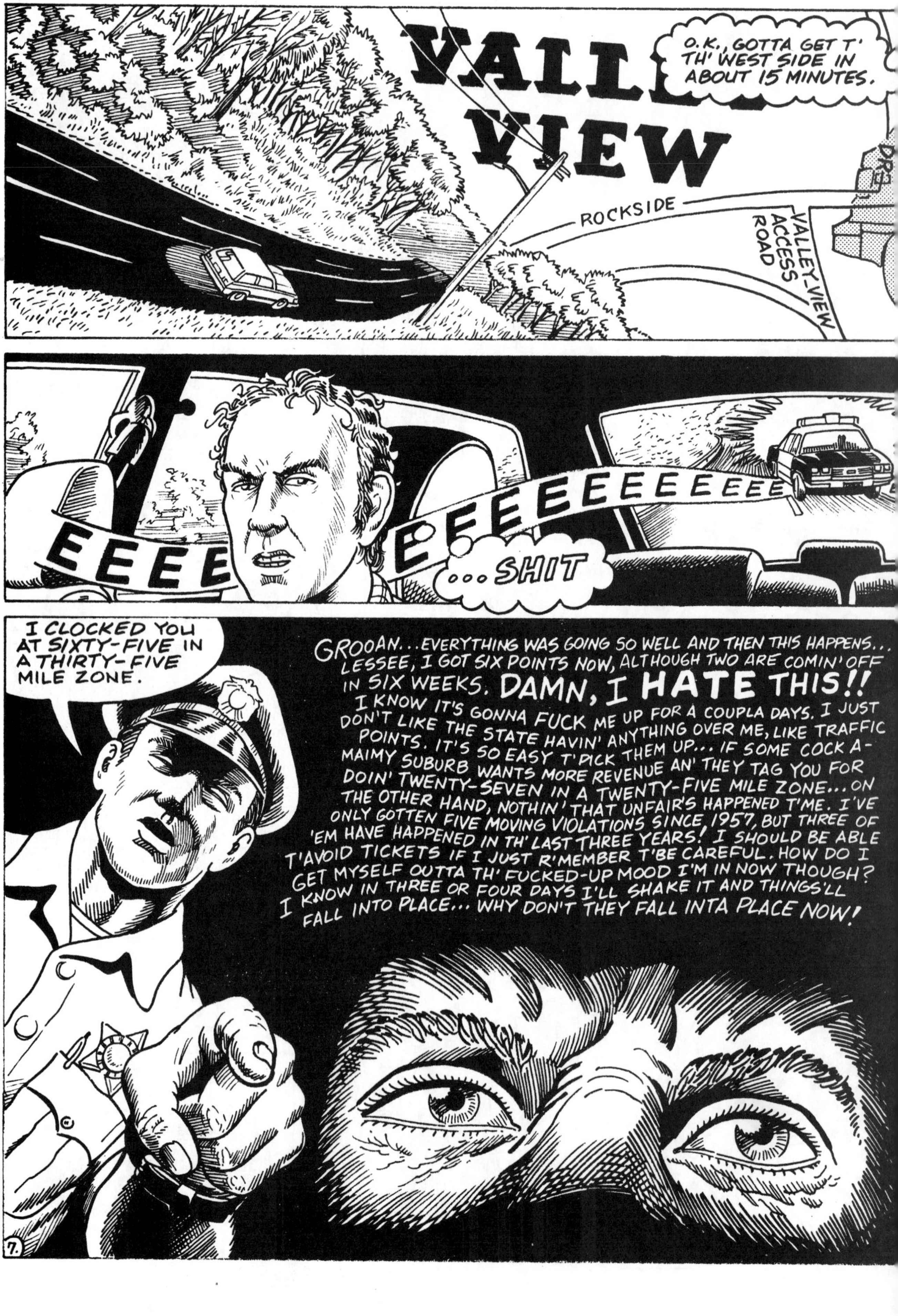
VALLEY VIEW
O.K., GOTTA GET T' TH' WEST SIDE IN ABOUT 15 MINUTES.
ROCKSIDE
VALLEY VIEW ACCESS ROAD
EEEEEEEEEEEEEEEEEEEE
...SHIT
I CLOCKED YOU AT SIXTY-FIVE IN A THIRTY-FIVE MILE ZONE.
GROOAN... EVERYTHING WAS GOING SO WELL AND THEN THIS HAPPENS... LESSEE, I GOT SIX POINTS NOW, ALTHOUGH TWO ARE COMIN' OFF IN SIX WEEKS. DAMN, I HATE THIS!! I KNOW IT'S GONNA FUCK ME UP FOR A COUPLA DAYS. I JUST DON'T LIKE THE STATE HAVIN' ANYTHING OVER ME, LIKE TRAFFIC POINTS. IT'S SO EASY T'PICK THEM UP... IF SOME COCK A-MAIMY SUBURB WANTS MORE REVENUE AN' THEY TAG YOU FOR DOIN' TWENTY-SEVEN IN A TWENTY-FIVE MILE ZONE... ON THE OTHER HAND, NOTHIN' THAT UNFAIR'S HAPPENED T'ME. I'VE ONLY GOTTEN FIVE MOVING VIOLATIONS SINCE 1957, BUT THREE OF 'EM HAVE HAPPENED IN TH' LAST THREE YEARS! I SHOULD BE ABLE T'AVOID TICKETS IF I JUST R'MEMBER T'BE CAREFUL. HOW DO I GET MYSELF OUTTA TH' FUCKED-UP MOOD I'M IN NOW THOUGH? I KNOW IN THREE OR FOUR DAYS I'LL SHAKE IT AND THINGS'LL FALL INTO PLACE... WHY DON'T THEY FALL INTA PLACE NOW!
7.

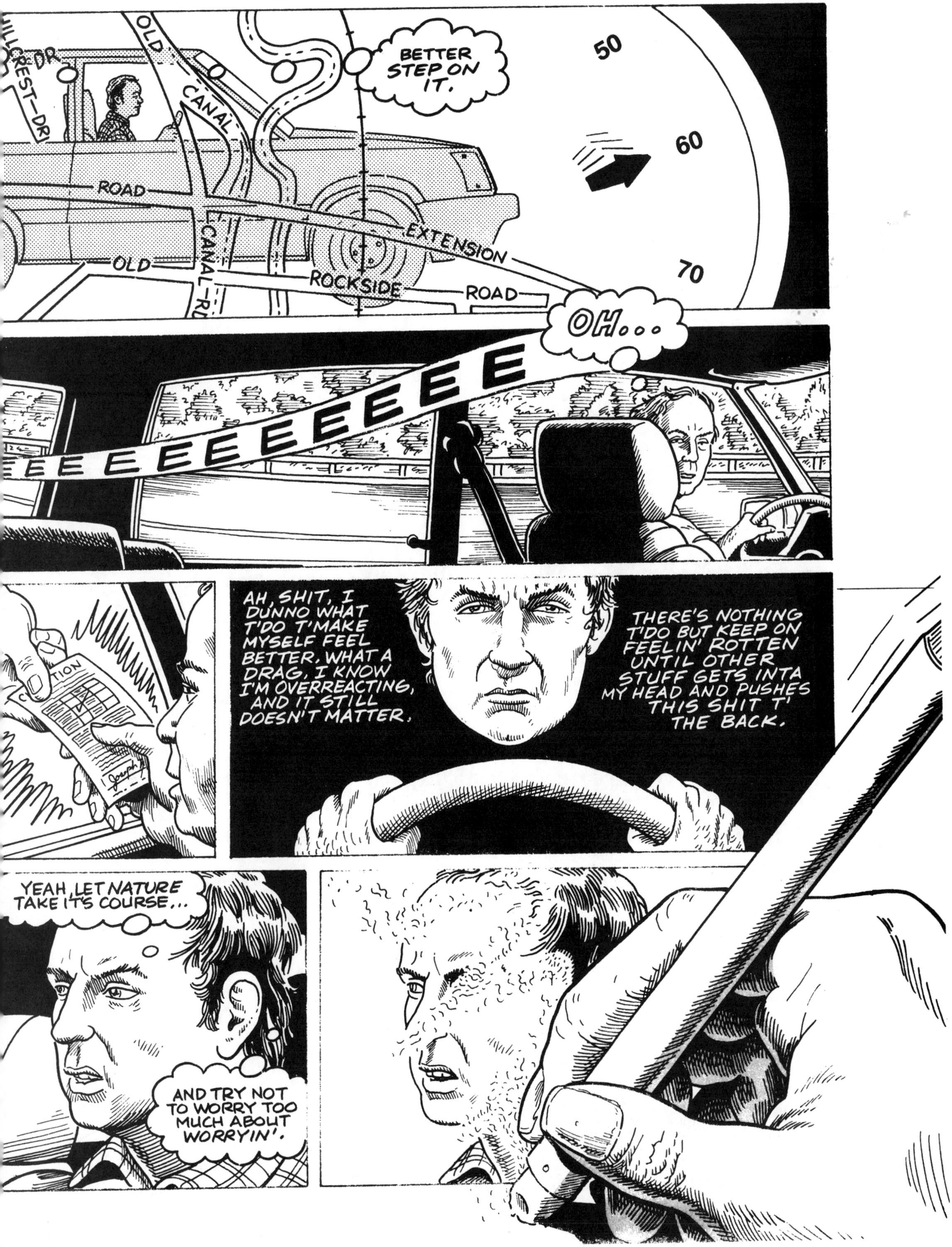
HILLCREST DR
HILLCREST—DR
OLD
CANAL
ROAD
CANAL RD
OLD
EXTENSION
ROCKSIDE
ROAD
BETTER STEP ON IT.
50
60
70
OH...
EEEEEEEEEEEEEE
AH, SHIT, I DUNNO WHAT T'DO T'MAKE MYSELF FEEL BETTER. WHAT A DRAG, I KNOW I'M OVERREACTING, AND IT STILL DOESN'T MATTER.
THERE'S NOTHING T'DO BUT KEEP ON FEELIN' ROTTEN UNTIL OTHER STUFF GETS INTA MY HEAD AND PUSHES THIS SHIT T' THE BACK.
YEAH, LET NATURE TAKE IT'S COURSE...
AND TRY NOT TO WORRY TOO MUCH ABOUT WORRYIN'.

the Greenhouse Effect

STORY BY *HARVEY PEKAR*
ART BY M.A. ZINGARELLI

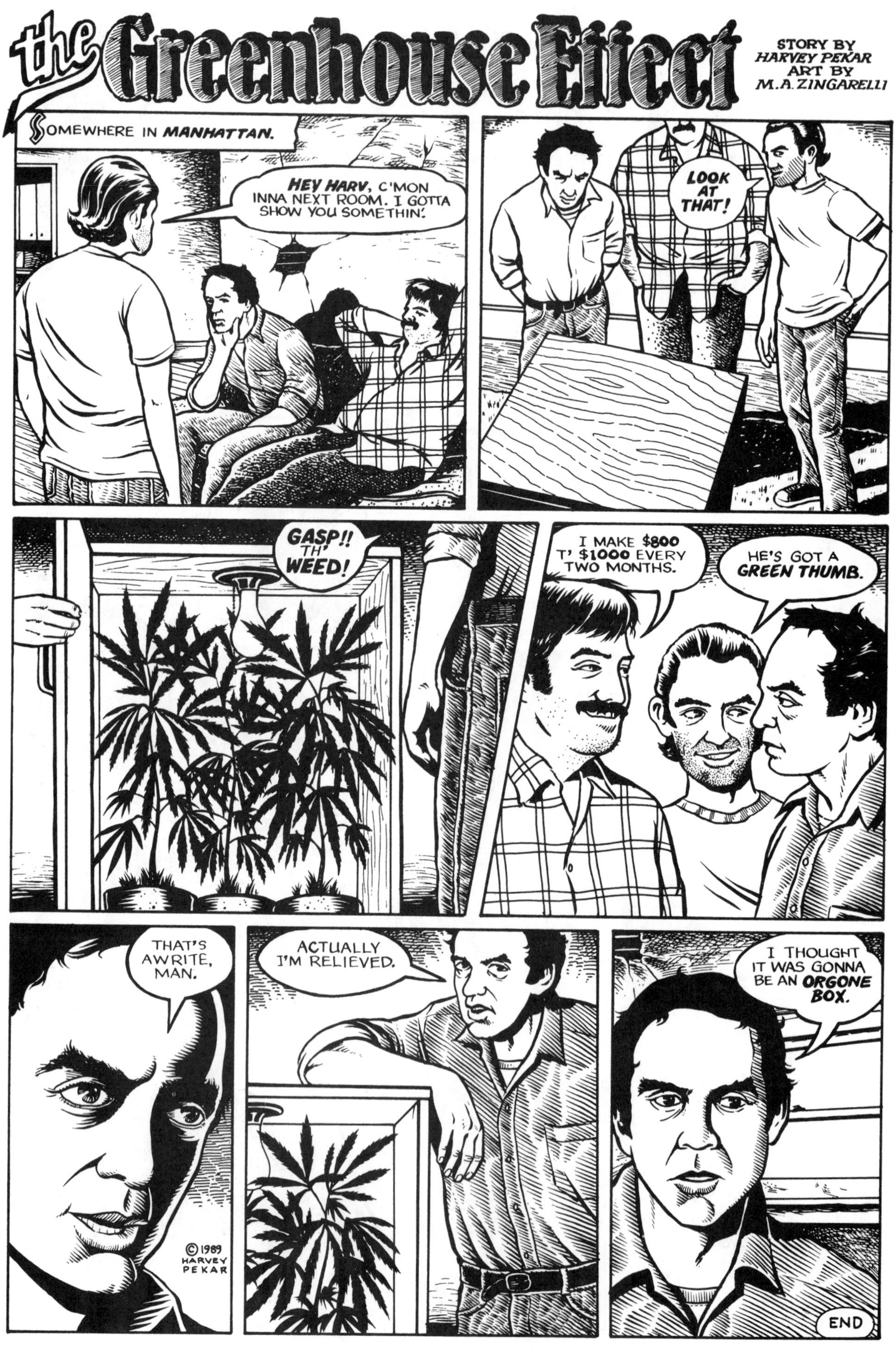
SOMEWHERE IN MANHATTAN.
HEY HARV, C'MON INNA NEXT ROOM. I GOTTA SHOW YOU SOMETHIN'.
LOOK AT THAT!
GASP!! TH' WEED!
I MAKE $800 T' $1000 EVERY TWO MONTHS.
HE'S GOT A GREEN THUMB.
THAT'S AWRITE, MAN.
©1989 HARVEY PEKAR
ACTUALLY I'M RELIEVED.
I THOUGHT IT WAS GONNA BE AN ORGONE BOX.
END

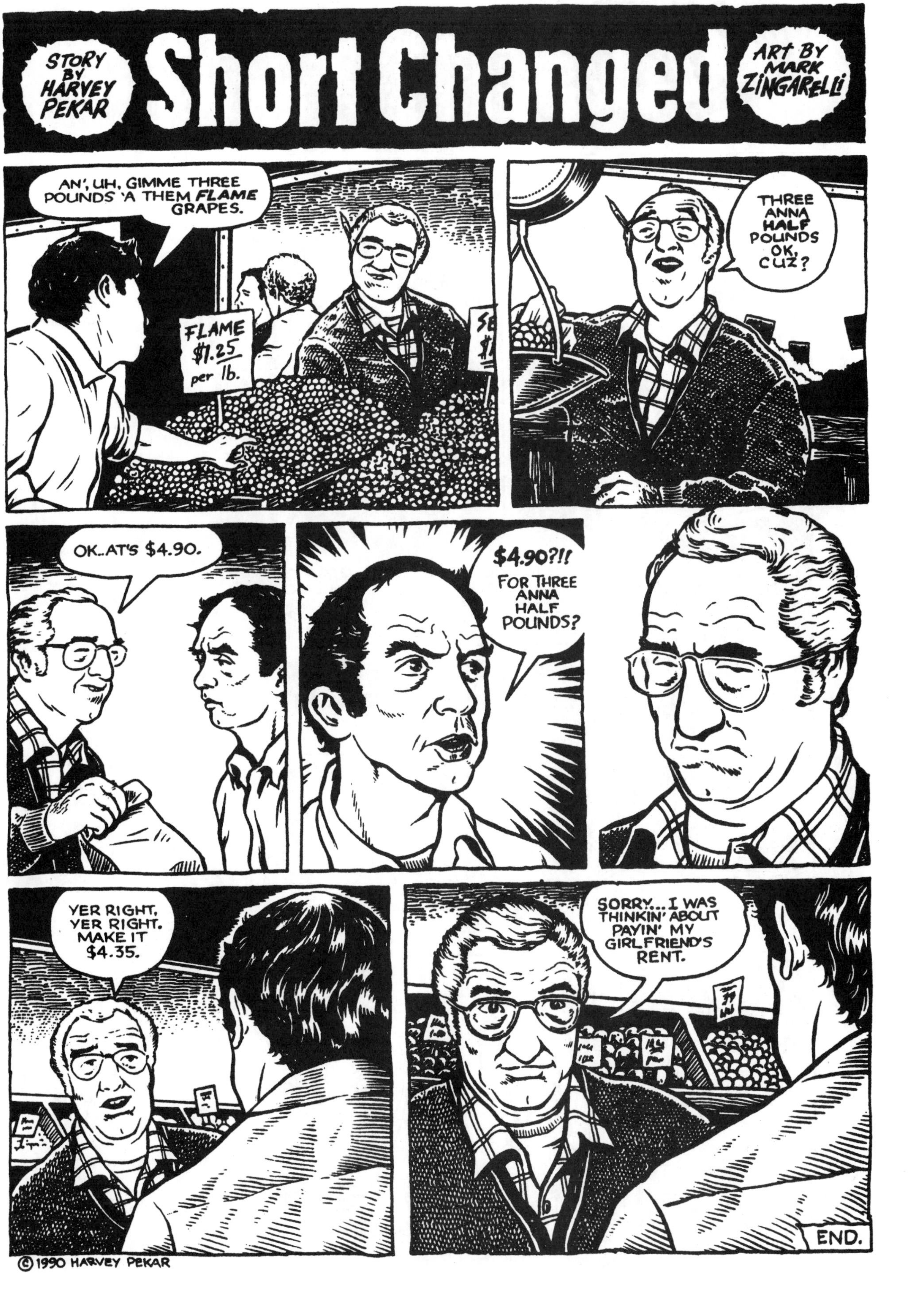
STORY BY HARVEY PEKAR
Short Changed
ART BY MARK ZINGARELLI
AN', UH, GIMME THREE POUNDS 'A THEM FLAME GRAPES.
FLAME $1.25 per lb.
THREE ANNA HALF POUNDS OK, CUZ?
OK..AT'S $4.90.
$4.90?!! FOR THREE ANNA HALF POUNDS?
YER RIGHT, YER RIGHT. MAKE IT $4.35.
SORRY... I WAS THINKIN' ABOUT PAYIN' MY GIRLFRIEND'S RENT.
END.

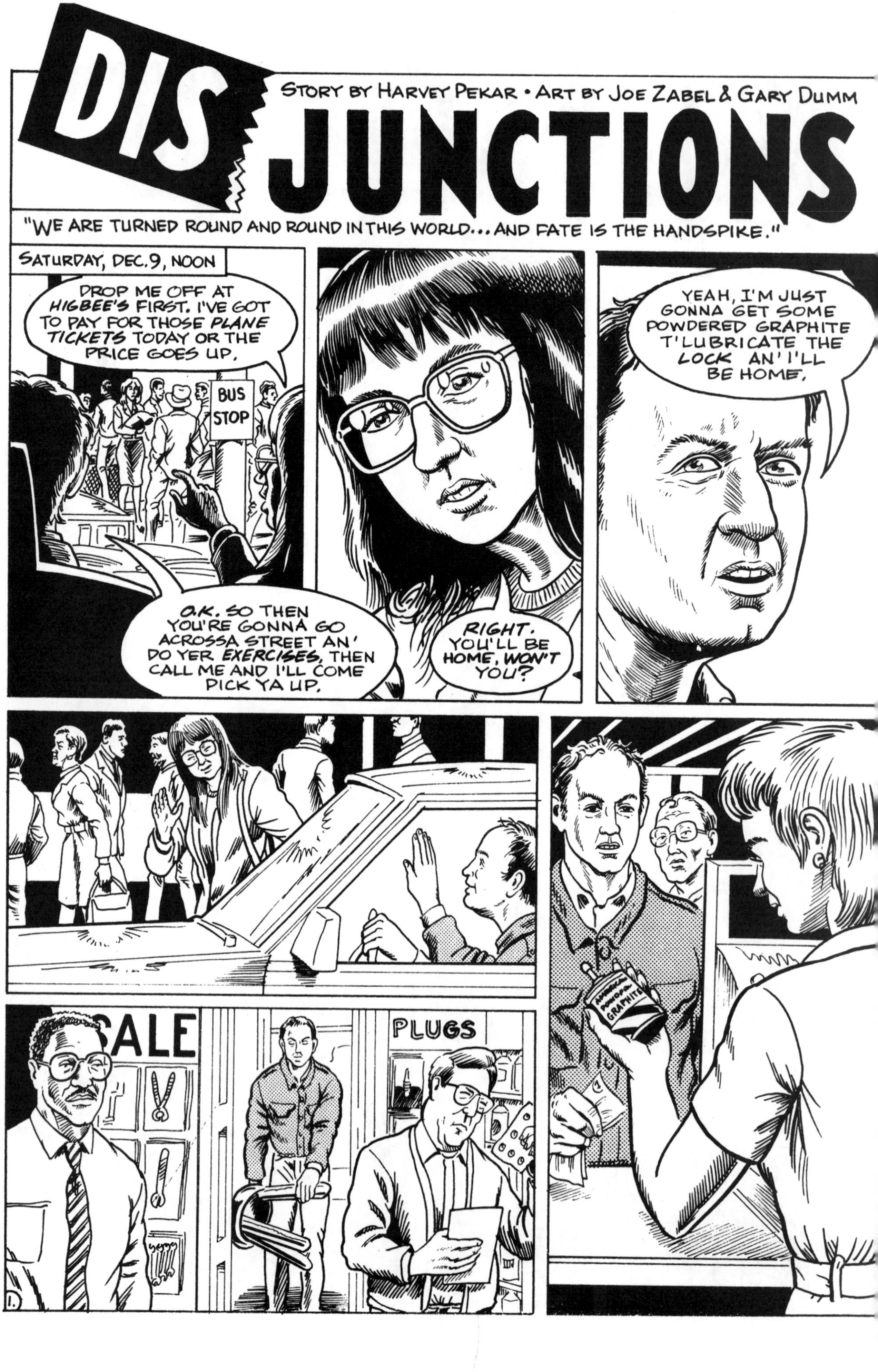
DIS JUNCTIONS
STORY BY HARVEY PEKAR • ART BY JOE ZABEL & GARY DUMM
"WE ARE TURNED ROUND AND ROUND IN THIS WORLD... AND FATE IS THE HANDSPIKE."
SATURDAY, DEC. 9, NOON
DROP ME OFF AT HIGBEE'S FIRST. I'VE GOT TO PAY FOR THOSE PLANE TICKETS TODAY OR THE PRICE GOES UP.
BUS STOP
O.K. SO THEN YOU'RE GONNA GO ACROSSA STREET AN' DO YER EXERCISES, THEN CALL ME AND I'LL COME PICK YA UP.
RIGHT. YOU'LL BE HOME, WON'T YOU?
YEAH, I'M JUST GONNA GET SOME POWDERED GRAPHITE T'LUBRICATE THE LOCK AN' I'LL BE HOME.
SALE
PLUGS
1.

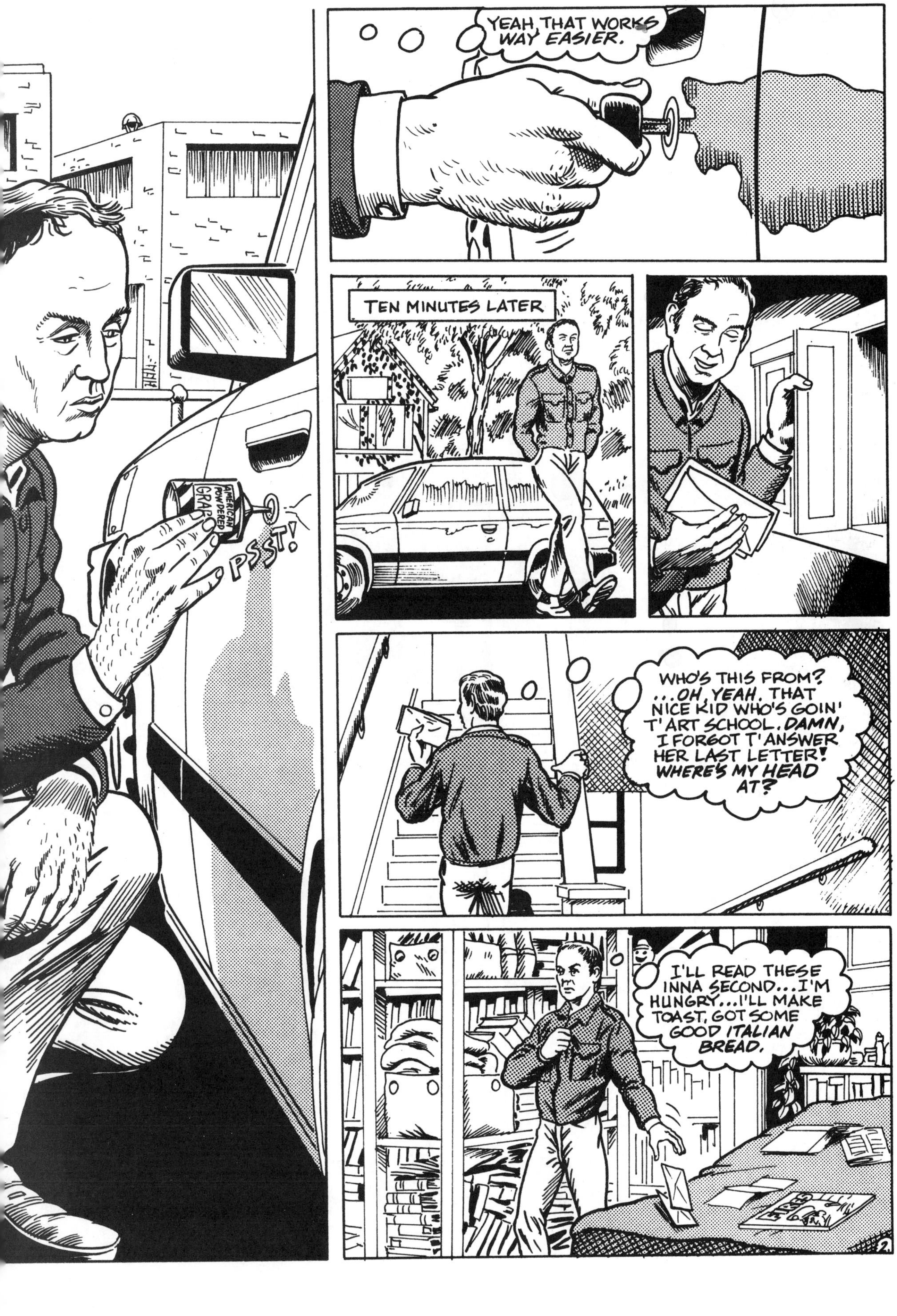
AMERICAN POWDERED GRAP
PSSST!
YEAH, THAT WORKS WAY EASIER.
TEN MINUTES LATER
WHO'S THIS FROM? ...OH, YEAH, THAT NICE KID WHO'S GOIN' T'ART SCHOOL. DAMN, I FORGOT T'ANSWER HER LAST LETTER! WHERE'S MY HEAD AT?
I'LL READ THESE INNA SECOND... I'M HUNGRY... I'LL MAKE TOAST, GOT SOME GOOD ITALIAN BREAD.
2.

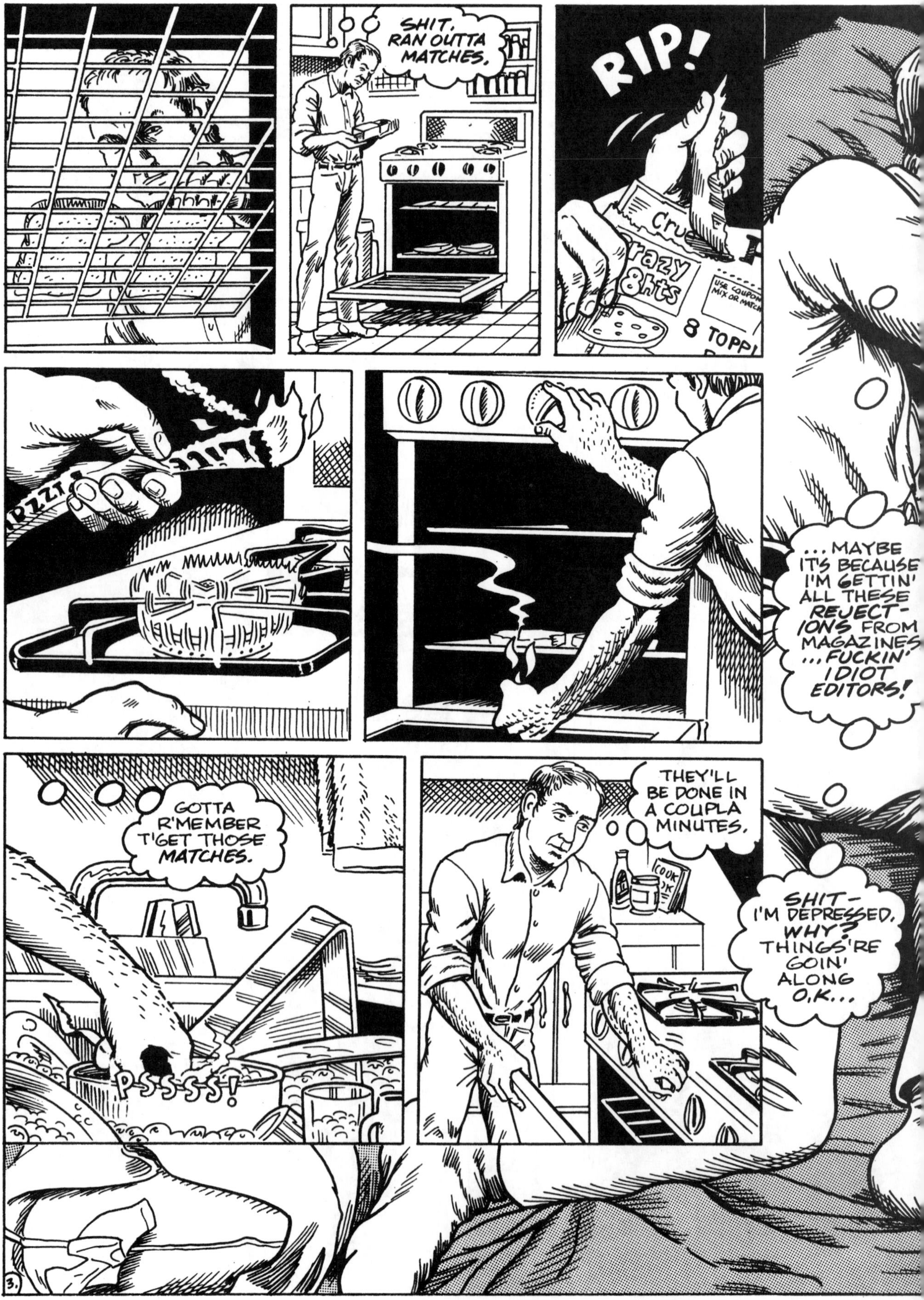
SHIT, RAN OUTTA MATCHES.
RIP!
Crazy 8hts
8 TOPPI
GOTTA R'MEMBER T'GET THOSE MATCHES.
PSSSSS!
THEY'LL BE DONE IN A COUPLA MINUTES.
SHIT- I'M DEPRESSED. WHY? THINGS'RE GOIN' ALONG O.K...
...MAYBE IT'S BECAUSE I'M GETTIN' ALL THESE REJECTIONS FROM MAGAZINES ...FUCKIN' IDIOT EDITORS!

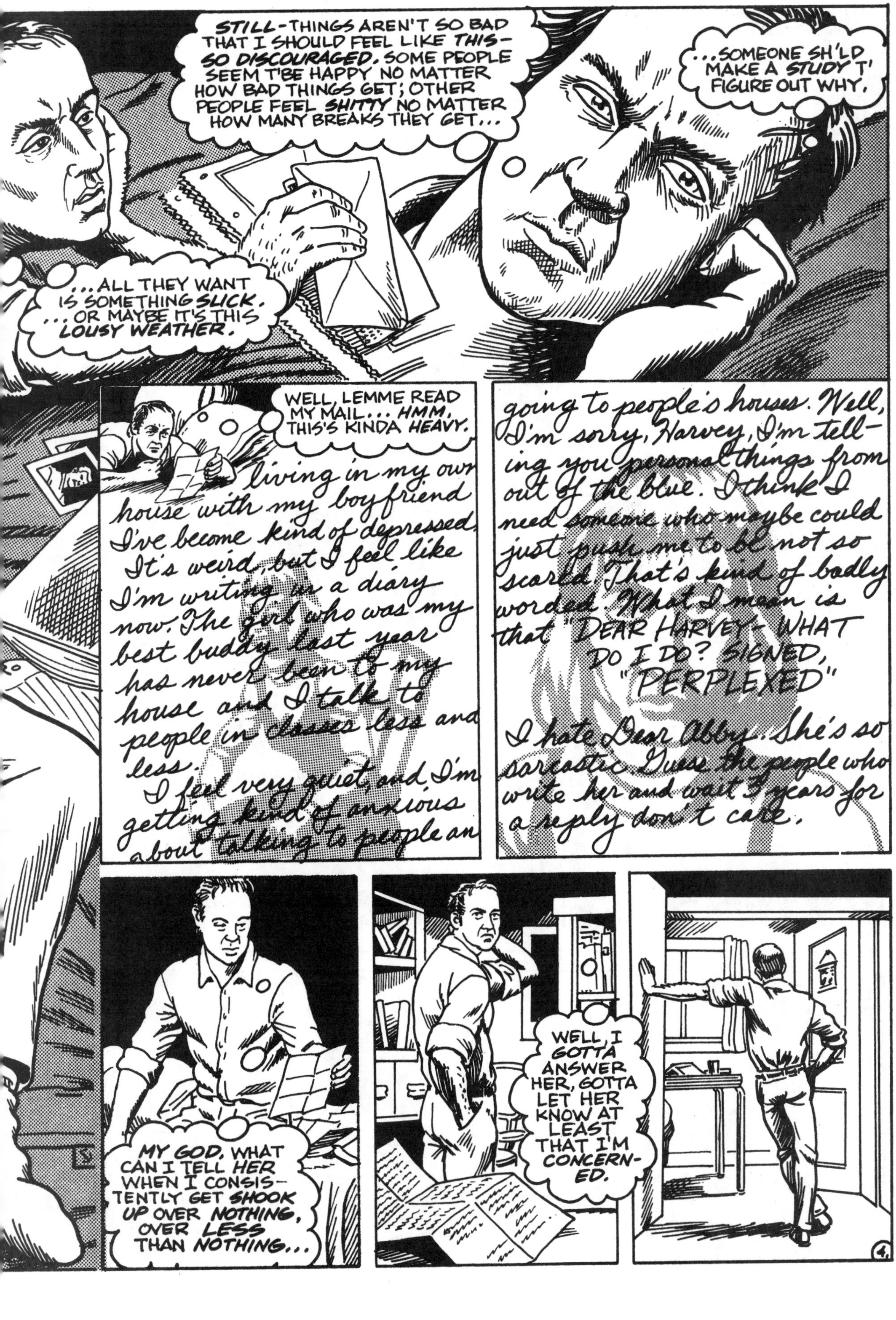

STILL-THINGS AREN'T SO BAD THAT I SHOULD FEEL LIKE THIS-SO DISCOURAGED. SOME PEOPLE SEEM T'BE HAPPY NO MATTER HOW BAD THINGS GET; OTHER PEOPLE FEEL SHITTY NO MATTER HOW MANY BREAKS THEY GET...
...SOMEONE SH'LD MAKE A STUDY T' FIGURE OUT WHY.
...ALL THEY WANT IS SOMETHING SLICK. ...OR MAYBE IT'S THIS LOUSY WEATHER.
WELL, LEMME READ MY MAIL... HMM, THIS'S KINDA HEAVY.
living in my own house with my boyfriend I've become kind of depressed. It's weird, but I feel like I'm writing in a diary now. The girl who was my best buddy last year has never been to my house and I talk to people in classes less and less.
I feel very quiet, and I'm getting kind of anxious about talking to people and
going to people's houses. Well, I'm sorry, Harvey, I'm telling you personal things from out of the blue. I think I need someone who maybe could just push me to be not so scared. That's kind of badly worded. What I mean is that "DEAR HARVEY- WHAT DO I DO? SIGNED, "PERPLEXED"
I hate Dear Abby. She's so sarcastic. Guess the people who write her and wait 3 years for a reply don't care.
MY GOD, WHAT CAN I TELL HER WHEN I CONSISTENTLY GET SHOOK UP OVER NOTHING, OVER LESS THAN NOTHING...
WELL, I GOTTA ANSWER HER, GOTTA LET HER KNOW AT LEAST THAT I'M CONCERNED.
4.

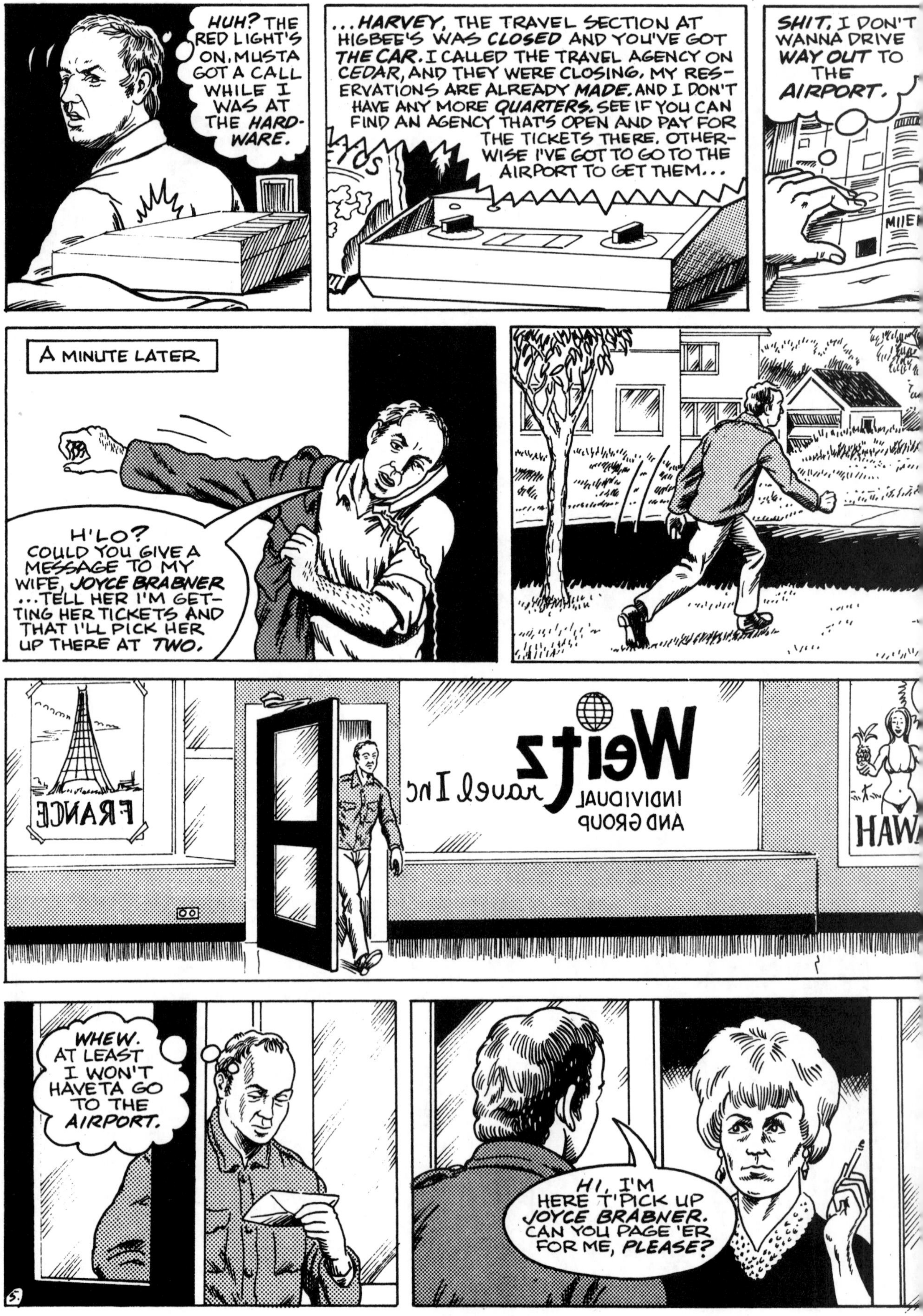
HUH? THE RED LIGHT'S ON, MUSTA GOT A CALL WHILE I WAS AT THE HARD-WARE.
...HARVEY, THE TRAVEL SECTION AT HIGBEE'S WAS CLOSED AND YOU'VE GOT THE CAR. I CALLED THE TRAVEL AGENCY ON CEDAR, AND THEY WERE CLOSING. MY RES-ERVATIONS ARE ALREADY MADE. AND I DON'T HAVE ANY MORE QUARTERS. SEE IF YOU CAN FIND AN AGENCY THAT'S OPEN AND PAY FOR THE TICKETS THERE. OTHER-WISE I'VE GOT TO GO TO THE AIRPORT TO GET THEM...
SHIT, I DON'T WANNA DRIVE WAY OUT TO THE AIRPORT.
A MINUTE LATER
H'LO? COULD YOU GIVE A MESSAGE TO MY WIFE, JOYCE BRABNER ...TELL HER I'M GET-TING HER TICKETS AND THAT I'LL PICK HER UP THERE AT TWO.
FRANCE
Weitz Travel Inc
INDIVIDUAL AND GROUP
WHEW. AT LEAST I WON'T HAVETA GO TO THE AIRPORT.
HI, I'M HERE T'PICK UP JOYCE BRABNER. CAN YOU PAGE 'ER FOR ME, PLEASE?
5.

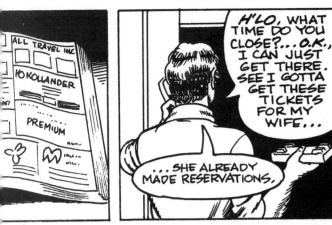

ALL TRAVEL INC
KOLLANDER
PREMIUM
H'LO. WHAT TIME DO YOU CLOSE?... O.K., I CAN JUST GET THERE. SEE I GOTTA GET THESE TICKETS FOR MY WIFE...
...SHE ALREADY MADE RESERVATIONS.
HUH? YEAH, HER NAME IS BRABNER. HOW DID YOU KNOW... HMM. SHE MUSTA CALLED YOU AFTER SHE CALLED ME... ANYWAY, I'LL BE RIGHT UP T' GET 'EM.
JAPAN
OI... I FORGOT TO GET THE TOAST OUTTA THE OVEN... IT'S STILL ON.
END.

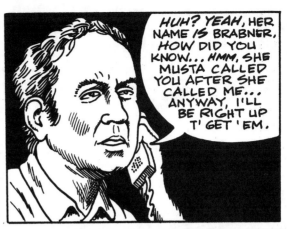

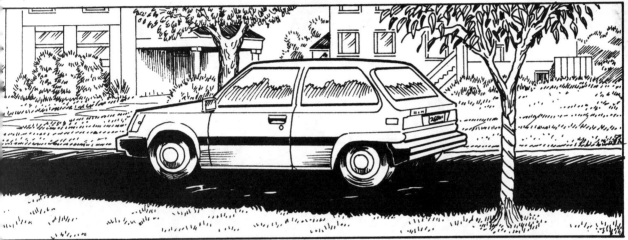

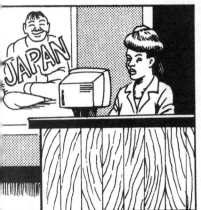

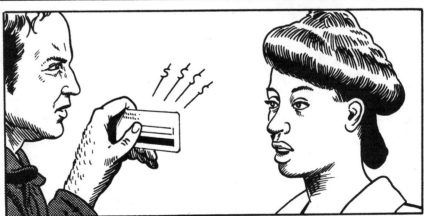

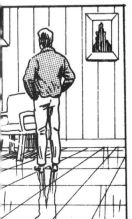

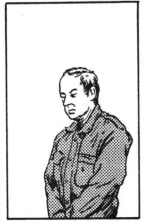

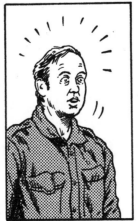

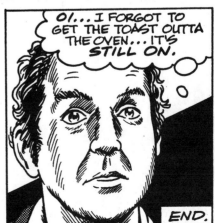

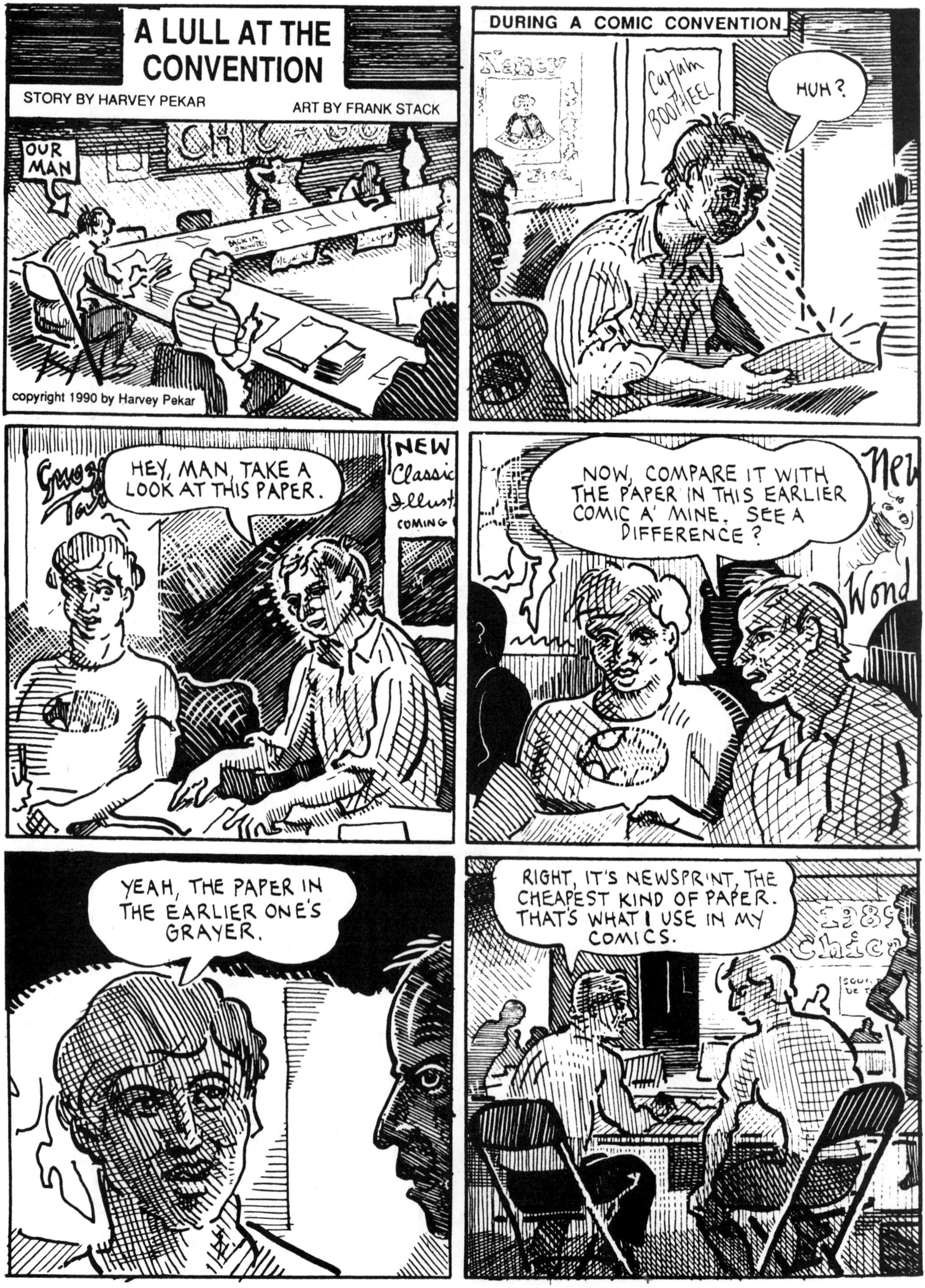
A LULL AT THE CONVENTION
STORY BY HARVEY PEKAR
ART BY FRANK STACK
OUR MAN
copyright 1990 by Harvey Pekar
DURING A COMIC CONVENTION
HUH?
HEY, MAN, TAKE A LOOK AT THIS PAPER.
NEW
NOW, COMPARE IT WITH THE PAPER IN THIS EARLIER COMIC A' MINE. SEE A DIFFERENCE?
YEAH, THE PAPER IN THE EARLIER ONE'S GRAYER.
RIGHT, IT'S NEWSPRINT, THE CHEAPEST KIND OF PAPER. THAT'S WHAT I USE IN MY COMICS.

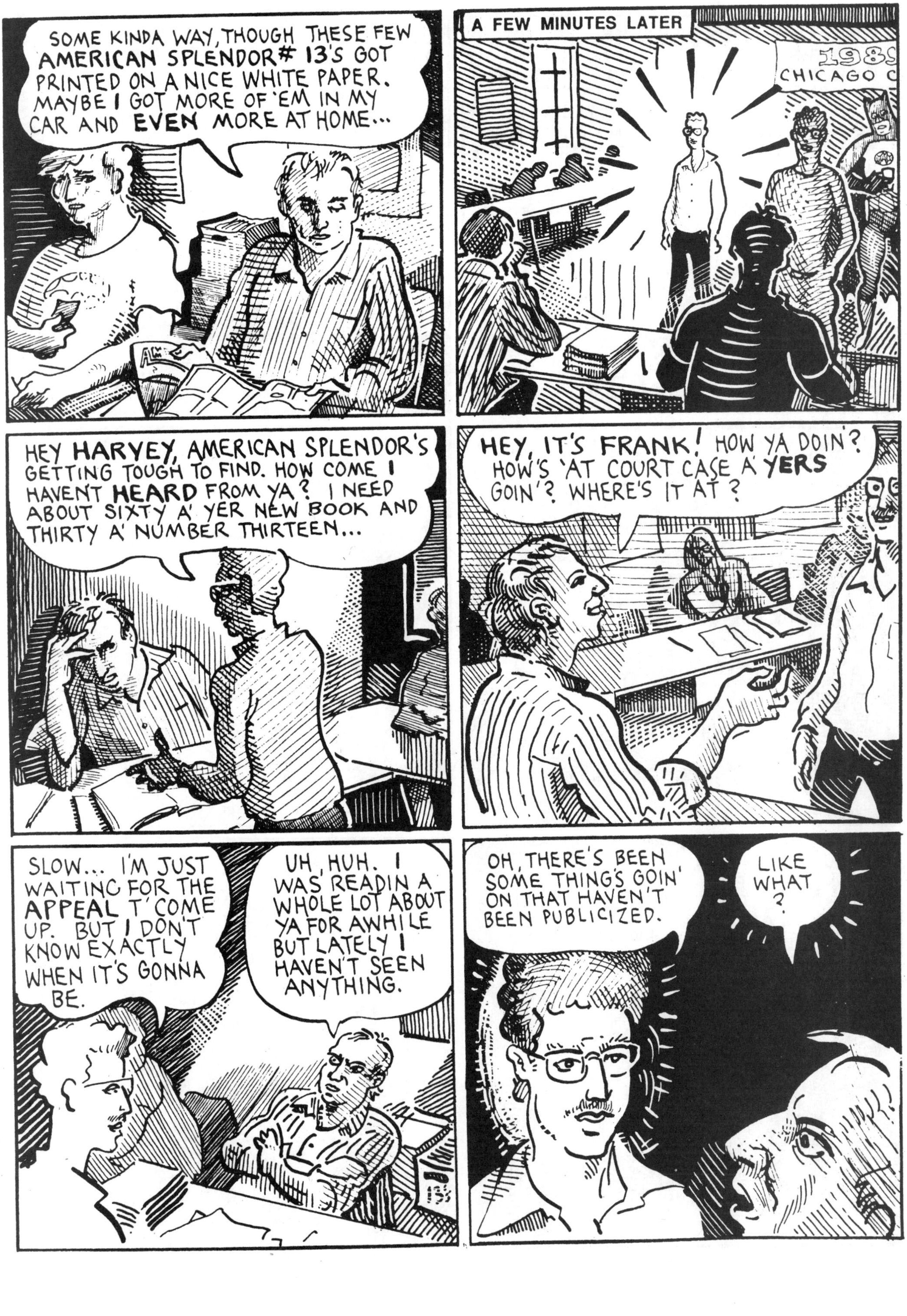
SOME KINDA WAY, THOUGH THESE FEW AMERICAN SPLENDOR # 13'S GOT PRINTED ON A NICE WHITE PAPER. MAYBE I GOT MORE OF 'EM IN MY CAR AND EVEN MORE AT HOME...
A FEW MINUTES LATER
1989
CHICAGO C
HEY HARVEY, AMERICAN SPLENDOR'S GETTING TOUGH TO FIND. HOW COME I HAVEN'T HEARD FROM YA? I NEED ABOUT SIXTY A' YER NEW BOOK AND THIRTY A' NUMBER THIRTEEN...
HEY, IT'S FRANK! HOW YA DOIN'? HOW'S 'AT COURT CASE A YERS GOIN'? WHERE'S IT AT?
SLOW... I'M JUST WAITING FOR THE APPEAL T' COME UP. BUT I DON'T KNOW EXACTLY WHEN IT'S GONNA BE.
UH, HUH. I WAS READIN A WHOLE LOT ABOUT YA FOR AWHILE BUT LATELY I HAVEN'T SEEN ANYTHING.
OH, THERE'S BEEN SOME THINGS GOIN' ON THAT HAVEN'T BEEN PUBLICIZED.
LIKE WHAT?

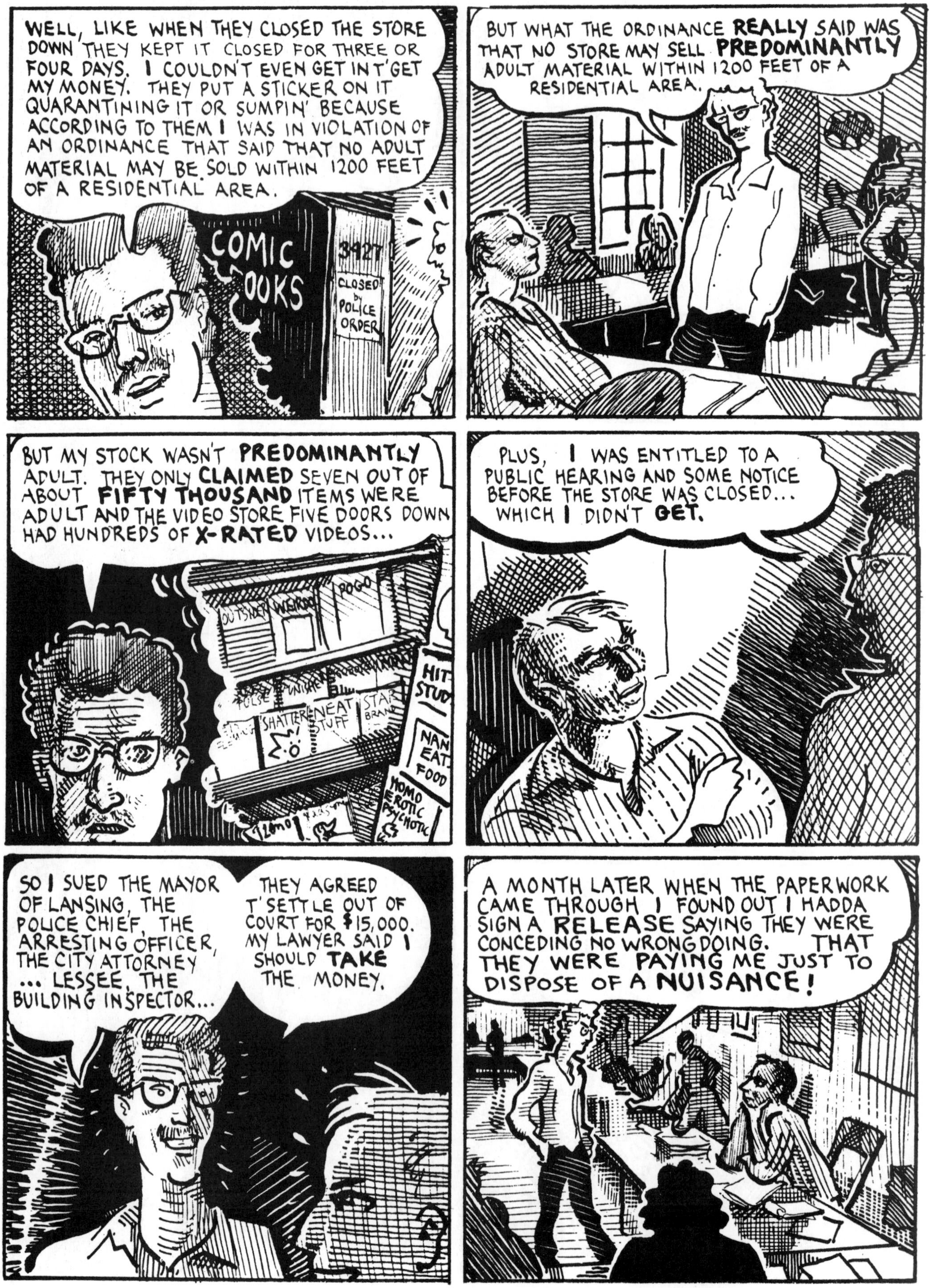

WELL, LIKE WHEN THEY CLOSED THE STORE DOWN THEY KEPT IT CLOSED FOR THREE OR FOUR DAYS. I COULDN'T EVEN GET IN T'GET MY MONEY. THEY PUT A STICKER ON IT QUARANTINING IT OR SUMPIN' BECAUSE ACCORDING TO THEM I WAS IN VIOLATION OF AN ORDINANCE THAT SAID THAT NO ADULT MATERIAL MAY BE SOLD WITHIN 1200 FEET OF A RESIDENTIAL AREA.
3927
CLOSED by POLICE ORDER
BUT WHAT THE ORDINANCE REALLY SAID WAS THAT NO STORE MAY SELL PREDOMINANTLY ADULT MATERIAL WITHIN 1200 FEET OF A RESIDENTIAL AREA.
BUT MY STOCK WASN'T PREDOMINANTLY ADULT. THEY ONLY CLAIMED SEVEN OUT OF ABOUT FIFTY THOUSAND ITEMS WERE ADULT AND THE VIDEO STORE FIVE DOORS DOWN HAD HUNDREDS OF X-RATED VIDEOS...
WEIRDO
POGO
NEAT STUFF
SHATTER
HOMO EROTIC PSYCHOTIC
PLUS, I WAS ENTITLED TO A PUBLIC HEARING AND SOME NOTICE BEFORE THE STORE WAS CLOSED... WHICH I DIDN'T GET.
SO I SUED THE MAYOR OF LANSING, THE POLICE CHIEF, THE ARRESTING OFFICER, THE CITY ATTORNEY ... LESSEE, THE BUILDING INSPECTOR...
THEY AGREED T'SETTLE OUT OF COURT FOR $15,000. MY LAWYER SAID I SHOULD TAKE THE MONEY.
A MONTH LATER WHEN THE PAPERWORK CAME THROUGH I FOUND OUT I HADDA SIGN A RELEASE SAYING THEY WERE CONCEDING NO WRONGDOING. THAT THEY WERE PAYING ME JUST TO DISPOSE OF A NUISANCE!

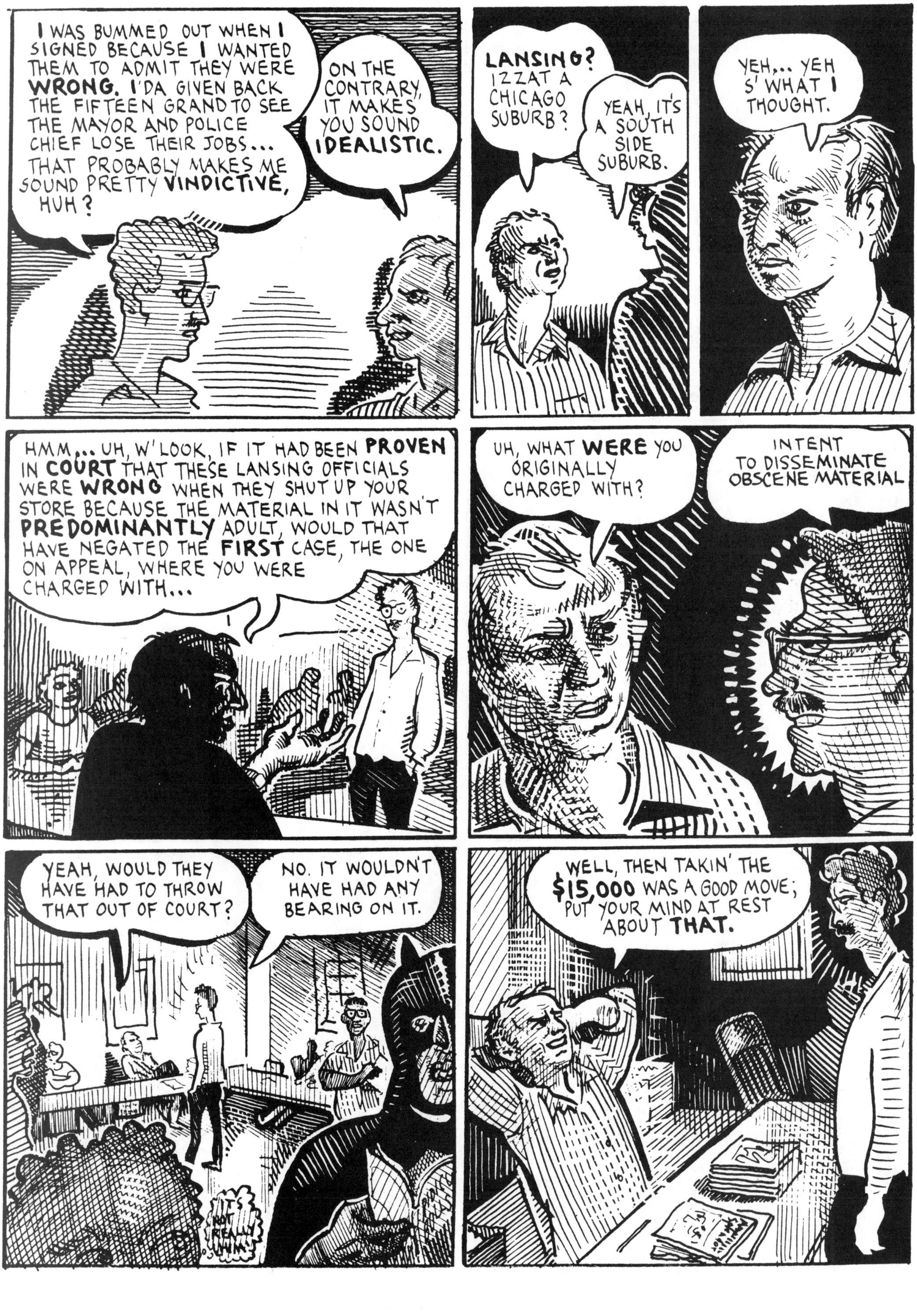
I WAS BUMMED OUT WHEN I SIGNED BECAUSE I WANTED THEM TO ADMIT THEY WERE WRONG. I'DA GIVEN BACK THE FIFTEEN GRAND TO SEE THE MAYOR AND POLICE CHIEF LOSE THEIR JOBS... THAT PROBABLY MAKES ME SOUND PRETTY VINDICTIVE, HUH?
ON THE CONTRARY, IT MAKES YOU SOUND IDEALISTIC.
LANSING? IZZAT A CHICAGO SUBURB?
YEAH, IT'S A SOUTH SIDE SUBURB.
YEH,... YEH S' WHAT I THOUGHT.
HMM,.. UH, W' LOOK, IF IT HAD BEEN PROVEN IN COURT THAT THESE LANSING OFFICIALS WERE WRONG WHEN THEY SHUT UP YOUR STORE BECAUSE THE MATERIAL IN IT WASN'T PREDOMINANTLY ADULT, WOULD THAT HAVE NEGATED THE FIRST CASE, THE ONE ON APPEAL, WHERE YOU WERE CHARGED WITH...
I
UH, WHAT WERE YOU ORIGINALLY CHARGED WITH?
INTENT TO DISSEMINATE OBSCENE MATERIAL
YEAH, WOULD THEY HAVE HAD TO THROW THAT OUT OF COURT?
NO. IT WOULDN'T HAVE HAD ANY BEARING ON IT.
IT'S NOT REALLY HIM!
WELL, THEN TAKIN' THE $15,000 WAS A GOOD MOVE; PUT YOUR MIND AT REST ABOUT THAT.

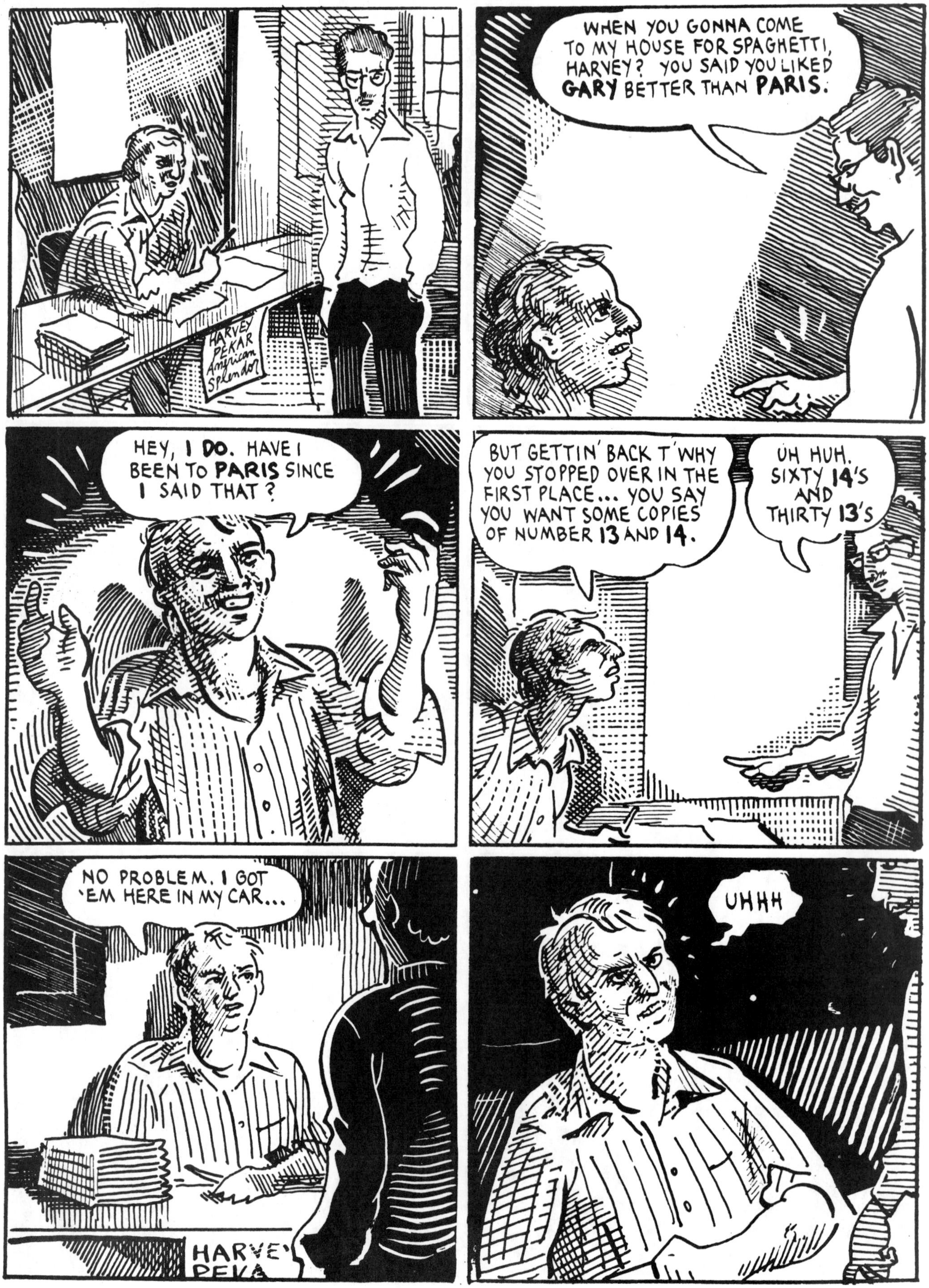
HARVEY PEKAR American Splendor
WHEN YOU GONNA COME TO MY HOUSE FOR SPAGHETTI, HARVEY? YOU SAID YOU LIKED GARY BETTER THAN PARIS.
HEY, I DO. HAVE I BEEN TO PARIS SINCE I SAID THAT?
BUT GETTIN' BACK T'WHY YOU STOPPED OVER IN THE FIRST PLACE... YOU SAY YOU WANT SOME COPIES OF NUMBER 13 AND 14.
UH HUH. SIXTY 14'S AND THIRTY 13'S
NO PROBLEM. I GOT 'EM HERE IN MY CAR...
HARVE PEKA
UHHH

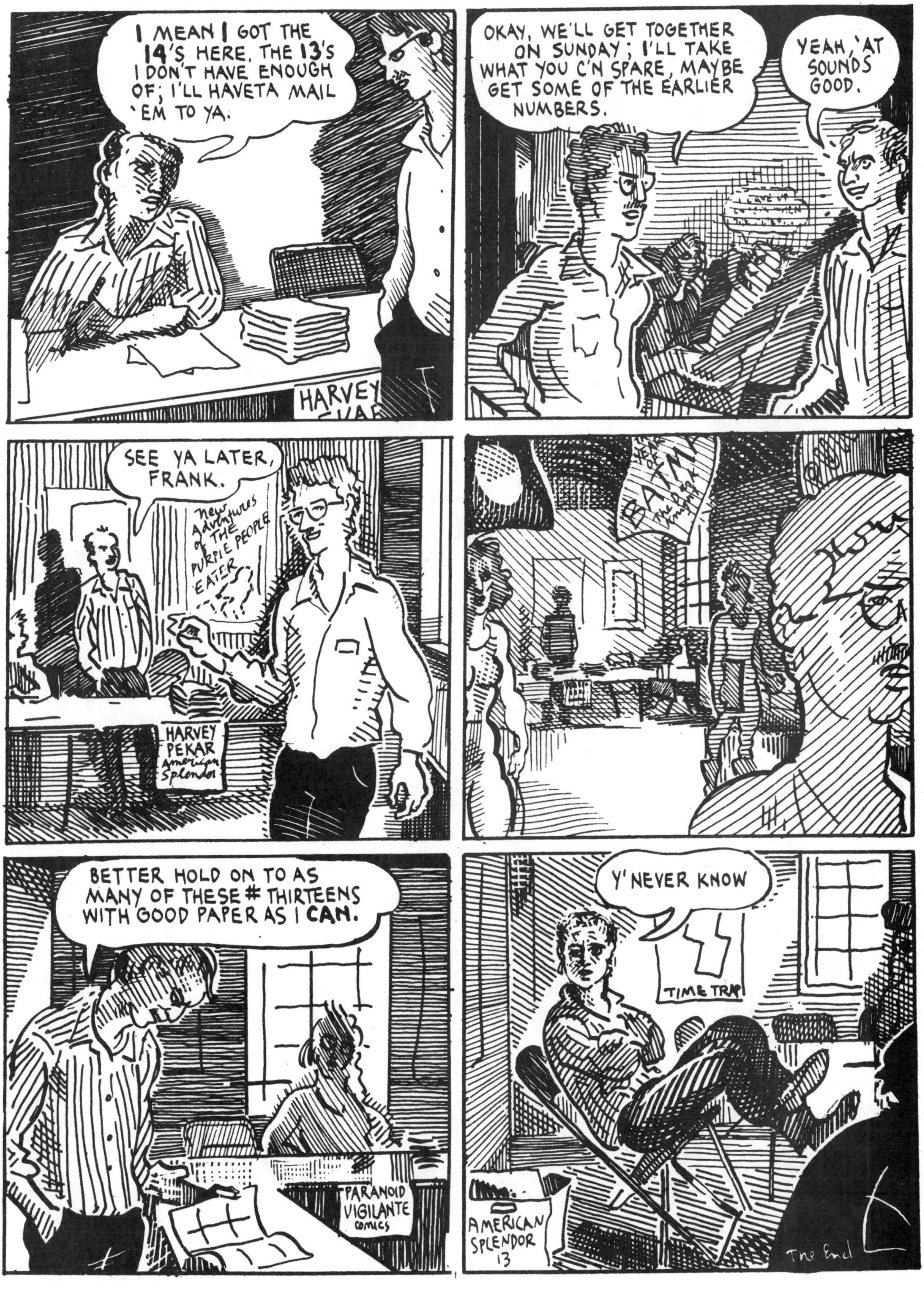
I MEAN I GOT THE 14'S HERE. THE 13'S I DON'T HAVE ENOUGH OF; I'LL HAVETA MAIL 'EM TO YA.
HARVEY
OKAY, WE'LL GET TOGETHER ON SUNDAY; I'LL TAKE WHAT YOU C'N SPARE, MAYBE GET SOME OF THE EARLIER NUMBERS.
YEAH, 'AT SOUNDS GOOD.
SEE YA LATER, FRANK.
New Adventures of THE PURPLE PEOPLE EATER
HARVEY PEKAR American Splendor
BETTER HOLD ON TO AS MANY OF THESE # THIRTEENS WITH GOOD PAPER AS I CAN.
PARANOID VIGILANTE comics
Y'NEVER KNOW
TIME TRIP
AMERICAN SPLENDOR 13
The End

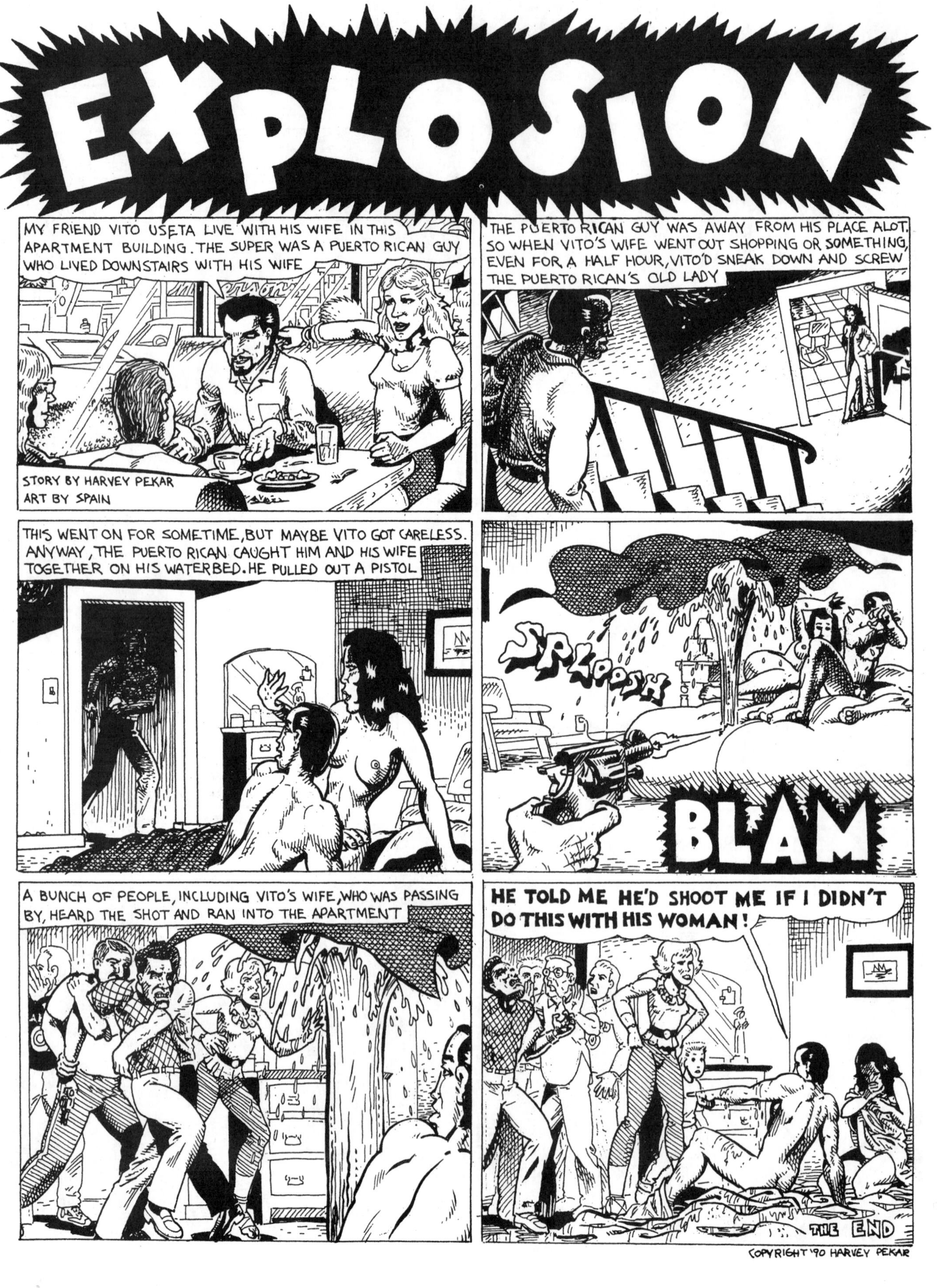
EXPLOSION
MY FRIEND VITO USETA LIVE WITH HIS WIFE IN THIS APARTMENT BUILDING. THE SUPER WAS A PUERTO RICAN GUY WHO LIVED DOWNSTAIRS WITH HIS WIFE
STORY BY HARVEY PEKAR
ART BY SPAIN
THE PUERTO RICAN GUY WAS AWAY FROM HIS PLACE ALOT. SO WHEN VITO'S WIFE WENT OUT SHOPPING OR SOMETHING, EVEN FOR A HALF HOUR, VITO'D SNEAK DOWN AND SCREW THE PUERTO RICAN'S OLD LADY
THIS WENT ON FOR SOMETIME, BUT MAYBE VITO GOT CARELESS. ANYWAY, THE PUERTO RICAN CAUGHT HIM AND HIS WIFE TOGETHER ON HIS WATERBED. HE PULLED OUT A PISTOL
SPLOOSH
BLAM
A BUNCH OF PEOPLE, INCLUDING VITO'S WIFE, WHO WAS PASSING BY, HEARD THE SHOT AND RAN INTO THE APARTMENT
HE TOLD ME HE'D SHOOT ME IF I DIDN'T DO THIS WITH HIS WOMAN!
THE END

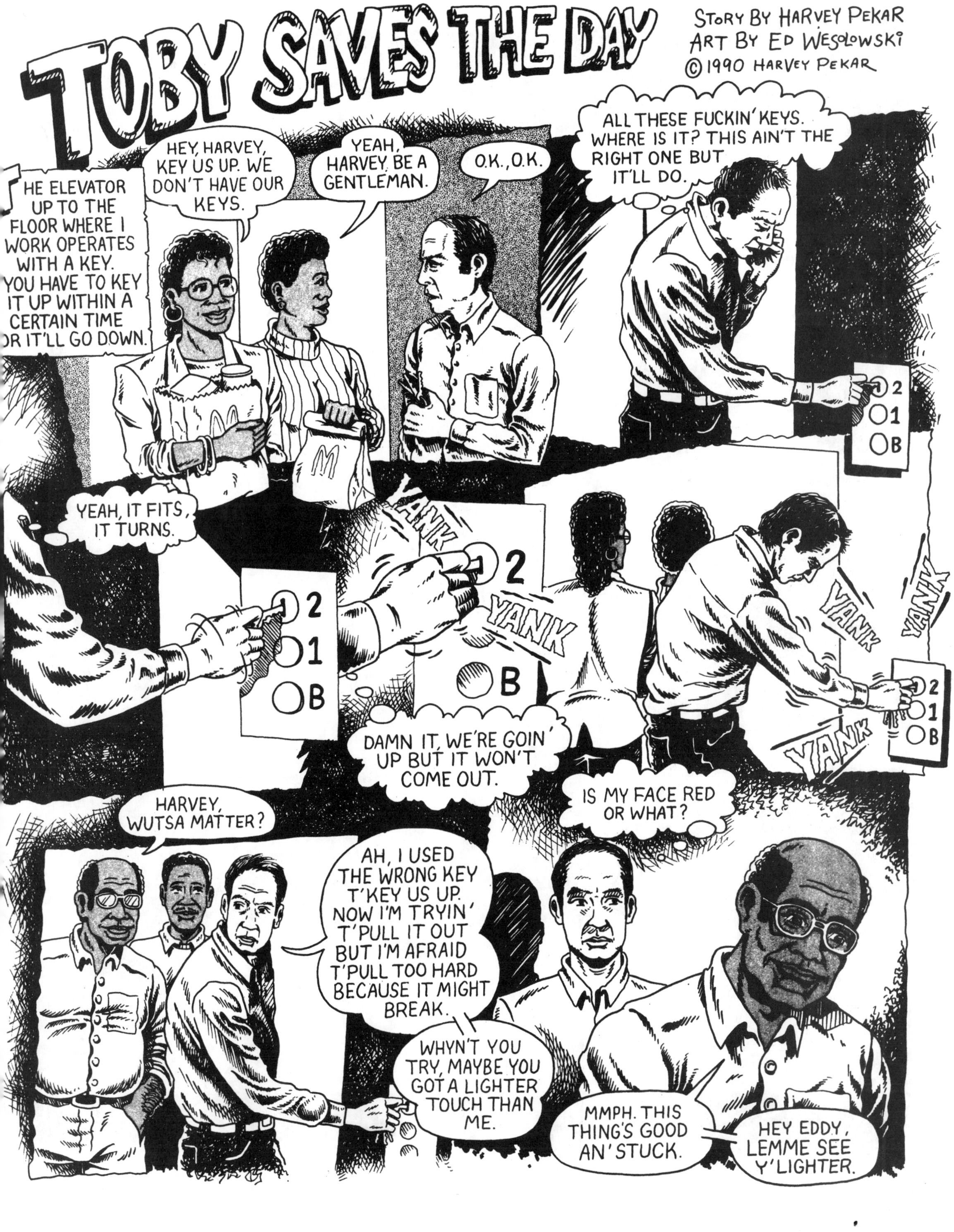
TOBY SAVES THE DAY
STORY BY HARVEY PEKAR
ART BY ED WESOLOWSKI
© 1990 HARVEY PEKAR
THE ELEVATOR UP TO THE FLOOR WHERE I WORK OPERATES WITH A KEY. YOU HAVE TO KEY IT UP WITHIN A CERTAIN TIME OR IT'LL GO DOWN.
HEY, HARVEY, KEY US UP. WE DON'T HAVE OUR KEYS.
YEAH, HARVEY, BE A GENTLEMAN.
O.K., O.K.
ALL THESE FUCKIN' KEYS. WHERE IS IT? THIS AIN'T THE RIGHT ONE BUT IT'LL DO.
2
1
B
YEAH, IT FITS, IT TURNS.
2
1
B
YANK
YANK
2
B
YANK
YANK
YANK
2
1
B
DAMN IT, WE'RE GOIN' UP BUT IT WON'T COME OUT.
IS MY FACE RED OR WHAT?
HARVEY, WUTSA MATTER?
AH, I USED THE WRONG KEY T'KEY US UP. NOW I'M TRYIN' T'PULL IT OUT BUT I'M AFRAID T'PULL TOO HARD BECAUSE IT MIGHT BREAK.
WHYN'T YOU TRY, MAYBE YOU GOT A LIGHTER TOUCH THAN ME.
MMPH. THIS THING'S GOOD AN' STUCK.
HEY EDDY, LEMME SEE Y'LIGHTER.

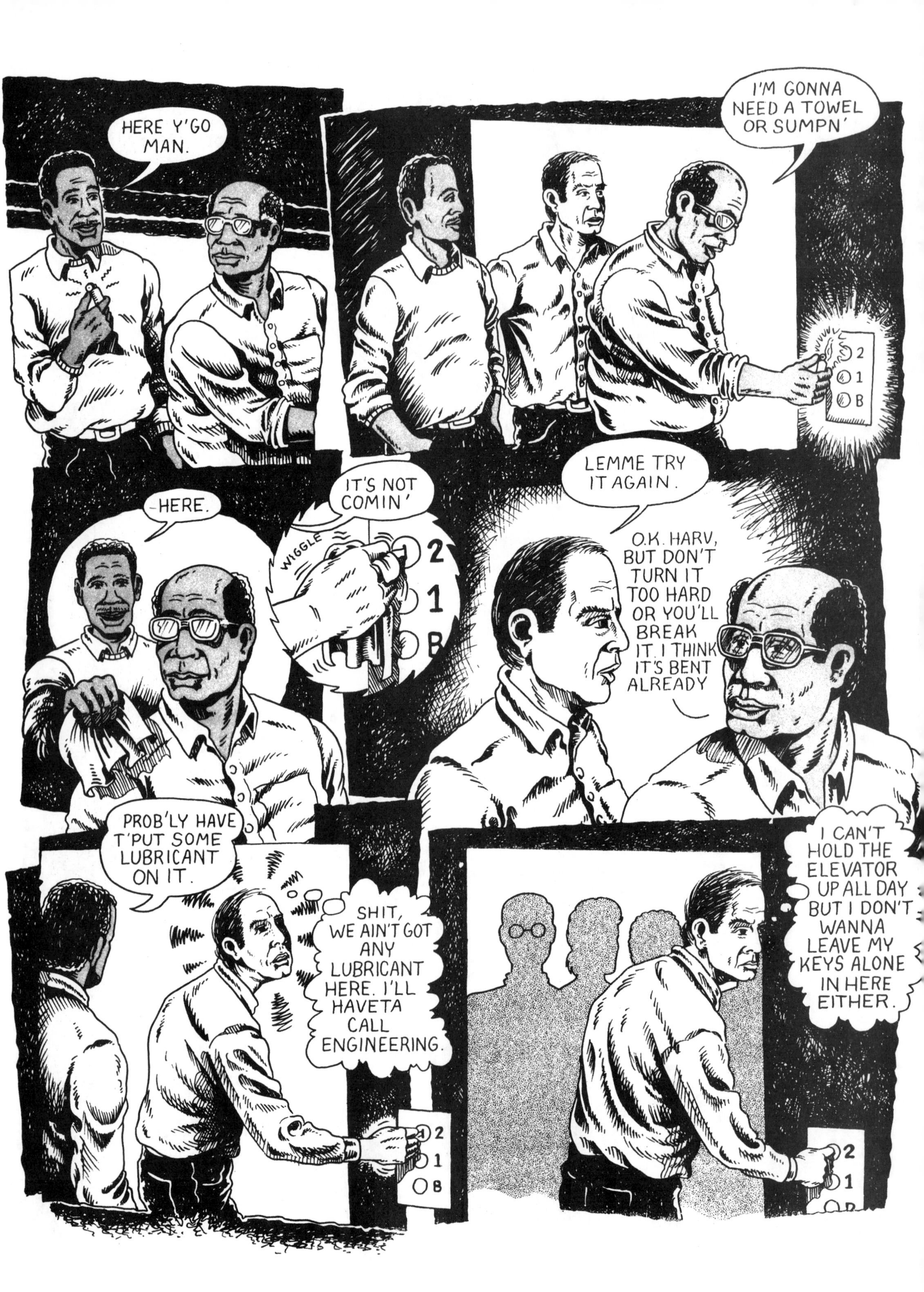
HERE Y'GO MAN.
I'M GONNA NEED A TOWEL OR SUMPN'
2
1
B
-HERE.
IT'S NOT COMIN'
WIGGLE
2
1
B
LEMME TRY IT AGAIN.
O.K. HARV, BUT DON'T TURN IT TOO HARD OR YOU'LL BREAK IT. I THINK IT'S BENT ALREADY
PROB'LY HAVE T'PUT SOME LUBRICANT ON IT.
SHIT, WE AIN'T GOT ANY LUBRICANT HERE. I'LL HAVETA CALL ENGINEERING.
2
1
B
I CAN'T HOLD THE ELEVATOR UP ALL DAY BUT I DON'T WANNA LEAVE MY KEYS ALONE IN HERE EITHER.
2
1

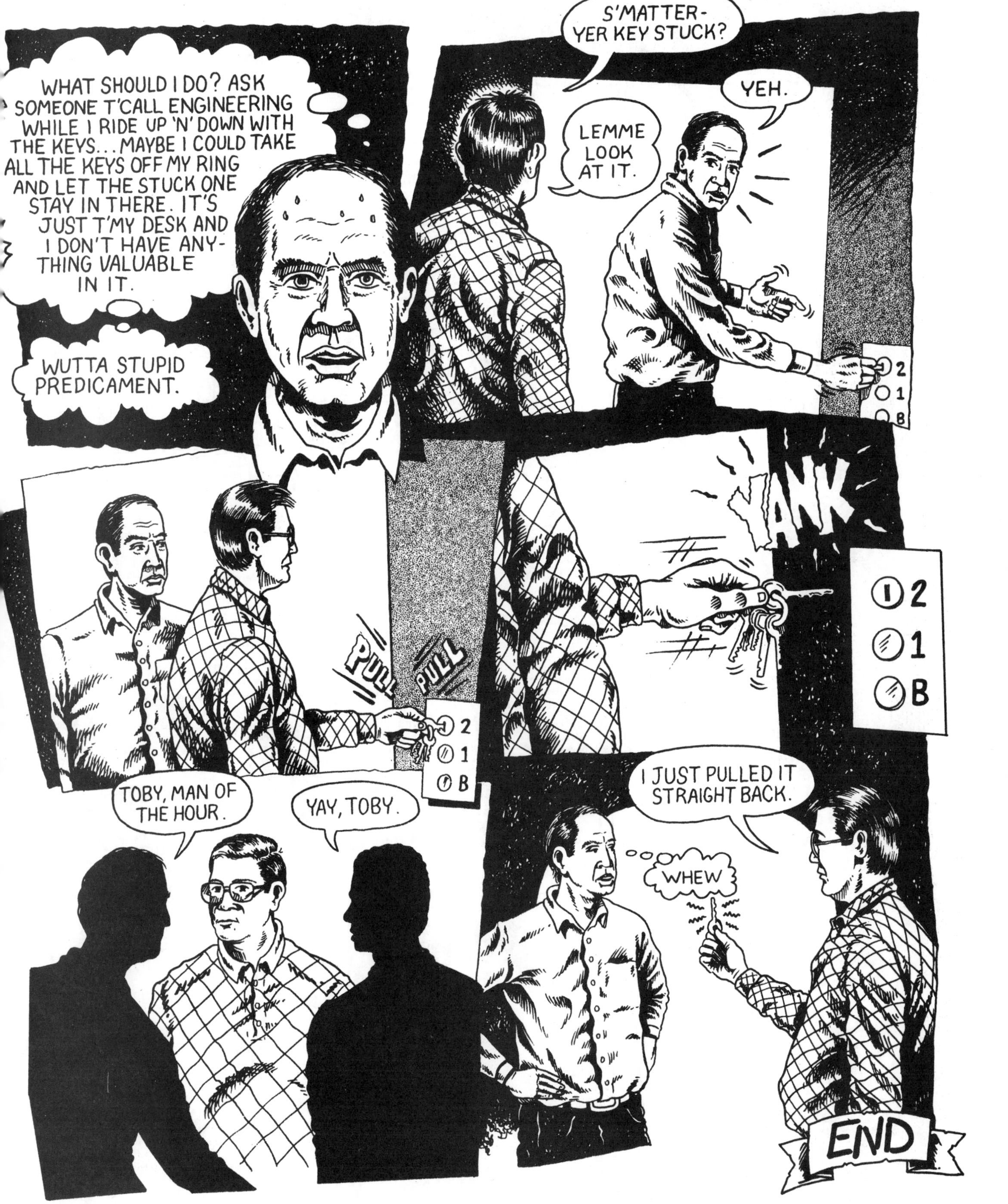
WHAT SHOULD I DO? ASK SOMEONE T'CALL ENGINEERING WHILE I RIDE UP 'N' DOWN WITH THE KEYS... MAYBE I COULD TAKE ALL THE KEYS OFF MY RING AND LET THE STUCK ONE STAY IN THERE. IT'S JUST T'MY DESK AND I DON'T HAVE ANYTHING VALUABLE IN IT.
WUTTA STUPID PREDICAMENT.
S'MATTER- YER KEY STUCK?
YEH.
LEMME LOOK AT IT.
2
1
B
PULL
PULL
2
1
B
YANK
2
1
B
TOBY, MAN OF THE HOUR.
YAY, TOBY.
I JUST PULLED IT STRAIGHT BACK.
WHEW
END

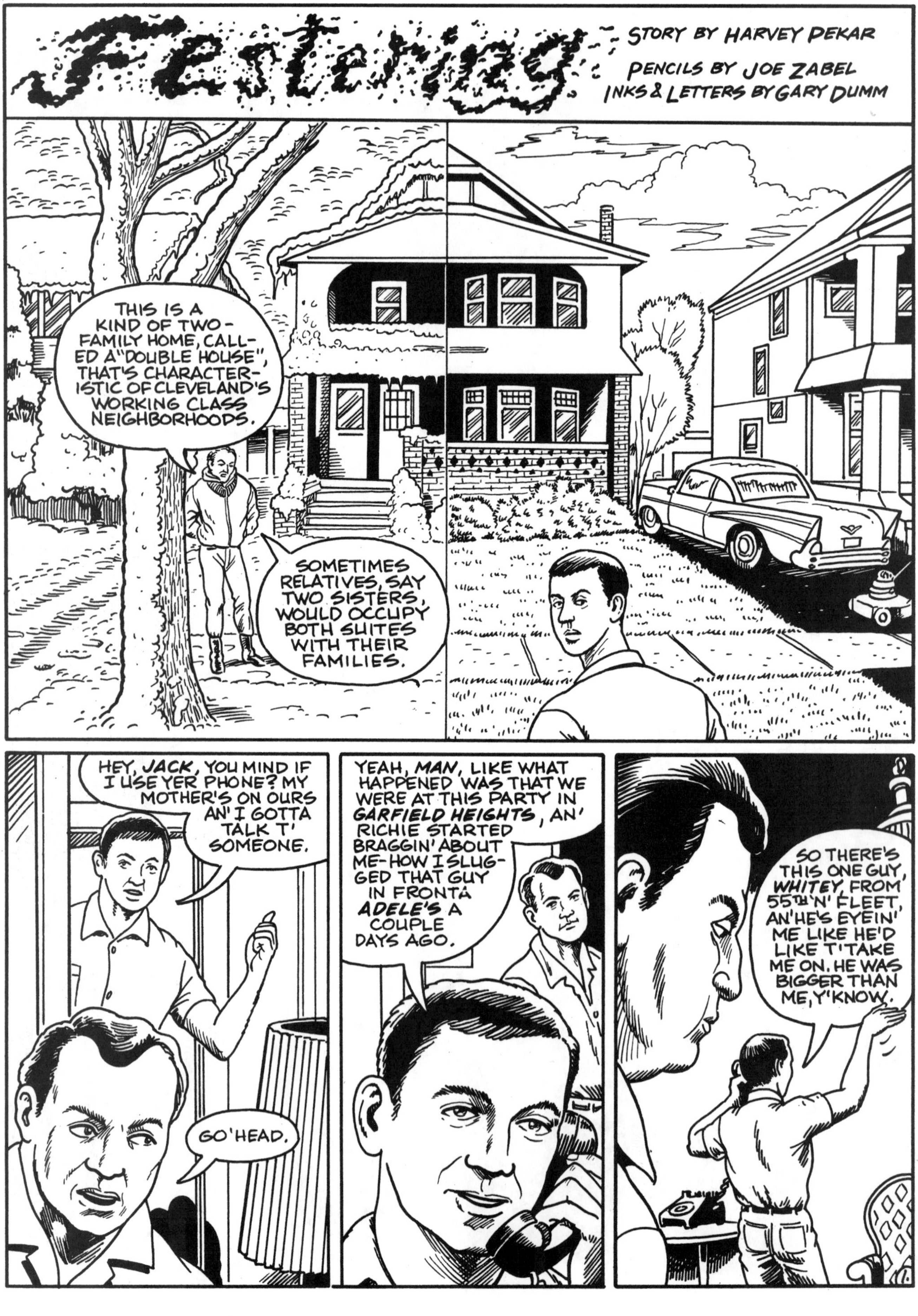
Festering
STORY BY HARVEY PEKAR
PENCILS BY JOE ZABEL
INKS & LETTERS BY GARY DUMM
THIS IS A KIND OF TWO-FAMILY HOME, CALLED A "DOUBLE HOUSE", THAT'S CHARACTERISTIC OF CLEVELAND'S WORKING CLASS NEIGHBORHOODS.
SOMETIMES RELATIVES, SAY TWO SISTERS, WOULD OCCUPY BOTH SUITES WITH THEIR FAMILIES.
HEY, JACK, YOU MIND IF I USE YER PHONE? MY MOTHER'S ON OURS AN' I GOTTA TALK T' SOMEONE.
GO'HEAD.
YEAH, MAN, LIKE WHAT HAPPENED WAS THAT WE WERE AT THIS PARTY IN GARFIELD HEIGHTS, AN' RICHIE STARTED BRAGGIN' ABOUT ME-HOW I SLUGGED THAT GUY IN FRONTA ADELE'S A COUPLE DAYS AGO.
SO THERE'S THIS ONE GUY, WHITEY, FROM 55TH 'N' FLEET, AN' HE'S EYEIN' ME LIKE HE'D LIKE T' TAKE ME ON. HE WAS BIGGER THAN ME, Y'KNOW.
1.

I FIGURED SUM'P'N MIGHT HAPPEN B'FORE TH' NIGHT WAS OVER. A-ROUND 11:00 I GO T' GET A CHAIR FROM NEXT T'HIM.

I SAY, 'ANY-BODY USIN' 'IS CHAIR?' AN' HE SAYS 'YEAH, DON'T TOUCH IT.'

I FIGURE IT'S GONNA START SOONER OR LATER—WHY NOT SOONER?

I GOT ON TOP OF 'IM, BUT THEY PULLED ME OFF.

I KNEW I COULD FLATTEN THIS GUY, SO I FOLLOWED HIM OUTSIDE AND KNOCKED 'IM DOWN AGAIN. THIS TIME RICHIE HELD THE DOOR CLOSED SO NO ONE COULD STOP ME.

I GOT ON TOP OF 'IM AN' STARTED SOCKIN' 'IM.

HE TRIED T'GOUGE MY EYES, SO I BIT ONE A' HIS FINGERS AN' WOULDN' LET GO.

AN' HE STARTS SCREAMIN', 'AAAH. SOMEONE HELP! THIS GUY'S BITIN' ME!

I KICKED HIS ASS, MAN. THAT'LL TEACH 'IM ...HEH, HEH.

2.

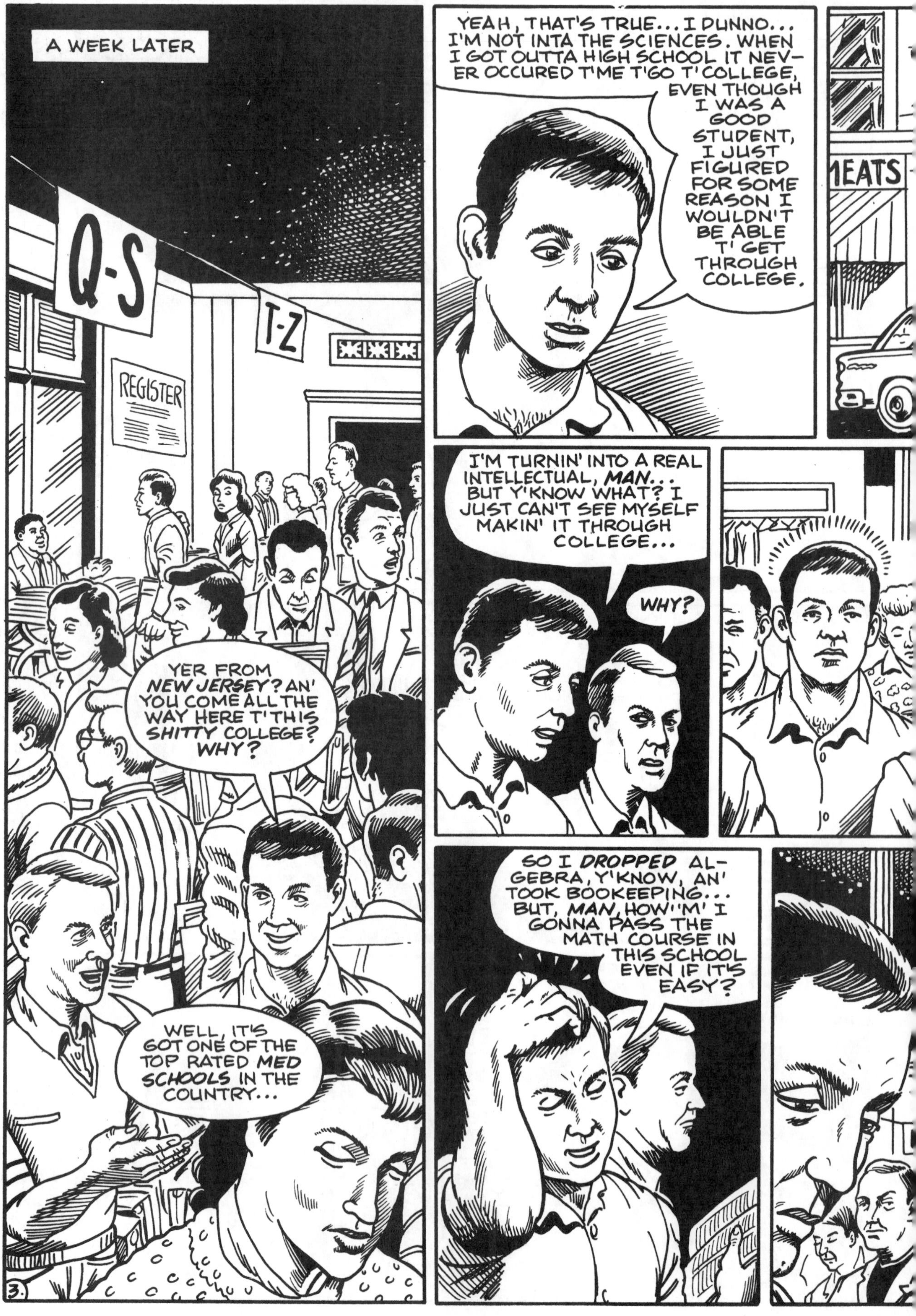
A WEEK LATER
Q-S
T-Z
REGISTER
YER FROM NEW JERSEY? AN' YOU COME ALL THE WAY HERE T'THIS SHITTY COLLEGE? WHY?
WELL, IT'S GOT ONE OF THE TOP RATED MED SCHOOLS IN THE COUNTRY...
YEAH, THAT'S TRUE... I DUNNO... I'M NOT INTA THE SCIENCES. WHEN I GOT OUTTA HIGH SCHOOL IT NEVER OCCURED T'ME T'GO T'COLLEGE, EVEN THOUGH I WAS A GOOD STUDENT, I JUST FIGURED FOR SOME REASON I WOULDN'T BE ABLE T'GET THROUGH COLLEGE.
MEATS
I'M TURNIN' INTO A REAL INTELLECTUAL, MAN... BUT Y'KNOW WHAT? I JUST CAN'T SEE MYSELF MAKIN' IT THROUGH COLLEGE...
WHY?
SO I DROPPED ALGEBRA, Y'KNOW, AN' TOOK BOOKEEPING... BUT, MAN, HOW'M' I GONNA PASS THE MATH COURSE IN THIS SCHOOL EVEN IF IT'S EASY?
3.

BUT, Y'KNOW, IN THE YEAR I WAS OUTTA SCHOOL I COULDN'T FIND ANY WORK I COULD LIVE WITH. SO I WENT BACK T' SCHOOL. THERE WAS NOTHING LEFT T'DO, NOWHERE ELSE T'GO.

SO IT TURNS OUT THAT I'M DOIN' *GOOD.* LIKE, I'VE FINISHED THREE SEMESTERS NOW, AN' I'VE GOT A 3.5 AVERAGE AN' LIKE, I'VE DEVELOPED THIS INTEREST IN *WRITING.* I EVEN GOT AN ARTICLE ACCEPTED BY THIS JAZZ MAGAZINE.

I REALLY LOVE JAZZ.... GOT A NICE RECORD COLLECTION.

JAZZ MUSIC

UH, WELL, THIS IS GONNA SEEM *CRAZY* TO YOU, BUT SEE, IN ORDER TO GRADUATE FROM THIS COLLEGE YOU GOTTA PASS SOME KINDA MATH COURSE

AND I GOT THIS PHOBIA ABOUT MATH.

IT WAS ALWAYS MY *WORST* SUBJECT. I DID O.K. IN IT THO'. USETA GET "C'S". SO THEN IN 9TH GRADE I WAS TAKING BEGINNING ALGEBRA AND RIGHT NEAR THE END OF THE SCHOOL YEAR EVERYTHING CAME *TOGETHER.* I REALLY UNDERSTOOD WHAT I WAS DOIN'... I GOT A "B".

85

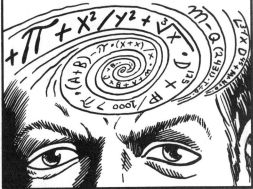

SO I TOOK ANOTHER ALGEBRA CLASS IN TENTH GRADE AND ALL OF A SUDDEN IT SEEMED LIKE I LOST IT. I DIDN'T UNDERSTAND THE STUFF *ANYMORE.* WHEN I TRIED TO THINK ABOUT IT I JUST GOT *NERVOUS, PANICKY.*

SIGN-IN

I *DUNNO,* GUESS I'LL PUT OFF THAT MATH CLASS AS LONG AS I CAN. MAYBE IN A COUPLA YEARS THEY WON'T REQUIRE IT ANYMORE.

FAT CHANCE, HUH?

4.

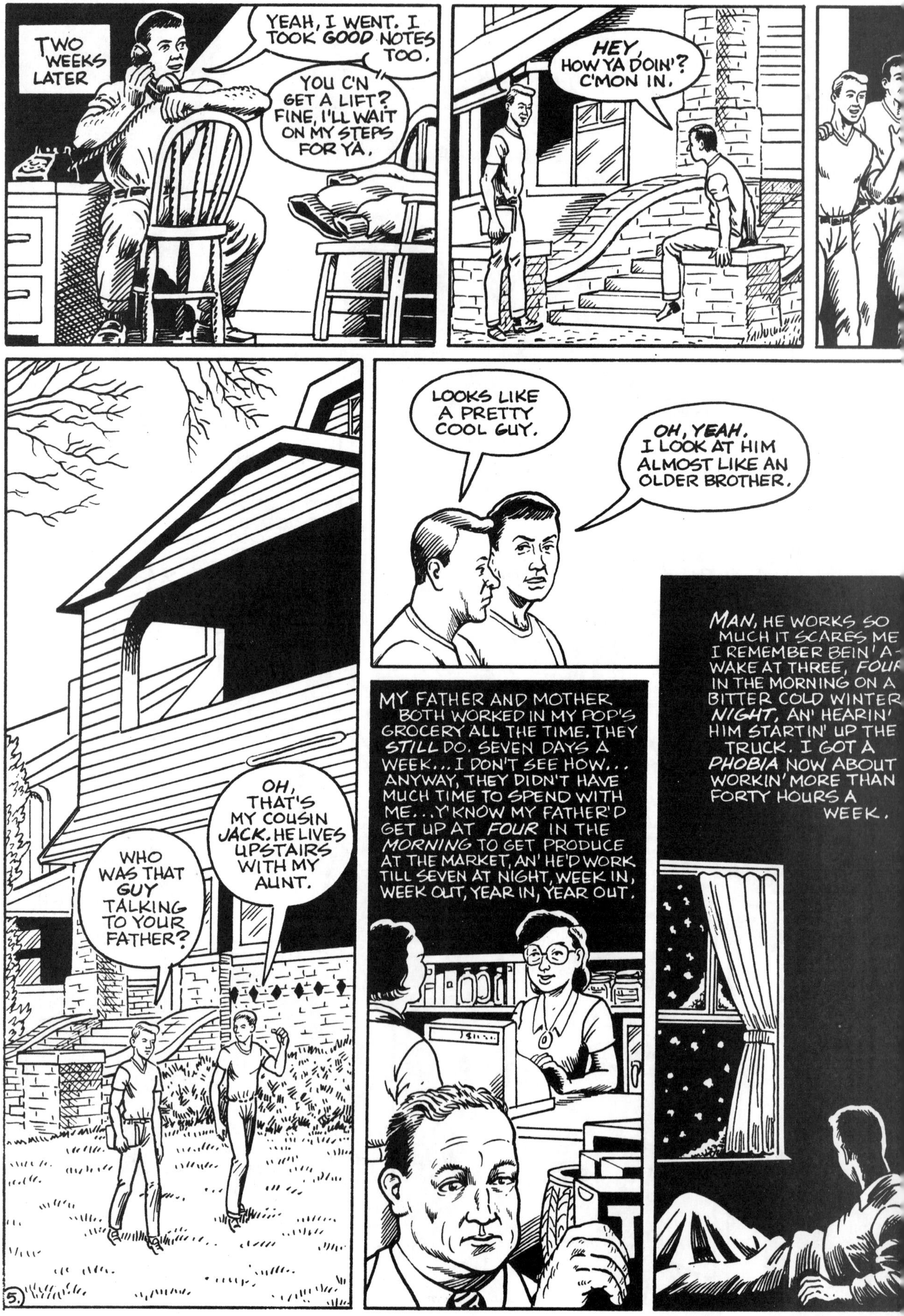
TWO WEEKS LATER
YEAH, I WENT. I TOOK GOOD NOTES TOO.
YOU C'N GET A LIFT? FINE, I'LL WAIT ON MY STEPS FOR YA.
HEY, HOW YA DOIN'? C'MON IN.
WHO WAS THAT GUY TALKING TO YOUR FATHER?
OH, THAT'S MY COUSIN JACK. HE LIVES UPSTAIRS WITH MY AUNT.
LOOKS LIKE A PRETTY COOL GUY.
OH, YEAH. I LOOK AT HIM ALMOST LIKE AN OLDER BROTHER.
MY FATHER AND MOTHER BOTH WORKED IN MY POP'S GROCERY ALL THE TIME. THEY STILL DO. SEVEN DAYS A WEEK... I DON'T SEE HOW... ANYWAY, THEY DIDN'T HAVE MUCH TIME TO SPEND WITH ME... Y'KNOW MY FATHER'D GET UP AT FOUR IN THE MORNING TO GET PRODUCE AT THE MARKET, AN' HE'D WORK TILL SEVEN AT NIGHT, WEEK IN, WEEK OUT, YEAR IN, YEAR OUT.
MAN, HE WORKS SO MUCH IT SCARES ME. I REMEMBER BEIN' A-WAKE AT THREE, FOUR IN THE MORNING ON A BITTER COLD WINTER NIGHT, AN' HEARIN' HIM STARTIN' UP THE TRUCK. I GOT A PHOBIA NOW ABOUT WORKIN' MORE THAN FORTY HOURS A WEEK.
5.

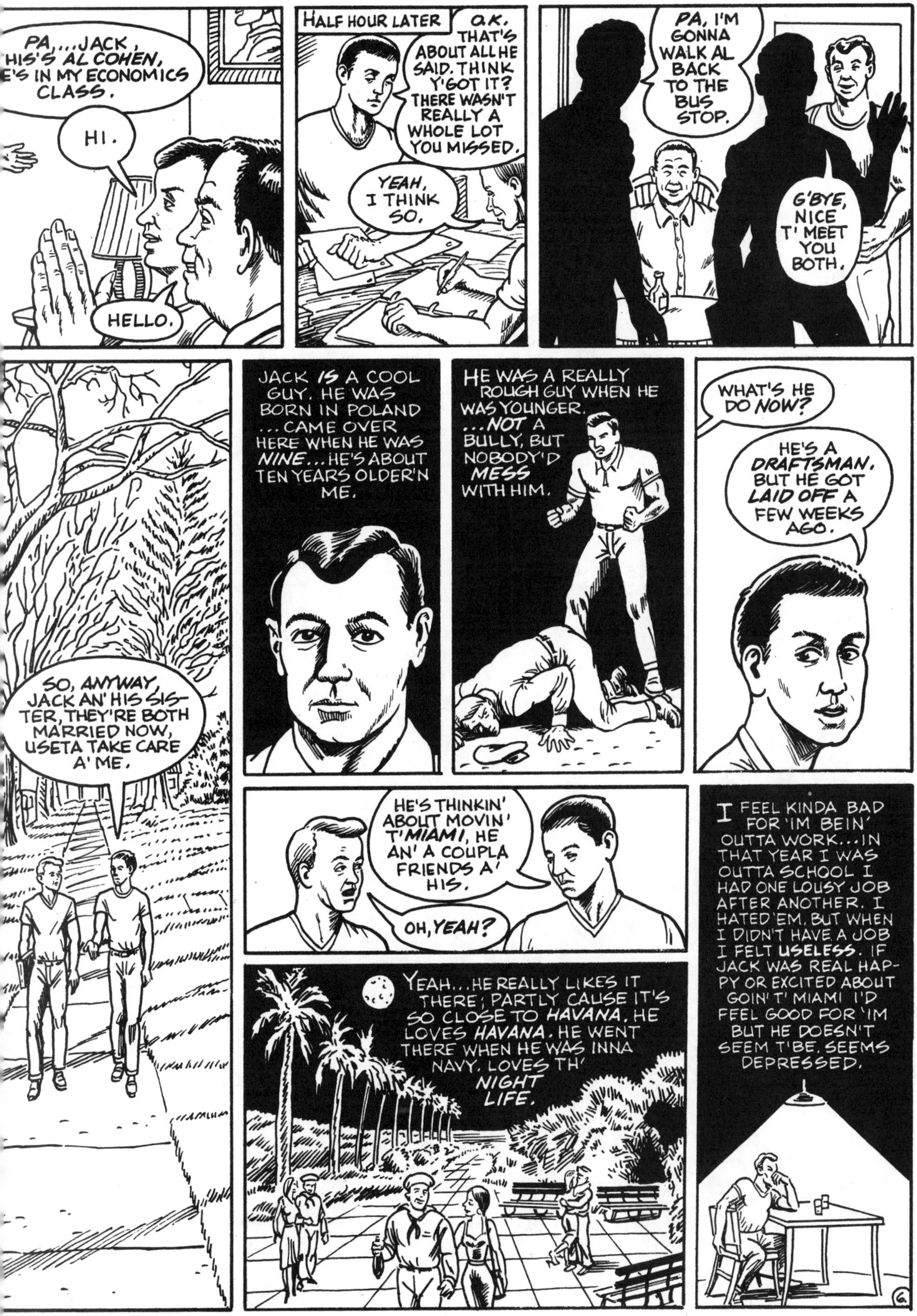

PA,...JACK, THIS'S AL COHEN, HE'S IN MY ECONOMICS CLASS.
HI.
HELLO.
HALF HOUR LATER
O.K. THAT'S ABOUT ALL HE SAID. THINK Y'GOT IT? THERE WASN'T REALLY A WHOLE LOT YOU MISSED.
YEAH, I THINK SO.
PA, I'M GONNA WALK AL BACK TO THE BUS STOP.
G'BYE, NICE T' MEET YOU BOTH.
SO, ANYWAY, JACK AN' HIS SISTER, THEY'RE BOTH MARRIED NOW, USETA TAKE CARE A' ME.
JACK IS A COOL GUY. HE WAS BORN IN POLAND ...CAME OVER HERE WHEN HE WAS NINE... HE'S ABOUT TEN YEARS OLDER'N ME.
HE WAS A REALLY ROUGH GUY WHEN HE WAS YOUNGER. ...NOT A BULLY, BUT NOBODY'D MESS WITH HIM.
WHAT'S HE DO NOW?
HE'S A DRAFTSMAN, BUT HE GOT LAID OFF A FEW WEEKS AGO.
HE'S THINKIN' ABOUT MOVIN' T'MIAMI, HE AN' A COUPLA FRIENDS A' HIS.
OH, YEAH?
YEAH... HE REALLY LIKES IT THERE; PARTLY CAUSE IT'S SO CLOSE TO HAVANA. HE LOVES HAVANA. HE WENT THERE WHEN HE WAS INNA NAVY. LOVES TH' NIGHT LIFE.
I FEEL KINDA BAD FOR 'IM BEIN' OUTTA WORK... IN THAT YEAR I WAS OUTTA SCHOOL I HAD ONE LOUSY JOB AFTER ANOTHER. I HATED 'EM, BUT WHEN I DIDN'T HAVE A JOB I FELT USELESS. IF JACK WAS REAL HAPPY OR EXCITED ABOUT GOIN' T' MIAMI I'D FEEL GOOD FOR 'IM BUT HE DOESN'T SEEM T'BE. SEEMS DEPRESSED.
6

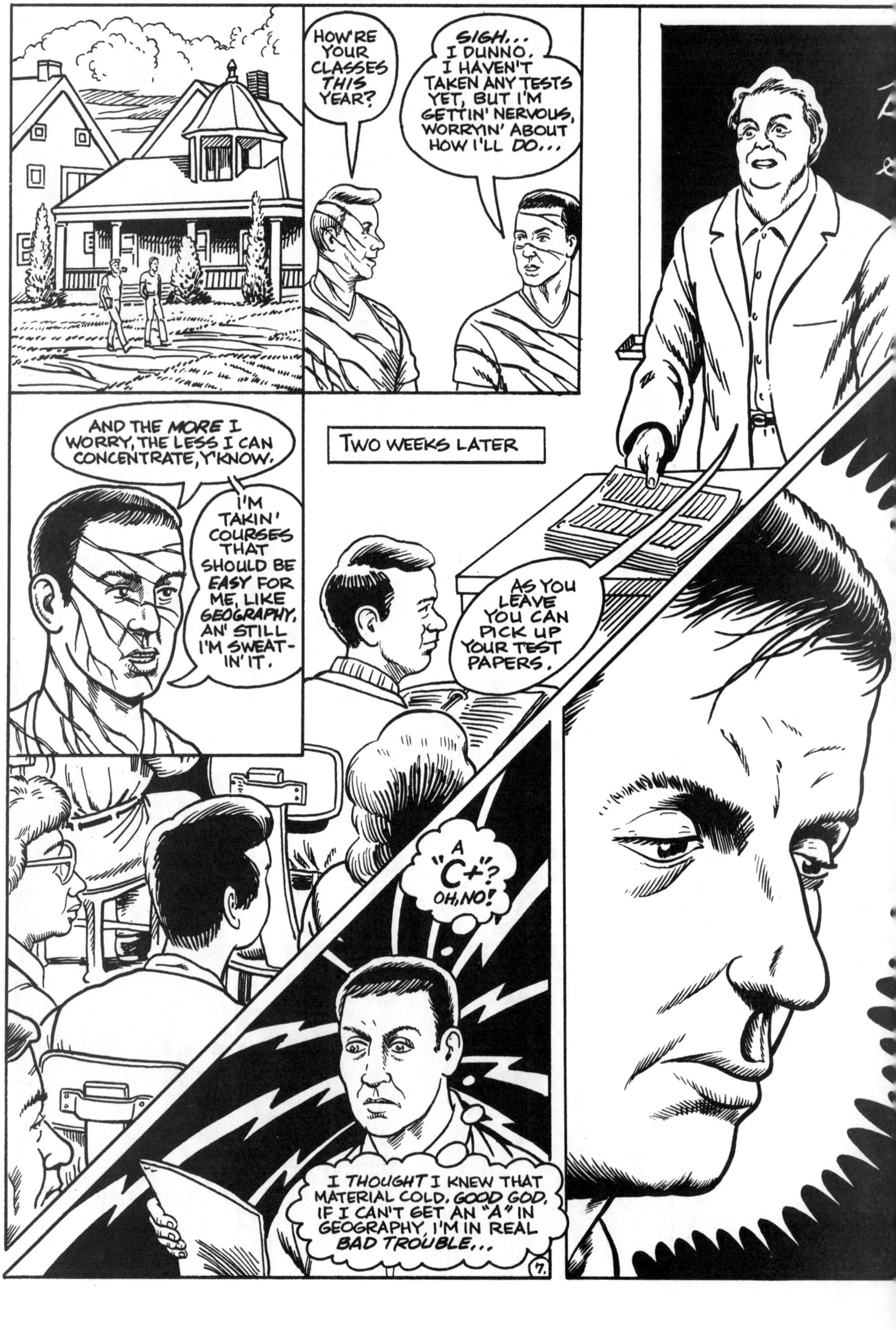
HOW'RE YOUR CLASSES THIS YEAR?
SIGH... I DUNNO. I HAVEN'T TAKEN ANY TESTS YET, BUT I'M GETTIN' NERVOUS, WORRYIN' ABOUT HOW I'LL DO...
AND THE MORE I WORRY, THE LESS I CAN CONCENTRATE, Y'KNOW.
I'M TAKIN' COURSES THAT SHOULD BE EASY FOR ME, LIKE GEOGRAPHY, AN' STILL I'M SWEAT-IN' IT.
TWO WEEKS LATER
AS YOU LEAVE YOU CAN PICK UP YOUR TEST PAPERS.
A "C+"? OH, NO!
I THOUGHT I KNEW THAT MATERIAL COLD. GOOD GOD. IF I CAN'T GET AN "A" IN GEOGRAPHY, I'M IN REAL BAD TROUBLE...
7.

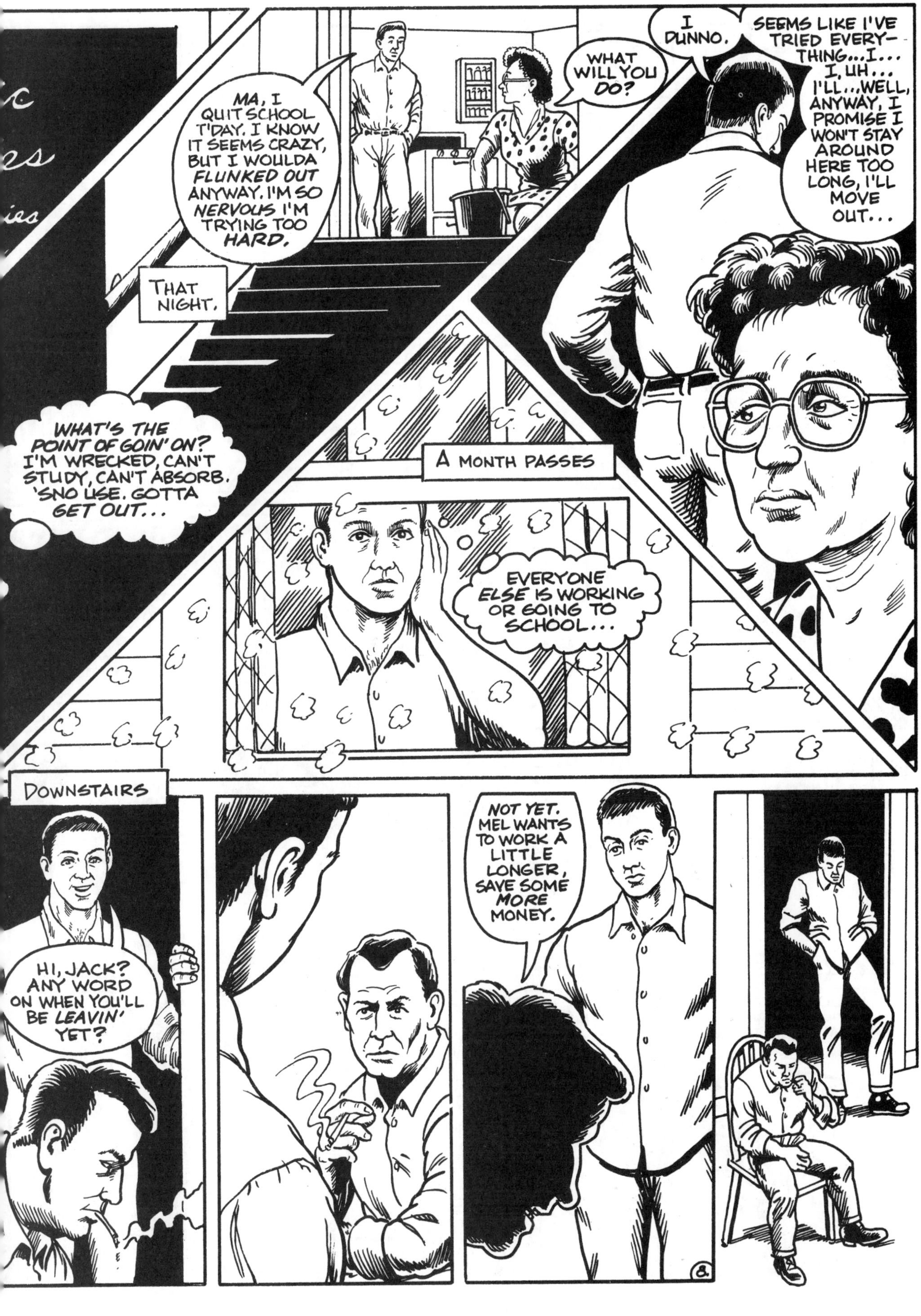
MA, I QUIT SCHOOL T'DAY. I KNOW IT SEEMS CRAZY, BUT I WOULDA FLUNKED OUT ANYWAY. I'M SO NERVOUS I'M TRYING TOO HARD.
WHAT WILL YOU DO?
I DUNNO.
SEEMS LIKE I'VE TRIED EVERY-THING... I... I, UH... I'LL... WELL, ANYWAY, I PROMISE I WON'T STAY AROUND HERE TOO LONG, I'LL MOVE OUT...
THAT NIGHT.
WHAT'S THE POINT OF GOIN' ON? I'M WRECKED, CAN'T STUDY, CAN'T ABSORB. 'SNO USE. GOTTA GET OUT...
A MONTH PASSES
EVERYONE ELSE IS WORKING OR GOING TO SCHOOL...
DOWNSTAIRS
HI, JACK? ANY WORD ON WHEN YOU'LL BE LEAVIN' YET?
NOT YET. MEL WANTS TO WORK A LITTLE LONGER, SAVE SOME MORE MONEY.
8.

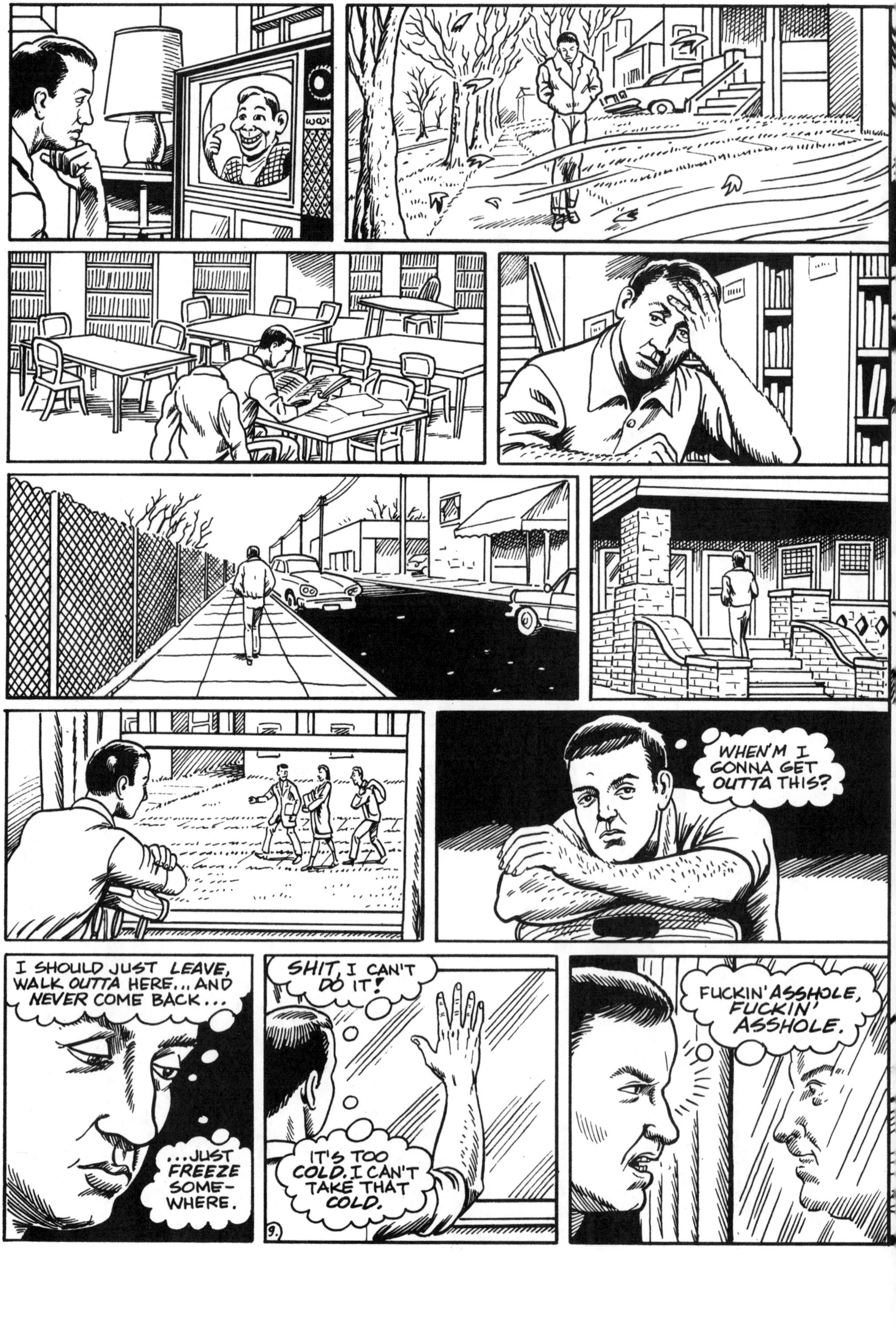
WHEN'M I GONNA GET OUTTA THIS?
I SHOULD JUST LEAVE, WALK OUTTA HERE... AND NEVER COME BACK...
...JUST FREEZE SOME-WHERE.
SHIT, I CAN'T DO IT!
IT'S TOO COLD. I CAN'T TAKE THAT COLD.
FUCKIN' ASSHOLE, FUCKIN' ASSHOLE.

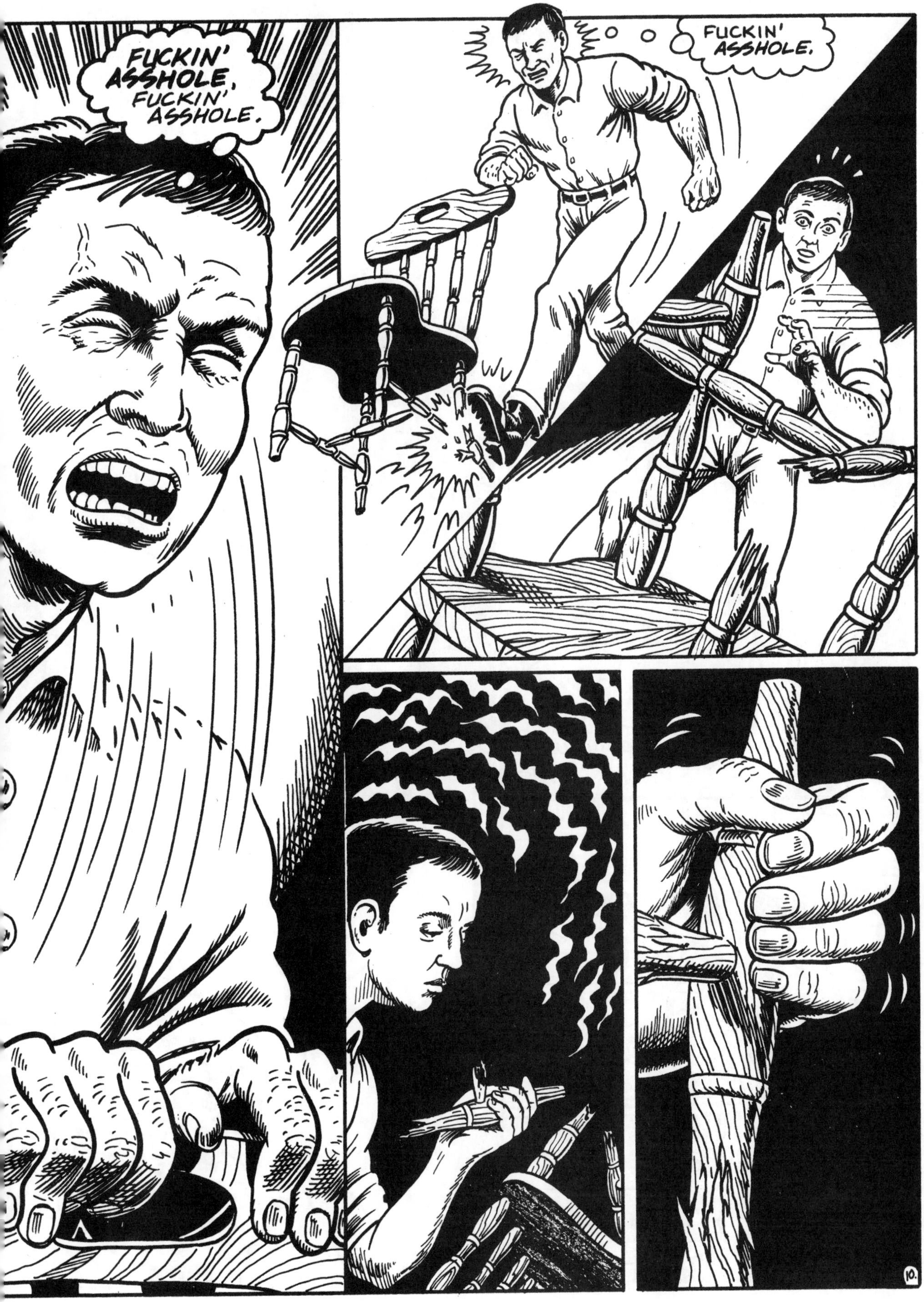
FUCKIN' ASSHOLE. FUCKIN' ASSHOLE.
FUCKIN' ASSHOLE.

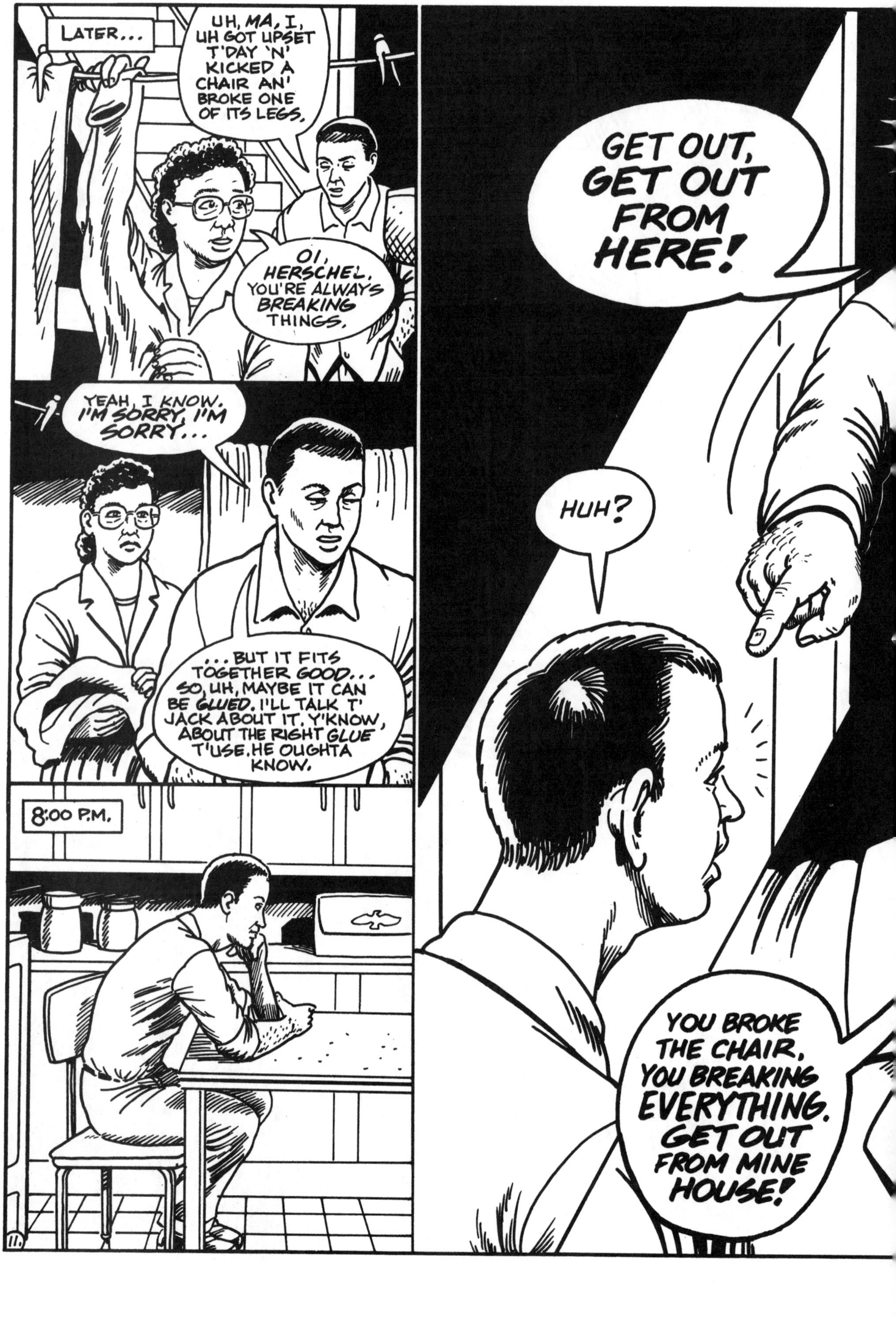
LATER...
UH, MA, I, UH GOT UPSET T'DAY 'N' KICKED A CHAIR AN' BROKE ONE OF ITS LEGS.
OI, HERSCHEL. YOU'RE ALWAYS BREAKING THINGS.
YEAH, I KNOW. I'M SORRY, I'M SORRY...
...BUT IT FITS TOGETHER GOOD... SO, UH, MAYBE IT CAN BE GLUED. I'LL TALK T' JACK ABOUT IT. Y'KNOW, ABOUT THE RIGHT GLUE T'USE. HE OUGHTA KNOW.
8:00 P.M.
GET OUT, GET OUT FROM HERE!
HUH?
YOU BROKE THE CHAIR, YOU BREAKING EVERYTHING. GET OUT FROM MINE HOUSE!

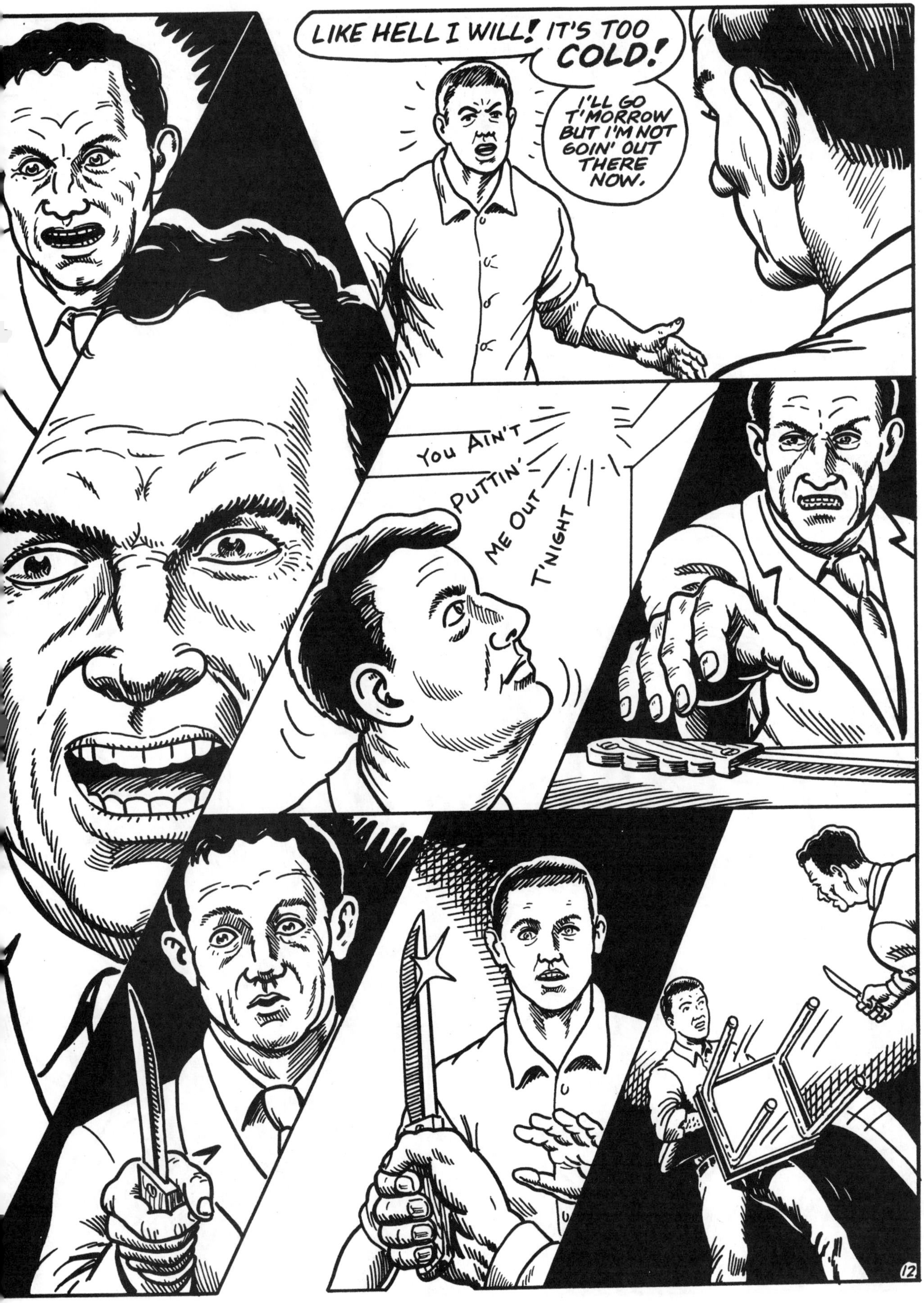

LIKE HELL I WILL! IT'S TOO COLD!
I'LL GO T'MORROW BUT I'M NOT GOIN' OUT THERE NOW.
YOU AIN'T PUTTIN' ME OUT T'NIGHT

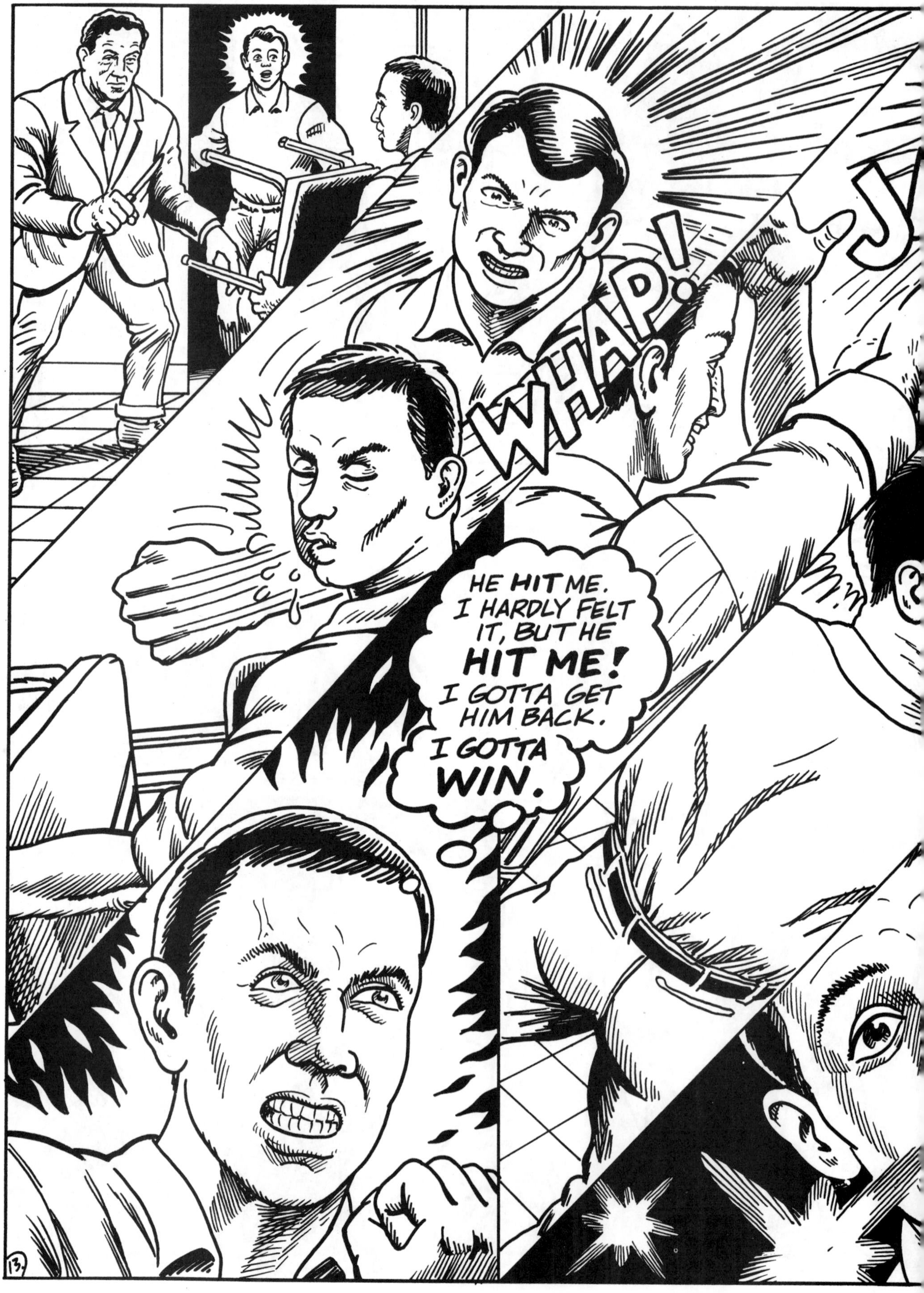
WHAP!
HE HIT ME. I HARDLY FELT IT, BUT HE HIT ME! I GOTTA GET HIM BACK. I GOTTA WIN.

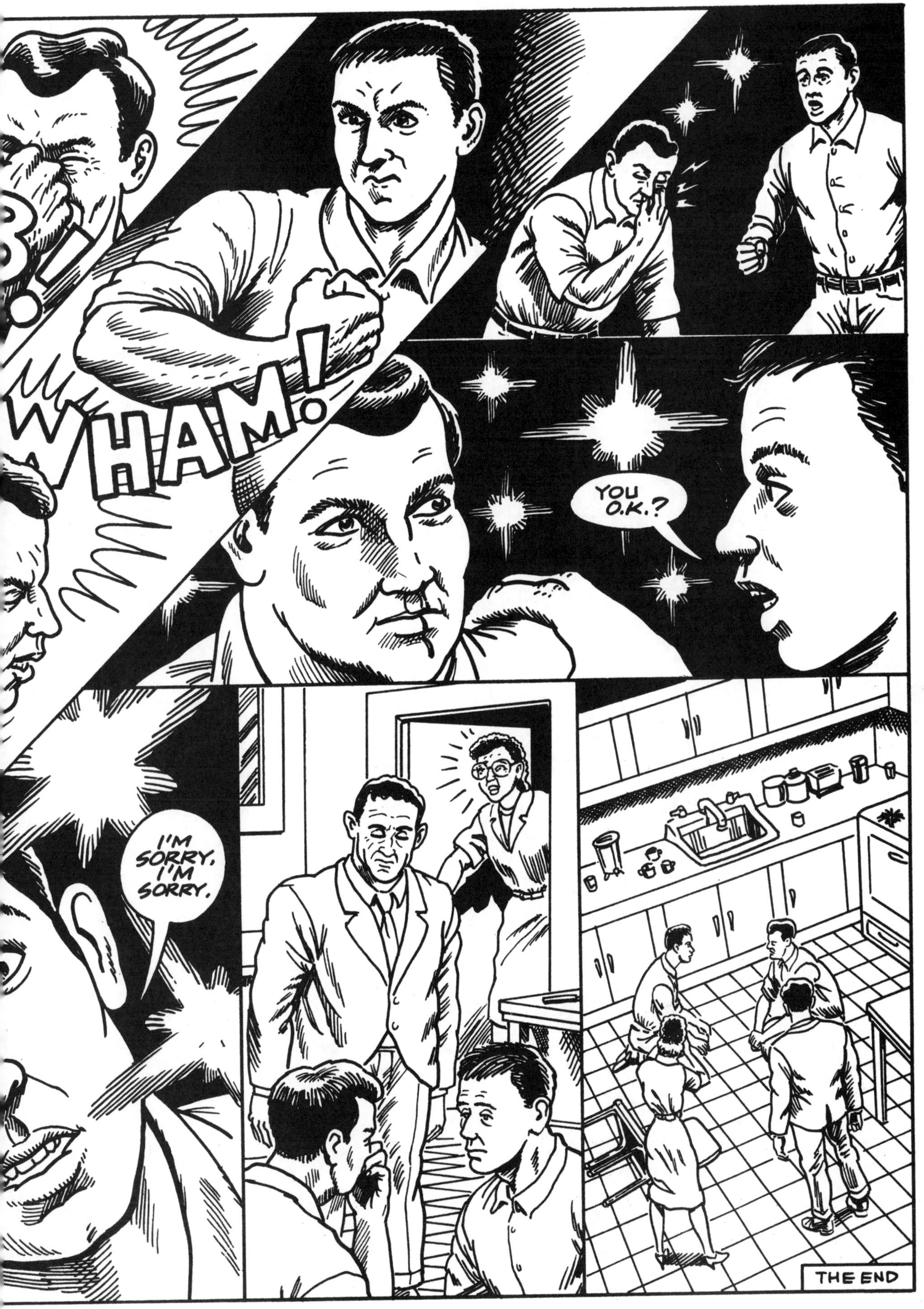
WHAM!
YOU O.K.?
I'M SORRY. I'M SORRY.
THE END

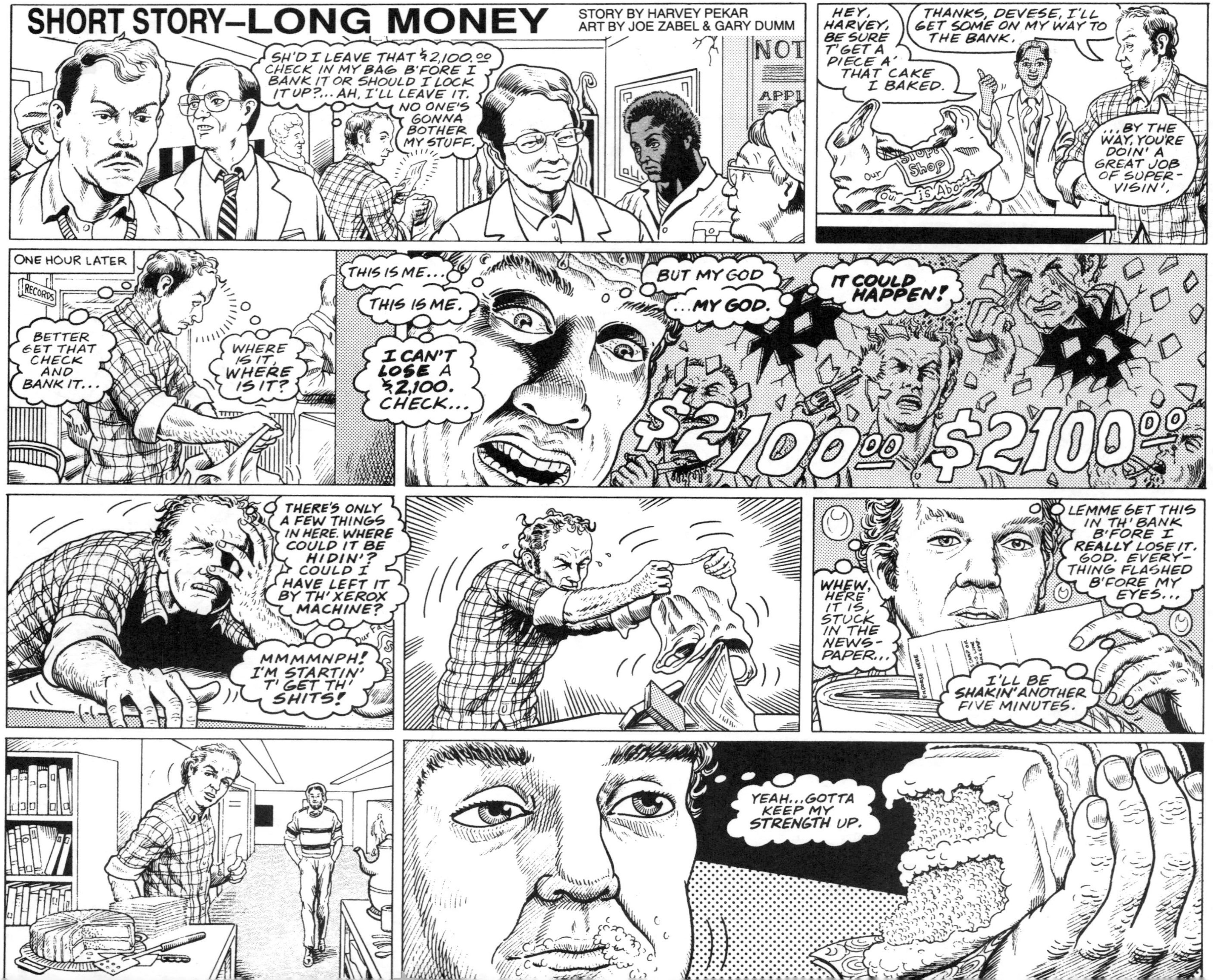
SHORT STORY–LONG MONEY
STORY BY HARVEY PEKAR
ART BY JOE ZABEL & GARY DUMM
SH'D I LEAVE THAT $2,100.00 CHECK IN MY BAG B'FORE I BANK IT OR SHOULD I LOCK IT UP?... AH, I'LL LEAVE IT. NO ONE'S GONNA BOTHER MY STUFF.
HEY, HARVEY, BE SURE T'GET A PIECE A' THAT CAKE I BAKED.
THANKS, DEVESE, I'LL GET SOME ON MY WAY TO THE BANK.
...BY THE WAY, YOU'RE DOIN' A GREAT JOB OF SUPER-VISIN'.
ONE HOUR LATER
RECORDS
BETTER GET THAT CHECK AND BANK IT...
WHERE IS IT, WHERE IS IT?
THIS IS ME...
THIS IS ME.
I CAN'T LOSE A $2,100. CHECK...
BUT MY GOD
...MY GOD.
IT COULD HAPPEN!
$2100.00 $2100.00
THERE'S ONLY A FEW THINGS IN HERE. WHERE COULD IT BE HIDIN'? COULD I HAVE LEFT IT BY TH' XEROX MACHINE?
MMMMNPH! I'M STARTIN' T' GET TH' SHITS!
WHEW, HERE IT IS, STUCK IN THE NEWS-PAPER...
LEMME GET THIS IN TH' BANK B'FORE I REALLY LOSE IT. GOD, EVERY-THING FLASHED B'FORE MY EYES...
I'LL BE SHAKIN' ANOTHER FIVE MINUTES.
YEAH... GOTTA KEEP MY STRENGTH UP.

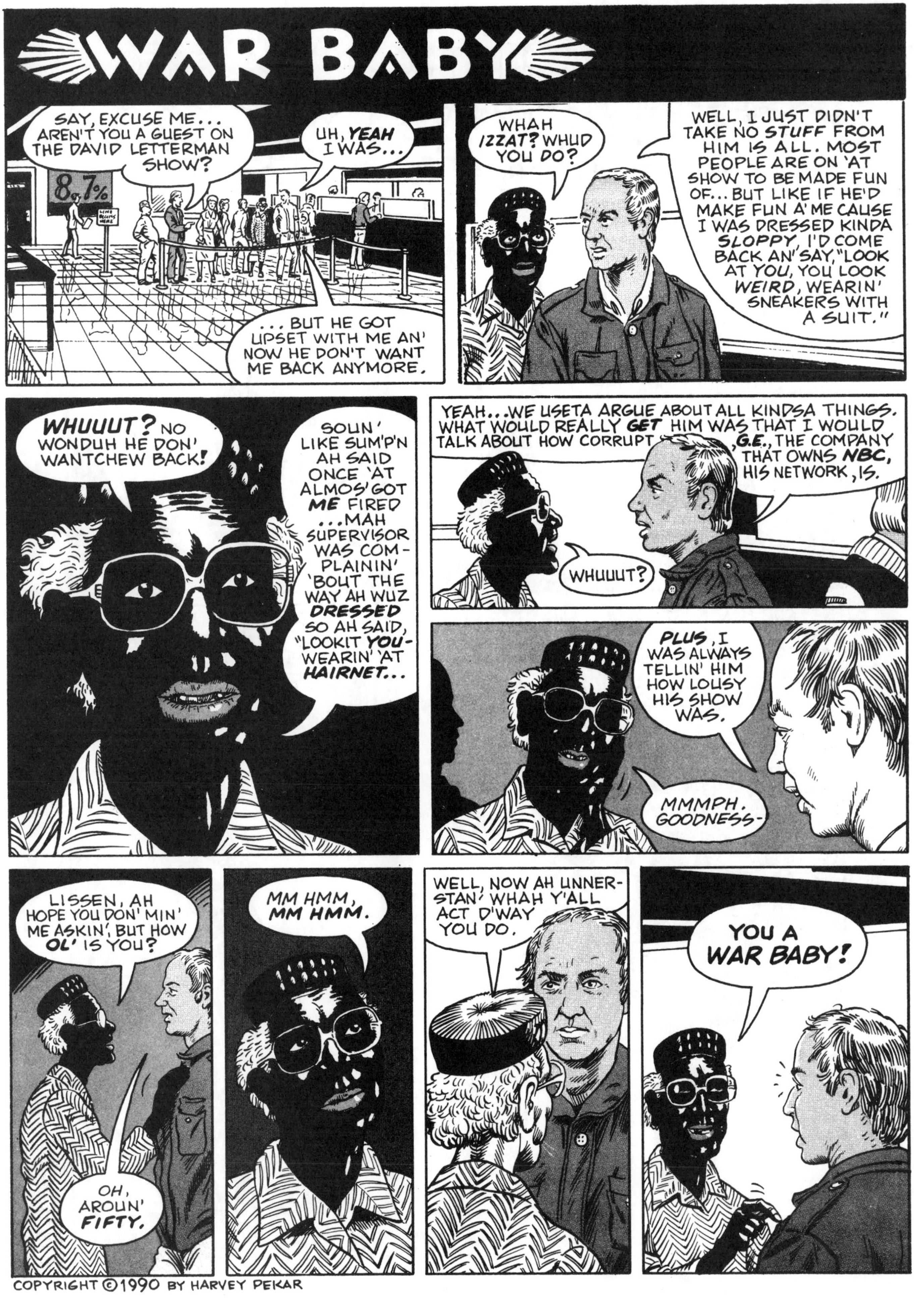
WAR BABY
SAY, EXCUSE ME... AREN'T YOU A GUEST ON THE DAVID LETTERMAN SHOW?
UH, YEAH I WAS...
8.7%
...BUT HE GOT UPSET WITH ME AN' NOW HE DON'T WANT ME BACK ANYMORE.
WHAH IZZAT? WHUD YOU DO?
WELL, I JUST DIDN'T TAKE NO STUFF FROM HIM IS ALL. MOST PEOPLE ARE ON 'AT SHOW TO BE MADE FUN OF... BUT LIKE IF HE'D MAKE FUN A'ME CAUSE I WAS DRESSED KINDA SLOPPY, I'D COME BACK AN' SAY, "LOOK AT YOU, YOU LOOK WEIRD, WEARIN' SNEAKERS WITH A SUIT."
WHUUUT? NO WONDUH HE DON' WANTCHEW BACK!
SOUN' LIKE SUM'P'N AH SAID ONCE 'AT ALMOS' GOT ME FIRED ...MAH SUPERVISOR WAS COMPLAININ' 'BOUT THE WAY AH WUZ DRESSED SO AH SAID, "LOOKIT YOU-WEARIN' 'AT HAIRNET...
YEAH...WE USETA ARGUE ABOUT ALL KINDSA THINGS. WHAT WOULD REALLY GET HIM WAS THAT I WOULD TALK ABOUT HOW CORRUPT G.E., THE COMPANY THAT OWNS NBC, HIS NETWORK, IS.
WHUUUT?
PLUS, I WAS ALWAYS TELLIN' HIM HOW LOUSY HIS SHOW WAS.
MMMPH. GOODNESS-
LISSEN, AH HOPE YOU DON' MIN' ME ASKIN', BUT HOW OL' IS YOU?
OH, AROUN' FIFTY.
MM HMM, MM HMM.
WELL, NOW AH UNNERSTAN' WHAH Y'ALL ACT D'WAY YOU DO.
YOU A WAR BABY!

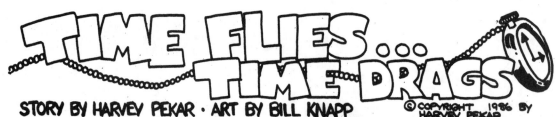

TIME FLIES... TIME DRAGS

STORY BY HARVEY PEKAR · ART BY BILL KNAPP

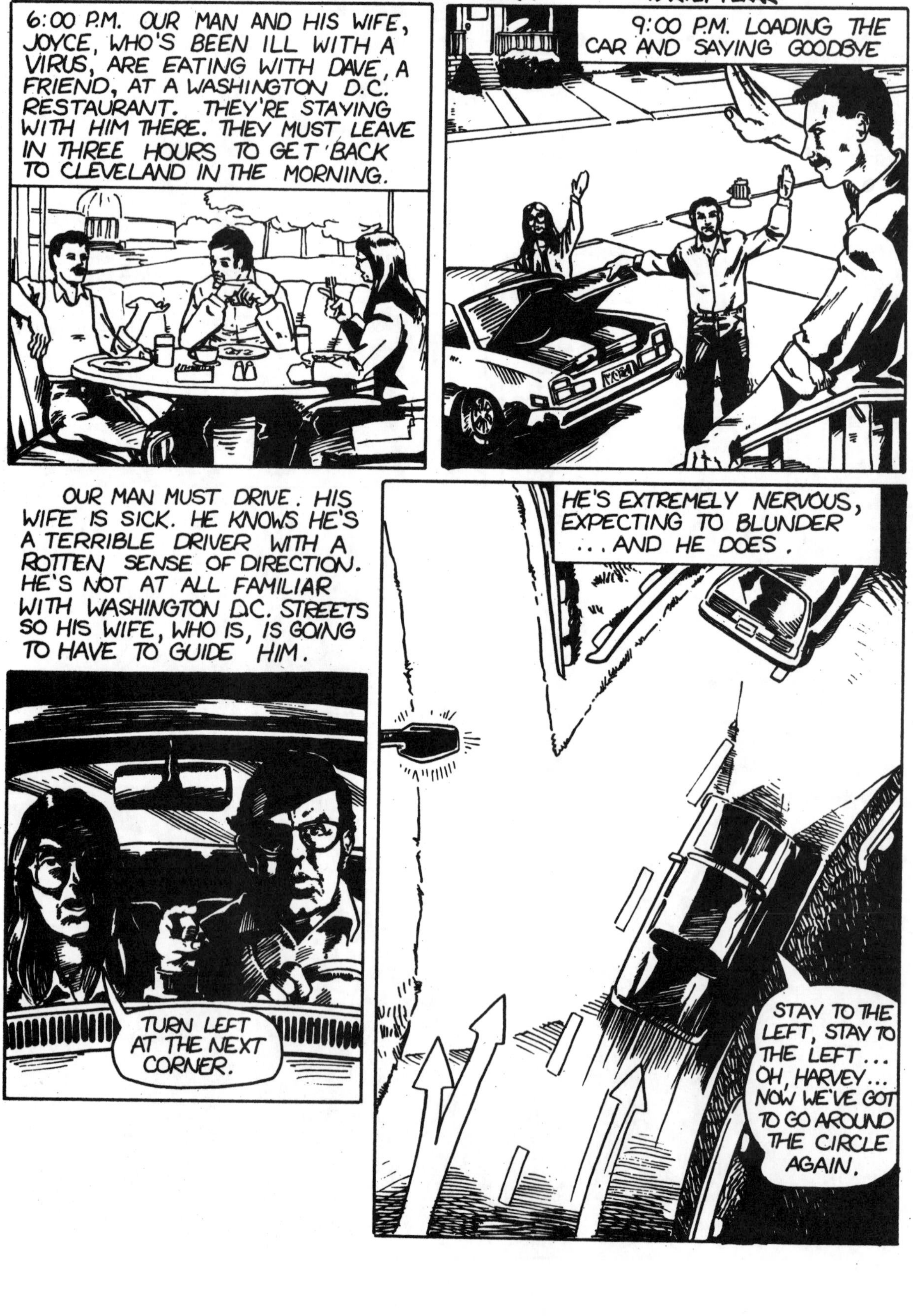
6:00 P.M. OUR MAN AND HIS WIFE, JOYCE, WHO'S BEEN ILL WITH A VIRUS, ARE EATING WITH DAVE, A FRIEND, AT A WASHINGTON D.C. RESTAURANT. THEY'RE STAYING WITH HIM THERE. THEY MUST LEAVE IN THREE HOURS TO GET BACK TO CLEVELAND IN THE MORNING.
9:00 P.M. LOADING THE CAR AND SAYING GOODBYE
OUR MAN MUST DRIVE. HIS WIFE IS SICK. HE KNOWS HE'S A TERRIBLE DRIVER WITH A ROTTEN SENSE OF DIRECTION. HE'S NOT AT ALL FAMILIAR WITH WASHINGTON D.C. STREETS SO HIS WIFE, WHO IS, IS GOING TO HAVE TO GUIDE HIM.
TURN LEFT AT THE NEXT CORNER.
HE'S EXTREMELY NERVOUS, EXPECTING TO BLUNDER ...AND HE DOES.
STAY TO THE LEFT, STAY TO THE LEFT... OH, HARVEY... NOW WE'VE GOT TO GO AROUND THE CIRCLE AGAIN.

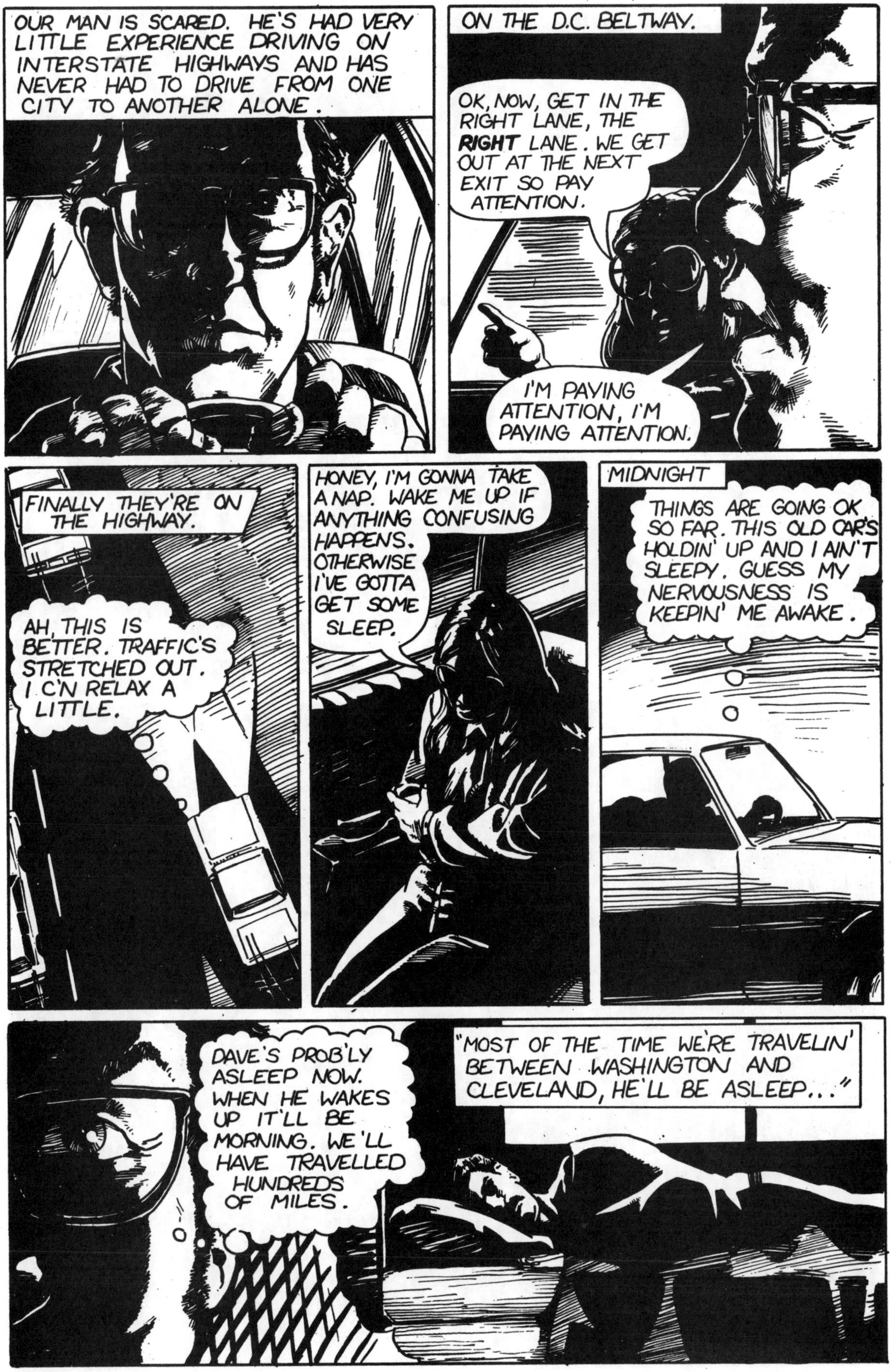
OUR MAN IS SCARED. HE'S HAD VERY LITTLE EXPERIENCE DRIVING ON INTERSTATE HIGHWAYS AND HAS NEVER HAD TO DRIVE FROM ONE CITY TO ANOTHER ALONE.
ON THE D.C. BELTWAY.
OK, NOW, GET IN THE RIGHT LANE, THE **RIGHT** LANE. WE GET OUT AT THE NEXT EXIT SO PAY ATTENTION.
I'M PAYING ATTENTION, I'M PAYING ATTENTION.
FINALLY THEY'RE ON THE HIGHWAY.
AH, THIS IS BETTER. TRAFFIC'S STRETCHED OUT. I C'N RELAX A LITTLE.
HONEY, I'M GONNA TAKE A NAP. WAKE ME UP IF ANYTHING CONFUSING HAPPENS. OTHERWISE I'VE GOTTA GET SOME SLEEP.
MIDNIGHT
THINGS ARE GOING OK SO FAR. THIS OLD CAR'S HOLDIN' UP AND I AIN'T SLEEPY. GUESS MY NERVOUSNESS IS KEEPIN' ME AWAKE.
DAVE'S PROB'LY ASLEEP NOW. WHEN HE WAKES UP IT'LL BE MORNING. WE'LL HAVE TRAVELLED HUNDREDS OF MILES.
"MOST OF THE TIME WE'RE TRAVELIN' BETWEEN WASHINGTON AND CLEVELAND, HE'LL BE ASLEEP..."

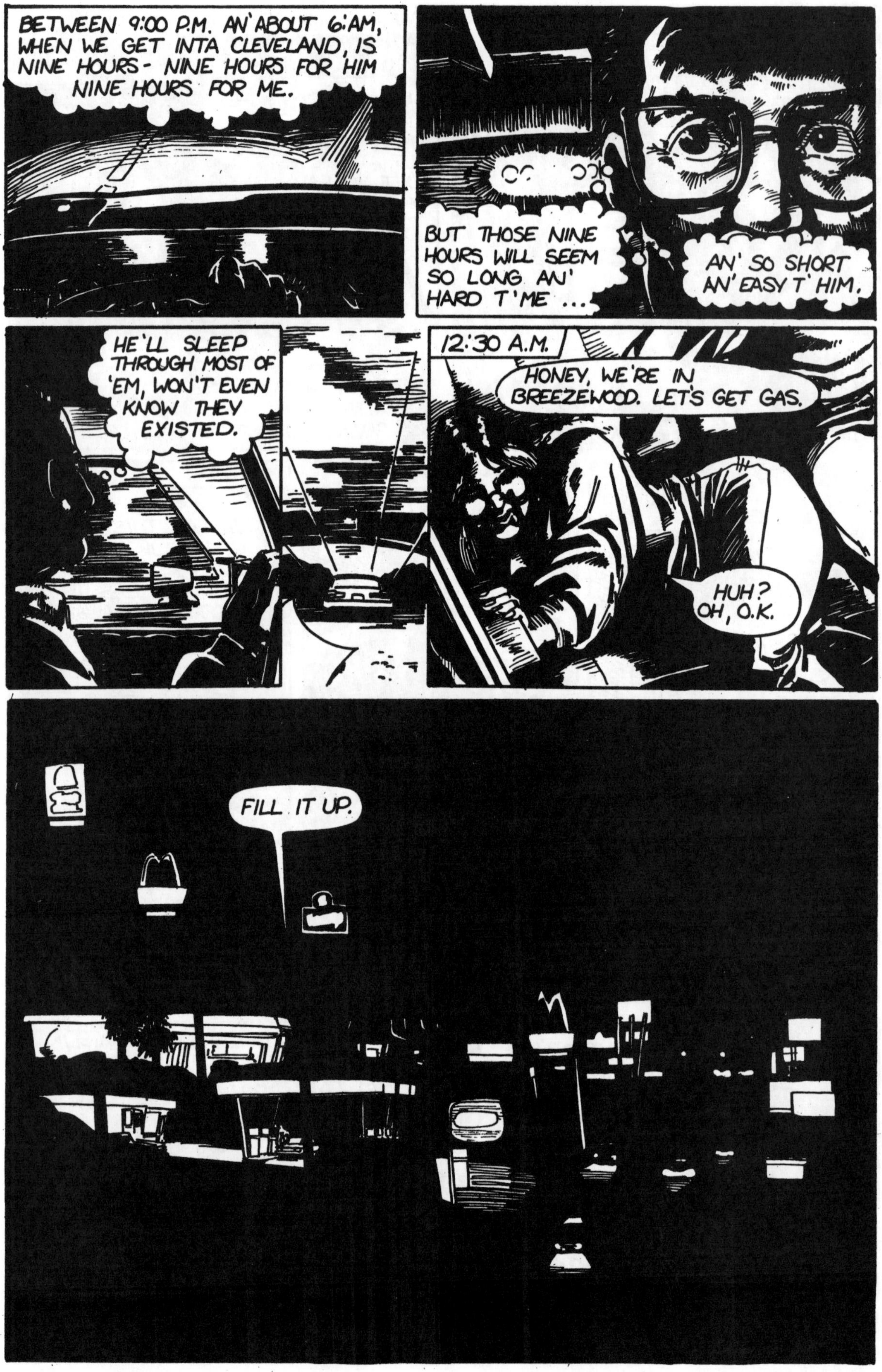
BETWEEN 9:00 P.M. AN' ABOUT 6:AM, WHEN WE GET INTA CLEVELAND, IS NINE HOURS- NINE HOURS FOR HIM NINE HOURS FOR ME.
BUT THOSE NINE HOURS WILL SEEM SO LONG AN' HARD T'ME ...
AN' SO SHORT AN' EASY T' HIM.
HE'LL SLEEP THROUGH MOST OF 'EM, WON'T EVEN KNOW THEY EXISTED.
12:30 A.M.
HONEY, WE'RE IN BREEZEWOOD. LET'S GET GAS.
HUH? OH, O.K.
FILL IT UP.

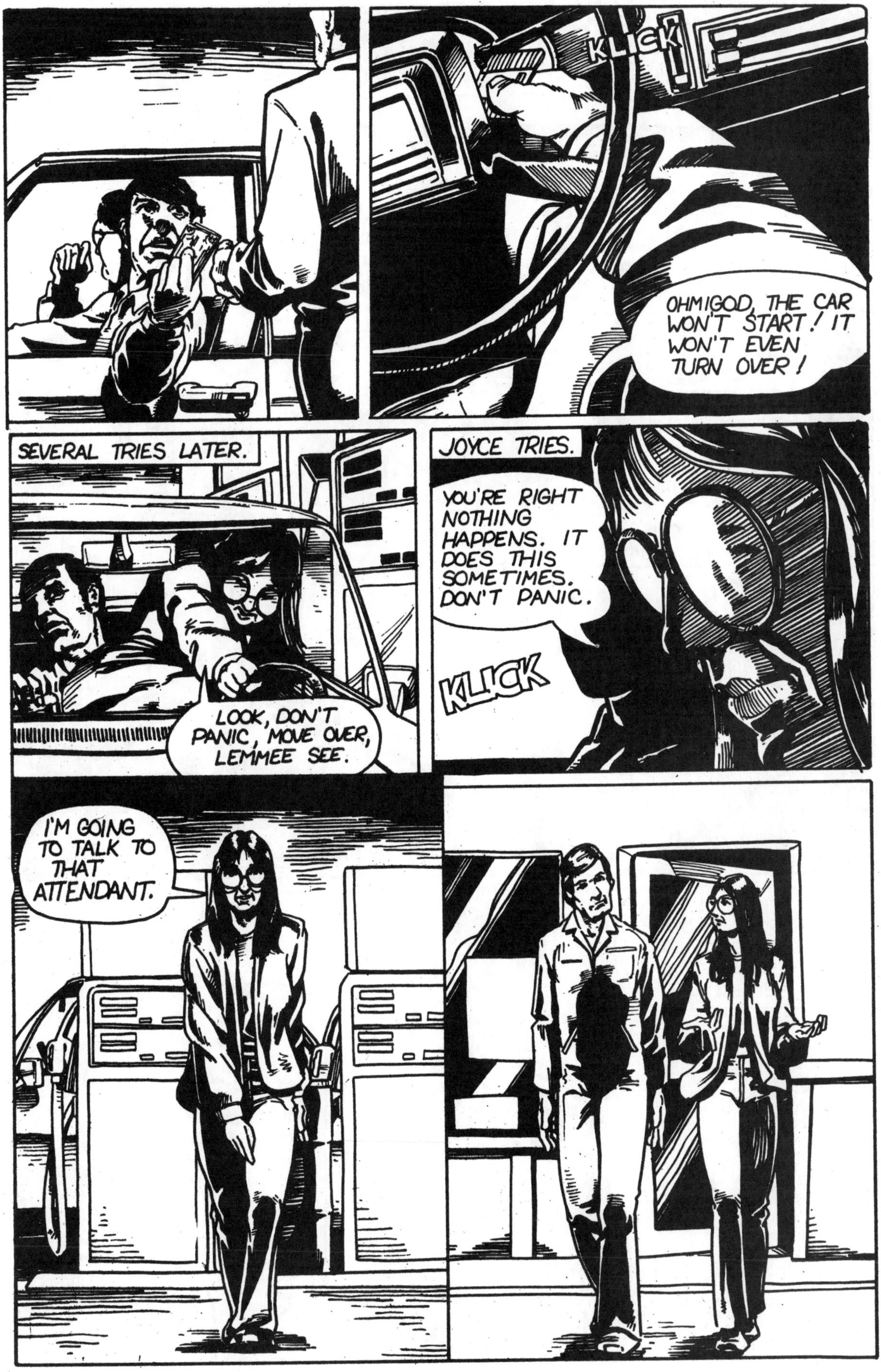
KLICK
OHMIGOD, THE CAR WON'T START! IT WON'T EVEN TURN OVER!
SEVERAL TRIES LATER.
LOOK, DON'T PANIC, MOVE OVER, LEMMEE SEE.
JOYCE TRIES.
YOU'RE RIGHT NOTHING HAPPENS. IT DOES THIS SOMETIMES. DON'T PANIC.
KLICK
I'M GOING TO TALK TO THAT ATTENDANT.

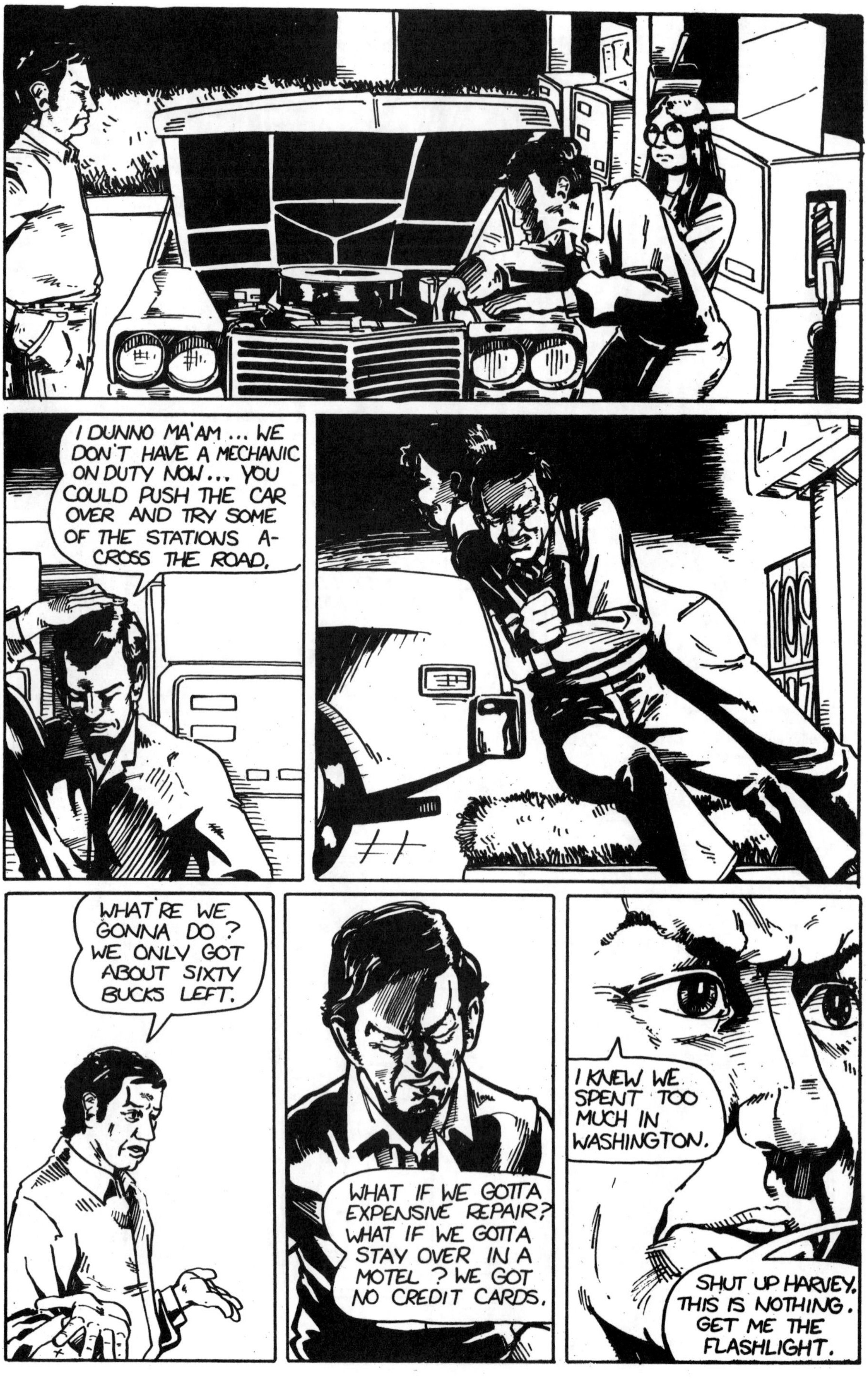
I DUNNO MA'AM ... WE DON'T HAVE A MECHANIC ON DUTY NOW... YOU COULD PUSH THE CAR OVER AND TRY SOME OF THE STATIONS A-CROSS THE ROAD.
WHAT'RE WE GONNA DO? WE ONLY GOT ABOUT SIXTY BUCKS LEFT.
WHAT IF WE GOTTA EXPENSIVE REPAIR? WHAT IF WE GOTTA STAY OVER IN A MOTEL? WE GOT NO CREDIT CARDS.
I KNEW WE SPENT TOO MUCH IN WASHINGTON.
SHUT UP HARVEY. THIS IS NOTHING. GET ME THE FLASHLIGHT.

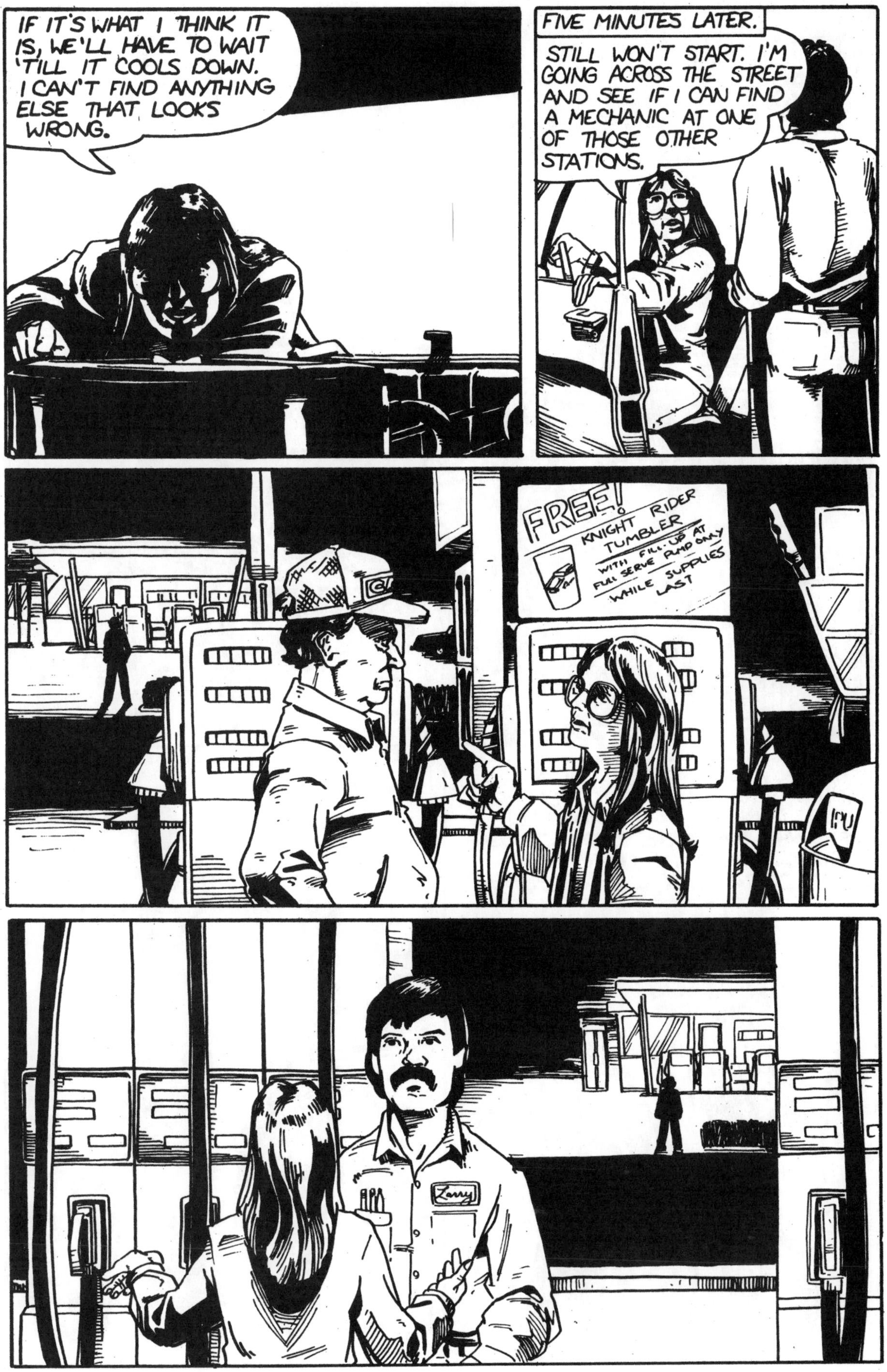
IF IT'S WHAT I THINK IT IS, WE'LL HAVE TO WAIT 'TILL IT COOLS DOWN. I CAN'T FIND ANYTHING ELSE THAT LOOKS WRONG.
FIVE MINUTES LATER.
STILL WON'T START. I'M GOING ACROSS THE STREET AND SEE IF I CAN FIND A MECHANIC AT ONE OF THOSE OTHER STATIONS.
FREE!
KNIGHT RIDER TUMBLER
WITH FILL-UP AT FULL SERVE PUMP ONLY
WHILE SUPPLIES LAST
Larry

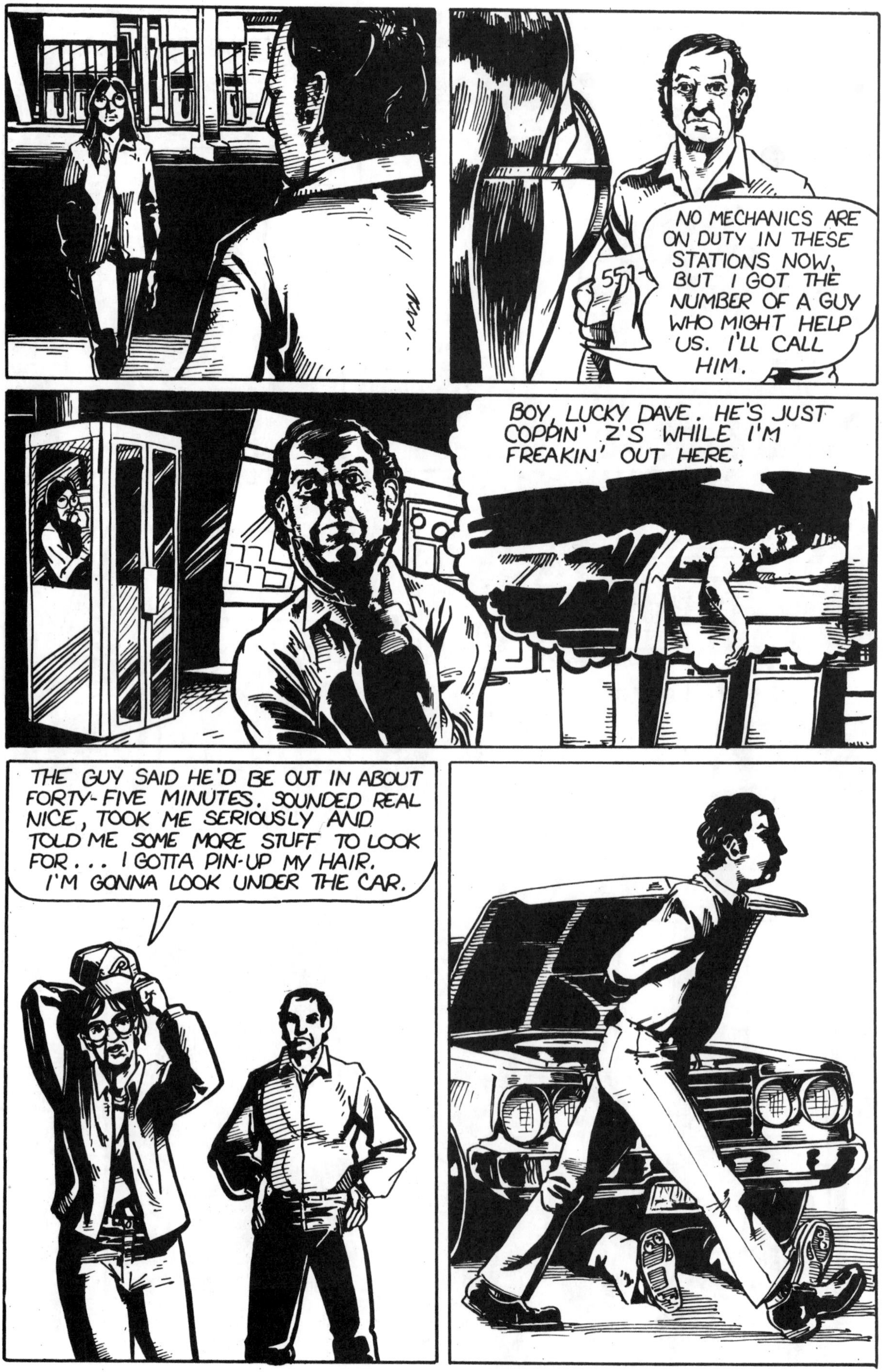
NO MECHANICS ARE ON DUTY IN THESE STATIONS NOW, BUT I GOT THE NUMBER OF A GUY WHO MIGHT HELP US. I'LL CALL HIM.
BOY, LUCKY DAVE. HE'S JUST COPPIN' Z'S WHILE I'M FREAKIN' OUT HERE.
THE GUY SAID HE'D BE OUT IN ABOUT FORTY-FIVE MINUTES. SOUNDED REAL NICE, TOOK ME SERIOUSLY AND TOLD ME SOME MORE STUFF TO LOOK FOR... I GOTTA PIN-UP MY HAIR. I'M GONNA LOOK UNDER THE CAR.

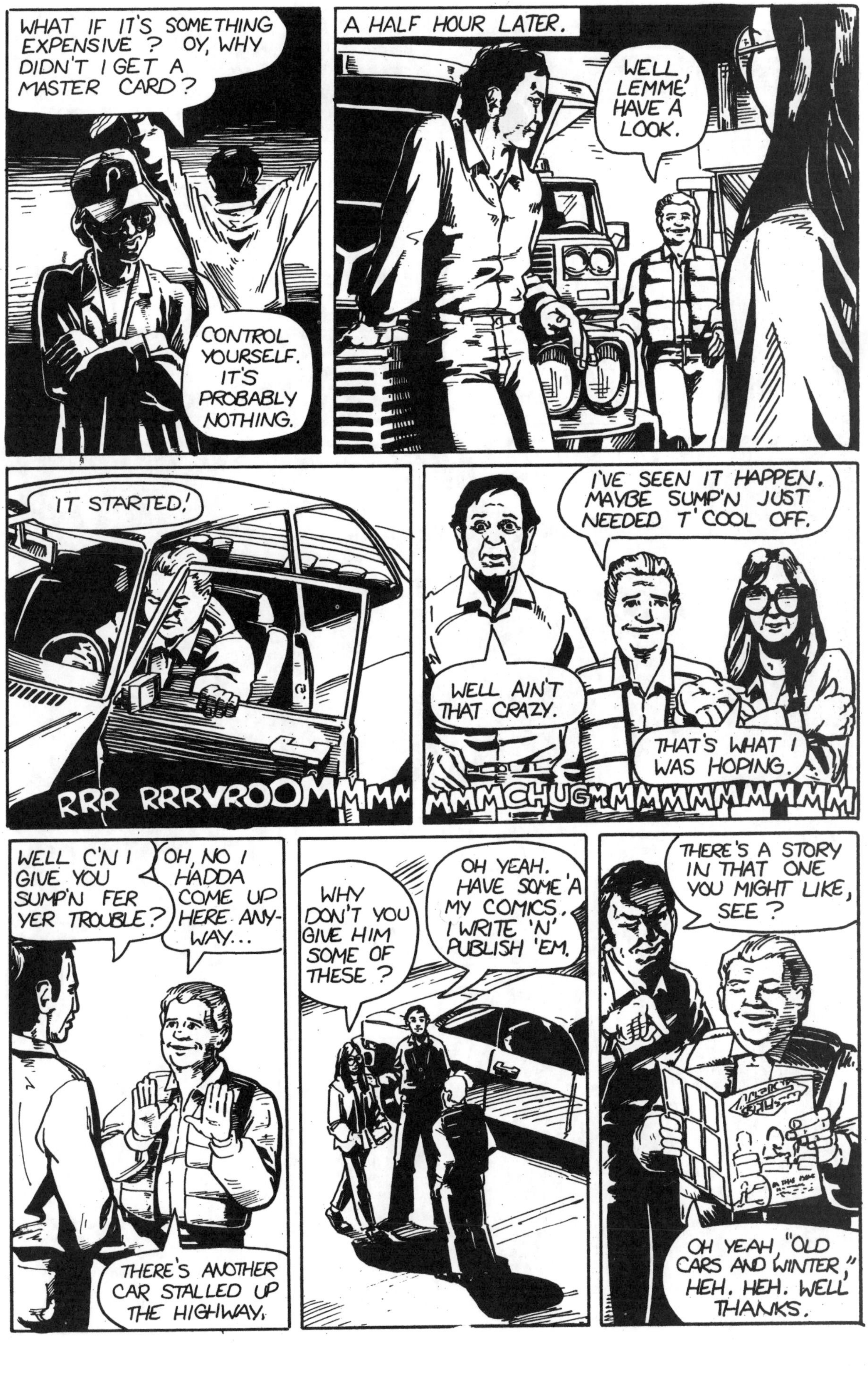
WHAT IF IT'S SOMETHING EXPENSIVE ? OY, WHY DIDN'T I GET A MASTER CARD ?
CONTROL YOURSELF. IT'S PROBABLY NOTHING.
A HALF HOUR LATER.
WELL, LEMME HAVE A LOOK.
IT STARTED!
RRR RRRVROOMMMM
I'VE SEEN IT HAPPEN. MAYBE SUMP'N JUST NEEDED T' COOL OFF.
WELL AIN'T THAT CRAZY.
THAT'S WHAT I WAS HOPING.
MMMCHUGMMMMMMMMMMM
WELL C'N I GIVE YOU SUMP'N FER YER TROUBLE?
OH, NO I HADDA COME UP HERE ANY-WAY...
THERE'S ANOTHER CAR STALLED UP THE HIGHWAY.
WHY DON'T YOU GIVE HIM SOME OF THESE ?
OH YEAH. HAVE SOME 'A MY COMICS. I WRITE 'N' PUBLISH 'EM.
THERE'S A STORY IN THAT ONE YOU MIGHT LIKE, SEE ?
OH YEAH, "OLD CARS AND WINTER," HEH. HEH. WELL THANKS.

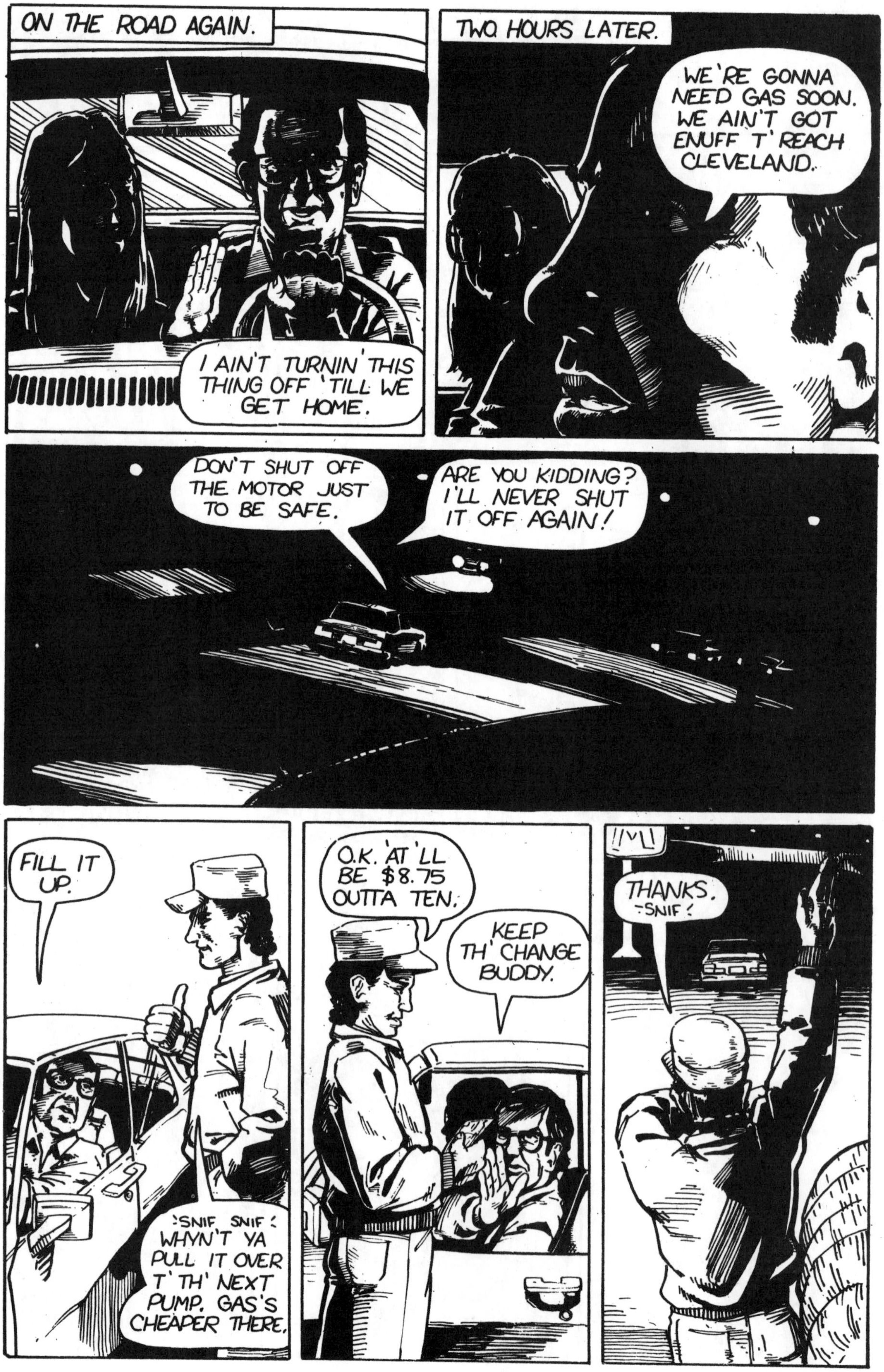
ON THE ROAD AGAIN.
I AIN'T TURNIN' THIS THING OFF 'TILL WE GET HOME.
TWO HOURS LATER.
WE'RE GONNA NEED GAS SOON. WE AIN'T GOT ENUFF T' REACH CLEVELAND.
DON'T SHUT OFF THE MOTOR JUST TO BE SAFE.
ARE YOU KIDDING? I'LL NEVER SHUT IT OFF AGAIN!
FILL IT UP.
-SNIF SNIF- WHYN'T YA PULL IT OVER T' TH' NEXT PUMP. GAS'S CHEAPER THERE.
O.K. AT'LL BE $8.75 OUTTA TEN.
KEEP TH' CHANGE BUDDY.
THANKS. -SNIF-

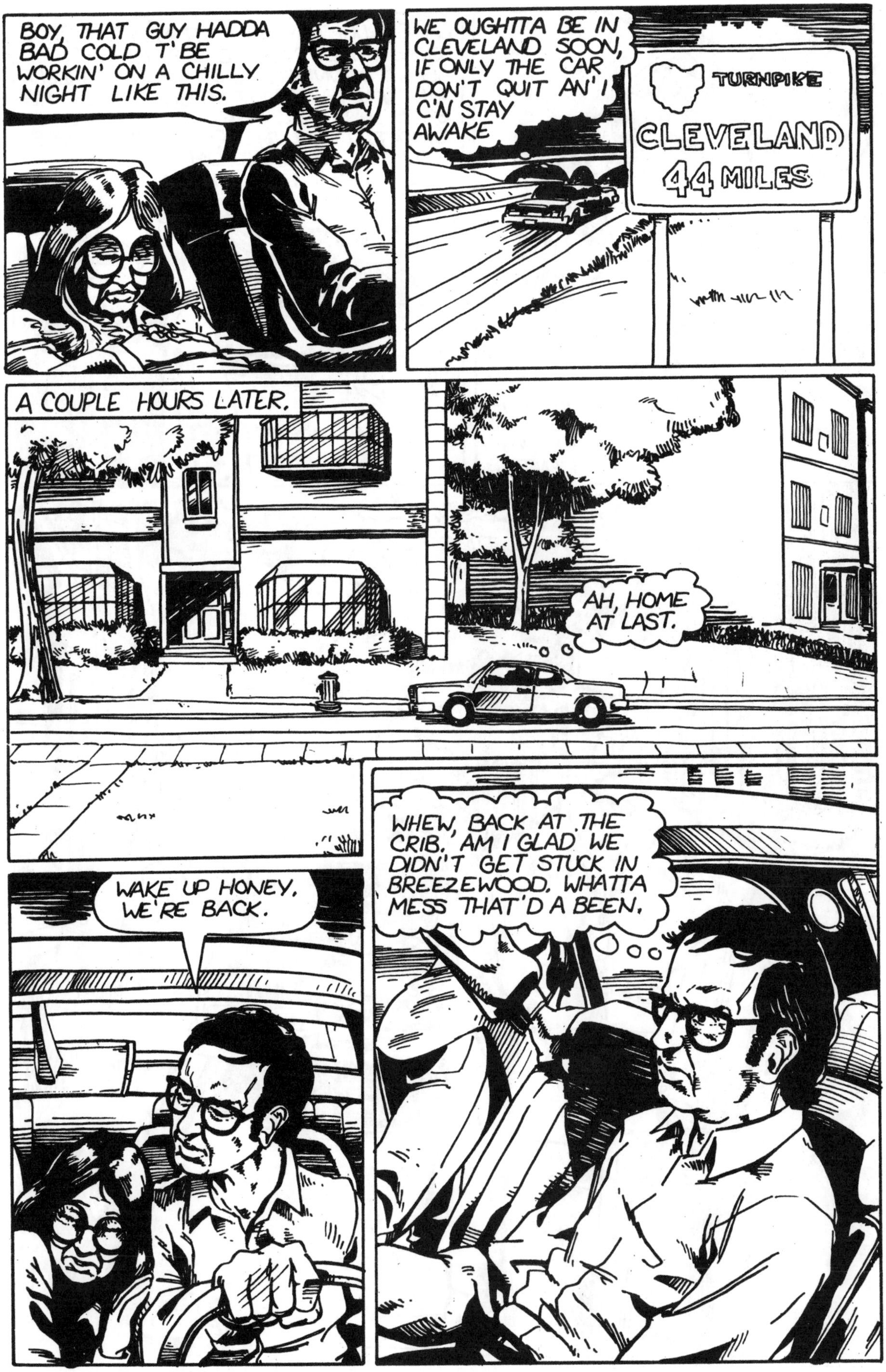
BOY, THAT GUY HADDA BAD COLD T'BE WORKIN' ON A CHILLY NIGHT LIKE THIS.
WE OUGHTTA BE IN CLEVELAND SOON, IF ONLY THE CAR DON'T QUIT AN' I C'N STAY AWAKE
TURNPIKE
CLEVELAND
44 MILES
A COUPLE HOURS LATER.
AH, HOME AT LAST.
WAKE UP HONEY, WE'RE BACK.
WHEW, BACK AT THE CRIB. AM I GLAD WE DIDN'T GET STUCK IN BREEZEWOOD. WHATTA MESS THAT'D A BEEN.

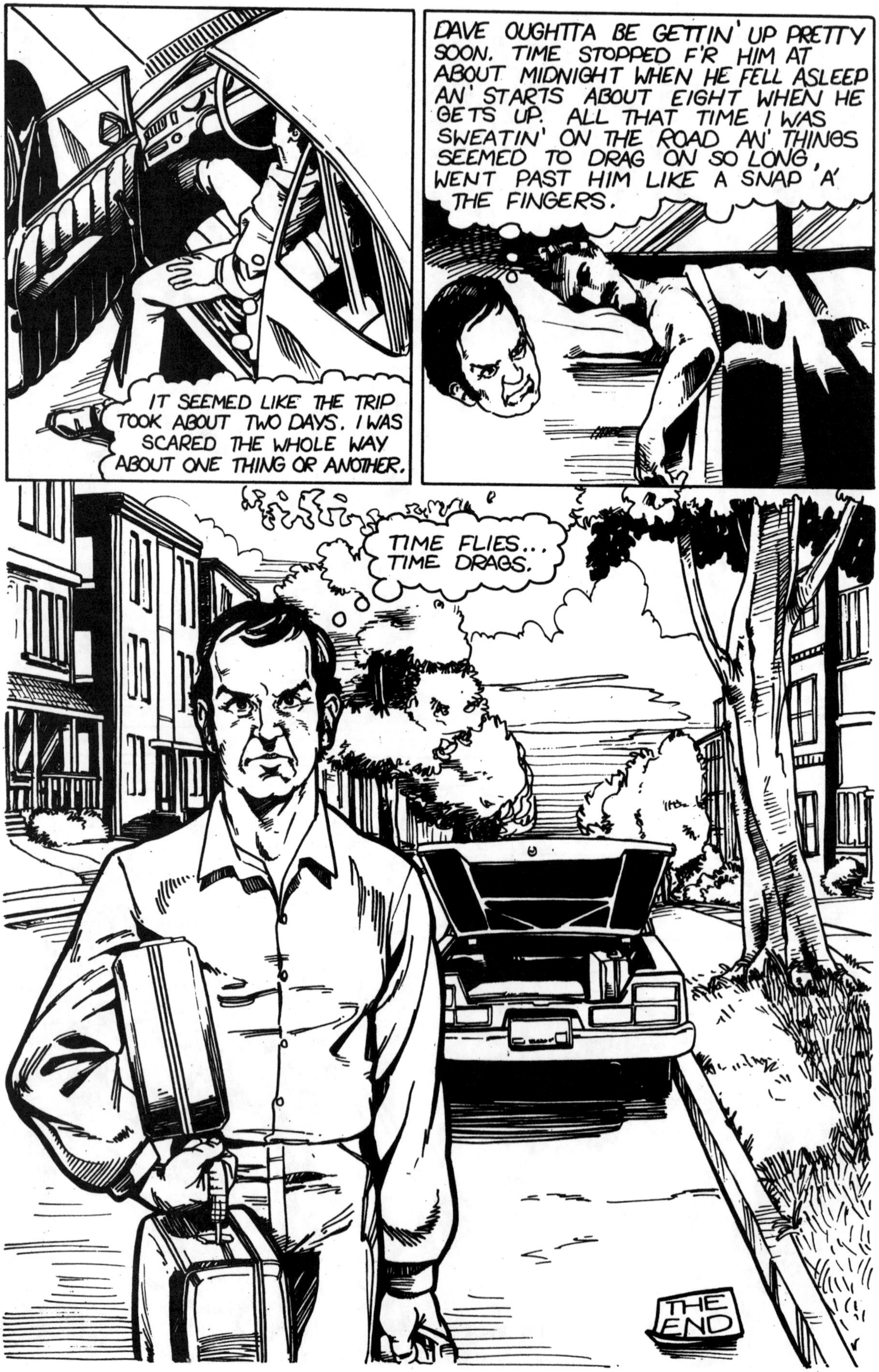
IT SEEMED LIKE THE TRIP TOOK ABOUT TWO DAYS. I WAS SCARED THE WHOLE WAY ABOUT ONE THING OR ANOTHER.
DAVE OUGHTTA BE GETTIN' UP PRETTY SOON. TIME STOPPED F'R HIM AT ABOUT MIDNIGHT WHEN HE FELL ASLEEP AN' STARTS ABOUT EIGHT WHEN HE GETS UP. ALL THAT TIME I WAS SWEATIN' ON THE ROAD AN' THINGS SEEMED TO DRAG ON SO LONG, WENT PAST HIM LIKE A SNAP 'A' THE FINGERS.
TIME FLIES... TIME DRAGS.
THE END

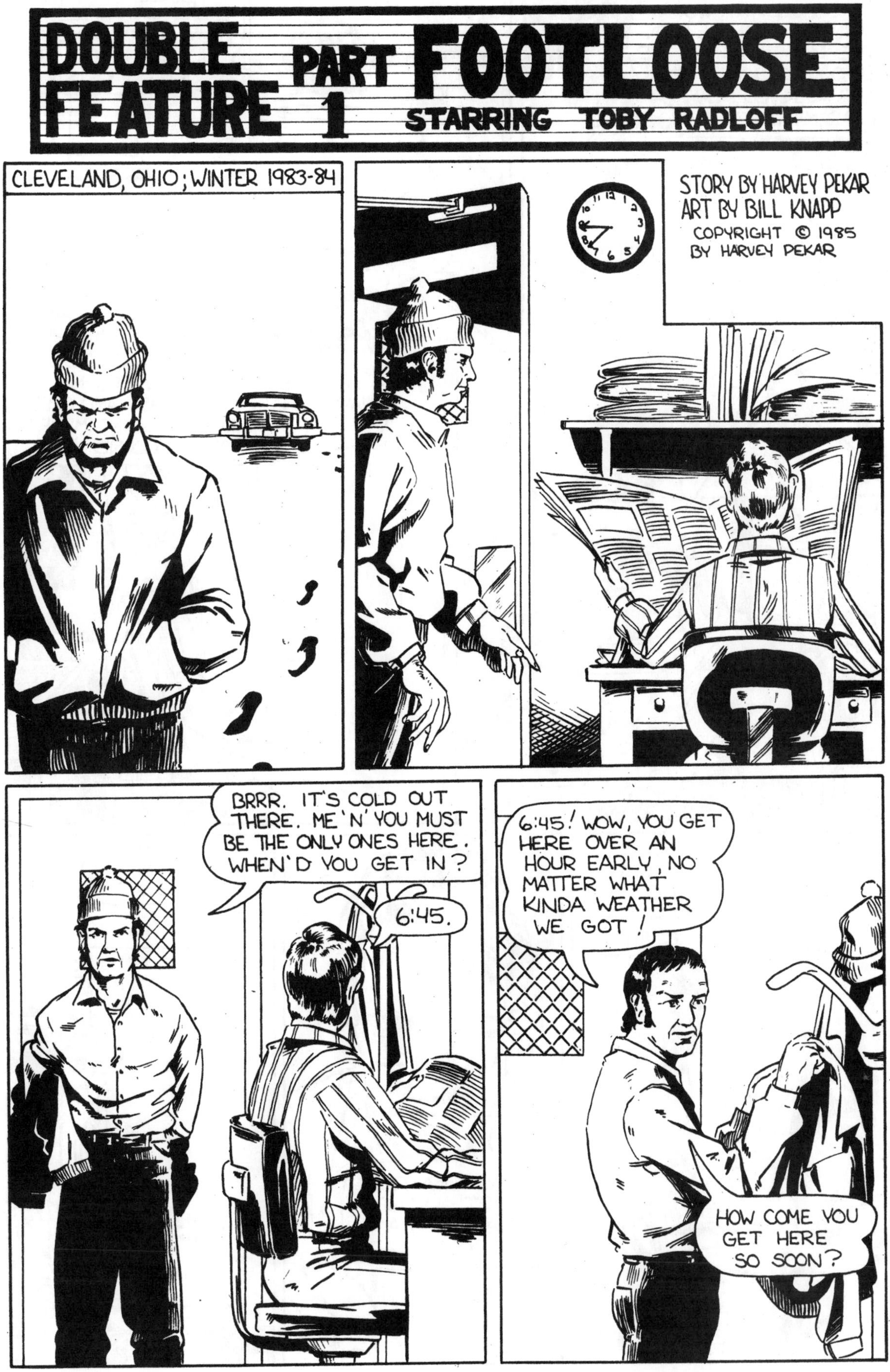

DOUBLE FEATURE
PART 1
FOOTLOOSE
STARRING TOBY RADLOFF
CLEVELAND, OHIO; WINTER 1983-84
STORY BY HARVEY PEKAR
ART BY BILL KNAPP
COPYRIGHT © 1985 BY HARVEY PEKAR
BRRR. IT'S COLD OUT THERE. ME 'N' YOU MUST BE THE ONLY ONES HERE. WHEN'D YOU GET IN?
6:45.
6:45! WOW, YOU GET HERE OVER AN HOUR EARLY, NO MATTER WHAT KINDA WEATHER WE GOT!
HOW COME YOU GET HERE SO SOON?

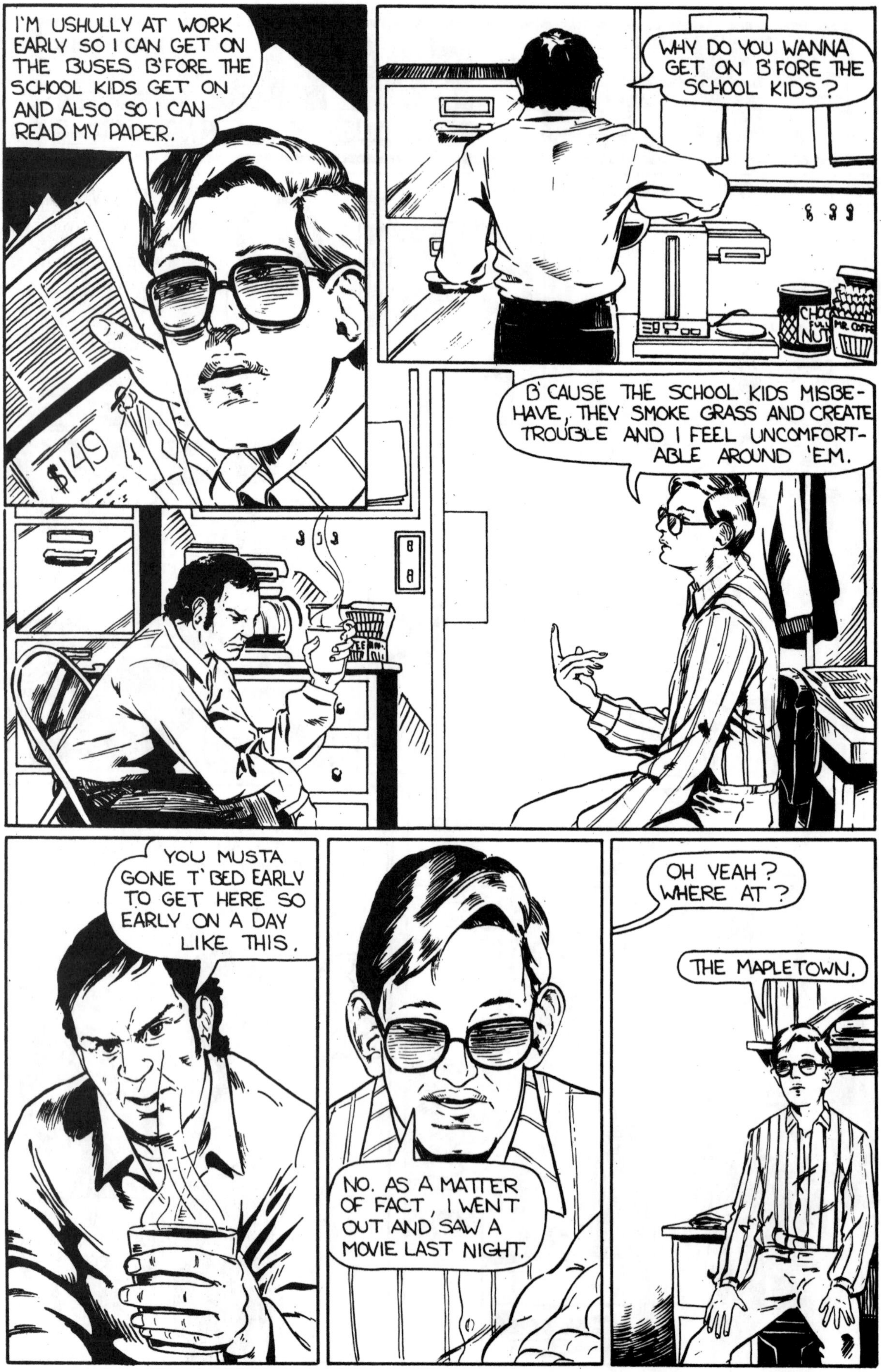
I'M USHULLY AT WORK EARLY SO I CAN GET ON THE BUSES B'FORE THE SCHOOL KIDS GET ON AND ALSO SO I CAN READ MY PAPER.
$149
WHY DO YOU WANNA GET ON B'FORE THE SCHOOL KIDS?
CHOCK FULL O NUTS
MR. COFFEE
B'CAUSE THE SCHOOL KIDS MISBE-HAVE, THEY SMOKE GRASS AND CREATE TROUBLE AND I FEEL UNCOMFORT-ABLE AROUND 'EM.
YOU MUSTA GONE T'BED EARLY TO GET HERE SO EARLY ON A DAY LIKE THIS.
NO. AS A MATTER OF FACT, I WENT OUT AND SAW A MOVIE LAST NIGHT.
OH YEAH? WHERE AT?
THE MAPLETOWN.

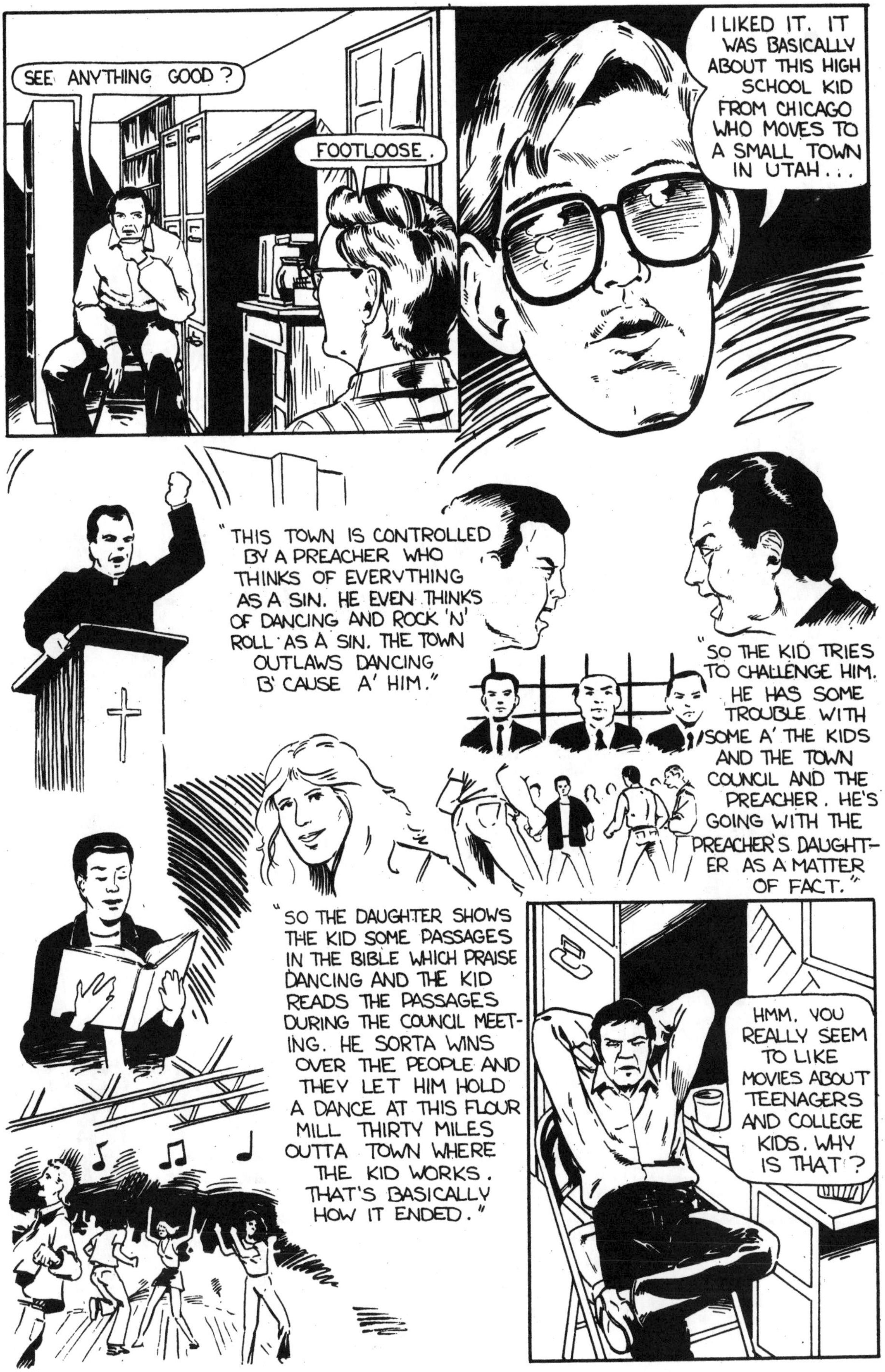
SEE ANYTHING GOOD?
FOOTLOOSE.
I LIKED IT. IT WAS BASICALLY ABOUT THIS HIGH SCHOOL KID FROM CHICAGO WHO MOVES TO A SMALL TOWN IN UTAH...
"THIS TOWN IS CONTROLLED BY A PREACHER WHO THINKS OF EVERYTHING AS A SIN. HE EVEN THINKS OF DANCING AND ROCK 'N' ROLL AS A SIN. THE TOWN OUTLAWS DANCING B' CAUSE A' HIM."
"SO THE KID TRIES TO CHALLENGE HIM. HE HAS SOME TROUBLE WITH SOME A' THE KIDS AND THE TOWN COUNCIL AND THE PREACHER. HE'S GOING WITH THE PREACHER'S DAUGHTER AS A MATTER OF FACT."
"SO THE DAUGHTER SHOWS THE KID SOME PASSAGES IN THE BIBLE WHICH PRAISE DANCING AND THE KID READS THE PASSAGES DURING THE COUNCIL MEETING. HE SORTA WINS OVER THE PEOPLE AND THEY LET HIM HOLD A DANCE AT THIS FLOUR MILL THIRTY MILES OUTTA TOWN WHERE THE KID WORKS. THAT'S BASICALLY HOW IT ENDED."
HMM, YOU REALLY SEEM TO LIKE MOVIES ABOUT TEENAGERS AND COLLEGE KIDS. WHY IS THAT?

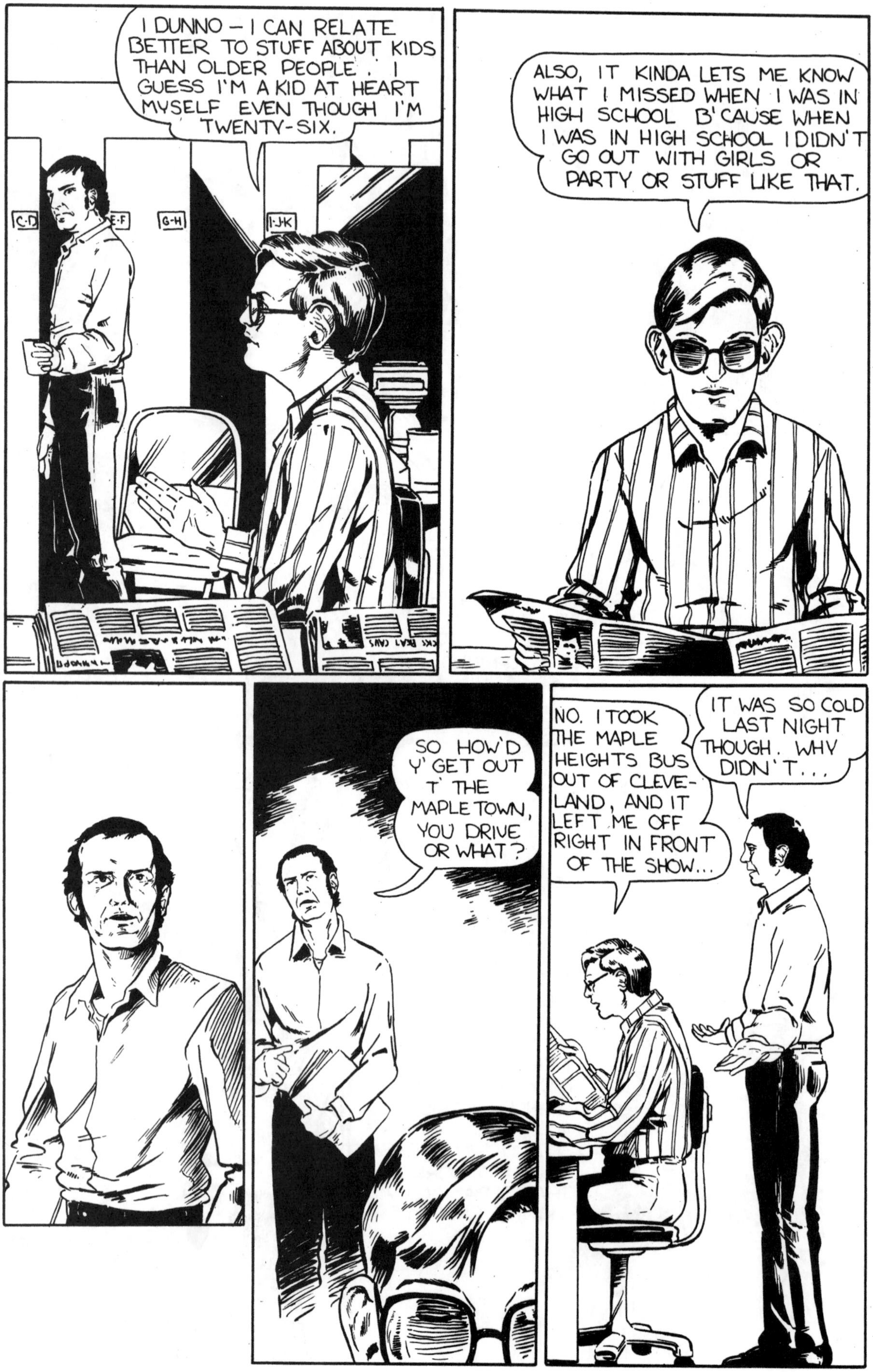

I DUNNO – I CAN RELATE BETTER TO STUFF ABOUT KIDS THAN OLDER PEOPLE. I GUESS I'M A KID AT HEART MYSELF EVEN THOUGH I'M TWENTY-SIX.
C-D
E-F
G-H
I-J-K
ALSO, IT KINDA LETS ME KNOW WHAT I MISSED WHEN I WAS IN HIGH SCHOOL B'CAUSE WHEN I WAS IN HIGH SCHOOL I DIDN'T GO OUT WITH GIRLS OR PARTY OR STUFF LIKE THAT.
SO HOW'D Y' GET OUT T' THE MAPLE TOWN, YOU DRIVE OR WHAT?
NO. I TOOK THE MAPLE HEIGHTS BUS OUT OF CLEVE-LAND, AND IT LEFT ME OFF RIGHT IN FRONT OF THE SHOW...
IT WAS SO COLD LAST NIGHT THOUGH. WHY DIDN'T...

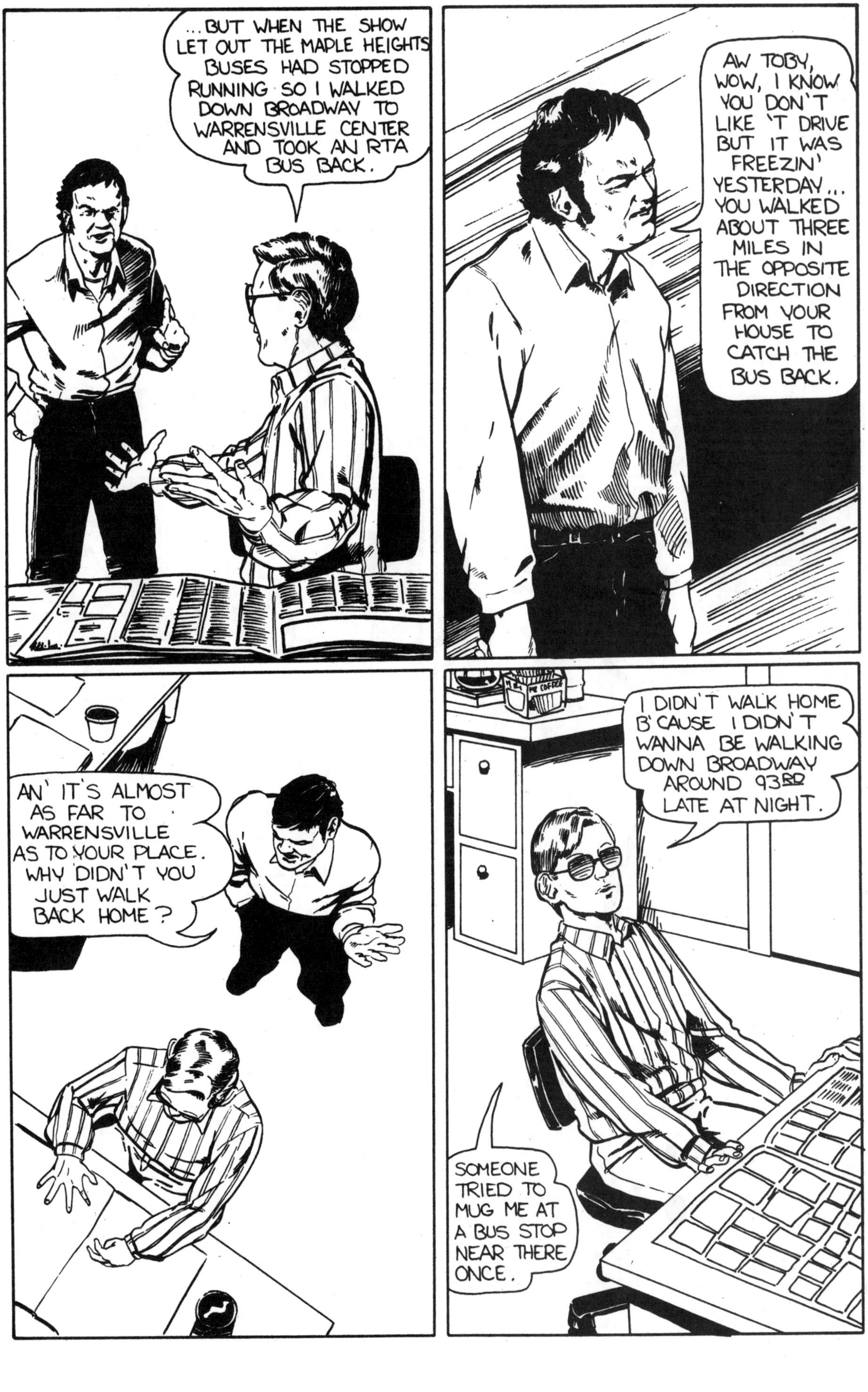
...BUT WHEN THE SHOW LET OUT THE MAPLE HEIGHTS BUSES HAD STOPPED RUNNING SO I WALKED DOWN BROADWAY TO WARRENSVILLE CENTER AND TOOK AN RTA BUS BACK.
AW TOBY, WOW, I KNOW YOU DON'T LIKE 'T DRIVE BUT IT WAS FREEZIN' YESTERDAY... YOU WALKED ABOUT THREE MILES IN THE OPPOSITE DIRECTION FROM YOUR HOUSE TO CATCH THE BUS BACK.
AN' IT'S ALMOST AS FAR TO WARRENSVILLE AS TO YOUR PLACE. WHY DIDN'T YOU JUST WALK BACK HOME?
I DIDN'T WALK HOME B'CAUSE I DIDN'T WANNA BE WALKING DOWN BROADWAY AROUND 93RD LATE AT NIGHT.
SOMEONE TRIED TO MUG ME AT A BUS STOP NEAR THERE ONCE.

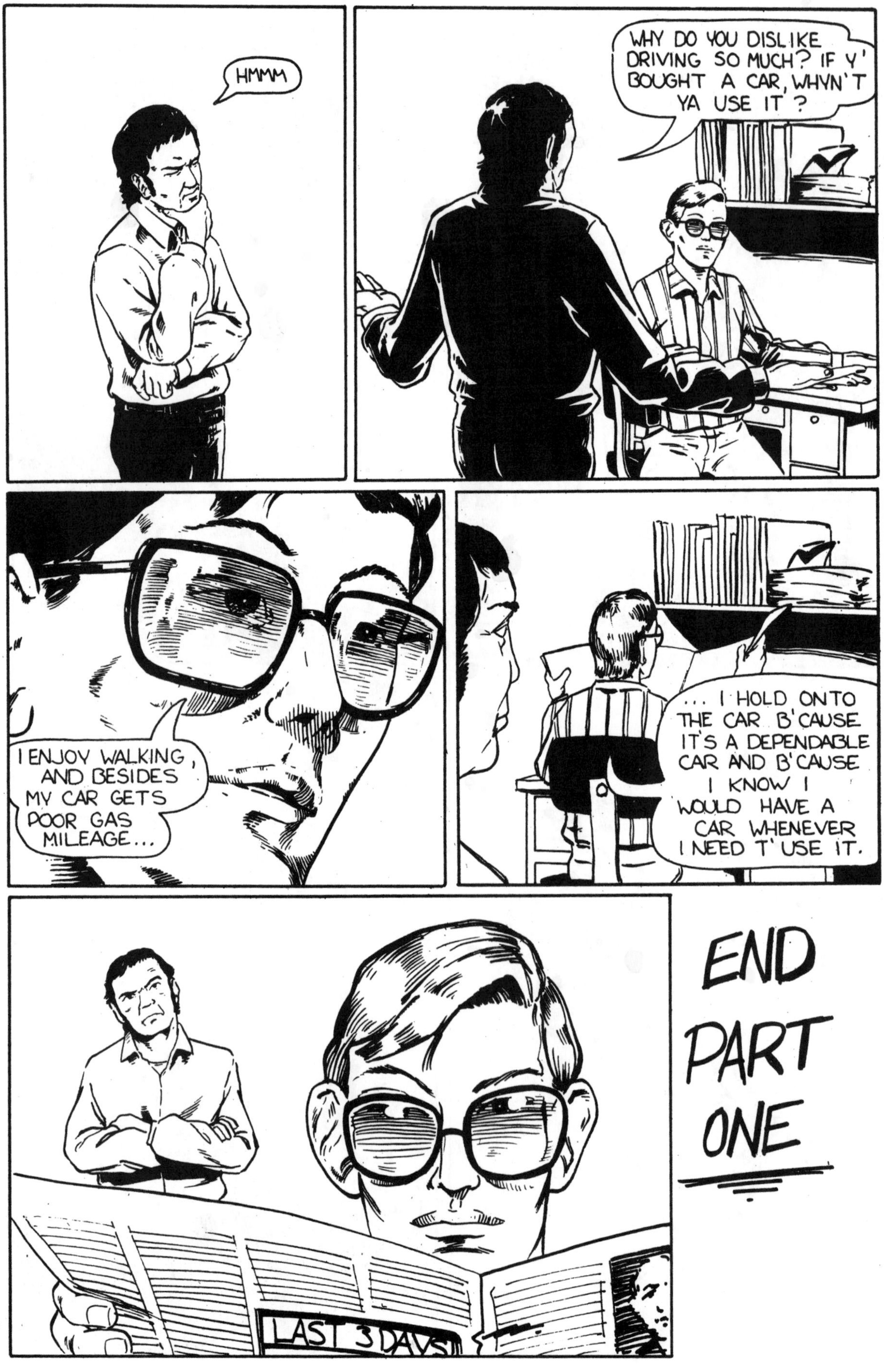
HMMM
WHY DO YOU DISLIKE DRIVING SO MUCH? IF Y' BOUGHT A CAR, WHYN'T YA USE IT ?
I ENJOY WALKING, AND BESIDES MY CAR GETS POOR GAS MILEAGE...
... I HOLD ONTO THE CAR B'CAUSE IT'S A DEPENDABLE CAR AND B'CAUSE I KNOW I WOULD HAVE A CAR WHENEVER I NEED T' USE IT.
LAST 3 DAYS
END PART ONE

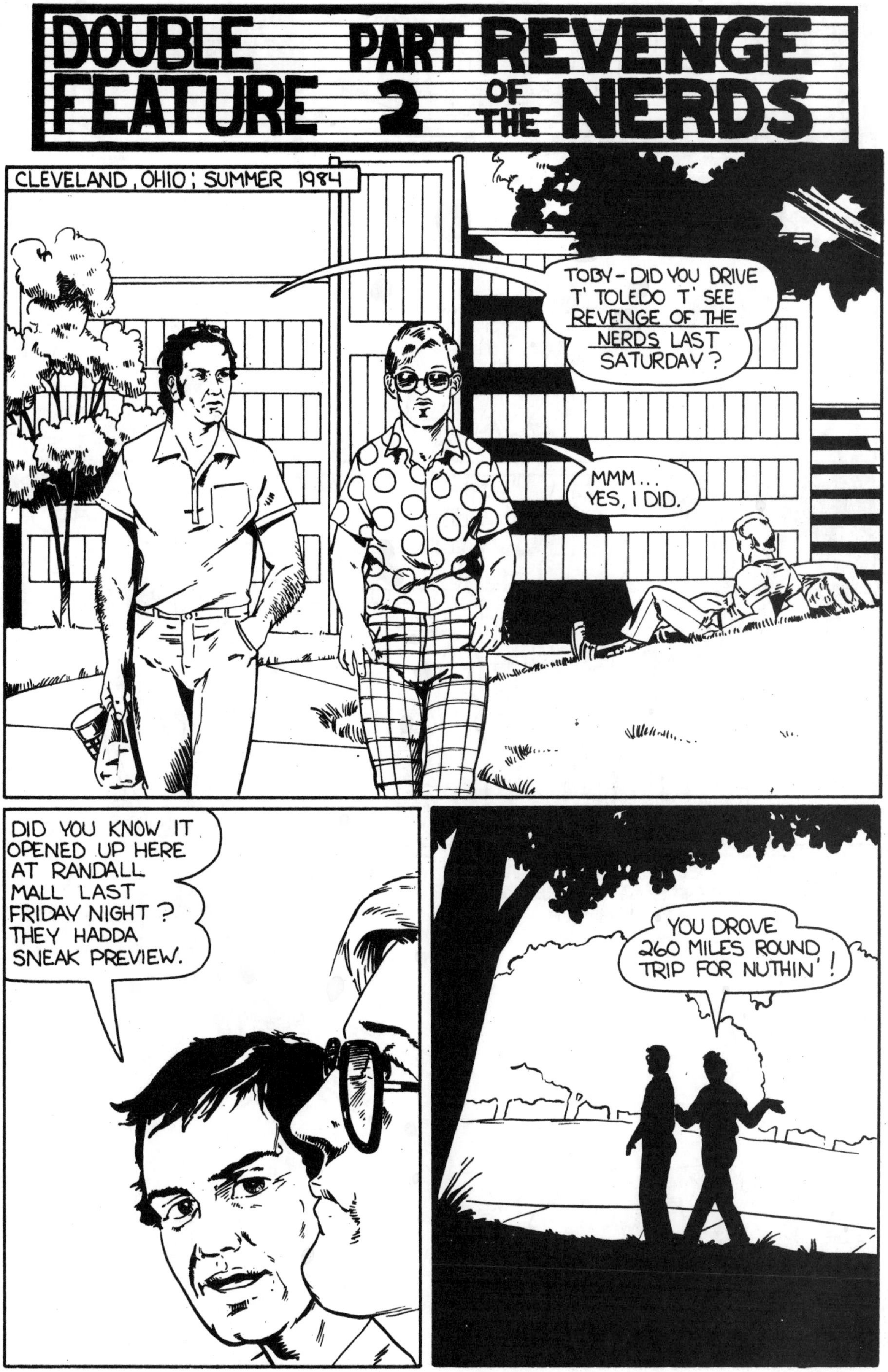
DOUBLE FEATURE PART 2 REVENGE OF THE NERDS
CLEVELAND, OHIO; SUMMER 1984
TOBY - DID YOU DRIVE T' TOLEDO T' SEE REVENGE OF THE NERDS LAST SATURDAY?
MMM... YES, I DID.
DID YOU KNOW IT OPENED UP HERE AT RANDALL MALL LAST FRIDAY NIGHT? THEY HADDA SNEAK PREVIEW.
YOU DROVE 260 MILES ROUND TRIP FOR NUTHIN'!

I KNOW. I HEARD ABOUT IT WHEN I GOT BACK. I'LL PROB'LY SEE IT A FEW TIMES WHEN IT'S HERE. STILL, A LOT OF MOVIES DON'T PLAY CLEVELAND AND I WANTED TO MAKE SURE I SAW IT.

BOY, YOU MUSTA, THE WAY YOU HATE T' DRIVE.

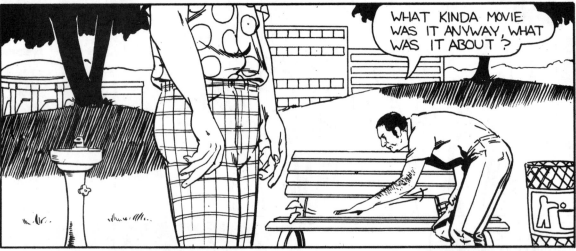

WHAT KINDA MOVIE WAS IT ANYWAY, WHAT WAS IT ABOUT?

MM... THERE WAS A GROUP OF NERD COLLEGE STUDENTS WHO WERE BEING PICKED ON ALL THE TIME BY THE JOCKS SO THEY DECIDED TO TAKE REVENGE ON THEM.

THEY POURED LIQUID HEAT IN THE JOCK'S JOCK STRAPS IN THE LOCKER ROOM AND THEY STAGED A PANTY RAID WHERE THE JOCKS' GIRL FRIENDS WERE STAYING AND BUGGED THEIR SORORITY HOUSE WITH HIDDEN TV CAMERAS.

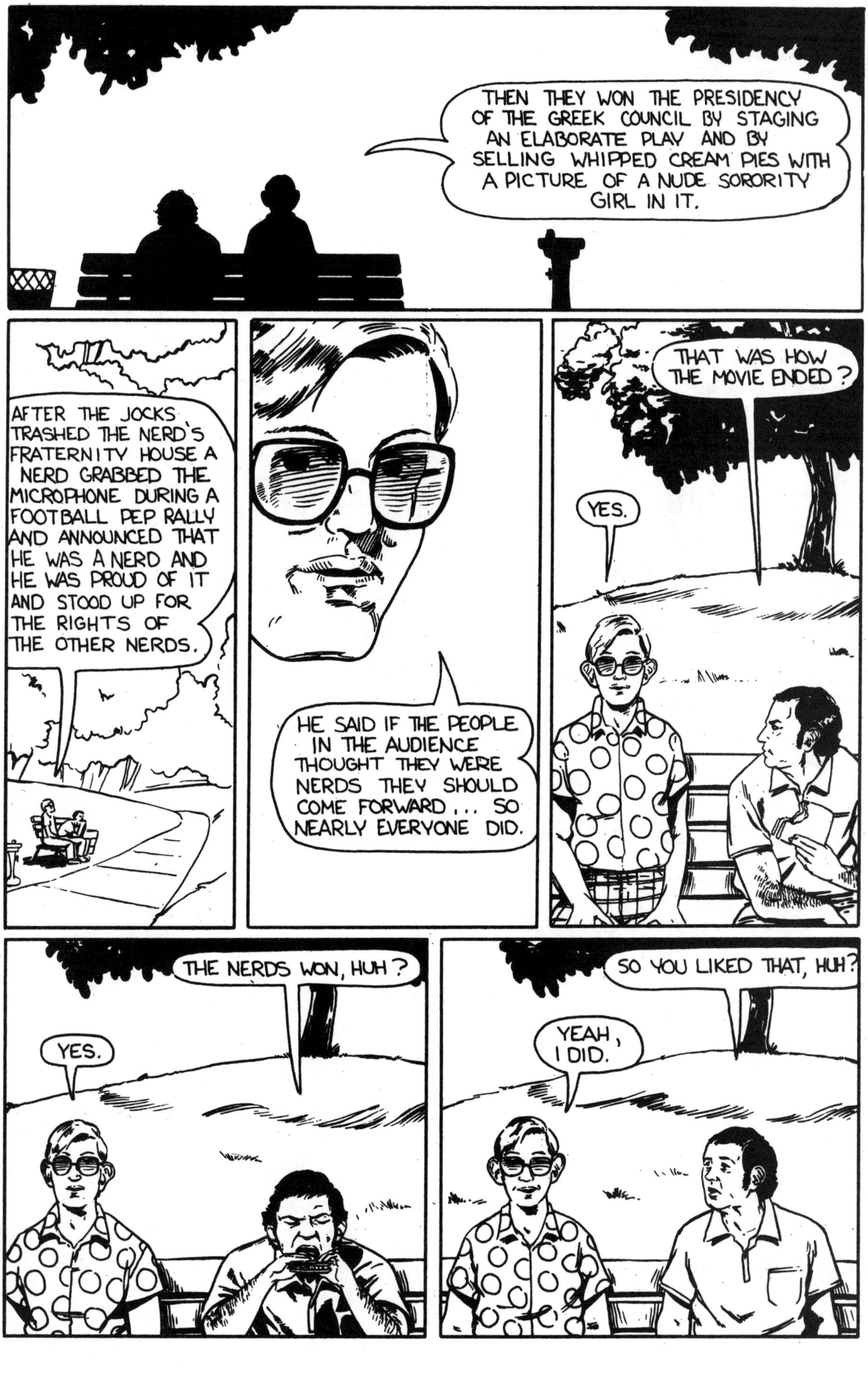
THEN THEY WON THE PRESIDENCY OF THE GREEK COUNCIL BY STAGING AN ELABORATE PLAY AND BY SELLING WHIPPED CREAM PIES WITH A PICTURE OF A NUDE SORORITY GIRL IN IT.
AFTER THE JOCKS TRASHED THE NERD'S FRATERNITY HOUSE A NERD GRABBED THE MICROPHONE DURING A FOOTBALL PEP RALLY AND ANNOUNCED THAT HE WAS A NERD AND HE WAS PROUD OF IT AND STOOD UP FOR THE RIGHTS OF THE OTHER NERDS.
HE SAID IF THE PEOPLE IN THE AUDIENCE THOUGHT THEY WERE NERDS THEY SHOULD COME FORWARD... SO NEARLY EVERYONE DID.
THAT WAS HOW THE MOVIE ENDED?
YES.
THE NERDS WON, HUH?
YES.
SO YOU LIKED THAT, HUH?
YEAH, I DID.

SO WHAT WERE THESE NERDS LIKE? HOW WOULDJA DESCRIBE 'EM?

HMM... NERDS ARE SMART BUT THEY LOOK AND ACT DIFFERENTLY THAN OTHER PEOPLE SO THEY GET PICKED ON ALL THE TIME...

"LIKE, NERDS MIGHT WEAR POLYESTER BUTTON-DOWN SHIRTS AND FLOOD PANTS, WHERE THEIR ANKLES AND THEIR SOCKS ARE SHOWING. THEY HAVE SHORT HAIR AND A LOT OF THEM WEAR GLASSES."

THEY CARRY POCKETS FULLA PENS OR A CALCULATOR. BUT THAT'S ONLY SOME...

NOT ALL OF 'EM DO.

A WEEK LATER.

HEY HARVEY, LOOK WHAT I GOT.

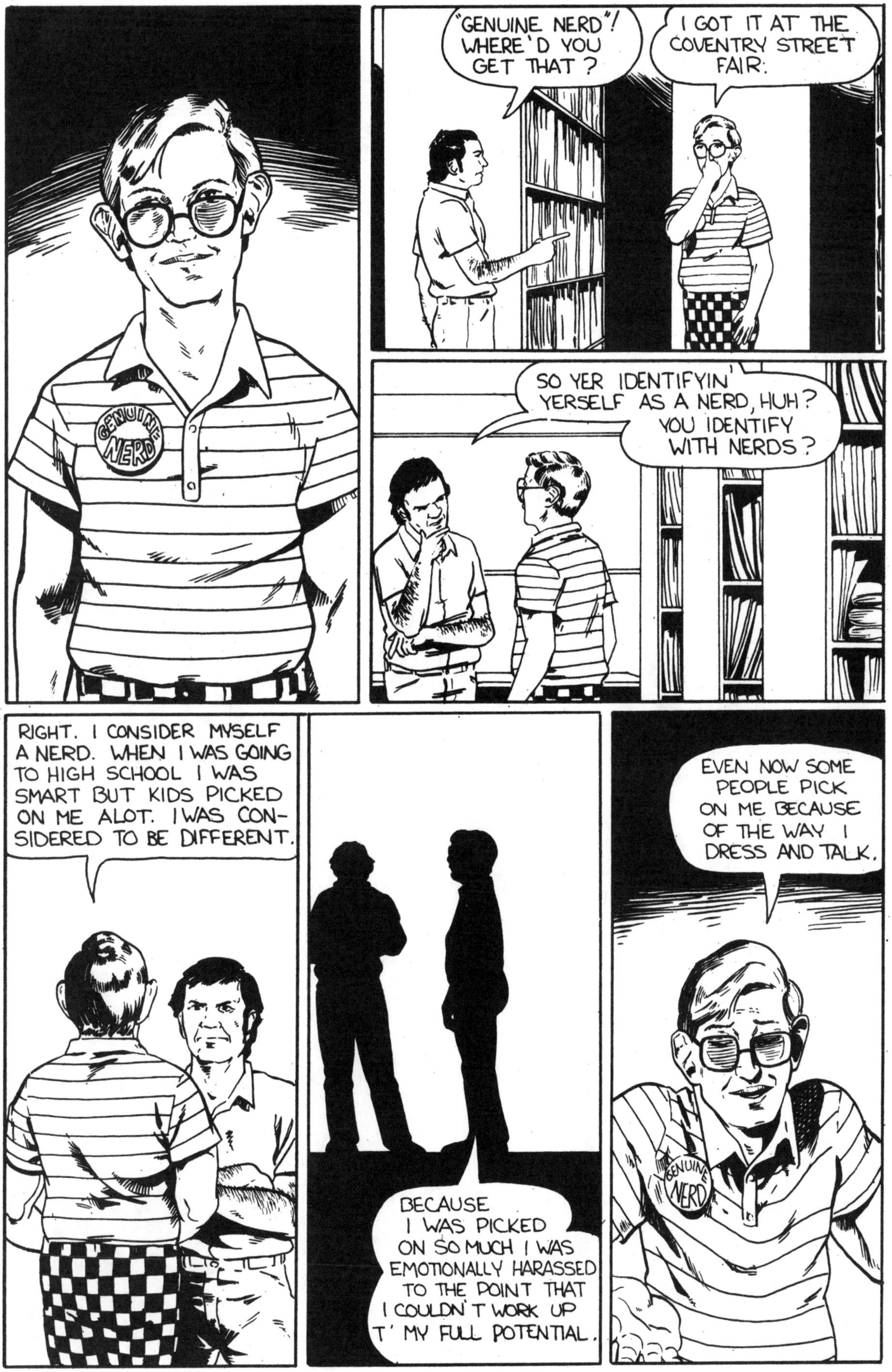

"GENUINE NERD"! WHERE'D YOU GET THAT?
I GOT IT AT THE COVENTRY STREET FAIR.
GENUINE NERD
SO YER IDENTIFYIN' YERSELF AS A NERD, HUH? YOU IDENTIFY WITH NERDS?
RIGHT. I CONSIDER MYSELF A NERD. WHEN I WAS GOING TO HIGH SCHOOL I WAS SMART BUT KIDS PICKED ON ME ALOT. I WAS CONSIDERED TO BE DIFFERENT.
BECAUSE I WAS PICKED ON SO MUCH I WAS EMOTIONALLY HARASSED TO THE POINT THAT I COULDN'T WORK UP T' MY FULL POTENTIAL.
EVEN NOW SOME PEOPLE PICK ON ME BECAUSE OF THE WAY I DRESS AND TALK.
GENUINE NERD

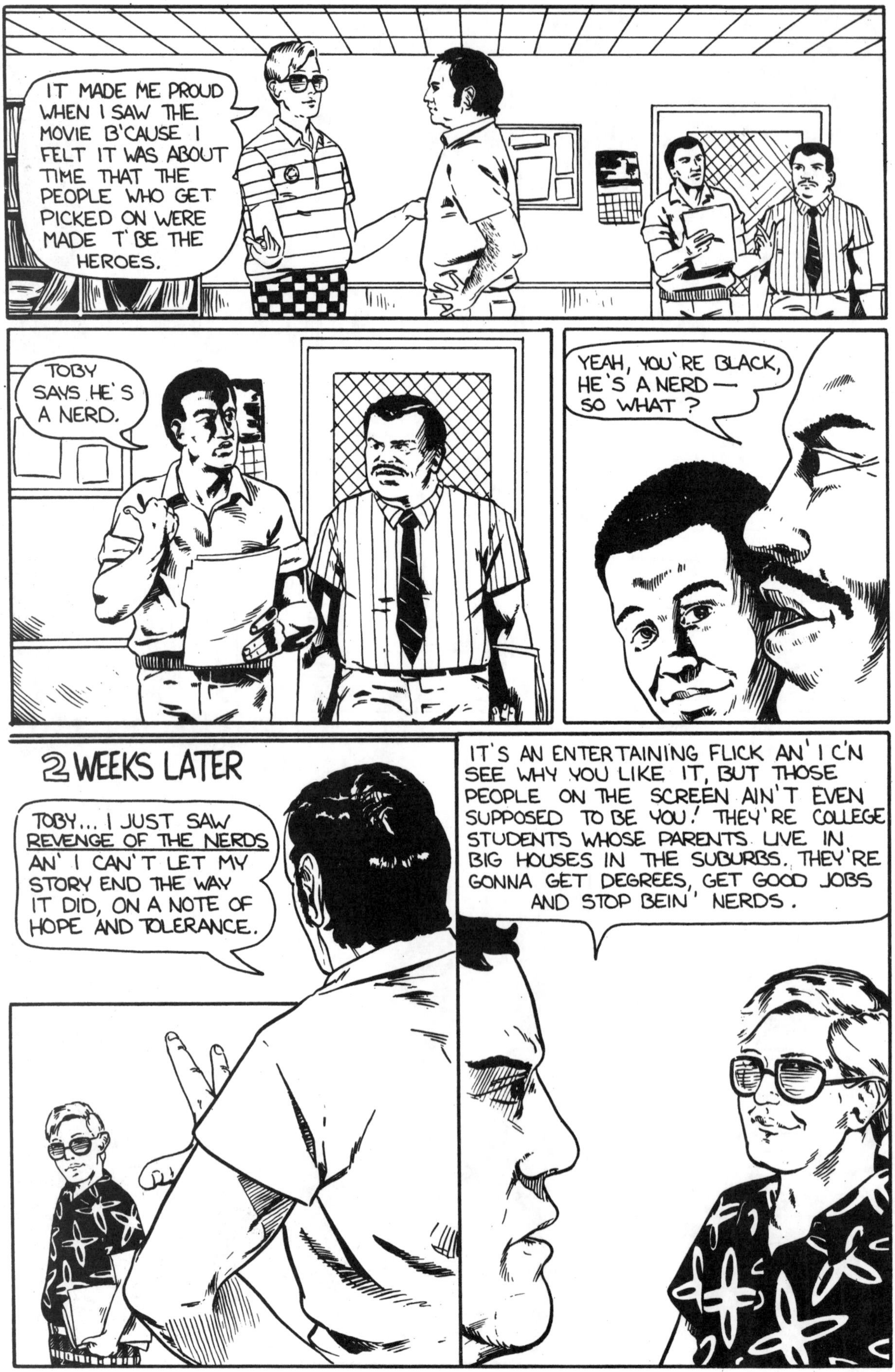
IT MADE ME PROUD WHEN I SAW THE MOVIE B'CAUSE I FELT IT WAS ABOUT TIME THAT THE PEOPLE WHO GET PICKED ON WERE MADE T'BE THE HEROES.
TOBY SAYS HE'S A NERD.
YEAH, YOU'RE BLACK, HE'S A NERD — SO WHAT?
2 WEEKS LATER
TOBY... I JUST SAW REVENGE OF THE NERDS AN' I CAN'T LET MY STORY END THE WAY IT DID, ON A NOTE OF HOPE AND TOLERANCE.
IT'S AN ENTERTAINING FLICK AN' I C'N SEE WHY YOU LIKE IT, BUT THOSE PEOPLE ON THE SCREEN AIN'T EVEN SUPPOSED TO BE YOU! THEY'RE COLLEGE STUDENTS WHOSE PARENTS LIVE IN BIG HOUSES IN THE SUBURBS. THEY'RE GONNA GET DEGREES, GET GOOD JOBS AND STOP BEIN' NERDS.

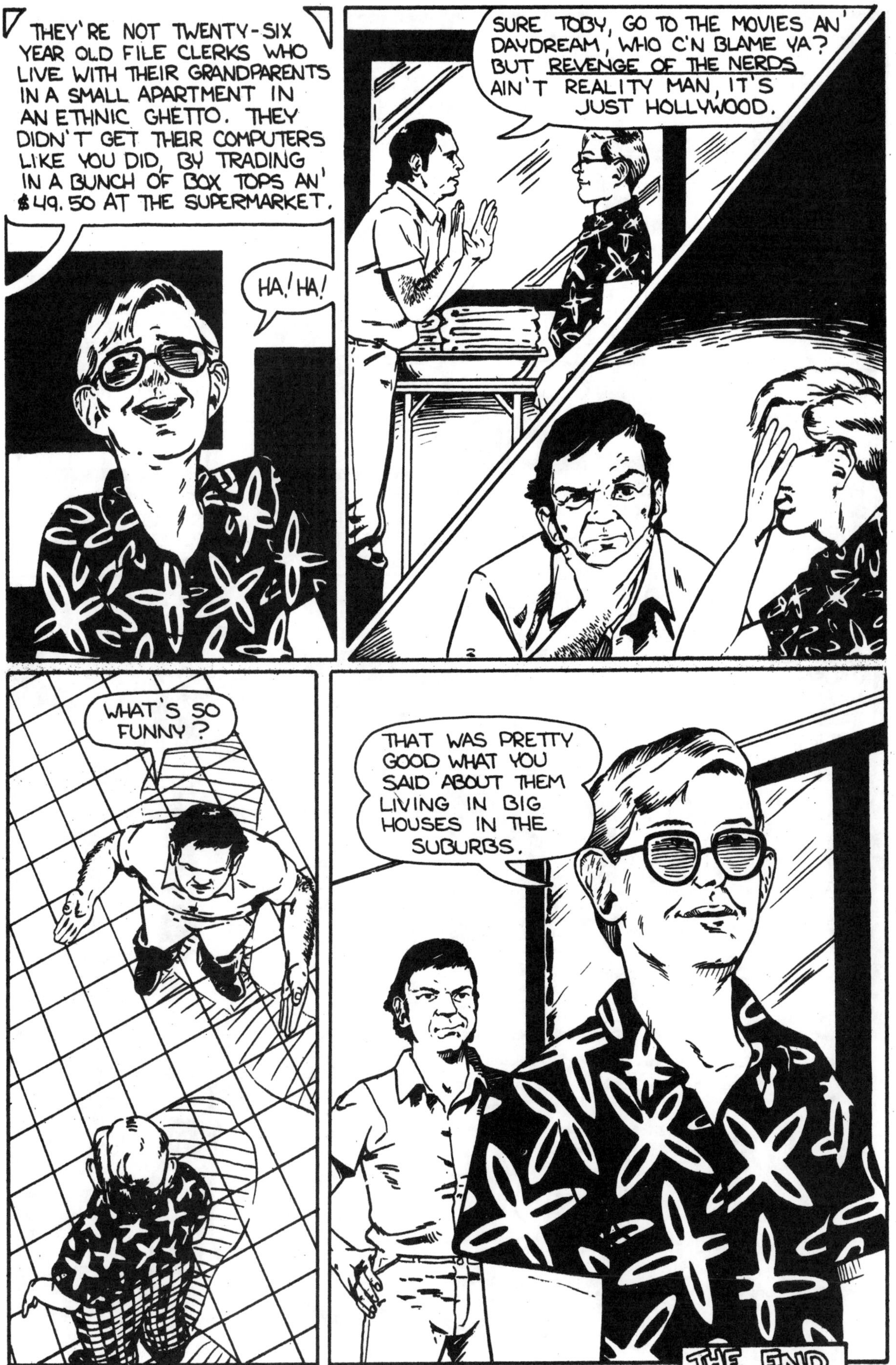
THEY'RE NOT TWENTY-SIX YEAR OLD FILE CLERKS WHO LIVE WITH THEIR GRANDPARENTS IN A SMALL APARTMENT IN AN ETHNIC GHETTO. THEY DIDN'T GET THEIR COMPUTERS LIKE YOU DID, BY TRADING IN A BUNCH OF BOX TOPS AN' $49.50 AT THE SUPERMARKET.
HA! HA!
SURE TOBY, GO TO THE MOVIES AN' DAYDREAM, WHO C'N BLAME YA? BUT REVENGE OF THE NERDS AIN'T REALITY MAN, IT'S JUST HOLLYWOOD.
WHAT'S SO FUNNY?
THAT WAS PRETTY GOOD WHAT YOU SAID ABOUT THEM LIVING IN BIG HOUSES IN THE SUBURBS.
THE END

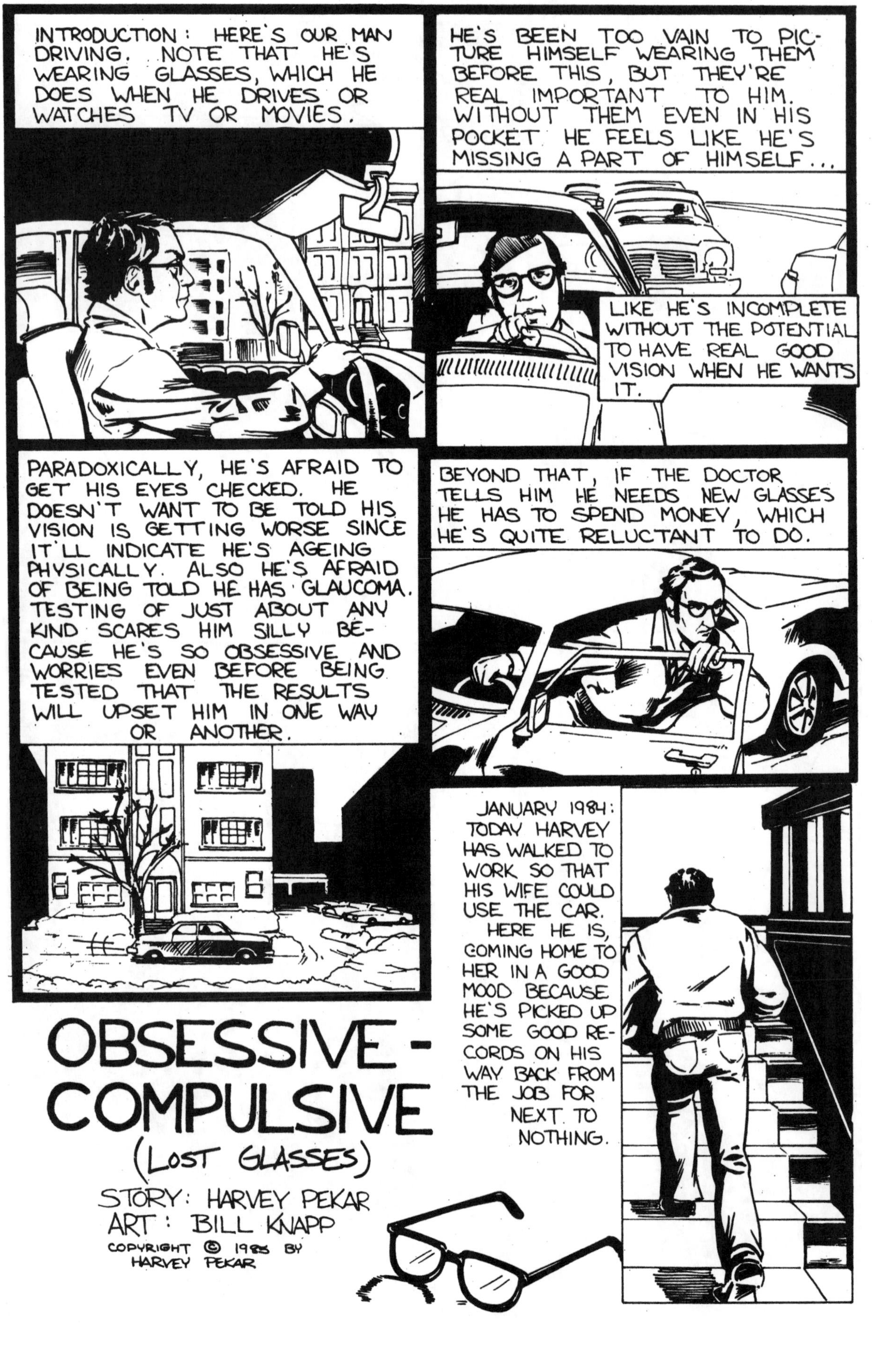
INTRODUCTION: HERE'S OUR MAN DRIVING. NOTE THAT HE'S WEARING GLASSES, WHICH HE DOES WHEN HE DRIVES OR WATCHES TV OR MOVIES.
HE'S BEEN TOO VAIN TO PICTURE HIMSELF WEARING THEM BEFORE THIS, BUT THEY'RE REAL IMPORTANT TO HIM. WITHOUT THEM EVEN IN HIS POCKET HE FEELS LIKE HE'S MISSING A PART OF HIMSELF...
LIKE HE'S INCOMPLETE WITHOUT THE POTENTIAL TO HAVE REAL GOOD VISION WHEN HE WANTS IT.
PARADOXICALLY, HE'S AFRAID TO GET HIS EYES CHECKED. HE DOESN'T WANT TO BE TOLD HIS VISION IS GETTING WORSE SINCE IT'LL INDICATE HE'S AGEING PHYSICALLY. ALSO HE'S AFRAID OF BEING TOLD HE HAS GLAUCOMA. TESTING OF JUST ABOUT ANY KIND SCARES HIM SILLY BECAUSE HE'S SO OBSESSIVE AND WORRIES EVEN BEFORE BEING TESTED THAT THE RESULTS WILL UPSET HIM IN ONE WAY OR ANOTHER.
BEYOND THAT, IF THE DOCTOR TELLS HIM HE NEEDS NEW GLASSES HE HAS TO SPEND MONEY, WHICH HE'S QUITE RELUCTANT TO DO.
JANUARY 1984: TODAY HARVEY HAS WALKED TO WORK SO THAT HIS WIFE COULD USE THE CAR.
HERE HE IS, COMING HOME TO HER IN A GOOD MOOD BECAUSE HE'S PICKED UP SOME GOOD RECORDS ON HIS WAY BACK FROM THE JOB FOR NEXT TO NOTHING.
OBSESSIVE-COMPULSIVE
(LOST GLASSES)
STORY: HARVEY PEKAR
ART: BILL KNAPP
COPYRIGHT © 1985 BY HARVEY PEKAR

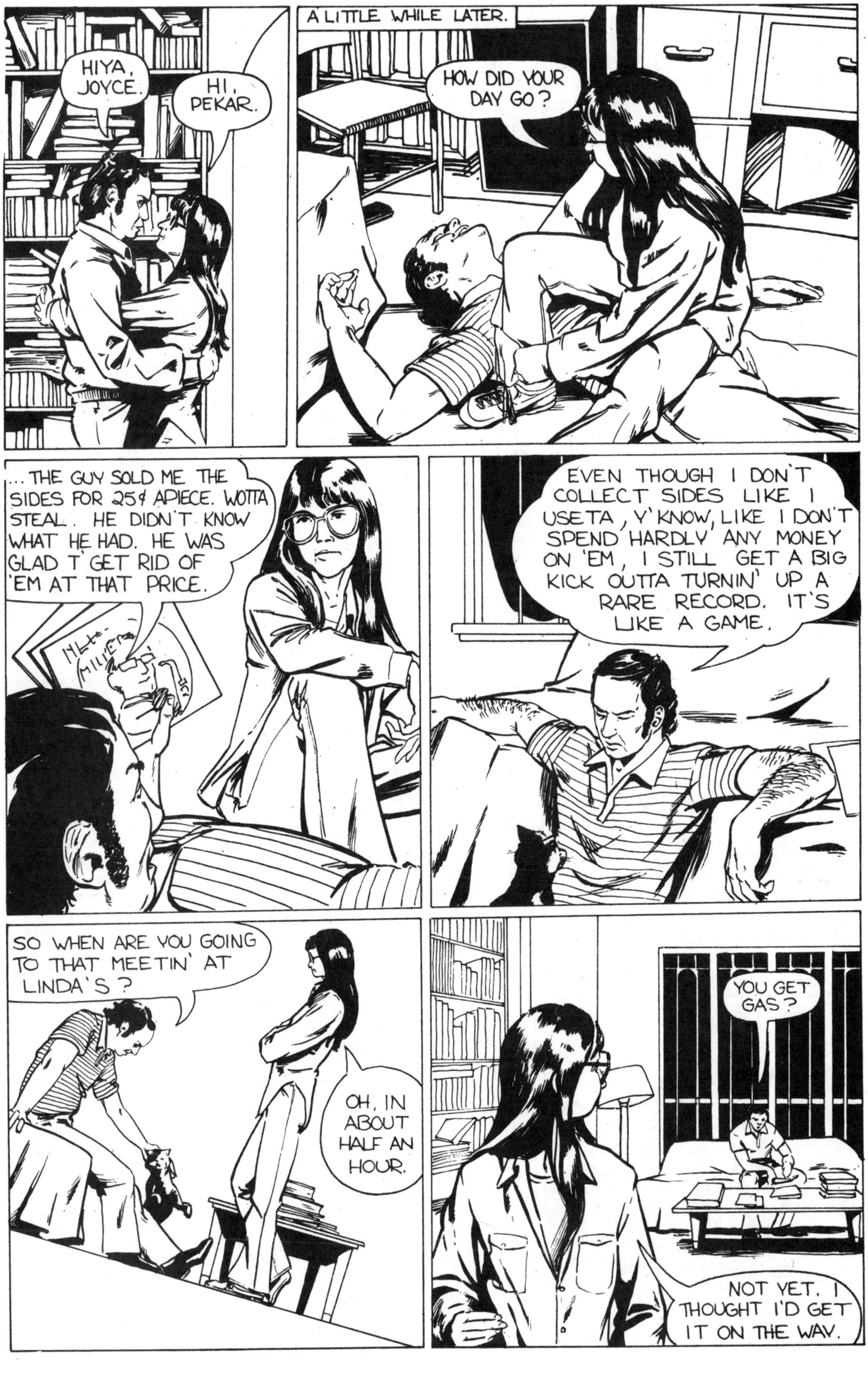
HIYA, JOYCE.
HI, PEKAR.
A LITTLE WHILE LATER.
HOW DID YOUR DAY GO?
...THE GUY SOLD ME THE SIDES FOR 25¢ APIECE. WOTTA STEAL. HE DIDN'T KNOW WHAT HE HAD. HE WAS GLAD T' GET RID OF 'EM AT THAT PRICE.
EVEN THOUGH I DON'T COLLECT SIDES LIKE I USETA, Y'KNOW, LIKE I DON'T SPEND HARDLY ANY MONEY ON 'EM, I STILL GET A BIG KICK OUTTA TURNIN' UP A RARE RECORD. IT'S LIKE A GAME.
SO WHEN ARE YOU GOING TO THAT MEETIN' AT LINDA'S?
OH, IN ABOUT HALF AN HOUR.
YOU GET GAS?
NOT YET. I THOUGHT I'D GET IT ON THE WAY.

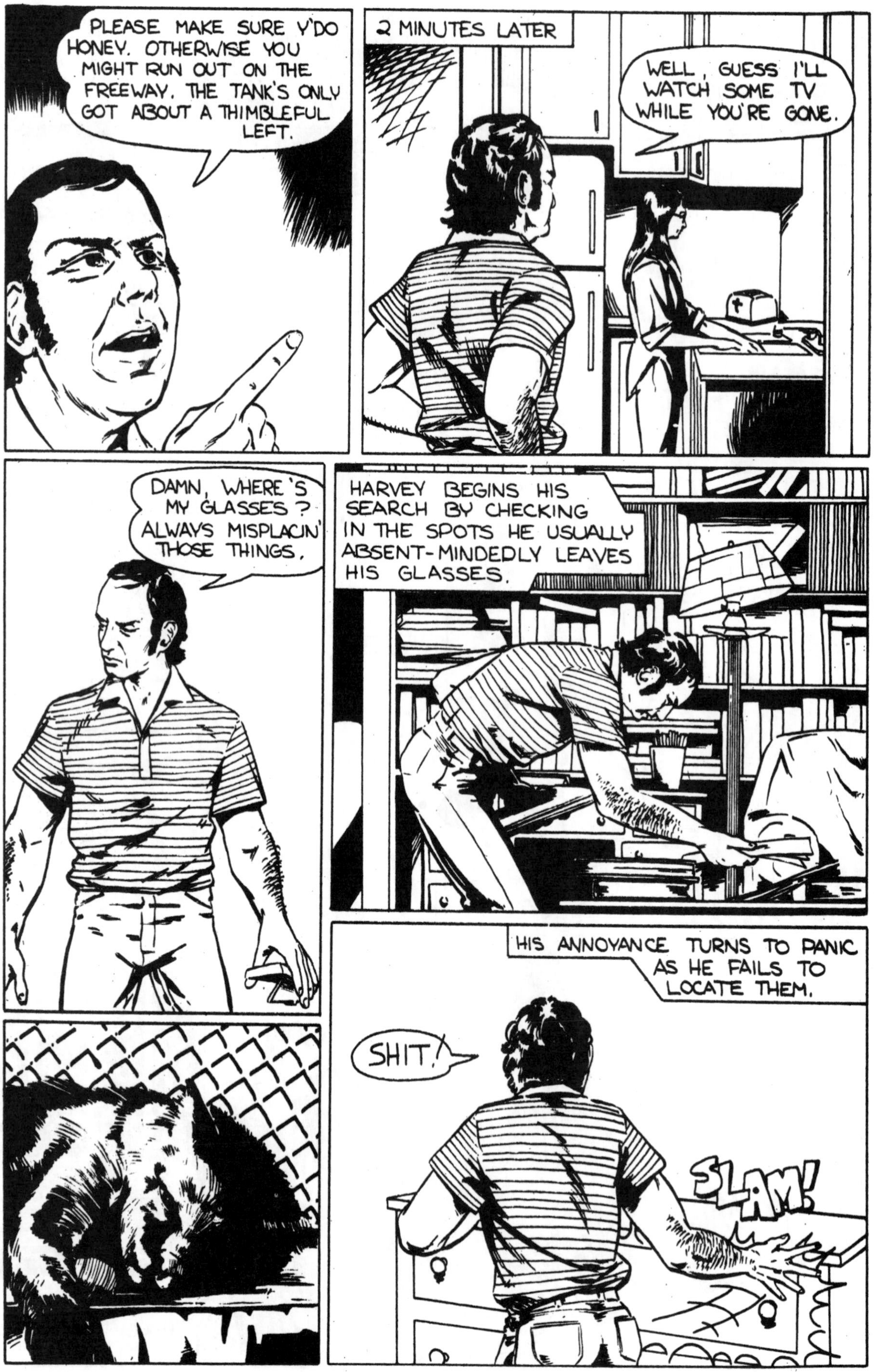
PLEASE MAKE SURE Y'DO HONEY. OTHERWISE YOU MIGHT RUN OUT ON THE FREEWAY. THE TANK'S ONLY GOT ABOUT A THIMBLEFUL LEFT.
2 MINUTES LATER
WELL, GUESS I'LL WATCH SOME TV WHILE YOU'RE GONE.
DAMN, WHERE'S MY GLASSES? ALWAYS MISPLACIN' THOSE THINGS.
HARVEY BEGINS HIS SEARCH BY CHECKING IN THE SPOTS HE USUALLY ABSENT-MINDEDLY LEAVES HIS GLASSES.
HIS ANNOYANCE TURNS TO PANIC AS HE FAILS TO LOCATE THEM.
SHIT!
SLAM!

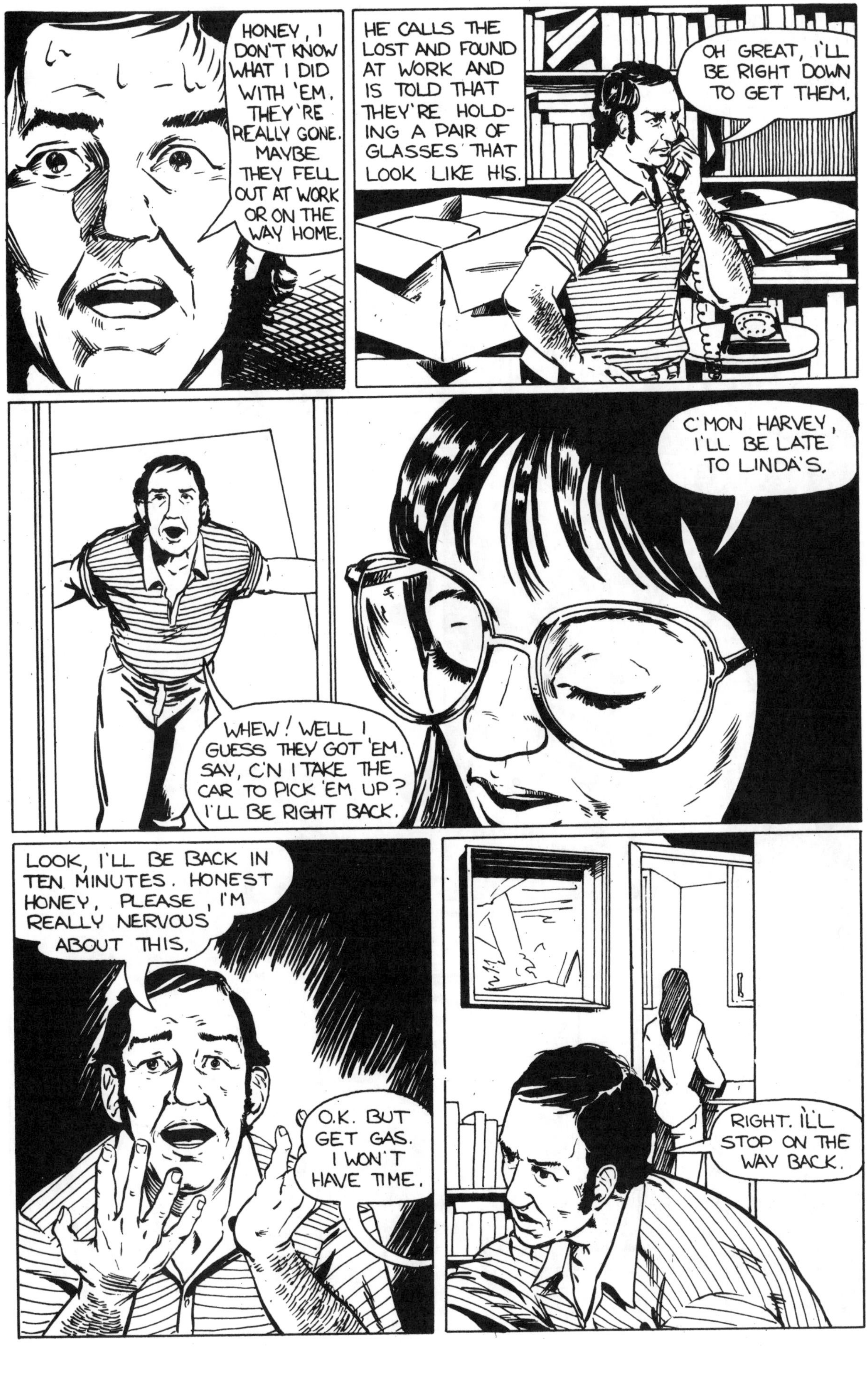
HONEY, I DON'T KNOW WHAT I DID WITH 'EM. THEY'RE REALLY GONE. MAYBE THEY FELL OUT AT WORK OR ON THE WAY HOME.
HE CALLS THE LOST AND FOUND AT WORK AND IS TOLD THAT THEY'RE HOLDING A PAIR OF GLASSES THAT LOOK LIKE HIS.
OH GREAT, I'LL BE RIGHT DOWN TO GET THEM.
C'MON HARVEY, I'LL BE LATE TO LINDA'S.
WHEW! WELL I GUESS THEY GOT 'EM. SAY, C'N I TAKE THE CAR TO PICK 'EM UP? I'LL BE RIGHT BACK.
LOOK, I'LL BE BACK IN TEN MINUTES. HONEST HONEY, PLEASE, I'M REALLY NERVOUS ABOUT THIS.
O.K. BUT GET GAS. I WON'T HAVE TIME.
RIGHT. I'LL STOP ON THE WAY BACK.

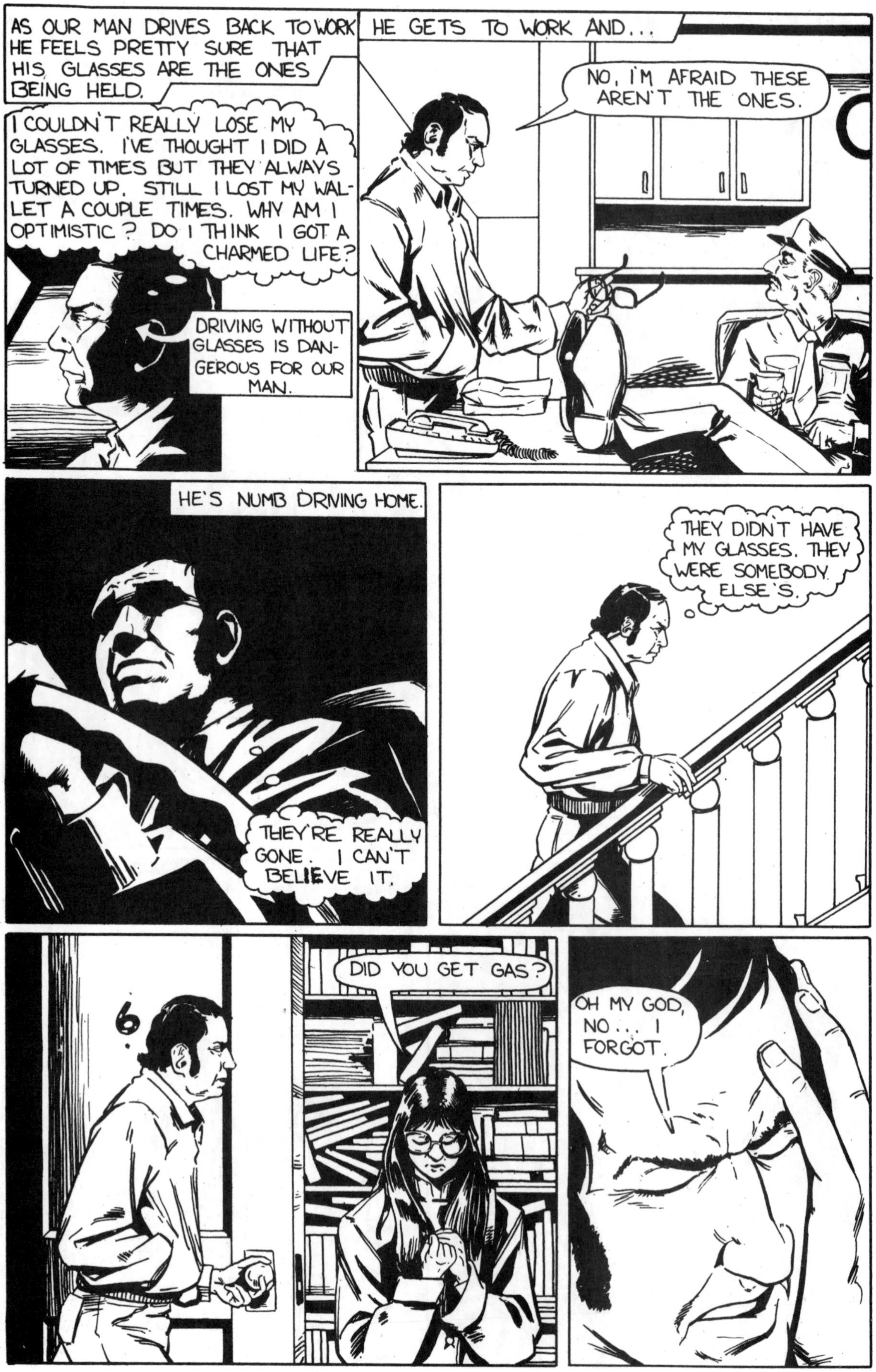
AS OUR MAN DRIVES BACK TO WORK HE FEELS PRETTY SURE THAT HIS GLASSES ARE THE ONES BEING HELD.
I COULDN'T REALLY LOSE MY GLASSES. I'VE THOUGHT I DID A LOT OF TIMES BUT THEY ALWAYS TURNED UP. STILL I LOST MY WALLET A COUPLE TIMES. WHY AM I OPTIMISTIC? DO I THINK I GOT A CHARMED LIFE?
DRIVING WITHOUT GLASSES IS DANGEROUS FOR OUR MAN.
HE GETS TO WORK AND...
NO, I'M AFRAID THESE AREN'T THE ONES.
HE'S NUMB DRIVING HOME.
THEY'RE REALLY GONE. I CAN'T BELIEVE IT.
THEY DIDN'T HAVE MY GLASSES. THEY WERE SOMEBODY ELSE'S.
6
DID YOU GET GAS?
OH MY GOD, NO... I FORGOT.

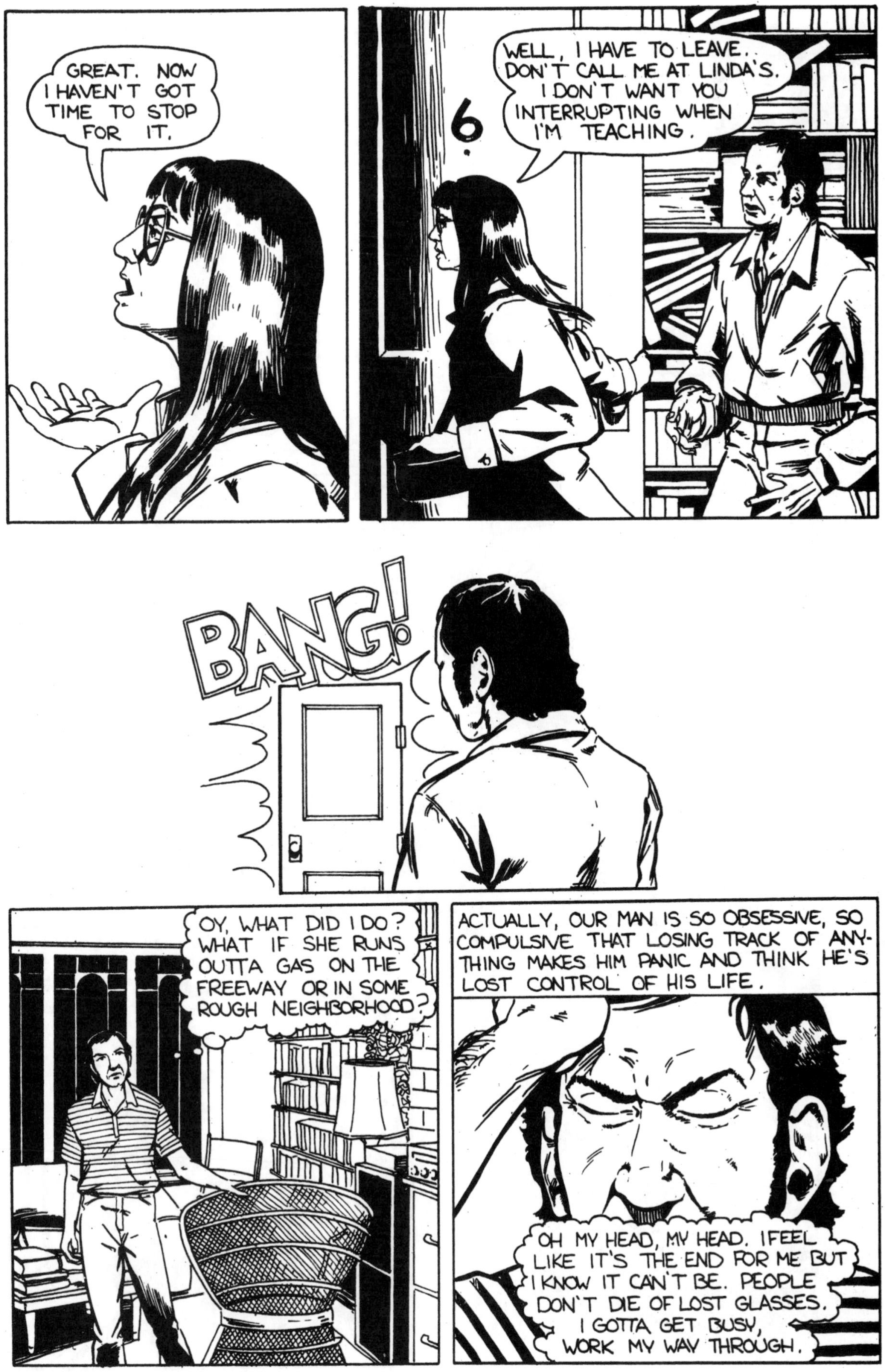

GREAT. NOW I HAVEN'T GOT TIME TO STOP FOR IT.
WELL, I HAVE TO LEAVE. DON'T CALL ME AT LINDA'S. I DON'T WANT YOU INTERRUPTING WHEN I'M TEACHING.
BANG!
OY, WHAT DID I DO? WHAT IF SHE RUNS OUTTA GAS ON THE FREEWAY OR IN SOME ROUGH NEIGHBORHOOD?
ACTUALLY, OUR MAN IS SO OBSESSIVE, SO COMPULSIVE THAT LOSING TRACK OF ANYTHING MAKES HIM PANIC AND THINK HE'S LOST CONTROL OF HIS LIFE.
OH MY HEAD, MY HEAD. I FEEL LIKE IT'S THE END FOR ME BUT I KNOW IT CAN'T BE. PEOPLE DON'T DIE OF LOST GLASSES. I GOTTA GET BUSY, WORK MY WAY THROUGH.

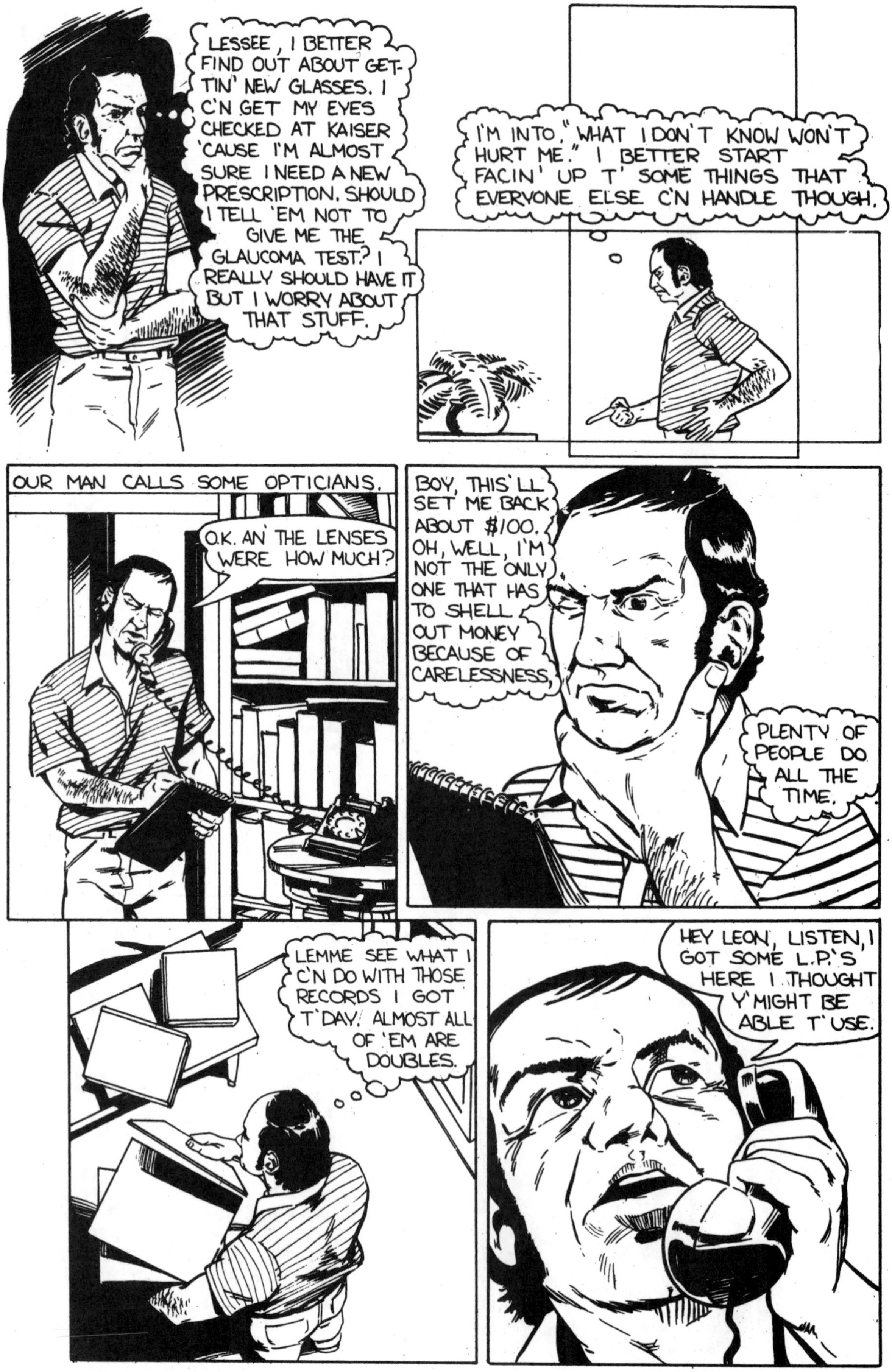
LESSEE, I BETTER FIND OUT ABOUT GET-TIN' NEW GLASSES. I C'N GET MY EYES CHECKED AT KAISER 'CAUSE I'M ALMOST SURE I NEED A NEW PRESCRIPTION. SHOULD I TELL 'EM NOT TO GIVE ME THE GLAUCOMA TEST? I REALLY SHOULD HAVE IT BUT I WORRY ABOUT THAT STUFF.
I'M INTO, "WHAT I DON'T KNOW WON'T HURT ME." I BETTER START FACIN' UP T' SOME THINGS THAT EVERYONE ELSE C'N HANDLE THOUGH.
OUR MAN CALLS SOME OPTICIANS.
O.K. AN' THE LENSES WERE HOW MUCH?
BOY, THIS'LL SET ME BACK ABOUT $100. OH, WELL, I'M NOT THE ONLY ONE THAT HAS TO SHELL OUT MONEY BECAUSE OF CARELESSNESS,
PLENTY OF PEOPLE DO ALL THE TIME.
LEMME SEE WHAT I C'N DO WITH THOSE RECORDS I GOT T'DAY. ALMOST ALL OF 'EM ARE DOUBLES.
HEY LEON, LISTEN, I GOT SOME L.P.'S HERE I THOUGHT Y'MIGHT BE ABLE T'USE.

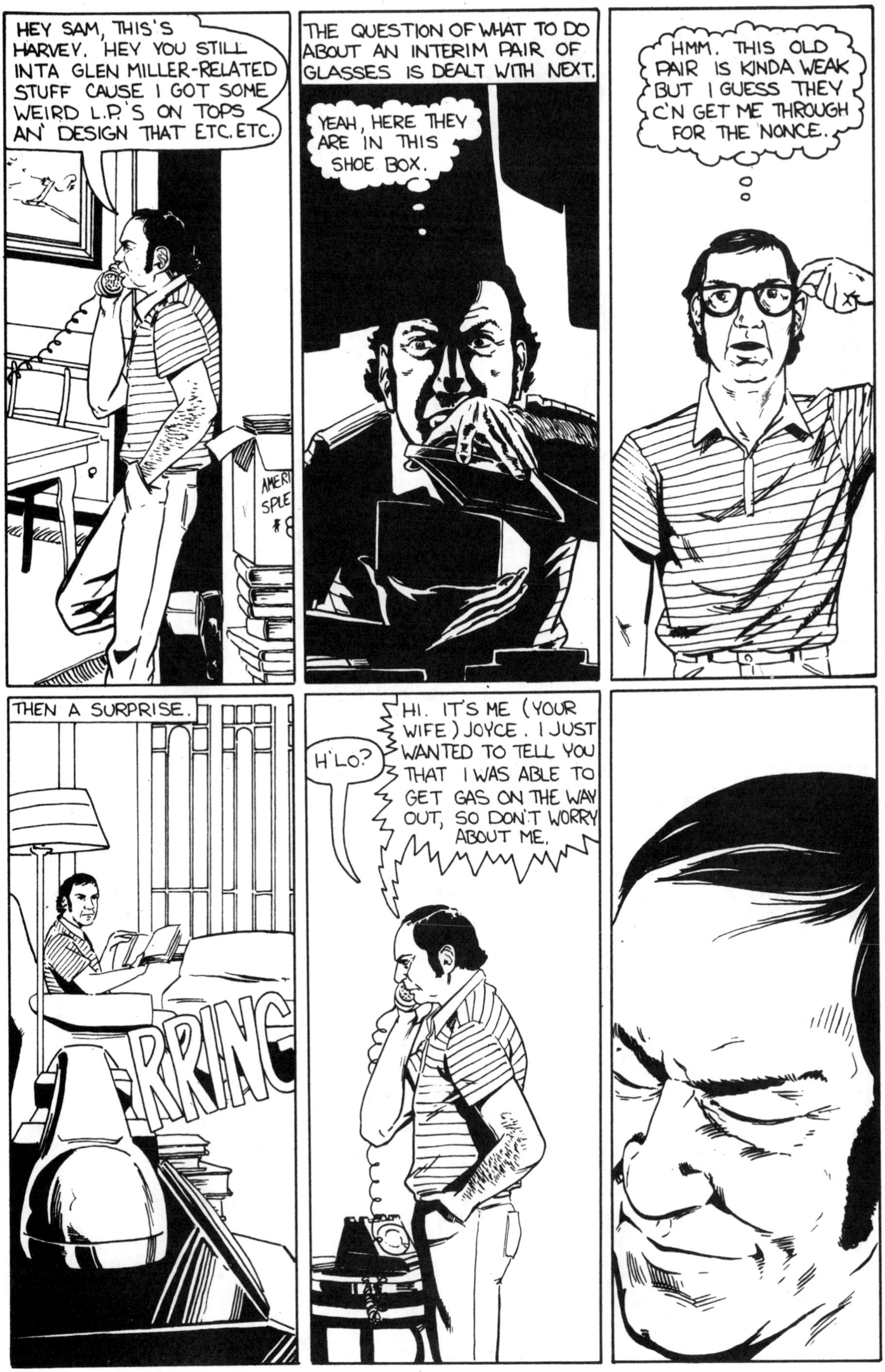

HEY SAM, THIS'S HARVEY. HEY YOU STILL INTA GLEN MILLER-RELATED STUFF CAUSE I GOT SOME WEIRD L.P.'S ON TOPS AN' DESIGN THAT ETC. ETC.
THE QUESTION OF WHAT TO DO ABOUT AN INTERIM PAIR OF GLASSES IS DEALT WITH NEXT.
YEAH, HERE THEY ARE IN THIS SHOE BOX.
HMM. THIS OLD PAIR IS KINDA WEAK BUT I GUESS THEY C'N GET ME THROUGH FOR THE NONCE.
THEN A SURPRISE.
RRING
H'LO?
HI. IT'S ME (YOUR WIFE) JOYCE. I JUST WANTED TO TELL YOU THAT I WAS ABLE TO GET GAS ON THE WAY OUT, SO DON'T WORRY ABOUT ME.

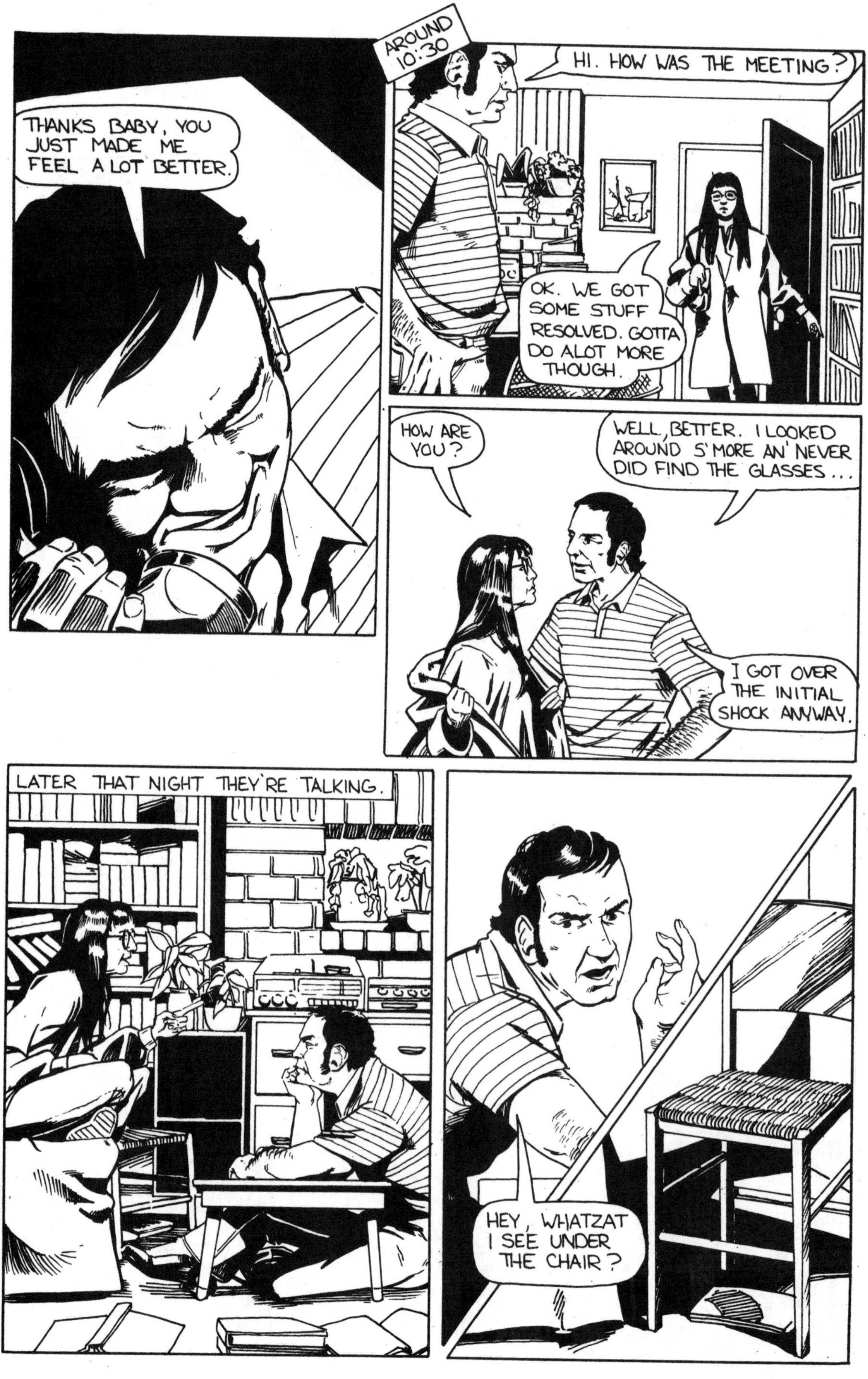
THANKS BABY, YOU JUST MADE ME FEEL A LOT BETTER.
AROUND 10:30
HI. HOW WAS THE MEETING?
OK. WE GOT SOME STUFF RESOLVED. GOTTA DO ALOT MORE THOUGH.
HOW ARE YOU?
WELL, BETTER. I LOOKED AROUND S'MORE AN' NEVER DID FIND THE GLASSES...
I GOT OVER THE INITIAL SHOCK ANYWAY.
LATER THAT NIGHT THEY'RE TALKING.
HEY, WHATZAT I SEE UNDER THE CHAIR?

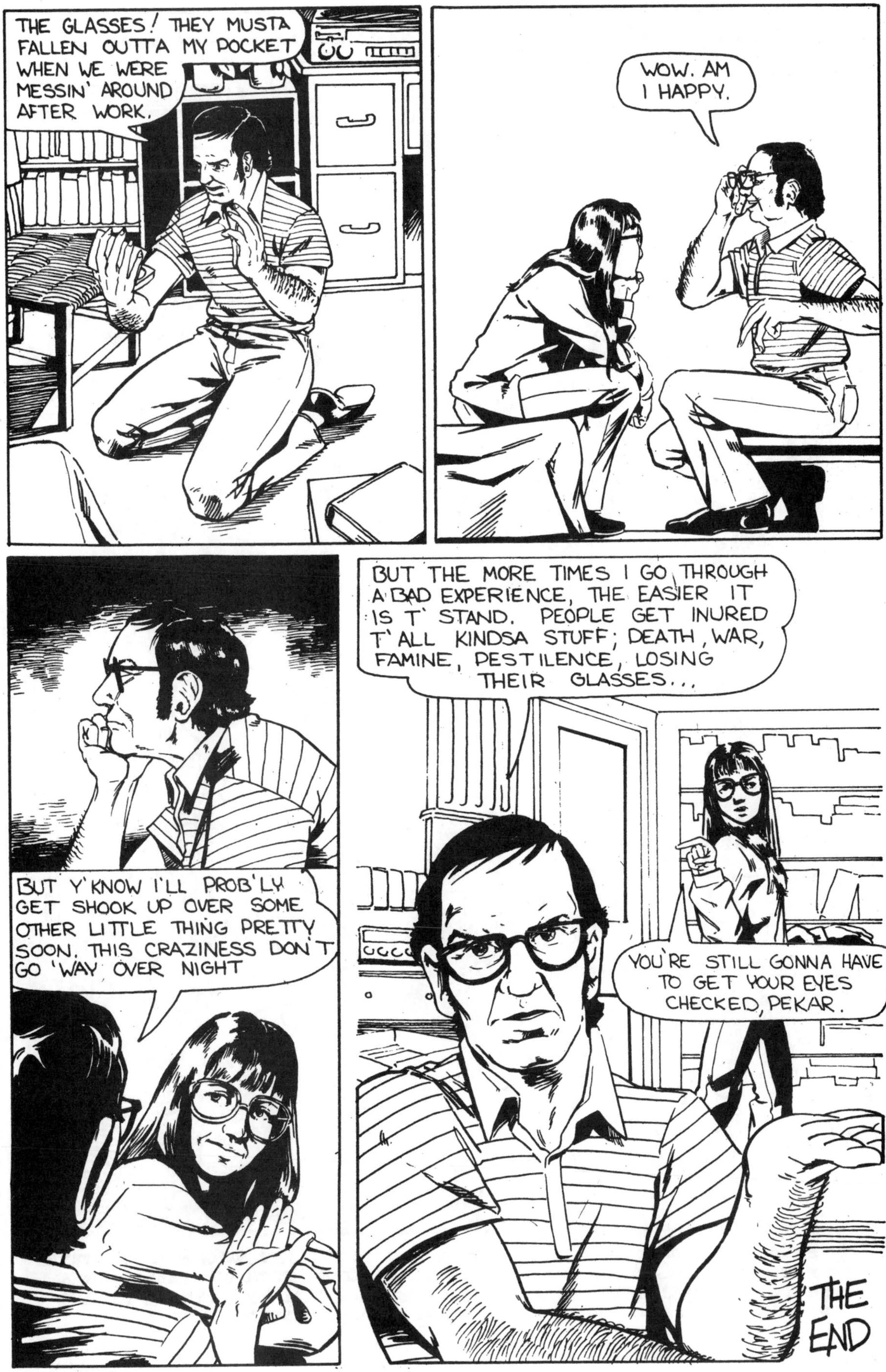
THE GLASSES! THEY MUSTA FALLEN OUTTA MY POCKET WHEN WE WERE MESSIN' AROUND AFTER WORK.
WOW. AM I HAPPY.
BUT Y'KNOW I'LL PROB'LY GET SHOOK UP OVER SOME OTHER LITTLE THING PRETTY SOON. THIS CRAZINESS DON'T GO 'WAY OVER NIGHT
BUT THE MORE TIMES I GO THROUGH A BAD EXPERIENCE, THE EASIER IT IS T' STAND. PEOPLE GET INURED T'ALL KINDSA STUFF; DEATH, WAR, FAMINE, PESTILENCE, LOSING THEIR GLASSES...
YOU'RE STILL GONNA HAVE TO GET YOUR EYES CHECKED, PEKAR.
THE END

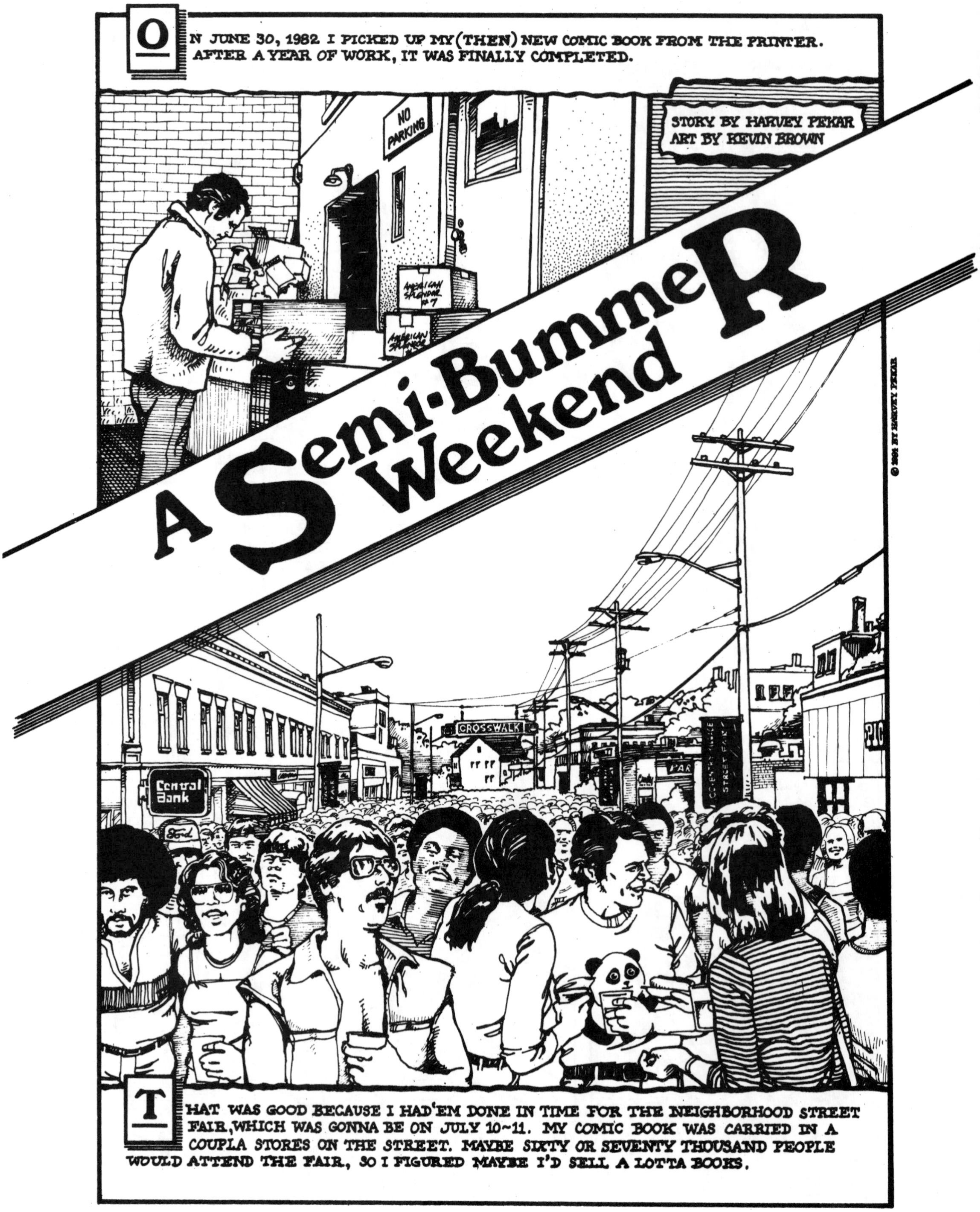
ON JUNE 30, 1982 I PICKED UP MY (THEN) NEW COMIC BOOK FROM THE PRINTER. AFTER A YEAR OF WORK, IT WAS FINALLY COMPLETED.
STORY BY HARVEY PEKAR
ART BY KEVIN BROWN
NO PARKING
A Semi-BummeR Weekend
CROSSWALK
Central Bank
THAT WAS GOOD BECAUSE I HAD'EM DONE IN TIME FOR THE NEIGHBORHOOD STREET FAIR, WHICH WAS GONNA BE ON JULY 10~11. MY COMIC BOOK WAS CARRIED IN A COUPLA STORES ON THE STREET. MAYBE SIXTY OR SEVENTY THOUSAND PEOPLE WOULD ATTEND THE FAIR, SO I FIGURED MAYBE I'D SELL A LOTTA BOOKS.

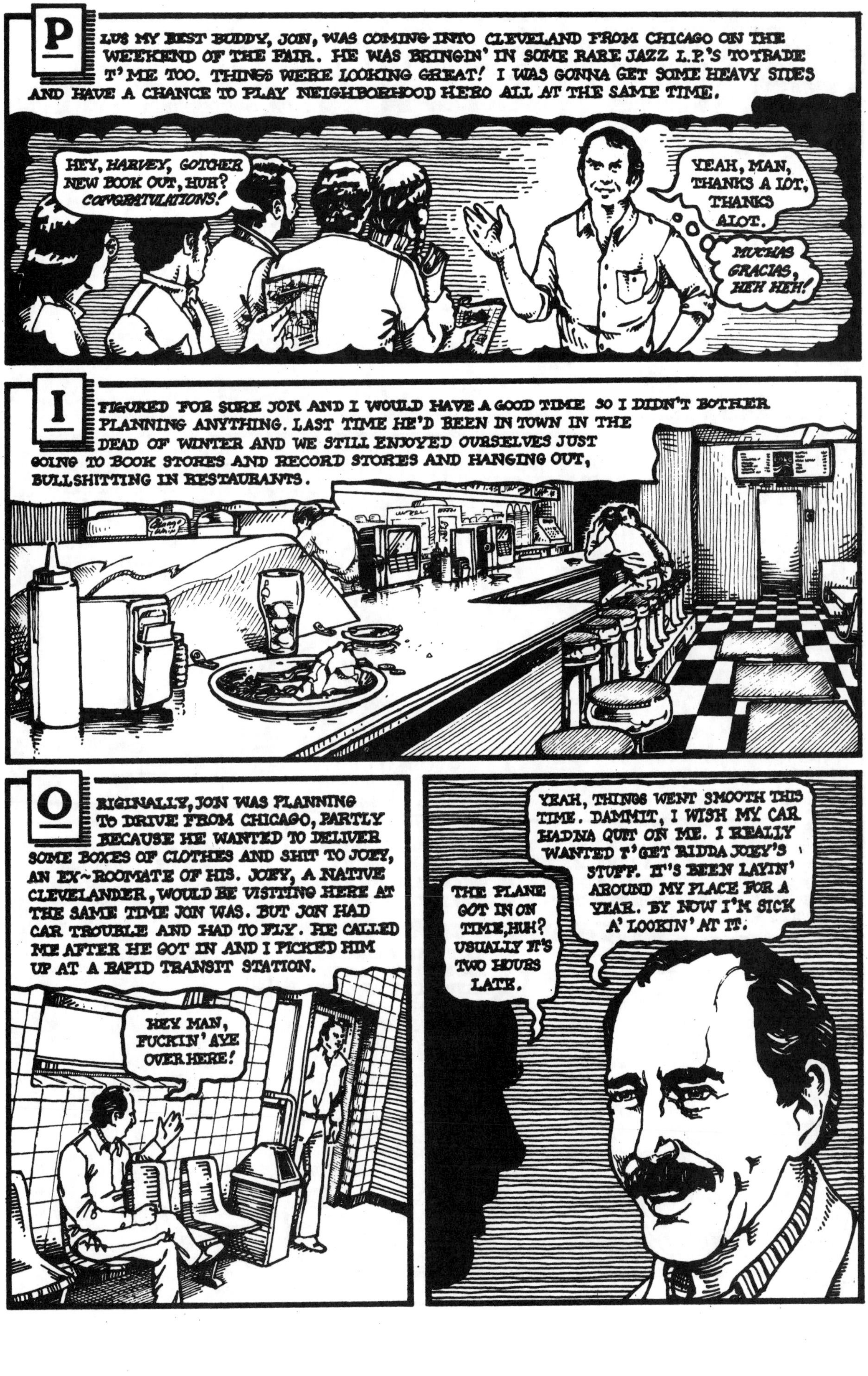
PLUS MY BEST BUDDY, JON, WAS COMING INTO CLEVELAND FROM CHICAGO ON THE WEEKEND OF THE FAIR. HE WAS BRINGIN' IN SOME RARE JAZZ L.P.'S TO TRADE T' ME TOO. THINGS WERE LOOKING GREAT! I WAS GONNA GET SOME HEAVY SIDES AND HAVE A CHANCE TO PLAY NEIGHBORHOOD HERO ALL AT THE SAME TIME.
HEY, HARVEY, GOTCHER NEW BOOK OUT, HUH? CONGRATULATIONS!
YEAH, MAN, THANKS A LOT, THANKS ALOT.
MUCHAS GRACIAS, HEH HEH!
I FIGURED FOR SURE JON AND I WOULD HAVE A GOOD TIME SO I DIDN'T BOTHER PLANNING ANYTHING. LAST TIME HE'D BEEN IN TOWN IN THE DEAD OF WINTER AND WE STILL ENJOYED OURSELVES JUST GOING TO BOOK STORES AND RECORD STORES AND HANGING OUT, BULLSHITTING IN RESTAURANTS.
ORIGINALLY, JON WAS PLANNING TO DRIVE FROM CHICAGO, PARTLY BECAUSE HE WANTED TO DELIVER SOME BOXES OF CLOTHES AND SHIT TO JOEY, AN EX~ROOMMATE OF HIS. JOEY, A NATIVE CLEVELANDER, WOULD BE VISITING HERE AT THE SAME TIME JON WAS. BUT JON HAD CAR TROUBLE AND HAD TO FLY. HE CALLED ME AFTER HE GOT IN AND I PICKED HIM UP AT A RAPID TRANSIT STATION.
HEY MAN, FUCKIN' AYE OVER HERE!
THE PLANE GOT IN ON TIME, HUH? USUALLY IT'S TWO HOURS LATE.
YEAH, THINGS WENT SMOOTH THIS TIME. DAMMIT, I WISH MY CAR HADNA QUIT ON ME. I REALLY WANTED T' GET RIDDA JOEY'S STUFF. IT'S BEEN LAYIN' AROUND MY PLACE FOR A YEAR. BY NOW I'M SICK A' LOOKIN' AT IT.

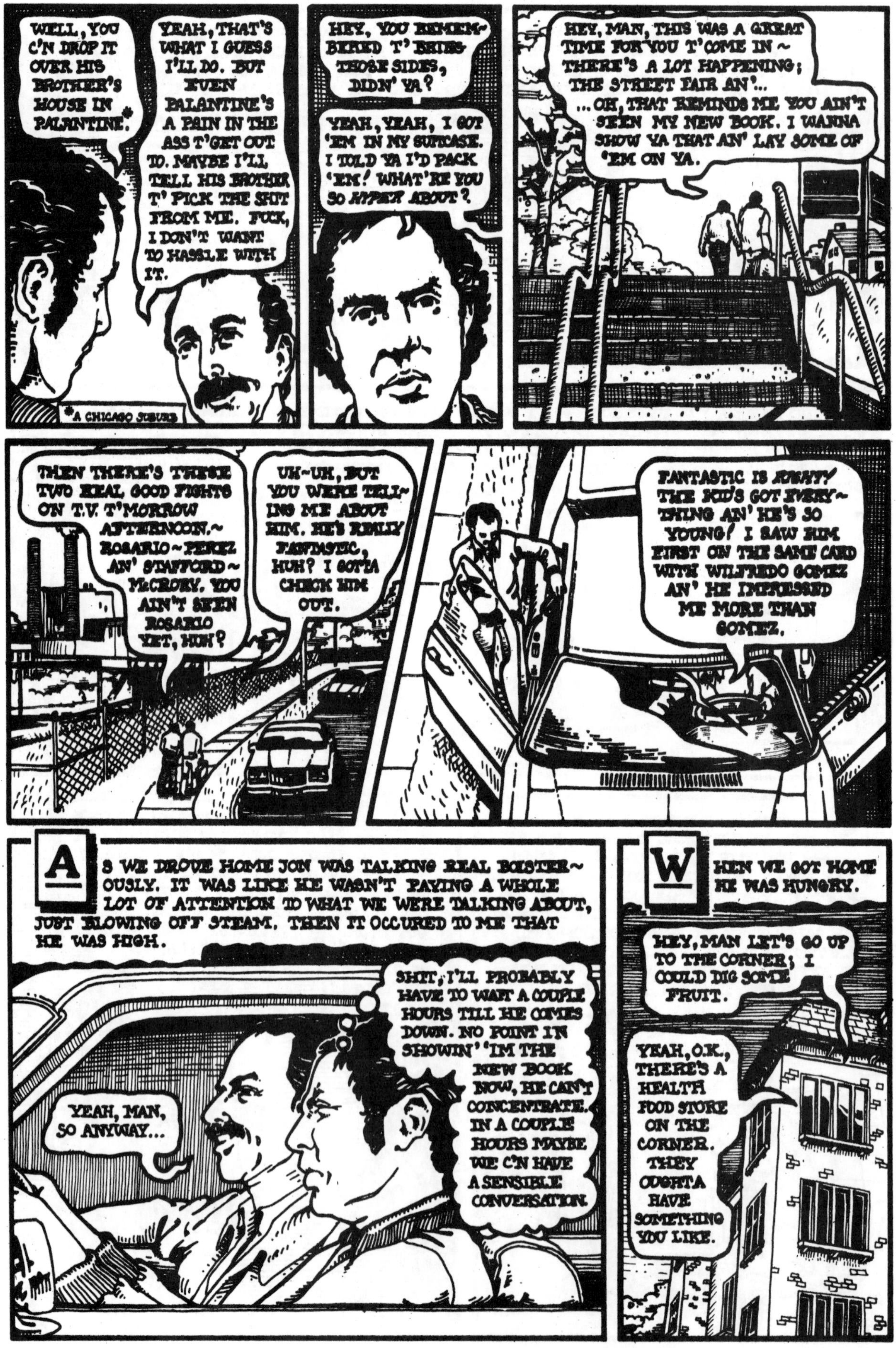
WELL, YOU C'N DROP IT OVER HIS BROTHER'S HOUSE IN PALANTINE.*
YEAH, THAT'S WHAT I GUESS I'LL DO. BUT EVEN PALANTINE'S A PAIN IN THE ASS T'GET OUT TO. MAYBE I'LL TELL HIS BROTHER T' PICK THE SHIT FROM ME. FUCK, I DON'T WANT TO HASSLE WITH IT.
*A CHICAGO SUBURB
HEY, YOU REMEMBERED T' BRING THOSE SIDES, DIDN' YA?
YEAH, YEAH, I GOT 'EM IN MY SUITCASE. I TOLD YA I'D PACK 'EM! WHAT'RE YOU SO HYPER ABOUT?
HEY, MAN, THIS WAS A GREAT TIME FOR YOU T'COME IN ~ THERE'S A LOT HAPPENING; THE STREET FAIR AN'... ...OH, THAT REMINDS ME YOU AIN'T SEEN MY NEW BOOK. I WANNA SHOW YA THAT AN' LAY SOME OF 'EM ON YA.
THEN THERE'S THESE TWO REAL GOOD FIGHTS ON T.V. T'MORROW AFTERNOON.~ ROSARIO~PEREZ AN' STAFFORD~ McCRORY. YOU AIN'T SEEN ROSARIO YET, HUH?
UH~UH, BUT YOU WERE TELL~ING ME ABOUT HIM. HE'S REALLY FANTASTIC, HUH? I GOTTA CHECK HIM OUT.
FANTASTIC IS RIGHT! THE KID'S GOT EVERY~THING AN' HE'S SO YOUNG! I SAW HIM FIRST ON THE SAME CARD WITH WILFREDO GOMEZ AN' HE IMPRESSED ME MORE THAN GOMEZ.
AS WE DROVE HOME JON WAS TALKING REAL BOISTER~OUSLY. IT WAS LIKE HE WASN'T PAYING A WHOLE LOT OF ATTENTION TO WHAT WE WERE TALKING ABOUT, JUST BLOWING OFF STEAM. THEN IT OCCURED TO ME THAT HE WAS HIGH.
SHIT, I'LL PROBABLY HAVE TO WAIT A COUPLE HOURS TILL HE COMES DOWN. NO POINT IN SHOWIN' 'IM THE NEW BOOK NOW, HE CAN'T CONCENTRATE. IN A COUPLE HOURS MAYBE WE C'N HAVE A SENSIBLE CONVERSATION.
YEAH, MAN, SO ANYWAY...
WHEN WE GOT HOME HE WAS HUNGRY.
HEY, MAN LET'S GO UP TO THE CORNER; I COULD DIG SOME FRUIT.
YEAH, O.K., THERE'S A HEALTH FOOD STORE ON THE CORNER. THEY OUGHTA HAVE SOMETHING YOU LIKE.

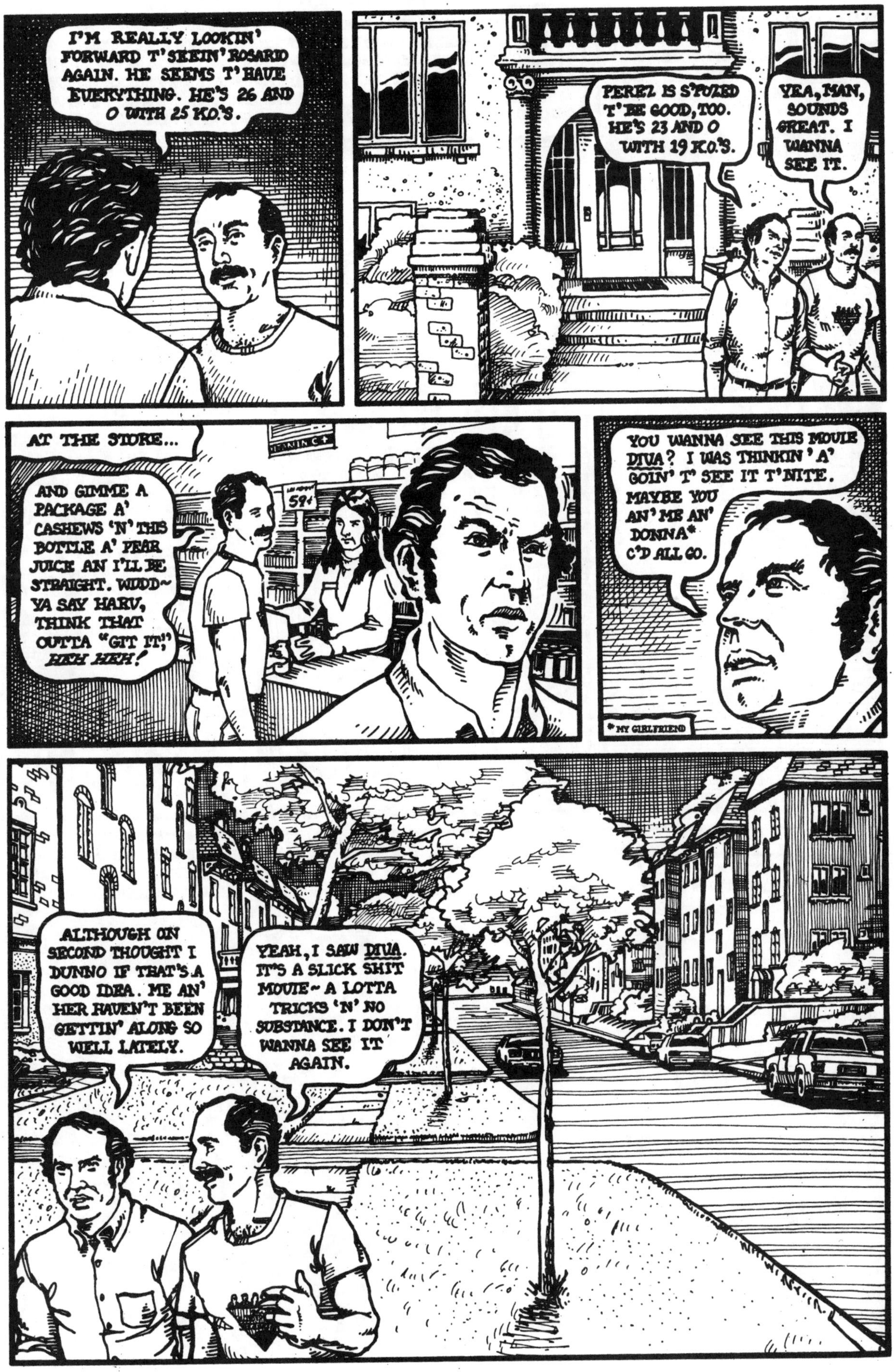
I'M REALLY LOOKIN' FORWARD T'SEEIN' ROSARIO AGAIN. HE SEEMS T'HAVE EVERYTHING. HE'S 26 AND O WITH 25 K.O.'S.
PEREZ IS S'POZED T'BE GOOD, TOO. HE'S 23 AND O WITH 19 K.O.'S.
YEA, MAN, SOUNDS GREAT. I WANNA SEE IT.
AT THE STORE...
AND GIMME A PACKAGE A' CASHEWS 'N' THIS BOTTLE A' PEAR JUICE AN I'LL BE STRAIGHT. WUDD~YA SAY HARV, THINK THAT OUTTA "GIT IT," HEH HEH!
59¢
YOU WANNA SEE THIS MOVIE DIVA? I WAS THINKIN' 'A' GOIN' T' SEE IT T'NITE. MAYBE YOU AN' ME AN' DONNA* C'D ALL GO.
*MY GIRLFRIEND
ALTHOUGH ON SECOND THOUGHT I DUNNO IF THAT'S A GOOD IDEA. ME AN' HER HAVEN'T BEEN GETTIN' ALONG SO WELL LATELY.
YEAH, I SAW DIVA. IT'S A SLICK SHIT MOVIE~ A LOTTA TRICKS 'N' NO SUBSTANCE. I DON'T WANNA SEE IT AGAIN.

10:00 AM SATURDAY MORNING
WHEN WE GOT BACK JON WAS COMING DOWN OFF HIS HIGH SO WE HAD A GOOD DISCUSSION BEFORE GOING TO SLEEP.
I'VE BEEN READIN' A LOTTA MAILER LATELY. RIGHT NOW I'M IN THE MIDDLE OF "A FIRE ON THE MOON." DAMN, I SHOULDA THOUGHT T' BRING IT WITH ME. HE'S GOT IMPORTANT THINGS TO SAY ABOUT THE IMPACT OF TECH~NOLOGY ON SOCIETY IN THE 70'S.
WE REALLY HADN'T FIGURED WHAT WE WERE GOING TO DO ON SATURDAY NIGHT. WE THOUGHT THINGS WOULD NATUR~ALLY WORK OUT. IN THE MORNING WE CALLED A MUTUAL MUSICIAN FRIEND OF OURS THAT JON WANTED T' SEE BUT THAT DIDN'T WORK OUT BECAUSE I HATE GOING TO BARS.
HE'S GOT A GIG TONIGHT. HE WANTS ME T'GO OUT THERE WITH 'IM BUT I CAN'T SEE STAYIN' OUT THERE ALL NIGHT IF YOU DON'T WANNA GO.
WHEN WE WORKED OUT A TRADE ON THE L.P.'S. I WAS REAL HAPPY WITH WHAT I GOT FROM JON BUT HE THOUGHT MAYBE I'D RIPPED HIM OFF.
I DUNNO MAN, IF I'D HELD ON T' THOSE SIDES A LITTLE LONGER MAYBE I'D A' DONE BETTER ON 'EM... BUT HELL, YOU'RE A BUDDY...
JUST REMEMBER WHERE YOU GOT THOSE SIDES, THOUGH. I'M TAKIN' TH' STUFF YOU'RE GIVING ME FOR 'EM BUT I WANTCHA T'KNOW THAT I KNOW YOU'RE GETTIN' OFF REAL CHEAP!
warne marsh quartet
WE LOOKED IN THE PAPERS TO SEE IF THERE WERE ANY GOOD MOVIES AROUND, BUT NOTHING APPEALED TO JON.
RELIGION
THEN JON COULDN'T FIND HIS SUN~GLASSES. HE THOUGHT MAYBE HE'D LEFT 'EM IN THE HEALTH FOOD STORE.
SHIT!

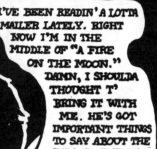

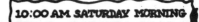

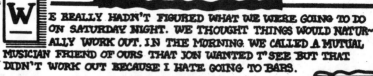

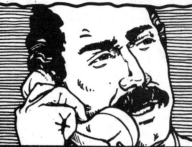

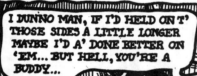

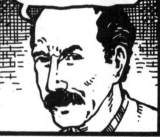

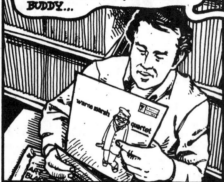

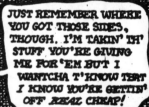

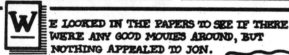

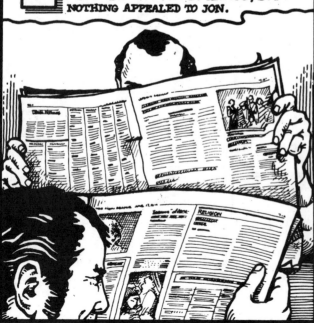

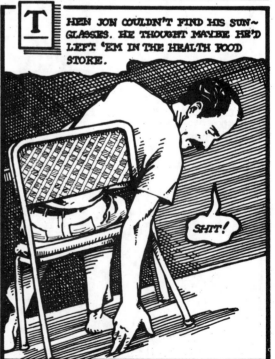

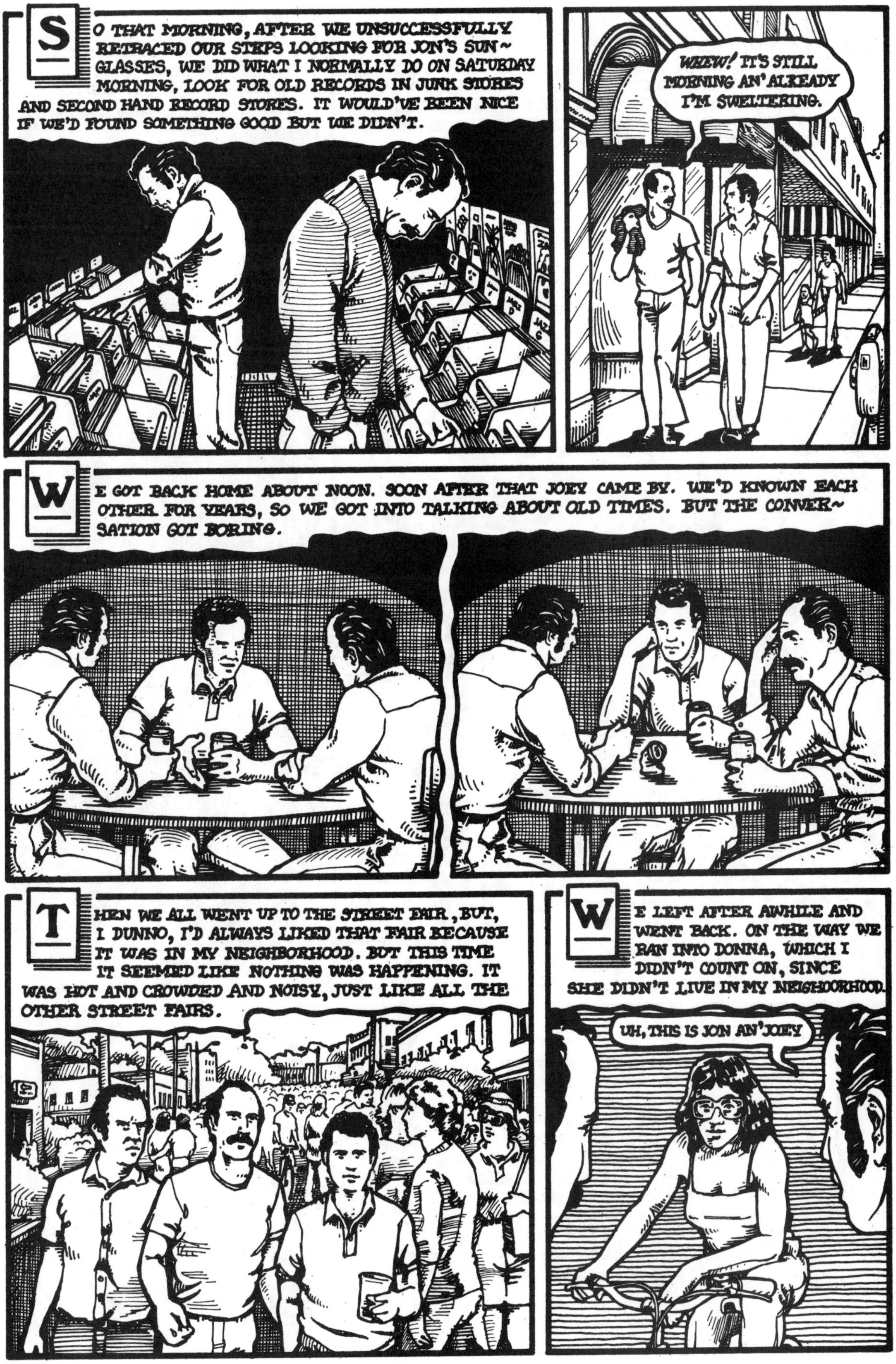
SO THAT MORNING, AFTER WE UNSUCCESSFULLY RETRACED OUR STEPS LOOKING FOR JON'S SUN~GLASSES, WE DID WHAT I NORMALLY DO ON SATURDAY MORNING, LOOK FOR OLD RECORDS IN JUNK STORES AND SECOND HAND RECORD STORES. IT WOULD'VE BEEN NICE IF WE'D FOUND SOMETHING GOOD BUT WE DIDN'T.
WHEW! IT'S STILL MORNING AN' ALREADY I'M SWELTERING.
WE GOT BACK HOME ABOUT NOON. SOON AFTER THAT JOEY CAME BY. WE'D KNOWN EACH OTHER FOR YEARS, SO WE GOT INTO TALKING ABOUT OLD TIMES. BUT THE CONVER~SATION GOT BORING.
THEN WE ALL WENT UP TO THE STREET FAIR, BUT, I DUNNO, I'D ALWAYS LIKED THAT FAIR BECAUSE IT WAS IN MY NEIGHBORHOOD. BUT THIS TIME IT SEEMED LIKE NOTHING WAS HAPPENING. IT WAS HOT AND CROWDED AND NOISY, JUST LIKE ALL THE OTHER STREET FAIRS.
WE LEFT AFTER AWHILE AND WENT BACK. ON THE WAY WE RAN INTO DONNA, WHICH I DIDN'T COUNT ON, SINCE SHE DIDN'T LIVE IN MY NEIGHBORHOOD.
UH, THIS IS JON AN' JOEY

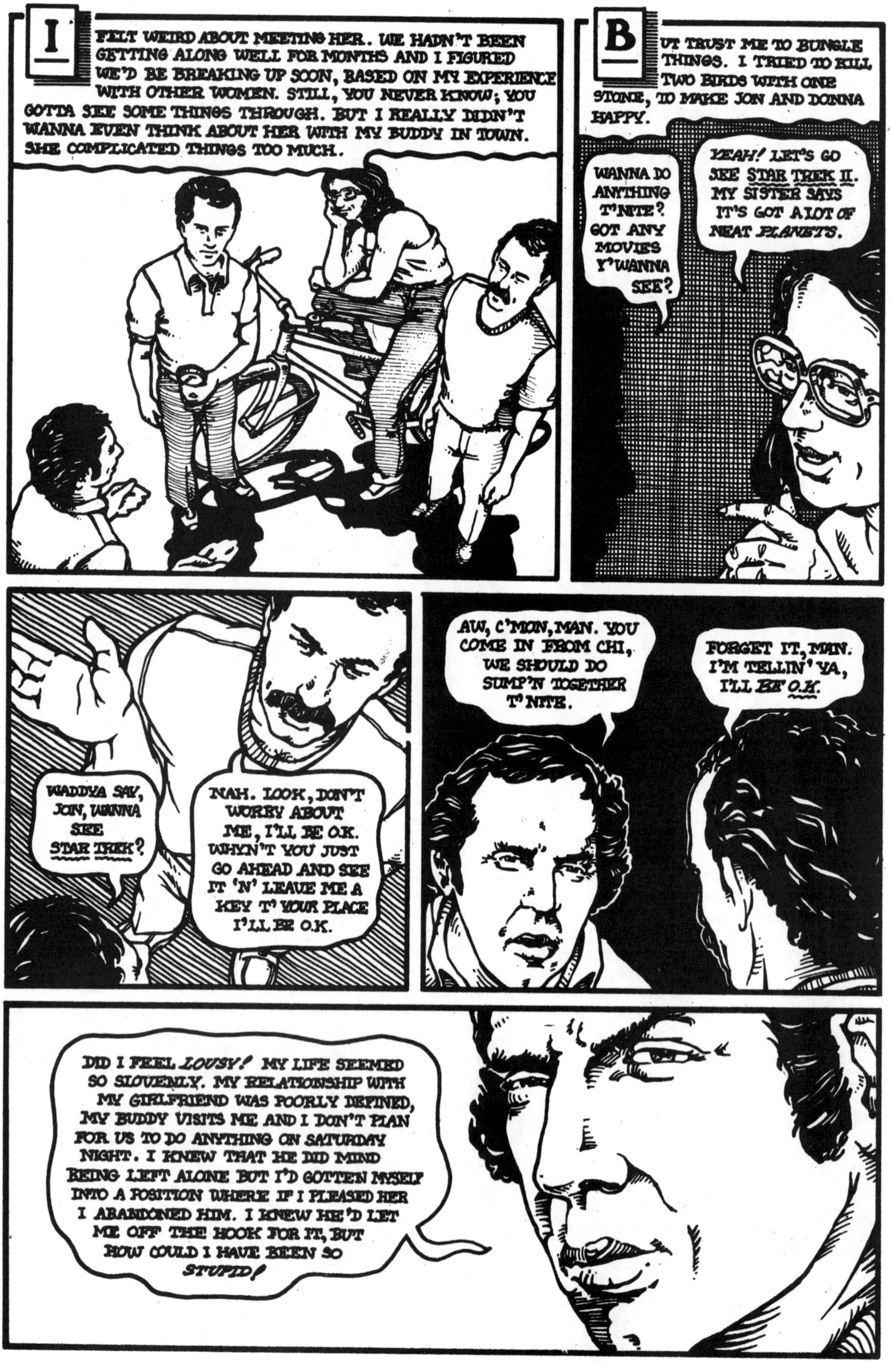
I FELT WEIRD ABOUT MEETING HER. WE HADN'T BEEN GETTING ALONG WELL FOR MONTHS AND I FIGURED WE'D BE BREAKING UP SOON, BASED ON MY EXPERIENCE WITH OTHER WOMEN. STILL, YOU NEVER KNOW; YOU GOTTA SEE SOME THINGS THROUGH. BUT I REALLY DIDN'T WANNA EVEN THINK ABOUT HER WITH MY BUDDY IN TOWN. SHE COMPLICATED THINGS TOO MUCH.
BUT TRUST ME TO BUNGLE THINGS. I TRIED TO KILL TWO BIRDS WITH ONE STONE, TO MAKE JON AND DONNA HAPPY.
WANNA DO ANYTHING T'NITE? GOT ANY MOVIES Y'WANNA SEE?
YEAH! LET'S GO SEE STAR TREK II. MY SISTER SAYS IT'S GOT A LOT OF NEAT PLANETS.
WADDYA SAY, JON, WANNA SEE STAR TREK?
NAH. LOOK, DON'T WORRY ABOUT ME, I'LL BE O.K. WHYN'T YOU JUST GO AHEAD AND SEE IT 'N' LEAVE ME A KEY T' YOUR PLACE I'LL BE O.K.
AW, C'MON, MAN. YOU COME IN FROM CHI, WE SHOULD DO SUMP'N TOGETHER T'NITE.
FORGET IT, MAN. I'M TELLIN' YA, I'LL BE O.K.
DID I FEEL LOUSY! MY LIFE SEEMED SO SLOVENLY. MY RELATIONSHIP WITH MY GIRLFRIEND WAS POORLY DEFINED, MY BUDDY VISITS ME AND I DON'T PLAN FOR US TO DO ANYTHING ON SATURDAY NIGHT. I KNEW THAT HE DID MIND BEING LEFT ALONE BUT I'D GOTTEN MYSELF INTO A POSITION WHERE IF I PLEASED HER I ABANDONED HIM. I KNEW HE'D LET ME OFF THE HOOK FOR IT, BUT HOW COULD I HAVE BEEN SO STUPID!

 WAS HOPING SEEING THE FIGHT THAT AFTERNOON WOULD PUT ME IN A BETTER MOOD. JON & I BOTH REALLY DUG BOXING AN' ROSARIO WAS A PHENOMENAL PROSPECT. BUT DIG WHAT HAPPENED:

WE'RE SORRY TO ANNOUNCE THAT TODAY'S BOUT BETWEEN EDWIN ROSARIO AND "CUBANITO" PEREZ HAS BEEN CANCELLED DUE TO ROSARIO'S BREAKING HIS HAND. INSTEAD, WE BRING YOU A TEN-ROUND BOUT BETWEEN...

SHIT!!

T HAT REALLY WAS A KILLER. I WAS FIGURING THAT FIGHT WOULD BE THE HIGHLIGHT OF THE WEEKEND FOR JON. IF NOTHING WORKED OUT IT'D STILL BE GOOD, BE SOMETHING T' TALK ABOUT. AND THEN ROSARIO GOES AND *BREAKS* HIS *HAND!*

T HAT NIGHT I WENT TO SEE *STAR TREK II* WITH DONNA.

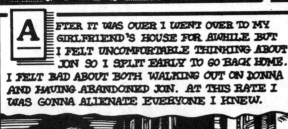

I T WAS AN ABSURD FLICK. RICARDO MONTALBAN PLAYED SOME OUTER SPACE VILLIAN NAMED KHAN DRESSED UP LIKE A TWENTY-FIFTH CENTURY BIKER. THE SPECIAL EFFECTS WERE CHINTZY.

A FTER IT WAS OVER I WENT OVER TO MY GIRLFRIEND'S HOUSE FOR AWHILE BUT I FELT UNCOMFORTABLE THINKING ABOUT JON SO I SPLIT EARLY TO GO BACK HOME. I FELT BAD ABOUT BOTH WALKING OUT ON DONNA AND HAVING ABANDONED JON. AT THIS RATE I WAS GONNA ALIENATE EVERYONE I KNEW.

W HEN I GOT BACK JON WAS THERE BUT HE WASN'T IN A REAL GREAT MOOD (I FOUND OUT LATER HE WAS REALLY PISSED.).

WUD'D YOU DO?

I WENT UP T' THE STREET FAIR AGAIN. I TRIED T' GET OF A FIRE ON THE MOON AT TH' BOOKSTORE BUT THEY DIDN'T HAVE IT.

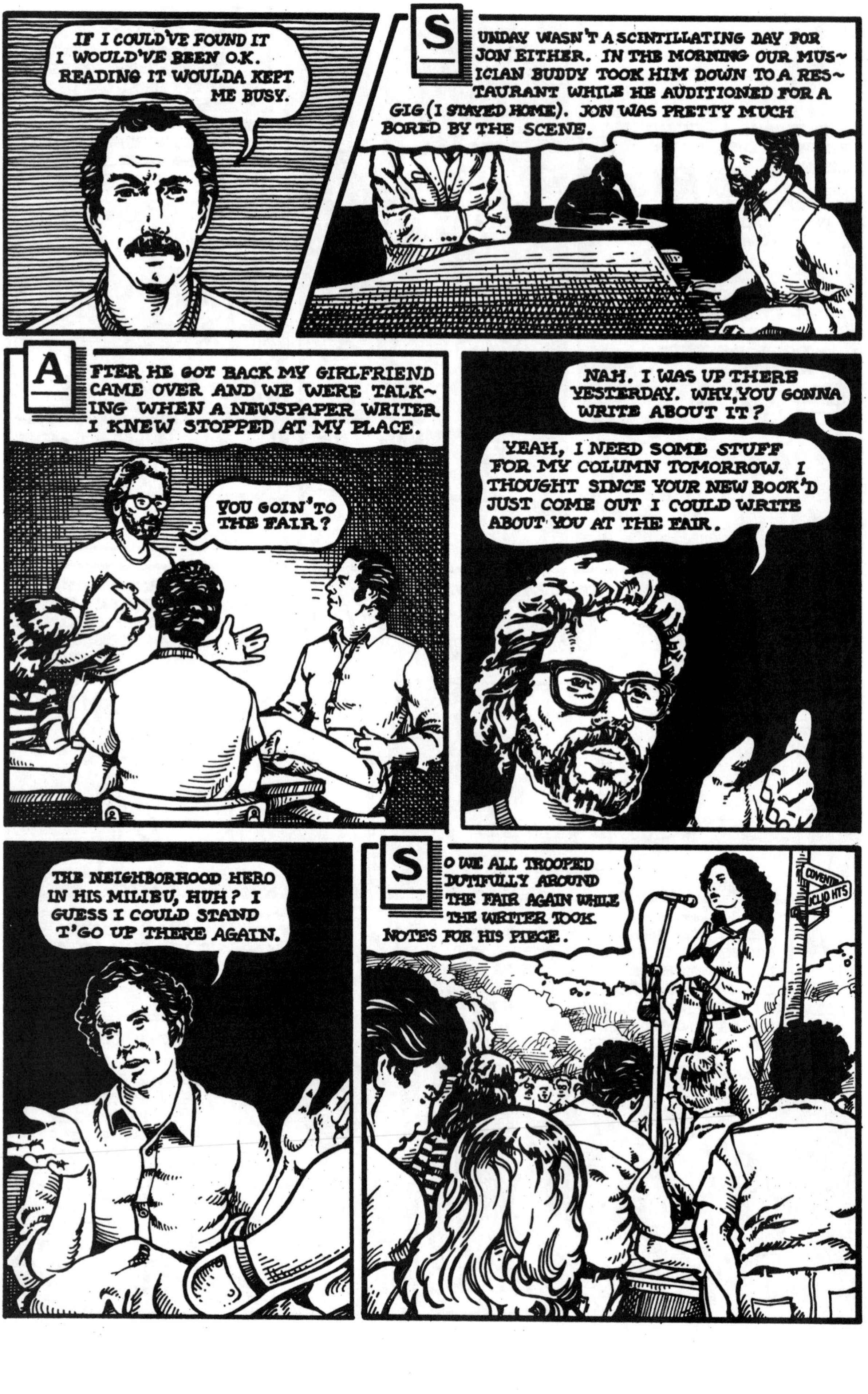
IF I COULD'VE FOUND IT I WOULD'VE BEEN O.K. READING IT WOULDA KEPT ME BUSY.
SUNDAY WASN'T A SCINTILLATING DAY FOR JON EITHER. IN THE MORNING OUR MUS~ICIAN BUDDY TOOK HIM DOWN TO A RES~TAURANT WHILE HE AUDITIONED FOR A GIG (I STAYED HOME). JON WAS PRETTY MUCH BORED BY THE SCENE.
AFTER HE GOT BACK MY GIRLFRIEND CAME OVER AND WE WERE TALK~ING WHEN A NEWSPAPER WRITER I KNEW STOPPED AT MY PLACE.
YOU GOIN' TO THE FAIR?
NAH. I WAS UP THERE YESTERDAY. WHY, YOU GONNA WRITE ABOUT IT?
YEAH, I NEED SOME STUFF FOR MY COLUMN TOMORROW. I THOUGHT SINCE YOUR NEW BOOK'D JUST COME OUT I COULD WRITE ABOUT YOU AT THE FAIR.
THE NEIGHBORHOOD HERO IN HIS MILIBU, HUH? I GUESS I COULD STAND T'GO UP THERE AGAIN.
SO WE ALL TROOPED DUTIFULLY AROUND THE FAIR AGAIN WHILE THE WRITER TOOK NOTES FOR HIS PIECE.
COVENTRY
EUCLID HTS

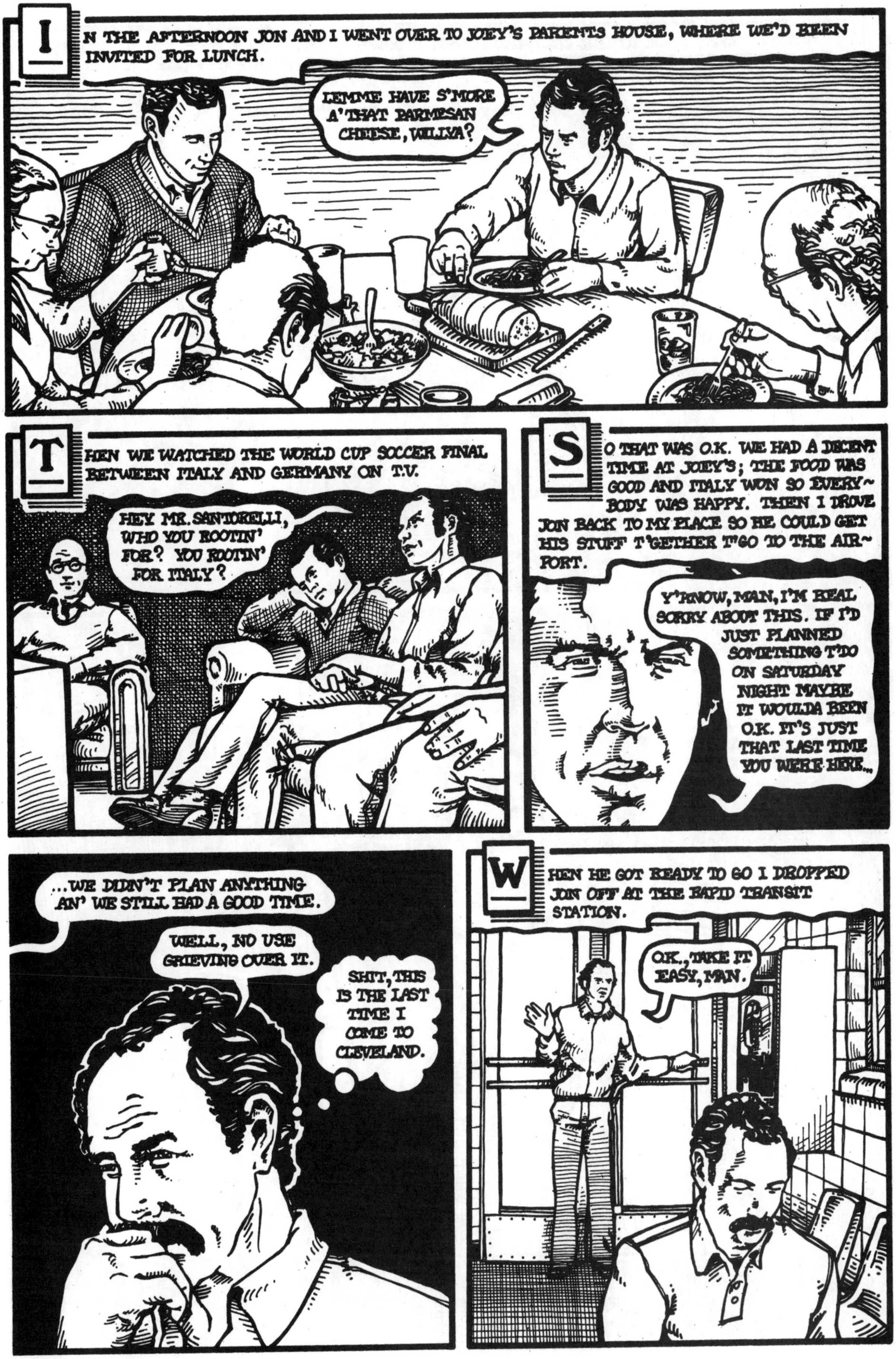
IN THE AFTERNOON JON AND I WENT OVER TO JOEY'S PARENTS HOUSE, WHERE WE'D BEEN INVITED FOR LUNCH.
LEMME HAVE S'MORE A'THAT PARMESAN CHEESE, WILLYA?
THEN WE WATCHED THE WORLD CUP SOCCER FINAL BETWEEN ITALY AND GERMANY ON T.V.
HEY MR. SANTORELLI, WHO YOU ROOTIN' FOR? YOU ROOTIN' FOR ITALY?
SO THAT WAS O.K. WE HAD A DECENT TIME AT JOEY'S; THE FOOD WAS GOOD AND ITALY WON SO EVERY~BODY WAS HAPPY. THEN I DROVE JON BACK TO MY PLACE SO HE COULD GET HIS STUFF T'GETHER T'GO TO THE AIR~PORT.
Y'KNOW, MAN, I'M REAL SORRY ABOUT THIS. IF I'D JUST PLANNED SOMETHING T'DO ON SATURDAY NIGHT MAYBE IT WOULDA BEEN O.K. IT'S JUST THAT LAST TIME YOU WERE HERE...
...WE DIDN'T PLAN ANYTHING AN' WE STILL HAD A GOOD TIME.
WELL, NO USE GRIEVING OVER IT.
SHIT, THIS IS THE LAST TIME I COME TO CLEVELAND.
WHEN HE GOT READY TO GO I DROPPED JON OFF AT THE RAPID TRANSIT STATION.
O.K., TAKE IT EASY, MAN.

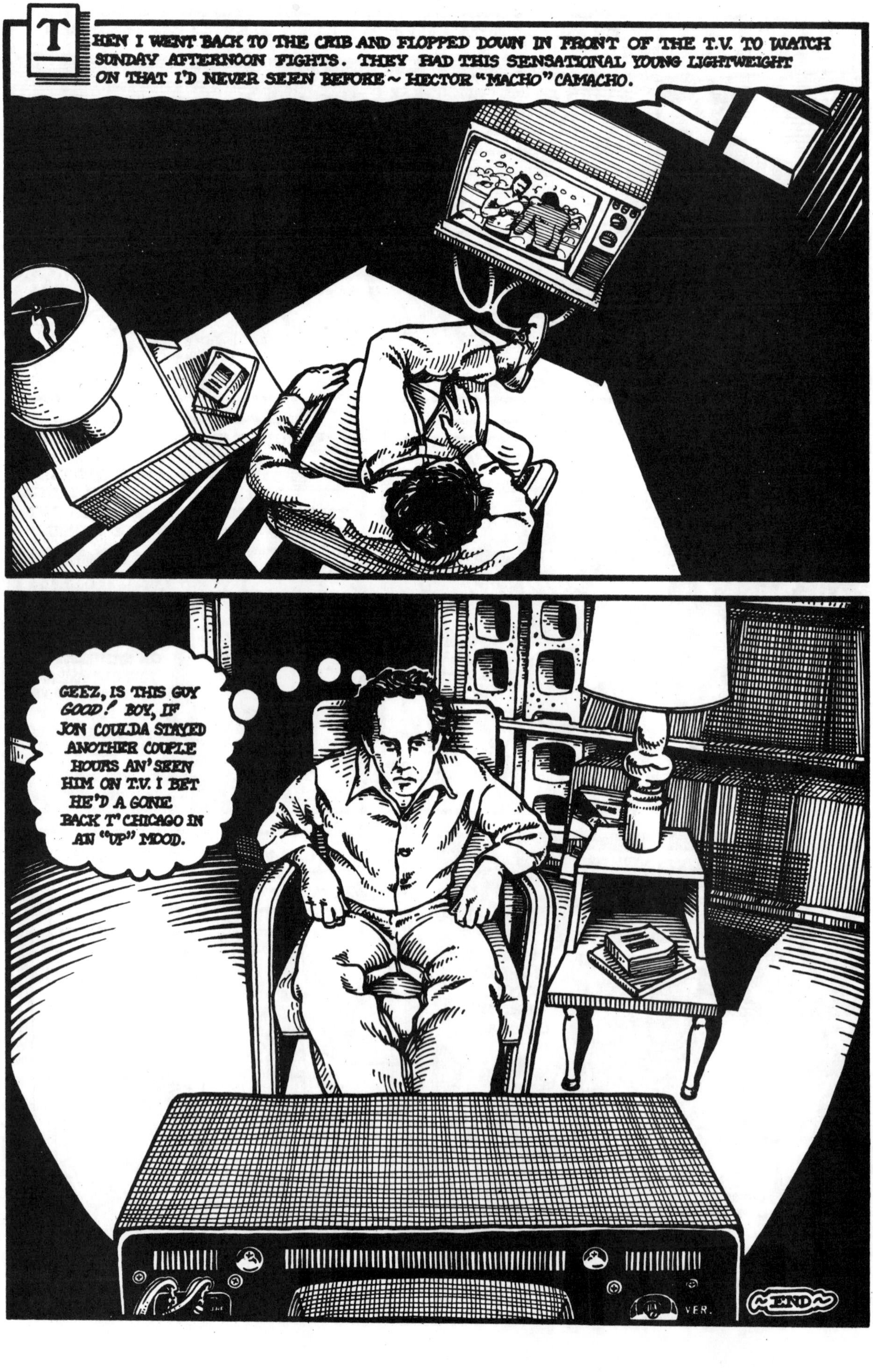
THEN I WENT BACK TO THE CRIB AND FLOPPED DOWN IN FRONT OF THE T.V. TO WATCH SUNDAY AFTERNOON FIGHTS. THEY HAD THIS SENSATIONAL YOUNG LIGHTWEIGHT ON THAT I'D NEVER SEEN BEFORE ~ HECTOR "MACHO" CAMACHO.
GEEZ, IS THIS GUY GOOD! BOY, IF JON COULDA STAYED ANOTHER COUPLE HOURS AN' SEEN HIM ON T.V. I BET HE'D A GONE BACK T' CHICAGO IN AN "UP" MOOD.
VER.
~END~

A HARVEY PEKAR STORY

AS TOLD BY JON GOLDMAN

STORY BY HARVEY PEKAR
ART BY VAL MAYERIK

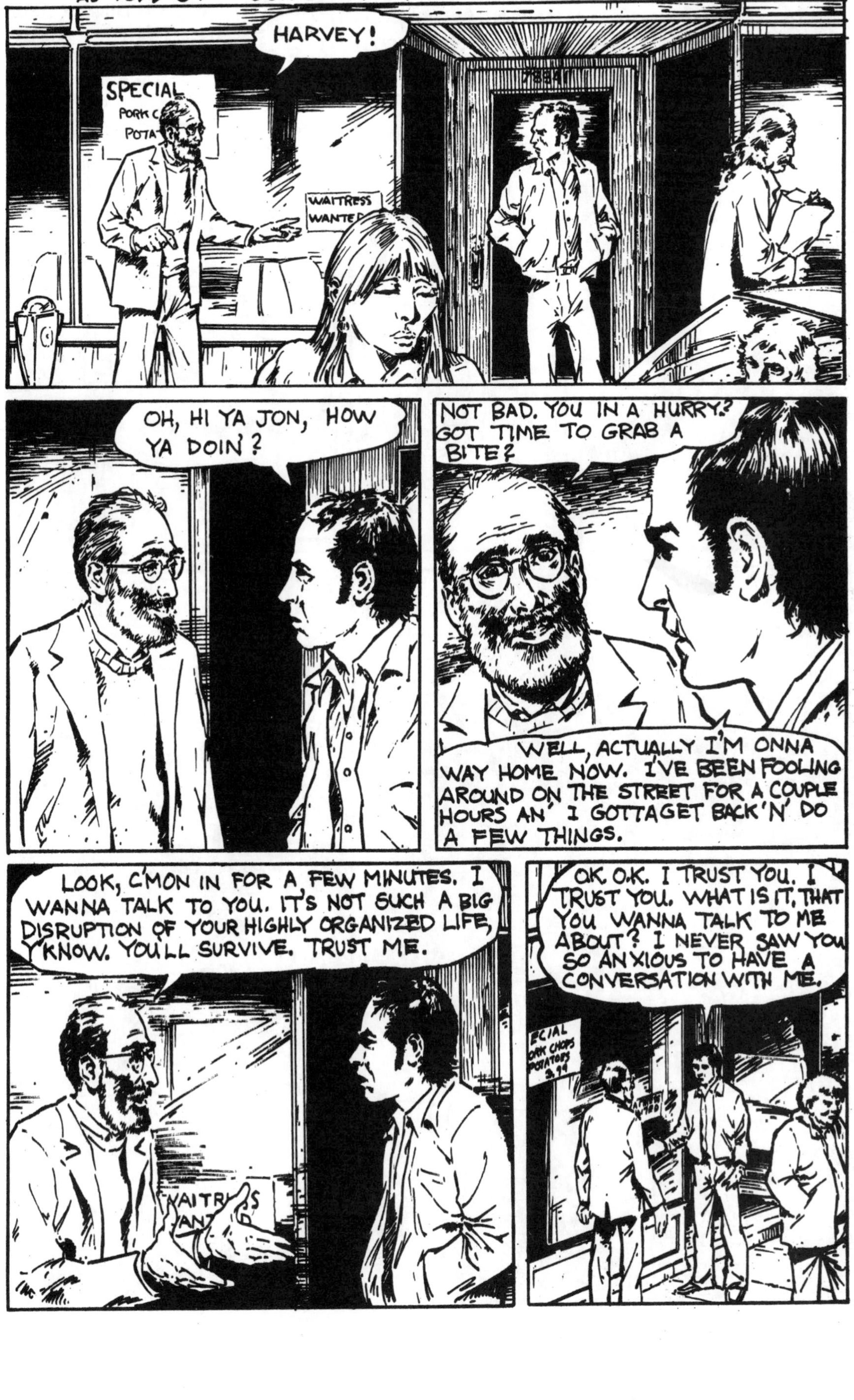
HARVEY!
SPECIAL
OH, HI YA JON, HOW YA DOIN'?
NOT BAD. YOU IN A HURRY? GOT TIME TO GRAB A BITE?
WELL, ACTUALLY I'M ONNA WAY HOME NOW. I'VE BEEN FOOLING AROUND ON THE STREET FOR A COUPLE HOURS AN' I GOTTAGET BACK 'N' DO A FEW THINGS.
LOOK, C'MON IN FOR A FEW MINUTES. I WANNA TALK TO YOU. IT'S NOT SUCH A BIG DISRUPTION OF YOUR HIGHLY ORGANIZED LIFE, Y'KNOW. YOU'LL SURVIVE. TRUST ME.
O.K. O.K. I TRUST YOU. I TRUST YOU. WHAT IS IT, THAT YOU WANNA TALK TO ME ABOUT? I NEVER SAW YOU SO ANXIOUS TO HAVE A CONVERSATION WITH ME.

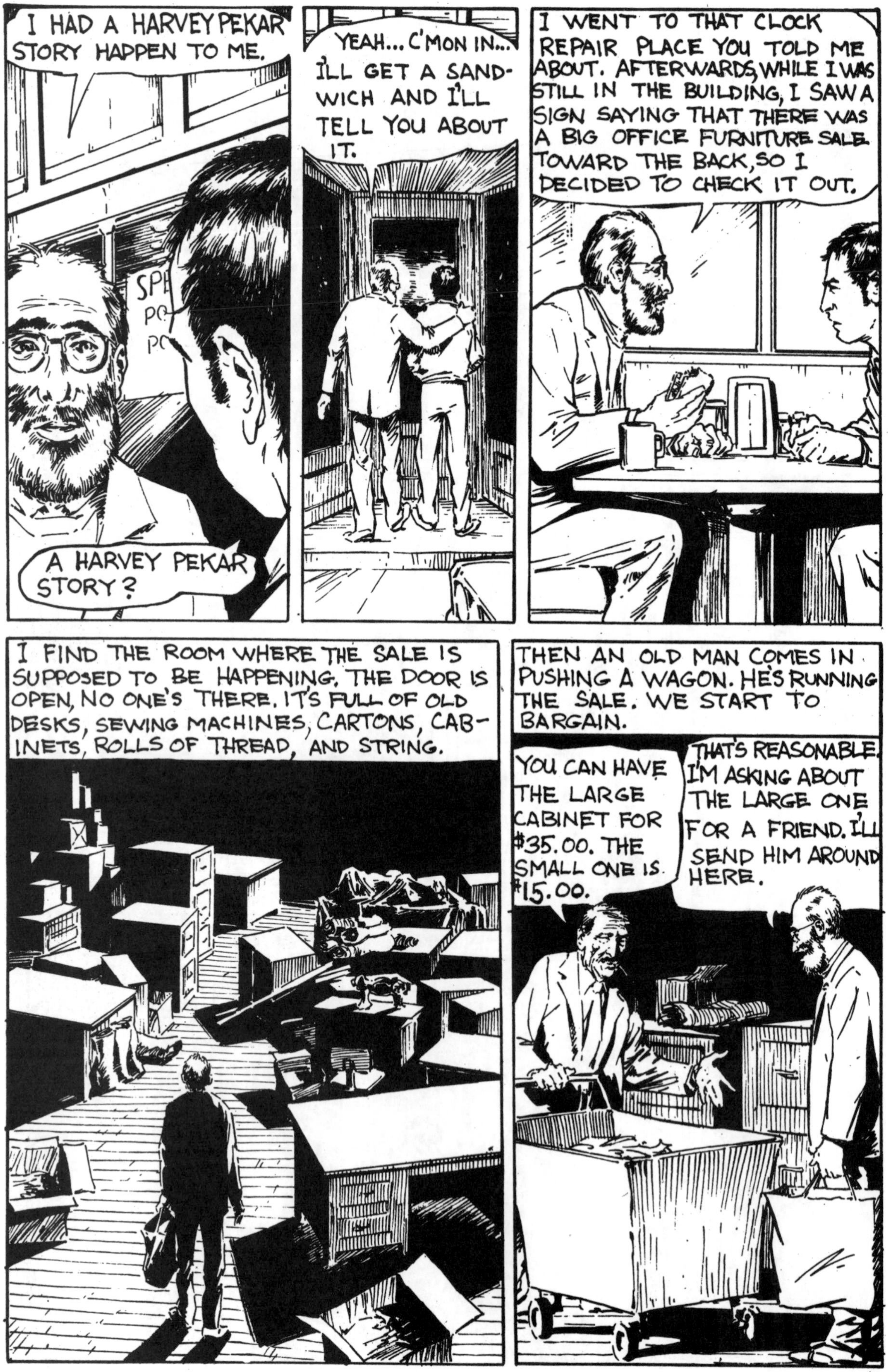
I HAD A HARVEY PEKAR STORY HAPPEN TO ME.
A HARVEY PEKAR STORY?
YEAH... C'MON IN... I'LL GET A SANDWICH AND I'LL TELL YOU ABOUT IT.
I WENT TO THAT CLOCK REPAIR PLACE YOU TOLD ME ABOUT. AFTERWARDS, WHILE I WAS STILL IN THE BUILDING, I SAW A SIGN SAYING THAT THERE WAS A BIG OFFICE FURNITURE SALE TOWARD THE BACK, SO I DECIDED TO CHECK IT OUT.
I FIND THE ROOM WHERE THE SALE IS SUPPOSED TO BE HAPPENING. THE DOOR IS OPEN, NO ONE'S THERE. IT'S FULL OF OLD DESKS, SEWING MACHINES, CARTONS, CABINETS, ROLLS OF THREAD, AND STRING.
THEN AN OLD MAN COMES IN PUSHING A WAGON. HE'S RUNNING THE SALE. WE START TO BARGAIN.
YOU CAN HAVE THE LARGE CABINET FOR $35.00. THE SMALL ONE IS $15.00.
THAT'S REASONABLE. I'M ASKING ABOUT THE LARGE ONE FOR A FRIEND. I'LL SEND HIM AROUND HERE.

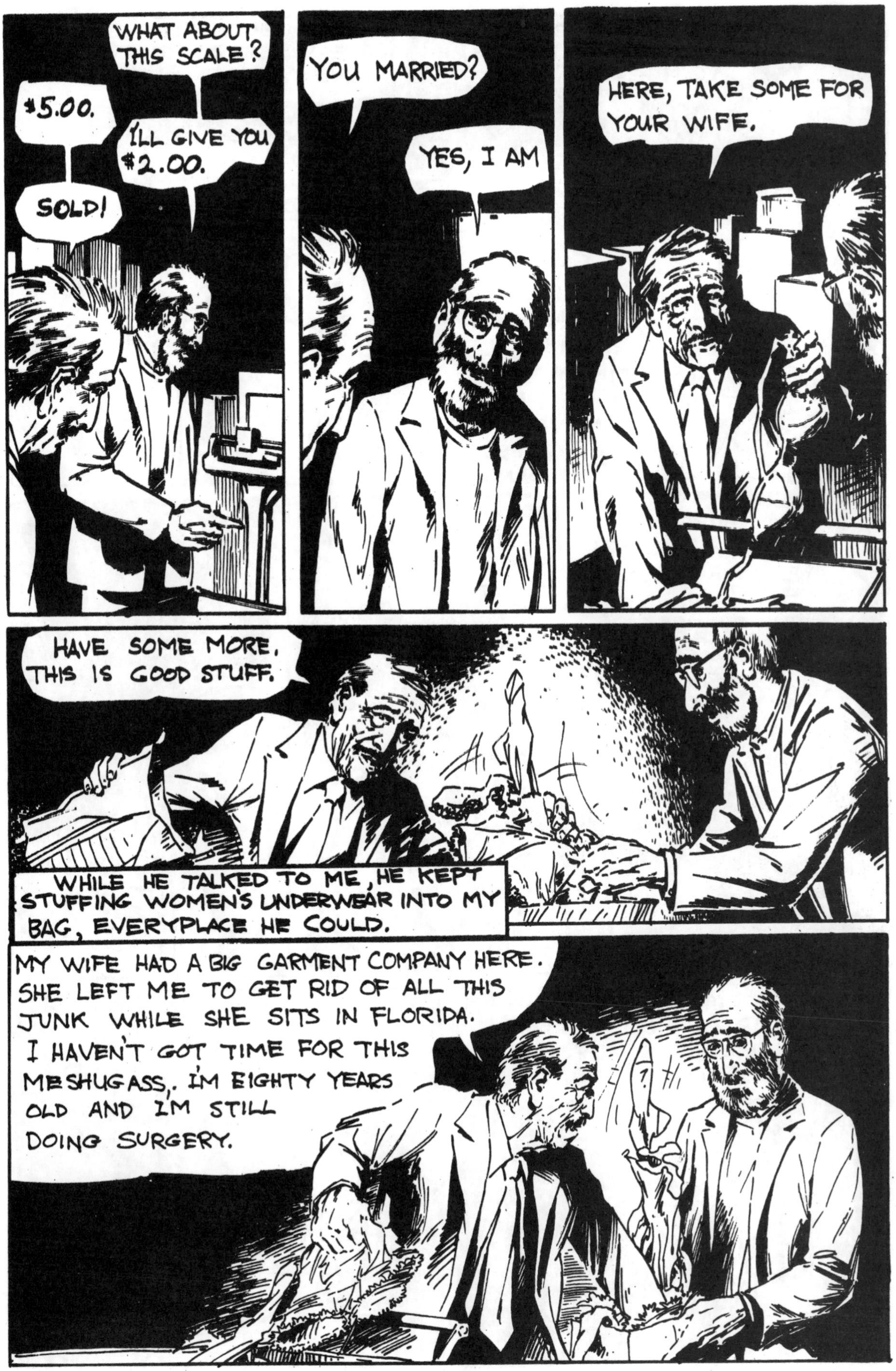
WHAT ABOUT THIS SCALE?
$5.00.
I'LL GIVE YOU $2.00.
SOLD!
YOU MARRIED?
YES, I AM
HERE, TAKE SOME FOR YOUR WIFE.
HAVE SOME MORE. THIS IS GOOD STUFF.
WHILE HE TALKED TO ME, HE KEPT STUFFING WOMEN'S UNDERWEAR INTO MY BAG, EVERYPLACE HE COULD.
MY WIFE HAD A BIG GARMENT COMPANY HERE. SHE LEFT ME TO GET RID OF ALL THIS JUNK WHILE SHE SITS IN FLORIDA. I HAVEN'T GOT TIME FOR THIS MESHUGASS. I'M EIGHTY YEARS OLD AND I'M STILL DOING SURGERY.

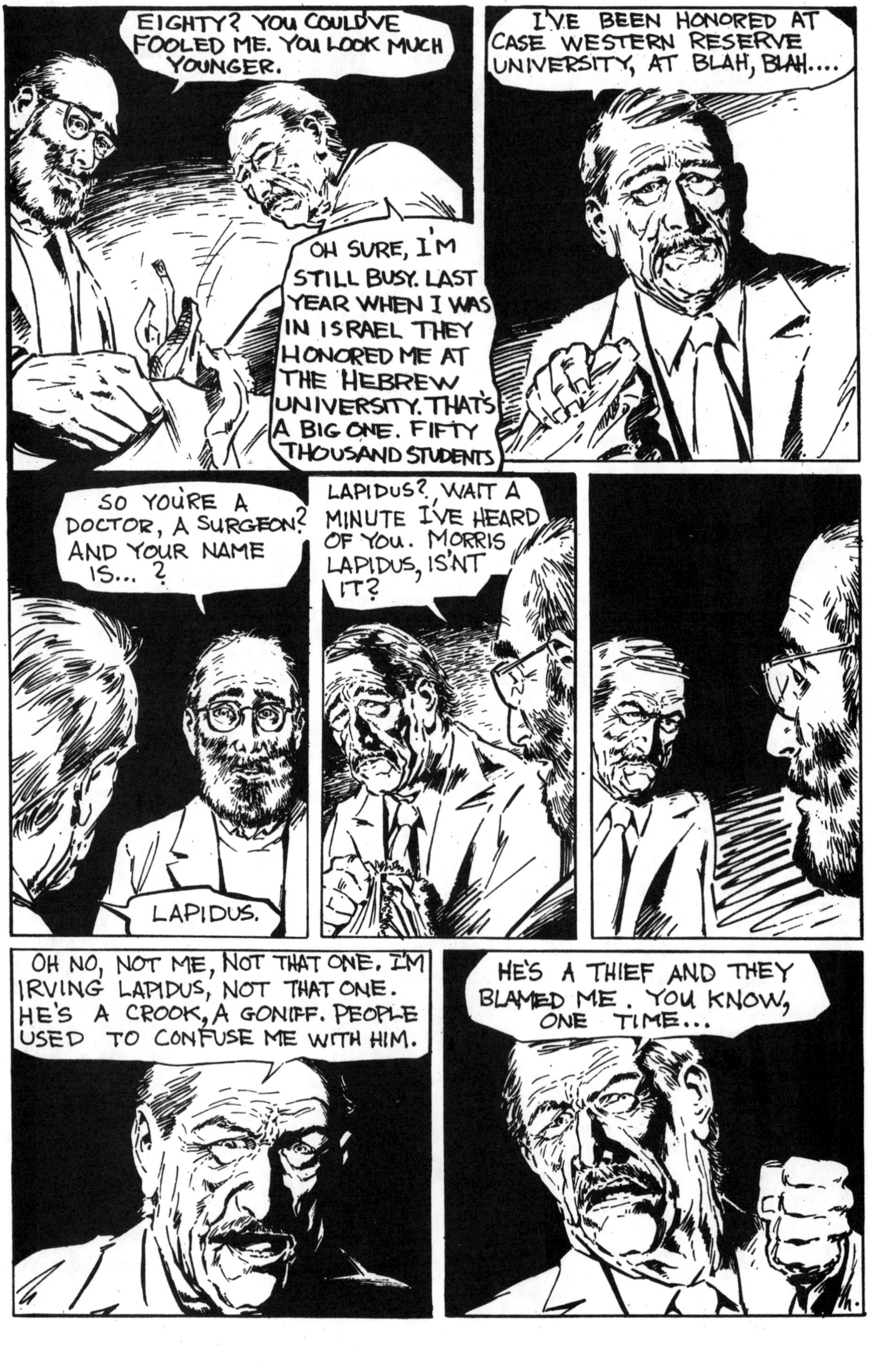
EIGHTY? YOU COULD'VE FOOLED ME. YOU LOOK MUCH YOUNGER.
OH SURE, I'M STILL BUSY. LAST YEAR WHEN I WAS IN ISRAEL THEY HONORED ME AT THE HEBREW UNIVERSITY. THAT'S A BIG ONE. FIFTY THOUSAND STUDENTS
I'VE BEEN HONORED AT CASE WESTERN RESERVE UNIVERSITY, AT BLAH, BLAH....
SO YOU'RE A DOCTOR, A SURGEON? AND YOUR NAME IS... ?
LAPIDUS.
LAPIDUS?, WAIT A MINUTE I'VE HEARD OF YOU. MORRIS LAPIDUS, IS'NT IT?
OH NO, NOT ME, NOT THAT ONE. I'M IRVING LAPIDUS, NOT THAT ONE. HE'S A CROOK, A GONIFF. PEOPLE USED TO CONFUSE ME WITH HIM.
HE'S A THIEF AND THEY BLAMED ME. YOU KNOW, ONE TIME...

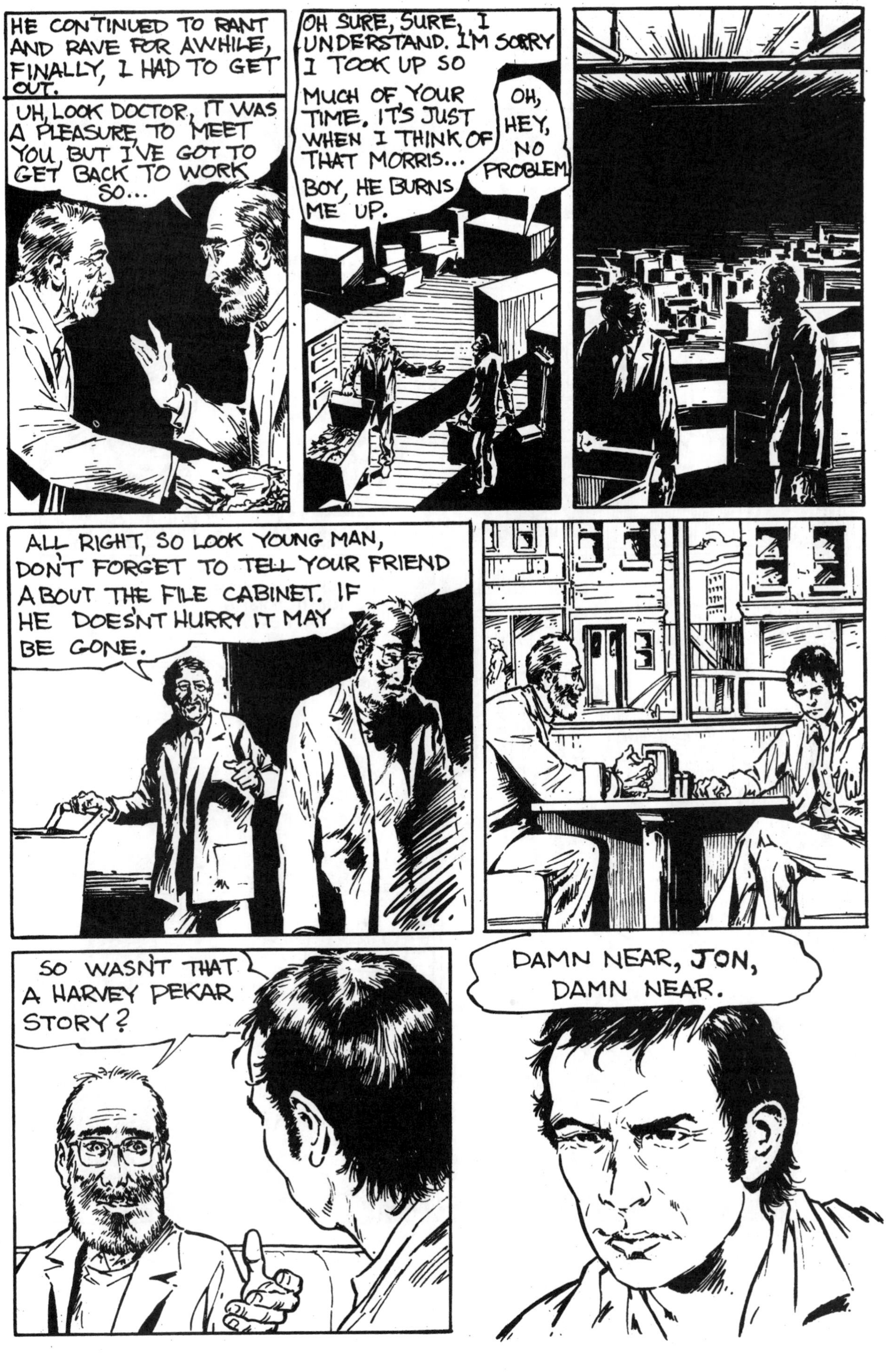
HE CONTINUED TO RANT AND RAVE FOR AWHILE, FINALLY, I HAD TO GET OUT.
UH, LOOK DOCTOR, IT WAS A PLEASURE TO MEET YOU, BUT I'VE GOT TO GET BACK TO WORK SO...
OH SURE, SURE, I UNDERSTAND. I'M SORRY I TOOK UP SO
MUCH OF YOUR TIME. IT'S JUST WHEN I THINK OF THAT MORRIS... BOY, HE BURNS ME UP.
OH, HEY, NO PROBLEM.
ALL RIGHT, SO LOOK YOUNG MAN, DON'T FORGET TO TELL YOUR FRIEND ABOUT THE FILE CABINET. IF HE DOESN'T HURRY IT MAY BE GONE.
SO WASN'T THAT A HARVEY PEKAR STORY?
DAMN NEAR, JON, DAMN NEAR.

The Last Supper

STORY BY HARVEY PEKAR
ART BY R. CRUMB

HEY, RUDY! YER A LITTLE LATE T'DAY.
YEAH, YOU KEEPIN' BANKERS' HOURS?
AH... THERE'S A LOTTA CONFUSION OVER MY HOUSE T'DAY... MY FATHER DIED LAST NIGHT.
REALLY?! WOW, I'M SORRY T'HEAR THAT, RUDY!
YUP, IT HAPPENED RIGHT DURING SUPPER...
MY MOM'S REAL MAD AT ME TOO...
WHY?
UH... I ASKED IF I COULD FINISH HIS PUDDING...

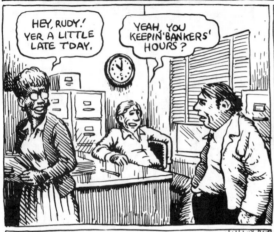

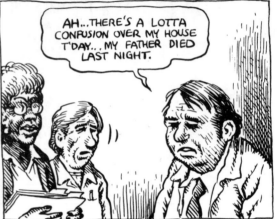

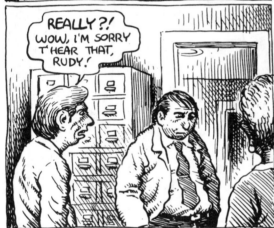

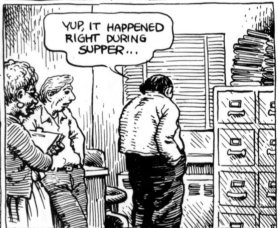

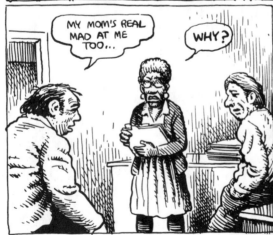

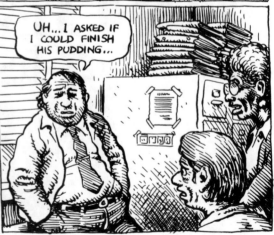

COLD WORLD

STORY BY HARVEY PEKAR ILLUSTRATED BY GERRY SHAMRAY

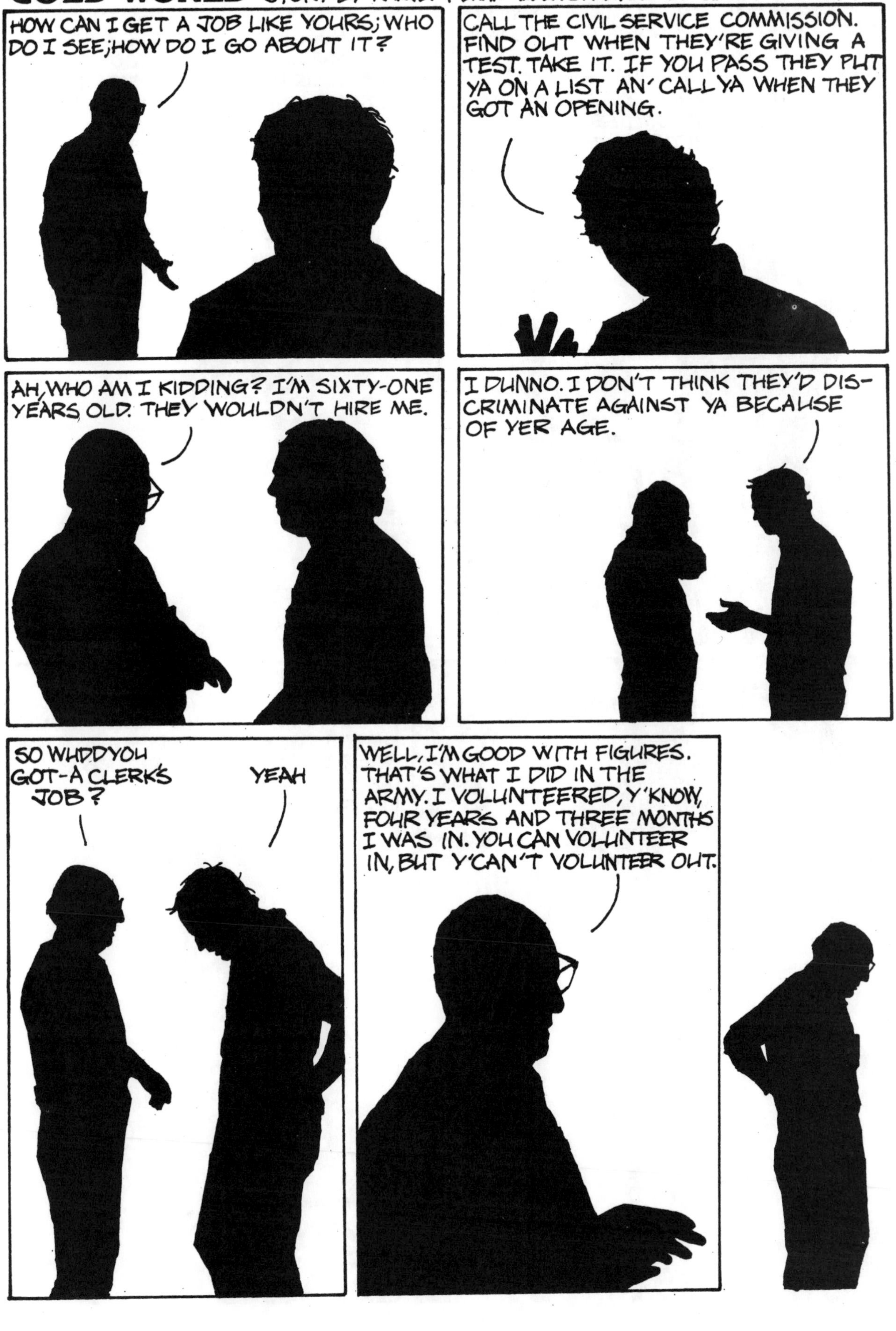
HOW CAN I GET A JOB LIKE YOURS; WHO DO I SEE; HOW DO I GO ABOUT IT?
CALL THE CIVIL SERVICE COMMISSION. FIND OUT WHEN THEY'RE GIVING A TEST. TAKE IT. IF YOU PASS THEY PUT YA ON A LIST AN' CALL YA WHEN THEY GOT AN OPENING.
AH, WHO AM I KIDDING? I'M SIXTY-ONE YEARS OLD. THEY WOULDN'T HIRE ME.
I DUNNO. I DON'T THINK THEY'D DISCRIMINATE AGAINST YA BECAUSE OF YER AGE.
SO WHDDYOU GOT-A CLERK'S JOB?
YEAH
WELL, I'M GOOD WITH FIGURES. THAT'S WHAT I DID IN THE ARMY. I VOLUNTEERED, Y'KNOW, FOUR YEARS AND THREE MONTHS I WAS IN. YOU CAN VOLUNTEER IN, BUT Y'CAN'T VOLUNTEER OUT.

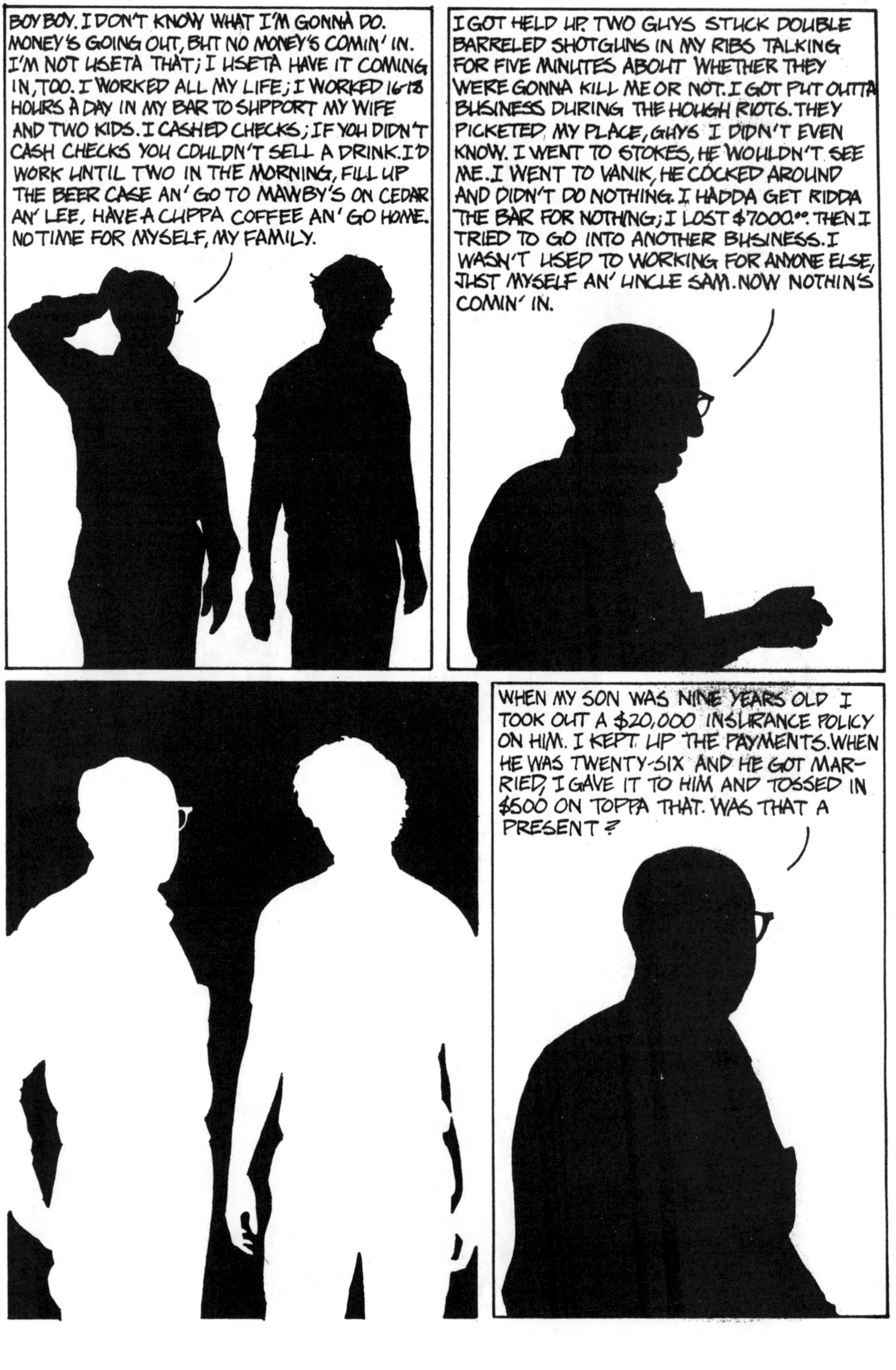
BOY BOY. I DON'T KNOW WHAT I'M GONNA DO. MONEY'S GOING OUT, BUT NO MONEY'S COMIN' IN. I'M NOT USETA THAT; I USETA HAVE IT COMING IN, TOO. I WORKED ALL MY LIFE; I WORKED 16-18 HOURS A DAY IN MY BAR TO SUPPORT MY WIFE AND TWO KIDS. I CASHED CHECKS; IF YOU DIDN'T CASH CHECKS YOU COULDN'T SELL A DRINK. I'D WORK UNTIL TWO IN THE MORNING, FILL UP THE BEER CASE AN' GO TO MAWBY'S ON CEDAR AN' LEE, HAVE A CUPPA COFFEE AN' GO HOME. NO TIME FOR MYSELF, MY FAMILY.
I GOT HELD UP. TWO GUYS STUCK DOUBLE BARRELED SHOTGUNS IN MY RIBS TALKING FOR FIVE MINUTES ABOUT WHETHER THEY WERE GONNA KILL ME OR NOT. I GOT PUT OUTTA BUSINESS DURING THE HOUGH RIOTS. THEY PICKETED MY PLACE, GUYS I DIDN'T EVEN KNOW. I WENT TO STOKES, HE WOULDN'T SEE ME. I WENT TO VANIK, HE COCKED AROUND AND DIDN'T DO NOTHING. I HADDA GET RIDDA THE BAR FOR NOTHING; I LOST $7000.00. THEN I TRIED TO GO INTO ANOTHER BUSINESS. I WASN'T USED TO WORKING FOR ANYONE ELSE, JUST MYSELF AN' UNCLE SAM. NOW NOTHIN'S COMIN' IN.
WHEN MY SON WAS NINE YEARS OLD I TOOK OUT A $20,000 INSURANCE POLICY ON HIM. I KEPT UP THE PAYMENTS. WHEN HE WAS TWENTY-SIX AND HE GOT MARRIED, I GAVE IT TO HIM AND TOSSED IN $500 ON TOPPA THAT. WAS THAT A PRESENT?

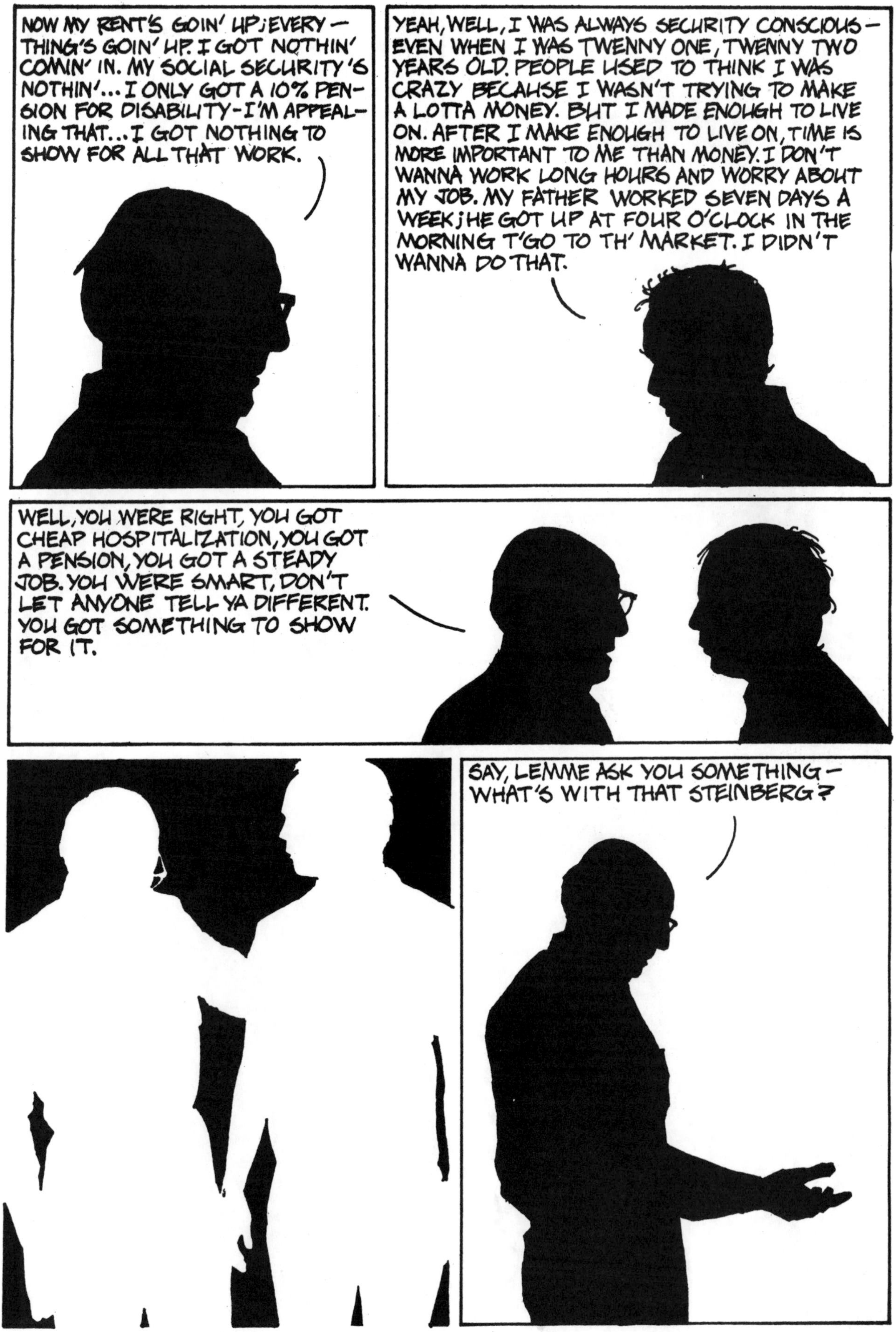
NOW MY RENT'S GOIN' UP; EVERY-THING'S GOIN' UP. I GOT NOTHIN' COMIN' IN. MY SOCIAL SECURITY'S NOTHIN'... I ONLY GOT A 10% PENSION FOR DISABILITY-I'M APPEALING THAT... I GOT NOTHING TO SHOW FOR ALL THAT WORK.
YEAH, WELL, I WAS ALWAYS SECURITY CONSCIOUS-EVEN WHEN I WAS TWENNY ONE, TWENNY TWO YEARS OLD. PEOPLE USED TO THINK I WAS CRAZY BECAUSE I WASN'T TRYING TO MAKE A LOTTA MONEY. BUT I MADE ENOUGH TO LIVE ON. AFTER I MAKE ENOUGH TO LIVE ON, TIME IS MORE IMPORTANT TO ME THAN MONEY. I DON'T WANNA WORK LONG HOURS AND WORRY ABOUT MY JOB. MY FATHER WORKED SEVEN DAYS A WEEK; HE GOT UP AT FOUR O'CLOCK IN THE MORNING T'GO TO TH' MARKET. I DIDN'T WANNA DO THAT.
WELL, YOU WERE RIGHT, YOU GOT CHEAP HOSPITALIZATION, YOU GOT A PENSION, YOU GOT A STEADY JOB. YOU WERE SMART, DON'T LET ANYONE TELL YA DIFFERENT. YOU GOT SOMETHING TO SHOW FOR IT.
SAY, LEMME ASK YOU SOMETHING-WHAT'S WITH THAT STEINBERG?

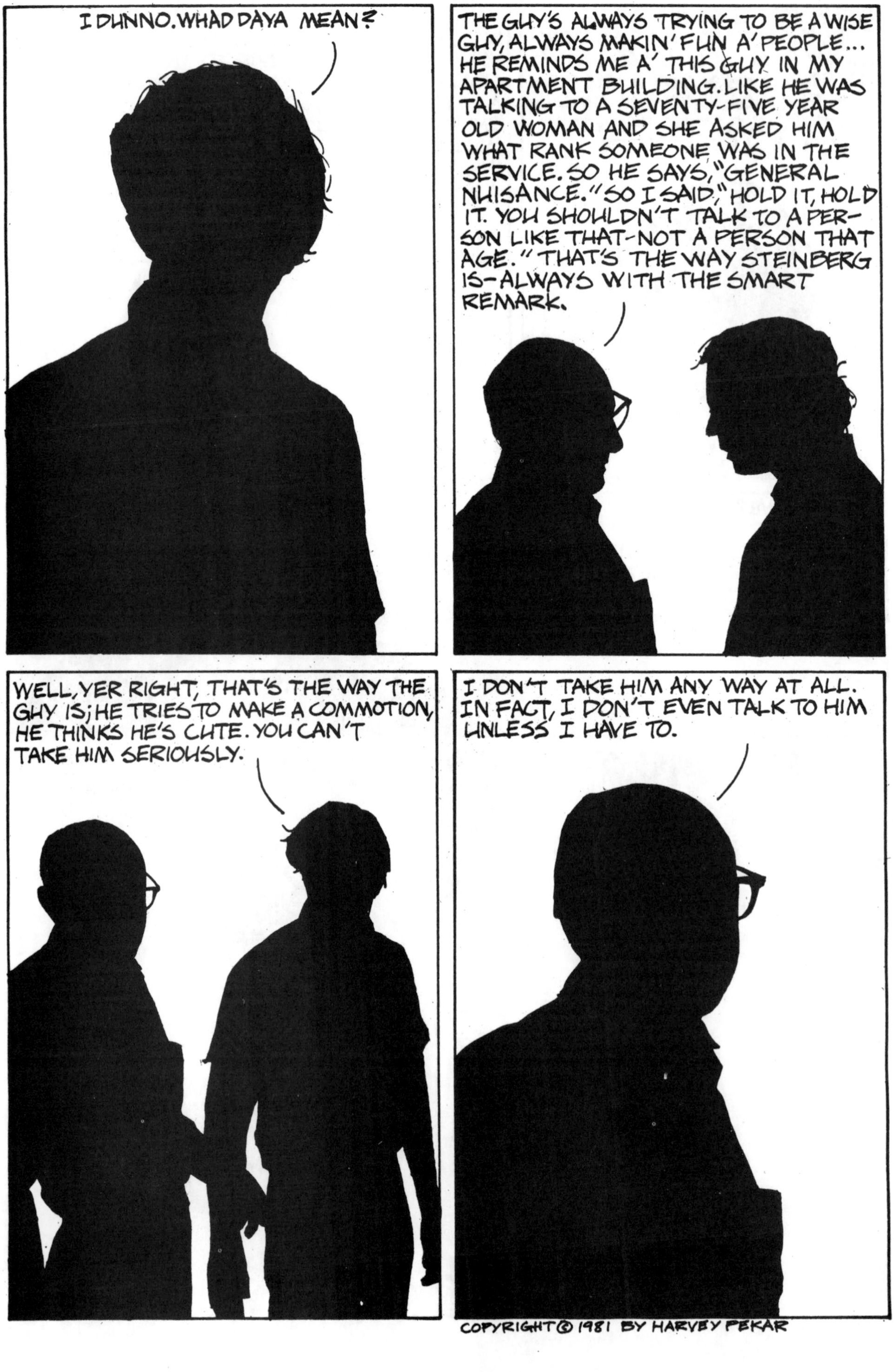
I DUNNO. WHAD DAYA MEAN?
THE GUY'S ALWAYS TRYING TO BE A WISE GUY, ALWAYS MAKIN' FUN A' PEOPLE... HE REMINDS ME A' THIS GUY IN MY APARTMENT BUILDING. LIKE HE WAS TALKING TO A SEVENTY-FIVE YEAR OLD WOMAN AND SHE ASKED HIM WHAT RANK SOMEONE WAS IN THE SERVICE. SO HE SAYS, "GENERAL NUISANCE." SO I SAID, "HOLD IT, HOLD IT. YOU SHOULDN'T TALK TO A PERSON LIKE THAT- NOT A PERSON THAT AGE." THAT'S THE WAY STEINBERG IS- ALWAYS WITH THE SMART REMARK.
WELL, YER RIGHT, THAT'S THE WAY THE GUY IS; HE TRIES TO MAKE A COMMOTION, HE THINKS HE'S CUTE. YOU CAN'T TAKE HIM SERIOUSLY.
I DON'T TAKE HIM ANY WAY AT ALL. IN FACT, I DON'T EVEN TALK TO HIM UNLESS I HAVE TO.

EXCERPT

STORY BY: HARVEY PEKAR
ART BY: R. CRUMB

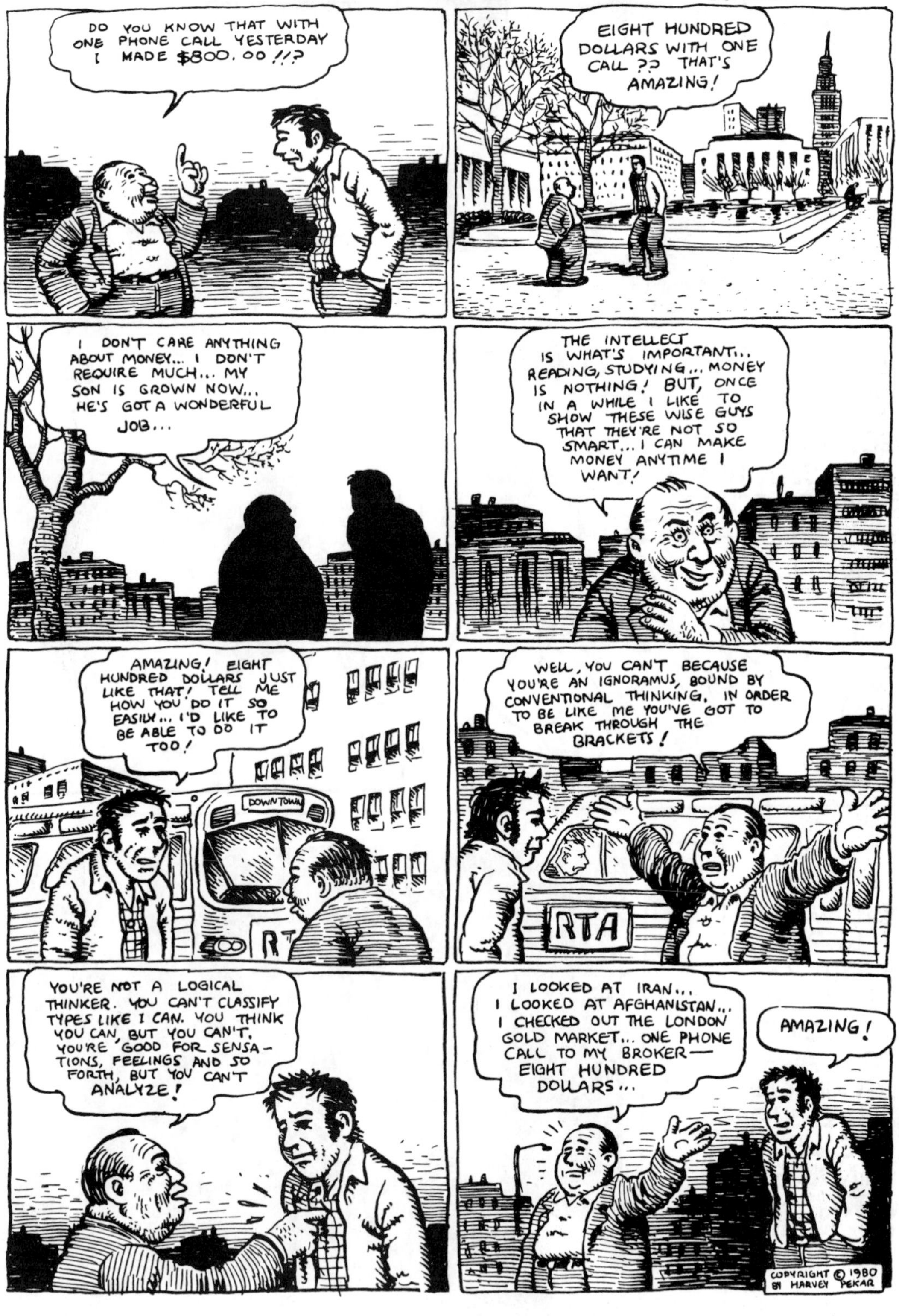
DO YOU KNOW THAT WITH ONE PHONE CALL YESTERDAY I MADE $800.00 !!?
EIGHT HUNDRED DOLLARS WITH ONE CALL ?? THAT'S AMAZING!
I DON'T CARE ANYTHING ABOUT MONEY... I DON'T REQUIRE MUCH... MY SON IS GROWN NOW... HE'S GOT A WONDERFUL JOB...
THE INTELLECT IS WHAT'S IMPORTANT... READING, STUDYING... MONEY IS NOTHING! BUT, ONCE IN A WHILE I LIKE TO SHOW THESE WISE GUYS THAT THEY'RE NOT SO SMART... I CAN MAKE MONEY ANYTIME I WANT!
AMAZING! EIGHT HUNDRED DOLLARS JUST LIKE THAT! TELL ME HOW YOU DO IT SO EASILY... I'D LIKE TO BE ABLE TO DO IT TOO!
DOWNTOWN
WELL, YOU CAN'T BECAUSE YOU'RE AN IGNORAMUS, BOUND BY CONVENTIONAL THINKING. IN ORDER TO BE LIKE ME YOU'VE GOT TO BREAK THROUGH THE BRACKETS!
RTA
YOU'RE NOT A LOGICAL THINKER. YOU CAN'T CLASSIFY TYPES LIKE I CAN. YOU THINK YOU CAN, BUT YOU CAN'T. YOU'RE GOOD FOR SENSATIONS, FEELINGS AND SO FORTH, BUT YOU CAN'T ANALYZE!
I LOOKED AT IRAN... I LOOKED AT AFGHANISTAN... I CHECKED OUT THE LONDON GOLD MARKET... ONE PHONE CALL TO MY BROKER— EIGHT HUNDRED DOLLARS...
AMAZING!
COPYRIGHT © 1980 BY HARVEY PEKAR

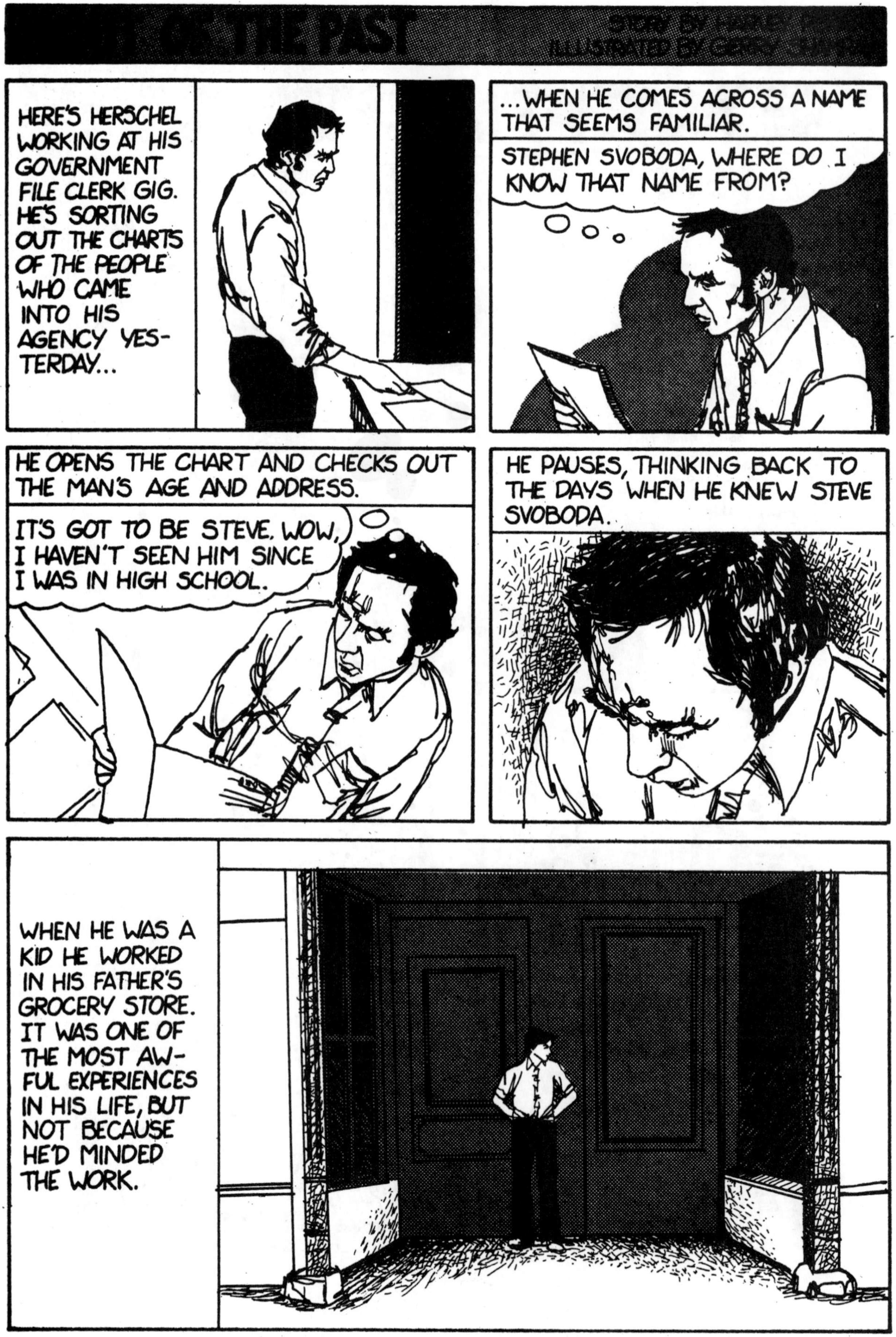

OF THE PAST
STORY BY
ILLUSTRATED BY
HERE'S HERSCHEL WORKING AT HIS GOVERNMENT FILE CLERK GIG. HE'S SORTING OUT THE CHARTS OF THE PEOPLE WHO CAME INTO HIS AGENCY YES-TERDAY...
...WHEN HE COMES ACROSS A NAME THAT SEEMS FAMILIAR.
STEPHEN SVOBODA, WHERE DO I KNOW THAT NAME FROM?
HE OPENS THE CHART AND CHECKS OUT THE MAN'S AGE AND ADDRESS.
IT'S GOT TO BE STEVE. WOW, I HAVEN'T SEEN HIM SINCE I WAS IN HIGH SCHOOL.
HE PAUSES, THINKING BACK TO THE DAYS WHEN HE KNEW STEVE SVOBODA.
WHEN HE WAS A KID HE WORKED IN HIS FATHER'S GROCERY STORE. IT WAS ONE OF THE MOST AW-FUL EXPERIENCES IN HIS LIFE, BUT NOT BECAUSE HE'D MINDED THE WORK.

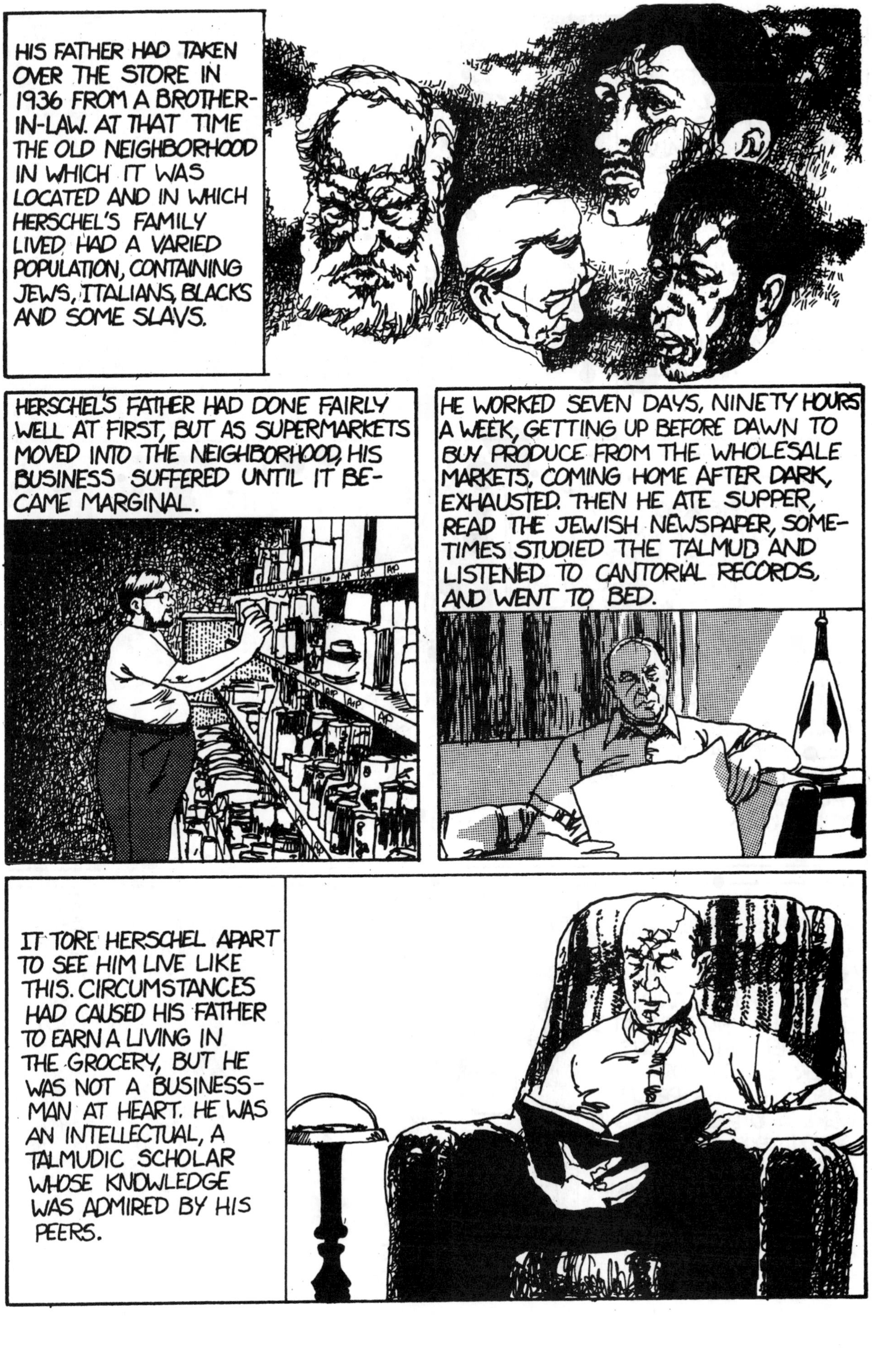
HIS FATHER HAD TAKEN OVER THE STORE IN 1936 FROM A BROTHER-IN-LAW. AT THAT TIME THE OLD NEIGHBORHOOD IN WHICH IT WAS LOCATED AND IN WHICH HERSCHEL'S FAMILY LIVED HAD A VARIED POPULATION, CONTAINING JEWS, ITALIANS, BLACKS AND SOME SLAVS.
HERSCHEL'S FATHER HAD DONE FAIRLY WELL AT FIRST, BUT AS SUPERMARKETS MOVED INTO THE NEIGHBORHOOD, HIS BUSINESS SUFFERED UNTIL IT BE-CAME MARGINAL.
HE WORKED SEVEN DAYS, NINETY HOURS A WEEK, GETTING UP BEFORE DAWN TO BUY PRODUCE FROM THE WHOLESALE MARKETS, COMING HOME AFTER DARK, EXHAUSTED. THEN HE ATE SUPPER, READ THE JEWISH NEWSPAPER, SOME-TIMES STUDIED THE TALMUD AND LISTENED TO CANTORIAL RECORDS, AND WENT TO BED.
IT TORE HERSCHEL APART TO SEE HIM LIVE LIKE THIS. CIRCUMSTANCES HAD CAUSED HIS FATHER TO EARN A LIVING IN THE GROCERY, BUT HE WAS NOT A BUSINESS-MAN AT HEART. HE WAS AN INTELLECTUAL, A TALMUDIC SCHOLAR WHOSE KNOWLEDGE WAS ADMIRED BY HIS PEERS.

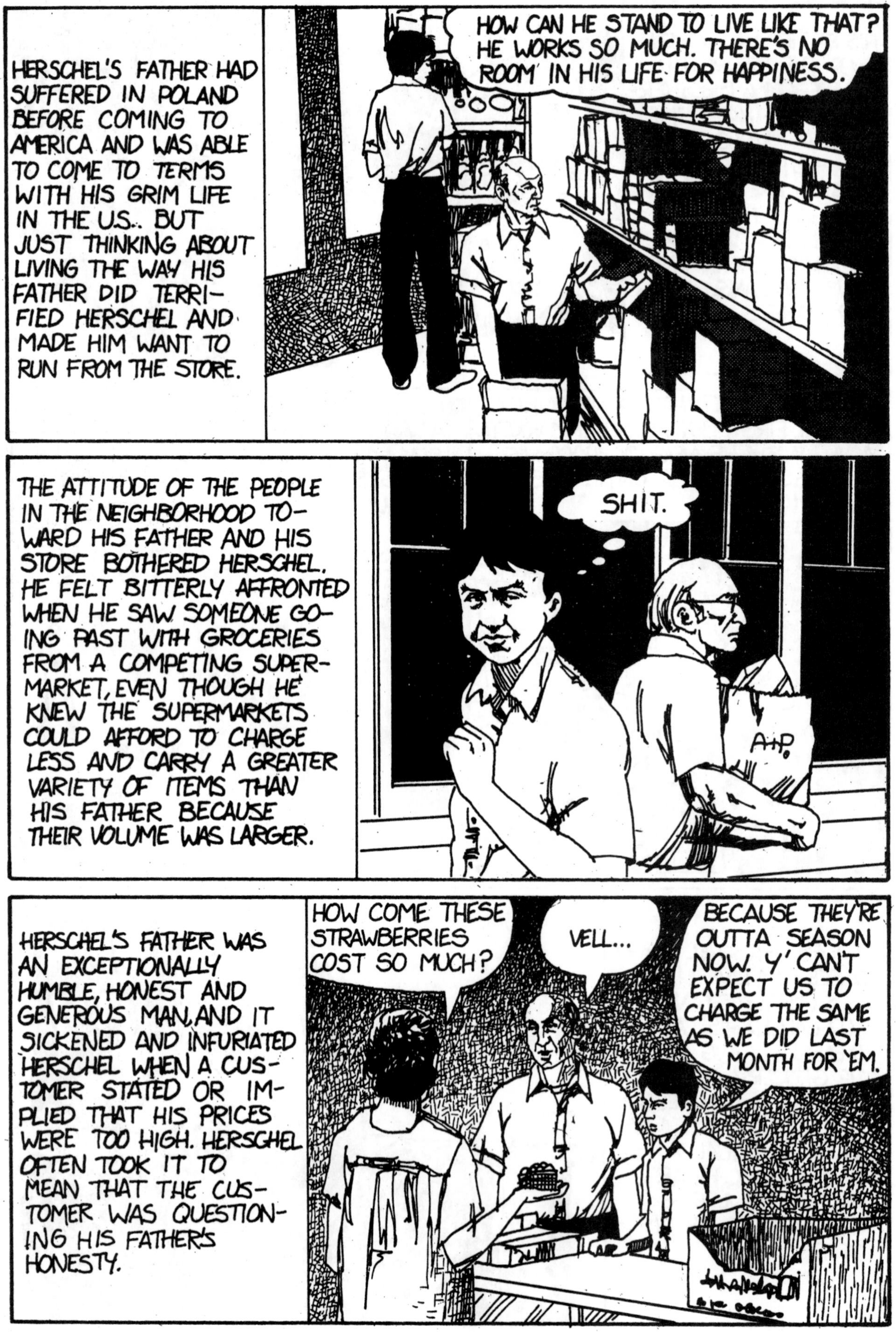
HERSCHEL'S FATHER HAD SUFFERED IN POLAND BEFORE COMING TO AMERICA AND WAS ABLE TO COME TO TERMS WITH HIS GRIM LIFE IN THE U.S.. BUT JUST THINKING ABOUT LIVING THE WAY HIS FATHER DID TERRIFIED HERSCHEL AND MADE HIM WANT TO RUN FROM THE STORE.
HOW CAN HE STAND TO LIVE LIKE THAT? HE WORKS SO MUCH. THERE'S NO ROOM IN HIS LIFE FOR HAPPINESS.
THE ATTITUDE OF THE PEOPLE IN THE NEIGHBORHOOD TOWARD HIS FATHER AND HIS STORE BOTHERED HERSCHEL. HE FELT BITTERLY AFFRONTED WHEN HE SAW SOMEONE GOING PAST WITH GROCERIES FROM A COMPETING SUPERMARKET, EVEN THOUGH HE KNEW THE SUPERMARKETS COULD AFFORD TO CHARGE LESS AND CARRY A GREATER VARIETY OF ITEMS THAN HIS FATHER BECAUSE THEIR VOLUME WAS LARGER.
SHIT.
A+P
HERSCHEL'S FATHER WAS AN EXCEPTIONALLY HUMBLE, HONEST AND GENEROUS MAN, AND IT SICKENED AND INFURIATED HERSCHEL WHEN A CUSTOMER STATED OR IMPLIED THAT HIS PRICES WERE TOO HIGH. HERSCHEL OFTEN TOOK IT TO MEAN THAT THE CUSTOMER WAS QUESTIONING HIS FATHER'S HONESTY.
HOW COME THESE STRAWBERRIES COST SO MUCH?
VELL...
BECAUSE THEY'RE OUTTA SEASON NOW. Y' CAN'T EXPECT US TO CHARGE THE SAME AS WE DID LAST MONTH FOR 'EM.

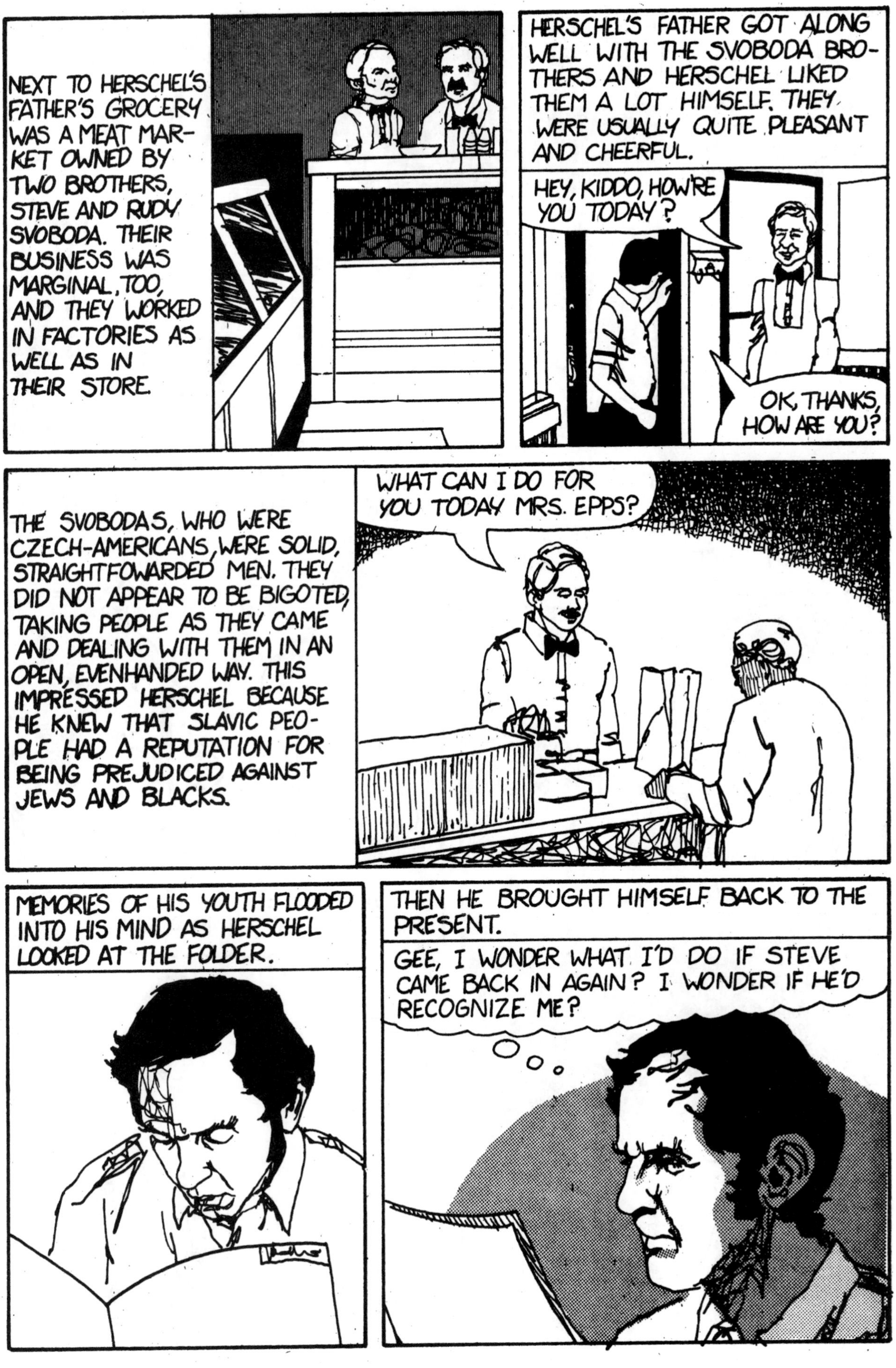
NEXT TO HERSCHEL'S FATHER'S GROCERY WAS A MEAT MARKET OWNED BY TWO BROTHERS, STEVE AND RUDY SVOBODA. THEIR BUSINESS WAS MARGINAL, TOO, AND THEY WORKED IN FACTORIES AS WELL AS IN THEIR STORE.
HERSCHEL'S FATHER GOT ALONG WELL WITH THE SVOBODA BROTHERS AND HERSCHEL LIKED THEM A LOT HIMSELF. THEY WERE USUALLY QUITE PLEASANT AND CHEERFUL.
HEY, KIDDO, HOW'RE YOU TODAY?
OK, THANKS, HOW ARE YOU?
THE SVOBODAS, WHO WERE CZECH-AMERICANS, WERE SOLID, STRAIGHTFOWARDED MEN. THEY DID NOT APPEAR TO BE BIGOTED, TAKING PEOPLE AS THEY CAME AND DEALING WITH THEM IN AN OPEN, EVENHANDED WAY. THIS IMPRESSED HERSCHEL BECAUSE HE KNEW THAT SLAVIC PEOPLE HAD A REPUTATION FOR BEING PREJUDICED AGAINST JEWS AND BLACKS.
WHAT CAN I DO FOR YOU TODAY MRS. EPPS?
MEMORIES OF HIS YOUTH FLOODED INTO HIS MIND AS HERSCHEL LOOKED AT THE FOLDER.
THEN HE BROUGHT HIMSELF BACK TO THE PRESENT.
GEE, I WONDER WHAT I'D DO IF STEVE CAME BACK IN AGAIN? I WONDER IF HE'D RECOGNIZE ME?

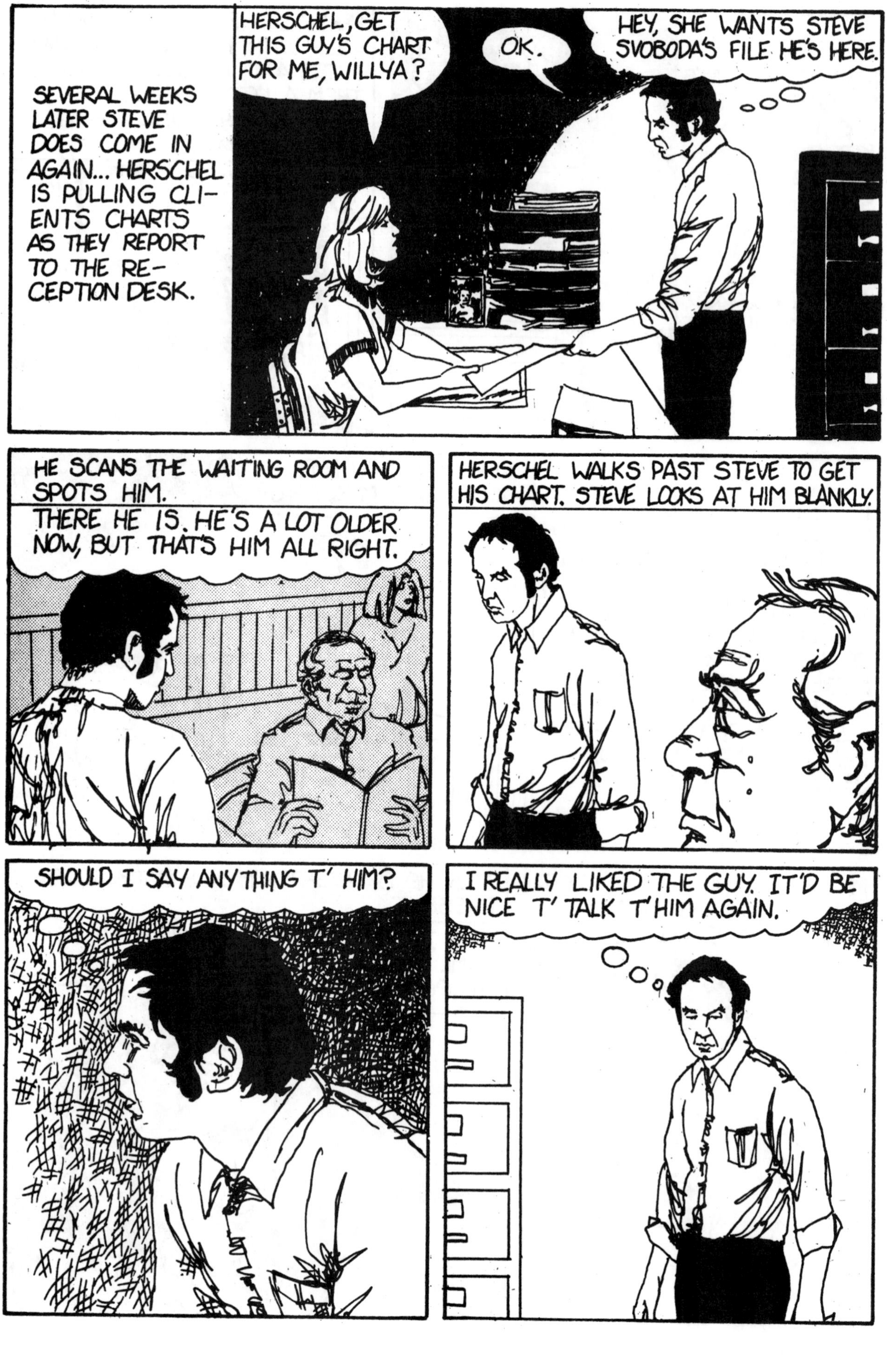
SEVERAL WEEKS LATER STEVE DOES COME IN AGAIN... HERSCHEL IS PULLING CLI-ENTS CHARTS AS THEY REPORT TO THE RE-CEPTION DESK.
HERSCHEL, GET THIS GUY'S CHART FOR ME, WILLYA?
OK.
HEY, SHE WANTS STEVE SVOBODA'S FILE HE'S HERE.
HE SCANS THE WAITING ROOM AND SPOTS HIM.
THERE HE IS. HE'S A LOT OLDER NOW, BUT THAT'S HIM ALL RIGHT.
HERSCHEL WALKS PAST STEVE TO GET HIS CHART. STEVE LOOKS AT HIM BLANKLY.
SHOULD I SAY ANYTHING T' HIM?
I REALLY LIKED THE GUY. IT'D BE NICE T' TALK T'HIM AGAIN.

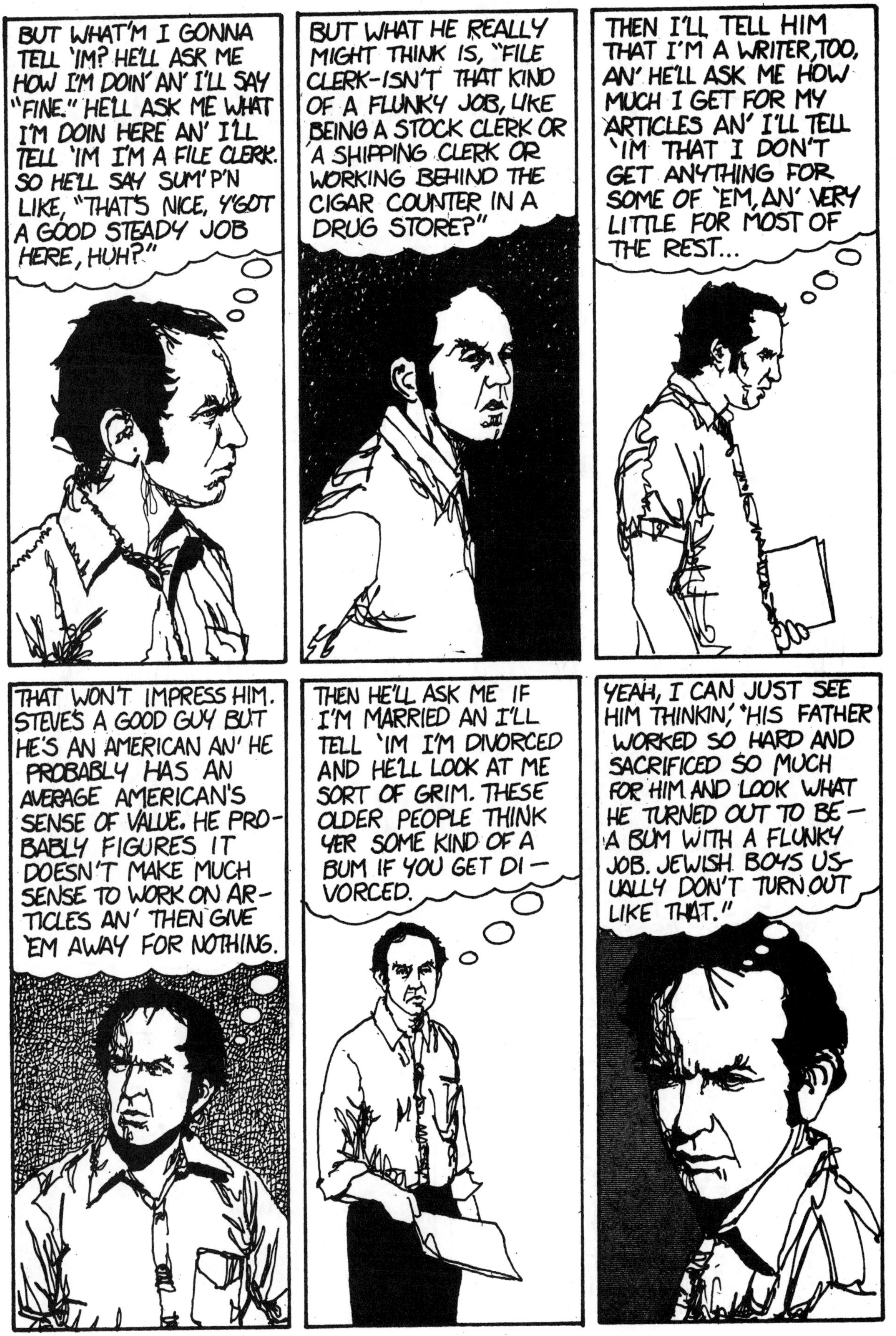
BUT WHAT'M I GONNA TELL 'IM? HE'LL ASK ME HOW I'M DOIN' AN' I'LL SAY "FINE." HE'LL ASK ME WHAT I'M DOIN HERE AN' I'LL TELL 'IM I'M A FILE CLERK. SO HE'LL SAY SUM'P'N LIKE, "THAT'S NICE, Y'GOT A GOOD STEADY JOB HERE, HUH?"
BUT WHAT HE REALLY MIGHT THINK IS, "FILE CLERK-ISN'T THAT KIND OF A FLUNKY JOB, LIKE BEING A STOCK CLERK OR A SHIPPING CLERK OR WORKING BEHIND THE CIGAR COUNTER IN A DRUG STORE?"
THEN I'LL TELL HIM THAT I'M A WRITER, TOO, AN' HE'LL ASK ME HOW MUCH I GET FOR MY ARTICLES AN' I'LL TELL 'IM THAT I DON'T GET ANYTHING FOR SOME OF 'EM, AN' VERY LITTLE FOR MOST OF THE REST...
THAT WON'T IMPRESS HIM. STEVE'S A GOOD GUY BUT HE'S AN AMERICAN AN' HE PROBABLY HAS AN AVERAGE AMERICAN'S SENSE OF VALUE. HE PROBABLY FIGURES IT DOESN'T MAKE MUCH SENSE TO WORK ON ARTICLES AN' THEN GIVE 'EM AWAY FOR NOTHING.
THEN HE'LL ASK ME IF I'M MARRIED AN I'LL TELL 'IM I'M DIVORCED AND HE'LL LOOK AT ME SORT OF GRIM. THESE OLDER PEOPLE THINK YER SOME KIND OF A BUM IF YOU GET DIVORCED.
YEAH, I CAN JUST SEE HIM THINKIN,' "HIS FATHER WORKED SO HARD AND SACRIFICED SO MUCH FOR HIM AND LOOK WHAT HE TURNED OUT TO BE-A BUM WITH A FLUNKY JOB. JEWISH BOYS USUALLY DON'T TURN OUT LIKE THAT."

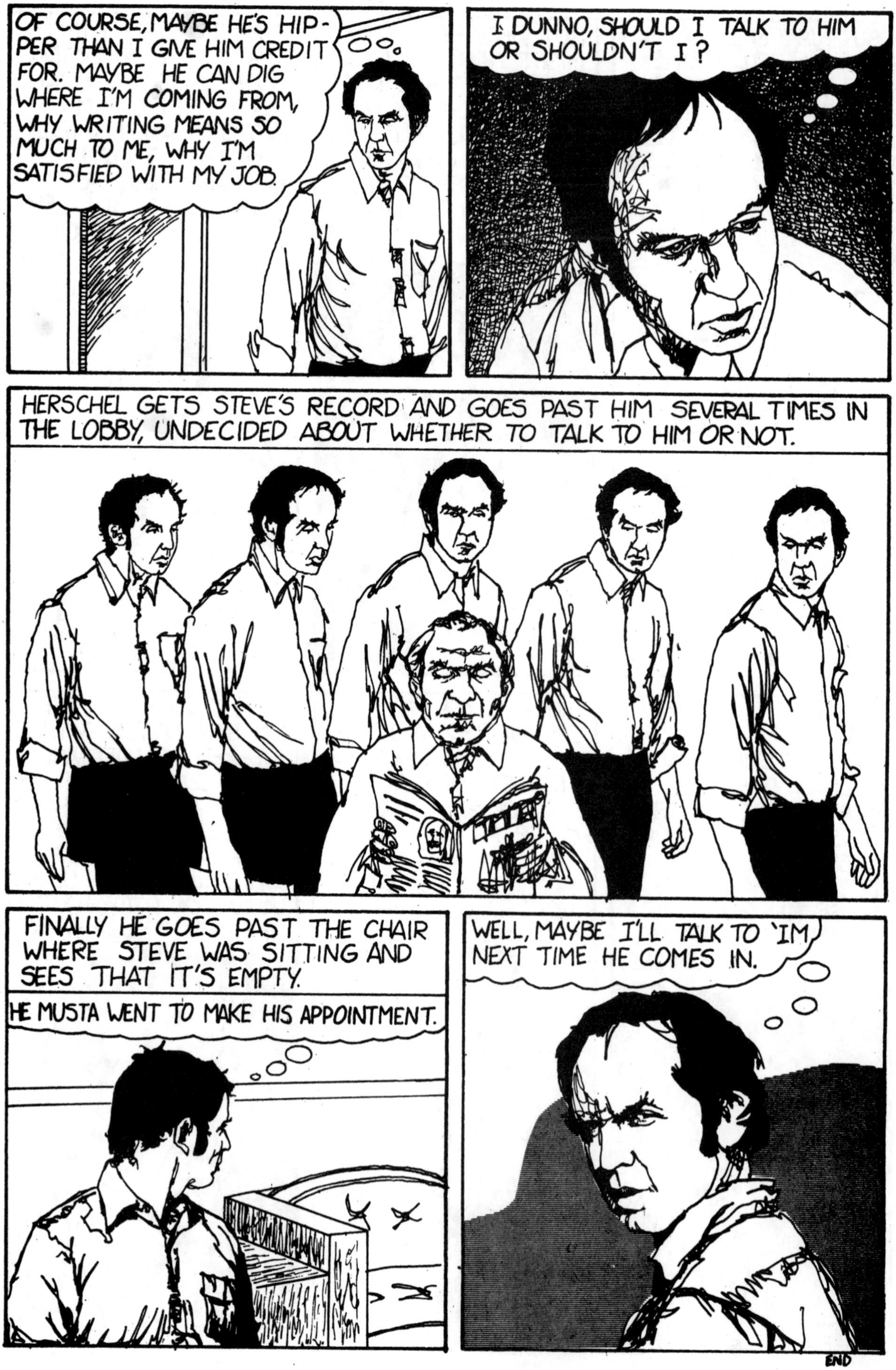
OF COURSE, MAYBE HE'S HIP-PER THAN I GIVE HIM CREDIT FOR. MAYBE HE CAN DIG WHERE I'M COMING FROM, WHY WRITING MEANS SO MUCH TO ME, WHY I'M SATISFIED WITH MY JOB.
I DUNNO, SHOULD I TALK TO HIM OR SHOULDN'T I?
HERSCHEL GETS STEVE'S RECORD AND GOES PAST HIM SEVERAL TIMES IN THE LOBBY, UNDECIDED ABOUT WHETHER TO TALK TO HIM OR NOT.
FINALLY HE GOES PAST THE CHAIR WHERE STEVE WAS SITTING AND SEES THAT IT'S EMPTY.
HE MUSTA WENT TO MAKE HIS APPOINTMENT.
WELL, MAYBE I'LL TALK TO 'IM NEXT TIME HE COMES IN.
END

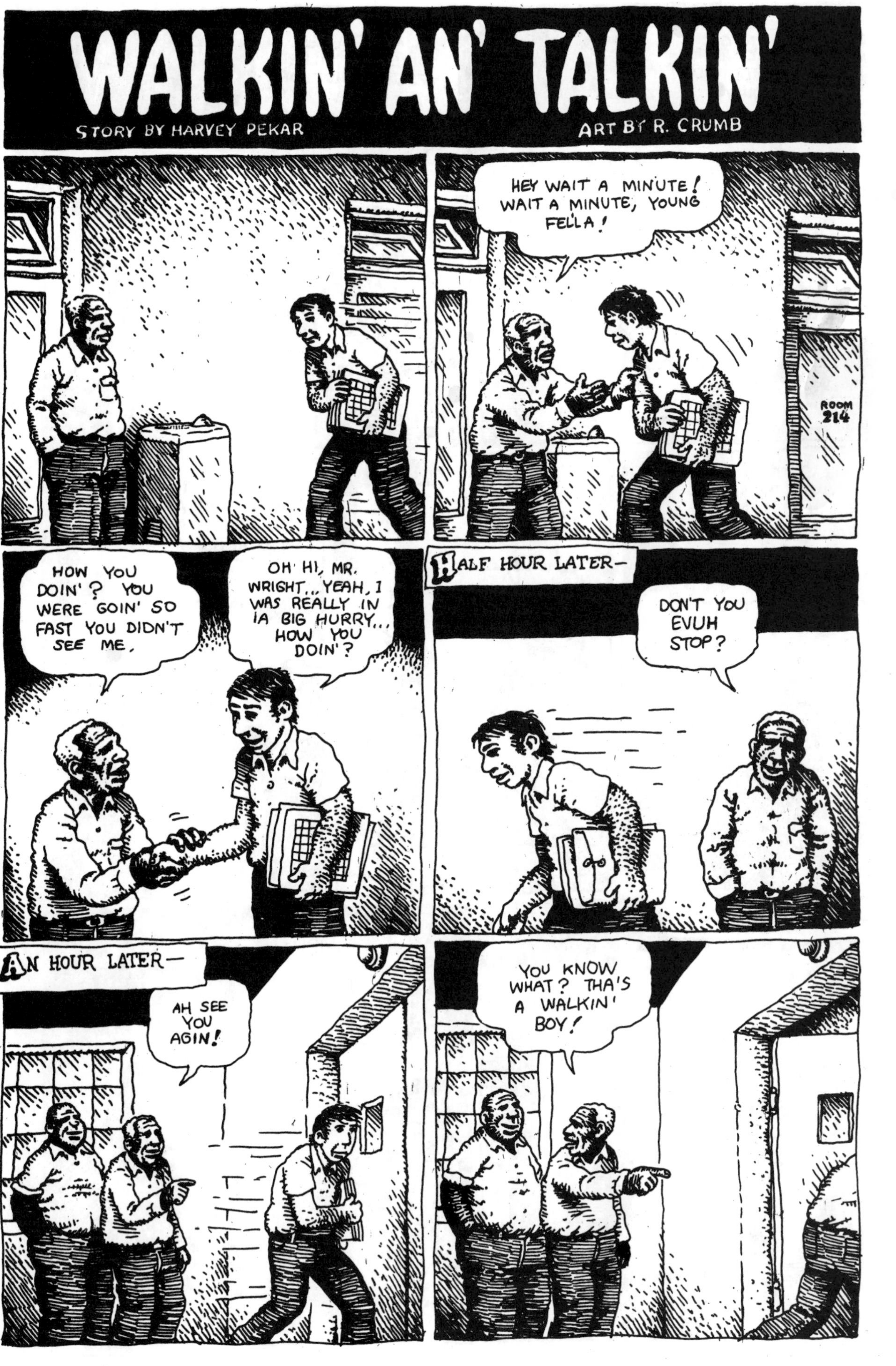
WALKIN' AN' TALKIN'
STORY BY HARVEY PEKAR
ART BY R. CRUMB
HEY WAIT A MINUTE! WAIT A MINUTE, YOUNG FELLA!
ROOM 214
HOW YOU DOIN'? YOU WERE GOIN' SO FAST YOU DIDN'T SEE ME.
OH HI, MR. WRIGHT... YEAH, I WAS REALLY IN A BIG HURRY... HOW YOU DOIN'?
HALF HOUR LATER—
DON'T YOU EVUH STOP?
AN HOUR LATER—
AH SEE YOU AGIN!
YOU KNOW WHAT? THA'S A WALKIN' BOY!

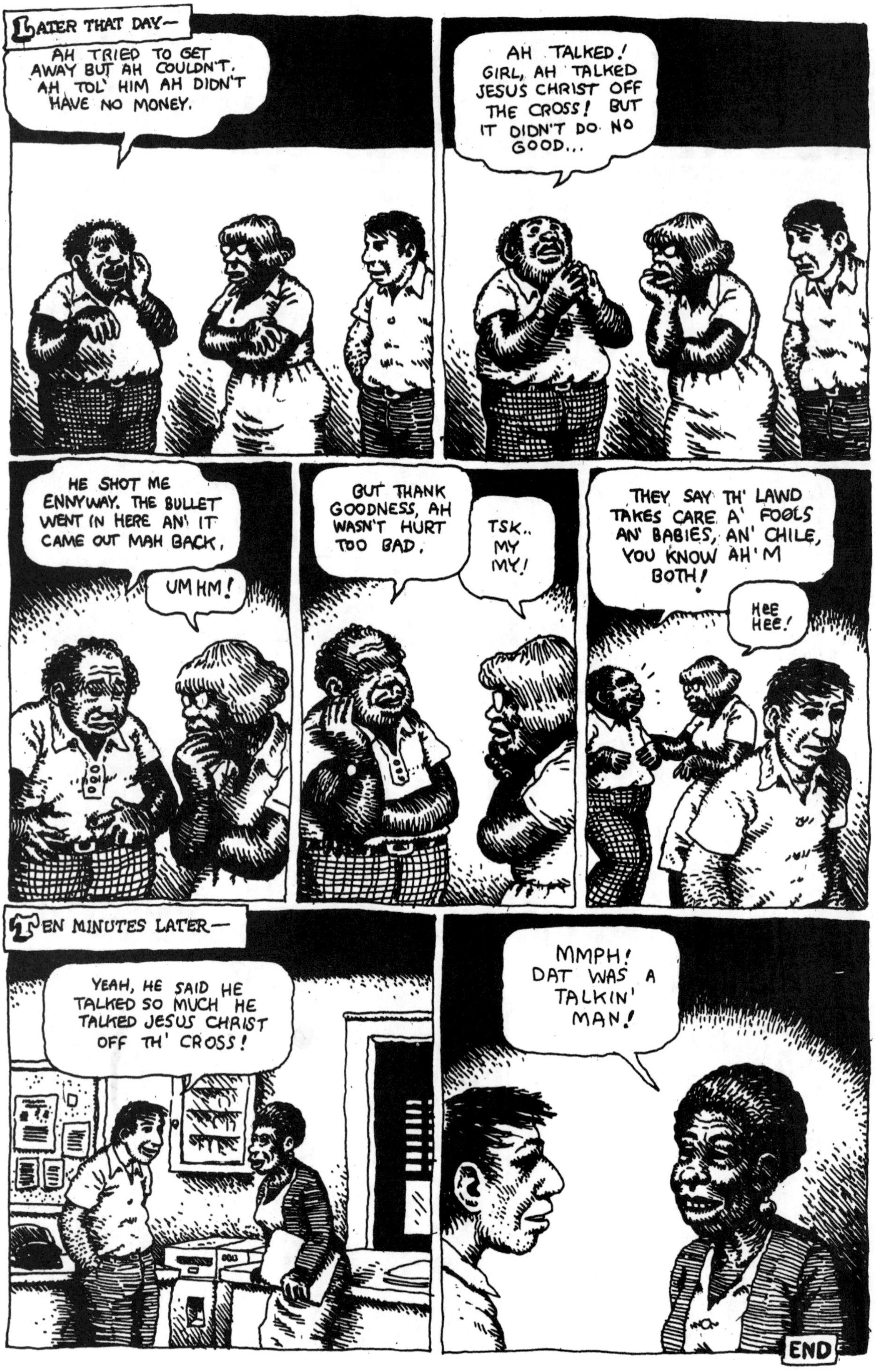
LATER THAT DAY—
AH TRIED TO GET AWAY BUT AH COULDN'T. AH TOL' HIM AH DIDN'T HAVE NO MONEY.
AH TALKED! GIRL, AH TALKED JESUS CHRIST OFF THE CROSS! BUT IT DIDN'T DO NO GOOD...
HE SHOT ME ENNYWAY. THE BULLET WENT IN HERE AN' IT CAME OUT MAH BACK.
UMHM!
BUT THANK GOODNESS, AH WASN'T HURT TOO BAD.
TSK.. MY MY!
THEY SAY TH' LAWD TAKES CARE A' FOOLS AN' BABIES, AN' CHILE, YOU KNOW AH'M BOTH!
HEE HEE!
TEN MINUTES LATER—
YEAH, HE SAID HE TALKED SO MUCH HE TALKED JESUS CHRIST OFF TH' CROSS!
MMPH! DAT WAS A TALKIN' MAN!
END

Traditional Male Chauvinism

STORY BY HARVEY PEKAR   ART BY GREG BUDGETT + GARY DUMM

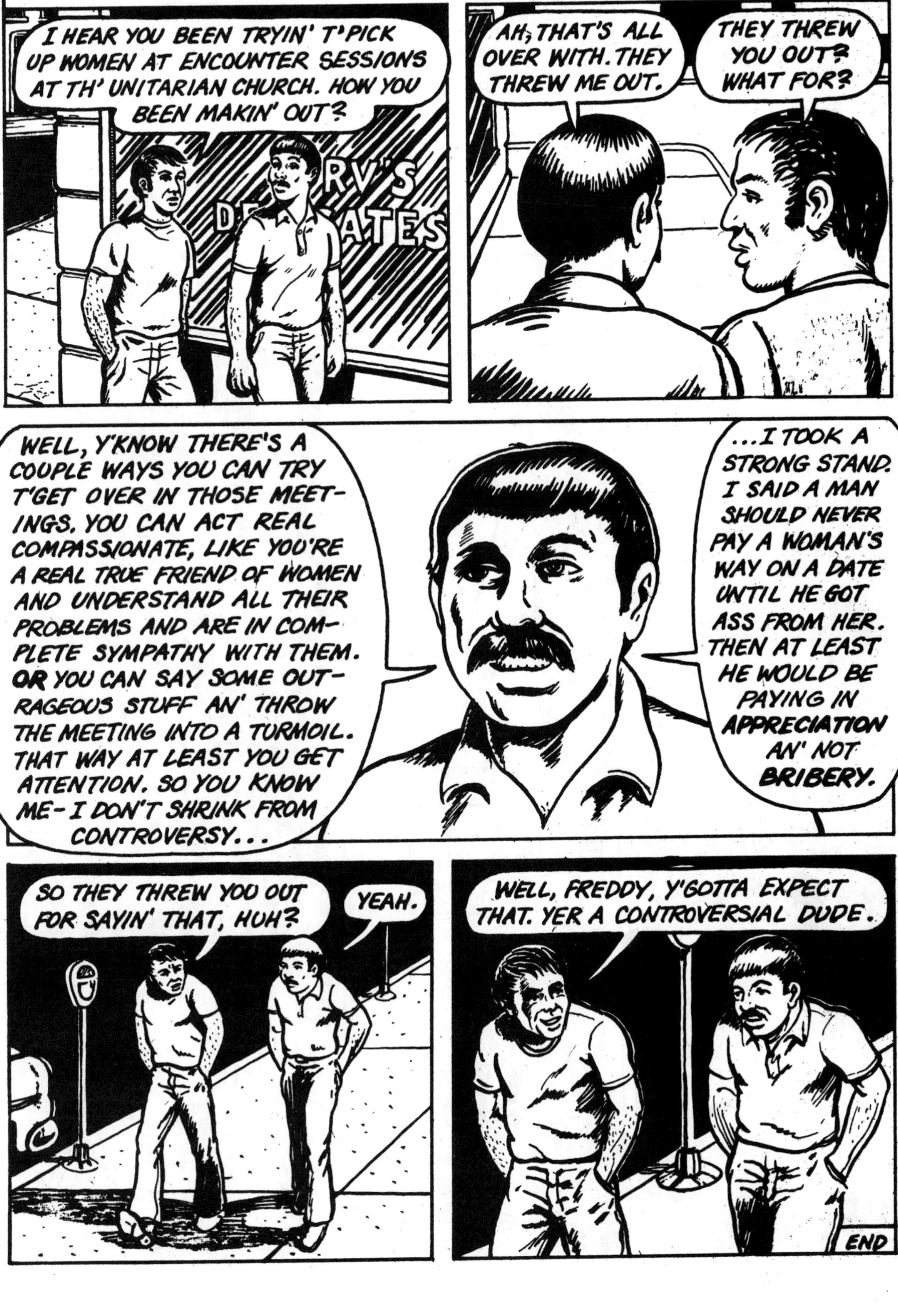
I HEAR YOU BEEN TRYIN' T'PICK UP WOMEN AT ENCOUNTER SESSIONS AT TH' UNITARIAN CHURCH. HOW YOU BEEN MAKIN' OUT?
AH, THAT'S ALL OVER WITH. THEY THREW ME OUT.
THEY THREW YOU OUT? WHAT FOR?
WELL, Y'KNOW THERE'S A COUPLE WAYS YOU CAN TRY T'GET OVER IN THOSE MEETINGS. YOU CAN ACT REAL COMPASSIONATE, LIKE YOU'RE A REAL TRUE FRIEND OF WOMEN AND UNDERSTAND ALL THEIR PROBLEMS AND ARE IN COMPLETE SYMPATHY WITH THEM. OR YOU CAN SAY SOME OUTRAGEOUS STUFF AN' THROW THE MEETING INTO A TURMOIL. THAT WAY AT LEAST YOU GET ATTENTION. SO YOU KNOW ME - I DON'T SHRINK FROM CONTROVERSY...
...I TOOK A STRONG STAND. I SAID A MAN SHOULD NEVER PAY A WOMAN'S WAY ON A DATE UNTIL HE GOT ASS FROM HER. THEN AT LEAST HE WOULD BE PAYING IN APPRECIATION AN' NOT BRIBERY.
SO THEY THREW YOU OUT FOR SAYIN' THAT, HUH?
YEAH.
WELL, FREDDY, Y'GOTTA EXPECT THAT. YER A CONTROVERSIAL DUDE.
END

The End of Innocence

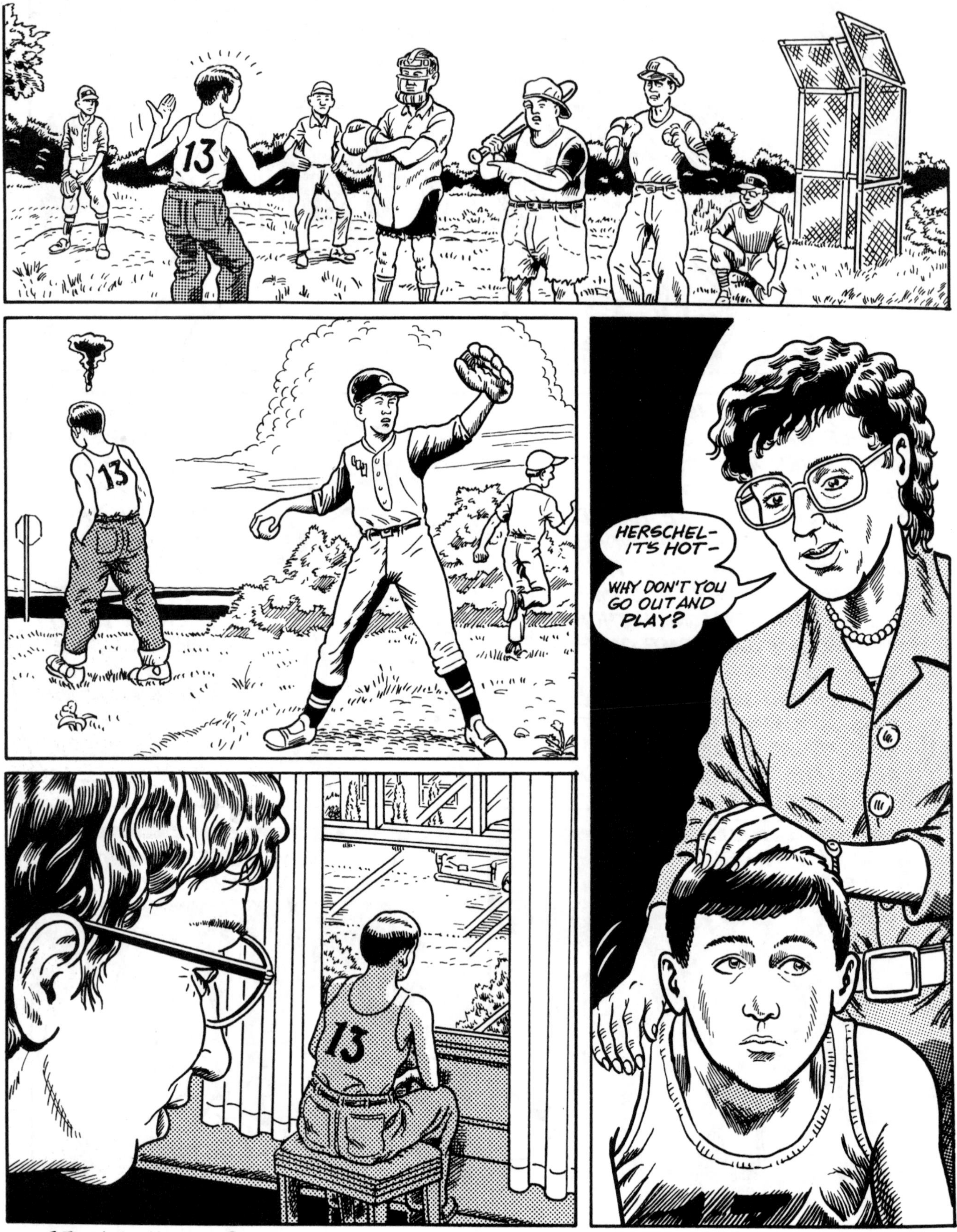
HERSCHEL- IT'S HOT-
WHY DON'T YOU GO OUT AND PLAY?

STORY BY HARVEY PEKAR

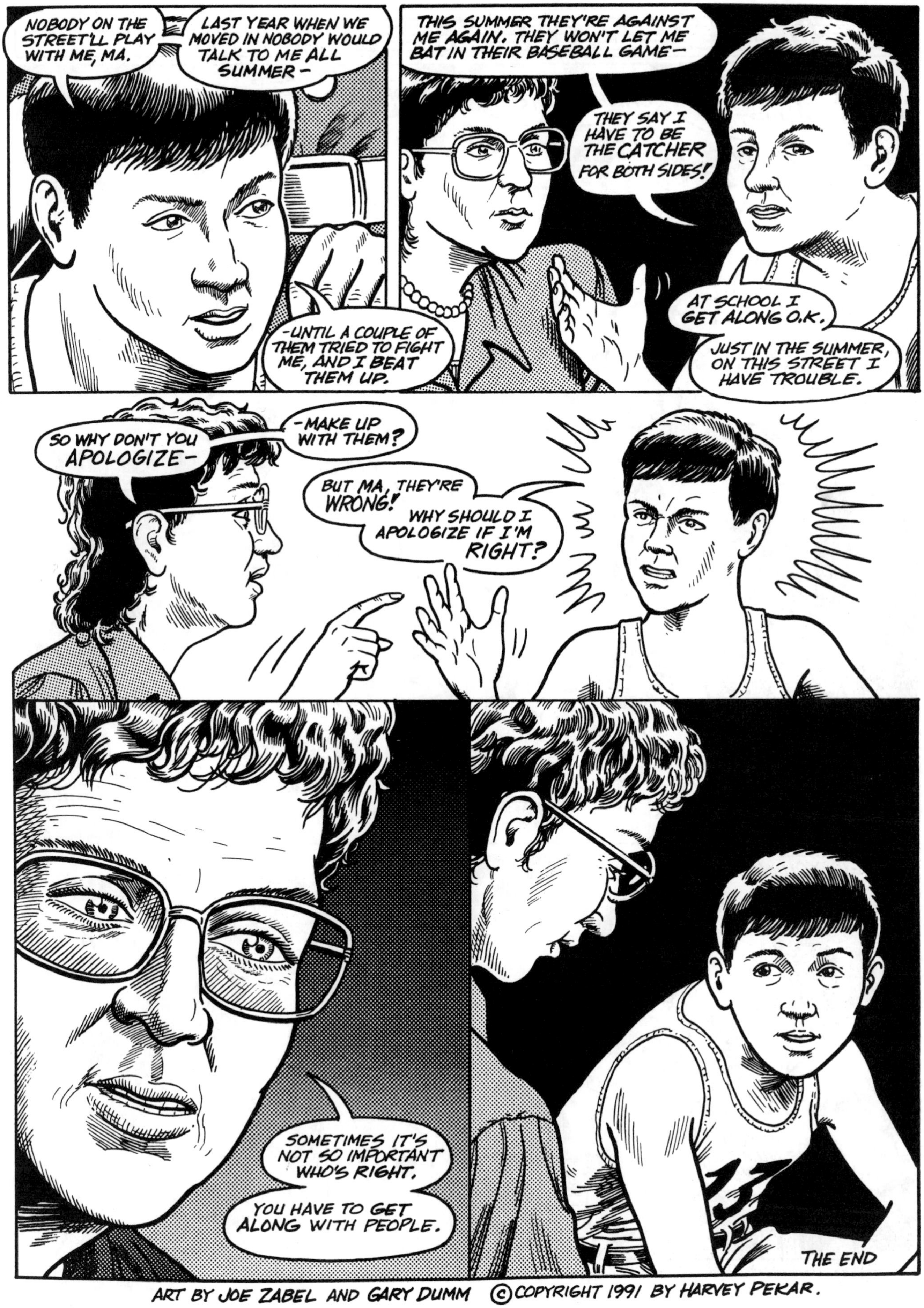
NOBODY ON THE STREET'LL PLAY WITH ME, MA.
LAST YEAR WHEN WE MOVED IN NOBODY WOULD TALK TO ME ALL SUMMER -
-UNTIL A COUPLE OF THEM TRIED TO FIGHT ME, AND I BEAT THEM UP.
THIS SUMMER THEY'RE AGAINST ME AGAIN. THEY WON'T LET ME BAT IN THEIR BASEBALL GAME—
THEY SAY I HAVE TO BE THE CATCHER FOR BOTH SIDES!
AT SCHOOL I GET ALONG O.K.
JUST IN THE SUMMER, ON THIS STREET I HAVE TROUBLE.
SO WHY DON'T YOU APOLOGIZE—
-MAKE UP WITH THEM?
BUT MA, THEY'RE WRONG!
WHY SHOULD I APOLOGIZE IF I'M RIGHT?
SOMETIMES IT'S NOT SO IMPORTANT WHO'S RIGHT.
YOU HAVE TO GET ALONG WITH PEOPLE.
THE END

ART BY JOE ZABEL AND GARY DUMM

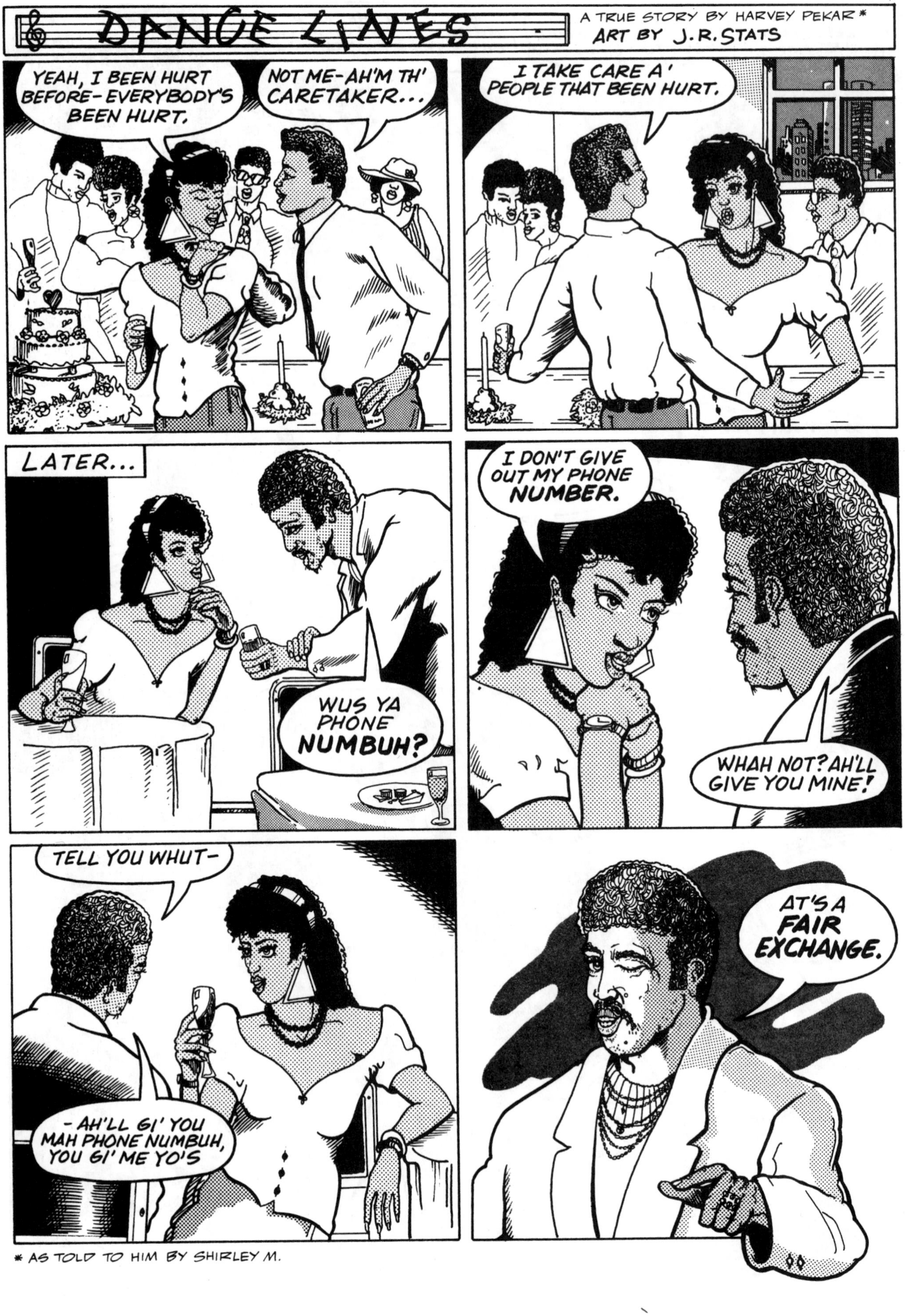

DANCE LINES
A TRUE STORY BY HARVEY PEKAR*
ART BY J.R. STATS
YEAH, I BEEN HURT BEFORE-EVERYBODY'S BEEN HURT.
NOT ME-AH'M TH' CARETAKER...
I TAKE CARE A' PEOPLE THAT BEEN HURT.
LATER...
WUS YA PHONE NUMBUH?
I DON'T GIVE OUT MY PHONE NUMBER.
WHAH NOT? AH'LL GIVE YOU MINE!
TELL YOU WHUT-
-AH'LL GI' YOU MAH PHONE NUMBUH, YOU GI' ME YO'S
AT'S A FAIR EXCHANGE.
* AS TOLD TO HIM BY SHIRLEY M.

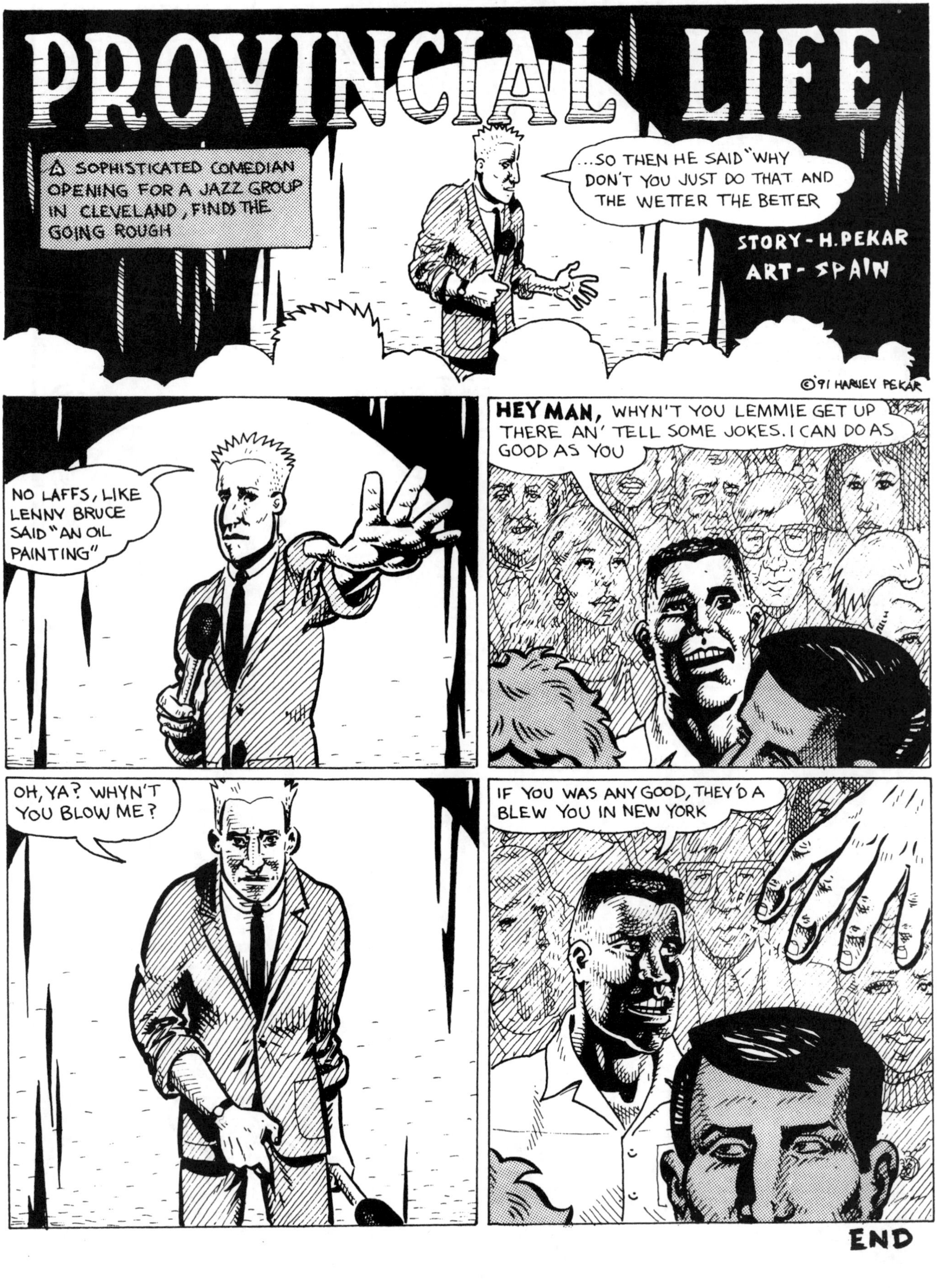
PROVINCIAL LIFE
A SOPHISTICATED COMEDIAN OPENING FOR A JAZZ GROUP IN CLEVELAND, FINDS THE GOING ROUGH
...SO THEN HE SAID "WHY DON'T YOU JUST DO THAT AND THE WETTER THE BETTER
STORY - H. PEKAR
ART - SPAIN
©'91 HARVEY PEKAR
NO LAFFS, LIKE LENNY BRUCE SAID "AN OIL PAINTING"
HEY MAN, WHYN'T YOU LEMMIE GET UP THERE AN' TELL SOME JOKES. I CAN DO AS GOOD AS YOU
OH, YA? WHYN'T YOU BLOW ME?
IF YOU WAS ANY GOOD, THEY'D A BLEW YOU IN NEW YORK

END

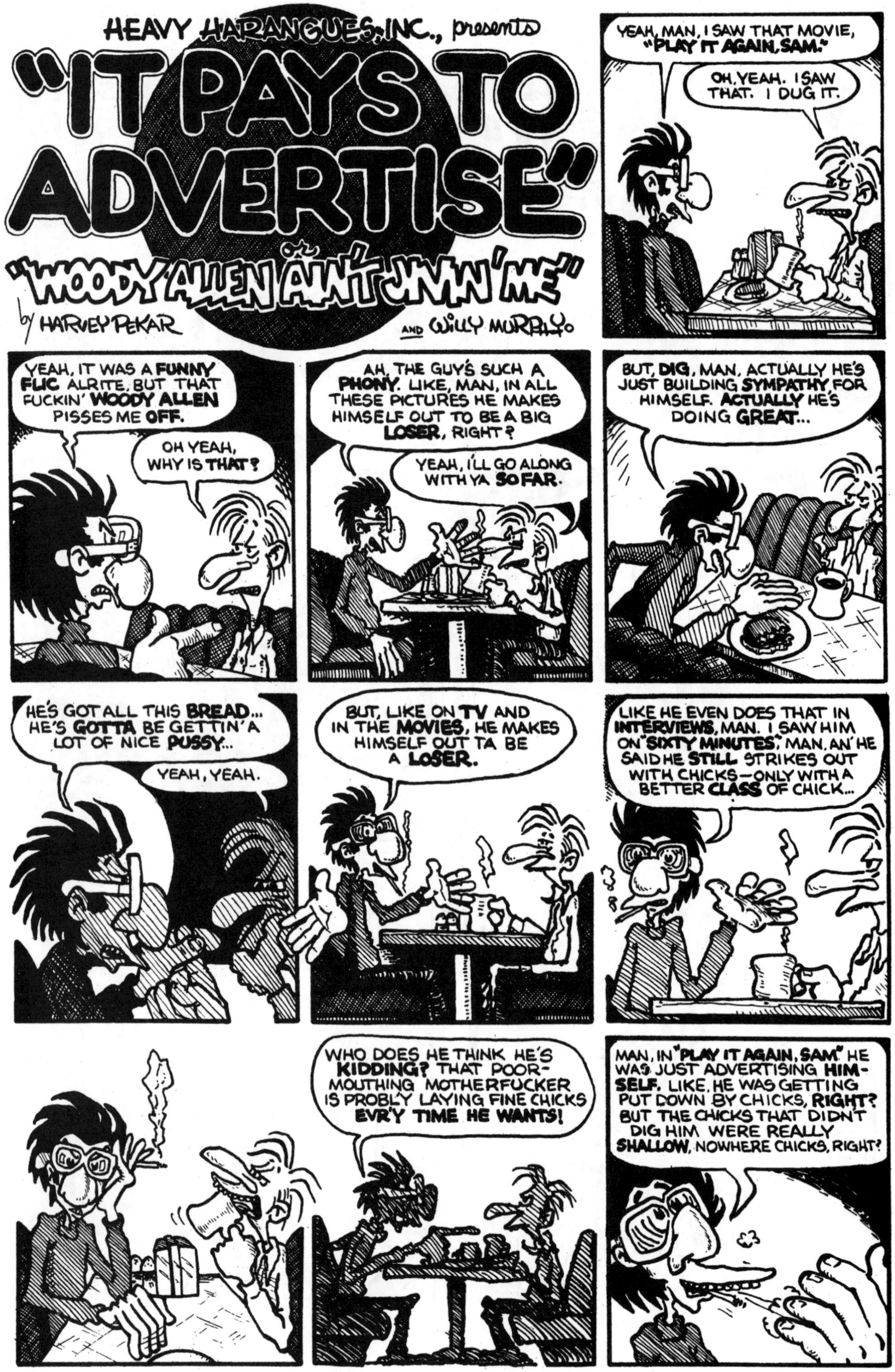
HEAVY HARANGUES, INC., presents
"IT PAYS TO ADVERTISE"
or
"WOODY ALLEN AIN'T JIVIN' ME"
by HARVEY PEKAR
AND WILLY MURPHY
YEAH, MAN, I SAW THAT MOVIE, "PLAY IT AGAIN, SAM."
OH, YEAH. I SAW THAT. I DUG IT.
YEAH, IT WAS A FUNNY FLIC ALRITE, BUT THAT FUCKIN' WOODY ALLEN PISSES ME OFF.
OH YEAH, WHY IS THAT?
AH, THE GUY'S SUCH A PHONY. LIKE, MAN, IN ALL THESE PICTURES HE MAKES HIMSELF OUT TO BE A BIG LOSER, RIGHT?
YEAH, I'LL GO ALONG WITH YA SO FAR.
BUT, DIG, MAN, ACTUALLY HE'S JUST BUILDING SYMPATHY FOR HIMSELF. ACTUALLY HE'S DOING GREAT...
HE'S GOT ALL THIS BREAD... HE'S GOTTA BE GETTIN' A LOT OF NICE PUSSY...
YEAH, YEAH.
BUT, LIKE ON TV AND IN THE MOVIES, HE MAKES HIMSELF OUT TA BE A LOSER.
LIKE HE EVEN DOES THAT IN INTERVIEWS, MAN. I SAW HIM ON "SIXTY MINUTES," MAN, AN' HE SAID HE STILL STRIKES OUT WITH CHICKS—ONLY WITH A BETTER CLASS OF CHICK...
WHO DOES HE THINK HE'S KIDDING? THAT POOR-MOUTHING MOTHERFUCKER IS PROBLY LAYING FINE CHICKS EVR'Y TIME HE WANTS!
MAN, IN "PLAY IT AGAIN, SAM," HE WAS JUST ADVERTISING HIMSELF. LIKE, HE WAS GETTING PUT DOWN BY CHICKS, RIGHT? BUT THE CHICKS THAT DIDN'T DIG HIM WERE REALLY SHALLOW, NOWHERE CHICKS, RIGHT?

BUT, THE **HEAVIEST** CHICK IN THE MOVIE **DIGS** WOODY, RIGHT? SHE SEES THROUGH THAT UGLY **EXTERIOR**. SHE REALIZES HE'S REALLY A **GEM**... A SWEET, BRIGHT, WITTY GUY...

AN' MAN...**THAT'S** WHAT WOODY ALLEN **REALLY** THINKS A' HIMSELF... HE THINKS HE'S **TOO MUCH!**

SEE HOW HE **PROMOTES** HIMSELF? HOW HE GETS **BROADS** FEELIN' **SORRY** FOR 'IM?

MAN, REMEMBER HOW HUMPHREY BOGART IS **ADVISIN'** HIM THE WHOLE MOVIE?

THEN, AT THE **END**, WHEN WOODY PERFORMS THAT NOBLE ACT OF FRIENDSHIP AN' HUMPHREY **BOWS OUT** AN' SEZ HE CAN'T TEACH WOODY ANYTHING ANYMORE...

MAN, I WANTED TA **PUKE**

THERE I WAS, I HAVEN'T BEEN LAID FOR **MONTHS** AN' I HAVE TA WATCH THAT **SCHMUCK** PROMOTE HIMSELF.

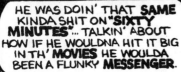

HE WAS DOIN' THAT **SAME** KINDA SHIT ON "SIXTY MINUTES"... TALKIN' ABOUT HOW IF HE WOULDNA HIT IT BIG IN TH' **MOVIES** HE WOULDA BEEN A FLUNKY **MESSENGER**.

THERE I AM... A GUY WHO'S BEEN A **FILE CLERK** FOR SIX YEARS... **LISTENING** TO THIS SCHMUCK...

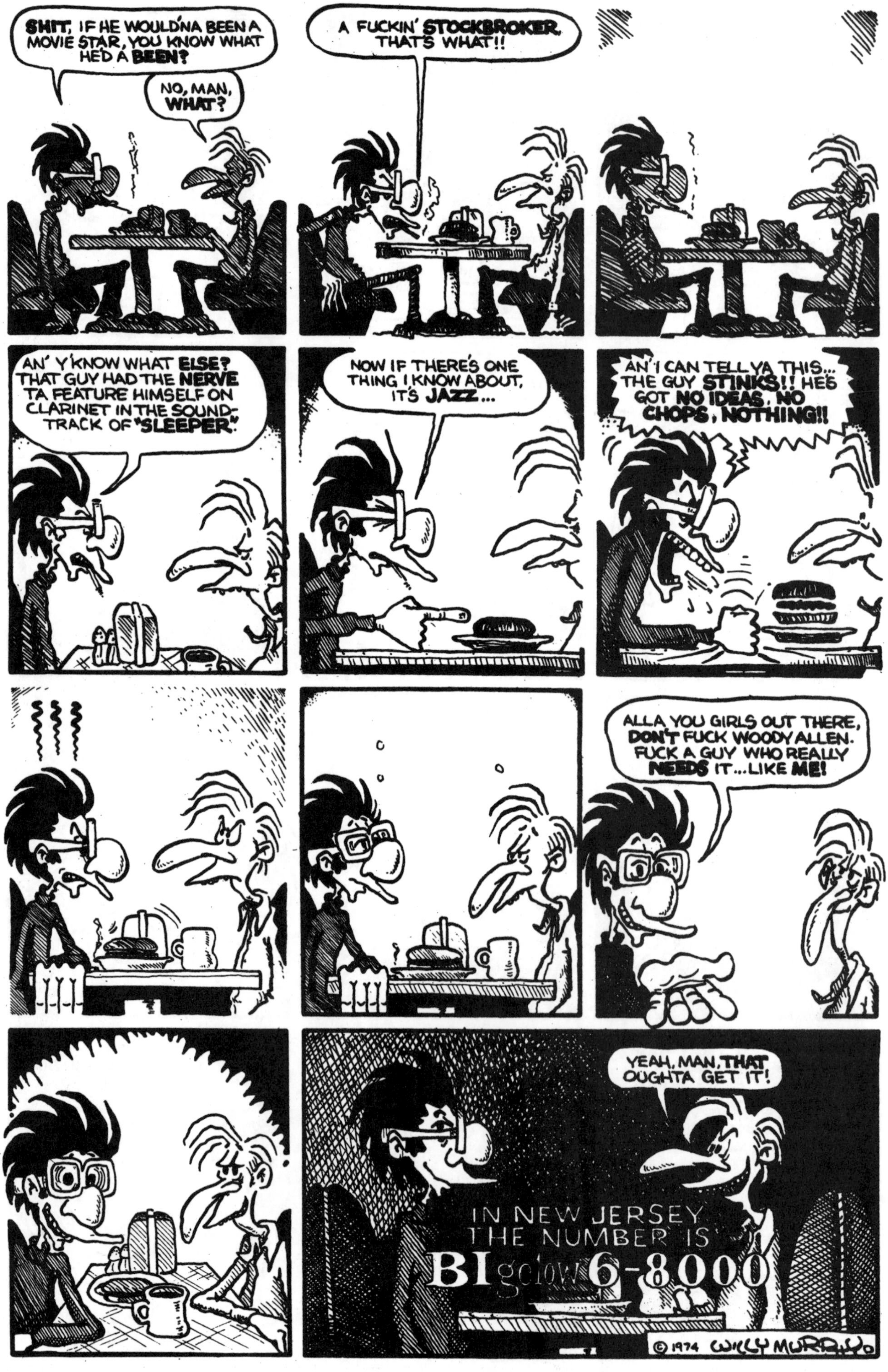
SHIT, IF HE WOULD'NA BEEN A MOVIE STAR, YOU KNOW WHAT HE'D A BEEN?
NO, MAN, WHAT?
A FUCKIN' STOCKBROKER, THAT'S WHAT!!
AN' Y'KNOW WHAT ELSE? THAT GUY HAD THE NERVE TA FEATURE HIMSELF ON CLARINET IN THE SOUND-TRACK OF "SLEEPER".
NOW IF THERE'S ONE THING I KNOW ABOUT, IT'S JAZZ...
AN' I CAN TELL YA THIS... THE GUY STINKS!! HE'S GOT NO IDEAS, NO CHOPS, NOTHING!!
ALLA YOU GIRLS OUT THERE, DON'T FUCK WOODY ALLEN. FUCK A GUY WHO REALLY NEEDS IT... LIKE ME!
YEAH, MAN, THAT OUGHTA GET IT!
IN NEW JERSEY THE NUMBER IS
BIgelow 6-8000
© 1974 WILLY MURPHY

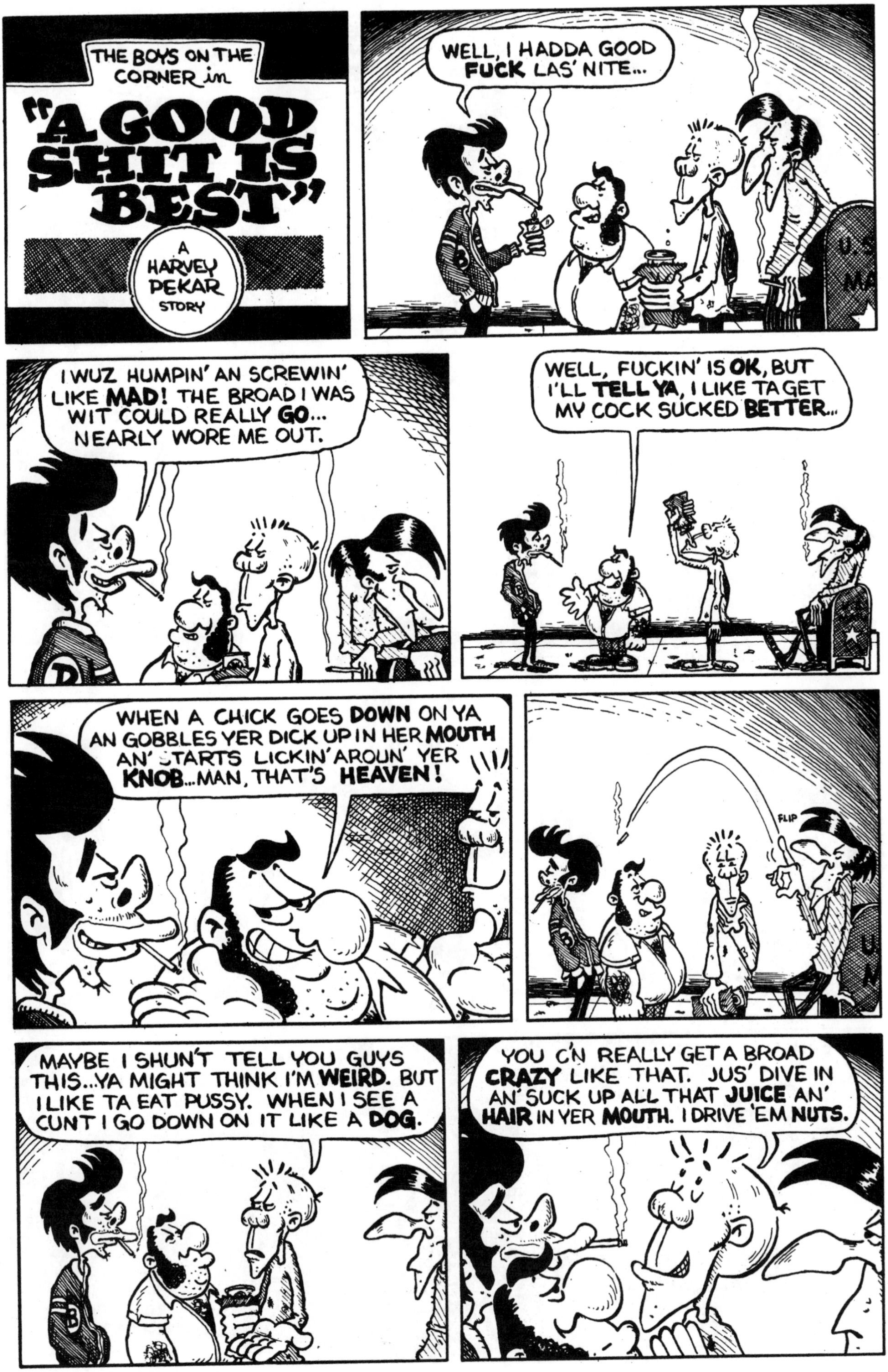
THE BOYS ON THE CORNER in
"A GOOD SHIT IS BEST"
A HARVEY PEKAR STORY
WELL, I HADDA GOOD FUCK LAS' NITE...
I WUZ HUMPIN' AN SCREWIN' LIKE MAD! THE BROAD I WAS WIT COULD REALLY GO... NEARLY WORE ME OUT.
WELL, FUCKIN' IS OK, BUT I'LL TELL YA, I LIKE TA GET MY COCK SUCKED BETTER...
WHEN A CHICK GOES DOWN ON YA AN GOBBLES YER DICK UP IN HER MOUTH AN' STARTS LICKIN' AROUN' YER KNOB...MAN, THAT'S HEAVEN!
FLIP
MAYBE I SHUN'T TELL YOU GUYS THIS...YA MIGHT THINK I'M WEIRD. BUT I LIKE TA EAT PUSSY. WHEN I SEE A CUNT I GO DOWN ON IT LIKE A DOG.
YOU C'N REALLY GET A BROAD CRAZY LIKE THAT. JUS' DIVE IN AN' SUCK UP ALL THAT JUICE AN' HAIR IN YER MOUTH. I DRIVE 'EM NUTS.

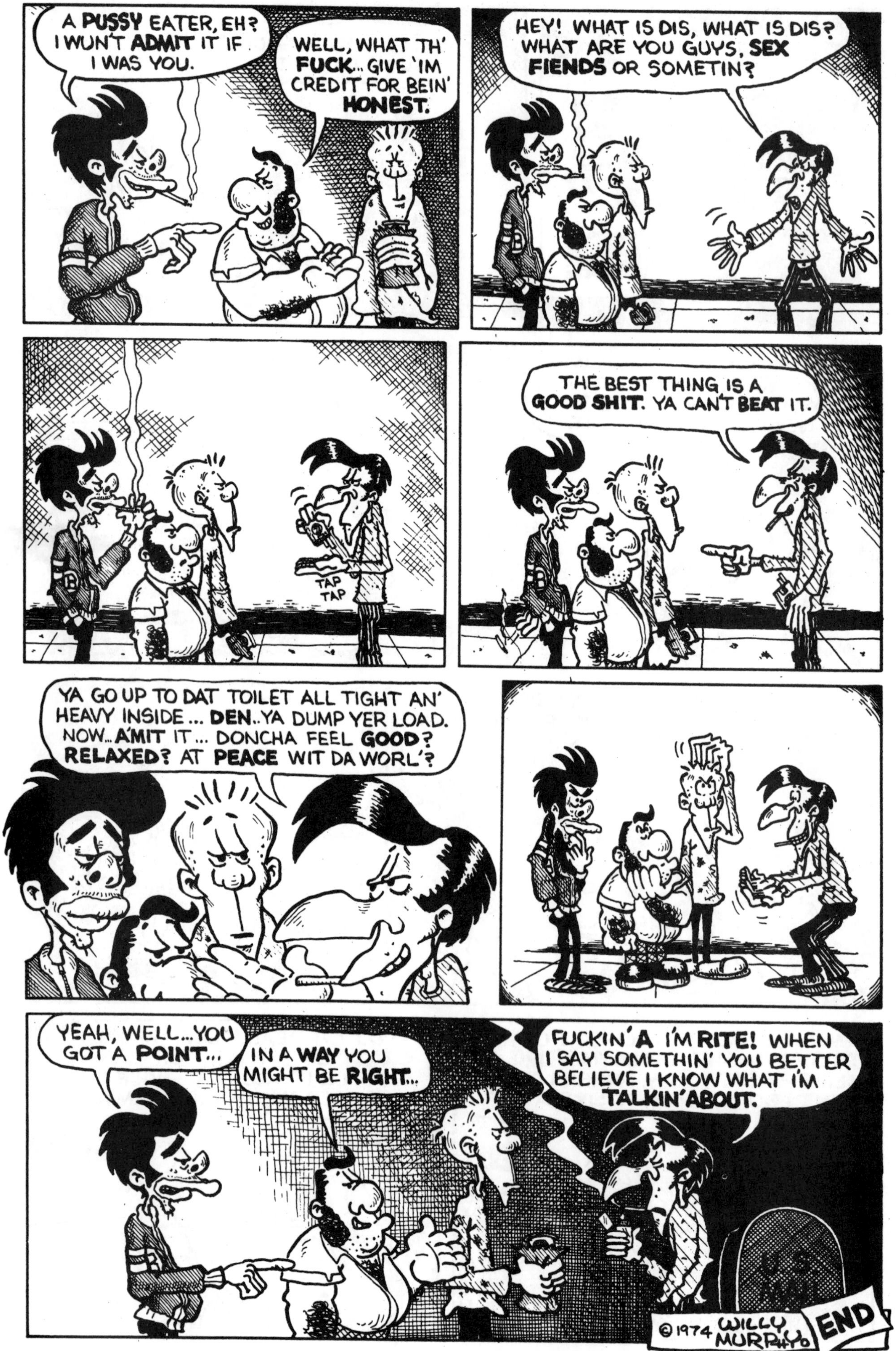
A PUSSY EATER, EH? I WUN'T ADMIT IT IF I WAS YOU.
WELL, WHAT TH' FUCK... GIVE 'IM CREDIT FOR BEIN' HONEST.
HEY! WHAT IS DIS, WHAT IS DIS? WHAT ARE YOU GUYS, SEX FIENDS OR SOMETIN?
TAP TAP
THE BEST THING IS A GOOD SHIT. YA CAN'T BEAT IT.
YA GO UP TO DAT TOILET ALL TIGHT AN' HEAVY INSIDE... DEN.. YA DUMP YER LOAD. NOW... A'MIT IT... DONCHA FEEL GOOD? RELAXED? AT PEACE WIT DA WORL'?
YEAH, WELL... YOU GOT A POINT...
IN A WAY YOU MIGHT BE RIGHT...
FUCKIN' A I'M RITE! WHEN I SAY SOMETHIN' YOU BETTER BELIEVE I KNOW WHAT I'M TALKIN' ABOUT.
© 1974 WILLY MURPHY
END

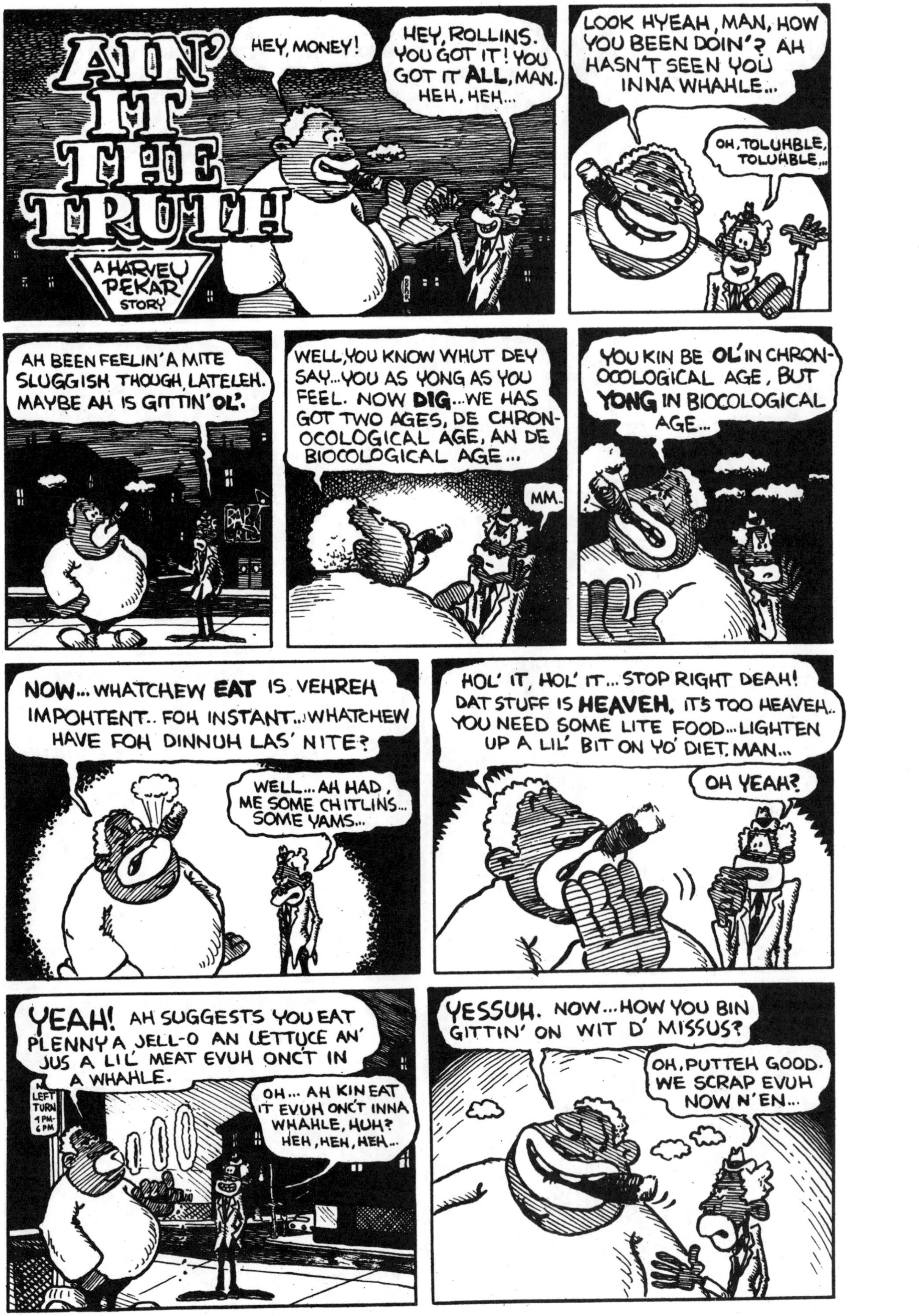
AIN' IT THE TRUTH
A HARVEY PEKAR STORY
HEY, MONEY!
HEY, ROLLINS. YOU GOT IT! YOU GOT IT ALL, MAN. HEH, HEH...
LOOK HYEAH, MAN, HOW YOU BEEN DOIN'? AH HASN'T SEEN YOU INNA WHAHLE...
OH, TOLUHBLE, TOLUHBLE...
AH BEEN FEELIN' A MITE SLUGGISH THOUGH, LATELEH. MAYBE AH IS GITTIN' OL'.
WELL, YOU KNOW WHUT DEY SAY... YOU AS YONG AS YOU FEEL. NOW DIG... WE HAS GOT TWO AGES, DE CHRON-OCOLOGICAL AGE, AN DE BIOCOLOGICAL AGE...
MM.
YOU KIN BE OL' IN CHRON-OCOLOGICAL AGE, BUT YONG IN BIOCOLOGICAL AGE...
NOW... WHATCHEW EAT IS VEHREH IMPOHTENT.. FOH INSTANT... WHATCHEW HAVE FOH DINNUH LAS' NITE?
WELL... AH HAD, ME SOME CHITLINS... SOME YAMS...
HOL' IT, HOL' IT... STOP RIGHT DEAH! DAT STUFF IS HEAVEH. IT'S TOO HEAVEH.. YOU NEED SOME LITE FOOD... LIGHTEN UP A LIL' BIT ON YO' DIET, MAN...
OH YEAH?
YEAH! AH SUGGESTS YOU EAT PLENNY A JELL-O AN LETTUCE AN' JUS A LIL' MEAT EVUH ONC'T IN A WHAHLE.
LEFT TURN 4 PM-6 PM
OH... AH KIN EAT IT EVUH ONC'T INNA WHAHLE, HUH? HEH, HEH, HEH...
YESSUH. NOW... HOW YOU BIN GITTIN' ON WIT D' MISSUS?
OH, PUTTEH GOOD. WE SCRAP EVUH NOW N' EN...

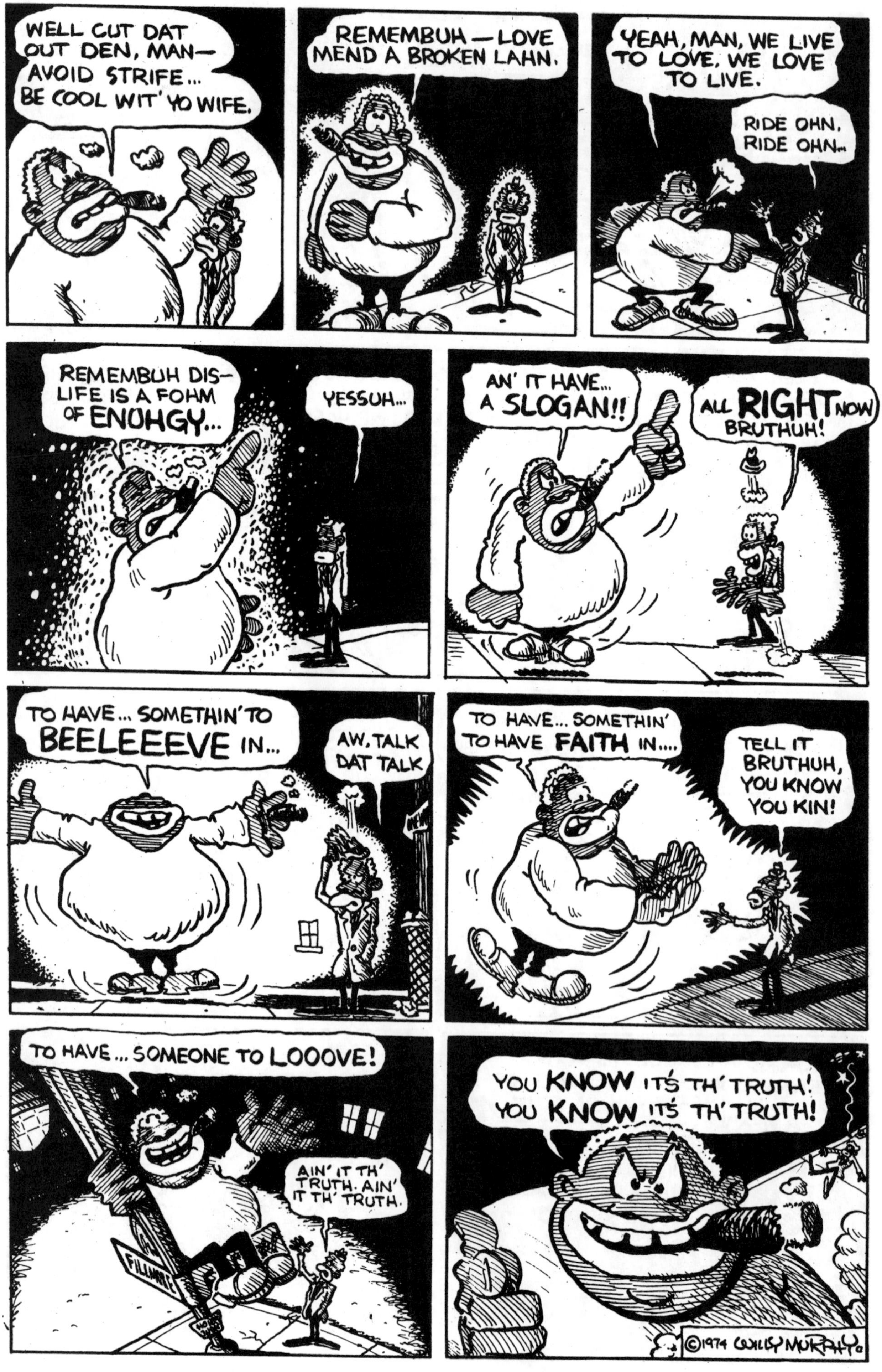
WELL CUT DAT OUT DEN, MAN— AVOID STRIFE... BE COOL WIT' YO WIFE.
REMEMBUH — LOVE MEND A BROKEN LAHN.
YEAH, MAN, WE LIVE TO LOVE, WE LOVE TO LIVE.
RIDE OHN, RIDE OHN...
REMEMBUH DIS-LIFE IS A FOHM OF ENUHGY...
YESSUH...
AN' IT HAVE... A SLOGAN!!
ALL RIGHT NOW BRUTHUH!
TO HAVE... SOMETHIN' TO BEELEEEVE IN...
AW, TALK DAT TALK
TO HAVE... SOMETHIN' TO HAVE FAITH IN....
TELL IT BRUTHUH, YOU KNOW YOU KIN!
TO HAVE... SOMEONE TO LOOOVE!
AIN' IT TH' TRUTH. AIN' IT TH' TRUTH.
FILLMORE
YOU KNOW IT'S TH' TRUTH! YOU KNOW IT'S TH' TRUTH!
©1974 WILLY MURPHY

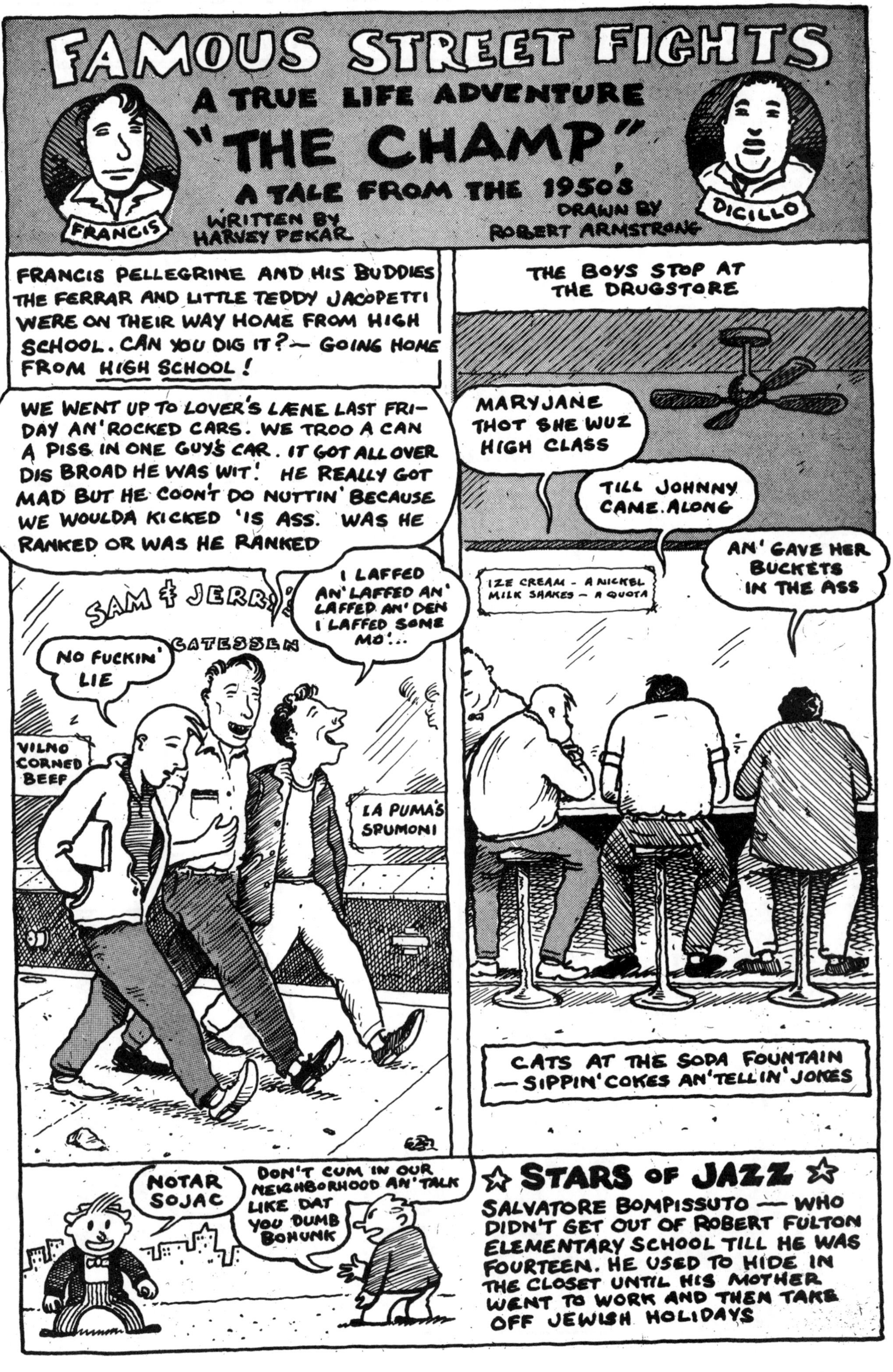

FAMOUS STREET FIGHTS
A TRUE LIFE ADVENTURE
"THE CHAMP"
A TALE FROM THE 1950'S
FRANCIS
DICILLO
WRITTEN BY HARVEY PEKAR
DRAWN BY ROBERT ARMSTRONG
FRANCIS PELLEGRINE AND HIS BUDDIES THE FERRAR AND LITTLE TEDDY JACOPETTI WERE ON THEIR WAY HOME FROM HIGH SCHOOL. CAN YOU DIG IT? — GOING HOME FROM HIGH SCHOOL!
WE WENT UP TO LOVER'S LAENE LAST FRIDAY AN' ROCKED CARS. WE TROO A CAN A PISS IN ONE GUY'S CAR. IT GOT ALL OVER DIS BROAD HE WAS WIT! HE REALLY GOT MAD BUT HE COON'T DO NUTTIN' BECAUSE WE WOULDA KICKED 'IS ASS. WAS HE RANKED OR WAS HE RANKED
SAM & JERRY'S
CATESSEN
I LAFFED AN' LAFFED AN' LAFFED AN' DEN I LAFFED SOME MO'...
NO FUCKIN' LIE
VILNO CORNED BEEF
LA PUMA'S SPUMONI
THE BOYS STOP AT THE DRUGSTORE
MARYJANE THOT SHE WUZ HIGH CLASS
TILL JOHNNY CAME ALONG
AN' GAVE HER BUCKETS IN THE ASS
IZE CREAM - A NICKEL
MILK SHAKES - A QUOTA
CATS AT THE SODA FOUNTAIN — SIPPIN' COKES AN' TELLIN' JOKES
NOTAR SOJAC
DON'T CUM IN OUR NEIGHBORHOOD AN' TALK LIKE DAT YOU DUMB BOHUNK
☆ STARS OF JAZZ ☆
SALVATORE BOMPISSUTO — WHO DIDN'T GET OUT OF ROBERT FULTON ELEMENTARY SCHOOL TILL HE WAS FOURTEEN. HE USED TO HIDE IN THE CLOSET UNTIL HIS MOTHER WENT TO WORK AND THEN TAKE OFF JEWISH HOLIDAYS

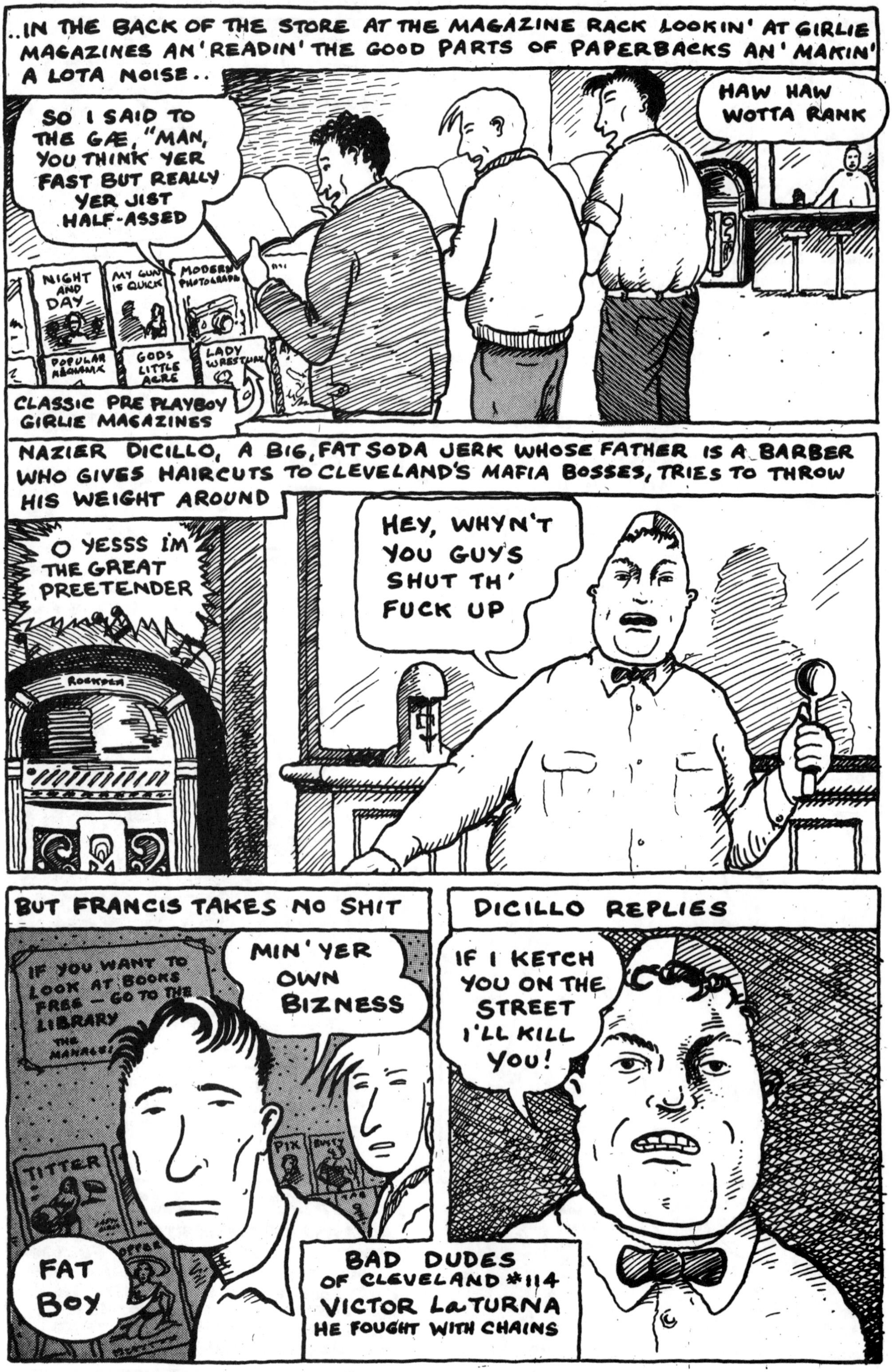

..IN THE BACK OF THE STORE AT THE MAGAZINE RACK LOOKIN' AT GIRLIE MAGAZINES AN' READIN' THE GOOD PARTS OF PAPERBACKS AN' MAKIN' A LOTA NOISE..
SO I SAID TO THE GÆ, "MAN, YOU THINK YER FAST BUT REALLY YER JIST HALF-ASSED
HAW HAW WOTTA RANK
NIGHT AND DAY
MY GUN IS QUICK
MODERN PHOTOGRAPHY
POPULAR MECHANIX
GODS LITTLE ACRE
LADY WRESTLING
CLASSIC PRE PLAYBOY GIRLIE MAGAZINES
NAZIER DICILLO, A BIG, FAT SODA JERK WHOSE FATHER IS A BARBER WHO GIVES HAIRCUTS TO CLEVELAND'S MAFIA BOSSES, TRIES TO THROW HIS WEIGHT AROUND
O YESSS I'M THE GREAT PREETENDER
HEY, WHYN'T YOU GUYS SHUT TH' FUCK UP
BUT FRANCIS TAKES NO SHIT
IF YOU WANT TO LOOK AT BOOKS FREE — GO TO THE LIBRARY THE MANAGER
MIN' YER OWN BIZNESS
TITTER
FAT BOY
DICILLO REPLIES
IF I KETCH YOU ON THE STREET I'LL KILL YOU!
BAD DUDES OF CLEVELAND #114
VICTOR LaTURNA
HE FOUGHT WITH CHAINS

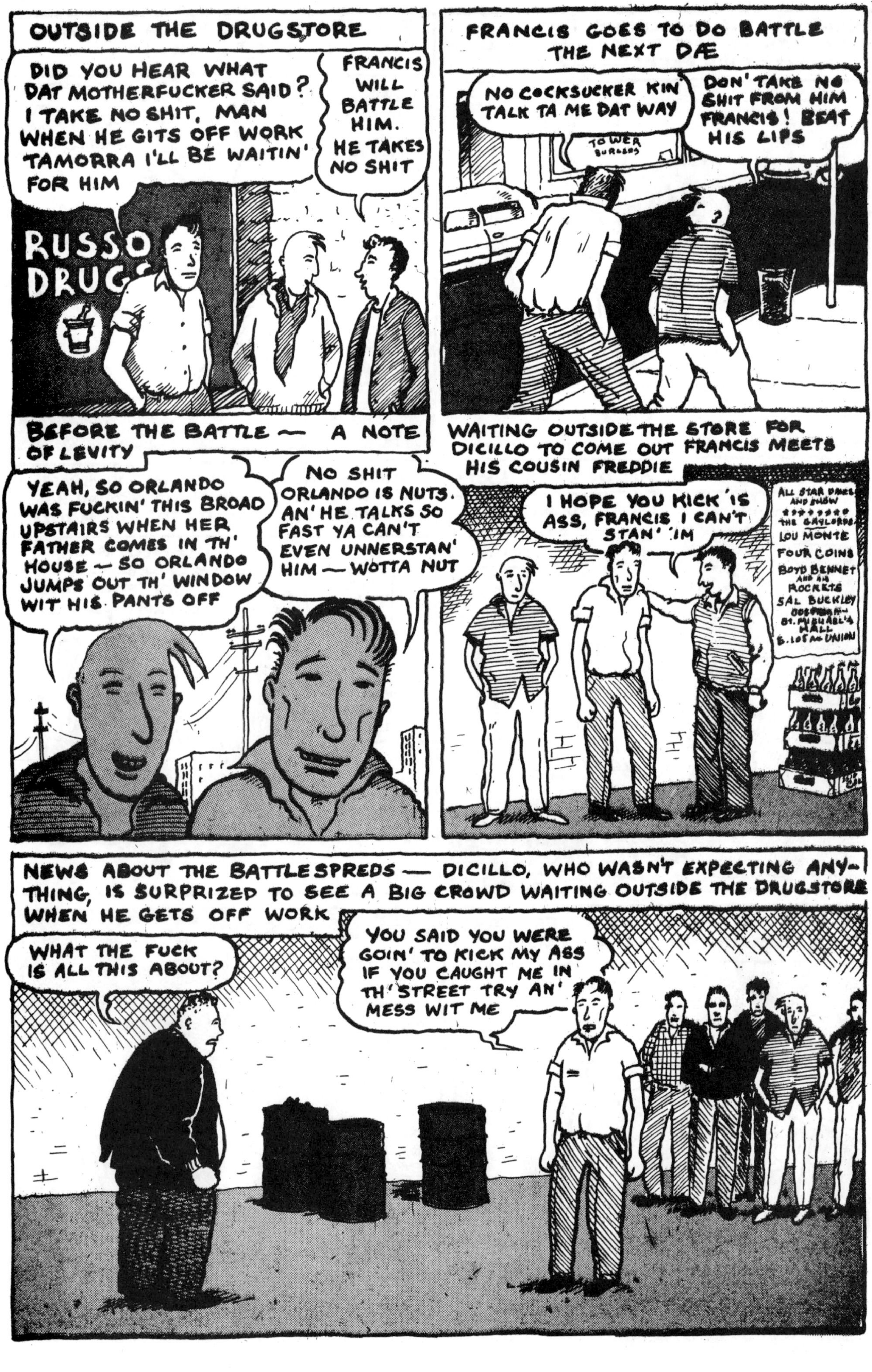
OUTSIDE THE DRUGSTORE
DID YOU HEAR WHAT DAT MOTHERFUCKER SAID? I TAKE NO SHIT, MAN WHEN HE GITS OFF WORK TAMORRA I'LL BE WAITIN' FOR HIM
FRANCIS WILL BATTLE HIM. HE TAKES NO SHIT
RUSSO DRUG
FRANCIS GOES TO DO BATTLE THE NEXT DÆ
NO COCKSUCKER KIN TALK TA ME DAT WAY
DON'T TAKE NO SHIT FROM HIM FRANCIS! BEAT HIS LIPS
TOWER BURGERS
BEFORE THE BATTLE — A NOTE OF LEVITY
YEAH, SO ORLANDO WAS FUCKIN' THIS BROAD UPSTAIRS WHEN HER FATHER COMES IN TH' HOUSE — SO ORLANDO JUMPS OUT TH' WINDOW WIT HIS PANTS OFF
NO SHIT ORLANDO IS NUTS. AN' HE TALKS SO FAST YA CAN'T EVEN UNNERSTAN' HIM — WOTTA NUT
WAITING OUTSIDE THE STORE FOR DICILLO TO COME OUT FRANCIS MEETS HIS COUSIN FREDDIE
I HOPE YOU KICK 'IS ASS, FRANCIS I CAN'T STAN' 'IM
ALL STAR DANCE AND SHOW
THE GAYLORDS
LOU MONTE
FOUR COINS
BOYD BENNET AND HIS ROCKETS
SAL BUCKLEY
ST. MICHAEL'S HALL
E. 105 AND UNION
NEWS ABOUT THE BATTLE SPREDS — DICILLO, WHO WASN'T EXPECTING ANYTHING, IS SURPRIZED TO SEE A BIG CROWD WAITING OUTSIDE THE DRUGSTORE WHEN HE GETS OFF WORK
WHAT THE FUCK IS ALL THIS ABOUT?
YOU SAID YOU WERE GOIN' TO KICK MY ASS IF YOU CAUGHT ME IN TH' STREET TRY AN' MESS WIT ME

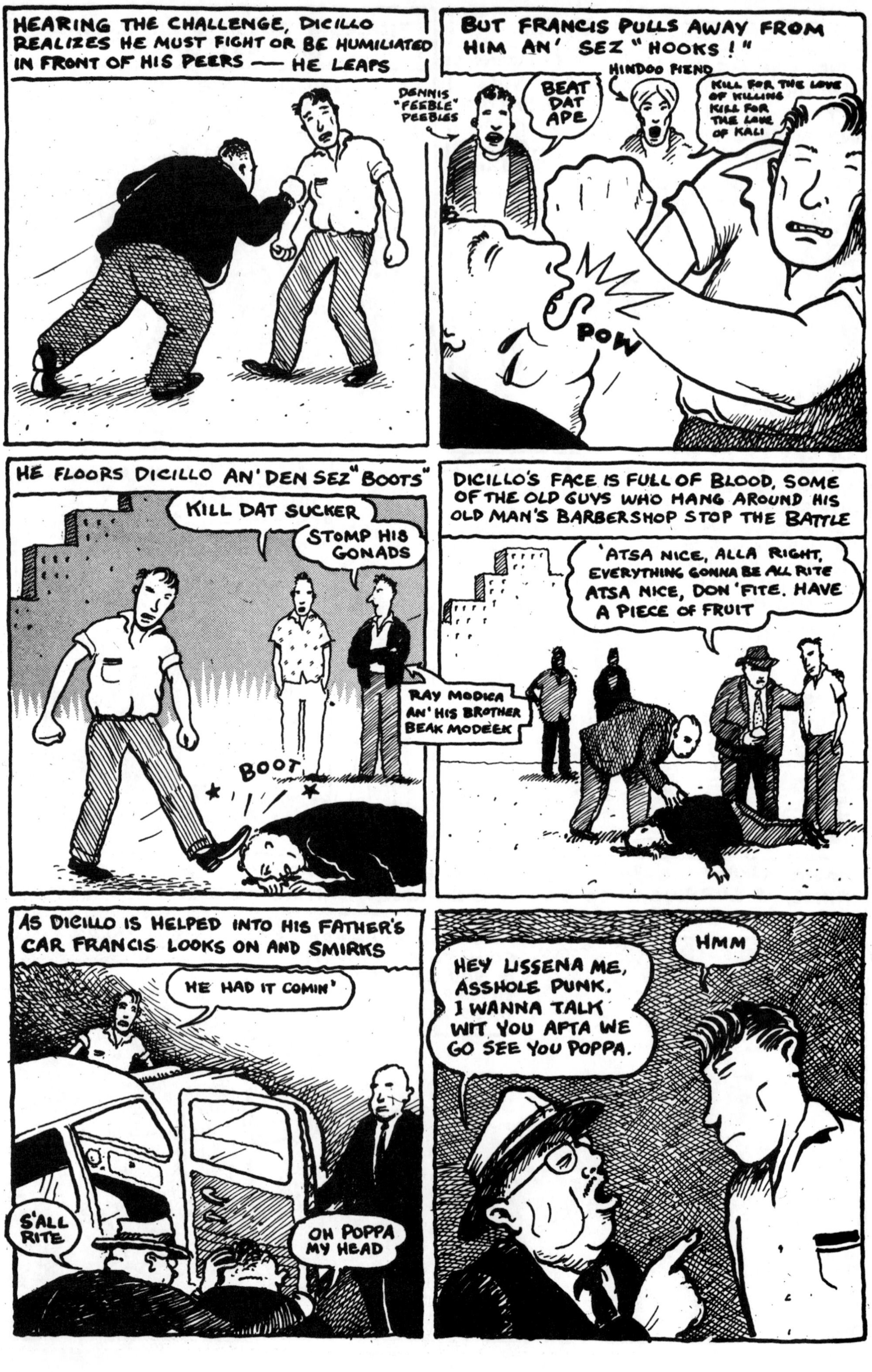
HEARING THE CHALLENGE, DICILLO REALIZES HE MUST FIGHT OR BE HUMILIATED IN FRONT OF HIS PEERS — HE LEAPS
BUT FRANCIS PULLS AWAY FROM HIM AN' SEZ "HOOKS!"
DENNIS "FEEBLE" PEEBLES
BEAT DAT APE
HINDOO FIEND
KILL FOR THE LOVE OF KILLING KILL FOR THE LOVE OF KALI
POW
HE FLOORS DICILLO AN' DEN SEZ "BOOTS"
KILL DAT SUCKER
STOMP HIS GONADS
RAY MODICA AN' HIS BROTHER BEAK MODEEK
BOOT
DICILLO'S FACE IS FULL OF BLOOD, SOME OF THE OLD GUYS WHO HANG AROUND HIS OLD MAN'S BARBERSHOP STOP THE BATTLE
'ATSA NICE, ALLA RIGHT, EVERYTHING GONNA BE ALL RITE ATSA NICE, DON'FITE. HAVE A PIECE OF FRUIT
AS DICILLO IS HELPED INTO HIS FATHER'S CAR FRANCIS LOOKS ON AND SMIRKS
HE HAD IT COMIN'
S'ALL RITE
OH POPPA MY HEAD
HMM
HEY LISSENA ME, ASSHOLE PUNK, I WANNA TALK WIT YOU APTA WE GO SEE YOU POPPA.

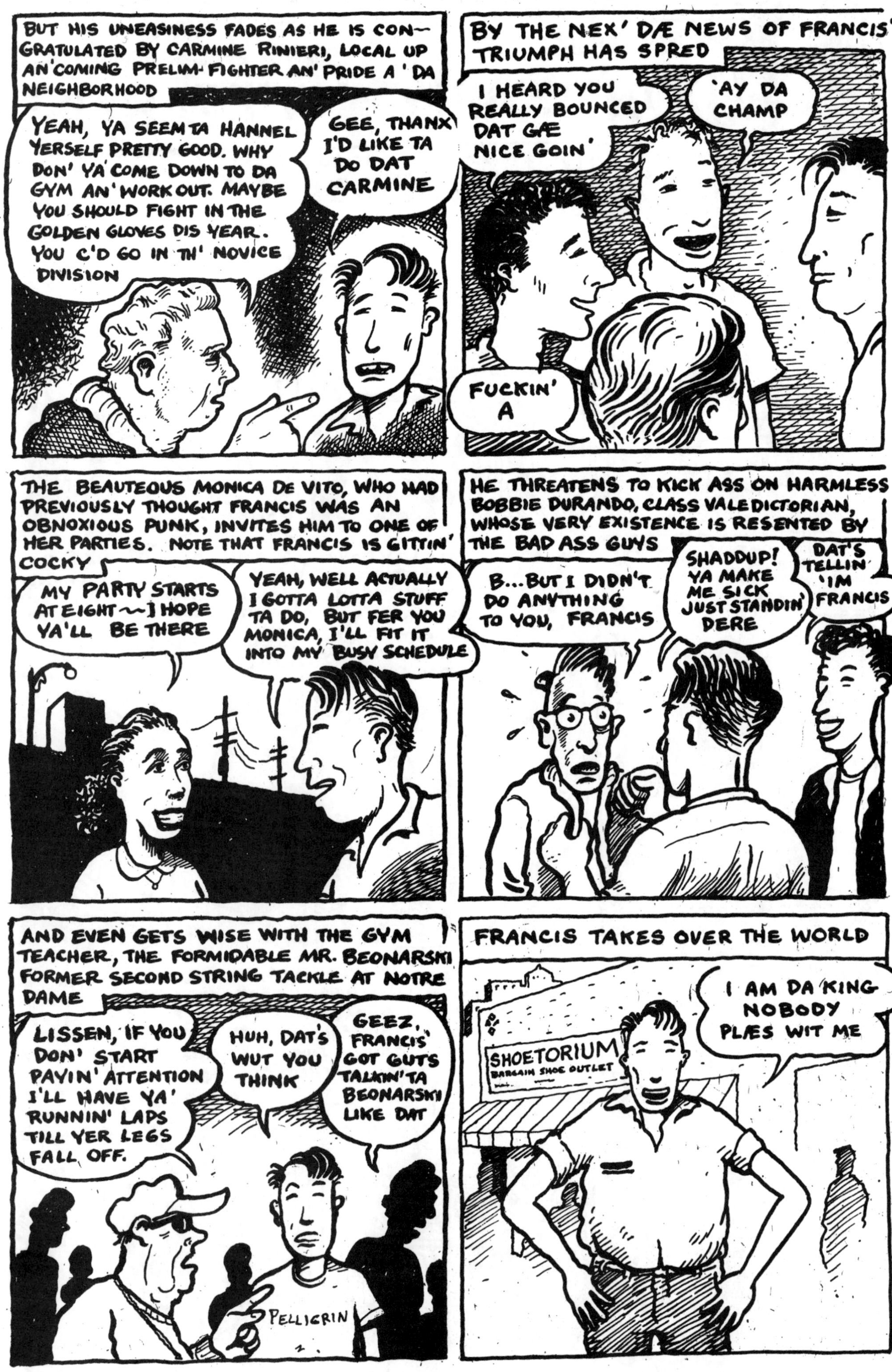
BUT HIS UNEASINESS FADES AS HE IS CON-GRATULATED BY CARMINE RINIERI, LOCAL UP AN'COMING PRELIM-FIGHTER AN' PRIDE A 'DA NEIGHBORHOOD
YEAH, YA SEEM TA HANNEL YERSELF PRETTY GOOD. WHY DON' YA COME DOWN TO DA GYM AN' WORK OUT. MAYBE YOU SHOULD FIGHT IN THE GOLDEN GLOVES DIS YEAR. YOU C'D GO IN TH' NOVICE DIVISION
GEE, THANX I'D LIKE TA DO DAT CARMINE
BY THE NEX' DÆ NEWS OF FRANCIS' TRIUMPH HAS SPRED
I HEARD YOU REALLY BOUNCED DAT GÆ NICE GOIN'
'AY DA CHAMP
FUCKIN' A
THE BEAUTEOUS MONICA DE VITO, WHO HAD PREVIOUSLY THOUGHT FRANCIS WAS AN OBNOXIOUS PUNK, INVITES HIM TO ONE OF HER PARTIES. NOTE THAT FRANCIS IS GITTIN' COCKY
MY PARTY STARTS AT EIGHT~~I HOPE YA'LL BE THERE
YEAH, WELL ACTUALLY I GOTTA LOTTA STUFF TA DO, BUT FER YOU MONICA, I'LL FIT IT INTO MY BUSY SCHEDULE
HE THREATENS TO KICK ASS ON HARMLESS BOBBIE DURANDO, CLASS VALEDICTORIAN, WHOSE VERY EXISTENCE IS RESENTED BY THE BAD ASS GUYS
B...BUT I DIDN'T DO ANYTHING TO YOU, FRANCIS
SHADDUP! YA MAKE ME SICK JUST STANDIN' DERE
DAT'S TELLIN' 'IM FRANCIS
AND EVEN GETS WISE WITH THE GYM TEACHER, THE FORMIDABLE MR. BEONARSKI FORMER SECOND STRING TACKLE AT NOTRE DAME
LISSEN, IF YOU DON' START PAYIN' ATTENTION I'LL HAVE YA' RUNNIN' LAPS TILL YER LEGS FALL OFF.
HUH, DAT'S WUT YOU THINK
GEEZ, FRANCIS' GOT GUTS TALKIN' TA BEONARSKI LIKE DAT
PELLIGRIN
FRANCIS TAKES OVER THE WORLD
SHOETORIUM
BARGAIN SHOE OUTLET
I AM DA KING NOBODY PLÆS WIT ME

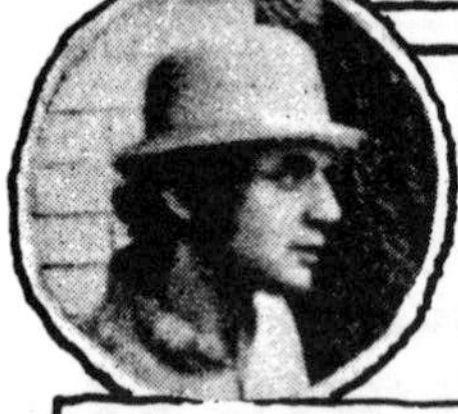

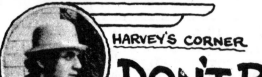

HARVEY'S CORNER

WRITTEN by HARVEY PEKAR
DRAWN by L.B. ARMSTRONG

DON'T RAIN ON MY PARADE

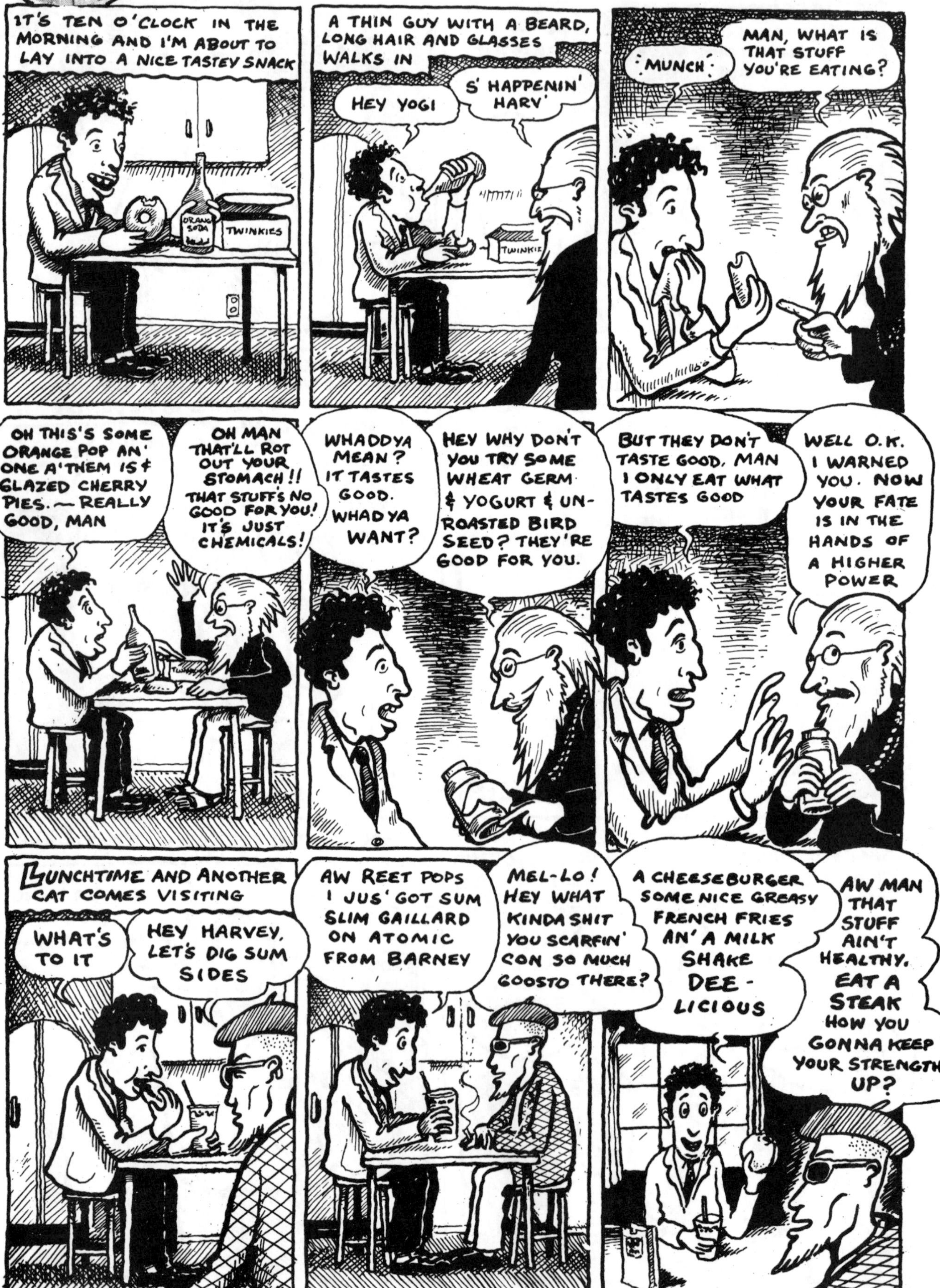
IT'S TEN O'CLOCK IN THE MORNING AND I'M ABOUT TO LAY INTO A NICE TASTEY SNACK
ORANGE SODA
TWINKIES
A THIN GUY WITH A BEARD, LONG HAIR AND GLASSES WALKS IN
HEY YOGI
S' HAPPENIN' HARV'
TWINKIES
MUNCH
MAN, WHAT IS THAT STUFF YOU'RE EATING?
OH THIS'S SOME ORANGE POP AN' ONE A'THEM IS & GLAZED CHERRY PIES. — REALLY GOOD, MAN
OH MAN THAT'LL ROT OUT YOUR STOMACH!! THAT STUFF'S NO GOOD FOR YOU! IT'S JUST CHEMICALS!
WHADDYA MEAN? IT TASTES GOOD. WHADYA WANT?
HEY WHY DON'T YOU TRY SOME WHEAT GERM & YOGURT & UN-ROASTED BIRD SEED? THEY'RE GOOD FOR YOU.
BUT THEY DON'T TASTE GOOD, MAN I ONLY EAT WHAT TASTES GOOD
WELL O.K. I WARNED YOU. NOW YOUR FATE IS IN THE HANDS OF A HIGHER POWER
LUNCHTIME AND ANOTHER CAT COMES VISITING
WHAT'S TO IT
HEY HARVEY, LET'S DIG SUM SIDES
AW REET POPS I JUS' GOT SUM SLIM GAILLARD ON ATOMIC FROM BARNEY
MEL-LO! HEY WHAT KINDA SHIT YOU SCARFIN' CON SO MUCH GOOSTO THERE?
A CHEESEBURGER SOME NICE GREASY FRENCH FRIES AN' A MILK SHAKE DEE-LICIOUS
AW MAN THAT STUFF AIN'T HEALTHY. EAT A STEAK HOW YOU GONNA KEEP YOUR STRENGTH UP?

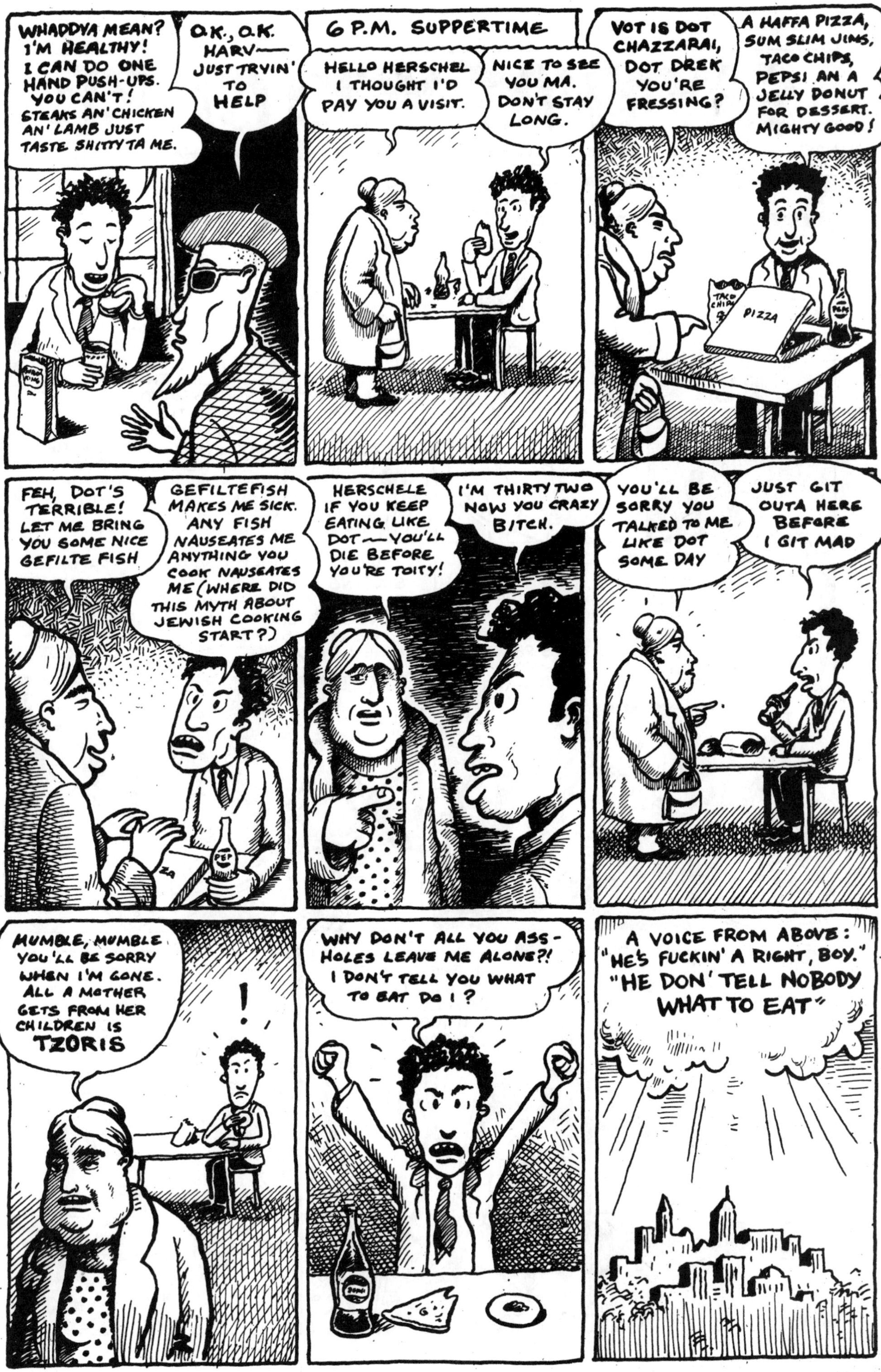
WHADDYA MEAN? I'M HEALTHY! I CAN DO ONE HAND PUSH-UPS. YOU CAN'T! STEAKS AN' CHICKEN AN' LAMB JUST TASTE SHITTY TA ME.
O.K., O.K. HARV—— JUST TRYIN' TO HELP
6 P.M. SUPPERTIME
HELLO HERSCHEL I THOUGHT I'D PAY YOU A VISIT.
NICE TO SEE YOU MA. DON'T STAY LONG.
VOT IS DOT CHAZZARAI, DOT DREK YOU'RE FRESSING?
A HAFFA PIZZA, SUM SLIM JIMS, TACO CHIPS, PEPSI AN A JELLY DONUT FOR DESSERT. MIGHTY GOOD!
PIZZA
FEH, DOT'S TERRIBLE! LET ME BRING YOU SOME NICE GEFILTE FISH
GEFILTEFISH MAKES ME SICK. ANY FISH NAUSEATES ME ANYTHING YOU COOK NAUSEATES ME (WHERE DID THIS MYTH ABOUT JEWISH COOKING START?)
HERSCHELE IF YOU KEEP EATING LIKE DOT —— YOU'LL DIE BEFORE YOU'RE TOITY!
I'M THIRTY TWO NOW YOU CRAZY BITCH.
YOU'LL BE SORRY YOU TALKED TO ME LIKE DOT SOME DAY
JUST GIT OUTA HERE BEFORE I GIT MAD
MUMBLE, MUMBLE YOU'LL BE SORRY WHEN I'M GONE. ALL A MOTHER GETS FROM HER CHILDREN IS TZORIS
!
WHY DON'T ALL YOU ASS-HOLES LEAVE ME ALONE?! I DON'T TELL YOU WHAT TO EAT DO I?
A VOICE FROM ABOVE: "HE'S FUCKIN' A RIGHT, BOY." "HE DON' TELL NOBODY WHAT TO EAT"

SAY THAT YOU CARE

STORY BY HARVEY PEKAR · ART BY PAUL MAVRIDES · © 1988 BY HARVEY PEKAR

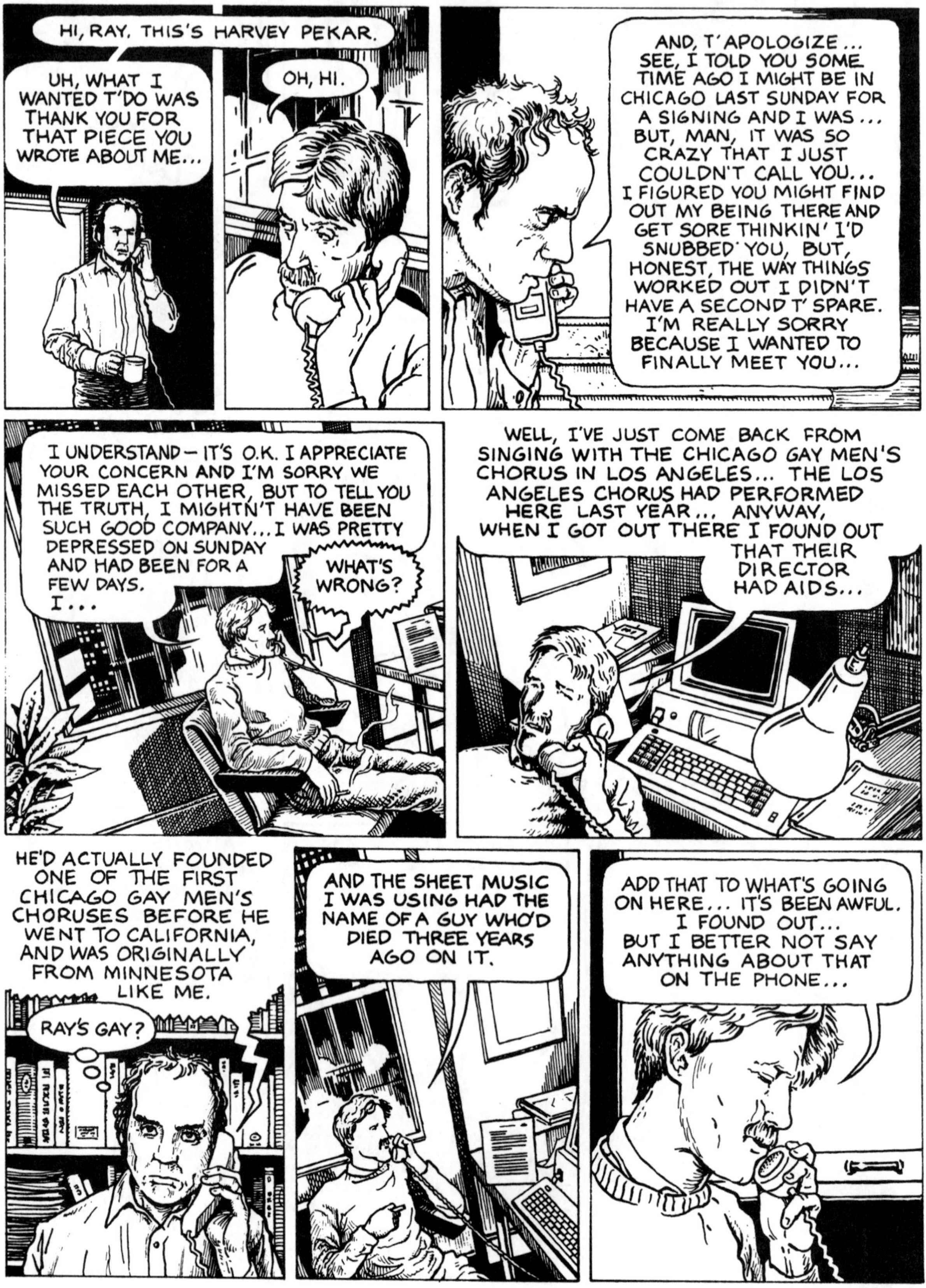

HI, RAY. THIS'S HARVEY PEKAR.
UH, WHAT I WANTED T'DO WAS THANK YOU FOR THAT PIECE YOU WROTE ABOUT ME...
OH, HI.
AND, T'APOLOGIZE... SEE, I TOLD YOU SOME TIME AGO I MIGHT BE IN CHICAGO LAST SUNDAY FOR A SIGNING AND I WAS... BUT, MAN, IT WAS SO CRAZY THAT I JUST COULDN'T CALL YOU... I FIGURED YOU MIGHT FIND OUT MY BEING THERE AND GET SORE THINKIN' I'D SNUBBED YOU, BUT, HONEST, THE WAY THINGS WORKED OUT I DIDN'T HAVE A SECOND T' SPARE. I'M REALLY SORRY BECAUSE I WANTED TO FINALLY MEET YOU...
I UNDERSTAND — IT'S O.K. I APPRECIATE YOUR CONCERN AND I'M SORRY WE MISSED EACH OTHER, BUT TO TELL YOU THE TRUTH, I MIGHTN'T HAVE BEEN SUCH GOOD COMPANY... I WAS PRETTY DEPRESSED ON SUNDAY AND HAD BEEN FOR A FEW DAYS. I...
WHAT'S WRONG?
WELL, I'VE JUST COME BACK FROM SINGING WITH THE CHICAGO GAY MEN'S CHORUS IN LOS ANGELES... THE LOS ANGELES CHORUS HAD PERFORMED HERE LAST YEAR... ANYWAY, WHEN I GOT OUT THERE I FOUND OUT THAT THEIR DIRECTOR HAD AIDS...
HE'D ACTUALLY FOUNDED ONE OF THE FIRST CHICAGO GAY MEN'S CHORUSES BEFORE HE WENT TO CALIFORNIA, AND WAS ORIGINALLY FROM MINNESOTA LIKE ME.
RAY'S GAY?
AND THE SHEET MUSIC I WAS USING HAD THE NAME OF A GUY WHO'D DIED THREE YEARS AGO ON IT.
ADD THAT TO WHAT'S GOING ON HERE... IT'S BEEN AWFUL. I FOUND OUT... BUT I BETTER NOT SAY ANYTHING ABOUT THAT ON THE PHONE...

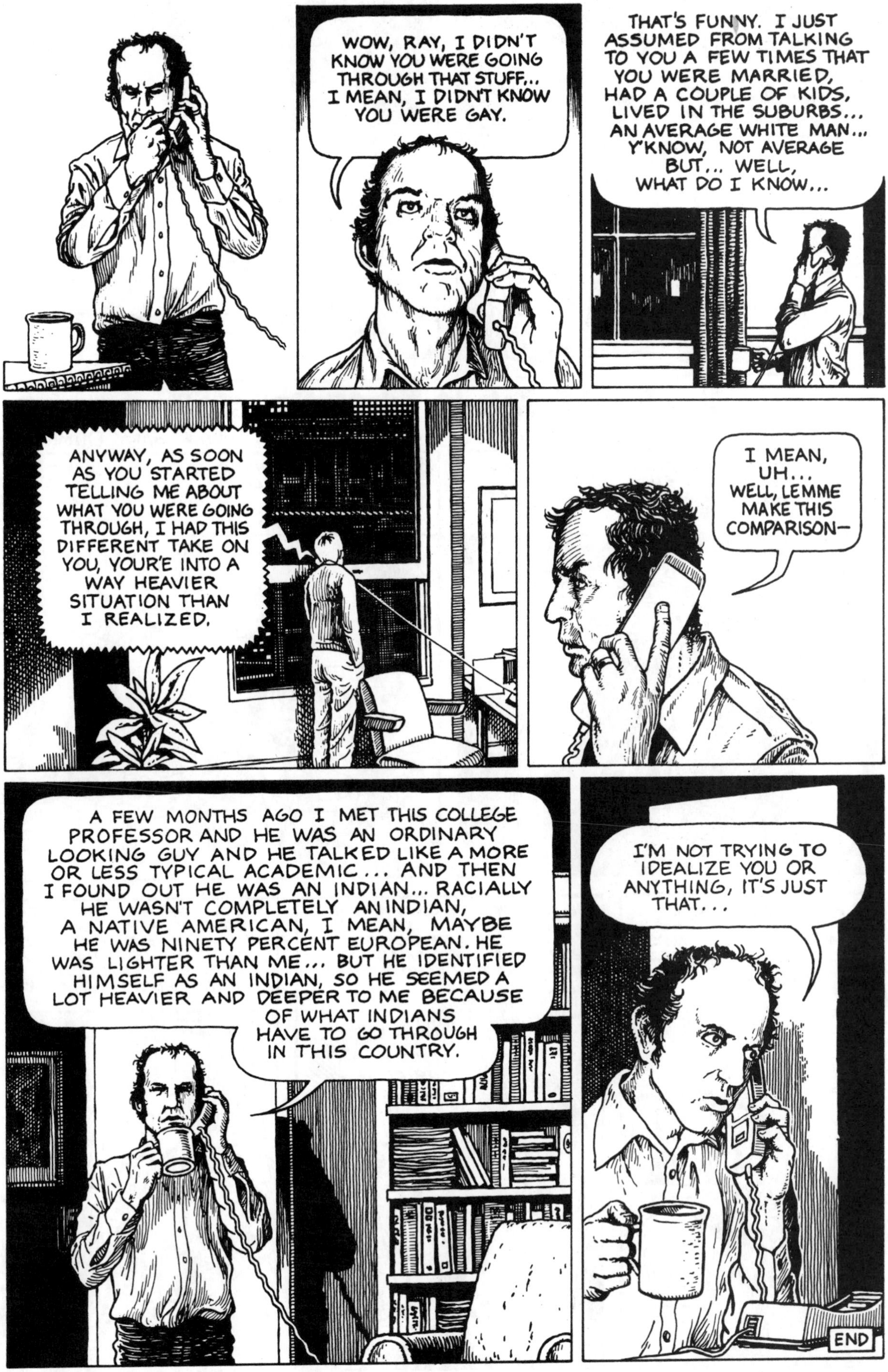
WOW, RAY, I DIDN'T KNOW YOU WERE GOING THROUGH THAT STUFF... I MEAN, I DIDN'T KNOW YOU WERE GAY.
THAT'S FUNNY. I JUST ASSUMED FROM TALKING TO YOU A FEW TIMES THAT YOU WERE MARRIED, HAD A COUPLE OF KIDS, LIVED IN THE SUBURBS... AN AVERAGE WHITE MAN... Y'KNOW, NOT AVERAGE BUT... WELL, WHAT DO I KNOW...
ANYWAY, AS SOON AS YOU STARTED TELLING ME ABOUT WHAT YOU WERE GOING THROUGH, I HAD THIS DIFFERENT TAKE ON YOU, YOUR'E INTO A WAY HEAVIER SITUATION THAN I REALIZED.
I MEAN, UH... WELL, LEMME MAKE THIS COMPARISON—
A FEW MONTHS AGO I MET THIS COLLEGE PROFESSOR AND HE WAS AN ORDINARY LOOKING GUY AND HE TALKED LIKE A MORE OR LESS TYPICAL ACADEMIC... AND THEN I FOUND OUT HE WAS AN INDIAN... RACIALLY HE WASN'T COMPLETELY AN INDIAN, A NATIVE AMERICAN, I MEAN, MAYBE HE WAS NINETY PERCENT EUROPEAN. HE WAS LIGHTER THAN ME... BUT HE IDENTIFIED HIMSELF AS AN INDIAN, SO HE SEEMED A LOT HEAVIER AND DEEPER TO ME BECAUSE OF WHAT INDIANS HAVE TO GO THROUGH IN THIS COUNTRY.
I'M NOT TRYING TO IDEALIZE YOU OR ANYTHING, IT'S JUST THAT...
END

Harvey Pekar Gary Dumm Joe Zabel

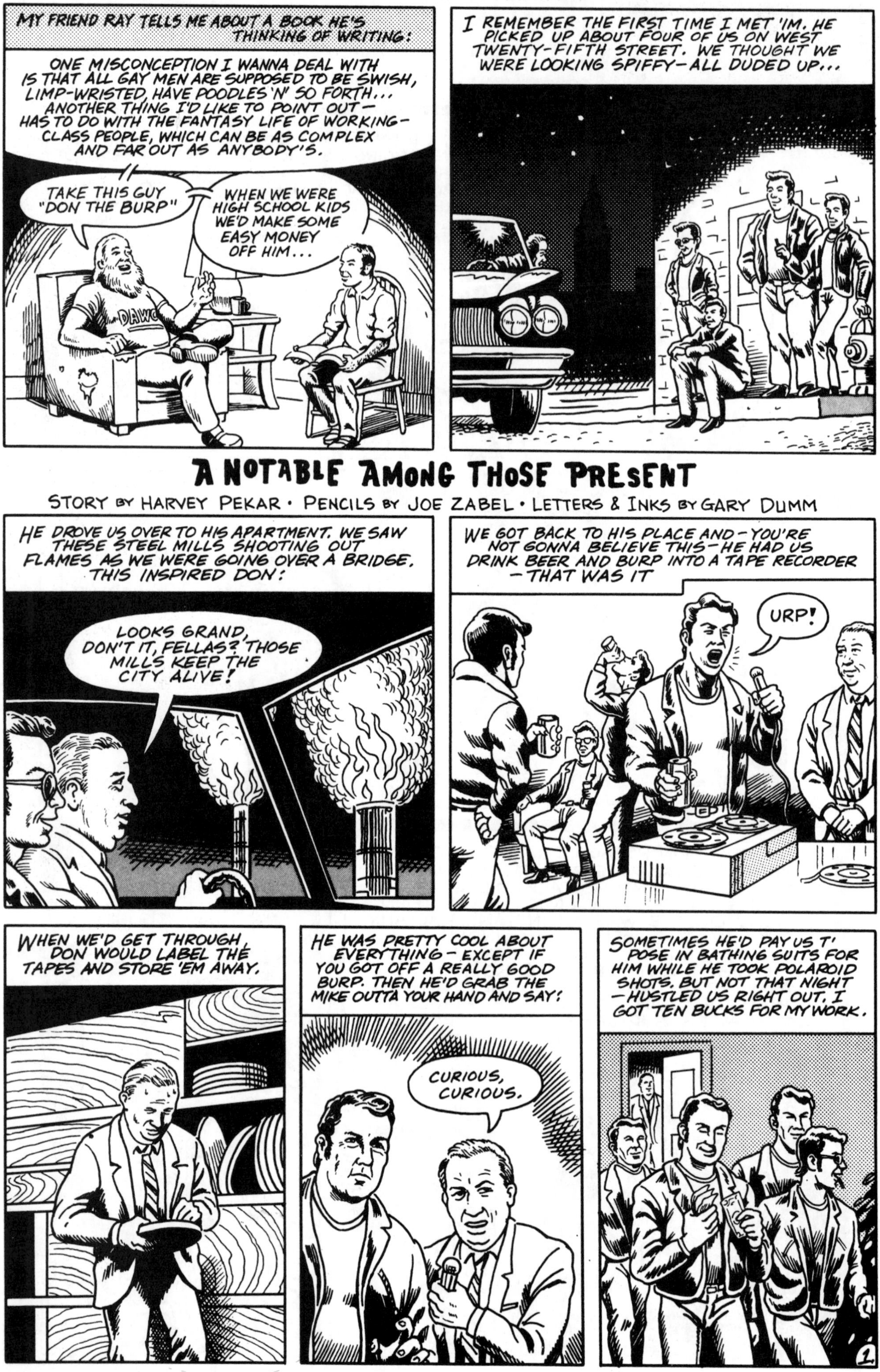

MY FRIEND RAY TELLS ME ABOUT A BOOK HE'S THINKING OF WRITING:
ONE MISCONCEPTION I WANNA DEAL WITH IS THAT ALL GAY MEN ARE SUPPOSED TO BE SWISH, LIMP-WRISTED, HAVE POODLES 'N' SO FORTH... ANOTHER THING I'D LIKE TO POINT OUT—HAS TO DO WITH THE FANTASY LIFE OF WORKING-CLASS PEOPLE, WHICH CAN BE AS COMPLEX AND FAR OUT AS ANYBODY'S.
TAKE THIS GUY "DON THE BURP"
WHEN WE WERE HIGH SCHOOL KIDS WE'D MAKE SOME EASY MONEY OFF HIM...
DAWG
I REMEMBER THE FIRST TIME I MET 'IM. HE PICKED UP ABOUT FOUR OF US ON WEST TWENTY-FIFTH STREET. WE THOUGHT WE WERE LOOKING SPIFFY—ALL DUDED UP...
A NOTABLE AMONG THOSE PRESENT
STORY BY HARVEY PEKAR · PENCILS BY JOE ZABEL · LETTERS & INKS BY GARY DUMM
HE DROVE US OVER TO HIS APARTMENT. WE SAW THESE STEEL MILLS SHOOTING OUT FLAMES AS WE WERE GOING OVER A BRIDGE. THIS INSPIRED DON:
LOOKS GRAND, DON'T IT, FELLAS? THOSE MILLS KEEP THE CITY ALIVE!
WE GOT BACK TO HIS PLACE AND—YOU'RE NOT GONNA BELIEVE THIS—HE HAD US DRINK BEER AND BURP INTO A TAPE RECORDER —THAT WAS IT
URP!
WHEN WE'D GET THROUGH, DON WOULD LABEL THE TAPES AND STORE 'EM AWAY.
HE WAS PRETTY COOL ABOUT EVERYTHING—EXCEPT IF YOU GOT OFF A REALLY GOOD BURP. THEN HE'D GRAB THE MIKE OUTTA YOUR HAND AND SAY:
CURIOUS, CURIOUS.
SOMETIMES HE'D PAY US T' POSE IN BATHING SUITS FOR HIM WHILE HE TOOK POLAROID SHOTS. BUT NOT THAT NIGHT—HUSTLED US RIGHT OUT. I GOT TEN BUCKS FOR MY WORK.
1

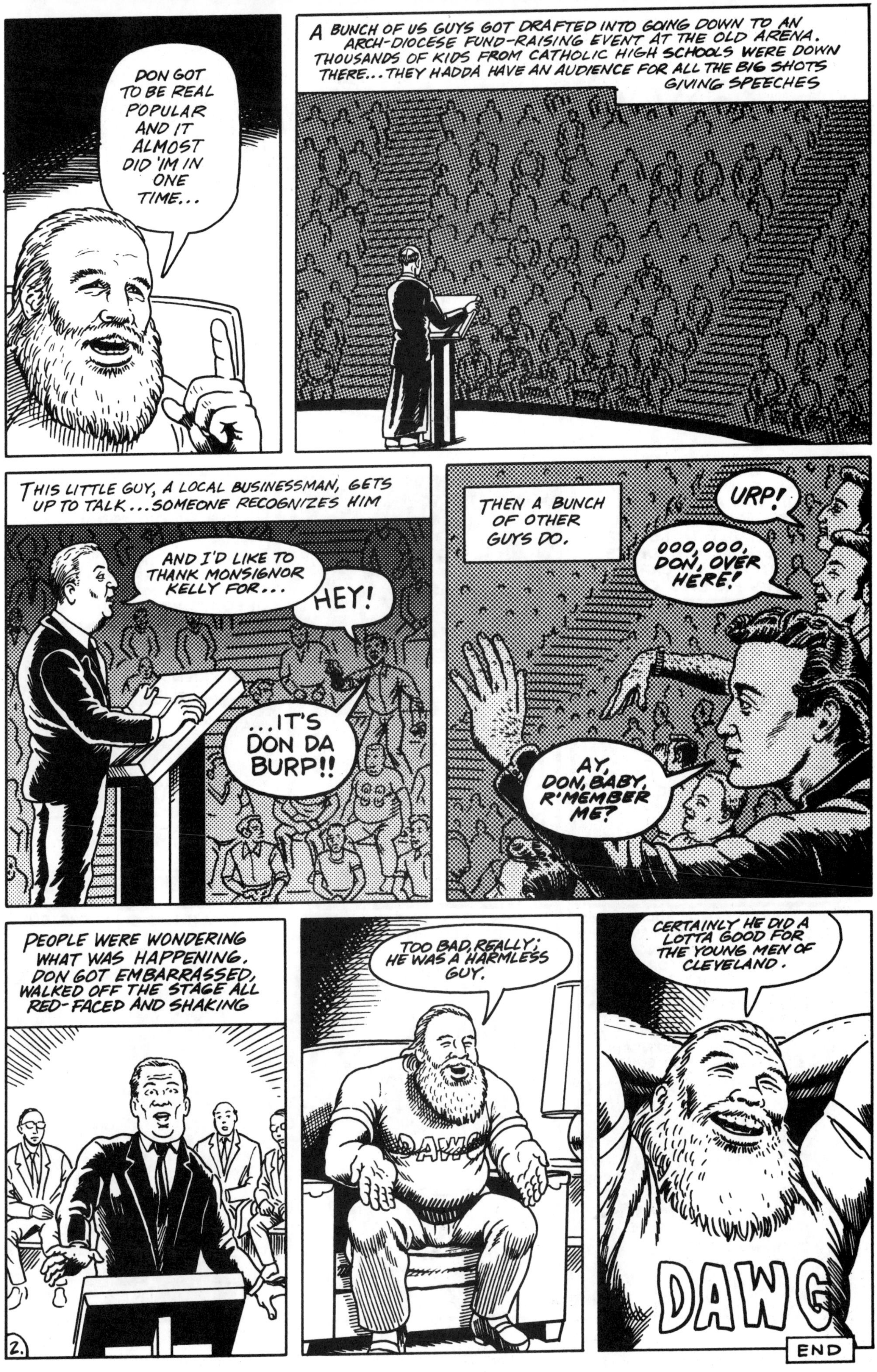
DON GOT TO BE REAL POPULAR AND IT ALMOST DID 'IM IN ONE TIME...
A BUNCH OF US GUYS GOT DRAFTED INTO GOING DOWN TO AN ARCH-DIOCESE FUND-RAISING EVENT AT THE OLD ARENA. THOUSANDS OF KIDS FROM CATHOLIC HIGH SCHOOLS WERE DOWN THERE... THEY HADDA HAVE AN AUDIENCE FOR ALL THE BIG SHOTS GIVING SPEECHES
THIS LITTLE GUY, A LOCAL BUSINESSMAN, GETS UP TO TALK... SOMEONE RECOGNIZES HIM
AND I'D LIKE TO THANK MONSIGNOR KELLY FOR...
HEY!
...IT'S DON DA BURP!!
THEN A BUNCH OF OTHER GUYS DO.
URP!
OOO,OOO, DON, OVER HERE!
AY, DON, BABY, R'MEMBER ME?
PEOPLE WERE WONDERING WHAT WAS HAPPENING. DON GOT EMBARRASSED, WALKED OFF THE STAGE ALL RED-FACED AND SHAKING
TOO BAD, REALLY; HE WAS A HARMLESS GUY.
DAWG
CERTAINLY HE DID A LOTTA GOOD FOR THE YOUNG MEN OF CLEVELAND.
DAWG
END

HOW THIS FOREWORD GOT WRITTEN

STORY BY HARVEY PEKAR!

DRAWINGS BY CHESTER

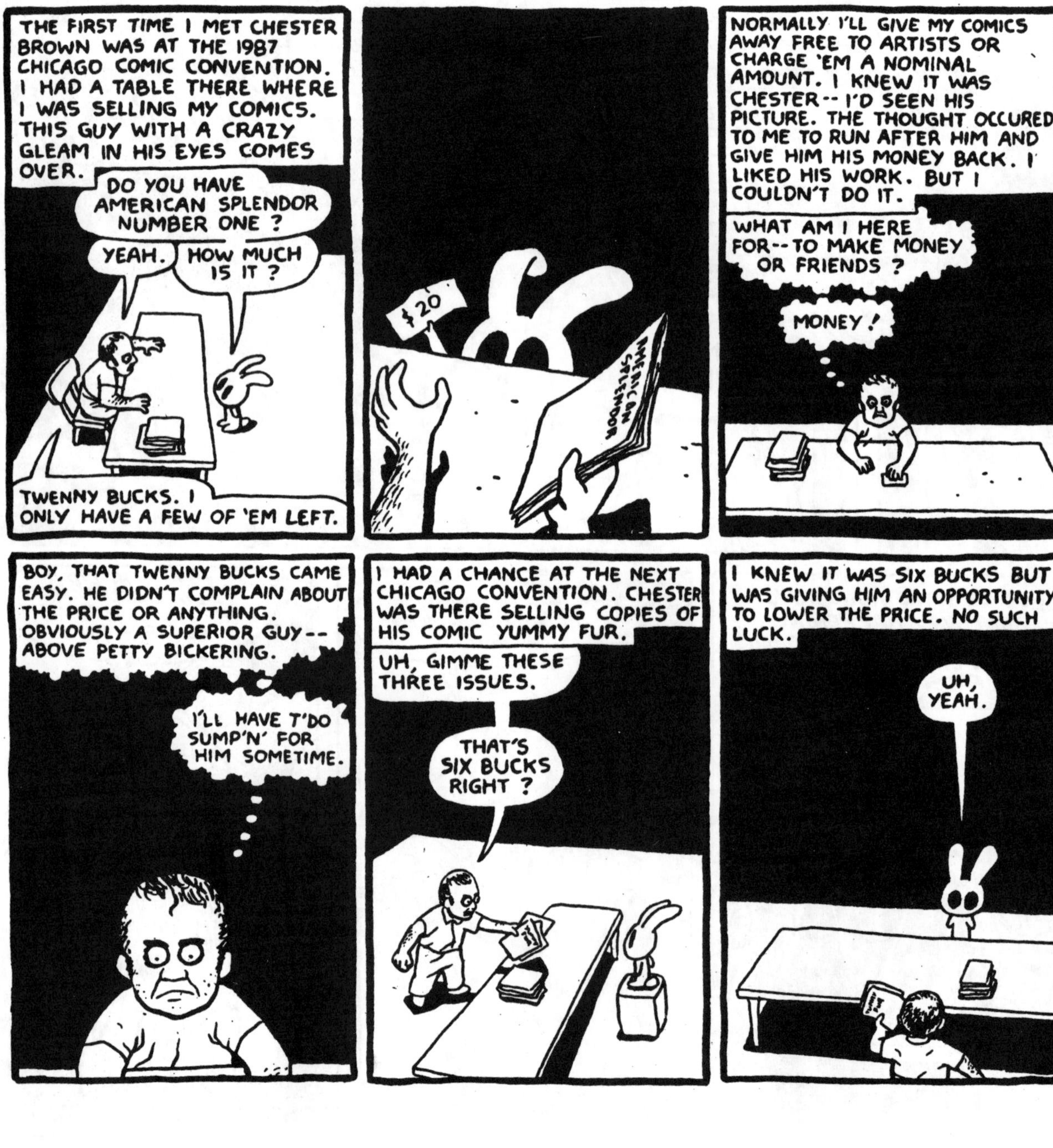
THE FIRST TIME I MET CHESTER BROWN WAS AT THE 1987 CHICAGO COMIC CONVENTION. I HAD A TABLE THERE WHERE I WAS SELLING MY COMICS. THIS GUY WITH A CRAZY GLEAM IN HIS EYES COMES OVER.
DO YOU HAVE AMERICAN SPLENDOR NUMBER ONE?
YEAH.
HOW MUCH IS IT?
TWENNY BUCKS. I ONLY HAVE A FEW OF 'EM LEFT.
$20
AMERICAN SPLENDOR
NORMALLY I'LL GIVE MY COMICS AWAY FREE TO ARTISTS OR CHARGE 'EM A NOMINAL AMOUNT. I KNEW IT WAS CHESTER -- I'D SEEN HIS PICTURE. THE THOUGHT OCCURED TO ME TO RUN AFTER HIM AND GIVE HIM HIS MONEY BACK. I LIKED HIS WORK. BUT I COULDN'T DO IT.
WHAT AM I HERE FOR -- TO MAKE MONEY OR FRIENDS?
MONEY!
BOY, THAT TWENNY BUCKS CAME EASY. HE DIDN'T COMPLAIN ABOUT THE PRICE OR ANYTHING. OBVIOUSLY A SUPERIOR GUY -- ABOVE PETTY BICKERING.
I'LL HAVE T'DO SUMP'N' FOR HIM SOMETIME.
I HAD A CHANCE AT THE NEXT CHICAGO CONVENTION. CHESTER WAS THERE SELLING COPIES OF HIS COMIC YUMMY FUR.
UH, GIMME THESE THREE ISSUES.
THAT'S SIX BUCKS RIGHT?
I KNEW IT WAS SIX BUCKS BUT WAS GIVING HIM AN OPPORTUNITY TO LOWER THE PRICE. NO SUCH LUCK.
UH, YEAH.

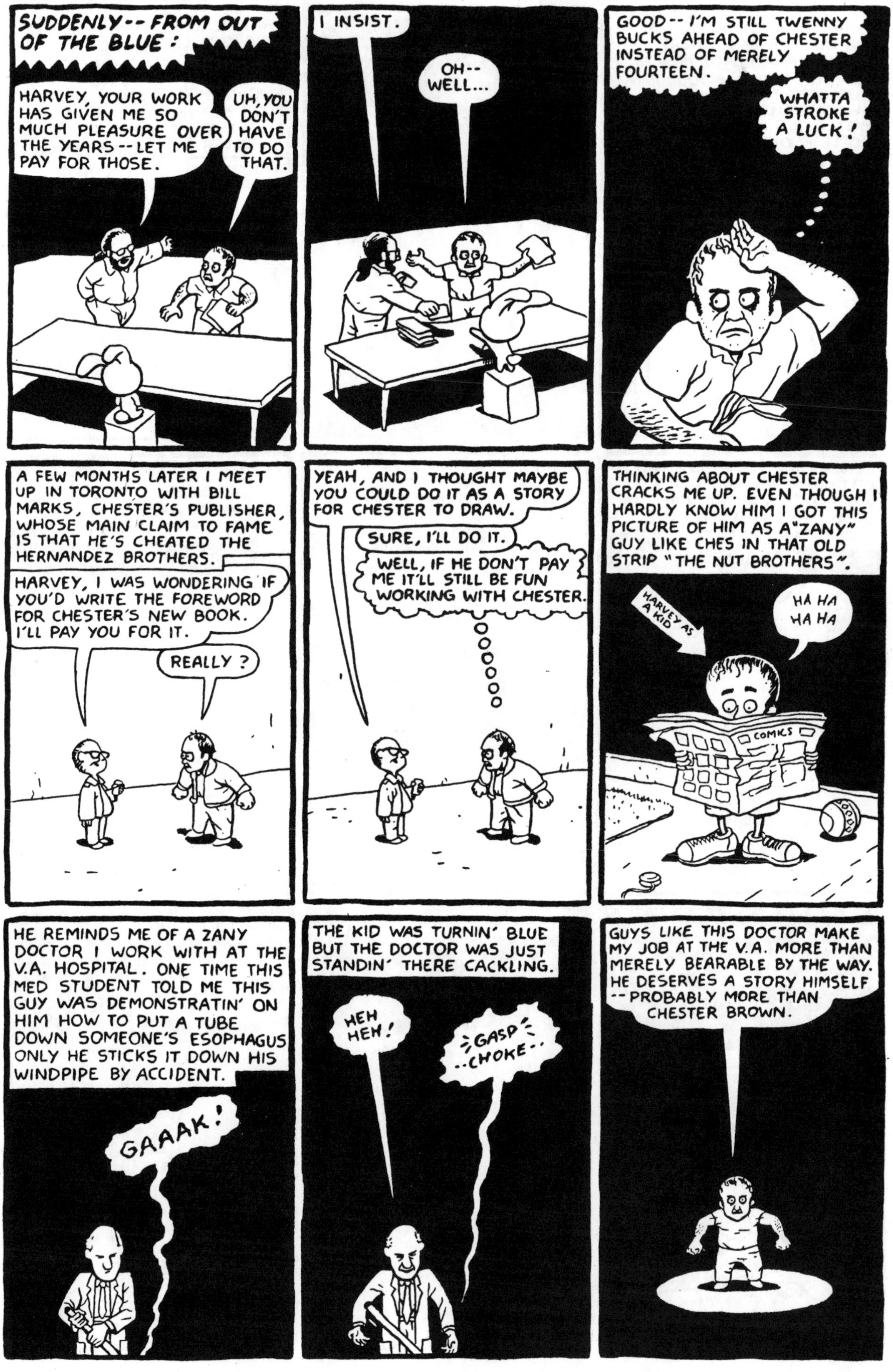
SUDDENLY -- FROM OUT OF THE BLUE:
HARVEY, YOUR WORK HAS GIVEN ME SO MUCH PLEASURE OVER THE YEARS -- LET ME PAY FOR THOSE.
UH, YOU DON'T HAVE TO DO THAT.
I INSIST.
OH -- WELL...
GOOD -- I'M STILL TWENNY BUCKS AHEAD OF CHESTER INSTEAD OF MERELY FOURTEEN.
WHATTA STROKE A LUCK!
A FEW MONTHS LATER I MEET UP IN TORONTO WITH BILL MARKS, CHESTER'S PUBLISHER, WHOSE MAIN CLAIM TO FAME IS THAT HE'S CHEATED THE HERNANDEZ BROTHERS.
HARVEY, I WAS WONDERING IF YOU'D WRITE THE FOREWORD FOR CHESTER'S NEW BOOK. I'LL PAY YOU FOR IT.
REALLY?
YEAH, AND I THOUGHT MAYBE YOU COULD DO IT AS A STORY FOR CHESTER TO DRAW.
SURE, I'LL DO IT.
WELL, IF HE DON'T PAY ME IT'LL STILL BE FUN WORKING WITH CHESTER.
THINKING ABOUT CHESTER CRACKS ME UP. EVEN THOUGH I HARDLY KNOW HIM I GOT THIS PICTURE OF HIM AS A "ZANY" GUY LIKE CHES IN THAT OLD STRIP "THE NUT BROTHERS".
HARVEY AS A KID
HA HA HA HA
COMICS
HE REMINDS ME OF A ZANY DOCTOR I WORK WITH AT THE V.A. HOSPITAL. ONE TIME THIS MED STUDENT TOLD ME THIS GUY WAS DEMONSTRATIN' ON HIM HOW TO PUT A TUBE DOWN SOMEONE'S ESOPHAGUS ONLY HE STICKS IT DOWN HIS WINDPIPE BY ACCIDENT.
GAAAK!
THE KID WAS TURNIN' BLUE BUT THE DOCTOR WAS JUST STANDIN' THERE CACKLING.
HEH HEH!
GASP --CHOKE--
GUYS LIKE THIS DOCTOR MAKE MY JOB AT THE V.A. MORE THAN MERELY BEARABLE BY THE WAY. HE DESERVES A STORY HIMSELF -- PROBABLY MORE THAN CHESTER BROWN.

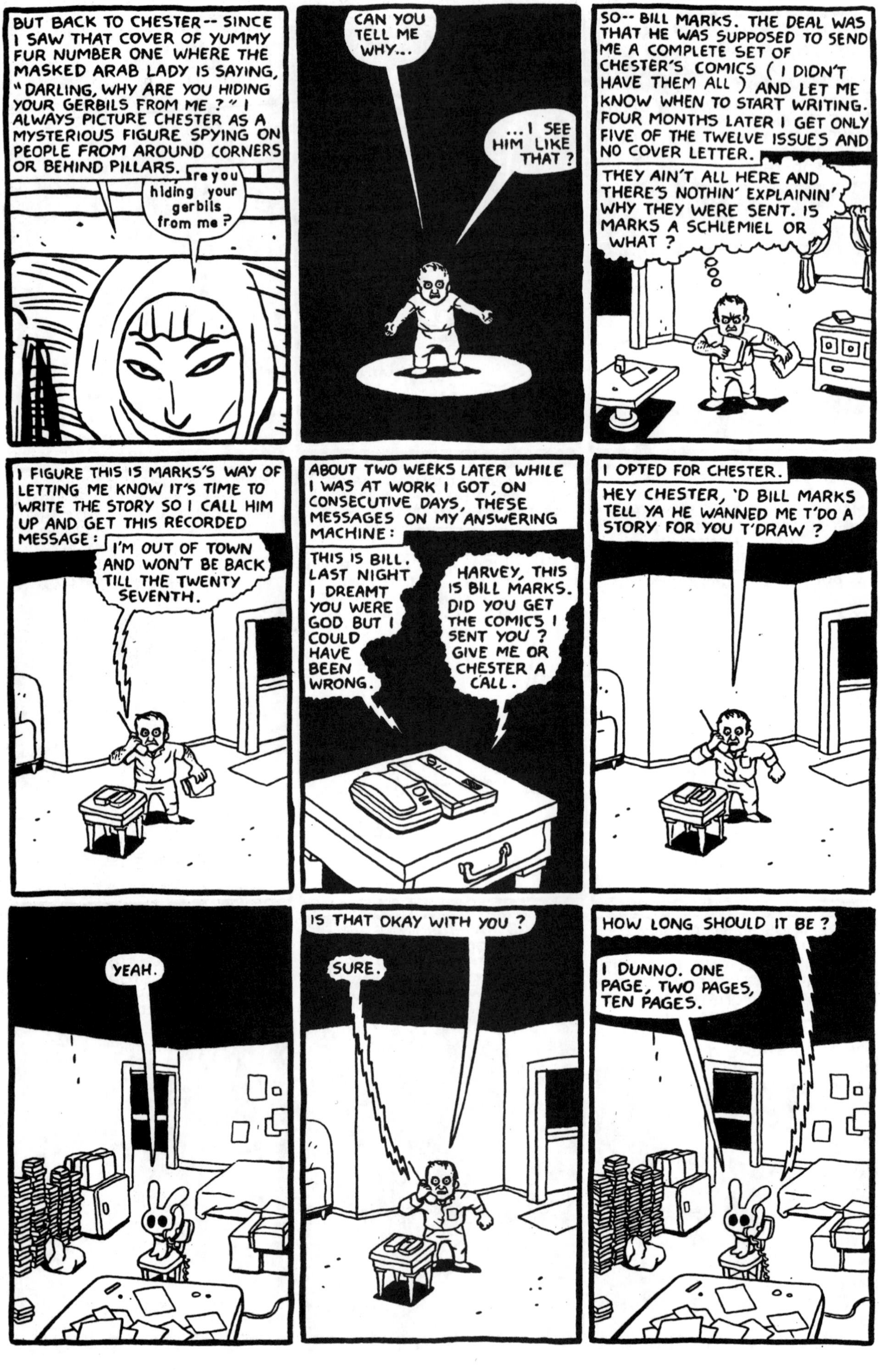
BUT BACK TO CHESTER -- SINCE I SAW THAT COVER OF YUMMY FUR NUMBER ONE WHERE THE MASKED ARAB LADY IS SAYING, "DARLING, WHY ARE YOU HIDING YOUR GERBILS FROM ME ?" I ALWAYS PICTURE CHESTER AS A MYSTERIOUS FIGURE SPYING ON PEOPLE FROM AROUND CORNERS OR BEHIND PILLARS.
are you hiding your gerbils from me ?
CAN YOU TELL ME WHY...
...I SEE HIM LIKE THAT ?
SO-- BILL MARKS. THE DEAL WAS THAT HE WAS SUPPOSED TO SEND ME A COMPLETE SET OF CHESTER'S COMICS (I DIDN'T HAVE THEM ALL) AND LET ME KNOW WHEN TO START WRITING. FOUR MONTHS LATER I GET ONLY FIVE OF THE TWELVE ISSUES AND NO COVER LETTER.
THEY AIN'T ALL HERE AND THERE'S NOTHIN' EXPLAININ' WHY THEY WERE SENT. IS MARKS A SCHLEMIEL OR WHAT ?
I FIGURE THIS IS MARKS'S WAY OF LETTING ME KNOW IT'S TIME TO WRITE THE STORY SO I CALL HIM UP AND GET THIS RECORDED MESSAGE :
I'M OUT OF TOWN AND WON'T BE BACK TILL THE TWENTY SEVENTH.
ABOUT TWO WEEKS LATER WHILE I WAS AT WORK I GOT, ON CONSECUTIVE DAYS, THESE MESSAGES ON MY ANSWERING MACHINE :
THIS IS BILL. LAST NIGHT I DREAMT YOU WERE GOD BUT I COULD HAVE BEEN WRONG.
HARVEY, THIS IS BILL MARKS. DID YOU GET THE COMICS I SENT YOU ? GIVE ME OR CHESTER A CALL.
I OPTED FOR CHESTER.
HEY CHESTER, 'D BILL MARKS TELL YA HE WANNED ME T'DO A STORY FOR YOU T'DRAW ?
YEAH.
IS THAT OKAY WITH YOU ?
SURE.
HOW LONG SHOULD IT BE ?
I DUNNO. ONE PAGE, TWO PAGES, TEN PAGES.

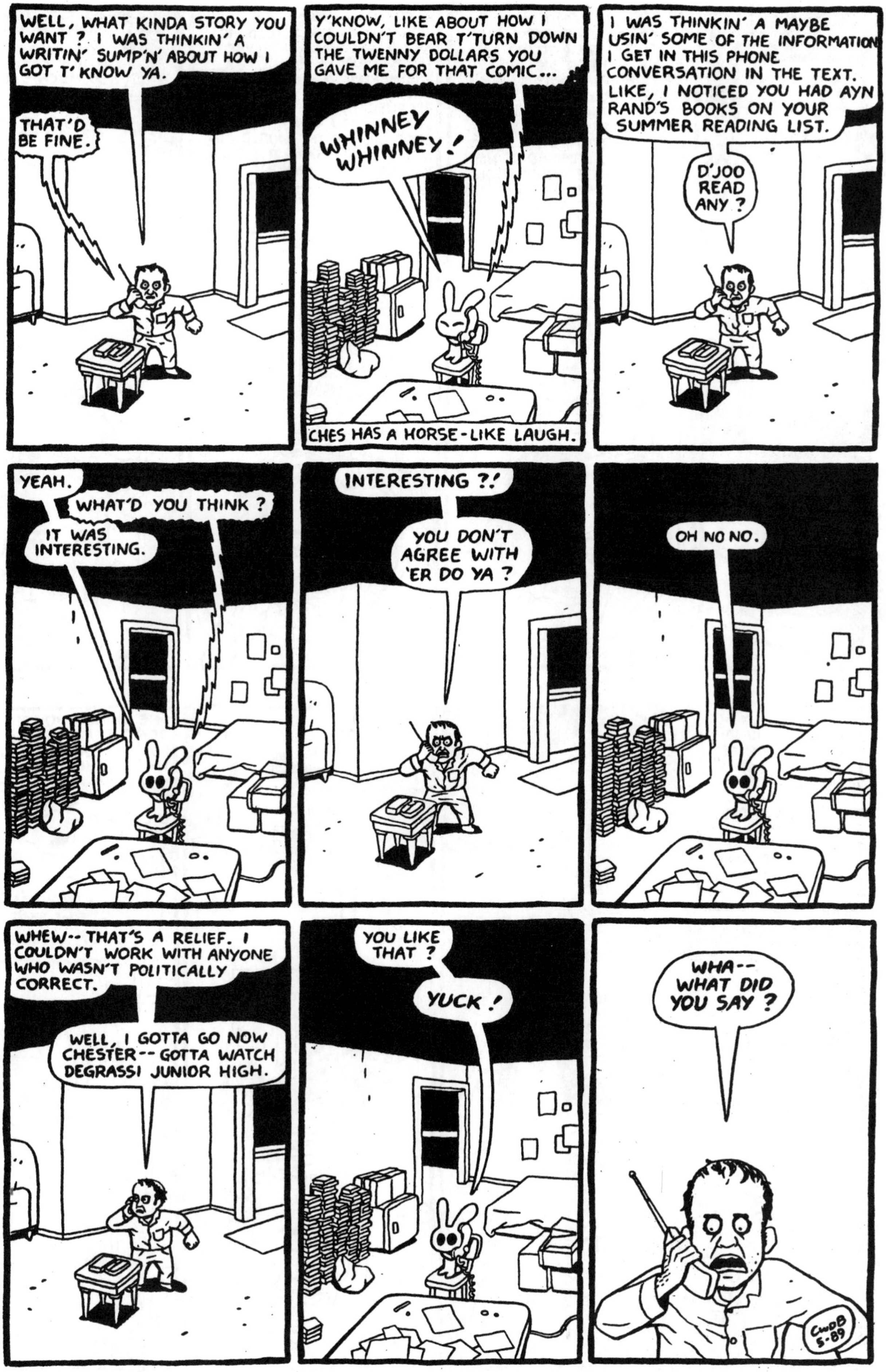
WELL, WHAT KINDA STORY YOU WANT ? I WAS THINKIN' A WRITIN' SUMP'N' ABOUT HOW I GOT T' KNOW YA.
THAT'D BE FINE.
Y'KNOW, LIKE ABOUT HOW I COULDN'T BEAR T'TURN DOWN THE TWENNY DOLLARS YOU GAVE ME FOR THAT COMIC...
WHINNEY WHINNEY !
CHES HAS A HORSE-LIKE LAUGH.
I WAS THINKIN' A MAYBE USIN' SOME OF THE INFORMATION I GET IN THIS PHONE CONVERSATION IN THE TEXT. LIKE, I NOTICED YOU HAD AYN RAND'S BOOKS ON YOUR SUMMER READING LIST.
D'JOO READ ANY ?
YEAH.
WHAT'D YOU THINK ?
IT WAS INTERESTING.
INTERESTING ?!
YOU DON'T AGREE WITH 'ER DO YA ?
OH NO NO.
WHEW-- THAT'S A RELIEF. I COULDN'T WORK WITH ANYONE WHO WASN'T POLITICALLY CORRECT.
WELL, I GOTTA GO NOW CHESTER-- GOTTA WATCH DEGRASSI JUNIOR HIGH.
YOU LIKE THAT ?
YUCK !
WHA-- WHAT DID YOU SAY ?
CWDB 5-89

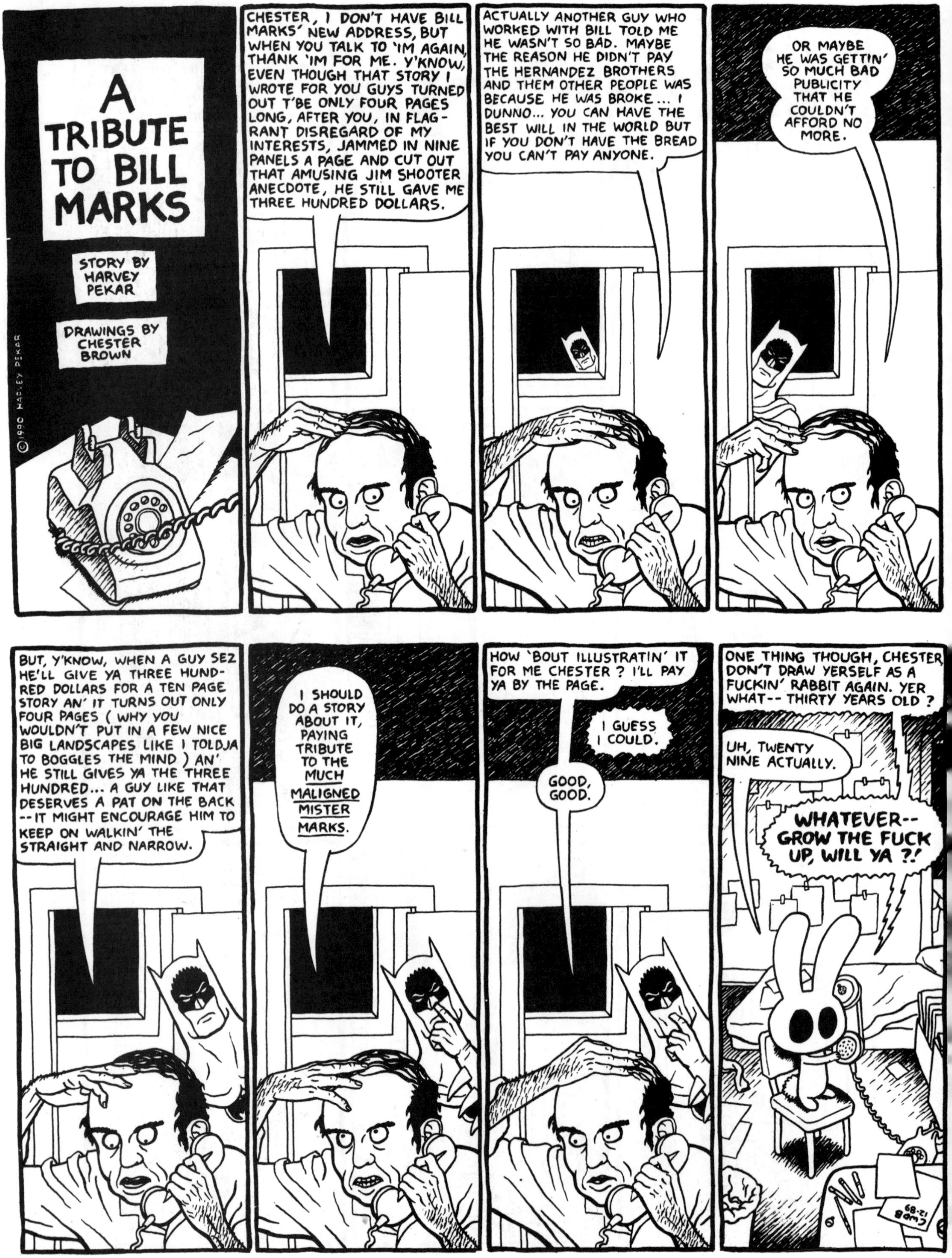
A TRIBUTE TO BILL MARKS
STORY BY HARVEY PEKAR
DRAWINGS BY CHESTER BROWN
©1990 HARVEY PEKAR
CHESTER, I DON'T HAVE BILL MARKS' NEW ADDRESS, BUT WHEN YOU TALK TO 'IM AGAIN, THANK 'IM FOR ME. Y'KNOW, EVEN THOUGH THAT STORY I WROTE FOR YOU GUYS TURNED OUT T'BE ONLY FOUR PAGES LONG, AFTER YOU, IN FLAG-RANT DISREGARD OF MY INTERESTS, JAMMED IN NINE PANELS A PAGE AND CUT OUT THAT AMUSING JIM SHOOTER ANECDOTE, HE STILL GAVE ME THREE HUNDRED DOLLARS.
ACTUALLY ANOTHER GUY WHO WORKED WITH BILL TOLD ME HE WASN'T SO BAD. MAYBE THE REASON HE DIDN'T PAY THE HERNANDEZ BROTHERS AND THEM OTHER PEOPLE WAS BECAUSE HE WAS BROKE... I DUNNO... YOU CAN HAVE THE BEST WILL IN THE WORLD BUT IF YOU DON'T HAVE THE BREAD YOU CAN'T PAY ANYONE.
OR MAYBE HE WAS GETTIN' SO MUCH BAD PUBLICITY THAT HE COULDN'T AFFORD NO MORE.
BUT, Y'KNOW, WHEN A GUY SEZ HE'LL GIVE YA THREE HUND-RED DOLLARS FOR A TEN PAGE STORY AN' IT TURNS OUT ONLY FOUR PAGES (WHY YOU WOULDN'T PUT IN A FEW NICE BIG LANDSCAPES LIKE I TOLDJA TO BOGGLES THE MIND) AN' HE STILL GIVES YA THE THREE HUNDRED... A GUY LIKE THAT DESERVES A PAT ON THE BACK --IT MIGHT ENCOURAGE HIM TO KEEP ON WALKIN' THE STRAIGHT AND NARROW.
I SHOULD DO A STORY ABOUT IT, PAYING TRIBUTE TO THE MUCH MALIGNED MISTER MARKS.
HOW 'BOUT ILLUSTRATIN' IT FOR ME CHESTER ? I'LL PAY YA BY THE PAGE.
I GUESS I COULD.
GOOD, GOOD.
ONE THING THOUGH, CHESTER DON'T DRAW YERSELF AS A FUCKIN' RABBIT AGAIN. YER WHAT-- THIRTY YEARS OLD ?
UH, TWENTY NINE ACTUALLY.
WHATEVER-- GROW THE FUCK UP, WILL YA ?!
CWDB 12-89

INTRODUCING DENNIS EICHHORN

STORY BY HARVEY PEKAR   ART BY JIM WOODRING

DENNIS P. EICHHORN? DENNY EICHHORN? WUTTA GUY! SAY — I COULD GO ON FOREVER ABOUT HIM. TALK ABOUT A PAL! WHEN I WAS OUT IN VICTORIA B.C. ONE TIME, GIVIN' A TALK AT A COLLEGE — WHO COMES OVER FROM SEATTLE T'SEE IT? S'RIGHT, DENNY! NEVER EVEN MET ME B'FORE AN' HE COMES ALL THAT WAY. SOLIDARITY, BROTHER, NOTHIN' BUT SOLIDARNOSC!!

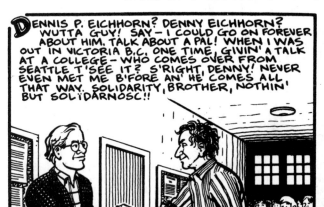

LATER DENNY WENT AN' STARTED HIS OWN NEWSPAPER — THE NORTHWEST EXTRA! WONDERFUL PAPER, BUT THE PEOPLE IN WASHINGTON WOULDN'T SUPPORT IT. I WROTE FOR THE EXTRA! DENNY WAS THE BEST EDITOR I EVER WORKED FOR. HE KNEW I KNEW MY STUFF, SO HE LET ME WRITE ANYTHING I WANTED TO. 'COURSE I REPAID HIS CONFIDENCE WITH SOME ARTICLES THAT WILL LIVE FOREVER!!

FELIPE ALFAU BY HARVEY PEKAR

HEY, DENNY'S HAD A HARD LIFE. I TOL' YA HOW THE SUPPOSEDLY HIP PEOPLE OF WASHINGTON STATE LET 'IM DOWN ABOUT THE N.W. EXTRA! HE LOST THOUSANDS ON IT. THEN HE'S BEEN IN JAIL, BEEN IN THE MIDDLE OF ALL THESE SEX, VIOLENCE AND DOPE SCENES, AND HAD T'SUFFER ALL THESE INDIGNITIES, LIKE ALINE KOMINSKY PUTTIN' 'IM DOWN BECAUSE HE WAS A LITTLE OVERWEIGHT. 'AY ALINE, DENNY'S LOST THIRTY POUNDS NOW; HE'S LOOKIN' TRIM ATHLETIC. WHEN YOU GET BACK FROM FRAWNCE OR WHEREVER YOU ARE AND YOU SEE 'IM, YOU'RE GONNA BE SORRY YOU WEREN'T MORE DIPLOMATIC ...PROB'LY BE ASHAMED OF YERSELF.

OH, DENNIS P.— CAN YOU EVER FORGIVE ME?

OF COURSE, WOMAN — BUT GET UP OFF YOUR KNEES, CAWN'T YOU SEE YOU'RE EMBARRASSING ME?

YEAH, THE WASHINGTON STATERS CRAPPED OUT ON DENNIS AND ME TOO, SINCE I PUT SO MUCH INTO N.W. EXTRA! QUIET AS IT'S KEPT, THE HIPPEST NORTHWESTERNERS ARE PROBABLY FROM IDAHO, DENNY'S ORIGINAL HOME. EVEN THERE AND IN ALASKA HE LITERALLY GOT SHIT ON, COVERED WITH SHIT, AS YOU FIND OUT IN NOT ONE BUT TWO STORIES HERE. BUT NOT EVEN A RIVER OF SHIT CAN STOP THIS GUY — HE'S A MAN WITH A MISSION.

GRRRR!

PHEW!!

IT'S HARD WORK, BUT HE'LL MAKE IT.

DENNY GOT A WIDE VARIETY OF GIFTED ARTISTS WORKING FOR HIM HERE, THEIR WORK ALONE IS WORTH MANY TIMES THE PRICE OF THIS COMIC. LIKE CHECK OUT WHAT JIM WOODRING DOES HERE IN THIS SPECIAL "JIM WOODRING SHOWCASE" PANEL!

HEY, I'M THIRSTY!

GIMME A DRINK, BITCH!

YES SIR!

WHAT CAN I TELL YA? DENNY'S A FRESH NEW FACE ON THE COMICS SCENE. HE'S GOIN' PLACES. BETTER JUMP ON THE DENNY EICHHORN BANDWAGON NOW, OR BE CONDEMNED TO THE ASHCAN OF HISTORY.

SQUARE!

FUCKIN' CRETIN!

REAL STUFF

DARK KNIGHT

END!

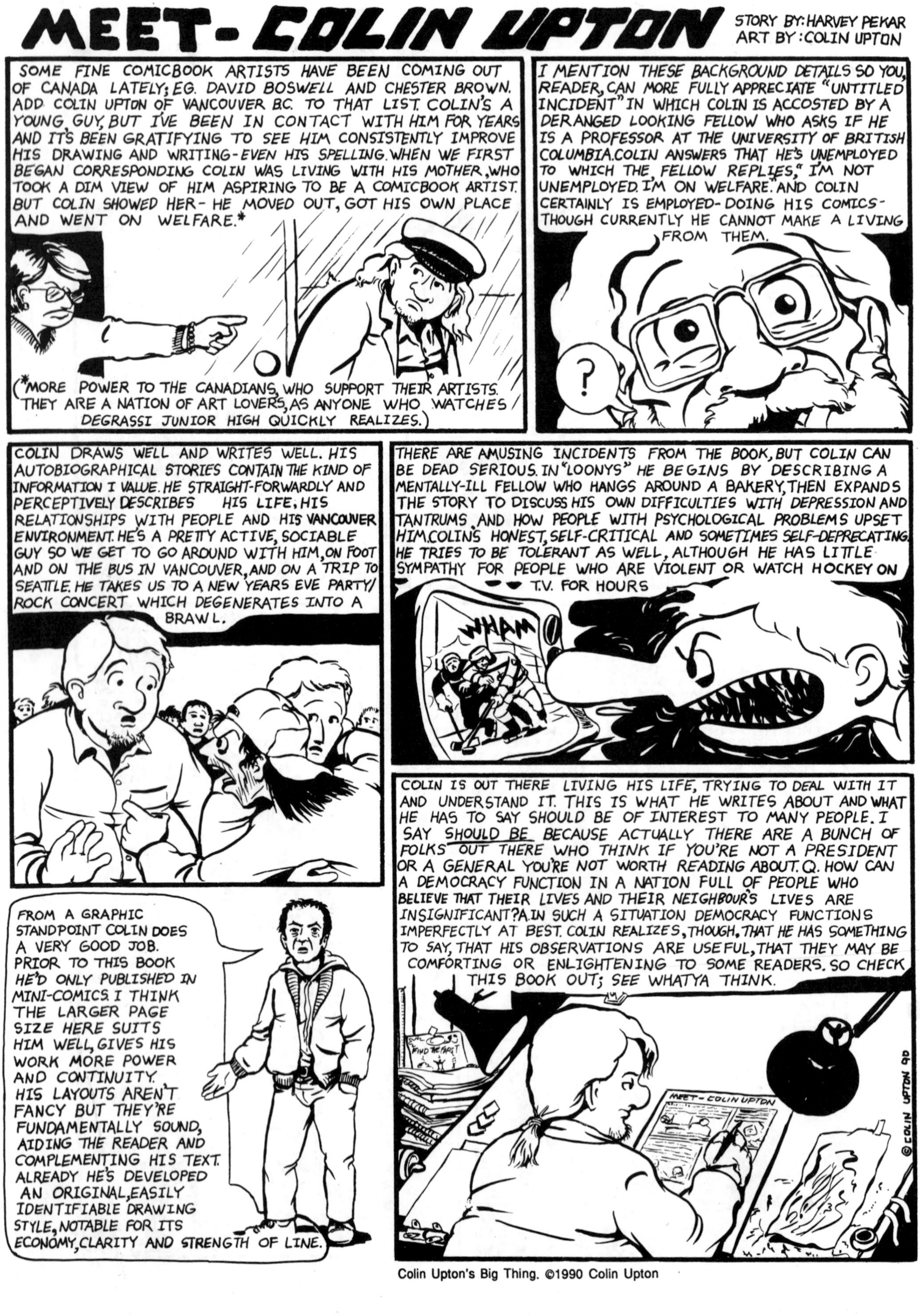
MEET - COLIN UPTON
STORY BY: HARVEY PEKAR
ART BY: COLIN UPTON
SOME FINE COMICBOOK ARTISTS HAVE BEEN COMING OUT OF CANADA LATELY; EG. DAVID BOSWELL AND CHESTER BROWN. ADD COLIN UPTON OF VANCOUVER B.C. TO THAT LIST. COLIN'S A YOUNG GUY, BUT I'VE BEEN IN CONTACT WITH HIM FOR YEARS AND IT'S BEEN GRATIFYING TO SEE HIM CONSISTENTLY IMPROVE HIS DRAWING AND WRITING - EVEN HIS SPELLING. WHEN WE FIRST BEGAN CORRESPONDING COLIN WAS LIVING WITH HIS MOTHER, WHO TOOK A DIM VIEW OF HIM ASPIRING TO BE A COMICBOOK ARTIST. BUT COLIN SHOWED HER - HE MOVED OUT, GOT HIS OWN PLACE AND WENT ON WELFARE.*
(*MORE POWER TO THE CANADIANS, WHO SUPPORT THEIR ARTISTS. THEY ARE A NATION OF ART LOVERS, AS ANYONE WHO WATCHES DEGRASSI JUNIOR HIGH QUICKLY REALIZES.)
I MENTION THESE BACKGROUND DETAILS SO YOU, READER, CAN MORE FULLY APPRECIATE "UNTITLED INCIDENT" IN WHICH COLIN IS ACCOSTED BY A DERANGED LOOKING FELLOW WHO ASKS IF HE IS A PROFESSOR AT THE UNIVERSITY OF BRITISH COLUMBIA. COLIN ANSWERS THAT HE'S UNEMPLOYED TO WHICH THE FELLOW REPLIES, "I'M NOT UNEMPLOYED. I'M ON WELFARE." AND COLIN CERTAINLY IS EMPLOYED - DOING HIS COMICS - THOUGH CURRENTLY HE CANNOT MAKE A LIVING FROM THEM.
?
COLIN DRAWS WELL AND WRITES WELL. HIS AUTOBIOGRAPHICAL STORIES CONTAIN THE KIND OF INFORMATION I VALUE. HE STRAIGHT-FORWARDLY AND PERCEPTIVELY DESCRIBES HIS LIFE, HIS RELATIONSHIPS WITH PEOPLE AND HIS VANCOUVER ENVIRONMENT. HE'S A PRETTY ACTIVE, SOCIABLE GUY SO WE GET TO GO AROUND WITH HIM, ON FOOT AND ON THE BUS IN VANCOUVER, AND ON A TRIP TO SEATTLE. HE TAKES US TO A NEW YEARS EVE PARTY/ ROCK CONCERT WHICH DEGENERATES INTO A BRAWL.
THERE ARE AMUSING INCIDENTS FROM THE BOOK, BUT COLIN CAN BE DEAD SERIOUS. IN "LOONYS" HE BEGINS BY DESCRIBING A MENTALLY-ILL FELLOW WHO HANGS AROUND A BAKERY, THEN EXPANDS THE STORY TO DISCUSS HIS OWN DIFFICULTIES WITH DEPRESSION AND TANTRUMS AND HOW PEOPLE WITH PSYCHOLOGICAL PROBLEMS UPSET HIM. COLIN'S HONEST, SELF-CRITICAL AND SOMETIMES SELF-DEPRECATING. HE TRIES TO BE TOLERANT AS WELL, ALTHOUGH HE HAS LITTLE SYMPATHY FOR PEOPLE WHO ARE VIOLENT OR WATCH HOCKEY ON T.V. FOR HOURS
WHAM
COLIN IS OUT THERE LIVING HIS LIFE, TRYING TO DEAL WITH IT AND UNDERSTAND IT. THIS IS WHAT HE WRITES ABOUT AND WHAT HE HAS TO SAY SHOULD BE OF INTEREST TO MANY PEOPLE. I SAY SHOULD BE BECAUSE ACTUALLY THERE ARE A BUNCH OF FOLKS OUT THERE WHO THINK IF YOU'RE NOT A PRESIDENT OR A GENERAL YOU'RE NOT WORTH READING ABOUT. Q. HOW CAN A DEMOCRACY FUNCTION IN A NATION FULL OF PEOPLE WHO BELIEVE THAT THEIR LIVES AND THEIR NEIGHBOUR'S LIVES ARE INSIGNIFICANT? A. IN SUCH A SITUATION DEMOCRACY FUNCTIONS IMPERFECTLY AT BEST. COLIN REALIZES, THOUGH, THAT HE HAS SOMETHING TO SAY, THAT HIS OBSERVATIONS ARE USEFUL, THAT THEY MAY BE COMFORTING OR ENLIGHTENING TO SOME READERS. SO CHECK THIS BOOK OUT; SEE WHATYA THINK.
FROM A GRAPHIC STANDPOINT COLIN DOES A VERY GOOD JOB. PRIOR TO THIS BOOK HE'D ONLY PUBLISHED IN MINI-COMICS. I THINK THE LARGER PAGE SIZE HERE SUITS HIM WELL, GIVES HIS WORK MORE POWER AND CONTINUITY. HIS LAYOUTS AREN'T FANCY BUT THEY'RE FUNDAMENTALLY SOUND, AIDING THE READER AND COMPLEMENTING HIS TEXT. ALREADY HE'S DEVELOPED AN ORIGINAL, EASILY IDENTIFIABLE DRAWING STYLE, NOTABLE FOR ITS ECONOMY, CLARITY AND STRENGTH OF LINE.
FIND THE PARTY
MEET - COLIN UPTON
©COLIN UPTON 90